W9-BIM-768

sexual secrets

GANESHA
The elephant-headed deity is considered the embodiment of the Tantric mysteries. The graceful strength of the Elephant Lord represents the vast powerhouse of sexual energy. The highly adaptable trunk and sensuous mouth of the elephant suggest the male and female sex organs. Ruler of the sexual center, Ganesha is always evoked at the commencement of Hindu rites. Drawing from a stone sculpture, Hoysala, South India, twelfth–thirteenth century.

SEXUAL SECRETS

*the alchemy
of ecstasy*

NIK DOUGLAS
PENNY SLINGER

DESTINY BOOKS
New York

Destiny Books
377 Park Avenue South
New York, NY 10016

First published 1979

Editorial Director: Ehud C. Sperling

Book Design: David Laufer

Layout: Empty-Eye

Typography: J. M. Post Graphics

Cover Concept: Ehud C. Sperling

Cover Photography: Harry Giglio

Mechanicals and Chart Artist: Alden Cole

Copy-editing and Proofing:
Deborah Forman, Carole Freddo,
Kendra Crossen, Lisa Sperling

Set in V.I.P. Cartier and Helvetica Light; Typositor Jana

16 17 18 19 20 21 22 23 24 25

Library of Congress Cataloging in Publication Data
Douglas, Nik.
    Sexual secrets.

    Bibliography: p.
    Includes index.
    1. Sex customs-Asia. 2. Sex. 3. Erotica.
I. Slinger, Penelope, joint author. II. Title.
HQ18.A8D68   301.41'8   79-9497
ISBN 0-89281-010-6
ISBN 0-89281-011-4 pbk.

Text and illustrations copyright © 1979
by Nik Douglas & Penny Slinger
All rights reserved. No part of this book may be
reproduced or utilized in any form or by any means,
electronic or mechanical, including photocopying and
recording, or by any information storage and retrieval
system, without permission in writing from the
publisher. Inquiries should be addressed to Destiny Books.

Printed in the United States of America
Destiny Books is a division of Inner Traditions International.

Sexual union is an auspicious Yoga which, though involving enjoyment of all the sensual pleasures, gives release. It is a Path to Liberation.

KAULARAHASYA

The union of man and woman is like the mating of Heaven and Earth. It is because of their correct mating that Heaven and Earth last forever. Humans have lost this secret and have therefore become mortal. By knowing it the Path to Immortality is opened.

SHANG-KU-SAN-TAI

contents

Sexual union is an auspicious Yoga which,
though involving enjoyment of all the
sensual pleasures, gives release. It is a
Path to Liberation.

KAULARAHASYA

The union of man and woman is like the
mating of Heaven and Earth. It is because of
their correct mating that Heaven and Earth last
forever. Humans have lost this secret and have
therefore become mortal. By knowing it the
Path to Immortality is opened.

SHANG-KU-SAN-TAI

contents

the power of sex, the meaning of transcendence, the force of Brahma, the force of Vishnu, the force of Shiva, the triad of forces, understanding the sexual secrets, the realm of Brahma, the realm of Vishnu, the realm of Shiva, the three Shaktis, the goddess triad and the god triad, the meaning of Kali, her nakedness, her four arms, Parvati, one with Kali, Kali's mantras, Kali's yantra, sexual exchange, the best times for sexual initiation, chakra puja, bhairavi chakra, yogini chakra, the symbolic level of the yogini chakra, consonants and vowels, Kali-consonants, ali-vowels, contraction and expansion, the role of the guru, worldly gurus, spiritual gurus, Tantric gurus, the role of Tantric gurus, vehicles of liberation, mystic forms, erotic fantasy, the emotions, nine sentiments, conjuring forth emotions, emotions are focused in the heart, sentiments and colors, channeling emotions, sexual roles, role playing, old age, sex and transcendence, menopause, impotence, sex and pregnancy, the mystic child, astrology, sexual positions and astrology, sex and rejuvenation, magical powers, siddhis, siddhas, the power of drugs, drugs as sacraments, marijuana, fasting, abstinence, celibacy, Ganesha, Ganesha mantras, Ganesha's role, the creation of Ganesha, climax and orgasm, surrender, wave of ecstasy, exchange, the descent, the ascent, four levels of ascent, sex magic, secret breathing, womb breathing, storing sexual energy, transformed sexual energy, secret language, Tantric codes, secret signs, three levels of teaching, reality is paradoxical, five mudras, five families, symbolic language, mudra, shudra and rudra, the fifth Veda, Vasistha in China, Chinese rites

Mamaki, Locana, Pandara, Tara, Ishvari

daughters of earth, the dark girl, the elected girl, the plain girl, roles of heaven and earth, emperor's secrets, emperor's duty, illicit affairs, adultery in the heart, self-worship, narcissism, auto-eroticism, bondage, fetishism, feet, foot worship. heavenly and earthly net, melody of the five elements, the tripod of immortality

PART THREE:
VISHNU THE PRESERVER

acknowledgments

The authors would like to thank the following for their contribution to this project:

Gangotri Giri, for his constant guidance, support and example.
Durga Das Shastri, for inspiring our interest in these secrets.
Pagala Baba, for his Yogic demonstrations and sound advice.
Dr. Bindu Joshi, for his insights into Indian medicine and alchemy.
Dr. Jyotir Mitra, for his erudite scholarship and alchemical advice.
Yogiraja Vaidyaraja, for sharing personal Yogic experiences with us.
Yogini Rajyalakshmi Devi, for demonstrating advanced Yogic techniques.
Mahamahopadhyaya Gopinath Kaviraj, for his generosity and scholarship.
Swami Pratyagatmananda Saraswati, for his help and encouragement.
Dr. Ramesh Khandelwal, for sharing sources and information.
C. M. Chen Yogi, for his generosity and spontaneity.
Yogini Ma Bhairavi, for practical and direct advice.
The Gyalwa Karmapa, Rangjung Rigpe Dorje, for his generosity and help.
Lama Dudjom Rinpoche, for his encouragement.
Lama Kunzang Rinzing, for sharing many secrets.
Lama Dodrup Chen, for his generosity and guidance.
Lama Tulku Tsewang, for his willingness to discuss difficult topics.

Ehud Sperling, for his belief in the project and for his dedication and participation in all stages of its creation. Without his commitment, this work would never have been completed.
Lisa Sperling, for her belief in and support of this project.
Donald Weiser, for pointing us in the right direction.
Michael Rubinstein, for sound advice when we needed it.
Sir Roland Penrose, for support and encouragement.
Albion Jennings, for support and good advice.
Bhaskar Bhattacharya, for constructive suggestions and assistance.
Mark Dyczkowski, for the contribution of material.
Dr. A. Powell, for translations from Latin.
Dr. Andrija Puharich, for technical advice.
Richard Ravenal, for help and encouragement.
The following have generously contributed original material on which illustrations have been based:
David Salmon, Victor Lownes, Ravi Kumar, Navin Kumar, Firouzeh Diba, Michael Hudson, Meryl White, Caterine Milinaire, Dr. Stephen Fulder, David Tremayne Ltd., The British Museum, The Victoria and Albert Museum, Bharat Kala Bhavan, The British Library Board, The Art Institute of Chicago, The Royal Ontario Museum, The Bhaktapur Museum, The National Museum of New Delhi, The Benares Hindu University and The Kronhausen Erotic Art Collection, as well as others who wish to remain anonymous.

We would also like to thank Claudine Fischer and all those at Destiny Books who have selflessly contributed to this project. To all those who have in any way helped bring this book to completion, we extend our thanks and deep appreciation.

Nik Douglas & Penny Slinger

publisher's preface

In man and woman are found all the materials and experiences of the world. When they unite, these experiences and materials can be distilled into a vision of and a harmonization with the dynamic unity underlying all of reality. For centuries this vision of unity has been obscured by individuals and institutions that have promoted a schism between body and mind, between religious feelings and sexuality. The fear of mysticism has only been overshadowed by the fear of the inherent liberating power of human sexuality. The very repression of both mysticism and sexuality in the West serve only to reflect their secret marriage. For it is in sexual union that the ecstatic and uplifting experience of the mystic comes within reach of all who love. This ecstatic experience feeds a spontaneous spiritual awareness that dissolves conventions and frees the spirit to seek its origin.

SEXUAL SECRETS: *The Alchemy of Ecstasy* is the definitive study on sex and mysticism. No book of this magnitude has ever appeared on this subject, representing as it does a major as well as a vital contribution to our understanding of sexuality. It explores the path of love and mysticism, drawing upon the heritage and wisdom of the great cultures of the East. Created by a couple (writer and artist), it is meant to be experienced as well as read.

Nik Douglas studied Oriental art, philosophy, medicine and related sexual practices while living for eight years in the Himalayas. He studied with Indian physicians, adepts of Tantra and Tibetan lamas and at the same time mastered Sanskrit as well as the Tibetan language. He has organized numerous exhibitions of Eastern art, and is called upon by leading museums and private collectors to authenticate Oriental art and writings. SEXUAL SECRETS is based on more than two thousand years of authoritative Oriental texts on medicine, philosophy and sexual practices, many never before seen, let alone translated, in the West. The author has drawn upon a unique blend of living experience and a facility with ancient tongues to make these texts as vital and contemporary as they were when first written.

Penny Slinger has created more than six hundred illustrations to enhance the experience of the text. Exhibited widely throughout Europe, her work has been hailed as "dynamic, progressive eroticism, an exploration of female sexuality." More than two hundred sexual postures are illustrated, after the finest examples in collections throughout the world. Included is a complete illustrated KAMA SUTRA, ANANGA RANGA and the major Taoist love treatises, all of which have been newly translated. The illustrator has also drawn from some of the finest examples of Tantric art, which have never before been published. Working from life, she has created a completely new style of erotica that blends the images of the West with the sentiments of the East. This artistic achievement crowns the greatest and most diverse collection of illustrations expressing the erotic sentiment ever to be published.

The fruit of more than a decade of research, SEXUAL SECRETS heralds the marriage of love and mysticism, presenting a natural lifestyle, philosophy and practice in which the alchemy of love produces the ecstasy of liberation.

Ehud C. Sperling

Three indeed are the pursuits that should be followed by every person. These are the pursuit of life, the pursuit of transcendence and the pursuit of prosperity.

CHARAKA SAMHITA

King Nadir Shah in union with a favorite concubine. From a miniature painting in the collection of the King of Nepal, *circa* 1830.

In India, Nepal, Tibet, China and Japan, sexuality has long been regarded as both an art and a science worthy of detailed study and practice. Indeed, the Eastern view is that no learning is complete without a thorough knowledge of the sexual principles underlying all existence. Eastern metaphysical traditions make use of the mystery of sexuality as a means to the transcendental experience of Unity. The feeling of Oneness, achieved during or following the sexual act, is the most universally accessible mystical experience.

The sexual secrets, here revealed for the first time in a concise contemporary context, are the legacy of several converging traditions. These secrets are mentioned or implied in the early magical texts of the ancient Egyptians, as also in the mystical writings of the Hebrews, Greeks and Arabs. A study of the alchemical books of mediaeval Europe reveals a continuation of this tradition and experience, often taking the form of inspired romantic or mystical poetry, generally couched in allegory. Arabian songs and writings on the theme of love are replete with sexual elements which can best be understood by tracing in them the influences of the East. It is evident that all Occidental teachings of transcendence through actual or allegorical eroticism find their origin in the Orient.

We have been particularly fortunate in having had the opportunity to explore the theoretical and practical aspects of the sexual secrets with Eastern masters. Furthermore, we have drawn on our own personal experience, believing it valid as a touchstone by which to evaluate both the practical and theoretical truth of the teaching. We have translated texts directly from the Sanskrit, Tibetan and Chinese, and wherever possible have scrupulously sought out authentic sources. The alchemy of ecstasy is extremely simple, and at the same time, intricately complex. This paradox should not dissuade the earnest seeker, since the sexual secrets are here presented in a sequence helpful to practical use.

The sexual secrets for consciously inducing and maximizing the experience of ecstasy are most eloquently presented in the Taoist tradition of China. The Tantric teachings of India evolved synchronously and there was a two-way exchange of techniques and ideas. Tibet received the teachings from both India and China, perfecting the mysteries over a millennium. We consider the Taoist and Tantric traditions as representing the most clear and directly relevant sexual secrets for the present-day needs of the West.

The decision to compile and synthesize the sexual secrets in this form was inspired by our observation of the changing attitudes toward sexuality in our society. The growing interest in the expansion of consciousness and self-awareness has led many to search for liberation through sexuality. Sexual taboos and inhibitions have been broken through in an effort to free sensual enjoyment from feelings of guilt. We are sure that this is a step in the right direction, but dangerous unless accompanied by emotional maturation.

Liberation, especially sexual liberation, must be oriented in a positive spiritual direction. If not, when the novelty of new sexual experiences has worn off, emptiness and meaninglessness inevitably result. Western psychiatrists and psychologists have remarked on the increasing incidence of this feeling of emptiness as the root of neurosis in our all-permissive society, and are aware of the need to help re-establish meaning and creative direction in the life of the individual. Partly in response to the feeling of spiritual emptiness, the West has become conscious of the validity and profound insight of Eastern mystical practices. Yoga and meditation have become household words in little more than a decade. Encounter groups, sensitivity training, T'ai Chi, Transcendental Meditation, Gestalt Therapy, est and other awareness therapies abound throughout the United States and Europe. The proliferation of these movements has resulted from an authentic need to recover a deeper, more conscious experience of life.

The long-established norms of sexual behavior in the West have created psychological barriers that restrict inner growth. These "hang-ups," inculcated by parents and social institutions, have doomed many people to lives of permanent frustration. A desperate attempt to conform to a conventional, though possibly unnatural, "norm" of sexual behavior restricts individual development and may lead to furtive perversion and damaging guilt feelings. Yet an honest breaking with the expected standard, in a bid for personal liberation, might have led, up until recently, to alienation or even ostracism. Thus, many have seen the need to expand the parameters of the norm, to cut away the restrictions of convention and the limitations of habit. By exploring the sexual potential of ourselves and others, we can come to consciously know the alchemy of ecstasy. It is our opinion, and the philosophical assumption of this work, that this process of self-development should be undertaken in a spiritual context, with a sense of purpose and higher direction.

Only in the past few years has the West become aware of the depth of wisdom expressed in the Tantric and Taoist teachings concerning sexuality. Unfortunately, however, the sudden surge of interest in this largely esoteric literature has brought with it numerous misconceptions about sexual practices. These misconceptions have arisen from an ignorance of the subtle or allegorical meanings of many parts of the original texts, which were a carefully guarded secret only revealed to those who had successfully passed initiation rites. Furthermore, the bulk of the literature has only been accessible to scholars, with the result that lay people have had insufficient opportunity to explore the original material. A secondhand and often inaccurate acquaintance with the teachings has led Western sexologists and popular writers on sexual occultism to jump to premature and often erroneous conclusions.

The core experience of Tantra is the sexual secrets. Tantra is a philosophy, a science, an art and a way of life whereby sexual energy is consciously and creatively utilized. The mystical treatises, known as the Tantras, contain a broad spectrum of practical techniques for enhancing sexual awareness and achieving transcendence. The hidden potency of the sexual act is the seed of all creativity. Through an understanding of the practical teachings of Tantra, a whole new experience of life opens up.

Emperors, kings and queens had one standard of sexuality for themselves and another standard for their subjects. The sexual secrets were in the past reserved for rulers and initiates, who needed to wield power intelligently. Power was achieved through sexual experiences that served to strengthen vitality. The energy found in these practices was consciously channeled to enhance integrity, clarity and wisdom.

The well-being and prosperity of a country was once believed to be directly related to the vitality of the king. The sexual secrets were not readily available to the masses, although they did find expression in Spring festivals, fertility rites and forms of pagan worship. Paganism had sexual energy as its firm foundation; many of the rites and rituals were based on a profound understanding of sexuality.

We did not write this book for those who wish to gain power over others by manipulating or using the power of sex for purely worldly ends. The sexual secrets should not be used selfishly. Many of these secrets have been jealously guarded to protect against their misuse. This concealment has resulted in the gradual dispersion of half-truths about mystic sexuality, Tantra and Taoism, which, in the long run, has done more harm than good. Therefore, we are revealing knowledge that in the past has required initiation, as we believe the ethical cornerstone of this teaching is individual responsibility. Ultimately, progress in Tantric evolution is barred to those who have not shouldered this responsibility.

This is a book for couples or individuals wanting to become couples. It is for those who wish to use the sexual bond as a means to liberation and who desire to transcend the limits of the individual self. It is especially for those to whom love and trust are synonymous and who wish to give, as well as take. The sharing of the ecstatic experience is the key that unlocks the sexual secrets.

structure of this book

We have divided our book into three parts, which correspond to the Hindu triad of forces that pervades all activity. This triad is the Creative, the Transcendental and the Preserver. In our existence these principles correspond to birth, death and life. They occur at both material and psychological levels and are the underlying basis of the universe, which is in a constant state of flux. In the Tantric cosmology these forces are formalized as three aspects of one single Divine Unity. Separately they are known as Brahma, the Creative, Shiva, the Transcendental, and Vishnu, the Preserver. Each of these forces is understood as inseparable from a feminine Energy counterpart or *Shakti*. According to Tantra, every higher principle can only exist through a combination of male and female.

The Shaktis of Brahma, Shiva and Vishnu are known as Saraswati, Kali and Lakshmi respectively. Saraswati is the patroness of the arts, Kali the initiatress into transcendence and Lakshmi the embodiment of preservation and prosperity. The following chart is a convenient arrangement of their relationships.

PRINCIPLE	RELATIONSHIP	DIVINE ASPECT	DIVINE ENERGY
The Creative	Birth	Brahma	Saraswati
The Transcendental	Death	Shiva	Kali
The Preserver	Life	Vishnu	Lakshmi

Brahma, Shiva and Vishnu, symbolic of the creative, transcendental and preserving powers, respectively. Linked to birth, death and life, these three forces together evoke the Subtle Body of Tantra. From a stone sculpture, Hoysala, Halebid, India, *circa* twelfth century.

Padmasambhava, the Indian Tantric master who established Tantric Buddhism in Tibet in the eighth century, in ecstatic union with his consort. This mystic form celebrates the unity of celestial Voidness with terrestial Wisdom. From a Tibetan painting of the nineteenth century.

consider the senses in this role and explicate the cosmic function of such mundane activities as seeing, smelling, hearing and touching. We tell of the important ancient traditions concerning self-examination, psychological attitude, Yoga technology, food, drink, exercise, bathing, sleep, dreams, circulation of energy, massage, meditation and ritual acts. The context of sexuality is constantly brought to bear.

This first part of the book is intended to open the reader to higher possibilities. Some of the concepts will no doubt be familiar, while others will seem unusual or even extraordinary. However, we believe that, with the intuition open, everyone is able to receive the understanding of the sexual secrets. Theory is always enhanced by practical application, so try to adapt your lifestyle to enable the teaching to take on a personal meaning. The sexual secrets are best received in the spirit of initiation.

The central part of this book considers the theme of the Transcendental and takes the form of an intimate dialogue between a Tantric couple spontaneously producing the sexual secrets from the ecstasy of union. After a prolonged period of love-making, the couple identify themselves, through self-worship, with their divine counterparts, Shiva and Shakti. The couple are now exalted to god and goddess, and begin the transmission of the sexual secrets.

Generally it is the woman (Shakti, representing intuitive Wisdom-energy) who in the Tantras asks the man (Shiva, symbolic of transcendental power) to reveal the sexual secrets. His viewpoint is that of a "Lord over Death," the Supreme Yogi who has known everything. In the Buddhist Tantric tradition it is Buddha who converses with a Wisdom-goddess; in the Chinese Taoist counterpart, a mythical emperor talks with his Celestial-lady. The message is the same: an esoteric transmission of the function and practices of sexuality.

Traditionally, in Tantra, the innermost secrets are revealed and conveyed through the form of intimate dialogue. This practice ensures that the meaning of the teaching is understood spontaneously. Often, in texts of such dialogues, the meaning is concealed by allegory or a kind of "twilight language" of riddles. All lovers share an intimate vocabulary, the meaning

The Tantric neophyte should come to grips with these three basic principles. Their anthropomorphic conceptualization should not present an obstacle to understanding. The triadic conception of the Divine is an archetype found in Christianity, Buddhism, Taoism, Islam and even in Kabbalistic Judaism. Folk myths throughout the world contain references to threefold forces underlying all phenomena and evolution.

The first part of this book deals with the theme of the Creative and examines the positive attitudes and actions necessary to the seeker after Liberation. The creative is like a seed containing the potential for growth into a fully realized life. It is symbolized by a golden aura, an "egg," of positive energy. The preparations and proper mental attitudes for beginning on a Tantric lifestyle are clearly outlined. Here we tell of the "Sixty-four Arts" and their role in delighting the senses. Foremost of the arts is the "Art of Love," without which no creative activity would be possible. The medium of this noblest of arts is the human body and its sense organs. We therefore of which is often known only to themselves. An outsider, hearing their conversation, would be at a loss to understand them. In Tantra this protects against misuse of potent information.

In Part II of the book we explore the sexuality of the couple. The meaning of sexuality and the power of transcendence are discussed. The sexual secrets revealed include the meaning of the Shiva and Kali archetypes, mystic forms, sexual fantasy, magical practices, visualization, teachings on fasting, abstinence, orgasm, drugs and sexual alchemy. There are other topics covered also, in answer to questions raised by reading the first and third parts of the book. Part II will serve as a second initiation to the reader. Here is "heart talk," direct and spontaneous.

The third and final part of the book concerns the theme of the Preserver. In Hindu cosmology Lord Vishnu preserves everything that Brahma has created. As the Lord of all cosmic play, it is Vishnu's constant desire to preserve life and stimulate eros; the goddess Lakshmi, embodiment of all prosperity, is his wife. Here we consider the path of love in all its manifold activities and explore the joy of sexual awareness.

The practical applications of secret techniques for maintaining a heightened sensuous awareness are outlined and the entire repertory of love-making positions is explored in detail, illustrated wherever possible. We examine the natural cycles of love-making, the esoteric teachings and rituals of love, retention, mutual absorption, ejaculation, oral sex, sapphism, homosexuality and other aspects of sexuality included within the vast literature of Tantra and Taoism. Our aim has been to update and simplify the information contained in esoteric traditions and make it available in a form practicable for the present time.

Throughout this book we quote extensively from authoritative texts to support or illustrate our theme. Wherever possible we have consulted the manuscripts in their original language and compared texts of different periods. In most cases we have retranslated rather than use existing English renderings. We consulted numerous rare books, texts, manuscripts and paintings to bring together the material for this work.

Though the sources are varied, there is a consistency of tone, a direct and spontaneous awareness of the cosmic function of sex, which carries the ring of truth. Tantric and Taoist teachings are generally free of sexual inhibition or repression. It is remarkable that such esoteric material, preserved in so many independent traditions, should have this common ground.

Illustrations have been created to augment the experience of the text and help in the transmission of the sexual secrets. Many of the illustrations we have drawn from were originally commissioned by kings and emperors and now are in private collections or museums throughout the world. Others are from traditional Chinese, Japanese or Indian sources.

Numerous published collections have been consulted and the elements pertaining to the Tantric and Taoist teaching extracted. In doing this we have covered a vast time spectrum, from the ancient to the contemporary, encompassing a variety of media, from temple carvings to Tibetan paintings, employed to express the erotic sentiment.

Some of the illustrations have grown directly out of our involvement with the exploration of material for this book. We have researched modern forms of sexual expression and created new images that are conducive to the elevation of the senses. The drawings are unique works in themselves and represent, as does the text, a gathering together of many streams leading to the same source.

The present time calls for the sexual secrets to be made available to all without distinction, clearing the way for responsible seekers to experience their latent potentials. Each one of us has come into this world through the power of a sexual act. Every person who has experienced sexual love has had at least the taste of ecstasy.

Our own journey into the sexual secrets has deepened and enriched our relationship. By becoming aware of the sexual secrets and applying them to practical everyday life, we hope that our readers will fully experience the alchemy and ecstasy of love. We offer the fruit of our work to those who recognize the futility of existence without spiritual fulfillment.

Nik Douglas and Penny Slinger

Ganesha with his consort Siddhi (representing supernormal power). This Tantric form of the Elephant Lord symbolizes the awakening of sexuality and spiritual ideals. From a stone carving, South India, *circa* fourteenth century.

part one

BRAHMA

the creative

A form of Brahma, the creative force of evolution, seated on a lotus within an effulgent ovoid emanating rays. The lotus is an ancient symbol of spirituality; rising from the muddy depths, it blooms upward majestically. From a seventeenth-century south Indian sculpture.

Each person should cultivate a creative attitude in order to successfully advance along the path of love. This is a positive mental attitude, a dynamically charged state of mind, which derives its potency from the recognition that there is meaning and purpose to life. This attitude might best be called cosmic optimism. It consists in recognizing and identifying with the primal energy that has created all things. The creative attitude puts us in touch with the source of our being and endows us with a limitless capacity for evolution.

The creative attitude should remain with us always and be the touchstone by which we gauge our actions in the world. It is a feeling of self-confidence, a recognition of the Divine within each of us, a conviction that we are projections of higher principles that we can come to know. It is part of the process of evolution.

One lesson this book will endeavor to teach is that worldly or physical limitations can be overcome by invoking the creative attitude and making it work for us. Such mental attitudes have been utilized to achieve success in the world of commerce. Salesmen and top company executives are trained to imagine themselves as filled with positive energy, which creates an impenetrable barrier to any doubts or negativity.

In the area of Tantric sexuality there are many barriers to be overcome. A creative attitude works wonders in eliminating doubts or uncertainty, while at the same time acting as a potent virilific. Impotency and sexual frustration are direct effects of a lack of self-confidence, which in turn stems from a feeling of emptiness, that life has no purpose. By looking to high spiritual ideals for inspiration, we strengthen the creative attitude. An exquisite joyfulness accompanies this state of mind, so remember to evoke it at all times. Open yourself to the marvelous possibilities that will manifest. When the creative attitude is brought to bear during love-making, a wealth of variety unfolds.

Brahma, the Creator, desired that it should be so and he willed forth the Principle of the Universe; from this came the Primal Energy and from that the Mind. Then there evolved the subtle elements and from these the many worlds. From the acts performed by beings in those worlds the chain of cause and effect was established.

MUNDAKA UPANISHAD

Saraswati, the consort of Brahma, has a bodily luster more powerful than the light of ten million moons. Her garments are purified by celestial fire. She is the Mother of the Vedas, the very embodiment of Nature and the Patroness of the Arts and Sciences. She is always smiling and is exceedingly beautiful; her body is decorated with jewels and pearls.

SARASWATI STOTRA

Brahma and Saraswati

Brahma is the name of the creative aspect of the Divine. The symbol of Brahma is a golden egg or aura, the substance of which is infinite positive energy. In Tantric cosmology, Brahma is the embodiment of all creativity. Since Brahma rules over destiny and the things of the world, it is considered imperative to "become Brahma" or "have Brahma on your side." The Eastern teachings state that one can become a thing by identifying with it. Through identification, the power of creativity can work in the individual at all times.

Recognizing the reality of the creative as co-essential with one's own being, a new awareness emerges like radiance from the central "seed" of the Golden Egg. A useful and very effective technique for identifying with Brahma and the creative universal energy is to visualize yourself surrounded by a golden egg or aura of positively charged energy. See yourself radiating golden sunbeams, warming and invigorating, illuminating life itself.

The senses are the instruments of the Creative. Originating in the subtle inner realm of Brahma, they manifest on the surface of reality and are expressed in the sense organs, the eyes, ears, nose, mouth and skin. These instruments must be finely tuned to serve as sensitive conduits to the Divine Principle within. Esoteric traditions consider mind the instrument of the sixth sense. When the mind assumes the creative attitude, it functions as the organ of the sixth sense.

Saraswati is the Indian name given to the feminine Energy counterpart of Brahma, the Creative. She is always referred to as "Patroness of the Sixty-four Arts," of which the Art of Love is considered foremost. The feminine Energy or "Shakti" is the power of the Creative, without which no act of creation can proceed. So it is that Brahma and Saraswati are the creative Cosmic Couple, inseparable as the Creative Aspect and the Creative Energy. This dualism is found in all worldly relationships. The unity of these two principles is of particular significance to the path of Tantric love. When couples identify themselves with these high ideals, all relative aspects of their intimate relationship take on an inner and absolute significance. This is of great importance in the Art of Love.

The symbol of Saraswati is an Indian seven-stringed musical instrument known

Brahma is depicted in human form, seated on lotus petals and holding a lotus flower. Golden rays of light emanate outward from the cosmic egg of Brahma. The lotus is a universal symbol of spirituality. From an Indian painting of the eighteenth century.

as the Vina. The Vina has gourds as sounding boxes at each end of a fretted fingerboard. Its sensual shape is evocative of the body of a woman; the sound it makes is like a beautiful voice. It is the "instrument of the senses," the pleasure of Brahma. By playing on the Vina the goddess Saraswati expresses her joy in creation.

The seven strings of Saraswati's Vina symbolize the sevenfold nature of evolution, the seven rays of creation, the natural order of change found in all worldly phenomena. In science we find this sevenfold division of elements in the Periodic Table, based on relative atomic weights. In music it occurs in the scale; a ray of light is naturally divided into seven

The Patroness of the Arts. From a Japanese painting of the seventeenth century.

colors and in the Subtle Body of Tantra there are also seven stages. This sevenfold principle occurs throughout all esoteric literature.

Both Brahma and Saraswati should be visualized as golden and radiant. Like the sun, they emit creative, invigorating light, producing growth and evolution. Through identification with these higher Cosmic Truths, the couple can derive tremendous benefits. It is an abstract and at the same time a specific meditation, a support and an inner strength of vast potential. By "becoming Brahma and Saraswati" the couple can evoke the creative archetype of their existence.

Mystic form of Saraswati, depicted playing the Vina. Her four arms symbolize that she is the embodiment of the four Vedas, the branches of all knowledge. From a nineteenth-century Nepalese painting.

Out of Brahma, which is the Higher Self, came space; out of space, air; out of air, fire; out of fire, water; out of water, earth; out of earth, vegetation; out of vegetation, food; out of food, the body of all humanity.   TAITTRIYA UPANISHAD

When one becomes Saraswati all the Sixty-four Arts are immediately knowable. She is the Mother of the Vedas, the Auspicious One.   SARASWATI STOTRA

Brahma began the process of creation. Dividing into man and woman, they made love. Together Brahma and Saraswati begat the whole race of mortals.   SHIVA PURANA

the sixty-four arts

BRAHMA

the creative

The *Kama Sutra*, the classical Indian treatise on the Art of Love, enumerates the Sixty-four Arts. The text advises that these should be studied along with the *Kama Sutra*, preferably under the guidance of a teacher. These arts and sciences (for no distinction between them was then made) include singing, music, dancing, writing, drawing, painting, sewing, reading, recitation, poetry, sculpture, gymnastics, games, flower arranging, cooking, decoration, perfumery, gardening, mimicry, mental exercises, languages, etiquette, carpentry, magic, chemistry, minerology, gambling, architecture, logic, charm-making, religious rites, household management, disguise, physical sports, and martial arts plus many specialized activities related to the culture and time. The accomplishments expected of young women in Victorian times echoed this idea. To update this, the arts related to more recent technical innovations, such as photography, could be added.

The Indian treatises on love suggest that both men and women should be well versed in as many of the Sixty-four Arts as possible. Three arguments as to why these arts should be studied are presented in the texts. First, a person who is accomplished in them is automatically given an honorable place in society. Second, through the application of these arts one can more easily win over the object of desire, be it husband, wife or lover, and provide more fulfillment. Third, a single person can easily be self-supporting by the application of these skills. Even a bare knowledge of these arts adds to the charm and interest of a person.

In the West today, over-specialization is a problem, which tends to inhibit the mind's capacity to intuitively express the many facets of knowledge. Yet the Art of Love relies on the other arts for its support. Without these modes of expression our existence would be boring and restrictive. Humanity depends upon these arts as a means of communication and self-expression.

There is no Western equivalent of the *Kama Sutra*, and perhaps for this reason, sex as an art form has yet to mature in the West. Social repression and internalized guilt have prevented Westerners from a frank and joyous exploration of sexuality, today's "liberated attitudes" notwithstanding. Practically all that the Occident offers in this area is pornography, or clinical sex manuals, so filled with anatomical details and "techniques" that they would be sufficient to put a person off sex for life. One result of this repression is inhuman sexual perversion, a subject we will treat in more detail later. The sexual act is rarely tastefully portrayed in Western art or literature. We either reject sex altogether as a subject proper to art or, in lieu of better, accept mediocre treatment of it.

The Orient did not consider sex apart from, or opposed to, spirituality or religion. The sex act was given a place of honor and was intimately connected with the other arts. Men and women alike studied the *Kama Sutra* and similar texts. In the temples,

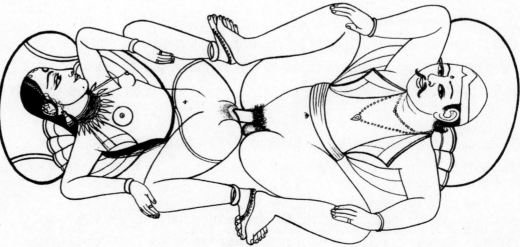

A Hindu maharaja in Tantric union with his consort. This unusual posture is particularly suitable for circulating energy during prolonged love-making. From a miniature painting in the collection of the King of Nepal, *circa* 1830.

all variations of sexual postures were openly portrayed and venerated as ideals. In the privacy of the home, the entire range of erotic art and literature was considered a normal and respectable subject of study.

The parameters of sexual behavior in the East extend way beyond the West's narrow spectrum of normalcy, without the least debasement of the sexual function. Celibacy, monogamy, polygamy and polyandry all had a place in Oriental culture.

The Sixty-four Arts should be conceived as the Paths of creative Energy. They are the emanations of the goddess Saraswati, the "anima" of Jungian psychology. They can be likened to the flames of an inner sun, blazing from the solar plexus. Burning up all negativity, these flames of the creative attitude purify the psyche and bring about an inner transformation. As practical skills of the outer world, they delight others and fulfill the talented practitioner.

A royal couple kneeling in mutual adoration. From a miniature painting in collection of the King of Nepal, *circa* 1830.

A person should study the Sixty-four Arts and sciences, as also the sixty-four aspects of sexual union.
KAMA SUTRA

At the navel region of the body there is a subtle center of transformation. It can be considered like a lotus with sixty-four petals, or a vital sun with sixty-four flames. The color of it is golden and it is turned upward.
SECRET TEACHING OF NAROPA

the temple of the body

The physical body is the temple of the soul, the microcosm of the universe. Within this temple are found all of the cosmic principles. The Tantras teach that no temple surpasses in sanctity the "Temple of the Body." All the elements, space, air, fire, water and earth, are found within the body, together with their properties. The bodily temple has its "gardens," "rivers," "sanctuaries" and "gates." By definition, a temple is a place of worship, an edifice dedicated to the service of God. This God, according to Tantra, is our highest self or soul, to be known and served through the Temple of the Body.

Tantra teaches that there are nine "gates" to the bodily temple. These are divided between the upper part and the lower part. The "lower gates" are the orifices of the anus and the sexual organ. The "upper gates" are the mouth, nose, two eyes, two ears and the fontanel opening at the top of the head. The fontanel is clearly visible as an opening at the time of birth, but it gradually closes up during the first year of life. Eastern esoteric tradition tells us that through this opening, known as the "Aperture of Brahma," the soul enters and leaves the bodily temple. Though the other gates may be used by the soul in its journeys, it is the uppermost one that leads to the higher spiritual realms.

The Temple of the Subtle Body contains three main "rivers," from which branch out innumerable tributaries. One Great River or "psychic pathway" runs from the region of the lower gates, the perineum, up the spine to the uppermost gate at the top of the head. This is sometimes referred to as the Great Axis, the Holy Mount Meru, or just the Great Pathway. It connects the individual with the cosmos.

At either side of the central Great River are two "rivers" that emanate from the same source and lead to the upper "gates." These are associated with the solar and lunar energies, related to the right and left sides of the body respectively. They are conceived of as crossing the central Great River at stages in the ascent, like twin snakes wound around a central staff. This symbol, known as the caduceus, or wand of Mercury, has been adopted as an emblem by the medical profession.

Twin snakes around a central column. This ancient Hermetic symbol, the caduceus, clearly illustrates the basic concept of the Subtle Body. The rising swirling energies of the snakes produce an ascending vortex of power, used in Tantra for personal transformation.

Lovers depicted in a Tantric posture for channeling energy upward. Mutual adoration uplifts the senses and helps the circulation and transformation of energy. From a Rajasthan miniature painting, India, *circa* 1800.

The act of worship in the Temple of the Body consists in focusing the creative attitude by channeling the sex energy upward. The evolutionary process, experienced as an ecstatic thrill, rises up from the sexual region and flares at the solar plexus. The sixty-four vital flames burn up all negativity and purify the psychic pathways. The fire of love floods the three rivers and the solar and lunar energies unite, thus illuminating the temple. This psycho-cosmic process manifests as the ecstatic emotion, which no words can truly describe. Through knowledge of the psychic pathways, the sexual experience becomes more potent. By practicing the secret techniques of Tantra one can consciously experience orgasm and the ensuing transcendental delight.

The psycho-cosmic process or "self-worship" in the Temple of the Body takes place on every level, from the physical to the most subtle. It is important to really regard the body as a temple. Awareness of its physical and subtle condition is an integral part of the creative attitude. The bodily temple should be kept clean, healthy and harmonious, out of respect for the divinity within. Provide enjoyment and spare no effort to ensure the temple divinity's complete satisfaction. Do not hold back, for real worship is a spontaneous and total act of love. By worshipping in the Temple of the Body during love-making, all desires are fulfilled. That sensual love is an act of great magical and spiritual potency is one of the main principles of Tantra.

Here in this body are the sacred rivers; here are the sun and moon, as well as all the pilgrimage places. I have not encountered another temple as blissful as my own body.

SARAHA DOHA

When my beloved returns to the house, I shall make my body into a Temple of Gladness. Offering this body as an altar of joy, my let-down hair will sweep it clean. Then my beloved will consecrate this temple.

VAISNAV BAUL SONG

head and heart

The head and the heart are two distinct parts of the body that, in the West, are a cause of psychic disunity. But the Temple of the Body, though comprising many parts, is in fact a Divine Unity. We speak of the "heart ruling the head" when someone seems to have lost all common sense and is prey to emotions. The head is said to rule the heart when the mind is calculating and unmoved by human feeling. In both cases, one center dominates at the expense of the other. This dichotomy of head and heart always produces a breakdown of intimacy in a relationship. It is completely incompatible with the selfless ecstasy of Tantric love.

In Western mystical traditions, one frequently encounters the idea of "renouncing the flesh for the sake of the soul." This is, in reality, a hopeless endeavor. For whatever is repressed will inevitably erupt, usually at the most inopportune moment. The Tantric way teaches that we must use all our endowments of mind, body, head and heart, on the Path to Liberation. Through the consecration of all parts of our being to an exalted purpose, we integrate them into a whole. In this way, the emotions and passions of the heart can be transformed into the joy of transcendent ecstasy. This transformation takes place through the interplay of head and heart, reason and emotion. The Tantric image of this process is the heart's "fire of emotion" melting and distilling the head's "waters of wisdom."

The notion of exchange and mutual enrichment is an essential ingredient of Tantric love-making. It makes possible a true exchange between the lovers. The path of Tantric love encompasses all aspects of the emotions and intellect. It leads to an experience of cosmic ecstasy through awareness of the Universal Self in both partners.

A Tantric love-making posture. From an Indian miniature of the eighteenth century.

When there is only worldly enjoyment, there is no release. And when there is only release, there is no worldly enjoyment. But both worldly enjoyment and release are in the palm of the hand of those who are devoted to the Higher Being.

KAULARAHASYA

By those same deeds which create bondage for dualistically inclined beings, one can be liberated from the bondage of this world. The main principle is that the act must be accompanied by non-dualism between "head" and "heart."

ADVAYASIDDHI

breaking habits

Personal growth can be accelerated simply by changing one's habits. It is the condition of dependency inherent in habits that must be broken. When you find yourself saying or thinking, "But I can't change *that* . . . . I *always* do that," then *that* is undoubtedly the first habit to break. Freedom of choice results from mastering habit. Independence from habits in the area of sexuality should be cultivated, as sexual habits are the most restrictive. Any intentional act of will has a magical potency and is far more effective than a habitual or unintentional act. The human body is capable of quite extraordinary adaptation, even when it seems set in a rigid pattern. The potential for change is always there, but it is better not to wait for a moment of crisis before ridding ourselves of habits. Our very survival as a species is due to our ability to change and adapt.

Mental habits are more difficult to deal with than physical ones, as they are less obvious. Often enough, they are inherited from parents or acquired through social conditioning. They restrict our whole way of life, insidiously providing a false sense of security. By causing us to forget our Higher Selves, they obliterate our awareness and are fatal to an intimate relationship. Frequently, an unawareness of disagreeable habits or idiosyncrasies is a source of contention between people. Yet often, all that's needed to overcome this obstacle is the willingness, on the part of both people, to change, grow and evolve. When the initial fear of change is overcome, one can really begin to enjoy new experiences. Sexual habits are especially limiting and it is here that Tantra requires absolute adaptability. All Eastern teachings on the sexual mysteries point to the need for variety and uninhibited spontaneity.

Where there is ecstasy, there is Creation;
Where there is no ecstasy, there is no Creation.
In the Infinite, there is ecstasy;
There is no ecstasy in the finite.
CHANDOGYA UPANISHAD

The louse of habit-forming thoughts is both self-originated and self-destructive. Kill this louse and find the teaching.

TILOPA

Love resulting from the constant and continual performance of some act is called love acquired by habit.

KAMA SUTRA

self-examination

Self-examination is vital to the evolutionary path of love. Only in an atmosphere of complete honesty can unconscious psychic impediments to our growth be cleared away. When we turn our consciousness inward to reflect upon the self, a new sensitivity unfolds. Self-examination helps to renew and fine-tune the senses. Sexual habits are particularly dulling to the senses, and it is here that self-examination is of great value.

If one partner depends exclusively on the other for support and comfort rather than seeking these within, the result can be a burdensome imbalance in the relationship. Real love places no value on projection of selfish fantasies onto the other. This does not allow room for the play of ecstatic, spontaneous love, which is the goal of Tantra. Instead, a relationship becomes limiting; it may even drag both partners into an unresolvable conflict.

Failures in both love and marriage often result when one partner does not live up to the expectations of the other. This suggests that there is no real partnership, but rather that one partner is being selfish with the other. In this situation a couple lives together in an inner state of separation and hypocrisy.

In the *Tao Te Ching*, a Chinese philosophical work of the sixth century B.C., there is a beautiful and clear statement about self-knowledge. The author, Lao-tzu, declares: "Knowing others leads to Wisdom; knowing the self leads to Enlightenment. Mastering others requires force; mastering the self calls for inner strength."

Self-examination is both a touchstone and a support in life. It strengthens the mental attitude necessary for self-development. It is a very personal practice and should not be made a topic of general conversation, for doing so results in psychic dispersion and weakened self-confidence. Positive self-examination deepens the capacity for intuitive experiences. It creates a state of enhanced receptivity. By seeing ourselves in a clear light, we can eliminate negativity and doubt, which tend to pollute our relationships. Authenticity within the couple fosters spontaneity, thus liberating the relationship from the conventional and predictable. Invoke an earnest desire to know your true self. Put aside self-doubt and fears.

Self-examination is a prerequisite of any practice of meditation. It can be performed at any time and is an internal reflective process far removed from the mind's chatter and random thoughts.

Self-examination starts with the observation of one's relation to the things and events of the world. Try to view all experiences as connected to one another and to oneself; notice the fine details and

Meditation posture, traditionally referred to as *padmasana*, meaning "lotus seat." The second finger and thumb are linked, to aid channeling of psychic energy.

cultivate an inquisitive but detached attitude. Examine whatever comes to you and try to understand the causes behind each situation and your actions in it. A simple procedure for self-examination is to sit comfortably in front of a mirror, close your eyes and empty your mind of all thoughts. Then gradually begin to open your eyes, looking at the reflection in the mirror as if meeting that person for the first time. See what sort of impression you make on yourself. Notice how changes in your facial expressions are linked to thoughts and emotions. Gradually enter into rapport with your mirror image, gently relaxing your face while maintaining conscious control of breathing. If you notice negative qualities in your reflection, make a careful adjustment of attitude and emotion, using the breath to stabilize the psyche. Imagine that you are replacing a negative quality with a positive one, and try to feel the "new you" as real and lasting. Then gradually close your eyes and concentrate on assimilating the experience, imagining it as pervading your whole being.

The essence of meditation is using the mind to know the self. External objects can help in meditation, but should not be relied upon exclusively. A lit candle can, for example, be a helpful aid to self-examination. Study the flame and focus all thought upon it. Then compare qualities in yourself with the bright dancing candlelight. Imagine that the flames are burning away all the impurities in your psyche. Then mentally center an image of the candle flame between your eyes and keep it burning in your mind. Bathe your whole

being with this inner light of the mind and use it as a focus for self-examination.

By knowing yourself you can come to know others. Don't criticize others before correcting faults in yourself. Only through self-examination can you develop real insight. Real insight requires courage and rigorous honesty. An attitude of constant self-examination will quickly overcome inner obstacles to growth and generate a marvelous potential for Tantric love. Self-examination is the most direct path to the experience of non-duality and mystic awareness. Only in that experience can a physical relationship take on a lasting meaning.

Padmasana, the lotus posture of Hatha Yoga, a comfortable and balanced position that is described in the *Shiva Samhita* in the following way: "Cross the legs, carefully placing the feet on opposite thighs. Fix the eyes on the tip of the nose and press the tongue against the roof of the mouth, behind the teeth. Inhale and exhale slowly, in an unobstructed stream. By this practice the vital airs are balanced and the whole organism harmonized."

Constantly maintain alertness of consciousness in walking, sitting, eating, sleeping and in all other acts. Avoid concealing your own faults and speaking of the faults of others. Should thought processes be difficult to control, be sure to persevere in your efforts to overcome them. Know that the meditator, the object of meditation and the act of meditation constitute an inseparable unity.

GAMPOPA

The mind is wavering and restless, difficult to guard and hard to restrain; let the wise person straighten his mind, just as an arrow maker makes his arrows straight.

DHAMMAPADA

bhakti and shakti

BRAHMA

the creative

There are two important requirements for the person embarking on a journey of self-awareness. These are the provisions that sustain one on the journey. The first is Bhakti, meaning faith or devotion. This quality can make the impossible possible. On the spiritual path, faith dissolves self-doubt, and devotion speeds one rapidly to the goal. By maintaining faith in the higher direction of evolution, one will overcome all obstacles. Faith has no substance, but is a deep feeling; people generally cannot say *why* they have faith, they just *know* and believe.

The erotic sentiment stimulates faith and leads to commitment. Eroticism can create the awareness of a timeless state of non-duality. There is an Eastern saying that "in the unsteady mind enters time"; faith

The cosmic couple, Shiva and Shakti, seated together in spiritual ecstasy. As Animus and Anima, they symbolize the union of consciousness and energy by the power of faith and devotion. From an Indian painting, Kangra Hills, *circa* eighteenth century.

is a timeless and steadying experience that can transform an ordinary physical love relationship into the supersensual union of a "god" and "goddess," the highest attributes of our spirits. The truly erotic experience is always timeless; the couple evoke faith in each other and awaken the non-dual essence within. So it is with faith in the cosmic nature of our consciousness and in the highest spiritual ideals common to every inner tradition. Test your faith by the practice of self-examination; open in your heart a field within which lasting faith can grow. Be devoted to everything you believe in and especially to the transforming power of sexual energy. A couple who are united in faith and mutual devotion can experience their true natures as god and goddess.

The second provision for the journey is *Shakti*, the Divine Energy of Creation, the exalted feminine principle that pervades all things. The term "Shakti" has several connotations, all of which relate to creative energy. In the human body this energy is located primarily in the sexual region. It is the power of transformation, an uplifting and liberating force that, when awakened, leads to the ecstasy of fulfillment. It is the power of the orgasm, the thrill of sexual delight, the sudden flash of insight. Shakti exists on many different levels, from the physical to the very subtle. When Shakti is evoked during sexual love, the couple can

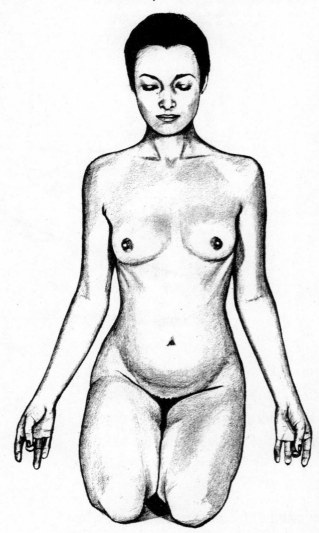

Virasana, or heroic posture, of Hatha Yoga is both easy and comfortable. It is ideal for meditation and breathing practices.

awaken to a new creative potential within themselves. Recognizing and honoring Shakti opens the path of love.

There is a well-known Tantric saying that "without Shakti the lover is but a corpse." Shakti is especially concentrated in woman and it is this power that enables her to give birth. The term "Shakti" therefore can also refer to the female partner, without whom no act of Tantric love can be completed. An "inner woman" exists in both men and women and manifests as sexual energy. This natural (bisexual) quality of all human beings results from our origin through the union of the two sexes. The attempt to suppress this natural androgyny in favor of an exaggerated "male" or "female" emphasis has created serious psychological imbalance in the West. Psychiatrists report sexual role confusion as one of the dominant neuroses in contemporary society.

A liberated attitude to sexuality demands an awareness of the natural bisexuality of all human beings. The couple should make full use of this kind of awareness during love-making and playfully exchange sex roles, recognizing that there is a female in every male and a male in every female. Both Taoist and Tantric teachings state that it is important to recognize the significance of role reversals when engaging in mystic sexual practices. This does not mean that a man needs to become "effeminate" or a woman "aggressive." Rather it means one should let go of preconceptions about sexual roles and allow spontaneity to enrich the relationship. Honor male and female qualities equally. Try to understand the mystery of life through the subtle interplay of male and female principles. All that is created is but an emanation of the one Creative Force of Nature. In this world the female principle, or *Adi Shakti* (Original Shakti), is particularly exalted and as such should be greatly honored.

A man's attitude toward women is a direct reflection of his attitude toward life. Therefore a man should always take care to honor the female principle in his partner, in other women and in himself. Likewise, a woman should recognize the qualities of the Goddess in herself and try to embody them. She should also try to relate to the "inner woman" of her partner, aiming to please both aspects of the One Creative

Lord Shiva the Supreme Yogi, seated with Parvati, his consort. This male/female icon, known as Bhairav Raga, tells of the power inherent in sexual harmonizaton. From an Indian miniature painting, Deccan, *circa* eighteenth century.

It is important for couples to explore sexual roles and positions spontaneously. From a contemporary photograph.

Power or Shakti. When a man spontaneously views his partner as an embodiment of Supreme Shakti, the Creative Goddess, she will respond with Bhakti, pure faith and devotion. She will become his high priestess and initiatress into the mysteries of love; he will then reveal himself as her Lord and Lover.

BRAHMA

the creative

The great goddess Kameshwari in the Yogic posture known as *bhagasana*, with feet together and Yogis making obeisance to a representation of the Yoni. Kameshwari is the Original Shakti or power principle of Tantra and is here portrayed in her lustful form. This image, from the sixty-four-Yogini Temple of Bheraghat, Madhya Pradesh, was totally disfigured by Moslem invaders who viewed the Hindu elevation of feminine energy as heretical. From a stone sculpture of the early twelfth century (we have restored some of the damaged details in this drawing).

Shakti is the essence of Bliss; she is the love-power. Bhakti or devotion is the uplifting force of faith.

DEVI PURANA

Shakti performs all the physical needs of Shiva. The bodiless Shiva, being of the nature of Pure Consciousness, must have the creative energy of Shakti for support.

KAMAKALAVILASA

Shiva and jiva

In the previous section we dealt with the relationship between faith and devotion and the Creative Energy. We introduced the concept of androgyny, the male and female within each of us. Any discussion of the Tantric view of Shakti as the exalted female principle automatically calls to mind her counterpart, Shiva, the exalted male principle. In the central part of this book we explore the meaning of Shiva from a transcendental viewpoint. Here we shall briefly examine the relationship between Shiva and Shakti, so the reader may recognize the exalted male principle within. Finally, the metaphysical meaning of Shiva will be presented. The Indian terminology may at first appear formidable, but a little patience will prove it useful, as the innate simplicity of the Tantric teaching becomes apparent.

Shiva, the exalted male principle, is found within both man and woman. Referred to in the ancient texts as the "Great God" or the "Immortal Divine Principle," Shiva's symbol is the erect phallus, the Lingam, which represents the Great Spirit in a state of excitement. The stimulus is the Creative Energy, the Shakti, swirling around Shiva's cosmic erection like an ocean of every-changing variety, a veritable sea of sensation.

The ancient Egyptians, Greeks, Romans and other pre-Christian peoples worshipped the phallus as the symbol of the exalted male principle. Shiva is the Yogic archetype par excellence, the evolutionary Lord of All Creatures. The Shiva-principle is directly related to the mental function and to the Eternal Spirit. In ancient mythology the god Shiva is referred to as "the One who conquers death." This conquest is achieved through the power of Tantric Yoga, the union of Shiva and Shakti. The whole universe is created out of the union of Shiva and Shakti, the cosmic male and female archetypes.

In Eastern iconography Shiva is portrayed as a Lingam, an abstract phallic form, a Lingam with a face, a column, a seated or standing Yogi with Lingam erect and in many multi-armed anthropomorphic forms. The Tantras teach that there is a Lingam within each Yoni. This observation refers anatomically to the clitoris, which is capable of erection when excited, and also reminds us of the inherent bisexuality of the female.

Knowledge of Shiva, the Transcendental, permits passage through the doorway to other worlds. Identify with the vital mind energy of Shiva during Tantric love-making. This will eventually cause an experience of transcendence beyond your normal worldly role or limitations. Shiva is experienced as a penetration into the depths of space, as being pulled out into the universe, beyond all knowable things or events. The *Shiva Samhita*, an important Hindu Tantric text, declares that "those who experience the Shiva-principle are heroic, enterprising, freed from the effects of blind emotions, skillful, persevering, talented, contented and firm-minded."

Lingam stone with face of Shiva carved on it. Known as Ekamukhalinga (One-Faced Lingam), this type of image is used as a focus in acts of worship and ritual. The Third Eye of Shiva is shown open and the face in ecstatic blissfulness. From a stone sculpture, Madhya Pradesh, *circa* fourth century.

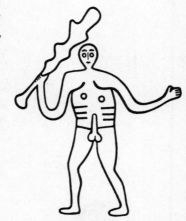

Giant primitive figure with phallus erect. Cut into the turf of a chalk hillside, this type of image indicates the sexual emphasis in pagan beliefs. Cerne Abbas, Dorset, England, probably of the time of the early Roman invasion of Britain.

Ityphallic figure of Shiva, the Supreme Yogi. He holds a club, signifying his all-powerful role as the Yogic ideal. Stone sculpture from Jageshwar, Uttar Pradesh, India, *circa* tenth century.

Yogic lotus posture with hands joined in salutation to the divine Shiva-principle within.

The Jiva dwells in the body of man and woman and is adorned with a garland of endless desires. The Jiva is chained to the body by the various Karmas amassed in previous lives. Whatever happens to an individual is born of Karma; all people enjoy or suffer according to the results of their actions. The Jiva that has accumulated an excess of virtuous actions receives a happy life and gets pleasant enjoyments from the world. The Jiva that has accumulated an excess of evil never rests in peace. Of whatever nature is the desire, that nature clings to and accompanies the Jiva through its various incarnations.

The concepts of Shiva and Jiva, the exalted male principle and the immortal individual soul, are of great significance to anyone who wishes to practice Tantric love. If you identify with Shiva, the Transcendental, you will realize a deeper insight into the essentially divine nature of the interplay between male and female. If you conceive your partner as the embodiment of the transcendental, beyond prediction and known limits, the experience of transcendence will enter your relationship. If you serve the loved one with faith and devotion, the creative Shakti-energy will awaken the Shiva-principle within. With Shakti as its counterpart, the Shiva-force of pure consciousness arises. Through the intimate union of Shiva and Shakti in ecstatic delight, the Jiva, the individual soul, becomes freed from the bondage of past lives. Then the couple can truly soar to the heights of Liberation.

When the male organ is honored as the Shiva Lingam, sex takes on a deep transcendental significance.

We cannot know the transcendental from our limited everyday viewpoint, as by definition it transcends the boundaries of the sense-perceptible universe. The Hindu term "Jiva" expresses a similar concept; the "Eternal, Unchangeable Essence, without beginning or end," the Immortal Soul, the very principle of life. Jiva is also used to refer to the individual soul and is likened to a single ray from the solar orb of Brahma, the Creative. Thus Hinduism does not consider the individual soul as in any way separate from its original Divine Source.

The *Shiva Samhita* gives a concise account of the nature and function of the Jiva. It states:

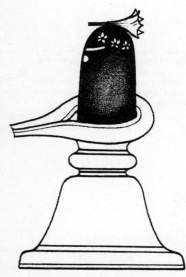

Natural Lingam stone installed in Yoni base. During rituals of worship flowers and other offerings are placed on top of the stone and milk, oil and holy water are poured over it. Here a datura flower, symbolic of divine intoxication, is offered on the Lingam. From an Indian painting, Kangra valley, *circa* eighteenth century.

There is a bridge between Time and Eternity; this bridge is the individual soul, the Jiva.

CHANDOGYA UPANISHAD

Shiva's love-play transforms the universe. The sexual activity of Shiva and Shakti makes the moon wax and wane. Shiva finds that his consort becomes a Yogini [female ascetic] whenever he practices Hatha Yoga, and when he is filled with the desire for making love, she becomes a lustful mistress.

SHIVA PURANA

The whole universe was created from the seed that poured from the erect Lingam of Shiva during his love-making. All the gods worship that Lingam, the symbol of Lord Shiva, the Supreme Yogi.

MAHABHARATA

There is a well-known saying that "breath is life." When the breathing process ceases, life is quickly extinguished; yet people take breathing very much for granted. When a baby is born, the first breath is vital. If there is any obstacle or delay, the child will die. At the other end of life, the last breath marks the individual's departure to another dimension. Between the points of birth and death, there is constant breathing, which in most people is totally unconscious.

The Yoga teachings stress the supreme importance of breath. According to ancient Yogic texts, the average healthy adult takes 21,600 breaths during the course of a complete day and night. This means an overall average of fifteen breaths per minute, or one breath every four seconds. In fact, a person generally breathes less frequently when at rest and more rapidly during extreme exertion. Love-making produces an increase in the rate of breathing, comparable to the effect of a hard run or prolonged jogging. A particularly energetic burst of love-making creates all the physical symptoms of an athletic breakthrough; the heart pounds and the blood rushes through the veins. Eastern mystic teachings stress the value of prolonged love-making in conjunction with deep and controlled breathing.

According to Yogic tradition, life expectancy is linked to the frequency of breathing. This certainly seems to be true of reptiles and mammals; the tortoise breathes very slowly and lives long, whereas the mouse breathes fast and has a very short life. According to the *Gheranda Samhita*, a Yogic source book of the mediaeval period, "By decreasing the frequency of breath, there takes place an increase of life energy; by increasing the breathing rate, life energy is decreased." Another important Hindu text, the *Shiva Samhita*, states: "The body of the person practicing the regulation of breath becomes harmoniously developed, emits sweet scent and becomes strong and beautiful. The wise practitioner surely destroys all his Karma, whether acquired in this life or in the past, through the regulation of breath." Many Yogis devote themselves exclusively to gaining conscious control of the breathing function, believing that by doing so, they can become masters of their destiny.

Right now, without changing your normal breathing, place one hand on the region of the abdomen, just below the solar plexus. See whether your breathing reaches down that far and notice whether the abdomen is distended on completion of inhalation. Natural breathing should work this way, with the lower region protruding as the breath is drawn in, and contracting as it is expelled. However, most people breathe contrary to the natural way. Generally, the breath is drawn in only to the region of the chest. Also, many people breathe only through the mouth, instead of through the nose, and under physical exertion, they pant through the open mouth. The long-term effect of such breathing is loss of the ability to concentrate, physical debility and heart trouble. Tantric teachings declare that if lovers breathe in an unnatural way and exert themselves excessively, there is a real danger of premature aging, impotence, inability to climax, emotional and mental problems, as well as general physical debility. Both Tantric and Taoist texts emphasize that love-breathing should preferably be deep, from the diaphragm, through the nose, with the consciousness focused on the assimilation and retention of life energy.

Many popular books are available that deal extensively with Yoga postures (asanas) and breathing techniques (*Pranayama*). Since we are covering this subject from the point of view of sexuality, we will not attempt a comprehensive teaching on Yogic breathing. However, it is helpful to consider one or two points here. First, be aware of the natural division of the breathing process. It has three parts: the in-breath, the retention and the out-breath.

The in-breath should be natural and never forced; air should flow into the body *as a result of* the expansion of the abdomen. When the breath is retained, the lower part of the body should take the shape of a pot; the Yoga term for this is *kumbhak*, meaning "container." The retention of breath is the point of greatest potency. During this period the inhaled air is partly absorbed by the lungs, vitalizing the whole body. The out-breath or exhalation rids the system of waste and surplus products. Tantric teachings advise that during inhalation one should imagine oneself absorbing the life-giving energies of Brahma. During retention one should focus on extracting the life force of the air and circulating it through the whole body. During exhalation one should imagine all negativity, physical ailments or tension leaving the body and returning to the earth for purification. These three parts of the breathing process should interact smoothly, without any harsh or jerky movements. Furthermore, one should cultivate mental awareness of the movement of breath in and out of the body.

It is the conscious retention of breath that is the most crucial element. Conscious breath retention strengthens the circulation and reinforces the subtle connections among all parts of the body. It also produces an increase in body secretions, particularly saliva, which, according to Yogic teachings, is vitalizing and nourishing. The *Goraksashatakam*, a Yogic text of the mediaeval period, aptly states: "One should inhale breath slowly and exhale it likewise, neither exceeding one's capacity to retain it nor exhaling too rapidly. Breath control frees the bonds of Karma and establishes harmony and balance throughout the organism."

The *complete breath*—conscious inhalation, retention and exhalation—is the first step toward using the breathing function as a means to Liberation. Having established a healthy and harmonious pattern of breath, one can then advance to specific breathing *rhythms*. The *healing breath*, for example, is extremely simple and can be practiced at any time. It consists of a conscious alteration of the proportions of time spent on each part of the breathing cycle. This new breath rhythm is particularly suited to the extraction of vital energy from the atmosphere. The new ratio will seem unnatural at first and the body will take time to adapt to it, so do not force things, but be patient.

In the *healing breath* the ratio of inhalation to retention to exhalation is 1:4:2, retention lasting four times as long as inhalation, and exhalation lasting twice as long as inhalation. The in-breath establishes the measure for determining the other two time periods. At first make the period of inhalation slightly longer than normal and proportion the periods of retention and exhalation

accordingly. Then gradually increase the measure of inhalation, adjusting to it the periods of the other parts. The result of this practice is a slowing down of the breathing process, which relaxes and heals both body and mind.

Never practice the technique of the healing breath to the point of physical strain. If you feel dizzy or tired, or if your heart starts beating rapidly, you are overdoing the practice, so take it easier. The proportion of the three parts can be measured either against the heartbeat (which can be noted by moving the fingers without counting) or a clock. But the proportions should never be mentally counted, for counting while meditating tends to negate the benefits of meditation. The reason is that the mind becomes filled with the logical process of counting and cuts itself off from the abstract process of meditation.

An ideal method of measuring the proportion of breaths is to focus the mind on the sounds of inhalation and exhalation, so creating a measure with an audio rhythm. Various Yogic texts refer to different sounds of breathing. For example, the *Gheranda Samhita* states:

In entering, the breath of every person makes the sound "SAH," and in coming out, the sound "HAM." These two sounds make the power words "SAHAM" (or "SOHAM," meaning "I am it") or "HAMSA" (meaning "Great Swan" or "Bird of the Soul"). Every living being performs this repetition, but normally it is unconscious. This subtle sound reverberates in three places; in the sexual center (between the anus and sexual organ), in the heart center (the heart) and in the Third Eye center (just above the point where the nostrils unite). The Yogi should perform this repetition consciously, measuring and changing the inhalation length and adjusting the retention and exhalation accordingly.

An additional and effective method of measuring the proportion of breathing is to make up a positively charged power phrase such as "I am surrounded by a positive protective aura," using its length as a measure while visualizing this aura as a golden light surrounding the body. Similarly, one can use a Mantra or power word repeated for each part of the breath cycle. Walking is an ideal time to practice and develop the healing breath, since you can use your pacing to measure the proportion of inhalation, retention and exhalation.

The correct practice of complete and healing breaths vitalizes and invigorates the whole body. The mind also benefits and can, by this practice, be brought under conscious control. According to the *Hathayoga Pradapika*, "When the breath is in motion, the mind is also in motion; if the breath is controlled, the mind is also controlled." The aim of all Yogic breathing exercises is, ultimately, the prolongation of retention, which leads to supernormal powers and the "burning up" of all Karmas.

When the vital forces in the body are brought under the power of the creative mind, an immediate effect is experienced in the sexual center. Suddenly, you feel an overall increase in energy and sensitivity. The senses are tuned up and are able to function more effectively. Any couple wishing to experience the ecstasies of Tantric love should first develop the complete breath until it becomes totally natural. Then the healing breath should be practiced, so the vital and subtle channels of the body are purified and strengthened. This prevents physical or emotional damage from the high intensity and energy levels of Tantric love.

Th motions of the vital air, the mind and sexual energy are all interdependent. Stopping the movement of any one of these three functions also checks the others. Here we can see how closely the flow of breath relates to the sexual function and to the subtle processes of the mind, such as thought and imagination. One of the most important aspects of sexual union is the sharing of a breathing experience, for emotions are directly linked to the breath. True physical love produces a total convergence of the breath rhythms of the couple. This experience holds the key to tremendous power.

Various other breathing techniques are also helpful in preparing a couple for Tantric love-making. One secret technique, known as the Crow-beak, consists in rolling the sides of the tongue inward and protruding it slightly, all the while inhaling air through the tongue and letting it fill the "pot" of the lungs and lower diaphragm. Retain for as long as possible and then exhale through both nostrils. According to the *Shiva Samhita*, "When a person drinks air through the Crow-beak at both the times of early morning and evening twilight, all diseases or

physical weaknesses are destroyed. This practice leads to the powers of clairvoyance and other miraculous abilities."

Crow-beak breathing exercise (*Kaki Mudra*) for cooling the body and eliminating disease. Air is inhaled slowly through the curled-up tongue. Another name for this exercise is *shitali*, meaning "cool." It helps activate liver and spleen, soothes eyes and ears and cools the whole bodily system.

Yoga traditions constantly refer to a fivefold division of breath, called *Prana* (life force). It is said that just as a king employs officials to rule over the different portions of his kingdom, so the original *Prana* contains four other *Pranas*, each assigned to rule over a specific bodily function. Of these five subtle breaths, the original *Prana*, which is upward moving, and the *Apana*, which is downward moving, are particularly important. Tantric Yoga aims to reverse the flow of these two life currents, causing them to combine and bring about a total transformation of the psycho-organism. The *Bhagavad Gita* declares: "Some Yogis offer the *Prana* breath into the *Apana*; others the *Apana* into the *Prana*." The *Goraksashatakam* states: "The Jiva [the individual soul] is in the thrall of *Prana* and *Apana*. He who knows and controls these two forces is a true knower of Yoga and quickly tastes the ecstasy of Liberation. Drawing up the *Apana*, one should unite it with the *Prana*."

The division of the inhaled breath into the five subtle breaths takes place during the period of retention. This natural process can be the basis of an important meditation. Imagine the air entering through the nostrils as if it were a fluid less dense than water. Draw it into the body by creating a pot shape in the lower abdomen. When the process of inhalation is complete, switch to retention and imagine that all the bodily openings (ears, eyes, nose, mouth, anus, etc.) are sealed. Imagine the air dividing into five parts, taking on the nature of the Five Great Elements (space, air, fire, water and earth) and nourishing the different parts of the body. Try to "see" this process with the mind's eye. During the period of conscious retention try to extract only the best parts of the inhaled breath. Then switch to exhalation and imagine all impurities, negativities or physical ailments leaving the body and returning to the earth for regeneration.

Breath control is vital to the correct practice of Tantric or Taoist love-techniques. Breathing exercises should never be practiced immediately after a meal or after heavy exertion. Generally, it is best to introduce conscious awareness of breathing into your life gradually. Don't be afraid of the power of breath; rather, learn to use it carefully. With the breath as your ally, ecstasy is within the reach of you and your partner.

Prana, the vital breath, is born of the Self. Like a person and his shadow, the Self and the Prana are inseparable. Prana enters the body at birth so the desires of the mind, continuing from past lives, can be fulfilled.

PRANA UPANISHAD

People of wisdom do not speak of a sense of speech, a faculty of sight or of hearing, or of meditation, but only of a group of Pranas, which do all these things. For these are all manifestations of Prana.

CHARAKA SAMHITA

The practitioner of Tantra aims at stopping the unconscious flow of micro-cosmic forces by getting control of the functions of breathing, which represents the outward aspect of vital energy. The initiate must master the breathing process until it becomes a most responsive and subtle tool.

VARAHI TANTRA

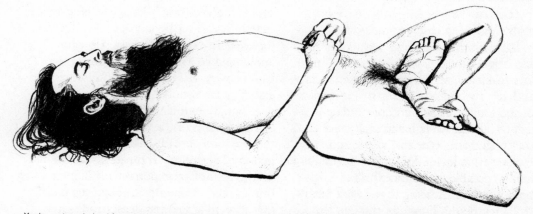

Yogic posture derived from the lotus position, lying flat, with both hands channeling energy back to the navel center of transformation. This is a very relaxing and energizing posture that helps control the upward and downward subtle energies in the body.

solar and lunar breathing

Eastern mystical teachings employ a symbolism that is derived from the belief that the components of man's inner nature are correlated with outer cosmic principles. Solar and lunar symbolism is found in all cultures based on a strong metaphysical belief structure. Since the most ancient times people have attributed specific qualities to the sun and moon. Thus, in the Hebrew tradition the sun is considered masculine in essence and is identified with the paternal archetype, whereas the moon is considered feminine and identified with the maternal archetype.

Solar and lunar symbolism is very much a part of the Yogic, Tantric and Taoist traditions. These teachings identify the right side of the body with the sun (solar forces) and the left with the moon (lunar forces). Tantra identifies solar energy with the masculine "fiery" psyche, the color red, the element fire and the intellectual processes. Conversely, lunar energy is linked to the feminine "cooling" quality (Soma), the color white, the element water and all intuitive processes.

Yogis who have spent years examining the idiosyncrasies of the breathing process have noticed that the breath changes from one side to the other at regular intervals. You can verify this right now by seeing from which nostril your breath is exhaled and inhaled. If you check this again after some time, you'll find that there has been a change over to the other nostril. The Tantras declare that the diurnal pattern of nostril breathing is caused by the influences of the sun, moon and stars.

Ancient Yogic teachings state that the dominance of breath naturally changes from one side to the other after about two hours and that the periods of change are linked directly to the passage of the moon through the zodiac. The breath sometimes comes out of the right nostril, sometimes out of the left nostril, and sometimes out of both nostrils. The science of breath (*Pranayama*) is the origin of Hatha Yoga, meaning the conjunction of the sun and moon. The term "Hatha" in Hatha Yoga refers to the HA breath of the sun and the THA breath of the moon. Since the breath is linked to celestial influences, when

breathing is controlled, these influences are also controlled. Many Tantric texts claim that by balancing the solar and lunar breaths, an individual can be freed from the influence of destiny. The synthesis of HA and THA breaths in a state of equilibrium is the inner goal of all Yogas.

In 1969 Dr. V. Pratap of the Kaivalyadhama Yoga Institute in Bombay conducted an experiment to determine patterns of diurnal nostril breathing. He found that there is a rhythmic pattern to alternate-nostril breathing, which differs from individual to individual and from day to day in the same individual. In his report he states:

The cause of the peculiar dominance of nostril breathing may pose a problem to physiologists. It is believed that it has something to do with sympathetic innervation. The author of this research paper feels that air currents which pass through the nose stimulate certain parts of the olfactory nerve filaments, and consequently the olfactory bulb, which is an extension of the brain, allowing impulses to continue after a stimulus has ceased. From the olfactory bulb, fibres pass towards the brain in the olfactory tract. Some terminate in the olfactory tubercle and others cross to the opposite cerebral hemisphere. It is possible that central mechanisms govern nostril breathing in order to maintain homeostasis of the organism. Therefore sometimes right nostril breathing is dominant, and sometimes left nostril breathing. Sometimes breathing takes place equally through both nostrils. It may be surmised that the air currents passing through the right nostril influence *excitatory* effects, while those passing through the other nostril produce *inhibitory* effects. As per the claim of this science of breath, it could be used in family planning, diagnosis, prognosis of diseases and their cure.

There is a very simple practice for gaining conscious control over the breath. It is known as *alternate-nostril breathing* or *solar-lunar breathing*, and the technique consists of blocking one nostril with a finger or thumb while slowly inhaling through the other. When the inhalation is complete, retain the breath for a while and then release the finger or thumb and exhale through the other nostril. Then repeat the process in the opposite way: inhale through the nostril you previously exhaled from, retain as before, and then exhale through the original nostril. This constitutes one complete "round" of alternate-nostril breathing. It balances the breath and greatly assists in gaining control over parasympathetic processes such as heartbeat, blood circulation and body temperature, so enabling a person to gain

Solar-lunar breathing, also known as alternate-nostril breathing. Highly regarded in all Yogic and Tantric texts, this type of exercise creates balance and harmony throughout the psycho-organism. The fingers are used to block each nostril in turn. The solar side (to the right) is linked to heat, expansion and all-consuming consciousness, whereas the lunar side (to the left) evokes coldness, contraction and intuitive Wisdom-energy.

ascendency over the life force itself.

The *Shiva Samhita* gives a beautiful and precise account of how the novice should practice solar-lunar breathing:

The wise beginner should keep the body firm and upright. Joining palms in supplication, salute the lineage of Gurus and the ancient Mother-goddesses on the left side and then honor the elephant-headed Ganesha on the right side. Then let the wise practitioner close the right nostril with the right thumb, inhale air through the left nostril and retain the air as long as possible without discomfort. Afterward breathe out slowly, not forcibly, through the right nostril. Again, draw in the breath through the right nostril and retain it as long as is comfortable; then release the air carefully through the left nostril. According to this method, try to practice twenty retentions of breath at each session, while keeping the mind free of all anxieties, doubts and dualities. This exercise should be practiced four times daily, early in the morning (preferably at sunrise), at midday, at sunset and at midnight. When it has been practiced daily for three months, all the subtle

channels of the body will be fully purified and Karmas will be destroyed.

Solar-lunar breathing can be practiced using equal measures for inhalation, retention and exhalation, or using the rhythm of the healing breath with its 1:4:2 proportion. The *Gheranda Samhita* gives a concise account of solar-lunar breathing using the healing breath proportions and including a simple meditation:

Contemplate the primordial seed-sound "YANG," which is linked to the air element and the heart center, and visualize this syllable as of a smoky color, filled with energy. Then draw in the breath through the left nostril, repeating the syllable mentally sixteen times. Restrain the breath while mentally repeating the syllable sixty-four times and then slowly exhale the air through the right nostril during the period required to mentally repeat the syllable "YANG" thirty-two times.

There are many other breathing techniques outlined in Yogic and Tantric texts, and all of them are designed to balance and unite the solar and lunar forces, the psyche and the Soma. *Pranayama* is an exact science and any breathing exercise should be undertaken with care and attention to detail.

The application of conscious solar and lunar breathing is a major key to the control of the sexual function. The solar breath is equated with the Shiva-principle of transcendental delight; the lunar breath is associated with the Shakti-principle of creative energy. When both breaths are working in balance, the life-force enters the "Great Axis," the central subtle psychic pathway that runs from the perineum at the base of the spine to the top of the head. When solar-lunar forces are in balance during love-making, an ecstatic thrill that "lifts up" the psyche and impels it in an evolutionary direction is experienced.

When a couple practice Tantric love, their Shiva and Shakti principles unite with each other and within themselves. At the same time there is a convergence and synchronization of their breaths. Their life-forces merge into a single vortex of pure ecstatic energy and an exchange of physical and subtle energies takes place.

The Tantric teachings contain a wealth of information on the different methods of utilizing solar and lunar breaths during love-making. First it is important to know that lying on one side causes the dominance of the opposite nostril's breath. While lying on the left side for example, the breath will automatically begin to flow through the right nostril. At night, when asleep or dreaming, most people toss and turn. This movement is the result of an unconscious attempt to help the solar and lunar breaths regain their natural balance, lost during the day.

Tantric texts declare that if at the moment of orgasm the solar breath dominates in the man and the lunar breath in the woman, and conception occurs, the child will be male. The opposite situation is said to produce female offspring. The texts further state that if the breath is dominant on the same side, either solar or lunar, in both partners, then any resultant child is likely to have strong homosexual tendencies. Hindu love-postures were created specifically to help stabilize irregularities of breath and create conditions suited to the birth of healthy and emotionally balanced children.

The teachings emphasize that if the man *consciously* draws in the exhaled air from the woman's *left* nostril through his *right* nostril, this will effect a great power of attraction between the couple. It is further stated that this effect is enhanced if the man exhales air from his *right* nostril and enables the woman to consciously inhale this air through her *left* nostril. This often happens naturally if a couple make love on their sides, facing each other, since then their breaths naturally work together in a complementary way.

In many ancient cultures breath had strong mystical connotations. In the East "savoring the exhaled breath of a friend" is still a gesture of deep friendship. The Eskimos do not use the kiss to show affection, but instead rub noses and exchange breaths.

Many Tantric and Taoist mystical treatises point to the binding power of complementary breaths. Rituals are outlined for developing a particular kind of breath dominance, in the belief that even destiny can be controlled through conscious breathing practices. Several Tantras declare

During love-making there is a natural convergence and synchronization of breathing between the couple. Tantra teaches that breathing should be consciously balanced, to enable ecstatic forces to be released and channeled upward. Here, the man is shown measuring his breathing with the help of beads, and his partner concentrates on the cooling lunar energy, so prolonging ecstasy. From a miniature painting, Kangra Hills, late eighteenth or early nineteenth century.

Alternate-nostril breathing, here practiced by a Jain master. From an Indian painting of the mid-eighteenth century.

that ecstatic love-making is most potent when the vital breaths are balanced and acting in a complementary way. One text states that "by meditating on the breath during love-making, one should seize the life-force of the other with the life-force of oneself and bestow the life-force of oneself on that of the other." This is the Tantric love pact, which binds souls together throughout Eternity. This love pact far transcends the vow "until death do us part,"

a concept of marriage that is cosmically pessimistic and limiting.

Love-making is a wonderful opportunity to bestow the best of oneself on one's partner. Breath control should be a natural part of foreplay, as should focusing awareness on the cosmic implications of breath exchange during intimacy. Observation of the subtle interplay of breaths can bring a new reality of mutual exchange, nourishment and commitment.

Sexual posture illustrating the spontaneous and joyous ecstasy of Tantra. From a Rajasthani miniature painting, *circa* eighteenth century.

The solar breath leads to transcendence; the lunar breath is a form-giving substance. Their union is evocative of the Eternal.
PRANA UPANISHAD

When the breath is unsteady, everything is unsteady; but when the breath is still, all else is still. So one should control the breath carefully. Inhale slowly and exhale likewise, neither retaining the breath excessively nor beyond your capacity. Do not exhale too rapidly. Inhalation gives strength and a controlled and purified body; retention gives steadiness of mind and longevity; and exhalation is totally purifying.
GORAKSASHATAKAM

The oracle of breath unfolds its secrets to those who know the keys. The elements in the breath are known as fire, water, earth, air and space.
SWARA CHINTAMANI

Kundalini: the serpent power

Most esoteric traditions refer to a great power inherent in the human psycho-organism. This power is referred to in the Tantras as an "inner woman" or *Kundalini Shakti*, and is likened to a dangerous coiled-up snake. This normally latent power can act either creatively or destructively, positively or negatively.

Kundalini can be understood on both a physical and a metaphysical level. The root word *Kunda* means "pool," and the Kundalini of the world is the molten pool of primordial elements at the core of the earth. This worldly Kundalini pulses at a regular frequency and occasionally wreaks havoc in the form of earthquakes and volcanoes.

The Kundalini of mankind is centered in the sexual region of each individual and is an "inner fire" with tremendous potential. This Kundalini Shakti is the power of sex, which can either bind or liberate a person. As the latent power necessary for spiritualization, the Kundalini is particularly significant to those who seek to understand the mysteries of sexuality.

The Tantras teach various methods for "awakening" and channeling the Kundalini-energy. According to the *Gheranda Samhita*, "The great goddess Kundalini, the primordial energy of the Self, sleeps in the sexual region of the body. She has a form rather like a serpent, having three and one half coils. As long as she remains asleep, the individual soul (Jiva) is limited and true knowledge does not arise. But just as the right key unlocks a particular door, so Hatha Yoga unlocks the door of Kundalini, allowing the self to experience Brahma and obtain Liberation." The same text goes on to explain how breath retention, visualization, mental repetition of specific sound vibrations and certain physical movements together awaken and control the all-powerful Kundalini:

Sit in a comfortable posture and inhale fully, visualizing the vital *Prana* [the evolutionary life energy] conjoining with the *Apana* [the downward-moving energy of the body]. Contract the rectum [by exercising the anal sphincter] and visualize the vital breaths entering the central Great Axis at the region just above the base of the spine. By restraining the inhaled breath, the serpentine Kundalini begins to feel cramped and suffocated. She begins to stir. Then awaken the sleeping goddess Kundalini by mentally repeating the all-powerful seed-sound "HUM" [pronounced "HOUNG"]. Say to yourself "SOHAM" [meaning 'I am it'] while imaging yourself as filled with Shakti and in union with Shiva. Draw up the Kundalini-energy from the lower region and contemplate the union of the pure Shiva-spirit with the primordial Shakti-energy.

Yogis often spend many years preparing themselves for the release of Kundalini. The conscious awakening and control of Kundalini-power requires strength of mind, awareness of the natural evolutionary upward movement of this raw sexual energy and a physical body in harmonious balance. Since physical well-being is linked to diet, exercise and mental attitude, these factors should be dealt with first and the necessary preparations in lifestyle made before allowing the Kundalini to transform one's life experience. Each stage of preparation is simple enough for any willing participant to follow. Once the principles are understood, only openness, earnest desire and application are necessary for the achievement of success.

Sexual contact is particularly liable to stimulate and awaken the Kundalini within. Lovers sometimes experience Kundalini spontaneously, through the natural convergence of life energies during love-making. Heavy physical exertion, particularly in the heterosexual acts of love, can replicate the conditions necessary for awakening the Kundalini; the deep breathing, movement of the sexual region, convergence and exchange of vital breaths, and the grunting and other noises of love (such as "Hm," "Hah," "Ouh") are all factors that play a role in stimulating the Serpent Power.

The experience of the awakened rising Kundalini is unmistakable; it is felt as an inner thrill, a "liquid fire," simultaneously hot and cold, electric, almost paralyzing, opening up the whole being, lightening and liberating, taking the breath away. Sometimes the awakening of Kundalini can be a fearful experience, but if the correct mental attitude is brought to bear, it is easy to channel the energy positively. Visualization, the creative imagination, bodily awareness and several physical techniques (see "Reverse Kundalini," Part

The Kundalini is likened to a dangerous coiled snake, ready to strike at any moment. Snake poison can be deadly, but if prepared correctly, it can be used to cure serious illnesses.

Kundalini, the Serpent Power, traditionally described as a coiled snake with heads at both ends. From a Gujarat miniature painting of the late seventeenth or early eighteenth century.

BRAHMA

the creative

Kundalini Yoga is the conscious awakening and channeling of sexual energy upward, to pierce through the subtle centers (Chakras) to unite the inner Shakti with the Shiva-principle of transcendence. Here the Chakras are depicted as open and effulgent, as the Kundalini-energy passes through. The Navel Chakra is the concentration point of solar energy, and the Head Chakra is the focus of lunar energy. From a Rajasthani painting of the eighteenth century.

III) all help overcome negative Kundalini experiences.

If the Kundalini is awakened through spontaneous, joyful love-making, it offers the couple a great opportunity to explore the heights of the spirit. For a couple engaged in Tantric love-making, the Kundalini is an ally that can help in the attainment of ecstasy and Liberation. Her potency transforms biological instincts into the urge for transcendence. Visualize the Kundalini in both yourself and your partner. Lead Her carefully and lovingly through Her journey upward. Lead Her in union from the sexual regions to the crown of the head and flood your hearts with the joyous energy of Shiva and Shakti. Visualize yourselves rising, freed from attachments and the duality of the world.

There has been much talk about Kundalini Yoga in recent years. Yet it is not a theoretical topic but a practical one, linked directly to sexuality. Even if Kundalini Yoga is practiced alone, it is sexual energy that is being channeled upward and the process always requires erotic visualization. In some people erotic fantasy is sufficient to awaken the Kundalini, but it is rare that such a person has the ability to use the energy creatively. The numerous texts known as the Tantras are particularly helpful in understanding how to control Kundalini and use her potent power in a truly creative way. Psychic phenomena such as clairvoyance and healing are instances in which the Serpent Power is being tapped and put to use. It is, however, in a physical heterosexual context that the Kundalinis of both partners can conjoin and truly reveal their potential for transformation. Such Kundalini Yoga experiences lead directly to cosmic consciousness, the joyous ecstasy of oneness with the universe, outside the limitations of time.

In Part III we describe a number of methods by which a couple can exalt physical love to a mystic dimension. The role of Kundalini is paramount to this process, for without her supersensual energy love-making cannot penetrate into the higher levels of consciousness. Mastery of Kundalini, the inner woman, should be

the goal of Yogis and lovers alike. For, in the words of a popular Tantric saying, "There is nothing in either this world or the next which is beyond the domain of Kundalini."

Visualize the Kundalini as a sensuous woman, a goddess, extremely beautiful and filled with eroticism. Try to fathom her special features and share in her all-powerful Wisdom-energy. The Kundalini is ever willing and able to transport the individual to the heights of cosmic oneness. Think of her often, talk to her, seduce her, share private desires with her and always try to please her; then she will grant fulfillment.

On her journey upward the Kundalini Shakti passes through psychic centers known as *Chakras*. These foci of subtle vibrations are transformed through contact with the rising Kundalini. They are aligned along the spine at the sexual region between genitals and anus, the spleen region above the genitals, the navel region, the heart region, the

throat region and finally in the head, between the eyebrows. These are subtle rather than physical centers and function as "transformers," converting impulses from one frequency to another. They play an important role in Tantric cosmology as well as in the evolution of the spirit. Anandagiri, a great Hindu teacher of the early mediaeval period, beautifully describes the ascent of Kundalini: "The inner woman, entering the 'royal road,' takes rest at intervals in the secret centers. Finally She embraces the Supreme Lord in the lotus of the head. From that union there flows an exquisite nectar that floods and permeates the body; then the Ineffable Bliss is experienced."

The Kundalini Shakti can be awakened by various techniques other than those described here. Drugs can awaken the

When a couple can learn to channel and converge their Kundalini-energy consciously, an ecstatic thrill uplifts their Spirit. Seated love-making positions are particularly helpful to the practice of Kundalini Yoga.

Kundalini, as can physical exercise, dancing (especially whirling), sudden shock or certain sounds that resonate in harmony with the Kundalini frequency. However, in such instances there is a danger that this powerful energy will get out of control and create psycho-physical problems. The safest way to channel Kundalini-energy is through deep commitment to transcendental love.

When the experience of Kundalini is prolonged, it becomes possible to "distill" some of Her energy into the heart center and store it there. The effect is that the emotions become empowered and compassionate love fills the heart center. Tantras teach that there is a subtle nerve linking the heart with the two eyes and that distilled Kundalini-energy can be channeled outward, through the eyes and directed at a person, awakening the Kundalini within that person. Such experiences are rarely lasting, unless the person can gain conscious control over the "inner woman" by him/herself.

When a couple learn to awaken and channel the Kundalini-energy consciously, their love-making takes on a totally new dimension. By treating the Kundalini as a friend and ally, the couple can be transported, in a moment of pure spontaneous joy, beyond the limits of ordinary consciousness to an experience of the mystic meaning of love.

Ecstatic love-making is likened to the opening and blossoming of lotuses. When the unconscious urge to orgasm can be consciously controlled at will, the Shiva and Shakti energies experience timeless Bliss and the Spirit is uplifted.

There are indications that a form of Kundalini Yoga was known to the ancient priestly religions of the Mediterranean during pre-Christian times. Here, a Cretan goddess is portrayed holding two snakes, indicating that she has tamed the Serpent Power. On her head is a cat, symbolic of occult attainment. Figure from the palace of Knossos, *circa* 1600 B.C.

The wise and excellent Yogi, rapt in ecstasy, should lead the Kundalini, along with the life-force, to consummate union with Her Lord, who stays in the Abode of Liberation in the pure lotus of the head center. When the Kundalini rises, all things become absorbed into her.   SATCHAKRANIRUPANA

When the sleeping goddess Kundalini is awakened through the grace of the teacher, then all the subtle lotuses and worldly bonds are readily pierced through and through. Let the wise person forcibly and firmly draw up the goddess Kundalini, for She is the giver of all miraculous powers.   SHIVA SAMHITA

The sleeping Kundalini is extremely fine, like the fiber of a lotus stalk. She is the world-bewilderer, gently covering the "door" to the central Great Axis. Like the spiral of a conch shell, Her shining snake-like form is coiled around three and a half times; Her luster is like a strong flash of lightning; Her sweet murmur is like an indistinct hum of swarms of love-mad bees. She maintains all beings of this world by means of inhalation and exhalation, and shines in the cavity of the sexual region.   SATCHAKRANIRUPANA

the subtle body

Esoteric teachings contend that men and women have an "auric" or Subtle Body as well as a physical body. Normally the various life energies in the body generate a kind of subtle "field" or aura, which can be seen by sensitives. The aura changes color and shape in resonance to the emotions and general physical condition, and also contracts or expands. A happy person has a "full" aura, whereas the aura of a sad person is contracted and colored by negative emotion.

In recent years scientific research has tended to support the traditional view of the aura. Color photographs taken using a technique known as Kirlian photography illustrate changes in the aura. Various theories explain telepathy and other ESP phenomena by the existence of an auric or "psi plasma" field. Dr. Andrija Puharich proved the biological and physical foundations of psi plasma field in his book *Beyond Telepathy*, which is a fine synthesis of traditional Shamanistic and Yogic teachings and scientific experimentation and analysis. His findings are supported by the most recent observations on the nature of subtle energy fields and throw light on the teachings on the Subtle Body as outlined in the Tantras.

The *Shiva Samhita* gives a clear account of the nature of the Subtle Body:

In this body the central Great Axis [Mount Meru, the spinal column] is surrounded by seven islands (the vital force, blood, flesh, fat, bones, marrow and semen/ovum). There are "rivers," "seas" and so on, as well as seers, sages, gods, goddesses, intelligences, all the stars and planets, sacred pilgrimage places, shrines and presiding deities. The sun and moon, the agents of creation and destruction, also move through the body, as do the Five Great Elements of space, air, fire, water and earth. All the beings that exist in all worlds are also to be found in the body, surrounding the central Great Axis.

In this body, which is called *Brahmanda* [the "egg" or "aura" of Brahma], the microcosm, there is the nectar-rayed moon, in its proper place, on top of the spinal column; it has its face *downward*, and rains nectar day and night. The ambrosia from the moon sub-divides into two subtle parts. One of these nourishes the body, like the waters of the heavenly river Ganges, and descends as a subtle channel on the left side. The other ray of ambrosia, brilliant as the purest milk, enters the central nerve of the spinal column in order to maintain and re-create the moon in its proper place on top of the central Great Axis.

At the lower region of the Great Axis of Meru is the sun, located within the body itself. From the

inner sun, situated at the navel, a subtle channel emanates to the right side of the body and carries the solar fluid upward by the power of its rays. This nerve on the right side is another form of the sun and moves through the body, swallowing up vital secretions and ultimately leading the spirit to Liberation. The Lord of Creation and Destruction is the sun, which moves through the vessel of the body.

In the human body there are several hundred thousand subtle channels, but the principle ones are fourteen in number. Of these, three are particularly important: *ida* (to the left), *pingala* (to the right) and *sushumna* (in the center). Of these three, *sushumna* alone is the highest and the most beloved of Yogis; all other subtle channels are subordinate to it. The nerve called *ida* is on the left side, coiling around the *sushumna* and going to the right nostril. The nerve *pingala* is on the right side, coiling around the central channel and entering the left nostril. He who knows this microcosm of the body and experiences its mysteries truly reaches the highest state.

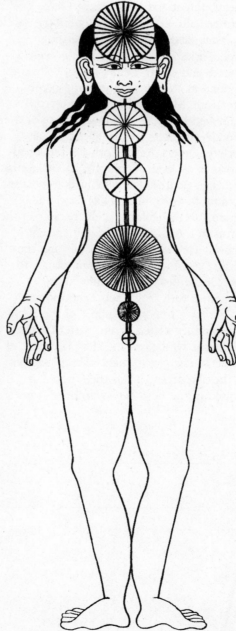

The Subtle Body of Tantra, according to the most ancient tradition. From a four-petaled Chakra at the sexual center, the Kundalini rises up, through the thirty-two petaled Chakra at the assimilative center, the sixty-four petaled Chakra at the navel center (the solar power of transformation), the eight-petaled Chakra at the heart center, the sixteen-petaled Chakra at the throat center, to the thirty-two-petaled Chakra at the head center (the lunar force of distillation). From a Tibetan painting of the seventeenth century.

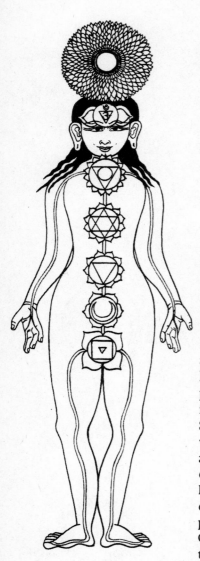

The Subtle Body of the later Hindu tradition, with symbolic representations of elements at each Chakra. This type of psycho-cosmogram illustrates the natural order of elements according to Yogic teachings. Subtle nerves leading from the feet to the sexual center, and from the hands to the throat center, are shown. From a Nepalese painting of the seventeenth century.

There are numerous similar accounts of the Subtle Body. All the most ancient Tantric treatises emphasize the solar-lunar symbolism, with the "moon" in the head center and the "sun" in the navel center, and, without exception, mention three principle subtle channels (*ida*, *pingala* and *sushumna*). In the *Gheranda Samhita*, for example, it is stated that "The sun dwells at the root of the navel, and the moon at the root of the palate." It is the Subtle Body that links mankind with the celestial bodies and serves as a bridge between this world and the next.

Tantric texts give varying accounts of the psychic centers, which are referred to as Chakras, meaning "wheels," located primarily in the sexual region, spleen, navel, heart, throat and head. These Chakras do not actually exist *in* the body but are subtle "plasma fields" vibrating at specific frequencies and taking on subtle shapes, sounds and colors. Descriptions of Chakras abound in Western esoteric and occult literature. Most are based on the account published by C. W. Leadbeater, one of the founder-members of the Theosophical Society. Others derive from the published works of Sir John Woodroffe, an Englishman and High Court judge who lived in India and commissioned translations of several later Hindu Tantras. Unfortunately, because of the errors in these later works, the current popular view of the Subtle Body and the Chakra system bears little resemblance to the concise descriptions outlined in numerous early Yogic and Tantric texts.

The most important aspect of the Subtle Body and its related Chakra system is the solar-lunar symbolism and the placement of heavenly energies in their correct locations in the microcosm. Thus, the "moon" is located in the head center and the "sun" is

at the navel center. The earliest Tantric texts refer to four main Chakras, located at the navel, heart, throat and head centers. Each of the Chakras has "petals," which symbolize the natural division of the force of that Chakra. The navel center is described as an upward-turned lotus of sixty-four petals, the heart center as a downward-turned lotus of eight petals, the throat center as an upward-turned lotus of sixteen petals and the head center is a downward-turned lotus of thirty-two petals. This is a very simple view of the Subtle Body system.

Centers located below the navel center are also described. These are the spleen and the sex center, both of which are traditionally considered predominantly *physical* rather than *subtle*, and thus are viewed as separate from the other four Chakras. According to most traditions, the sex center has four petals, facing upward, and the spleen center has thirty-two petals, facing downward. Tantric texts state that each of the petals of the heart center subdivides into three, to produce twenty-four petals, and similarly, that each of the petals of the sex center subdivides into three, to produce twelve petals.

Meditation on the Subtle Body as composed of these psychic centers helps the perception of the flow of energies through the psycho-organism. Kundalini Yoga requires the channeling of sex energy upward, through successive Chakras, to union with the Shiva-principle in the head center. The simplest meditation on the Subtle Body centers is to isolate the navel, heart and head centers, visualizing a simple lotus flowering in each location. Then perform the practices required to stimulate the Kundalini (contraction of anal sphincter, mental repetition of the seed-sound "HUNG," breath retention and erotic visualization) and draw her up through the Navel Chakra. Imagine that Brahma is born from this lotus and is empowered with the effulgence of Kundalini; visualize and identify with the multi-headed form of Brahma, the Creator, the solar orb, blazing bright. Then draw up the Kundalini to the Heart Chakra. Imagine her erotic energy piercing through the lotus to give birth to Vishnu (Lord of the waters, emotion and the flow of blood through the body); once again, visualize and identify with the multi-armed

THE ANCIENT VIEW OF THE SUBTLE BODY

SUBTLE

Force	Chakra	Petals	Facing	Divisions
Moon	Head Center	32	Down	—
—	Throat Center	16	Up	—
—	Heart Center	8	Down	24
Sun	Navel Center	64	Up	—

GROSS

Force	Chakra	Petals	Facing	Divisions
—	Spleen Center	32	Down	—
Kundalini	Sex Center	4	Up	12

form of Vishnu, the Preserver. Then draw up the Kundalini higher to the crown of the Head Chakra, piercing through the lotus and reaching the domain of Shiva, the Transcender. Retain the breath and, if in sexual union, refrain from climaxing. Try to become one with the union of the Kundalini Shakti and the Shiva-principle.

Several later Tantras give complex descriptions of Chakras, using shapes, colors, deities, seed-sounds, numbers of petals, elements and psychological qualities to form a synthesis of the inner-outer relationship. Unless one is following a single view of "reality" as taught by a teacher who is able to give direct guidance on the intricacies of his particular synthesis, such complex categorization can easily degenerate into dogma. Since the Subtle Body and the Chakra system are practical aids to Liberation, it is advisable to keep to the basic structure and allow the intuition to reveal the details.

Esoteric teachings declare that if one truly wishes to advance spiritually, one must work consciously to activate the Subtle Body. Though the basic ingredients and raw energies exist in everyone, they must be focused and channeled consciously. The body, emotions and mind should all be brought to bear on the conscious evocation of an all-powerful

Simple representation of the triad of forces within the Subtle Body: Brahma at the navel center, Vishnu at the heart center and Shiva at the head center. Meditating on these forces of creativity, preservation and transcendence at these Chakras resolves all dualitites and personal limitations. From an Indian painting of the nineteenth century.

Subtle Body, which can then serve as a source of strength, intelligence and transcendence. This is one of the most important secrets of the Tantric tradition.

The *Shiva Samhita* gives a beautiful meditation for awakening the Kundalini and the Subtle Body:

Fix the mind on the Sex Chakra and contract the anus while retaining the breath. Contemplate that the god of Love (Kama) resides at the Sex Chakra and that the Kundalini awakens as a brilliant but subtle flame, whose nature is intelligence. Visualize sexual union taking place between the Love-god and the Kundalini-flame, causing the sex energy to enter the central Subtle Nerve (*sushumna*) and rise through successive Chakras. Visualize the red and white Subtle Nerves of the left and right, converging on each Chakra in turn and emitting rosy pink effulgent light, which nourishes and harmonizes the whole being.

Tantric texts refer to a Chakra above the lunar head center. It is poetically described as the Thousand-Petaled Lotus, which the *Shiva Samhita* declares is "outside the microcosm of the body." All the great teachers of Tantric lineage are conceived of as inhabiting this Chakra, along with the original archetypal Shiva. Different traditions have different meditations on this uppermost Chakra, but all agree that by focusing the consciousness on this center, one links up with the source of the teachings.

By awakening the *natural* powers within, the self-transcendence techniques of Tantra help to bring the psyche into harmony with the cosmos. Over several thousand years individuals have practiced Tantric meditation techniques and many have become truly liberated. At the present time more people than ever are becoming familiar with these techniques and proving their effectiveness. The understanding of the Subtle Body is of tremendous importance for individuals wishing to explore their psyches.

Lovers need to explore more than each other's bodies. They need to plunge into each other's psyches and soar to the heights of the Spirit. Physical love offers numerous opportunities to discover new things about oneself. As the singularly significant act that has the power to endow life, sexual love has a deep mystic meaning. If a couple can learn to use the power of sex creatively, in areas other than procreation, they will discover mysteries beyond this world. The Subtle Body is the *vehicle* that allows participants to pass freely through this life to the next and share the joyous delights of the Spirit.

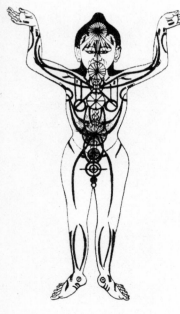

Tibetan medical view of the Subtle Body, with subtle nerves and centers clearly marked. Eastern medical systems consider both physical and subtle aspects of the being equally important in diagnosis. Recent medical research in the West has indicated the existence of subtle life energies and plexuses.

Contemplation is of three kinds: gross, luminous and subtle. When a particular figure, such as one's Guru or personal deity, is contemplated, it is known as gross contemplation. When Brahma or the Nature-principle is contemplated as a mass of light, it is called luminous contemplation. When the Kundalini-force is contemplated, it is said to be subtle contemplation. This third kind of contemplation lasts throughout all Eternity.

GHERANDA SAMHITA

The Subtle Body connects this world with the next. There is no single object or doctrine as important and lasting as the Subtle Body, which provides a constant doorway to Liberation.

KAULA TANTRA

A person practicing the higher teachings of Tantra becomes capable of letting all vibrations enter, stay and dissolve in the central pathway, the Great Axis, of the Subtle Body. When the four omens, a glittering before one's eyes, smoke, a glow and a cooling radiant lamp-like light, appear, that person becomes resurrected.

NARO CHOS DRUG

upper and lower

The "upper" and "lower" gates of the body have already been mentioned in the section "The Temple of the Body." To recapitulate briefly, the *upper gates* are the orifices of the head: the mouth, nose, two eyes, two ears and the fontanel opening. The *lower gates* are the orifices of the anus and sexual organ. These are the places through which the consciousness or life-force can pass, either when entering or leaving the body. The upper gates are generally considered to be more favorable than the lower ones, since they lead one to the higher evolutionary realms. Tantra teaches that the lower gates lead the consciousness to lower or sub-human forms of existence.

The life-force naturally divides into two main energy currents: the upward-moving *Prana* and the downward-moving *Apana*. The *Prana* usually moves in the region of the heart, residing there as an intelligent life-sustaining current. The *Apana* usually remains in the lower digestive region and extends to the anal orifice, performing its function as the instinctive excretory current. Three other primary life currents move in the region of the navel, the throat and around the whole body; their names are *Samana*, *Udana* and *Vyana*, respectively. Thus, the divisions of the five life currents are:

Prana : upward-moving, rests in the heart.
Apana : downward-moving, rests in the region of the anus.
Samana : encircles the navel region.
Udana : rests in the throat.
Vyana : pervades the whole body.

Each of the five life currents performs functions vital to the health of the body.

Yogic teachings state that, impelled by the *Prana* and *Apana* currents, the individual soul (the Jiva) moves up and down through the right and left channels of the Subtle Body. The *Goraksashatakam*, an important Yogic text, gives the following allegorical description of the movement of the Jiva through the body: "Just as a ball, when hit to the ground, rebounds again, when the Jiva is tossed about by the *Prana* and *Apana*, it follows after them." When one gains control over the movement of the individual soul (the Jiva) and focuses it in one place, then one truly governs one's own life. Tantras teach that in this way the individual can *make* his destiny rather than passively submitting to circumstances.

The Tantras teach that the upward and downward energy currents should be consciously controlled and united by the power of the Will and by physical techniques as well as visualizations. Certain postures of Hatha Yoga, such as the reverse positions and head stand, achieve this end.

The Yoga head stand (*shirsasana*) helps reverse the involuntary outward flow of energy. First the hands should form a comfortable support for the head, by interlocking the fingers. A triangular shape should be made with the hands and elbows, the upper part of the head placed carefully into the palms and the weight gradually taken. Slowly the feet should be brought up close to the elbows, lifted up and straightened. The Yoga head stand should not be rushed; the "base" of interlocked hands and the two elbows should be carefully held and breathing focused at the navel region. Practiced with care, the Yoga head stand ensures a proper blood supply to the pituitary, pineal and thyroid glands and tones up the whole body. It is particularly helpful in overcoming loss of memory, aging and sexual problems.

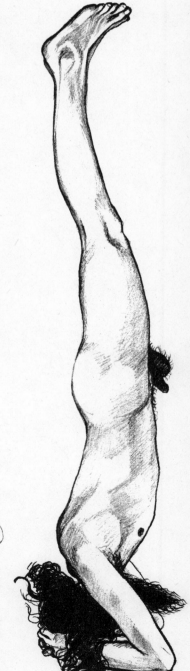

The *Gheranda Samhita* describes how inverse postures help to control the energy currents: "The solar force dwells normally at the navel center and the lunar force emanates from the head center; as the sun burns up the nectar that exudes from the moon, the individual becomes subject to death. By placing the head on the ground, steadying it with the hands and raising the legs, the flow is reversed. By the practice of this type of posture, the life energies are controlled and decay and death are held at bay."

Constriction of the anal sphincter muscles and abdominal contractions also help to draw up the downward-moving life energies, as does visualizing the energy flow reversed. When the *Apana* and *Prana* are united, the individual soul becomes centered in the heart region, where it is experienced by the intellect and emotions.

During extremes of eroticism the subtle life energies become vibrant, elated and expansive. This is experienced as an electric feeling, a thrill or expansive shock that almost takes the breath away: the heart beats faster and the face flushes; energy pours from the bodily orifices and the mystic moment of "soul sharing" is lost; the ecstatic vibrant feeling seems to "drain away" and the body feels cold and empty. Thoughts arise in the mind, where before there were none, a feeling of contraction pervades and the body jerks involuntarily. On occasions the couple feel almost near to death.

The "little death" is a theme that occurs in the erotic writings of both East and West. Though the experience has an attractive quality because of the taste of oblivion it seems to offer, Tantra teaches that the "little death" is a negative form of mysticism, linked to the *loss* of individual transcendence and soul communion. Texts explain that before the expansive experience is lost, the consciousness should be brought to bear on sealing the bodily orifices and circulating the life energies between the couple. Too often, lovers lose the full potential of ecstasy because the convergence of their consciousness is too brief.

The *secret of the lower gates* is in either constricting the anal orifice or placing a finger, foot or other body part over the opening. When in a seated position, the heel can be used to seal this lower orifice.

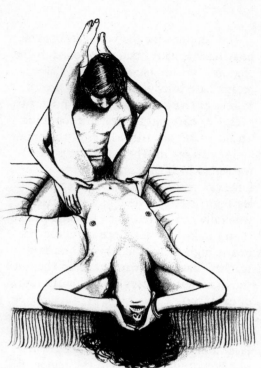

During love-making energy should be contained and circulated between the couple. When the upper and lower orifices of the body are sealed, ecstatic energy builds up.

When the Lingam and Yoni are in contact, they seal each other and exchange energies automatically.

The *secret of the upper gates* is to either physically or mentally close the orifices of mouth, nose, ears, eyes and fontanel. If the mouths of the couple are in contact, they seal each other. If the partners look straight into each other's eyes, energies will be exchanged rather than lost. The nose is sealed by retention or by close contact with the partner's nose, the ear orifices can be closed by positioning some part of the body over them, and the fontanel is best closed by a hand placed on the top of the head.

Yogic texts outline a "mystic seal" known as the *Yoni Mudra* and it is described in the *Gheranda Samhita* in the following way: "Close the ears with the thumbs, the eyes with the index fingers, the nostrils with the middle fingers, the upper lip with the ring fingers and the lower lip with the little fingers. Draw in the *Prana* and join it with the *Apana*; contemplate the Subtle Body and the Chakras, in order."

Though the Yoni Mudra is not essentially for lovers, it can be adapted to a sexual context. The important thing to remember is that as ecstasy approaches, there will be a tendency to energy loss, and this can be counteracted by sealing the bodily orifices. The best way is to do it for your partner, covering the top of the head with your hand and imagining an act of consecration or mystic initiation taking place. Then the ecstatic moment can be prolonged and mystic awareness will develop.

When ecstatic delight is contained within the bodies of the couple, the mind will begin to "see" visions and the heart will "feel" them. Both partners will share a mystic awareness of the meaning of their lives and beauteous visions will dawn in the mind's eye, helping to bind their souls together. A common mystic vision associated with sexual ecstasy is the *Island of Jewels*, an archetypal manifestation of souls in harmony. This vision can be developed and stabilized by adding to what appears in the mind. The *Gheranda Samhita* gives a beautiful visualization technique for developing the Island of Jewels.

Close the eyes and imagine that there is an ocean of nectar in the region of one's heart. In the middle of the ocean there is an island of precious jewels, with sands of pulverized diamonds, rocks of emeralds and rubies, and mountains of sapphires. Imagine that on all sides of the island there are trees laden with sweet-smelling flowers and lotuses covering select parts of the ground. In the middle of this auspicious garden let the Yogi imagine there stands the unique Wish-Granting Tree, with four branches representing the four Vedas (the ancient books of teaching), filled with fruit and flowers; bees buzz around this tree and sip nectar from it. All around and over the Wish-Granting Tree are miraculous birds and other flying creatures. Imagine that beneath the tree there is an exquisite platform built of the most precious of all the jewels on the island. See the different-colored lights sparkling from this wonderful platform and observe the reflections of it in the mind-sky and in the heart's ocean. Then visualize one's personal deity (or love-partner) seated on the precious platform, and contemplate the fine details.

If lovers become aware of the upper and lower gates of their bodies during love-making, they will be able to stop the leakage of life energies. When life energies are contained and circulated between the couple, the experience of union is intensified and exalted.

The upper and lower gates should be kept closed, so the life energies do not leave the body. By concentrating the ecstatic forces within, wonderful visions dawn in the mind-sky. This is a special secret, which shortens the journey of Liberation.

YOGINI TANTRA

Death is eaten by the person who reverses the flow of energies within the body. Energy flow can be reversed by postures, by "seals," by "drawing up," by breath control and by meditation.

KAULA TANTRA

Reverse sexual postures help channel sexual energy to the head and thus stimulate the glands, circulation, nerves and cells. From a Rajasthani miniature painting of the nineteenth century.

yoga

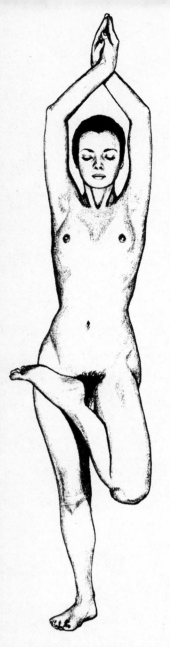

This type of standing position, with one leg up, is helpful to the development of balance and posture. Known as crane posture (*goldasana*) it stimulates all the internal organs and improves the hips and legs.

Yoga teachings have become quite familiar in the West. A large number of books cover Yoga's various aspects, from the theoretical to the physical. There are radio and television programs devoted entirely to Yoga in both Europe and America. It is now generally accepted that Hatha Yoga is healthful and there are numerous instances of severe diseases being counteracted by Yogic means.

The meaning of the word "Yoga" is "to join together," to "make union." In the Tantric tradition sexual union is considered the highest form of Yoga. When Yoga is practiced alone, an internal "marriage" takes place between the various complementary parts of the body, such as the upper and lower life energies, the solar and lunar vitalities, the head and the heart. Yoga is the practice of transcending duality through conscious action; as such, it takes place on both physical and metaphysical levels.

The Yoga of the physical body, or *Hatha Yoga*, dynamically promotes the health and well-being of the individual. Practiced consistently and correctly, it will eliminate most of the strains and stresses of modern life. Yoga rejuvenates the body and mind by relaxing tense muscles, soothing frayed nerves and toning the internal organs and glandular system, so preparing the whole body to be a fit vehicle for the experience of Tantric evolution. A radiantly healthy body is a prerequisite to the correct practice of Tantra.

Hatha Yoga can be learned from books, TV programs or classes, but whatever the mode of instruction, moderation and common sense must prevail. For example, one should never try to practice complex Yoga postures when physically ill, except under the guidance of a doctor or teacher, nor should one do so just before or after mealtimes. Yoga should be practiced neither immediately before nor just after extreme physical exertion. Reverse postures should not be practiced by a woman during menstruation.

The state of mind in which a person enters into any practice will largely determine the result. Therefore, do not be over-ambitious and force the postures, but let the body come to them gradually and naturally, when it is ready. The best times for Hatha Yoga practices are the early morning and early evening. Try to get into a regular routine. It really isn't necessary to spend hours each day on physical Yoga; ten minutes or half an hour is sufficient, provided it is practiced regularly and with concentration. Remember that the physical exercises of Hatha Yoga are not ends in themselves but means to develop and strengthen your body and mind.

Many people who embark on Yogic practices are too quickly disappointed by what they experience as their limitations. This is a mistake, for each individual's capacity is unlimited. Practices or postures that one day seem impossible may be accomplished easily and naturally a week later. It is, however, important to persevere and have faith in the long-term benefits. The powers of a creative attitude and Will are tremendous. Since all the techniques of Hatha Yoga are eminently suited to the human organism, it's the *unnatural* conditioning of the body and mind that we must strive to overcome. Each of us is a

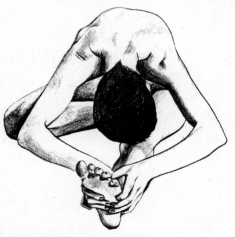

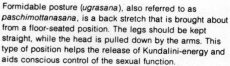

Formidable posture (*ugrasana*), also referred to as *paschimottanasana*, is a back stretch that is brought about from a floor-seated position. The legs should be kept straight, while the head is pulled down by the arms. This type of position helps the release of Kundalini-energy and aids conscious control of the sexual function.

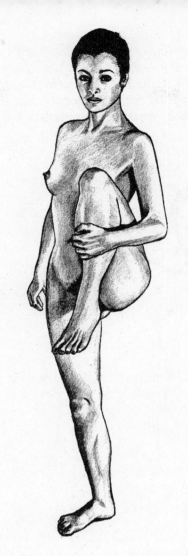

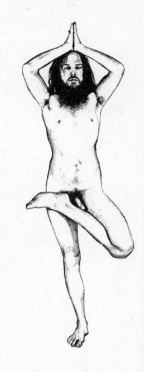

This type of standing posture requires balance and should be used to focus the mind and channel vital energy to different subtle centers (Chakras) by the placement of hand or hands. The "bound" position of the body creates a special circuit that concentrates energy. Both these positions tone up the internal organs (liver, spleen and intestines, especially) and aid the development of mental and spiritual intensity.

By drawing up the knees, in turn, and stretching the rest of the body, the abdominal muscles are strengthened, circulation is improved and the inner "fire" is stimulated. Sexual vigor is largely dependent on the healthy condition of the abdominal region and Navel Chakra.

Toe touching is a recommended starting procedure for any series of Hatha Yoga asanas. It helps the circulation, stretches the muscles and prepares the body for more complex positions. This series of illustrated exercises lengthens the tendons of the legs, enabling difficult postures to be attained.

natural Yogi or Yogini (female Yogi) if only we permit ourselves to be. Get to know your body and learn to discern its real from its imaginary needs. Be receptive and let your body speak to you directly. Above all, treat it as an intelligent friend and ally; get to know every part of it and, if necessary, coax or talk it into a state of harmony.

When two people live together, spontaneity is a crucial element to their survival as a couple. Yoga fosters this essential spontaneity and can be a shared and mutually appreciated practice. Yogic positions are evocative of natural elements or forces; many are named after animals, birds or other creatures. Hatha Yoga postures can be performed for your partner rather than for yourself alone. Watching your partner perform the different postures stimulates the erotic sentiment. When practiced with confidence and in the right spirit, they are certainly erotic.

Many of the sexual postures outlined in the third part of this book are facilitated by a grounding in Hatha Yoga. We recommend practicing Yoga either in the nude or with minimal clothing for the aesthetic value, as well as to allow for maximum freedom of movement. When the body is naked, the life energies circulate more freely than when it is clothed. Furthermore, naked Yoga creates an atmosphere charged with erotic energy. Naturally, if the temperature is cool, it is advisable to wear something light but unrestricting. Synthetic fabrics are not suitable because they obstruct the free flow of vital energies; natural fabrics such as cotton, light wool or silk are preferable. When Hatha Yoga becomes a natural part of your lifestyle, many obstacles to spiritual progress will be removed, allowing Tantric and Taoist Yogas of Love to be more easily mastered.

Hatha Yoga should always commence with simple stretching exercises to activate the circulation of blood and the flow of vital energy.

Human unhappiness results from mankind's acceptance of the lowest conditions of our minds. By the practice of Yoga, all such conditioning can be overcome.

PATANJALI YOGA SUTRAS

A person should resort to Yoga, which is like the fruit of the Wish-Granting Tree. The Yogi destroys diseases by the postures, Karmas by breath control, and mental disturbances by the withdrawal of the senses from the external world. A Yogi in the highest state of Samadhi is not affected by time or any other action.

GORAKSASHATAKAM

Calmness and steadiness of the body and senses are known as Yoga.

KATHA UPANISHAD

yoga asanas and techniques

"Asana" means a position that is both firm and pleasant. The practice of Yoga postures, or asanas, helps in the development of a stable and healthy body, tuning its capacity to withstand powerful ecstatic experiences. Though hundreds of thousands of postures are said to exist, the authoritative texts state that if only a few of them are practiced correctly, more than adequate results will be attained.

A posture may prove easy for one person and difficult for another. One person will find the lotus posture perfectly natural, whereas another will find it difficult or near impossible. One should not, therefore, feel discouraged if certain Yoga asanas seem out of reach. Practice those that come naturally and develop confidence. Leave the more difficult ones until later, when the muscles have become loosened and more flexible. Sometimes a new posture may be tried spontaneously. It's amazing how the body sometimes suddenly changes to accommodate a new form.

Many of the Yoga asanas were inspired by the flowers, animals and other creatures whose names they bear, for example, the lotus posture, the lion posture and the serpent posture. Yoga postures are a type of body language that communicates with the divinity within. There is a magical potency inherent in their form. Anyone who takes the trouble to practice Yoga asanas quickly becomes aware of this.

Many primitive tribes mimic the movements, postures and sounds of animals, believing that in so doing, they create a magical contact with them. It may well be that Yoga asanas, which mimic other creatures, allow us to contact earlier forms in our evolutionary heritage. Numerous sexual postures (described in the third part of this book) are based on life forms other than our own. When energies are exchanged and channeled through Tantric love-postures, they cause a resonance that travels beyond the dimensions of our world. Several Tantric texts refer to sexual postures as *vehicles* for supernormal or out-of-body travel.

The bow posture (*dhanurasana*) evolves from lying on the stomach, reaching back to hold the ankles and pulling up into a tension, as if the arms and legs are a bowstring. This posture is very effective in strengthening the gonads, which govern sexuality. It stretches the abdominal and back muscles and effectively relieves fatigue.

The posture known as head of a cow (*gomukhasana*) is created by linking the hands in turn, as shown. It creates a special energy circuit, opening up the heart and throat centers, effectively releasing tension. Several variations of this posture also involve the lower part of the body; in these the legs are either crossed in the lotus posture or directly over each other as in the heroic posture.

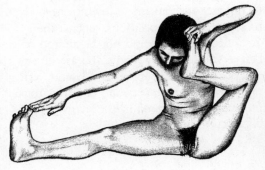

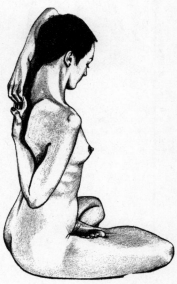

The near-ear bow posture (*akarna dhanurasana*) should be practiced with each leg extended in turn. It makes the legs and back very flexible, improving posture and aiding control of sexual energy. It should be practiced with the thought that one is an archer shooting arrows at a distant target. During the period of tension, when the posture is held, breathing should be natural and focused on the abdominal region.

The main purpose of the Yoga asana is to circulate subtle energies in a precise way. A well-balanced body, firmly positioned, does not encounter hindrances to meditation or conscious ecstasy. Postures create a particular *form* for the body that serves as a medium for communicaton with the Self. In advanced Tantric practices precise body postures are used during rituals to evoke particular archetypes and familiarize the Yogi with them.

As previously mentioned, the early part of the morning (especially sunrise) or the early evening (especially sunset) are particularly good times to practice Yoga asanas. First thing upon arising in the morning, drink a little pure fresh water to tone up the organs. Then take a bath or shower and clean the nostrils and tongue. The techniques for this are described in the section called "Bathing." Stretch the body and do a few light exercises. Proceed to the most simple asanas, such as the corpse posture (*shavasana*), which entails lying on one's back on the floor and relaxing completely. You can evolve your own order of practice or follow the instructions of a good Yoga manual. Generally, you should advance gradually to the more complex positions as you warm up during the session.

Breathing techniques are very much a part of Yoga asanas and should be practiced at the same time. But don't force them and always be sure to use your common sense. For example, don't move from an asana that requires exertion to a breathing technique, without first allowing the body to adjust. Reverse positions, such as the Yoga head stand, should not be attempted before you feel truly ready, and are best practiced with the support of a friend, wall or pillow. All the fine details of Hatha Yoga routines can be found in the many good books currently available.

People commonly perform Hatha Yoga postures without the benefit of visualizations to help loosen muscles and sinews and aid in the channeling of life currents through the body. Many Yoga asanas were developed largely to *release* latent energies, which are effective in causing physical and psychological transformations. It therefore benefits your practice to know the paths that the life energies take and to hold these in mind. Conscious visualization of the subtle pathways of the body while practicing Hatha Yoga postures will speed your progress. The more complex asanas can be easily achieved by first meditating and visualizing the form and flow of energy through the posture. Then, when you physically attempt the posture, you will be surprised to find a new ease and ability. The body opens up and becomes flexible once the mind has understood and gained ascendency over a posture.

For example, in the Yoga head stand it is helpful to imagine golden filaments streaming from the navel center and hooking onto the floor, ceiling or walls, providing support. This visualization should be mentally re-absorbed into the navel center when the body is accustomed to holding the position.

Hatha Yoga is best practiced as a creative activity rather than a mere task. Let the positions "speak" to you, and learn to flow naturally from one to the other. The practice of Yoga asanas will deepen your insight into the meaning of life, enable your body to function effectively and harmoniously, and help you to develop a deep awareness of the Subtle Body and its energies.

In all transcendental sexual experiences a healthy and relaxed body is an ally. A stiff torso is a real hindrance to sexual

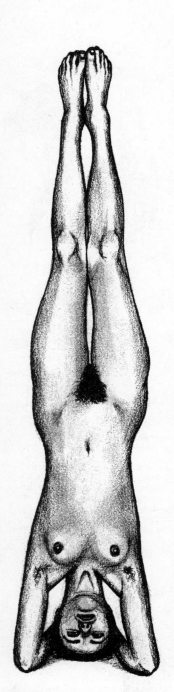

The yoga head stand (*shirsasana*) is one of the most effective postures for reversing the outward flow of sexual energy. When practicing it, one should visualize all energy flowing to the head.

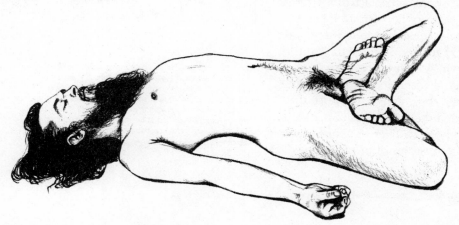

exploration; it reflects physicality, guilt and psychological retentiveness rather than ecstasy or liberation. Hatha Yoga is the antithesis of heavy physical exercise. A good Yogi is not muscle-bound; rather, his strength lies within, ready to be drawn on at any time.

The cow herder posture (*goraksasana*) is named after Guru Gorakhsa, an Indian Tantric teacher who, as a cow herder, gained Liberation through service to a Yogi prince called Chaurangi and to Mina, his own teacher. Legend has it that Chaurangi levitated in this posture. First the lotus posture should be attained; then one should jump up onto the knees and bring the hands together over the head. This posture creates a strong sense of balance, tones up the glands and aids the control of sexual energy.

The bound lotus posture (*bandha padmasana*) creates flexibility in the neck, shoulders and back. Once the position is achieved, the head should be thrown back and a number of deep breaths inhaled. Then bend forward while exhaling and touch the forehead to the ground. This helps awaken the latent Kundalini and should be accompanied by constriction of the anal sphincter muscles.

The fish posture (*matsyasana*) is ideal for total relaxation and meditation. First take up the full lotus posture and gradually lean back until the head rests on the floor. Practice arching up the back while keeping the head in position. This posture helps correct improper breathing, strengthens the lungs and stimulates the circulation. It is also helpful in regaining involuntarily lost sexual energy.

The supported complete body posture (*salamba sarvangasana*) or shoulder stand is an inverted position that has a direct beneficial effect on the whole glandular system, especially the thyroid. This posture aids the balance of hormonal levels in the body, tones up the organs and helps relieve asthma, bronchitis, colds and headaches. It invigorates the whole being and improves overall health and beauty.

Named after the cobra, the *bhujangasana* exercises the spine and tones up the internal organs. From a totally relaxed recumbent position, the body is stretched and tensed while the breath is held. The serpent posture (or cobra) creates conscious tension and relaxation, causing an expansion of consciousness and heightened sensual awareness. It improves circulation and stimulates the sexual organs.

The cat posture instills flexibility of body and mind, both of which are important to the correct practice of Tantric Yoga. The stretching and yawning antics of cats should be mimicked during this posture. Enter the pose while exhaling and relax the pose when inhaling.

The camel posture (*ushtrasana*) evolves from a bow-like shape, linking hands and feet. The hands are lifted up and brought together as illustrated. This posture is very beneficial to the back and stimulates the glandular system. It also helps one gain control of sexual energy.

The plow posture (*halasana*) should be practiced as slowly as possible. It is helpful to the muscles of the back and neck, increases the flow of blood to the legs and effectively reduces fatigue.

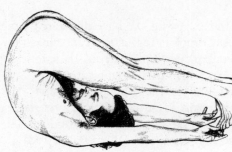

Forward-bending postures (variations of *paschimottanasana*, the back stretch) are essential to avoid premature aging. These postures stimulate the internal organs, release latent energies and aid the establishment of a creative mental attitude toward life.

In this variation of the plow posture (*halasana*) the legs are brought right over, while the hands give support. This position stimulates the internal organs and relieves fatigue.

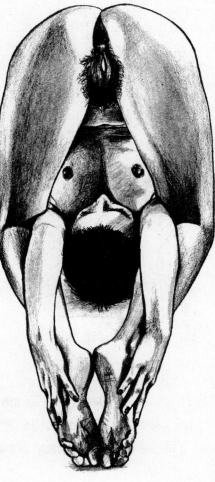

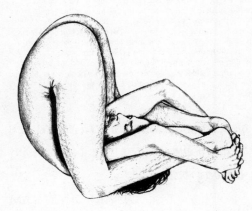

Once the forward-bending postures are perfected, the body will become flexible enough to reach the *yoganidrasana*, Vishnu's sleep posture (also known as posture of the intermediate state). This is extremely effective in balancing internal disharmony and stimulating sexuality.

Vishnu's sleep posture or *yoganidrasana*, though difficult to achieve, is extremely relaxing and stimulates all the glands, as well as the internal organs. It warms the body, releases latent energy and is sexually invigorating. The posture should never be rushed; each foot should be gently brought up to and over the shoulders in turn.

Sequence leading up to the peacock posture (*mayurasana*) from the lotus posture. The palms are placed on the floor, as shown, and the elbows bent into the abdominal region. The natural leverage created lifts the body into a horizontal position. The *mayurasana* is very effective in eliminating toxins from the body. It helps regulate digestion, tones up the internal organs and stimulates the sexual glands.
Named after the peacock, which has the power to digest poisons and is an enemy of snakes, the *mayurasana* should be maintained for only a few moments at a time, and then repeated. It aids the development of a strong Will and helps keep the body youthful.

62

BRAHMA

the creative

In this section we have illustrated some of the simplest Yoga asanas, as well as a few complex ones. Generally it is best to learn at least two sitting postures, several stretching positions, simple reclining positions, a squatting position, a reverse position (like the head stand), and at least one complex asana. When Hatha Yoga becomes a natural part of your life, you'll be amazed to find how much extra energy and spirit you have for day-to-day activities. For couples wishing to expand the parameters of their physical relationship, there is no greater preparation than shared participation in Hatha Yoga.

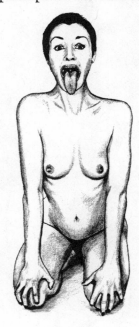

The lion posture (*simhasana*) evolves out of the kneeling heroic posture (*virasana*). The main feature is that the jaws should be wide open, the tongue extended as far as possible toward the chin and the hands stretched. This is a posture of tension, with the eyes widened and fixed either at the end of the nose or at the center of the brow. A feeling of "being a lion" should be evoked and the breath should be inhaled through the mouth. This posture instills psychological strength, tones up the senses and clears mucus.

There are as many Yoga asanas as there are species of animals and other creatures. Of these, eighty-four positions are particularly important. If one considers these, then the lotus posture and the half lotus posture are among the very best.

GORAKSASHATAKAM

Place the hands level and equipoised below the navel center. While thus sitting in the lotus posture, straighten the spinal column, throw out the diaphragm and bend the neck to the shape of a hook, pressing the chin near to the throat. Place the tongue against the roof of the mouth, just behind the teeth. All these factors help the practitioner of Yoga to experience true meditation.

SECRET DOCTRINES OF MAHAMUDRA

Sitting in the lotus posture, and becoming aware of the movements of Prana and Apana, the Yogi should perform breath control and visualize the flow of energy. Thus, Liberation becomes attainable.

SHIVA SAMHITA

One general principle that repeatedly appears in the Tantric teachings is to refrain from suppressing natural urges. Any suppression of our physical natures causes an inner reaction, a kind of distortion that destroys inner harmony. The whole range of physical, emotional and mental urges should be included in this admonition, even though such a statement may seem like an endorsement of self-indulgence. Self-indulgence is rarely the product of a natural urge. Rather, it results from a lack of emotional and psychological maturity. Of course it is all-important to be able to distinguish between the natural and the unnatural. Discernment is the key to putting this principle into practice. This point of view is unique to the Tantric tradition; almost without exception the other spiritual teachings prescribe strict rules for the suppression of natural functions such as hunger, sleep and, above all, sex. Tantra teaches that the suppression of natural urges is potentially harmful to both mental and physical health and can lead to neurosis or morbidity. Though suppression of natural urges may bring about desirable effects temporarily, the long-term result is limiting and true spiritual evolution is rarely achieved by this means.

There is a common misconception that the Tantric teachings condone licentiousness. On the contrary, Tantra requires great discipline. It enjoins, for example, a disciplined effort to uproot unnatural and unhealthy habits. As soon as a natural urge is understood, it can be either satisfied or transcended. Tantric texts state that unnatural urges should be *replaced* by natural ones rather than suppressed.

A Tibetan story concerns a man called Sarvabhaksha who had an obsessive compulsion to eat whatever he could lay his hands on. One day he met a Tantric Guru called Saraha and begged for some advice to help him with his problem. The Guru initiated him and taught him to visualize his belly as the empty sky and his digestive fire as the ultimate conflagration of all the worlds. He told him to view all food and drink as mere worldly phenomena and, while eating, to imagine himself devouring the whole universe. Finally the Guru advised him to meditate on the essential emptiness of all phenomena.

Sarvabhaksha followed his teacher's instructions and, instead of suppressing his urge to eat, replaced a gluttonous mental attitude with a meditation. After some years he achieved self-realization and became revered as a teacher, illustrating that it is not so much *what* we do but *how* we do it that transforms us.

Self-discipline should be undertaken willingly and consciously, and performed from a position of inner strength. Learn to distinguish the real from the unreal, the natural from the unnatural in yourself. For example, it is natural for the body to need food every few hours, but unnatural for it to crave food every ten minutes; the former urge should be gratified and the latter transformed. By indulging the unnatural urges of body and mind, one loses the capacity to recognize true needs.

Once again, don't suppress authentic physiological urges. If you have the urge to sneeze, vomit or go to the toilet, then by all means do so as soon as possible. If you don't obey these natural urges, the accumulation of pressure on the internal organs may lead to disease. The same principle applies to sexual urges, which should be viewed with similar common sense. If you wish to free yourself of an unwholesome habit, do so by degrees, replacing the negative habit with a positive one.

By degrees a person should become free of unwholesome and unnatural habits; similarly, one should try to develop wholesome natural habits. The way of doing this is to replace the unnatural with the natural. If withdrawal is gradual, addiction does not reappear; wholesome habits, gradually acquired, become firmly implanted.

CHARAKA SAMHITA

Taoism teaches that the force of Heaven rotates naturally to the left, whereas the force of Earth turns to the right. Sages saw this movement mirrored in the sexual act. From a Japanese woodblock print by Torii Kiyonobu, *circa* 1703.

heaven and earth

The mystic teachings of the East recognize the forces of Heaven and Earth as the two fundamental principles that pervade everything. Hinduism names them *Shiva* and *Shakti*, Tibetan Buddhists call them *Yab* (father) and *Yum* (mother), and Taoism refers to them as *Yang* and *Yin*. These two forces are operative throughout the phenomenal world: light and dark, hot and cold, dry and wet. They are interdependent and mutually sustaining.

The *Force of Heaven* determines the structure of the male sex organ, whereas the

Force of Earth creates the shape of the female sex organ. As the Yang-force of Heaven descends from above, it creates the outward shape of the Lingam. Conversely, as the Yin-force of Earth ascends from below, it creates the inward shape of the Yoni.

The *Yajur Veda*, an early Hindu text, contains the following account of the relative movement of Heaven and Earth: "This Earth revolves through the Heavens and space; it revolves with its mother, the waters. Turning and turning, it moves around its father, the sun." An ancient Taoist text links the rotation of the Heavens and the Earth to the sexual act performed by man and woman. The Japanese rendering of it, known as *Ishimpo*, states: "Just as Heaven rotates to the left and Earth turns to the right, so a man should move his body to the left and the woman to the right while making love. Sexual union performed in this manner is called *Heaven pacified and Earth resolved*."

When male and female forces are balanced, cosmic harmony results. Orgasm resolves the bipolarity of "outer" and "inner," expansion and contraction, positive and negative, solar and lunar. Rumi, a Sufi mystic of the thirteenth century, advised: "Heaven is man and Earth is woman; Earth fosters what Heaven lets fall. Regard Heaven and Earth as endowed with intelligence, since they do the work of intelligent beings." The esoteric function of sexual love is the resolution of the complementary intelligences of Heaven and Earth.

The Yang-force of Heaven is dominant in man and the Yin-force of Earth is dominant in woman. The former causes an outward penetrating shape to the Lingam, whereas the latter creates an inward receptive shape to the Yoni. Thus the forces of Heaven and Earth complement each other during sexual contact.

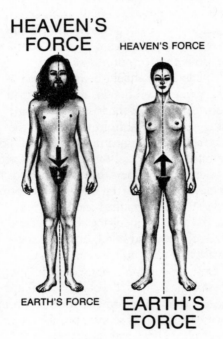

HEAVEN'S FORCE

HEAVEN'S FORCE

EARTH'S FORCE

EARTH'S FORCE

Heaven is lasting and Earth enduring. The reason for this is that they do not live for themselves alone; therefore they live long.

TAO TE CHING

The tree of Eternity has its roots in Heaven above and its branches hang down to Earth. It is the pure Immortal Spirit upon which all worlds rest.

KATHA UPANISHAD

The spending of the seed of Heaven and the giving shape to that seed by Earth are the natural way of man and woman, as natural as a fire blazing upward and water running downward. There is a method known as the Heavenly and Earthly "net," whereby men and women indulge in sexual intercourse like the birds and beasts in order thereby to avert worldly calamities.

TS'AN-T'UNG-CH'I / TAO AN

food: the supporter of life

Although food and drink are indispensable, being the primary physical supports of life, most people take them for granted. On the other hand, there is a current obsession with diet. Among the most popular diets today are health foods, zen macrobiotics and vegetarianism. Unfortunately the Yogic teachings on the subject of food and drink have not yet been fully explored in the West. Eastern-oriented health cults have emerged, but these tend to present only partial truths about the philosophy of food expounded in the Yoga texts.

Oriental medicine and Yoga have much to offer on the subject of diet. The unique feature of their dietary system is the categorization of foods by "taste." All the qualities inherent in food are believed to be represented by six primary tastes, which through various combinations create all the flavors we know. These six tastes—sweet, sour, salty, pungent, bitter and astringent—determine by their proportion, balance or imbalance the wholesomeness or unwholesomeness of food and its palatability to the individual.

Yogic teachings explain that the taste buds extract the essence of the food before it is passed on to the stomach, where the physical process of digestion takes place. We in the West concern ourselves with the protein, starch and vitamin content of the food we eat, but rarely consider the subtle transformation of food from physical matter to emotional, mental or spiritual energies.

In general, Westerners have a tendency to be overweight. We eat to excess and then become infatuated with diets. The Yoga tradition counsels eating in moderation, regularly and at the proper time; it teaches us to become aware of the digestive function and balance intake with the needs of our temperament.

According to Yogic texts, the taste of food has a direct effect on the feelings and sentiments and subtly influences the Spirit. One combination of tastes can cause elation and eroticism, while another can cause irritability or anger. The relationship between "taste" and "feelings" has been researched over a period of two thousand years, as well as expounded by Yogis, who have observed their bodily processes in a heightened state of awareness. Since we know that individuals vary in their temperaments, it seems logical to take this temperamental diversity into account in any study of nutrition. Yogis consider a finely tuned nutritional balance of great help in the achievement of spiritual development and, ultimately, Liberation.

Food is the chief of all material things. It is the medicine for all kinds of disease. From food all things are born.
TAITTRIYA UPANISHAD

One must eat in measure, and the measure of food is determined by the strength of one's gastric fire. A proper measure of food is that which is well digested in the appropriate time. The daily diet should be made up of food that not only helps to maintain well-being but also serves as a prophylactic against disease. From the moment of conception some people are equibalanced as regards the proportion of elemental principles in the body; others have a predominance of one element or another. The person who has an inner physical balance alone enjoys perfect health, while all others are ever liable to disease.
CHARAKA SAMHITA

A person who practices Hatha Yoga without moderating the diet falls prey to various diseases. The Yogi should eat rice, barley, beans, nuts, fruit and other wholesome things. Pure, sweet and cooling foods should be eaten to half fill the stomach. This is called moderation in diet.
GHERANDA SAMHITA

In India food is commonly still eaten with the hands, which are well washed before the meal. Meals are often served on plates made from leaves, as was the custom in ancient times. From an Indian miniature painting, Bilaspur, *circa*. eighteenth century.

food of the gods

Many diverse cultures have evolved rituals centering on the partaking of food as a sacrament. Sacramental food is generally normal food that is believed to possess spiritual qualitites because of a conscious identification by a priest, shaman or other religious figure of the food with a spiritual source. The concept of "empowering" food and taking it as a sacrament is found in the Christian as well as the Hebrew tradition and is usually associated with prayers or "grace" being said over the food. From another point of view, all wholesome food might be considered sacred because it is a life-sustaining gift. In Tantric philosophy all food is dedicated to nourishing spirituality.

Eating is also a highly erotic experience, akin to love-making in many respects. Take care to extract the very most from shared meals. Eat in moderation and choose food that is seasonal; learn from experience what is suitable or unsuitable. According to the *Gheranda Samhita*, at the beginning of Hatha Yoga practice one should refrain from eating excessively acid, bitter, salty or pungent foods. The same text gives good advice about *quantity*, advising that "Half the stomach should be filled with food, one quarter with water or other liquid, and one quarter should be kept empty to aid the practice of breath control."

The Yoga teachings point out that the mental attitude of the person who prepares food permeates the food in a subtle way. A good Yogi can tell the temperament of the person who has cooked a meal by eating the food. Likewise, the mental attitude of the person eating the food affects the digestive process, so don't brood or let yourself get irritable when either preparing or eating food. It's best to meditate, contemplate or sing while preparing food as these activities help to focus the mind and add to the sacramental quality of the meal. Try also to be aware of the properties of the food as you mix together the various ingredients. Above all, don't taste the food while you are preparing it, for this robs it of its sacramental quality. No meal can truly be served as an offering if it has already been tasted. In the East if a meal has been sampled, it is considered eaten and no

longer fit to be served. When cooking, the desires of the self should be set aside.

Yoga teachings categorize food into three main types, according to their effects on body and mind. These three types are related to the triad or *trinity of forces* that pervades all things. The first category is known as *sattvic*, which directly nourishes creative energy and attitude. *Sattvic* foods include milk, honey, butter, dairy products, nuts, grains, most fruits and all vegetables that grow above the ground. All these foods are related to the "sweet" primary taste in particular and are credited with the capacity to stimulate the creative and erotic sentiments. The higher nature of mind is also termed *sattvic*, and has *conscious awareness* as its essential property. All *sattvic* foods stimulate the primordial elements of space and air in the bodily vehicle, and therefore promote growth and creativity. This category is commonly termed the "Food of the Gods," the "milk and honey" of the Biblical tradition.

Indian medical texts declare that the taste essence of food is transformed successively into blood, flesh, fat, bone, marrow and finally semen or ovum. The taste of food thus influences the taste of sexual secretions. The texts suggest that "The best semen [for healthy offspring] is that which is sweet, non-irritant, and of a transparent white crystal-like appearance."

The second type of food, *rajasic*, induces the passionate sentiment. This category includes all foods that are heating and stimulating, such as the root vegetables, spices, salts, most fish, red meat and chicken. These foods are related to the salty and pungent primary tastes in particular, as well as to combinations of taste that include the sweet.

Animal products are considered suitable for human consumption only when very fresh and carefully prepared; otherwise long-term side effects are produced. *Rajasic* foods stimulate the senses, have heating and burning effects, are difficult to digest and produce many waste products. Yogic texts advise those who desire to eat birds or animals to hunt them, as this exercise stimulates both the gastric fire of digestion and the excretion of waste products through perspiration. The effect of such foods on the sexual secretions varies, depending on the ability of the individual to transform these morbid aspects. Generally, the semen becomes thick and slimy, with salty, fleshy or fetid qualities and odor. The secretions from the Yoni take on the same characteristics.

The third type of food, *tamasic*, is evocative of the furious and destructive sentiments. In this category are included all foods that derange or distort the senses, either through their excessively pungent, bitter or astringent tastes or through inner putrefactions. Particularly strong foods such as onions, garlic and chili peppers, as well as foods that are cooked in heavy oil or deep-fried, create destructive feelings unless prepared with great knowledge and care. The heavier meats and eggs fall into the *tamasic* group also; generally, any food that creates excessive body odors or flatulence is of this category.

Tamasic foods eventually bring about an increase in the elements of earth and water, which manifest in the body as mucus, fat and general physical heaviness. Sensitivity is greatly diminished and a very materialistic attitude to life predominates. Sexual secretions take on unpleasant characteristics and sexual intercourse ceases to be sensitive love-making and reverts to a blind striving for purely physical satisfaction.

The wise simplicity of this categorization of food makes it a useful and reliable system for determining what is suitable or unsuitable for consumption. Our choice of food should relate to our lifestyle and goals. A materialistic-minded person will find that the Food of the Gods tastes insipid, whereas a Yogically attuned individual will delight in the simple and subtle tastes of fruit and vegetables. The sportsman will usually prefer

Yogic cookery requires that all ingredients be carefully cleaned and prepared before being mixed. The mental attitude is believed to influence the subtle tastes of food. From an Indian miniature painting, Chamba, *circa* 1810.

to eat the animal protein foods, such as steak and eggs, since these are drawn upon and broken down by the extremes of physical exertion. *Sattvic* or "spiritual" food is best for the Tantric couple. Foodstuffs from the *rajasic* category can be added to this basic diet, especially when extra stimulation is needed. A basic blend of these two categories provides great range and variety, the secret being the correct balancing of the elements. Incorrectly balanced or stale food falls into the *tamasic* category. Experiment with different combinations and use the spicy elements delicately to create infinite and subtle variations of the Food of the Gods.

The wise person who seeks happiness in both this world and the next should exercise great care in selecting wholesome and invigorating food to eat. Light articles of food contain a predominance of the qualities of space, air and fire. The heavier foods contain a larger proportion of the properties of earth and water. CHARAKA SAMHITA

A wholesome diet promotes healthy physical and spiritual growth in a person. Indulgence in an unwholesome diet produces disease and worldly problems.

SUSHRUTA SAMHITA

water

Fresh water is necessary to the well-being of the body. Most water is fluorinated, chlorinated and contaminated from its passage through miles of metal pipe. Therefore, if you live in a city, it's well worth spending the money to purchase fresh spring or mineral water in bottles. On the average, we require about seven glasses of liquid a day. Fresh water is the most purifying and invigorating of all drinks. Taken first thing in the morning, its capacity to tone up the organs and senses has earned it the title of "nectar" in the Tantric tradition.

Rainwater is especially purifying and ancient Yogic teachings declare that the season of its collection changes the quality of the water and its therapeutic effect. Mineral water with high calcium or silica content is particularly suitable for the table, as is the naturally sparkling water from health springs. Avoid drinking large amounts of water near or during mealtimes. Doing so dilutes the digestive juices, and thus impairs the digestion of food. Drink only enough to purify your taste buds during the meal. Generally it is not advisable to drink water late at night, or water that is excessively cold. For digestive problems, a glass of warm water works wonders.

Fruit juices and liquid foods have a very high water content. As such, they are easily assimilated and are ideal for revitalizing and invigorating a tired body. Fresh fruit juices, rich in natural sugars, vitamins and minerals, are highly recommended for the Yogic way of life. Modern juice extractors make fresh fruit and vegetable juices easily available. Such liquid food is highly energizing and healing. The healthy habit of providing the body with wholesome liquids will prove a remarkable preventive measure against physical and mental illnesses of all types.

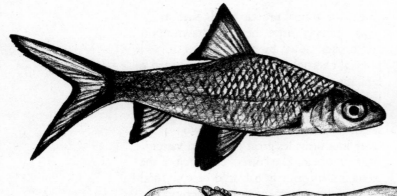

The fish posture (*matsyasana*) evolves from the lotus posture and is ideal for relaxation. It is particularly suited to follow bathing, prior to Tantric ritual. During practice of this posture meditate on yourself as a fish swimming against the current, while slightly moving the hips and pointing the fingers. It helps you gain control over watery elements in the body and endows your whole being with vitality.

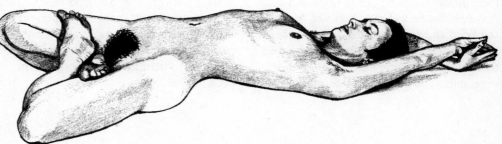

For all the six primary tastes, water is the common source; water and the sense of taste are intimately connected.
CHARAKA SAMHITA

Water nourishes and sustains the spirit as well as the physical body. Water is considered foremost among the elements, since it purifies and uplifts the individual from the mundane to the transcendental. Mountain water, spring water and collected rainwater are highly beneficial and are considered noble by the wise.
GARUDA PURANA

bathing

Water is a powerful agent of purification for the body and mind. Many religions have baptism rituals and also prescribe precise methods of bathing. In the West we shower or bathe every morning or evening, thinking nothing particular about it; it is a habit, practiced in the name of hygiene. Nevertheless, bathing, whether in a tub, shower, lake, pool or ocean, has both spiritual and erotic qualities.

Any intentional act has a power that far transcends the specific nature of the act itself. If you view bathing as a process of spiritual purification, and intentionally ritualize the practice, the benefits will be greater than if you bathe merely for the sake of hygiene. Start with the head and hands and finish with the feet, or contrariwise if you prefer, the point being to maintain an order. Always be sure to imagine that you are purifying more than just the physical body.

A cold shower produces a sudden charge of negative ions, which are healthful, invigorating and effective in creating a feeling of relaxation and psychic regeneration. Water is "negative" and "magnetic," and has a potent recharging effect on the psycho-organism. Use the natural qualities of water to help yourself overcome the stress and strain of city life. A bath or shower before Yoga is tremendously beneficial; its purificatory power restores the body to its natural responsiveness.

In the Bible there are many accounts of foot washing. Mary Magdalen, when washing the feet of Jesus, was giving the respect customary to an honored guest. It is still customary in the East to wash the hands and feet when entering the inner part of a house. A bowl and water are also provided for washing before and after a meal. The reasons for this are partly cultural, since most meals in the East are eaten with the hands, but the physical and psychic aspects of hygiene are also significant. This is reflected in most spiritual traditions, where the washing of hands and feet prior to prayer is obligatory.

After all worldly activities, washing is advisable, especially before any intimacy.

Bringing the office or kitchen "into the bedroom" dissipates the potency of love-making. The simple gesture of washing the hands and feet can make a great difference in your mental state, as well as discharging the accumulated tensions.

A simple Yogic trick to assist in maintaining natural equilibrium is to inhale a small quantity of cool or lukewarm water through each nostril separately, then blow it out again into a basin. First block one nostril with a finger and snort up water held in your cupped hand. Then blow it out and repeat for the other nostril. This clears the sinuses and balances the polarity of the breath. Another simple technique for restoring vitality is to put your feet under a running tap of cold water for a few minutes. This is particularly effective after a day spent walking around in shoes, and will cause an immediate discharge of tension.

Yogic texts refer to the importance of washing the anal orifice with cold water. This helps the contraction of the anus and also is commonsense hygiene. Since anal contraction is an essential practice of Tantric Yoga, aiding the drawing up of ecstatic energies, this practice is especially important.

Whenever taking a bath or shower, call on the Lord of the Waters to help maintain your inner vitality and joy. Do the same for your partner. In the Hindu tradition Vishnu, the Lord of the Waters, is also the Preserver and ruler over the erotic sentiment (see Part III). His counterpart is called Lakshmi, the goddess of prosperity and the provider of all material gain. When bathing in the sea, call on the waters to carry your spirit back to the source for replenishment. The main point is to imbue your daily ablutions with the sacred.

Many of the complex love-postures are best practiced in the sea or a pool, as water makes the body much lighter. If you do this, you will find it easier to attain these postures in the bedroom. Practicing love-postures in rivers and pools used to be a fairly common occurrence in the East, but with the advent of Western influence it became very rare.

Hot baths or showers are very relaxing and cause the physical and Subtle Body to expand. However, drowsiness can easily be

Bathing is invigorating and has both spiritual and erotic qualities. From a Chinese print of the eighteenth century.

Shared bathing helps establish deep and lasting communication. From a Chinese print of the Ming period.

produced and the mind can then become dull from the excessive heat. The action of hot water on the skin opens the pores and permits accumulated poisons to be expelled, purifying the body and clarifying the mind. The combination of hot baths and cold showers counteracts the tiring effect. After prolonged immersion in a hot tub, step out and pour cold water over your body. This will contract the body and sharpen the consciousness. It is a traditional practice for Yogis to dive into ice-cold waters in order to shock the body into wakefulness and concentrate the mind.

The common tendency to rush off to the bathroom to wash, douche or shower after love-making is condemned in the Eastern love treatises. The perspiration produced on bodies making love contains subtle minerals and vital secretions that are beneficial if absorbed. Yoga texts advise the couple not to bath or shower for at least an hour after climaxing. The absorption of love-secretions is of great benefit to the couple. These essences contain many vital elements that are beneficial to both body and mind. Certain Yoga techniques (see Part III) enhance the natural capacity of the sensitive membranes of the sexual organs to absorb love-juices.

Our bodies are composed mostly of water and the watery element covers the majority of our planet. Without water, we can live but a brief time. One of the most important elements to our well-being, water plays a sustaining and purifying role in our life. As such, it is worthy of honor for its symbolic as well as its physical qualities.

Hot tubs are very much a part of Japanese and Chinese hygiene. This humorous illustration, from a Japanese book of the late seventeenth century, shows a traditional tub in unorthodox use.

Water for bathing should be warm, rather than too cold or too hot, though this should be determined by circumstances. When the solar breath is dominant, it is good to remain in the water, and when the lunar breath prevails, it is best to come out. Protect the eyes from heat during steam baths, using a cool cloth for this purpose.

SWARA CHINTAMANI

One should first bathe the body properly with running water; then apply perfumes or ornaments. This type of bathing should be combined with breath control. The effect is to destroy both inner and outer dirt and make a person fit for spirituality.

LAKSHMI TANTRA

sacred fire

The use of fire by our primitive ancestors differentiated them from the animals. Thus, fire became recognized as sacred, an attribute that has influenced spiritual traditions everywhere. A well-known Greek myth describes how Prometheus and his brother were given the job of distributing knowledge among humans. When Prometheus noticed that whereas animals had ample protection from the elements, humans did not, he stole fire from the gods and gave it to mankind. The Greeks equated the gift of fire with the gift of culture, since fire is necessary for the development of the arts and sciences. The deity of fire, Hephaestus, was the son of Zeus (the ruler of the world) and Hera (goddess of all women), but was born ugly and lame. The last of his three wives, Aphrodite, was unfaithful to him; later she was associated with eroticism and became the goddess of Love. Fire is associated with erotic love in many ancient mythologies.

Hinduism includes a number of fiery gods in its pantheon; among these are Surya (the sun god), Mitra (the solar friend) and Agni (the fire god). Agni, the youngest of the Vedic gods, was the son of Heaven (Dyaus) and Earth (Prithivi), the brother of Indra (ruler of the world), and the guardian of this world. He was always portrayed as twin-headed, seven-tongued and red-colored. His wife is the dawn (Ushas) and he personified fire in a threefold way: as the blazing sun, the flashing lightning and the sacrificial flame. Inside man he represents the Navel Chakra (the solar plexus), the power of sight and the digestive fire.

Tantric texts frequently refer to fire as the origin and end of all phenomena. Western cosmologists speculate that fire is the main element at the moment of creation and the moment of final destruction of every sun. Fire has the power to level all that is created, so allowing for new acts of creation. Many great Yogis spent years seated in front of a fire, ultimately reaching transcendental perfection through a process of identification with and absorbtion into its flames.

With the advent of Christianity the West lost its sense of the sacred nature of fire. Instead, fire became merely a utilitarian aid or an aesthetic device. Most modern homes are heated by electricity, gas or fuel oil. People rarely sit in front of an open fire, and as a result the concept of a sacred fire has receded into the unconscious. This is unfortunate, for fire was long a source of inspiration to artists, poets, mystics, Yogis and lovers alike.

Eastern teachings refer to an inner fire as well as an outer one. They are equally sacred. The inner fire is the vital principle that, when stimulated by the breath, blazes up and consumes the impurities of both body and mind. Inner fire is also said to have the ability to devour destiny or Karma. When centered in the region of the stomach, it is the gastric fire that digests food and allows the body to assimilate life-sustaining ingredients. In the eyes inner fire manifests as the sparkle of clarity and delight; in the sexual region it is the primordial Kundalini, which flashes up the spine like lightning. The main focus of inner fire is at the navel center, where it blazes up; from this point of transformation the inner fire travels throughout the body and empowers consciousness.

When sitting in front of an open fire try to consider it as a living being. Regard fire as an awesome teacher from which much can be learned. Bearing in mind that fire is both sacred and transcendental will help the Spirit to evolve and mature. Treat fire carefully and with consideration. In the East Yogis and priests generally offer food to the sacred fire, even a small portion of every meal; this assists them in identifying their consciousness with fire. While watching a fire, meditate on your inner fire, centered at the navel region, imagining that it is burning up all physical impurities, mental confusion and psychic obstacles. Imagine your whole being filling up with spiritual fire and concentrate

Agni, the Indian Fire god, is two-headed, signifying inner and outer fire. His vehicle is the ram. From a South Indian carving of the eighteenth century.

Two heroes sit in front of a sacred fire. From an illustrated Ramayana, Kulu, *circa* 1670.

Fire is a potent object of meditation and is linked to the seed-sound "RANG" centered at the navel region of the body.

it in the Third Eye region of the forehead. Tantric texts state that when inner fire is spiritualized and concentrated in the brow, a vision of spiritual worlds is attained.

The flickering of firelight and the red glow of embers are conducive to meditation and visualization. Furthermore, fire can readily evoke the erotic sentiment and its radiant heat is effective in stimulating the Kundalini. Yogis often draw close to the glowing red embers of a long-burning fire and expose their genital region to its radiance, thereby deriving energy.

The *Gheranda Samhita* gives the following meditation and breathing practice as suited to the cultivation of inner fire:

While breathing in through the right nostril, mentally repeat the seed-sound "RANG" sixteen times and contemplate the navel center. Retain the breath through sixty-four repetitions of the same seed-sound and then expel the air through the left nostril during thirty-two repetitions. Next, fix the gaze on the tip of the nose and visualize the inner moon of the head center as reflected there. Repeat the whole process in reverse and imagine that a subtle nectar flows from the reflected moon at the tip of the nose and runs back through all the bodily channels, purifying and revitalizing them.

Tantric texts declare that firelight vibrates at specific frequencies, according to its color. The sacred fire can, in the Tantric view, be employed as a communication device and oracle. When precise vibrations of firelight are internalized, psychic powers result.

Eroticism is directly linked to the fiery element. The visualization of an inner fire blazing up from the navel center is stimulating to the glandular system and helps to heighten the erotic sentiment. Outer fire is also erotically stimulating. Let firelight flicker and play over your naked body whenever you get an opportunity; share this experience with your partner and allow it to enrich your love life. Allow the fires of passion to transform physical longing into spiritual fulfillment.

The inner fire is conceived of as a blazing sun centered in the navel region. From a Deccani painting of the eighteenth century.

The Imperishable is the Real. As sparks fly upward from the blazing fire, from the depths of the Imperishable arise all things, and to the depths of the Imperishable they in turn descend. To the fire, whence one came, whence one was born.

MUNDAKA/CHANDOGYA UPANISHADS

The Kundalini, blazing up at the navel center, burns up all psychic obstacles; the ego melts and becomes transformed.

CHANDAMAHAROSANA TANTRA

The pigmentation of the organism, the digestion of food, the vitalization and nutrition of cells, the origination and preservation of eyesight, the germination of heat and the maintenance of bodily temperature, and the origination of the intellectual faculty, all should be regarded as the functions of the five divisions of inner fire within the human body.

SUSHRUTA SAMHITA

karma and sex

The understanding and acceptance of the Eastern concept of *Karma* is particularly important to every person who wishes to apply the Tantric teachings in his or her life. The operation of Karma in everyday life should be constantly studied. The causes of events often seem mysterious, yet if we look carefully at the play of forces from a Karmic viewpoint, we can more easily understand the subtle workings of destiny. Although the general idea of Karma, the law of action and reaction, has been accepted in contemporary Western thought, a highly developed intuition of its precise workings is rarely found.

According to the Eastern view, Karma shapes reality; the events we are currently experiencing are a direct result of our past actions, either in this life or a previous one. And our present attitudes and actions likewise determine our future. This principle is as true for the world of physics as it is for the drama of individual and collective life.

According to Tantric teachings, the forces of Karma pervade the world. As already discussed in "Shiva and Jiva," desires cling to and accompany the individual soul (the Jiva) through its various incarnations. The Jiva enjoys or suffers the fruits of our action; bound into the chains of matter by their Karma, Jivas incarnate again and again, receiving various names and identities. Finally, when all its Karma has been extinguished, the Jiva is absorbed into its Source, which Sanskrit texts refer to as *Parabrahma* (beyond Brahma): the universal godhead.

Karmas migrate, like birds, from life to life, attaching themselves to the life-force. These Karmic forces are modified by conscious action during successive lifetimes. The *Prana Upanishad* declares that "Whatever is thought of at the moment of death unites a person with his or her primary *Prana*; then the *Prana* unites with the soul and leads the individual into rebirth in whatever realm is suitable." We have, in previous sections, referred to the upward- and downward-moving vitalities of the body, and also introduced the concept of the upper and lower gates of our bodily temple. These are the gates

through which *Prana* (life-force, breath) and Karma enter and leave this body; without a combination of these two, an individual would not be reincarnated.

Tantric love-posture for channeling energy. The feet are brought together, creating a closed circuit between the couple. From a Rajasthani miniature, *circa* eighteenth century.

The *Prana Upanishad*, an early Hindu text, states: "The *Prana* enters the body at birth, that the desires of the mind, continuing from past lives, may be fulfilled." Personal motivations are the "desires of the mind"; usually these unconscious motivations surface at times of agony or ecstasy. Tantras explain that an individual can learn to dissolve Karma by the action of the inner fire, by sense withdrawal, by meditation and absolute inner stillness, and by participating in the same activities that create the Karma, only with such care and consciousness that the original binding desires are transcended. Furthermore, if a person can live dynamically "in the present," past influences can be transcended. Karmic forces move through the channels of the Subtle Body and also pervade the outer world, manifesting in everyday events. Every moment is a Karmic experience; by contemplating and correlating these moments we can rediscover the Eternal Now within ourselves.

The lotus posture (*padmasana*) is ideally suited to meditation and contemplation. By visualizing a "lotus seat" and eliminating all desires from the mind, ascendency over the forces of destiny can be achieved.

The *Brihadaranyaka Upanishad*, another early text, gives us this interesting view of Karma: "The man who practices sexual intercourse *while knowing the formula of Karma and its action* takes to himself the accumulated good Karma of the woman; he who makes love *without knowing such a formula* stands the risk of losing his accumulated good Karma to her." During love-making the vital forces of the couple blend; their individual Karmas converge and an exchange takes place that can affect their individual or joint destinies. What actually happens depends on the degree of consciousness of the couple. If one is more aware than the other, selfishness will result in a negative Karmic exchange. On the other hand, if loving compassion dominates, a positive Karmic exchange is created. This is one of the subtle purposes behind sexual initiations, a secret practice common to most mystery teachings.

A Tibetan legend tells of a famous teacher called Gandapa (or Ghantapa) who inadvertently offended the king of the country by refusing to give him an initiation. The king decided to set a trap for the Yogi, in the hope of ridiculing him publicly. Knowing that Gandapa was practicing a discipline of celibacy, he paid a prostitute a great amount of money to arrange for the Yogi's seduction. The prostitute trained her young daughter for the task and sent a message to Gandapa to the effect that she was a widow and wanted to gain merit by preparing a feast for the Yogi, as was the custom.

The daughter's name was Darima and she was exquisite in every way. Her mother prepared an enormous feast, which was delivered to Gandapa by male attendants accompanied by Darima, who was to serve the delicacies. When the dishes were laid out, the attendants left, according to the prostitute's instructions.

Gandapa was a bit taken aback to find himself attended by such a young and beautiful virgin-girl; however, he didn't want to cause offense by making a fuss. Once his meal was finished, he told Darima to leave, but acting on instructions, she said, "It's going to rain. I'll wait awhile if you don't mind." She remained until dusk and then said, "Oh, I'm afraid of the dark. My mother promised to send an escort; I wonder when they'll come." As it got later, Gandapa told her she might as well spend the night outside his hut and provided her with blankets and a pillow. However, during the night Darima pretended to be afraid of demons and kept on crying out. Gandapa then told her to come into his hut and share his sleeping space.

The hut was so small that, inevitably, their bodies drew close together and intertwined. Spontaneously, Gandapa united with Darima and they made love passionately. Together they passed through the four levels of erotic ecstasy and together they traveled the path of Liberation to the very end. By her services to Gandapa, Darima cleared her own Karmic obstacles and became fully liberated. Later, when the king arrived with his retinue, instead of being able to expose Gandapa as a hypocrite, he witnessed a series of miracles that caused him to re-evaluate his point of view. Thus, the subtle Karmic exchange between Darima and Gandapa brought about a total change in Darima's destiny as well as in that of the king.

This story is in fact an allegory, illustrating how a single sexual act can, in the right circumstances, alter the course of destiny.

Selfish motivation should not be present during love-making, but rather a desire to benefit the loved one and attain spiritual ideals. In this way the relationship between Karma and sex is best served. Dedicate your union to the enrichment of your lover. Such an exchange happens spontaneously and naturally when two people find themselves totally and completely in love. However, a *conscious* awareness of the intermingling of the energies of Karma and sex will greatly assist the evolution of the couple.

Promiscuous sex causes Karma to be accumulated rapidly, which can, in turn, effect changes in character totally alien to one's basic nature. Another type of negative Karmic exchange takes the form of a kind of vampirism, in which positive Karma is deliberately tapped in the partner and replaced by negative Karma. Promiscuous sex rites of black magic make use of this type of vampirism to exalt one individual at the cost of another. Such practices are, fortunately, self-limiting, and lead to delusion and corruption.

Karmic exchanges take place when the life-force moves along the central Great Axis (the *Sushumna*) of the Subtle Body. Generally it is the emotions that cause this movement. Tantric texts state that when a person is truly angry, the life-force commonly enters the Great Axis and a Karmic exchange with the person at whom the anger is directed invariably results. Fear can likewise force the life energy into the Great Axis and create a condition of Karmic exchange. Anger and fear are facets of a similar experience, and when these emotions are brought into role playing, Karmic exchanges take place. Sadomasochistic relationships revolve around this type of exchange; glimpses of transcendental tranquility may be achieved through dominant/submissive role playing, but the long-term result is an unresolved Karmic imbalance that tends to manifest in self-destruction.

By developing an awareness of the subtle workings of Karma in human destiny, we evolve a frame of reference for understanding the seemingly erratic events of everyday life. Far too many relationships go wrong without any recognition of the real cause. It's no use blaming oneself or the other. Rather, the couple should share and discuss their hopes and fears, observing how their intertwined Karmas mold events. By channeling their desires consciously, the couple can become masters of their own destiny.

Karma leads, Karma moves, Karma takes, Karma follows; Karma binds, Karma releases, Karma gives, Karma never rests. The intelligent Yogi watches Karma and learns its ways; then, through the power of spirituality, steps aside from Karma.

VARAHI TANTRA

It is said that when a person very eagerly awaits the command of another, with a firm resolution that whatever is commanded must be carried out, then that person will, through the intensity of eagerness and resolution, attain a state of inner equilibrium. Through such a condition of mind the inhaling and exhaling breaths enter the central Great Axis. Then all mental states fade away and a tranquil consciousness emerges.

SPANDA KARIKA

If a person is falsely accused of something, then the merit of the accuser is transferred to that person and the bad Karma of the accused goes to the accuser. One must never mistreat a guest, for the guest then takes the good Karma of the host and leaves his or her own bad Karma behind.

PASHUPATA SUTRA / SHIVA PURANA

Love-posture for exchanging energy between the couple. The woman holds a rosary of flowers. From a Rajasthani miniature painting of the eighteenth century.

sleep

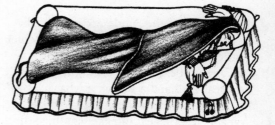

Sleeping on the left side makes the breath become dominant on the right side, and vice versa. Normally people toss and turn during sleep, as the breath tries to attain balance between right and left. From a Basohli miniature painting of the early eighteenth century.

The length of time one sleeps is less important than the *quality* of the sleep. Most modern-day city dwellers do not get as much relaxation and rest in their sleeping hours as they would in a natural environment. Because many environmental factors pollute and distort the quality of sleep, people often awake in the morning to find they've hardly rested at all. For this reason, many people take sleeping pills and tranquilizers to help them obtain the rest that is out of their reach. This, of course, is not a solution; sleep induced in this way is qualitatively different from natural sleep. Many problems in obtaining restful sleep can be overcome by a little conscious preparation. There is certainly no need to rely on pills.

It is not advisable to eat a large meal either late at night or just before sleep. The digestion functions best in harmony with the sun; in the morning, at midday or in the early evening there is plenty of digestive "fire" available. At night the body works at a different rhythm; it cannot break down food as easily as it can during the day.

While over-eating tends to induce sleep, this sleep is due to a condition of physical morbidity and, as such, is unhealthful. The toxins in the undigested food clog the system and stop the flow of vitality. Eventually over-eating leads to physical malfunctions and disease.

Mental and emotional conditions also affect the quality of sleep. Anyone who works in an office or with machinery should try to exorcise those "vibrations" from the body and mind before sleep. Take a bath or shower, "switch off" mentally from the day's work, stretch the body and do some Yoga, meditation or dance; do whatever you can to get back into your natural inner rhythm. If the day has been particularly difficult, with emotional upsets, try to correct any internal "damage" by consciously regulating the breathing. Solar-

lunar breathing is particularly helpful in such instances, as is the practice of the healing breath.

The creative attitude also has the power to transmute negative energies, thus allowing a natural entry into sleep. The Yoga asana known as *shavasana* (corpse position), which consists of lying on the back, without a pillow, and tensing and relaxing each part of the body in turn, is another very helpful method for preparing to sleep.

Sometimes it is difficult to get to sleep because the mind is "racing," turning over ideas or problems. When this happens, it helps to turn the mind backward. The technique is to try to trace *visually* (not verbally or mentally) whatever came to your mind last, then the thought before that, the one before that and so on. Eventually a kind of "neutral zone" will be reached and natural quiet will take over the mind and lead one into sleep.

Love-making is the most powerful way to relax the body and mind. Sharing the natural energies of love is a form of communion that clears the mind and restores the body. The time spent in bed just before going to sleep holds some of the most precious moments of the day. Removed from worldly concerns, you can contact your own and your partner's natural energies.

Sleep is a most natural activity and should never be viewed simply as an invitation to oblivion. By going to sleep *consciously*, one can enter the dream world and derive enjoyment and teaching from it.

The corpse posture (*shavasana*) requires total relaxation of each part of the body in turn. It clears tension and is a wonderful preparation for rejuvenating sleep.

When a person is entering deep sleep, then all the consciousness goes through the seventy-two thousand subtle channels that lead to the heart center from its circumference. At that time the soul rests in the covering around the heart.

BRIHADARANYAKA UPANISHAD

As, when embraced by the dear woman, one knows neither anything external nor internal, so also a man, when deeply embraced by the inner self, knows neither anything external nor internal.

BRIHADARANYAKA UPANISHAD

sweet dreams

Sleep and dreams are frequently spoken of as though they were the same thing, yet they are really quite distinct. During sleep the physical body rests and readjusts itself to the rhythms of nature. Eastern teachings state that at this time the consciousness settles into the region of the heart, focusing itself there from all parts of the body. The pattern of breathing is adjusted by the position of the body, which moves from one side to the other until sleep is obtained. While dreaming, the consciousness moves upward and, according to esoteric teachings, exits through the throat or head center. Rapid eye movements accompany most dream states, as do subtle movements of the face, mouth, throat and extremities.

We spend about one-third of our lives in either deep sleep or dream states, yet most of us are totally oblivious of the significance of this time. Sleep, like breath, is a natural vital function taken completely for granted. With the exception of remembering a vivid dream or enjoying a particularly refreshing sleep, we hardly give any thought to what transpires during all those years of sleep and dream. For the couple, this time is crucial as it may either bind them together or estrange them.

People generally are quite secretive about the dreams they do remember, but the vast majority of dreams are either never remembered or carelessly forgotten upon waking. Yet each dream conveys a message directly related to past or future events. In a dream the unconscious mind strives to become conscious. Tantra views our normal waking state as itself a kind of dream. To liberate ourselves we must awaken from this dream state and face reality as it is. So, too, must we gain a conscious awareness of our dreams. This can be achieved by learning to remember our dreams upon waking. Resolve before going to sleep that you will remember your dreams. In the morning try to wake up slowly, bringing some of your dream into waking consciousness. Most dreams are lost through too-sudden awakening.

Once you learn to remember your dreams, share them with your partner without concealing anything. A subtle understanding will develop between you, which will begin to permeate the dream world. At times you may even find yourselves sharing the same dream; at other times only some parts of your dreams will be in common. It's a wonderful

In Indian literature dream interpretation is given great importance. Tantra teaches that deep insights into both past and future can be attained through practice of Dream Yoga. Illustration from the Rasamanjari, Basohli school, *circa* 1695.

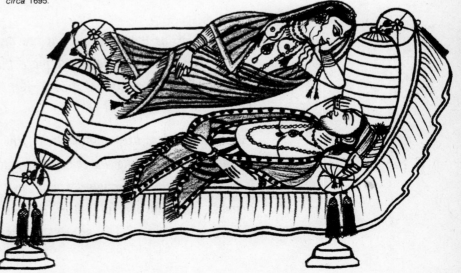

Fetal positions can be effective in gaining conscious control over dreams.

experience to share a dream with the one you love. It helps deepen understanding and gives new meaning to the relationship.

Try to exchange dreams immediately upon awakening, while they are still fresh. A Dream Book or diary of dreams is helpful and can lead to a deeper understanding of personal destiny. With a Dream Book you'll be able to watch the development of dreams over a period of time and gauge how they relate to your life. Try not to analyze your or your partner's dreams, but rather enjoy their drama and relive them as they are recounted. Let dream interpretation be on the light side; maintain the imagery of the dream instead of trying to explain it all away.

Listen and learn from the communications of the unconscious mind while teaching and gaining control of it. Don't view dream content in the light of personality or ego, because doing so will create problems for you both, leading to petty recriminations. It's amazing how jealous a partner can become of what the other is doing in his or her dreams. Rather than being hypocritical, it's best to totally familiarize each other with your inner worlds. Take care not to tell dreams carelessly, or to entertain casual acquaintances with them. Dreams should only be told to those with whom one has a bond of trust and commitment.

The dream world offers a rich treasure house of symbols, images and insights that should be shared with your partner rather than jealously guarded. Gaining conscious awareness of the dream experience helps a person to live a fuller life. Many revelations and sudden inspirations come directly from a remembered dream, a level of awareness outside the limitations of time and circumstance. Dreams can connect us with the past or future and teach us how to live more fully in the present. They are a wonderful source of insight into the nature of our spirit.

One particularly effective way of entering the dream world in a relaxed manner is through stimulation of the sense of smell. This old folk custom leads to "sweet dreams," and is both relaxing and therapeutic. Select a perfume, sweet-smelling herbs or flower petals. Flowers and herbs can fill a pillow or a small sachet and be kept near or under the head. Alternatively, perfume can be sprinkled directly on the bed cushions. Being wafted to sleep by the smell of sweet flowers and herbs is a marvelously relaxing experience. The sweet scent creates a form of psychic protection and leads the spirit to sweet dreams. Rose petals, lavender, rosemary, thyme, jasmine, lotus, sandalwood, marijuana leaves, patchouli and other exotic aromas are all relaxing and aid natural sleep.

The spirit of the human being has two distinct dwellings: this world and the timeless world beyond. There is also a third place, the ever-changing world of dreams. When the inner spirit is in the land of dreams, then all worlds belong to that spirit.

BRIHADARANYAKA UPANISHAD

At the time of deep sleep without dream, the consciousness stays in the region of the heart. At the time of dreaming, the consciousness moves to the neck. When one is not sleeping, it is located mainly in the navel region, and when male and female unite sexually in complete harmony and fulfillment, consciousness rests in the heads of the couple.

BRAHMOPANISHAD; ALSO, YIG CHUNG OF TSONGKHAPA

dream yoga

In a specialized branch of the Tantric teachings a number of specific techniques for gaining conscious control over the dream state are taught. These are referred to as *Dream Yoga* and the practices are connected directly with the mind's natural faculty for visualization.

These practices are simple, direct and especially suited to the highly developed intellectual capacities of the Western mind. In fact, it is surprising that no equivalent technique has emerged from contemporary schools of psychology. Dream analysis is quite different from Dream Yoga, and leads to complex speculation on the meaning of dreams rather than to simple release or transcendental insight. The net result of dream analysis is often more confusing than liberating.

The first principle of Dream Yoga is to regard *everything* as a dream. This means that while awake and seeing, eating, smelling, walking and so on, you should cultivate a kind of dream awareness, the thought that "this is all a dream." Of course one must continue to act with discrimination and responsibility. The object of Dream Yoga is to maintain an unbroken continuity of consciousness throughout both waking and dream states. A creative attitude and faith in your ultimate success are two crucial elements of this practice. It is best to avoid rich foods, over-eating and strenuous taxing of the body while practicing Dream Yoga. History records many instances of individuals receiving profound insights or even whole teachings while dreaming. Examples such as Coleridge's *Kublai Khan*, Edgar Cayce's medical diagnoses and Watson and Crick's vision of the structure of the DNA helix testify to the revelatory nature of dreams.

Before going to bed, take a bath or shower to relax the body. In addition, do some light breathing and meditation and then lie down on the right side. Lying on the right side creates a dominance of the lunar breath (linked to the left psychic channel), which is best suited to creative dreaming. The lunar breath, associated with the Shakti-power of creative energy and the intuitive faculty, enhances the learning of the arts and sciences, as well as all peaceful activities.

Use a scented pillow of suitable size, neither too hard nor too soft, to avoid strain on your neck. Be sure to keep your feet warm, either with bed socks or adequate covers. When you practice Dream Yoga with your partner, you both should lie on your right side, your bodies closely embracing. The man should then imagine the Kundalini, the "inner woman," awakening and taking the form of a goddess. Imagine that you are two sisters, the left and right subtle nerves, intertwined like the caduceus wand of Mercury, each enhancing the finest qualities of the other. Entwine your feet and hands, slightly bending the knees. Try to keep a slight pressure on the right side of the face and throat; this can be done either with the pillow or with the right hand or arm. You'll find that in this position profuse saliva is produced. Let the saliva collect in the mouth and slowly swallow it, all the while imagining that it is feeding and nourishing the Throat Chakra. Press the chin close to the neck and concentrate on the region of your throat. The most important factor during this stage of Dream Yoga is to fall asleep while maintaining an earnest desire to enter the dream world consciously.

Tibetan texts indicate that dream control can be achieved by lying on the right side, so the left breath is dominant, and focusing consciousness on the throat.

Concentrate on the Throat Chakra and imagine it in your mind's eye as colored red. Visualize a red trident or a red "OM" within the brilliantly radiating red throat center. This visualization stimulates the junction of nerves in the throat and helps fix the consciousness there, which in turn leads to conscious entry into the world of dreams. This concentration of mind will also assist the process of dream remembrance. Another technique found in Tantric texts is to visualize yourself in the form of a dancing red goddess or Dakini. The Dakini is an

The Sanskrit word "OM" can be written several different ways. All have a resemblance to the number 3.

The trident is a symbol of Shiva, the Supreme Yogi. It is also symbolic of the junction of nerves at each psychic center.

erotic Wisdom-archetype conceived of as a young girl, very sensual, with full breasts and hips and with a Third Eye blazing with passion. This red Dakini holds a bowl and mystic chopping knife, symbolic, respectively, of compassionate ecstatic non-attachment and cutting through egoistic limitations and dualities. You will find the emotions easily identify with this image, causing them to be aroused. By intentionally invoking the emotions in this manner, a predominantly unconscious emotional reaction is put under conscious control.

One reason for retaining consciousness while dreaming is to develop the faculty for transforming one dream image into another. Once you are conscious of your dream world, the ability to transform dream images will occur naturally. Through such practices a deep insight into the nature of existence will develop.

Various initiatory forms will begin to manifest in dreams as distinct entities with personalities. These may have a sexual implication, taking the form of extremely beautiful male or female figures; if you identify them with your human partner, rather than preserve them as a source of private fantasy, they will enrich the relationship. A number of Western magical texts refer to such male and female initiatory forms as incubi and succubi, evil spirits that seduce sleeping persons. The mediaeval wizards and witches (who were, essentially, sensitives or psychic mediums) were accused of associating with such phantom beings. Eastern teachings indicate that these spirits are related to past lives; they are protective entities, mystic forms of esoteric teachers or otherworldly beings. Western incubus/succubus folklore is found in connection with sexual superstitions, taboos, witchcraft and black magic. Involuntary emission of semen at night, or "wet dreams," was, until recently, associated with the devil or evil spirits. The Christian Church, with its emphasis on guilt and sexual repression, has been largely responsible for misconceptions about incubi and succubi.

Contemporary psychoanalysis fully accepts the sexual nature of most dreams. Whether sexual imagery stems from unfulfilled desires (the Freudian theory) or

from the collective unconscious (the Jungian theory), its significance is beyond doubt. The Tantras teach that through knowing and confronting these mystic dream entities one can, in effect, live out all future lifetimes, thus obviating the necessity for rebirth.

Try to identify dream entities with yourself and your partner rather than with a magical or extra-terrestial source. Above all, don't conceal such dream experiences from the one you love, for doing so may cause a feeling of separateness. The Dream Book and all discussion about dreams must be absolutely candid.

The classical Chinese text on Taoist sexual practices, *Yu-fang-pi-chuch*, describes an experiment for proving the existence of a succubus or incubus. The text advises:

One should go off to live alone, in a place far away from other humans. One should stay there in complete tranquility, staring into space and concentrating one's thoughts on sexual intercourse. After three days and nights the body will suddenly feel alternately cold and hot, the heart will be troubled and the vision will begin to blur. Then a man who is practicing this experiment will suddenly seem to meet a woman of great beauty, and if a woman is practicing, she will meet a handsome man. If one experiences sexual intercourse with such a succubus or incubus, it will seem that the pleasure is greater than with any normal human being. But at the same time a physical lethargy will be created, which will be hard to cure.

The text later explains that one should refrain from sexual intercourse and conserve sexual energy so that one can "make love to a human woman (or man) for a whole day and night, without ceasing. When the body is so weary that one is unable to continue with the act of sex, the sexual organs should remain united." This will ensure that any disease caused by the succubus or incubus will be cured.

When a dream nears its climax, the unifying thread of the dream should be determined. Select the most significant image or images that give a dream coherence. Try to retain this image and value it as initiation into the realm of the unconscious. This method will enable you to awaken with full knowledge of the dream and the subtle *meaning* of the experience. Dream Yoga is a source of inspiration and initiation outside the limitations of time and space.

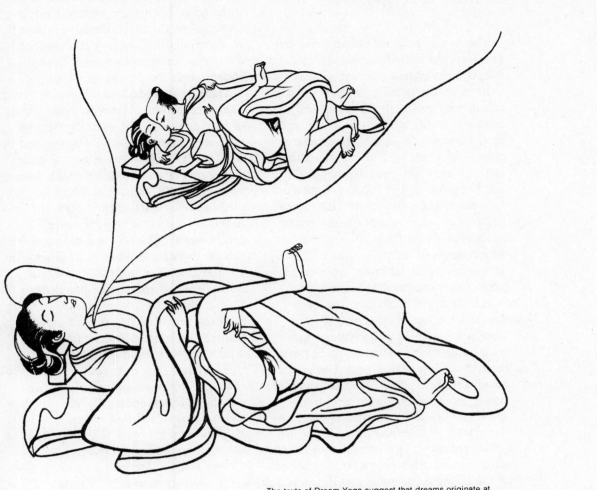

The texts of Dream Yoga suggest that dreams originate at the throat center (Chakra). This illustration depicts a lady having an erotic dream. From a Japanese print of the eighteenth century.

Going up and down in the dream state, the higher aspect of the dream spirit can assume many different forms; this may become enjoyment in the company of beautiful women, or laughing with companions, or even beholding wonderful or terrible sights.

BRIHADARANYAKA UPANISHAD

The Yogi who can recognize dreams fairly well should practice the transformation of dreams. This means that in the dream state you should try to change yourself into a bird, a tiger, a lion, a king, a forest, a house, or anything you like. Then transform into a Buddha-body, sitting or standing, large or small. Also, try to transform the things seen in dreams into different objects; for instance, an animal into a man, water into fire, earth into space, one into many, or many into one. Practice the various supernatural powers, such as shooting fire from the upper body and water from the lower part, trampling on the sun and moon, or multiplying your body into millions and billions, to fill the entire cosmos.

SIX YOGAS OF NAROPA

BRAHMA

the creative

The special relationship between sound and form has fascinated philosophers and scientists since the earliest times. Eastern spiritual teachings have included the study of this relationship in the science of metaphysics. In the East the whole visible universe is said to have evolved from a primordial sound that differentiated into approximately fifty "matrix energies" or vibrations during the process of outward expansion. Thus, everything that we can perceive is linked to a primordial sound.

The Tantric teachings refer to four distinct stages of sound emanation: unmanifest sound, becoming manifest sound, luminous enclosing sound and enclosed sound, the last of which also has form. Unmanifest sound is conceived of as "unstruck," without any vibration, and comparable to the moment just before a thought surfaces in the mind. The *Narada Purana*, a text that deals particularly with the properties of sound, states that "struck sound gives pleasure, whereas unstruck sound leads to Liberation."

Yogis of the distant past discovered many of the natural relationships between aspects of the phenomenal world and the source of all phenomena. Their years of solitary meditation helped them to abstract themselves from physical, emotional and mental activities, thus allowing them to perceive reality as it is. They recognized a number of primordial "seed-syllables" or *matrix-sound vibrations*, which could be combined to produce a series of Mantras.

A *Mantra* is a *protector of the mind*, used to augment consciousness. There are three stages in the use of a Mantra: the outer stage, in which sound is uttered aloud; the middle stage, in which it is uttered softly (barely audibly); and finally the inner stage, in which it is repeated silently in the mind. The third stage is the most powerful, but it is necessary to begin by repeating the

Mantra aloud so that its vibration resonates with and transforms the vibration within each Chakra. Gradually, the Mantra should be drawn inward, where it will potentiate the psyche and move the spirit toward reunion with the primordial source.

Traditionally, Mantras are received from a teacher or Guru. There are many kinds, of varying power and effect. Sometimes they are received intuitively or inspired by hearing a natural sound or animal noise. They can also be acquired through trance, vision, telepathy, dream or a state of prolonged Yogic absorption. They are used to protect the body from negative psychological influences and to concentrate the mind during day-to-day activities. They are also employed in ritual or magical works. It is said that a true practitioner of Tantra always has a Mantra in mind, even if it's not actually being uttered aloud. Mantras are used in association with breathing practices, meditation, ritual and love-making. They help awaken and channel the Kundalini, and also aid in controling sexual energy. "OM" is the best-known Mantra and is, in essence, the manifestation in sound of the creative attitude, the "sphere of Brahma."

Every element and entity is part of a specific evolutionary order, a cosmic "hierarchy." The *science of sound* (*Mantrayana*) and the subtle relationship of sound to form and color provide a key to understanding and contacting this hierarchy. Traces of this viewpoint are found in such Western mediaeval theories as the Doctrine of Signatures, in which herbs, fruits and minerals, among other natural things, were related by their color, shape and name to the parts of the human body as well as the celestial bodies. Thus, a walnut, resembling in form the cerebral cortex, was used to cure headaches and brain diseases. A number of important medical discoveries came out of this superficially simplistic view.

The Tantras declare that sound and form are directly related. Just as a musical note or

The Sanskrit Mantra "OM—BHUR—BHUWAH—SWA," written in traditional Devanagri script. Known as the shorter *Gayatri*, it evokes the Three Realms (this world, the next world and Eternity) and is effective in imparting spiritual direction to magical acts.

Eightfold Yantra of the heart center, with symbols of the elements located on the eight petals. This Yantra is a Tantric meditation device for creating natural harmony of emotions. From a Nepalese painting of the late seventeenth or early eighteenth century.

tone can be demonstrated to have a particular pattern, so every Mantra has a distinct form; this is known as its *Yantra*. So it is that a Mantra, or matrix form, is both the shape of a sound and a means of focusing thought on the subtle source from which all phenomena emerge. Tantras speak of our body as our personal Yantra and the sound of the breath as our personal Mantra. And if we follow an evolutionary path, how we live our life becomes our personal Tantra.

Our personal Yantra may alter when we

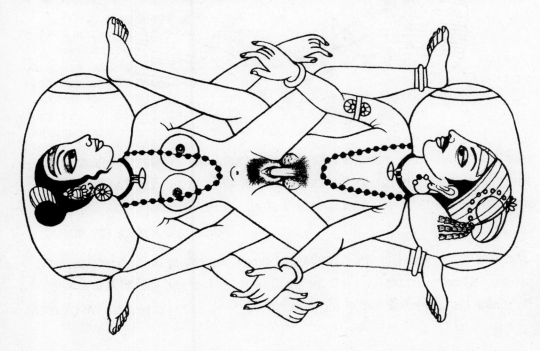

In the Tantric tradition postures are chosen to create harmonious shapes through which energy can be channeled and resonated. These love-positions are referred to as Yantras. From a Nepalese painting of the eighteenth century.

Complex love-posture of a Tantric type. The man is inverted, so energy is channeled to his head. His three female partners mimic the roles of the three main subtle nerves, which instill transcendence. This love-posture is a Yantra designed to create high energy channeling. From a stone sculpture, Khajuraho, India, *circa* eleventh century.

Love-positions evolved from mimicry of postures naturally practiced by animals and other creatures. Here a royal couple make love like moths. From a Jodhpur miniature painting, *circa* 1830.

change posture, and our breathing Mantra may alter when we exert ourselves excessively. However, each of us is distinguished by a characteristic form and sound. The Tantric viewpoint recommends continual awareness of both inner and outer sounds and form or posture. This applies particularly to the Mantra and Yantra of our body and mind. When standing, walking, sitting, lying, during all activities, remember to be aware of the shape of your body. Listen to the sound of your breathing and learn to recognize the subtle variations of breath. When making love, move consciously into position and reflect on the shape of your intertwined bodies. Notice the sounds of your breathing and try to practice either internal or external repetition of Tantric Mantras.

Concentrating the mind on the practice of a Mantra during love-making helps to make the experience both uplifting and liberating. Once again, it is the proper mental attitude that is important. Mantras are tools that aid in maintaining concentration and can be dispensed with if mental distraction is not a problem. But remember that a Mantra protects the mind

and don't hesitate to use one with this intent during love-making, especially if negative thoughts are disturbing you. It will bring clarity and direction to the experience.

Various love-making postures, which are described and illustrated in the last section of this book, are related to animals. Practice of these postures can be accompanied by the Mantras that evoke the sounds of the animals themselves. Remember to contemplate the link between a sexual posture and the special quality of the animal from which the posture was derived. Thus, butterflies and moths make love a certain way (generally reversed to each other) and have the special ability to metamorphose from one type of being into another. A similar Yantra endows us with some of these qualities.

There are many complex erotic postures in the Tantric tradition. Some of these are allegorical reminders of the Yantras that hold together the material world. Eastern teachings indicate that Mantra, Yantra and Tantra together form the key that unlocks the sexual secrets, enabling us to communicate directly with the divinity within.

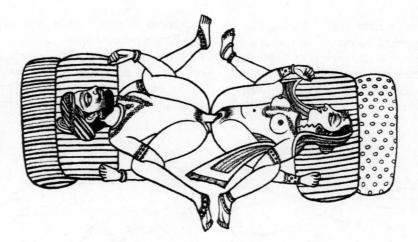

The source of all names is the word, for it is by the word that all names are spoken. The source of all forms is the eye, for it is by the eye that all forms are seen. The source of all action is the body, for it is by the body that all actions are done.

BRIHADARANYAKA UPANISHAD

The Yantra is ensouled by the Mantra and the personal deity is the expression of the personal Mantra. As the body is to the Jiva [the individual soul], as oil is to a lamp, so is Yantra the established seat of all divinities.

KULARNAVA TANTRA

the mantra "om"

In an early Hindu scripture, the *Mundaka Upanishad*, the following beautiful statement occurs: "OM is the bow, the arrow is the individual being, and Brahma is the target. With a tranquil heart, take aim; lose thyself in Brahma, even as the arrow is lost in the target." "OM" is the boat that enables one to cross over the rivers of fear, "OM" is the creative power in evolution, "OM" is the sound of true love; all other Mantras emerge from and recede back into the Supreme Mantra. Its form and power are certainly worth knowing and perfecting.

An analysis of this Mantra discloses a tripartite composition, the universal "three forces in one." These parts differentiate into the sounds "A" (pronounced "AH"), "U" (pronounced "OO") and finally "M" (pronounced "MM"). The last is intoned until the sound dies away completely. Thus, "OM" or "AH OO MM" should be carefully pronounced, using the whole mouth, with a deep tone for men and a high tone for women. The texts state that the first part, "AH," should be short, the next part, "OO," slightly longer, and the final "MM" should be longer still.

The Mantra "OM" precedes every complex group of Mantras. It is the *emanative support* of all created things, the original sound of Brahma, the Creator. It may be practiced either silently or vocally, but in either case the vibration of "OM" should be thought of as permeating your whole being. "OM" helps purify the physical, emotional, mental and subtle aspects of the self and brings with it many other benefits.

The traditional Sanskrit form of writing "OM" is rather like the number 3, or a trident turned clockwise a quarter-revolution. Its resemblance to the number 3 calls to mind the three subtle pathways that converge at the Chakras.

Traditionally, the emblem of a moon and sun, surmounted by a flame, is depicted above the Sanskrit or Tibetan word "OM." This glyph represents the full resolution of all dualities: male and female in harmonious union, sun and moon in eclipse, consonants and vowels returned to their original primordial point of emergence. For the Tantric couple it symbolizes the consummation of love.

"OM" is also a glyph of the Subtle Body. The sun symbolizes the solar energy at the Navel Chakra and its subtle nerve, the *pingala*, which reaches from the Sex Chakra, at the base, to the Head Chakra. The moon symbolizes the lunar effulgence of the Head Chakra and its subtle nerve, the *ida*, which reaches from the sex region to the head, on the left side of the body. The flame symbolizes the ascended Kundalini, dancing in ecstatic union. Thus, the sound of creation "OM" also evokes the cosmology of Liberation.

A Sanskrit version of the Mantra "OM."

The Mantra "OM," ornately drawn, with Brahma, Vishnu and Shiva depicted in the main body of the Sanskrit letters. Above, a Tantric form, known as *Sadashiva*, is shown ascending, with an androgynous Shiva/Shakti form in the silent "M" of this seed-sound. Traditional texts state that the Mantra "OM" contains the trinity of gods. Painting from Rajasthan, *circa* eighteenth century.

A Tibetan version of the Mantra "OM."

There are two ways of contemplation on Brahma, the Original Source. These are in sound and in silence. By sound we go to silence. The sound of Brahma is "OM." At the end of "OM" there is silence.

MAITRI UPANISHAD

Let the wise practitioner of Yoga destroy the multitude of Karmas by the Mantra "OM"; let him mystically rearrange his body functions. Thus, he will cease to participate in the consequences of action and need no longer be reborn again.

SHIVA SAMHITA

drops of wisdom

Because of the predominance of these two forces in the heavens, solar and lunar forces pervade all metaphysical treatises. When an awareness of the relationship between inner and outer, the microcosm and macrocosm, developed in man, it was natural to identify this relationship with solar and lunar forces. The solar forces reside in the navel center and are visualized as a lotus with sixty-four petals, or as a blazing sun with sixty-four flames, each of which has a particular function and characteristic. These "solar flares" are referred to as *Shaktis* or *Dakinis* and represent the transforming power of the psyche.

The inner moon is located in the Head Chakra. It is visualized as a lotus with thirty-two petals, or as effulgent rays emanating downward. The downward-pointing "inner moon" showers subtle secretions or "Soma drops," which nourish the psycho-organism. Tantric texts refer to these secretions as *Drops of Wisdom*, emphasizing that a Yogi should endeavor to prevent them from being "burnt up by the inner sun." The *Gheranda Samhita*, for example, states: "The sun dwells at the root of the navel, and the moon at the root of the palate. As the sun eats up the nectar secreted by the moon, humans become subject to death."

The concept of Drops of Wisdom can be understood as involving several different stages, from the purely physical to the subtle biological and finally the mystical. The first stage refers to the profuse secretions of saliva that accompany physical desire; food and sex are the two main agents that cause salivation. When food is eaten, it mixes with the saliva, which aids mastication, and is passed to the stomach for digestion. In the stomach the saliva helps the process of digestion and is itself assimilated by the action of the gastric juices, the "digestive fire."

The second stage, the subtle biological stage, is linked to the action of two glands, the pituitary and the pineal. Yogic texts that speak of the "melting of the inner moon" and the "opening of the Third Eye" are undoubtedly referring to the biophysical processes that occur in these two glands when consciousness is focused in the head center. It is interesting that Tantric descriptions of other psychic centers within the head center closely correspond to the physical structures of these two glands.

The pituitary gland is divided into two parts and is located in the middle of the brain ("above the palate," in the Yogic texts). It has an oval form and two lobes, and produces hormones that regulate sperm production, testosterone levels, ovulation, uterine contractions, secretion of breast milk and urine, and bodily growth. In addition, the pituitary governs and stimulates the thyroid gland (which controls metabolism, growth and development) and the adrenal glands (which control digestion, blood pressure, pulse rate and other vital functions). Hormones, which are produced by the glands, are biochemical "messengers" that enter the blood stream and travel to all parts of the body, controlling and governing through their catalytic action the various bodily processes.

The pineal gland is located further

forward than the pituitary and is conical in shape with two lobes. It is larger in a child than in an adult, and generally is of a greater size in women than in men. The function of the pineal gland is not understood by Western medicine; however, it contains structures very similar to those found in the human eyeball and secretes substances containing high levels of phosphorus salts. ESP activity has been observed in subjects with enlarged or highly active pineal glands. There are many indications that this gland is the "Third Eye" refered to so often in Yoga.

The third stage of the Soma drops is mystical, and acts on both inner and outer levels. On the inner level the action is a subtle communion with the lineage of transcended teachers, departed Wisdom-spirits of those who have liberated themselves from this world, but who still act as subtle guardians and guides, influencing humanity through the unconscious. It is their "Wisdom drops" that one receives as flashes of insight and inspiration. On the outer level, mystic Soma drops are tears shed out of loving communion, ecstasy and transcendence.

Yogis of the distant past understood the subtle workings of their bodies and used psycho-cosmic symbolism to explain their insights to others. Meditations and practices were developed to consciously cause the Drops of Wisdom to flow on all levels simultaneously. Thus, the physical body can be helped to digest food and control vital functions, the glandular system can serve its regulating and motivating role, the emotional system can participate in mystic release, and the lineage of "ancestors, guardians, spirit-guides and fully realized beings" can pervade and influence the psyche.

Several Tantric meditations were developed to stimulate the secretion of Drops of Wisdom from the Head Chakra. In most of these the inner fire of the Navel Chakra is first stimulated, usually through breathing techniques. As the psychic fire burns up all bodily impurities and Karmic obstacles, a pressure builds up, rises and "melts the moon" in the head. The *Chakrasambhara Tantra* gives the following description of one such process: "Imagine a dazzling white 'OM' in an inverted position, and upon that the first letter of the vowels, 'AH,' from which a lunar disc emerges. The

rising steam from the inner heat of the Navel Chakra causes the 'OM' and the lunar disc to drip nectar and emit rays of light. These one should conceive of as nourishing and transforming the whole psycho-system."

Yogic texts emphasize that one should try to stimulate the secretion of Drops of Wisdom and at the same time stop them from being wasted. The *Goraksashatakam* declares:

In the region of the navel there is a burning sun, while at the base of the palate there is an effulgent moon, full of nectar. The downward-looking inner moon showers nectar, and the sun, with his upturned

Depiction of the *Ajna* or "forehead *Chakra*" of later Hindu Tantras. It shows a two-petaled lotus containing a circle, a triangle, the syllable "OM" and a Lingam, symbolizing the pineal gland.

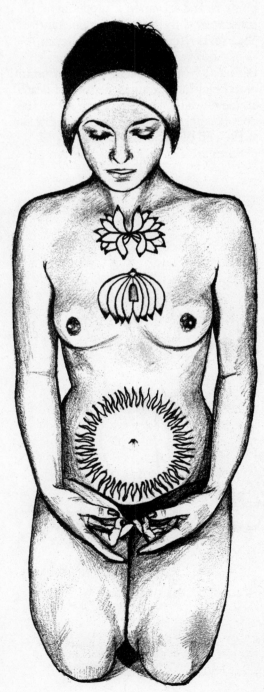

Simple representation of the Subtle Body. Four psychic centers are shown: a blazing sun at the navel, a downward-pointing lotus at the heart, an upward-pointing lotus at the throat and a moon in the head region. Spiritualization takes place when the psychic centers interact.

mouth, swallows it. In this connection those secret practices by which the nectar can be obtained and preserved should be known. If a person can retain the nectar of the moon, avoiding the open mouths of the inner sun, then the body ceases to be affected by physical decay and is outside the reaches of death. Furthermore, the semen of a Yogi whose body becomes filled with this nectar moves upward and gives rise to many miraculous powers.

The secret practices referred to are several. The most straightforward is the Yoga head stand (*shirsasana*), which reverses the natural flow of lunar and solar currents in the body. The pituitary and pineal glands become activated by such inverse postures, and salivation is produced and concentrated in the head region. Tantric Yoga texts refer to inverse postures as *viparitakarani* (reverse system) and the *Gheranda Samhita* states that "By the constant practice of such postures, decay and death are destroyed. One becomes an adept and does not perish, even at the conflagration at the end of an aeon." Inverse sexual postures are also included in this category.

Reverse postures stimulate the pineal and pituitary glands in the head. As a result, the whole body is invigorated. From a central Indian miniature painting, *circa* early nineteenth century.

Another of the secret practices, *khechari* (sky flier), consists in the gradual elongation of the tongue (over a period of weeks or months) and the reversal of it to cut off the loss of Soma drops. The *Gheranda Samhita* describes the technique as follows:

The tongue is milked and stretched until it becomes long enough to touch the space between the eyebrows. Then it is turned upward and backward until it reaches the nostril openings inside the head. These holes are sealed with the tongue, inhalation is stopped, and the gaze is fixed on the space between the eyebrows. When the tongue touches the holes inside the head, it obtains various juices and the person experiences new sensations; first a saltish taste, then alkaline, then bitter, then astringent, then of butter, then of clarified butter, then of milk, then of curds, then of whey, then of honey, then of palm juice; lastly arises the taste of nectar. This practice eliminates feelings of hunger, thirst, and laziness. It prevents disease, decay, and death. The body becomes divine and cannot be harmed by any elements.

Obviously such an evolved technique is out of the range of most people. It should not be attempted or practiced without the guidance of a skillful teacher, and presupposes a total control over the breathing function.

A Yogic technique known as *Jalandhara* (liquid holding) *Mudra* (seal) and linked to the *Nabho* (navel) *Mudra* is a far simpler secret practice for retaining the Drops of Wisdom from the inner moon. According to the *Gheranda Samhita*, the Jalandhara Mudra consists simply of "contracting the throat, by forming the neck into a hook shape and placing the chin near the chest." This effectively closes channels through which the Soma drops are lost. The Nabho Mudra should be practiced at the same time, and the *Gheranda Samhita* describes it as follows: "In whatever business the Yogi is engaged, wherever he be, let him always keep his tongue turned upward toward the palate, behind the upper front teeth, and restrain the breath consistently and consciously."

There are a number of secret practices specific to love-making. The most important recognize that the saliva produced during sexual excitement contains rich trace elements and should be exchanged with the partner. The Taoist teachings of China also refer to the importance of saliva to mystic love-making, claiming it contains a unique "wisdom property." The T'ang dynasty classic *Fang-nei-pu-i* recommends swallowing the saliva of the female partner during love-rites because of its ability to impart health and wisdom: "In order to live long, without growing old, a man should play with and excite the woman and drink in her saliva. He should imagine his essence as dividing itself into a sun and moon. When his sexual organ is deep inside the woman he should let it remain still, while above he sucks in the woman's saliva and below he absorbs her sexual secretions."

The Drops of Wisdom should be visualized as emanating from the Head Chakra, nourishing and transforming both body and mind. In a sexual context, they endow both oneself and one's partner with the power of transcendence. A healthy body, a clear mind, pure emotions and spiritual guidance are the benefits gained from recognizing and channeling the Drops of Wisdom within.

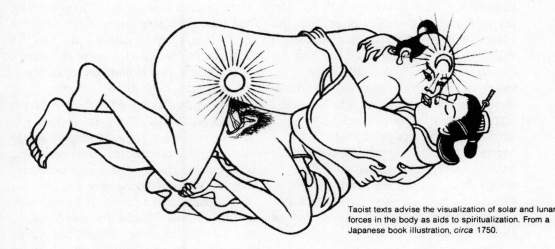

Taoist texts advise the visualization of solar and lunar forces in the body as aids to spiritualization. From a Japanese book illustration, *circa* 1750.

There is a curved duct from the inner moon to a hollow in the palatal region; this is known as the shankini nerve and leads to the upper lip. This is the curved duct through which the nectar or elixir of the moon can pass. It is described as being like a serpent with mouths at both ends; the mouth of this shankini nerve, through which the Soma pours down from the moon, is called the "tenth door" of the body. It is a great secret.

GORAKSAVIJAYA

The wise Yogi should practice the Khechari Mudra to enable him to drink the lunar secretions without loss. Reverse the tongue, fix it in the hollow of the throat and place it with great care on the mouth of the well of nectar within. Know this to be the source of all success. By this, one obtains power over the microcosm and all limiting things.

SHIVA SAMHITA

Let the Yogi contemplate the inner moon, located in the Head Chakra. Let him visualize the nectar-containing moon and then learn to drink the nectar flowing from it. By this practice the Drops of Wisdom are absorbed and Liberation is quickly attained.

SHIVA SAMHITA

Energy should ideally be channeled back and forth during love-making. Illustration from a Roman fresco, Museum of Naples.

circulation of energy

Oriental medical science views the harmonious circulation of life energies through the body as essential to health. When the life-force becomes stagnated or blocked, disease occurs. It is the natural flow of energy that rejuvenates and renews both body and mind. We all experience energy "lows" in our day-to-day lives and know that when we feel vital and "energized" we can accomplish almost anything. Indeed, it is the maintenance of vital energy that is the determining factor between youth and age. Energy should be circulated throughout the body so that no part of it is starved of vitality. A very simple method of doing this consists in moving rhythmically while visualizing vitality circulating and energizing the whole body. The secret is to keep the body moving continuously and harmoniously, as though dancing. Movement can be very subtle and should be linked to conscious visualization of the energy flow. The Chinese movements known as T'ai Chi are especially helpful in developing awareness of the natural flow of energy through the body.

One should first become aware of the Navel Chakra, visualizing vital forces moving and swirling within it, so producing a gyroscopic balance and emanating outward to the limbs, head and sex region. Breathe in rhythmically and deeply, focusing on the retention of breath and at the same time tracing the subtle channels from the navel outward to the four limbs and also up and down the body. Wherever the consciousness is directed, that part of the body will receive the energy of the navel center. Recent tests of Yogis have shown that the control of blood circulation is possible, and biofeedback makes use of these mental techniques. Western medicine has just recently started to make successful use of visualization techniques for treatment of cancer and also for psychological disorders such as deep depression.

Lovers can circulate energy for each other. Lie stretched out on the floor or bed. While breathing from the abdominal region, try to visualize the flow of energy, taking note of any tension points that seem to impede the flow. It's amazing how easily the mind can sense energy flow, provided you

allow your intuition to make contact with the body of your partner. The active partner should stand, sit beside or even straddle the other's body, passing over the energy pathways with a series of sweeping gestures with the fingertips extended. This is similar to the "mystic pass" used by mesmerists, hypnotists and psychic healers. It is very effective in channeling energy, provided a positive mental attitude is brought to bear and no self-doubt is allowed to enter the mind. You'll be surprised how quickly you can recharge your partner in this way. Sometimes it is helpful to verbalize the whole process, saying aloud, "I'm channeling vital energy, reaching out to all tired parts of the body and mind, relaxing and regenerating the organs and tissues, toning up the glands, harmonizing the emotions and bringing tranquility to the spirit."

The recipient should relax completely and trivial dialogue should be kept to the absolute minimum. Let your partner's subtle movements communicate to you, while you both visualize the flow of energy between and through you. At the same time, focus consciousness on the breath. A Mantra such as "OM—BHUR—BHUWAH—SWA" (an invocation of the three realms of this world, the next world, and Eternity) can be used to keep the mind from wandering.

Love-making is an ideal time for the conscious circulation of energy. Either you can circulate each other's energy simultaneously, or one partner can take over the active role. Energy is automatically circulated during love-making, but is often lost through lack of awareness. The important thing is to familiarize yourself with the *feeling* of free energy flow so you can consciously recognize it.

Deep breathing and breath retention will enable you to experience energy flow. You'll find that certain parts of the body feel awake, while other parts feel asleep or just "lazy." If you bring consciousness to bear on those parts, they'll become energized. Breath control and visualization effectively direct the vital flow of energy.

Hold in mind the idea of an all-powerful inner fire, the Kundalini. Imagine the Serpent Power awakening at the Sex Chakra and visualize the energy moving upward through the Spleen Chakra (the assimilative function) to the Navel Chakra. There it blazes up like an inner sun, sending purifying flares of light to all parts of the body. Imagine the subtle pathways and visualize their channels as thin radiant tubes through which the energy flows freely. Move the vitality upward, in the mind's eye, to the region of the heart and throat; awaken the Heart Chakra and imagine that the inner lotus turns upward and begins to glow radiantly, emanating love, the purified energy of the emotions. Awaken the Throat Chakra with the power of the heart, and imagine that the whole psycho-physical system is being purified and energized. Draw up the energy to the Head Chakra and see it opening to the timeless experience of ecstasy. Visualize the upper part of the head as a lunar orb, cooling and distilling the passionate psyche. Then focus on the Drops of Wisdom descending and enriching the soul.

Trace the flow of vitality up the back and along the arms and legs, using the fingers very lightly; visualize rays of vital energy emanating from the fingertips, all the while shaking them slightly to keep the energy vibrant. Weave a love-dance over the partner's body; open yourself to the circulation of energy and be receptive to its benefits. The subtle vitalities concentrate at the navel, heart, head and sexual regions, and flow from one to the other. So be sure to stimulate these areas when moving the energy through the partner's body. This practice is especially suitable as an addition to the art of massage and helps the harmonization of mood, an essential ingredient of foreplay.

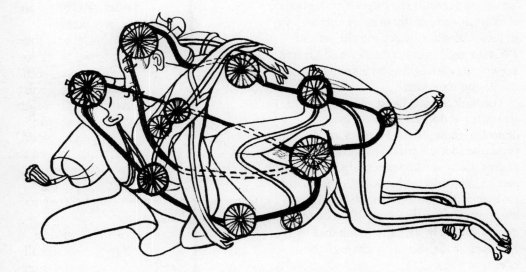

When lovers are in close embrace, subtle energies converge and exchange. Tantra teaches that life energies are concentrated into vortexes located from the sexual region to the head.

This hand contains all healing balms and integrates the whole body through the power of conscious touch. With the ten branches of the two hands, these healers of disease stroke away all sickness by their soft caress.

ATHARVA VEDA

The vital essence courses through the body in invisible currents of zigzag swirling patterns. These are like the waves of sound, in an upward direction like flames of fire, and in a downward direction like rivulets of water.

SUSHRUTA SAMHITA

The inner heart spreads out in a self-kindled glow. Externally this manifests in a vermilion-like light that surrounds the body; internally it is a five-colored radiant energy that is emitted and spread out in lines, like the tense string of a bow, vibrating silently.

SIX YOGAS OF NAROPA

hands and feet

The hands and feet are the "outer terminals" of the body. All the vital organs, the glands and nerves can be contacted and manipulated, via the many subtle pathways that lead from the hands and feet to the heart, head, throat, navel, spleen and sexual regions. These pathways, also known as *meridians*, are central to acupuncture, acupressure and Oriental medicine. They have stimulative and sedative properties and are categorized as either Yin or Yang, depending on whether the flow of energy through them is up, "from Earth to Heaven," or down, "from Heaven to Earth."

The hands and feet are considered microcosms of the body and may be used to make contact with the interior of the body. Shiatsu (Japanese finger-pressure therapy), Do-in (Oriental self-massage) and the related Western techniques of "zone" and "reflex" therapy are all founded on a knowledge and use of the meridians.

The Tantric and Taoist teachings utilize the outer terminals for consciously directing energy flow. Postures are prescribed for circulating the raw sexual energy along specific meridians, from one part of the body to the other, or from one partner to the other. Tantric and Taoist love-postures are designed to circulate energy precisely, and the hands and feet are often made use of to channel the energy.

Ritual gestures of the hands are found in all priestly cultures; they, too, are methods of short-circuiting and channeling energy through the meridians. They are potent Yantras, consciously created forms that act to concentrate forces in specific ways. The Tantras contain many teachings that can be transmitted through mystic gestures (Mudras). The inexpressible can at times be transmitted quite directly through mystic gestures, which concentrate and focus energy and reach areas of consciousness outside the range of words.

The lines in the hands and feet are said to reflect our destiny. Many people are familiar with the "head," "heart" and "life" lines of the hands, and it is widely known that each individual has a unique set of fingerprints. The feet also have

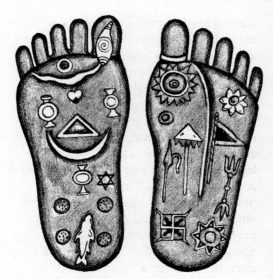

Mythological footprints of the gods, with auspicious symbols marked on the soles. From a Rajasthani miniature painting of the mid-eighteenth century.

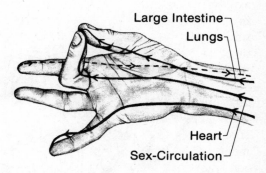

Subtle nerves connect the fingers with the internal organs. Tantra teaches that hand gestures are effective in creating circuits through which energies can be channeled. This gesture, common to Yogic meditation, links the outward flow of sexual energy back to the breathing function, so helping to stabilize the mind.

A type of mystic gesture (Mudra), used in Tantric meditation as an energy-channeling devices. From a contemporary photograph.

Taoist love-techniques include reverse positions that link hands and feet, allowing for sexual energy to be concentrated and controlled. From a Chinese print of the Ming period.

precise markings, which are entirely different in each individual. In ancient times it was a social convention to examine the hands and feet of a person in order to know that person better. These parts of the body would be washed by the host before a guest was seated or entertained.

Gentle but firm massage of the hands and feet, by stroking, caressing, tickling, or finger pressure, has a soothing and beneficial effect on the individual. Furthermore, by concentrating on specific parts of the body and applying pressure to the relevant zones of the hands and feet, it is possible to bring about a healing through adjustment of the inner balance of energies. Many sicknesses and malfunctions of body and mind can be corrected in this way. Beyond this, it is a thoroughly enjoyable and sensually stimulating experience. For the couple the oiling and massaging of hands and feet is a natural way of communicating as well as a basic tool in the art of love.

The feet are normally far more in need of massage than the hands because they are walked on all day, trapped in tight shoes and restricted by socks or hose. They make continual contact with hard pavements and floors and rarely have contact with organic surfaces such as earth, sand and grass. People whose employment forces them to use their hands excessively and those who are on their feet all day commonly suffer from internal malfunctions that may be caused by continual pressure on the outer terminals.

Internal blockages or constrictions can be released by massaging the hands and feet with single-minded concentration. The one being treated should remain open and relaxed and inform the other of any pain that is created by localized pressure. When pain occurs, it indicates an imbalance, stress or disorder in the internal organ or area corresponding to that point on the hand or foot (see charts).

Two Indian diagrams of the type known as *Hastakara Yantra*, illustrating relationships of subtle forces influencing the individual. The symbols are linked to cosmological forces. From Rajasthani paintings of the eighteenth century.

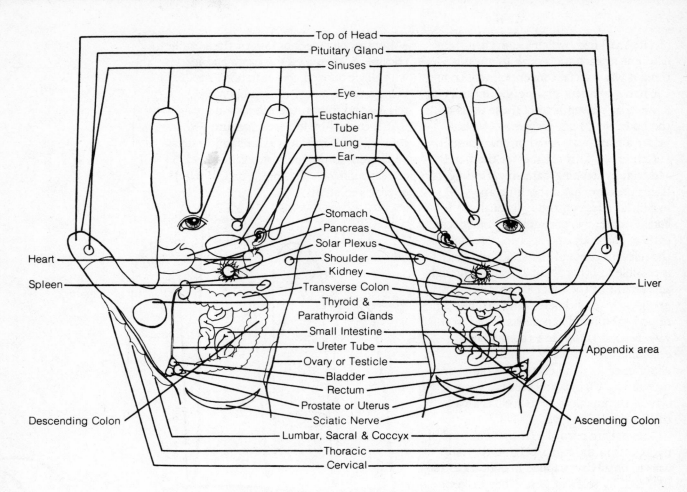

Top of Head
Pituitary Gland
Sinuses
Eye
Eustachian Tube
Lung
Ear

Stomach
Pancreas
Solar Plexus
Shoulder
Kidney
Transverse Colon
Thyroid & Parathyroid Glands
Small Intestine
Ureter Tube
Ovary or Testicle
Bladder
Rectum
Prostate or Uterus
Sciatic Nerve
Lumbar, Sacral & Coccyx
Thoracic
Cervical

Heart
Spleen
Descending Colon

Liver
Appendix area
Ascending Colon

Reflexology charts showing the relationship of internal organs to parts of the right and left palms. Firm pressure creates a reflex reaction in affected organs, causing healing to occur.

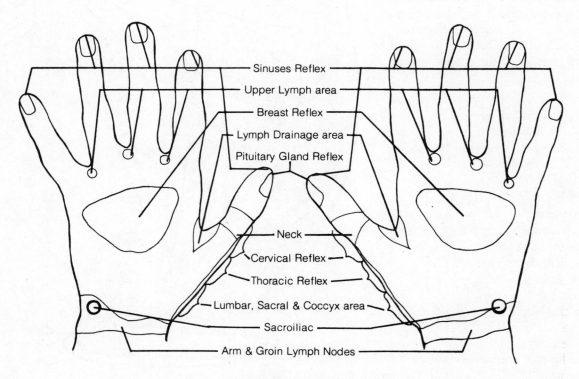

Sinuses Reflex
Upper Lymph area
Breast Reflex
Lymph Drainage area
Pituitary Gland Reflex

Neck
Cervical Reflex
Thoracic Reflex
Lumbar, Sacral & Coccyx area
Sacroiliac
Arm & Groin Lymph Nodes

Reflexology chart showing the relationship of internal organs to the back of the hands.

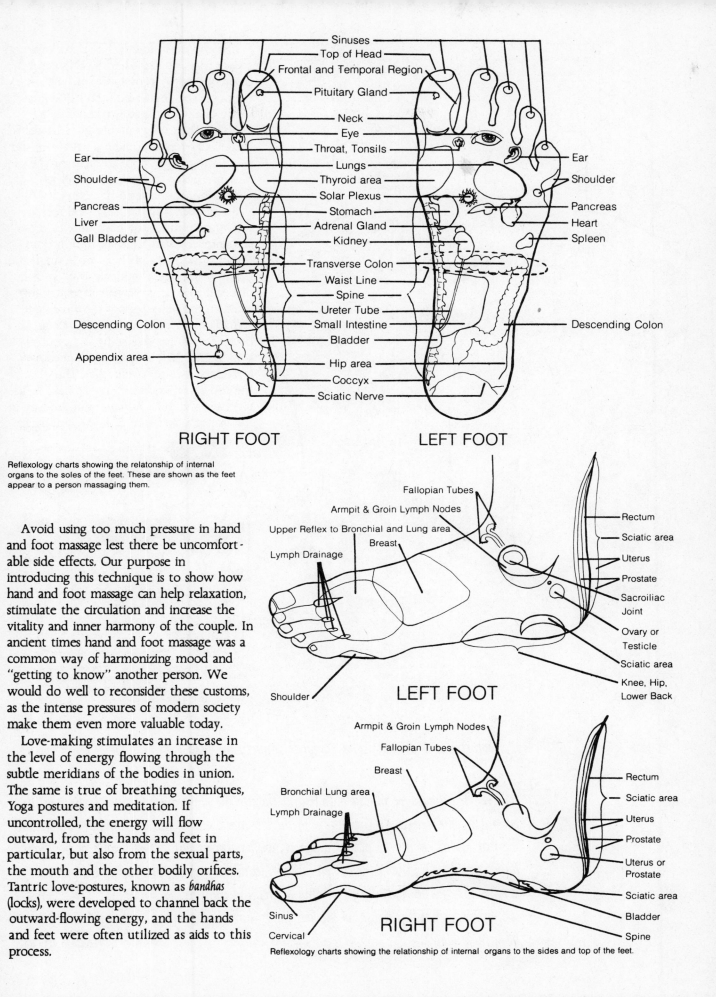

RIGHT FOOT

LEFT FOOT

Sinuses
Top of Head
Frontal and Temporal Region
Pituitary Gland
Neck
Eye
Throat, Tonsils
Lungs
Thyroid area
Solar Plexus
Stomach
Adrenal Gland
Kidney
Transverse Colon
Waist Line
Spine
Ureter Tube
Small Intestine
Bladder
Hip area
Coccyx
Sciatic Nerve

Ear
Shoulder
Pancreas
Liver
Gall Bladder
Descending Colon
Appendix area

Ear
Shoulder
Pancreas
Heart
Spleen
Descending Colon

Reflexology charts showing the relationship of internal organs to the soles of the feet. These are shown as the feet appear to a person massaging them.

Avoid using too much pressure in hand and foot massage lest there be uncomfortable side effects. Our purpose in introducing this technique is to show how hand and foot massage can help relaxation, stimulate the circulation and increase the vitality and inner harmony of the couple. In ancient times hand and foot massage was a common way of harmonizing mood and "getting to know" another person. We would do well to reconsider these customs, as the intense pressures of modern society make them even more valuable today.

Love-making stimulates an increase in the level of energy flowing through the subtle meridians of the bodies in union. The same is true of breathing techniques, Yoga postures and meditation. If uncontrolled, the energy will flow outward, from the hands and feet in particular, but also from the sexual parts, the mouth and the other bodily orifices. Tantric love-postures, known as *bandhas* (locks), were developed to channel back the outward-flowing energy, and the hands and feet were often utilized as aids to this process.

LEFT FOOT

Fallopian Tubes
Armpit & Groin Lymph Nodes
Upper Reflex to Bronchial and Lung area
Breast
Lymph Drainage
Shoulder

Rectum
Sciatic area
Uterus
Prostate
Sacroiliac Joint
Ovary or Testicle
Sciatic area
Knee, Hip, Lower Back

RIGHT FOOT

Armpit & Groin Lymph Nodes
Fallopian Tubes
Breast
Bronchial Lung area
Lymph Drainage
Sinus
Cervical

Rectum
Sciatic area
Uterus
Prostate
Uterus or Prostate
Sciatic area
Bladder
Spine

Reflexology charts showing the relationship of internal organs to the sides and top of the feet.

It is important to circulate sexual energy rather than letting it be lost; this can be accomplished by consciously placing the hands on the Sex Chakra, Navel Chakra, Heart Chakra or Head Chakra and directing the energy mentally to those Chakras. Lovers will find it a delightful and stimulating experience to discover the flow of energy in each other and its circulation from one to the other.

Remember that the hands and feet are the microcosms of the body and learn to recognize the signs of inner malfunctions through awareness of their condition. If the hands or feet seem suddenly swollen or hot or begin to ache in precise places, try to ascertain the inner reasons for these signs and adjust your life accordingly. It's far better to combat disease by slight outer adjustments than by prolonged, uncomfortable and costly medication. Thus, the hands and feet serve as guardians to the inner self and fulfill an important function in the diagnosis and cure of bodily imbalance.

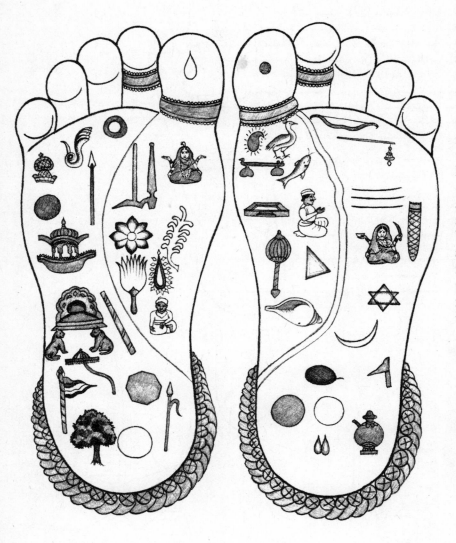

Mythological footprints, with auspicious symbols indicating celestial relationships between the macrocosm and microcosm. From a Rajasthani painting of the eighteenth century.

Tantric love-postures create subtle energy circuits for controlling involuntary orgasm. Positions of hands and feet play a vital role in this process. From a Nepalese painting of the mid-eighteenth century.

A footprint is a <u>Mandala</u>, *a complete universe in itself.*   HEVAJRA TANTRA

The left leg should be placed outside and close to the right one; this means the positive embracing the negative. The thumb of the left hand should touch its middle finger and the right hand should be placed under it, with palm upward. The thumb of the right hand should be bent over the left palm; this means the negative embracing the positive. It is what the ancients meant by "forming a circuit of eight psychic channels." The Taoist scriptures say that the linking of the four limbs shuts the four gates, so that the center can be held on to.

CHAO PI CH'EN

massage

Massage is one of the simplest ways of relaxing the body as well as one of the most direct methods of establishing deep communication with another. Massage is also a way of expressing love and compassion. As such, it holds an important position among the the arts of love.

An important principle to remember when massaging someone is that an equal balance should be created in the body; don't massage just one hand or foot and leave the other unattended, or stimulate meridians on one side of the body without stimulating the corresponding meridians on the other side. The reflexes of the left foot affect the various parts of the left side of the body up to the neck, at which point they cross over to the right side. Conversely, the reflexes of the right foot affect the right side up to the neck, where they begin to affect the left side.

The big toe connects through a meridian to the head; the center of the foot connects to the central part of the back, waistline, kidneys, stomach and pancreas; the area around the heel leads to the sexual region. The precise locations can be learned from the charts and, of course, by noticing the reflexes in the body. The whole head will benefit from simultaneous massage of both big toes; this kind of massage can cure headache and relieve discomforts of the eyes, ears and nose. Massage of both big toes is also erotically stimulating and causes profuse salivation in a relaxed subject.

For general fatigue or depression, the gland reflexes should be massaged; these are the meridians that connect to the pituitary, adrenal, spleen, pineal and sex areas. They are found in both hands and feet. Menstrual pains can be alleviated by massage of the meridians leading to the uterus, fallopian tubes and sex organ, and also by gentle but concentrated massage of the region of the lower back and base of the spine. Quite a number of good books dealing with therapeutic massage are available and we advise our readers to consult one for specific problems. The Japanese have developed massage therapy far more extensively than any other nationality. Excellent works detailing the specific Shiatsu points and the

Foot massage is a part of everyday Indian life. From a Guler painting *circa* 1810.

meridians for use in acupressure massage have been published recent!y. However, a demonstration by a knowledgeable person is by far the best method of learning massage techniques.

Foot massage certainly aids relaxation during childbirth and many instances of painless birth using these techniques have been documented. For menopause and sterility, there are precise methods of treatment. Constipation, which may greatly inhibit natural sexual activity, can be easily relieved by foot or hand massage. A regular attention to the art of massage helps the circulation of blood, freeing the body of toxic elements. Our society would benefit immensely if we developed the custom of exchanging relaxing and therapeutic hand and foot massage. In the Orient everyone learns some massage techniques; for simple village people and city dwellers, for maharajas' courtesans and Yogis, massage is part of the lifestyle.

Each toe is linked directly to the sinuses.

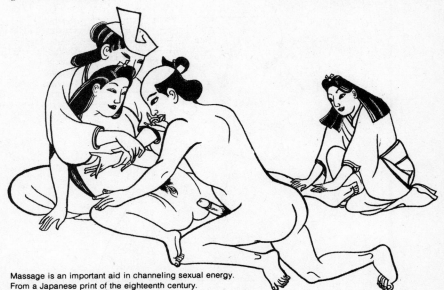

Massage is an important aid in channeling sexual energy. From a Japanese print of the eighteenth century.

Meridians also extend from the face to the internal organs. Thus, the inner condition of the organs can be diagnosed from a study of the facial features. The liver can be contacted by massaging between the eyes. There is a Yoga technique for this action known as *kapala randhra dhauti* (head cavity purification), which the *Gheranda Samhita* describes in the following way: "Rub the depression in the forehead, near the bridge of the nose, with the thumb of the right hand. If this exercise is practiced daily, diseases arising from vital imbalances will be cured. The internal vessels will become purified and clairvoyance will be induced. This exercise should be practiced daily, after awakening from sleep, after meals and in the evening also." It helps activate and invigorate the liver and other internal organs and is a great aid to health.

The spleen can be reached by massaging either side of the nose; the kidneys are affected by massage of the slight depressions under the eyes (the "bags" that indicate late nights, over-work and tired kidneys); the heart is contacted by light massage of the end of the nose; and the lungs by pressure on the nostrils, outward to the two cheeks. The sexual organ connects to the upper lip and slightly above it, up to the nose. This is one of the reasons why the kiss is a natural part of sexual foreplay.

The pituitary gland, which controls most hormonal secretions, can be stimulated by massage of the middle of the forehead, the pineal gland (the Third Eye) by massage of the crown of the head, and the thyroid gland by light massage around the neck. The temples can be lightly massaged to ease strain and mental tension. Most headaches can, in fact, be alleviated by considerate head massage. The cause of headaches is usually tensing of the muscles around the skull, which can easily be relaxed by massage of the scalp. The ears are also good massage points and are linked to the sex regions and the sciatic nerves. Thus, every part of the inner body is linked to outer terminals, which can be utilized to stimulate and relax all parts of the inner body. Since the brain controls sexual activity, this area is of great importance to lovers. A relaxing head massage can quickly alleviate tension, thus opening the body to erotic release.

Facial massage can be relaxing, invigorating and sexually stimulating. The different areas around the mouth are linked to different parts of the digestive system: the top of the upper lip to the stomach, the lower lip to the intestines and the corners of the mouth to the first part of the small intestines. In the East a good doctor can diagnose problems by studying the patient's face.

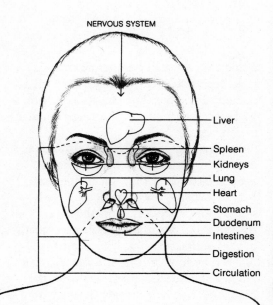

NERVOUS SYSTEM

— Liver
— Spleen
— Kidneys
— Lung
— Heart
— Stomach
— Duodenum
— Intestines
— Digestion
— Circulation

Reflexology chart showing the relationship of the internal organs to areas of the face. The upper part of the head is linked to the nervous system, the middle part to the circulation of blood and the lower part to digestion.

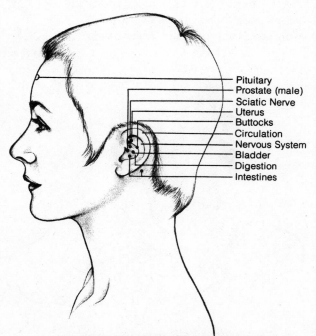

— Pituitary
— Prostate (male)
— Sciatic Nerve
— Uterus
— Buttocks
— Circulation
— Nervous System
— Bladder
— Digestion
— Intestines

Some main pressure points on the head and ear, which are linked to the internal organs through subtle meridians.

An all-over massage is one of the best tonics; it is also an excellent way to tune in to your lover's body and come to know the idiosyncrasies of his or her erogenous zones. All massage, like love-making, should be reciprocal. It's preferable to indicate places where massage would feel particularly good by inarticulate sounds rather than words, because specific directions like "left hand down a bit" can weaken the erotic effect. In time, a personal code of sound and movement will develop, and beyond that, an intuitive rapport. But affirmation *is* important to both the lover and the masseur or masseuse. In an intimate situation massage does not depend on prescribed rules or techniques. Competency is largely intuitive and will arise spontaneously provided a feeling of confidence prevails.

Healing and relaxing massage should become an integral part of your relationship. Used during foreplay, it will rid the body of accumulated tensions and bring it to that state of relaxation suitable for the practice of evolutionary love. Use massage to express your emotions; don't be afraid to pour out your feelings through your fingertips. Effective massage can range from deep muscular manipulation to a simple laying on of hands. The secret of its effectiveness lies in the *intention*, concentration and confidence of the person performing the massage, coupled with the trust and surrender of the person being massaged. The hands of healers emit a kind of "electric charge" that can positively affect the life energies of the "patient."

Use massage to awaken and tune up the physical and Subtle Body. Become aware of changes in the temperature of the skin over different areas of the body. Notice how these relate to imbalances and tensions and recognize them as signals that will aid in your intuitive knowledge of your partner's body.

Massage can be used to heal, relax and generally attune the bodies of the couple; it is also a powerful means of erotic arousal. It can be used to sublimate or concentrate sexual energy, as an integrated aspect of foreplay. In methods developed in the harems of the East the whole body is massaged with the bodies of others. This technique is referred to nowadays as

"Oriental," "Thai" or "full body" massage and involves the recipient body being rubbed all over by the active body. Both bodies are lubricated with perfumed oil or lather; then the masseur or masseuse lies on top and employs his or her body to stimulate and invigorate the body of the other. The elbows, knees, thighs, breasts, chin, forehead, feet and other bodily parts are all used. This manner of sensuous massage can culminate in love-making, or it can be an act of loving service in itself. It has long been a favorite of rulers, and, nowadays, of businessmen in the East. It can be practiced by the modern couple, preferably in an exotic environment, to the accompaniment of music, either taking turns or as a special treat for one's partner. Its benefits will be felt by both participants, whoever is taking the active role.

Treat massage as a ritual. Start with the head, feet or spine and mentally repeat your intention to clear away all obstacles or blockages in the partner and invigorate the body and charge it with positive energy. Try to harmonize your breathing and use breath control to aid your concentration. There is a special secret to creative massage. This is that the person massaging channels energy from his or her *whole body*, out through the hands. Consciously draw this energy up through the body and visualize it as being emitted through the fingertips.

Head massage is a very effective cure for headaches and nervous exhaustion.

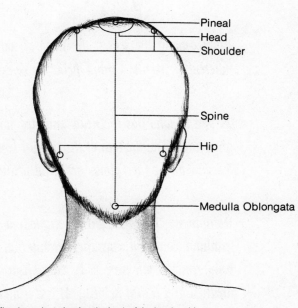

Pineal
Head
Shoulder

Spine

Hip

Medulla Oblongata

Reflexology chart showing the back of the head and its relationship to parts of the body.

Oils should be used during massage. Ideally they should be slightly heated, particularly in the winter. Many massage oils are available on the market, but very good results can be obtained with those you mix yourself. Choose a non-sticky base oil such as sesame seed oil, and add to this some essential oils of flowers or herbs; sandalwood, rose, jasmine, thyme, lavender, rosemary and patchouli are some of the possibilities. Baby oil is a good base to work with because it's easy to obtain and quite pure. Almond oil is good for the head, hands, feet and eyes, in particular.

An Indian massage oil known as Amla is particularly beneficial.

When massaging, be creative and truly inventive. Try visualizing the subtle channels and Chakras and concentrate on clarity of breath and thought. Mantras help to establish rhythm and reinforce concentration. Remember that touch has a great potential for healing and vitalization. Massage is a wonderful means of communicating feelings and is an ally in times of need. For the couple, the art of massage is a valuable way of serving each other.

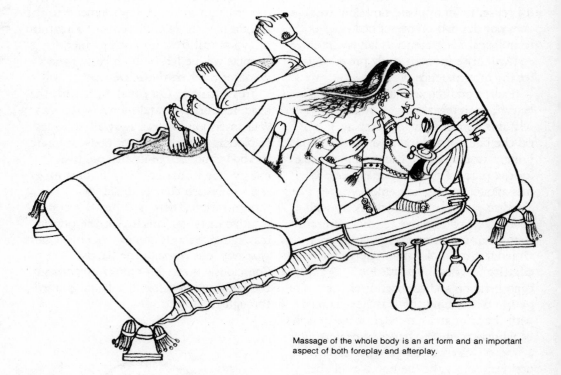

Massage of the whole body is an art form and an important aspect of both foreplay and afterplay.

From among the senses, the sense of touch pervades all the others and has the mind inherent in it; the "mind field" is co-extensive with the tactile sense.

CHARAKA SAMHITA

A person who has the head anointed with oil is not subject to headaches, baldness or gray hair. The strength of the cranial bones is increased, the sense organs become toned up, the skin of the face glows beautifully and the person sleeps well and becomes happy.

CHARAKA SAMHITA

Roughness, stiffness, dryness, fatigue and numbness of the feet are all quickly removed by regular oiling and massage; the internal organs also benefit. Massage of the rest of the body removes offensive body odor, heaviness, torpor, itching, loss of appetite, physical tiredness and sexual debility. It is a wonderful practice that helps overcome the problems of this world and the next.

SUSHRUTA SAMHITA

the perfumed garden

Yogic teachings stress the importance of the sense of smell, which is associated with the primary *Prana*, the upward-moving vitality, the Heart Chakra and the principle of cohesion. Sweet-smelling herbs, oils and incense are credited with the capacity to stimulate the creative attitude and uplift the spirit. It is these qualities that make scent an integral part of religious rites and rituals. The sweet odors of rose, jasmine, saffron, sandalwood, basil, cedar, patchouli and marijuana possess the same uplifting (*sattvic*) property as sweet tastes, which provoke the erotic and spiritual sentiments.

Pleasant-smelling perfumes and oils are an essential part of the Tantric lifestyle and are used to lift up the heart and the mind. Perfumes and fragrant oils also have the ability to create an atmosphere of psychic protection. A knowledgeable use of scents can help promote a harmonious emotional atmosphere in the home. Scent works mainly on the instinctive centers, stimulating many of man's primal urges.

In cultivating self-awareness one of the most important factors is conscious observation of bodily odors, which are associated with different physical, emotional or psychological states. Every person has a distinct odor, which, though constantly changing, is as special and unique as the color of the eyes or the way of walking. Body odor is directly related to diet and, to a certain extent, the general lifestyle of a person. A person who eats onions or garlic regularly will find that this odor permeates the breath, sweat and sexual secretions. Similarly, a meat eater, a vegetarian, a smoker and an alcohol drinker will have characteristically different body odors. Body odors are also affected by the spiritual qualities of a person.

The odor of a woman changes according to the time of her monthly cycle and the degree to which she is sexually excited. A man undergoes similar changes of odor with sudden excitement, anger, physical exercise, sexual longing or abstinence. In fact, a sensitive person can learn a great deal about a total stranger just from the sense of smell.

Primitive magical traditions throughout the world associate unpleasant smells with lower spirit forms and demons. Such bad smells are believed to have a "vibrational" property that attracts non-corporeal entities of a low evolutionary order that exhibit "possessive" characteristics. The rites of black magic often call for the use of noxious substances as burnt offerings; among these are dried blood, red pepper and asafoetida, all of which smell unpleasant.

When the internal forces of body and mind are in harmony, a subtle and delightful perfume is exuded from the pores of the skin. Yogis and spiritual leaders are commonly reported to have a naturally fragrant aura, which is a manifestation of their spiritual attainment. It has been recorded that a week after the great Hindu teacher Swami Yogananda died in America, his body still emanated the sweet fragrance of roses. This fact was attested to by many doctors, who were totally perplexed by the phenomenon, since a corpse normally decays very rapidly and begins to smell bad after just a few days. The Oriental custom of garlanding prominent teachers or highly respected friends with flowers is a way of acknowledging their inherent spirituality.

Many Eastern treatises on the Art of Love detail the different categories of sexual organs, classifying them according to their shape, taste and smell. In the Hindu text known as the *Ananga Ranga* the "Lotus-woman" is distinguished by her *Yoni*, which "resembles a lotus bud, perfumed like a sweet-smelling lily that has newly burst open," the "Art-woman" by her "sweet honey-smelling Yoni," the Conch-woman" by her "salty Yoni," and so forth. Likewise the "Hare-man" has "sweet-smelling,

Lotuses from a Bundi miniature painting, *circa* eighteenth century.

sweeting-tasting semen" and the "Horse-man" has "salty semen that smells of goats."

Sexual excitation causes all sorts of exotic odors to emanate from the body, from the breath, the skin and the sexual organs in particular. It is rightly said that the most exquisite scent a woman can wear is her own natural odor. A special trick of courtesans in mediaeval Europe was the use of their sexual secretions as perfume, behind their ears and around their necks, in order to attract customers. A great deal of human interaction occurs on the unconscious level and the sense of smell plays a significant role in this. One of the big drawbacks to the use of birth control pills is that they rob a woman of her copulins, the special sex scent of her Yoni secretions, which play a large part in stimulating the male sex drive.

Many well-known creations of perfumers rely on potent animal extracts to create a basic "tone" or "carrier vibration" upon which the more subtle fragrances can be imposed. Most commonly these basic ingredients come from the sex glands; musk is obtained from the secretion in a gland sack of a type of male deer, and civet from the anal gland of the civet cat. Most floral perfumes are derived from plant essences that are comparable to sexual secretions in animals.

Perfume and incense have been linked to sexuality at all times and in all cultures. Science long ago confirmed that the sexual instincts are stimulated by smell, in humans as well as animals. The sense of smell is much more acute in animals than in mankind, which has become desensitized through unnatural habits. A natural lifestyle significantly increases sensitivity to odors and opens up a whole new world of subtle fragrance, the very existence of which is unsuspected by the average person.

Sudden changes in body odor indicate changes in mood or emotions. Deep relaxation and the release of inner tensions cause the whole body chemistry to change; our odor also changes and we may notice that suddenly we seem to smell especially good. This is the sign that the bodily temple has become a Perfumed Garden in which the spirit is joyously experiencing inner harmony.

Scientific analysis of odors has established that it is the *shape* of the molecular structure of smells that determines their effect. Thus, all camphor types of smell have spherical molecules, musky smells have disc-shaped molecules, flowery smells have disc-shaped molecules with an extended tail, peppermint smells have wedge-shaped molecules and most alcohol smells have rod-shaped molecules. The inner part of the nose consists of cartilage, mucous membranes, olfactory nerves and tiny hairs. The mucous membranes bear a strong biochemical resemblance to some of the secretions produced by the pituitary gland, which governs the sex drive as well as metabolic functions. When we inhale an odor, the molecular vibration and shape cause changes in the mucous membranes, resonant with the tiny hairs and olfactory nerves, and stimulate the inner olfactory bulb of the brain. Thus, the sense of smell is multifaceted and linked directly to the chemistry of the body.

Above all, perfume, incense and fragrant oils create and enhance moods. They act on the sentiments and stimulate the supersensual faculties. Tantric practitioners employ this property in love rituals. Particular perfumes are specified for different rites. Before sexual union, the female partner is worshipped as the embodiment of the creative force, the Shakti or Wisdom-energy; her body parts are then anointed with different perfumes to honor her creative role and lift up her psyche so she can truly manifest as a goddess. In the sexual ritual known as the *Rite of the Five Essentials* (see Part III), the finest oil of jasmine is applied to the hands, oil of patchouli or keora to the neck and cheeks, essence of amber or hina musk to the breasts, extract of spikenard or valerian to the hair, musk from the musk deer to the sexual region, oil of sandalwood to the thighs and essence of saffron to the feet of the woman. For the male partner, sandalwood oil or paste is applied to the forehead, neck, chest, navel, sexual region, upper arms, thighs, hands and feet.

According to Islamic tradition, the Prophet Muhammad once declared: "Three things are especially dear to me. These are women, perfume and prayer." In the Arabic lands perfume is highly valued and is believed to strengthen the brain, the heart and the sexual organs. The spiritual significance of perfume was well known to the Arabs, Greeks, Babylonians and ancient Egyptians, who used numerous aromatic oils in daily life as well as for mummification of the dead.

Recently there has been an awakening of interest in the healing and beautifying properties of essential oils from flowers and herbs. Pure essences are readily available, so try to avoid using synthetic perfumes, for their effect is never the same as that of natural essences. Familiarize yourself with the different essential oils and learn to distinguish fine from inferior qualities. A good book for the beginner is

The Art of Aromatherapy by Robert Tisserand. Experiment with mixing your own scents, using almond or sesame seed oil as a base and adding essential oils as desired. Essence of lotus, rose, jasmine, night-queen, patchouli, rosemary, lavender, saffron, amber, myrrh and sandalwood are just some of the natural perfumes that are suitable for Tantric love-rites.

Use perfume as an aid to your natural sensuality. Whether applied to the body, burnt as incense, mixed in massage oil, used in saunas or mixed with water and sprayed into a room, natural perfumes will contribute much to the harmonization of body and mind. Use fragrant scents to enhance the outer atmosphere and stimulate the inner spirit.

In the Springtime the rounded hips of amorous women are adorned with silken garments reddened by the color of saffron. Languid with passion, they rub sandalwood paste mixed with sweet flowers, saffron and musk on their breasts. RITUSAMHARA

The harmful impurities of noxious things like onion and garlic are perceived in the four great realms. They produce an unclean smell in the Buddha-fields and displease the gods of space. The protective beings of pure lineage will not approach anywhere near a person who smells of such things. THE WAY OF SHEN/BON TEXT

Those who present Shiva with garlands of flowers, of the oleander or of the sweet-smelling jasmine, shall obtain the object of their wishes. KALIKAPURANA

environment

The environment sets the mood and should please the senses as well as the mind. With a little bit of work, almost any space can be transformed into an erotic temple. The hard lines and corners of Western architecture are easily altered by a careful selection of drapes, wall hangings, canopies, ornaments and lighting. By using such materials, an "inner sanctum" can be created within the home, a place that is truly in natural harmony with the spirit.

Eastern temples generally incorporate domes, arches and curved surfaces into their architecture. These shapes enhance the spiritual sentiments by their harmonious relationship with the forms of the human body. Colors are also important in the creation of a harmonious atmosphere. Red and purple are stimulating, deep blue and violet are relaxing and invigorating. Color directly affects the subtle centers of the psyche (the Chakras) and ideally one should choose color combinations that stimulate rather than inhibit sexuality.

Keeping the bed and furniture close to

Natural elements should be introduced into the home to help harmonize the environment and senses.

ground level helps to create a feeling of intimacy and is very practical for love-making. Carpets, rugs and cushions are musts for the modern Tantric love temple. Candles are easy to acquire and, when artfully placed, create a special ambiance. Open fires or fountains may not always be possible, but candlelight, fresh fruit, incense and flowers certainly are.

Plants and flowers are easy to tend, even in the city, and give an immediate feeling of naturalness. Ideally, as many natural elements as possible should be introduced into the home environment. Besides plants, organic materials such as silk hangings,

handwoven rugs and featherdown cushions can be used. The main point is to maintain contact with natural elements. Since both sound and light play a significant role in the environment, these factors should also be thoughtfully considered.

Candlelight is preferable to electric light because electric current has an inorganic frequency that is not harmonious with the subtle changes that occur in the body during erotic stimulation. The clear and soft light of candles can help to still and concentrate the mind and move it away from worldly thoughts. Candlelight is especially flattering to flesh tones and can be well used in conjunction with mirrors. Mirrors can help create a feeling of spaciousness and, when strategically placed, have great erotic potential. Naked bodies, colorful drapes, carpets, cushions, incense, mirrors and soft flickering candlelight all blend well to produce a theatre of erotic delight.

The five senses are the "instruments" of lovers; we must therefore learn to play them masterfully and with finesse. The sixth sense, the mind, is the connecting agent; it is the most discriminating of all the senses and by far the most sensitive. A fine environment frees the mind to commune with all the other senses.

Love-making in Nature's own environment is a totally different experience. There is a natural Shakti or energy inherent in all the creations of Nature. If the couple connect with this natural force, it will enhance their Shakti and act as a potent virilific. The transcendental aspects of physical love can be heightened by entering into mystical communion with the elements of Nature. Also, the unconventional and spontaneous aspects of love can be reawakened by such experiences in the country or on the beach. When you return to the city, you'll be able to hold the memory of union under the stars, in the fields or on the sand as a special token of your feeling for each other. A stone, rock, shell or other object brought back from such an encounter can take on deep significance in the confines of the home.

Yogis often go to cremation grounds to perform Tantric sexual rituals; the environment is said to be conducive to transcendence because it reminds the Yogi

An exotic Indian environment. From a Central Indian miniature painting of the late eighteenth century.

of death, the great doorway to the beyond.

Within your home, try to create a unique atmosphere where you customarily make love. If possible, keep this area private and separate so the chamber of love assumes a magical and sacred quality that enhances eroticism. Lovers need a private inner sanctum where they can relax and experiment without fear of disturbance.

Try to invest your environment with as much of your own spirit and creativity as possible. Doing so will help bring out the best in you and endow your home with a life and mood of its own.

Natural environments can be erotically stimulating.

The abode should ideally be situated near some water and divided into different compartments for different purposes. If possible, it should be surrounded by a garden and contain inner and outer rooms. The main room should be balmy with rich perfumes and contain a bed, soft, agreeable to the sight, covered with a clean cloth, low in the middle part, having garlands and bunches of flowers upon it, a canopy above it, and two pillows, one at the top and another at the bottom. There should also be a sort of couch, and at the head of this a stool on which should be placed fragrant ointments, perfume and flowers.

KAMA SUTRA

The bedstead was made ready, provided with luxuries, including a bronze censer for scenting the quilts. She let down the bed curtains to the floor. The mattresses and coverlets were piled up, the pointed pillows lay across them. She then shed her upper robe and took off her undergarment, revealing her white body, with thin bones and soft flesh. We then made love and her delicate body was soft and moist, like fine ointment.

MEI-JEN-FU

Decorate the beautiful walls of the love-chamber with pictures and other objects upon which the eye may dwell with delight. Scatter some musical instruments and refreshments, rosewater, essences, fans and books containing amorous songs and illustrations of love-postures. Splendid wall lights should gleam, reflected by wide mirrors, while both man and woman should not have any reserve or false shame, giving themselves up in complete nakedness to their unrestrained passions, upon a fine bed, ornamented with many useful pillows and covered with a canopy. The sheets should be sprinkled with flowers and scent, and sweet incense should be burned. In such an environment let the man, ascending the throne of love, enjoy the woman in ease and comfort, gratifying both his and her every wish and whim.

ANANGA RANGA

clothing

BRAHMA

the creative

Oriental clothing is generally loose and designed to allow freedom of movement and easy access. From a Chinese watercolor of the seventeenth century.

Most Western clothes tend to be restricting and uncomfortable. There are exceptions of course, but in general the over-tailored clothes of the present day, which tend to divide the body into separate segments, are neither healthy nor practical for love-making. Fumbling around with buttons and zippers is hardly conducive to spontaneous eroticism. So try to get into the habit of changing into loose, comfortable clothes once at home.

Most of the so-called erotic wear commercially available is made of synthetic materials. Boutiques generally produce expensive bedroom clothing that is geared more to fetishism than to comfort or natural beauty. But, fortunately, it's easy to create your own "fantasy range" of clothing using simple silks or satin, which need not even be sewn. There are also many Eastern clothing styles readily available, such as caftans, kimonos, "happy coats," loose "Thai" or "Indian" pajamas, "tie-around" tops, wraps and so on.

We are in the habit of wearing our "best" or most alluring clothes when we go out socially, to parties or to the theatre. This is fine, but concern with public appearance should not take precedence over how we appear to our loved one in the privacy of the home. The *Kama Sutra* states that "when a wife approaches her husband in private, her dress should consist of many ornaments, various flowers, a wrap or cloth of different colors, and some sweet-smelling ointments or unguents." The text goes on to advise that a woman reserve her best clothes for her husband, and that he do likewise. Every woman who wishes to constantly please and excite her partner should have a range of intimate clothing and should remember to dress up for him, as well as for social functions.

In the West the upper and lower parts of the body are usually separated by a tight belt. This is both uncomfortable and unhealthy since it restricts the free flow of energy throughout the body. Try to be kind to your body, particularly as it becomes more sensitive through a Yogic lifestyle. Loose garments are attractive, simple and inexpensive to make. They are also available ready-made and are often less expensive than regular tailored clothing.

Tie-around clothes give freedom of movement and naturally create erotically pleasing shapes.

Tight trousers are especially restricting and can actually cause damage to the sexual region. Eastern doctors commonly point to this as one of the main causes of such sexual problems as impotence and sterility, as well as cancers of the lower parts of the body. The psychic centers are upset by clothing that is too tight and the flow of vital energy from one part of the body to another is restricted. So try to get into the habit of changing from your working clothes to more flowing and comfortable apparel at home. Leave your body free to breathe and luxuriate in the soft sensual feeling of loose gowns.

Clothes should be fresh, aired and well cleaned. Perfume sachets give clothes a sensuous aura, and are extremely easy to

Caftans are comfortable, inexpensive and always look good.

make. The feel and smell of clothing, as well as its appearance, contribute to the erotic sentiment. Ornaments such as bracelets, necklaces, rings and flowers have a symbolic significance in the Tantric tradition; they function as psychic protection and serve to enhance beauty. In the East women adorn themselves with special jewelry for the delight of their lovers rather than for public show. The Art of Love demands that we make use of all erotically stimulating aids to captivate and uplift the senses.

In the Arabian love treatise *The Perfumed Garden*, which was translated into English by Sir Richard Burton and published in 1886, there is an example of a love-position that makes use of clothing as a sexual aid: "The woman wears a pair of harem trousers, which she lets drop upon her heels; she then stoops down, placing her head between her feet, so that her neck is in the trousers. At that moment the man should seize her legs and turn her on her back, making her perform a somersault; then with his legs curved under him, he should bring his sexual organ against hers, slipping it between her legs and inserting it fully."

Chinese women of the mediaeval period developed extraordinarily beautiful and erotic bedroom wear, devised to reveal and conceal at the same time, thus stimulating the imagination. Some of the most provocative and exquisite, in our opinion, are the loosely tied bodice of silk and the elaborately flared silk leggings, which normally trailed colored ribbons. Throughout the Orient there are many examples of simple yet erotically stimulating clothes that are both a pleasure to the eye and a delight to the body. Since clothing is so much a part of life, it should be designed to enhance the charms of the wearer rather than restrict freedom. Color and texture are as important as style and these should be chosen to stimulate the senses. Clothing should be an extension of the personality and heighten sensitivity rather than inhibit it.

Clothing is an integral part of Oriental erotic portrayals. From a Chinese painting on silk, *circa* eighteenth century.

The woman has her hair done up in a high chignon, she wears silk leggings and looks like a queen. The ladies-in-waiting wear green-blue silk girdles, plaited skirts and square-topped slippers.

CHANG CH'OU

Screens are placed in a circle around the couch and the pillows are laid out. The beautiful woman then takes off her silk bodice and unknots her red silk trousers, which are embroidered with flowers.

TA-LO-FU

the inner eye

The *subduing* gaze, linked to inhalation of breath.

The eyes have long been called the windows of the soul. They certainly indicate much about an individual's inner state, both physically and psychologically. For this reason, physicians are taught to inspect the eyes of their patients as an aid to diagnosis, and Tantric teachers examine the eyes of would-be students to help determine their needs.

We all receive impressions unconsciously, especially when meeting a person for the first time; it is the *look* in the eye that creates the "first impression." Sometimes a "twinkle" or a "flash" unaccountably creates a lasting impression; other times a "glare" or a certain "look" influences one's opinion of that person. Tantra holds such signs as significant and recognizes different categories of "looks."

The eyes create an intense *first impression*.

The Tantric teachings list four main types of "gazes" associated with different eye positions and breathing practices. In the *overthrowing* gaze of Tantra the eyes are directed upward, toward the forehead, while the breath is exhaled. In the *subduing* gaze the eyes look to the left, while the breath is inhaled. For *conjuring forth* the two eyes are turned to the right, slightly upward, while retaining the breath. Finally, for *petrifying* or "causing rigidity" the gaze is central, looking toward the tip of the nose, with the breath relaxed, but motionless. Such techniques, long known to Tantric Yogis, are familiar in the West only to professional hypnotists, magicians and the odd salesman or confidence trickster. For these gazes to be truly effective, prescribed meditation techniques must accompany them. Fortunately such techniques have remained largely secret.

The *overthrowing* gaze, linked to exhalation of breath.

The eyes have nerve structures very similar to those in the brain; they function in much the same way as a computer and can predict movements before they actually happen. The eyeballs are never still, even for a moment, and during dream experiences make very rapid movements. It seems there is a direct link between eye movements and fantasy; it's easy to tell when a person is listening just by looking at the eyes. Likewise, a lie or half-truth can easily be determined by studying eye movements.

The *Gheranda Samhita* gives a simple technique for gaining conscious control over the eyes. Known as *trataka* or "gazing," it is described in the text in the following way: "Gaze steadily, without blinking, at a small object held some distance away. Empty the mind and continue gazing until tears begin to flow. By practicing this, all eye diseases are destroyed and clairvoyance is induced." In the East "fixing the gaze on the tip of the nose" is a common meditation technique, serving to *still* the eye as well as the mind; it allows the sense of "seeing" to be drawn inward. In this exercise one should focus on breathing, noticing when one is breathing in, retaining and exhaling.

The *conjuring-forth* gaze, linked to retention of breath.

A clairvoyant can perceive the elements in the *breath* according to color and shape as the breath is inhaled. When the body is in balance and the mind at ease, an *inner vision* that transcends the normal limitations of time and place is awakened.

Sentiments are easily recognizable in the eyes, especially anger, joy, humor and eroticism. The "reflection" of emotions in the eyes is due to a subtle nerve connecting them with the Navel Chakra. You may consciously evoke a sentiment using breathing techniques and visualization; unconsciously, sentiments occur and change all the time. Retention of breath creates a subtle force that travels from the Navel Chakra to the eyes. When this force is linked to a visualization, the eyes show the relevant sentiment. If, for example, you wish to evoke the erotic, first stimulate the *inner fire* by a number of deep breaths, concentrating on retention and channeling the energy upward. Then, imagine something erotic and focus on all the details; you'll find yourself becoming "emotionally involved." By regulating breath, emotions and breathing, you'll be able to consciously channel erotic energy outward, through the eyes. Treat the force with care and try to instill it with deep, compassionate love. This is effectively achieved by visualizing another subtle nerve connecting the Heart Chakra with the eyes and channeling compassion outward, mixing it with the force from the Navel Chakra.

The right side of the brain is connected to the left eye, the left side of the brain to the right eye. A headache from over-work can often be cured by gentle finger pressure at points just above the eyeball, right up to the nose; sinus troubles or migraine can be alleviated by light massage of the region directly under the eyes, stroking outward, away from the nose. The eyes themselves are helped by head massage, cold water, fresh air and especially by inverted Yoga postures, which increase the flow of blood to the head.

Eastern teachings stress the importance of careful tending of the eyes. Since heat is considered especially harmful to the eyes, it is advisable to shield them with a cool cloth when taking a steam bath or a hot shower. The most ancient eye balm known to humanity is kohl, used by both men and women in the Near and Far East. Today there are many artificial kohls on the market. These "kohls" are merely black preparations made from dark substances mixed with a base; they have little beneficial effect and some preparations are actually dangerous. *Real* kohl is made by burning beneficial cooling herbs, oils or compounds and collecting the soot on a cool surface, such as the outer part of a pot filled with water. Some of the best kohl is made from camphor mixed with herbs and burned. When kohl is properly prepared, it cools, cleans and protects the eyes, at the same time darkening the rims in a dramatic and erotically pleasing way.

According to both Tantric and Taoist teachings, the eyes have a function that is directly related to control of the mind. For example, in order to control premature ejaculation, the eyes may be rolled several times, all the way around. Texts state that this effectively controls the "ascent of fire" at the Navel Chakra and creates a stabilization of the urge to orgasm. Another Tantric technique consists of turning the eyes upward while retaining the breath. This focuses the mind away from the senses and prevents involuntary orgasm.

Harmonious love-making is beneficial to the eyes and gives them luster and power. By becoming aware of the "inner" qualities of vision, the couple can acquire enhanced sensitivity and creativity. Instead of taking the eyes for granted, try to familiarize yourself with their secret power.

The *petrifying* gaze, with the breath relaxed but motionless.

Tantric diagram showing the subtle energy points around the eyes. Pressure on these areas eases eyestrain and also aids the development of clairvoyant vision. From a Rajasthani miniature painting of the late eighteenth century.

When worldly passion begins to subside, a wife does not look straight into the husband's eyes.

ANANGA RANGA

If a man makes love without ejaculating, his vital essence is strengthened, his body becomes harmonized and his subtle hearing and vision will become acute. Although such a man has repressed his passion, his love for the woman will increase; it is as if he cannot get enough of her.

YU-FANG-PI-CHUCH

Turning the eyes upward while retaining the breath focuses energy in a transcendental direction and aids control of orgasm. It is a technique familiar to both Taoism and Tantra.

Dissolve your whole body into vision, so to become seeing, seeing, seeing. . . .

RUMI

BRAHMA

the creative

The mind has tremendous powers of imagination, which are commonly lost in adulthood. This natural faculty can be reawakened and put to the service of the sexual secrets. All great poets, artists, scientists and philosophers have a natural faculty for creative imagination. Many of their greatest discoveries and works are the products of an imagined inner world. According to Eastern teachings, in this world of imagination contact is made with the true source of wisdom and intelligence. The mystic traditions prescribe specific techniques, to create an *inner scenery* in which creativity can flourish. When we think *visually* rather than through inner dialogue or "mental chatter," the opportunity for inner scenery to unfold is greatly enhanced.

The *Kena Upanishad*, an early Hindu text, states: "Through knowledge of the Self we obtain power; through the inner vision we attain Eternity." This metaphysical statement is helpful in understanding why Tantric teachings emphasize visualization as an aid to Liberation. Knowledge of the Self certainly awakens our enormous inner potential, but a developed visionary faculty is required to channel our inner power creatively. Fortunately, every individual is capable of developing inner vision as a tool of Self-discovery.

In Tantra the development of the visionary faculty is a twofold process: an open *introspection of images as they come to mind*, and an eager *stimulation of imagination through visualization*. Two basic philosophical principles serve as the foundation of Tantric visualization.

The first is the principle of *expansion and contraction*. All created things expand and, eventually, contract; the process is repeated over and over again. Stars, suns, whole galaxies, as well as atoms, compounds, inorganic and organic life forms, and individuals all exhibit the tendency to expand and contract. In the sexual act this expansion and contraction play an major role.

The second principle is that all phenomena are inherently "empty." However we view reality, emptiness is a consistent discovery. Tantra does not take a negative view of this "emptiness" but instead sees the qualities of consciousness and blissfulness rising out of the emptiness. This may seem a strange contradiction, yet the Tantric view is that in order for *emptiness to be experienced*, consciousness must be present. From about the second to third century A.D. Tantra emerged as a metaphysical teaching in its own right, with the threefold interaction of emptiness, consciousness and blissfulness as its philosophical base. No matter what internal or external object the mind focuses on, emptiness is found to be its first characteristic, consciousness its second, and blissfulness its third. Emptiness, or the "space element," permeates the object and is quantitatively greater than the other elements. For example, most of the universe is but empty space. Similarly, a single atom is composed largely of emptiness; the human body, if viewed under great magnification, would also seem to be a great expanse filled with small concentrations of pulsating energy. Emptiness also dominates the psyche, yet on introspection, emptiness is found to be filled with consciousness and bliss. This mystic view of reality is common to all evolved spiritual traditions and is but another way of saying that the universe is sustained by the blissful Will of God.

This saying is attributed to the Buddhist Tantric teacher Aryadeva: "Just as a clear gem is colored by the color of other objects around it, so also is the gem of the mind colored by the constructive imagination." If you wish to awaken and channel the visionary faculty, it's only necessary to color your mind with your own inner scenery.

Take a comfortable position, either seated or lying down, and relax the body by breathing deeply and fully. If you have a problem relaxing, concentrate the mind on different parts of the body in turn, from the feet up, tensing and relaxing each part. Tensing (contraction) and relaxing (expansion) help the psycho-organism to harmonize itself. Once the body feels at ease, slow the breathing and focus the mind on the air entering and leaving the body.

Imagine that the body is completely vacuous, as empty as the farthest reaches of

Intimate love-posture. From a Japanese woodblock print by Moronobu, seventeenth century.

Inner scenery is the mind's discovery of the relationships between microcosm and macrocosm. This drawing, from a contemporary Balinese painting, shows the mind contemplating itself as Meru, the Holy Mountain, with pilgrimage routes to the Third Eye and Aperture of Brahma.

outer space. See only the *surface* of the body, the outer skin, holding the *outer shape* of it in the mind's eye. Steadily concentrate on the inherent emptiness of the body and imagine that when you inhale, the outer surface expands, and when you exhale, it contracts. Watch this vision of yourself with the inner eye and try to keep calm and emotionally detached, all the time becoming more and more aware of the expansion and contraction. Recognizing that the outer universe expands and contracts also, see yourself as mirroring this process of interplay between Yang and Yin. Try to become absorbed in this mirroring process and feel that your heartbeat is the center of the universe. Imagine Brahma dwelling there as the innermost Self, sending out rays of visionary light to fill the "emptiness" within. Identify with Brahma (the creative spirit) as the sound

"OM" at the center of the body. Recognize that the *Brahma within* is not different from the *Brahma at the center of the macrocosm.*

Having contemplated Brahma both within the body and the universe, visualize inner scenery; just as the outer world is composed of elements, energies, heat and cold, fire and water, mountains, volcanoes, oceans, deserts, forests, hills, valleys, rivers, gardens and sanctuaries, so is the inner world. From the focus of the heart, emanate creative rays of effulgent light to the outer surface of the body. Think of the outer contours of the body as hills, the hairs as trees, the right and left eyes as the sun and the moon. Imagine the arteries and veins as rivers and streams, the internal organs as shrines and sanctuaries, the brain as Mount Meru, the peak of an inner holy mountain. Imagine the Subtle Body with its myriad subtle channels; think

Life Current	Color	Vital Body Function	Sense Faculty
Prana	Emerald-blue	Circulation and respiration	Smell
Udana	Red-violet	Sensations and swallowing	Touch
Samana	Solar red	Assimilation and digestion	Sight
Vyana	Blue-white	Muscles and posture	Hearing
Apana	Orange-red	All excretions	Taste

Dynamic love-posture. From a Rajasthan miniature painting of the eighteenth century.

of the Kundalini, the inner sun at the Navel Chakra and the inner moon at the Head Chakra. Try to visualize them *as if the Brahma residing in your heart is creating them.*

When you inhale, imagine the life-force entering the inner world of the body from the center of the universe. During the period of breath retention visualize the primordial vitality of Brahma dividing into the *Prana*, *Apana*, *Samana*, *Udana* and *Vyana* life currents. Each of these takes on the appearance of colored lights that illuminate and sustain the inner being, controlling the functioning of vital body functions and sense faculties. The chart above indicates the relationships.

Once you are able to evoke inner scenery at will, you can use it to enhance eroticism. Practice expanding and contracting the vision of inner scenery, increasing and decreasing the scale. Instead of hills or valleys, imagine rising crags and deep canyons; instead of rivers and pools, imagine torrents and rolling oceans. Link your emotions to these inner visions and they'll become stronger and more real.

Imagine that the body fills the universe, then visualize it as small as an atom. Concentrate on the fine details, always looking for more perfection in the vision. As you expand and contract the vision of the Self, it will become more concentrated, more controlled and transcendental. The *Prajnopaya*, a mediaeval Tantric text, gives some good advice about this process: "One must proceed in such a way that the mind does not swerve, for when a jewel-like mind swerves from the transcendental unity and lapses into contraries, perfection is not attained."

The visualization of inner scenery can serve an important function in eroticism. During love-making the person in the active role should visualize Yang things like fire, mountains and volcanoes, while the one in the passive role should hold in mind Yin things like water, valleys and pools. This has a very real and powerful effect on the quality of love-making. Most people fantasize while making love, but when this natural tendency is controlled and directed as outlined, the effects are quite different. Once the faculty for visualization has developed, it opens a new range of possibilities for creative love-making.

Brahma dwells within the heart's lotus, where, like the spokes of a wheel meeting the hub, the subtle nerves meet. Meditate on Brahma as "OM" and cross the ocean of darkness.

MUNDAKA UPANISHAD

The river of life impetuously rushes. It has five streams of sense feelings, which come from the five sources, the five great elements. Its waves are moved by five kinds of winds and its origin is the fivefold fountain of consciousness. The river has whirlpools and rapids.

SVETASVATARA UPANISHAD

These are the imaginary forms that appear in the mind's eye before the final vision of resolution; a mist, smoke, a sun, wind, fireflies, a fire, lightning, clear crystal, a moon.

SVETASVATARA UPANISHAD

visualization

Tantric teachings are largely expressed in visual terms, which naturally aid the understanding of deep intuitive truths. In coming to terms with our inherent nature we must learn how to "switch off" mental chatter and allow the mind to remain open. The *Chandogya Upanishad*, an important early Hindu text, declares: "Wherefrom do all these worlds emerge? They come from space. All beings and things emerge from space and into space they ultimately return; space is indeed their beginning and space is their final end." When we can consciously bring to mind the vastness of inner space, the ground is laid for the practice of visualization. By filling our inner space with creative visualization we effectively "make our own reality."

Though Tantric visualizations are of many different kinds, the common feature of them all is their origin in emptiness and space. As we have already explained in "Inner Scenery," the emptiness of Tantra is, paradoxically, filled with consciousness and bliss; it is a plenum void. A preliminary Tantric visualization sees the body as internally vacuous and externally as a surface with sense organs, elements and energies. Tantric texts outline different ways of developing enhanced receptivity and spontaneity through visualization techniques. The *Chakrasambhara Tantra*, an important metaphysical treatise that evolved in the sixth to eighth centuries A.D., gives the following visualization for awakening and enhancing the senses:

Find a quiet place and take up a comfortable position. Contemplate the inherent voidness of all phenomena and recognize that consciousness and blissfulness are to be found within the inner space. Visualize rays of light emerging from the heart center; these rays proceed through the body and reach out into space, shedding light on everything they encounter. Draw back the rays and gather them within; draw in the male and female breaths of the right and left and focus them in the region of the Heart Chakra. Imagine yourself as filled with heroism, fearless, and visualize a lineage of Tantric teachers above your head. Pray to them to aid the process of inner awakening and imagine a red and white disc resting on the junction of nerves in the Heart Chakra. On that disc imagine a point of light the size of a sesame seed and fix your mind intently on it. Regulate the breath, balancing the right and left until a gentle balance prevails. Hold the mind firm, so it doesn't run astray, and a blissful clarity

will result. Then transfer the imagination to the other sense organs.

Imagine two very fine bright *white* points within the pupils of the eyes. Close the eyes and imagine that the points are still there, and, when the mind is accustomed to it, focus on various objects, all the while keeping the bright points of light before the mind. With practice, the points will be ever more vivid, no matter what the eye falls upon. Having attained stability, draw in the points within the cavern of the heart and imagine the heart gaining brilliancy and clarity. Next, transfer the imagination to the two ears.

Imagine a fine *blue* point inside each ear and meditate on them, in a totally quiet place. When you have succeeded in fixing the mind upon them, move to a place where there are sounds, but always keep the mind fixed on the two fine blue points. With practice, the points will be more vivid, no matter what one hears. Having attained stability, draw in the points and focus them in the Heart Chakra. Then transfer the imagination to the nose.

Imagine a fine *yellow* point inside each nostril and meditate on them in a place totally free from odors. Concentrate the mind on them and, when the visualization does not waver, move to another place where there are odors. Keep the mind focused on the two fine yellow points no matter what, and they'll become more vivid. Having attained stability, draw them in the the Heart Chakra. Next transfer the imagination to the tongue.

Imagine a fine *red* point at the root of the tongue and meditate on it without tasting anything. Concentrate the mind on the red point and, when the visualization is steady, taste some different flavors. No matter what you taste, keep the mind focused on the point so it becomes more brilliant. Once stability is attained, draw it into the Heart Chakra.

Transfer the imagination to the body and focus on a fine *green* point at the sexual region, between the anus and the sexual organ. Fix your mind on it, without touching anything. When the mind has attained concentration on the green point, try touching various things, all the while keeping the mind focused so the point becomes even more brilliant. When vividness is attained, stabilize the concentration and draw in the point to the Heart Chakra.

Mix the different-colored effulgent points within the Heart Chakra and imagine them dissolving into one another and, finally, into nothingness. Then, rising up from the state of Innate Tranquility, imagine the colored points emerging simultaneously and spontaneously, reaching out and extending to the sense organs. By meditating thus, the whole being becomes purified and the senses exalted. This visualization evolves out of voidness, recedes into voidness, yet is truly filled with the conscious being-bliss experience.

This type of psycho-sensual visualization is typical of the Tantric method for gaining ascendency over faculties that normally remain purely mechanical. It leads to an expansion of consciousness and a heightened awareness. All visualization evolves from the play of the senses with the mind.

Yoga postures are helpful in the development of mental concentration and visualization.

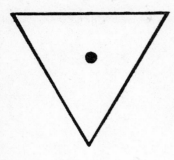

The base of the Yoga head stand is an equilateral triangular form made by the two elbows and interlocked hands. By visualizing this triangle as symbolizing the natural threefold division of all worldly phenomena, ascendency can be gained. The mind should be focused on an imagined dot at the center, physically located at the Third Eye region of the forehead.

Hatha Yoga is particularly helpful to visualization and many of the postures are linked directly to specific meditation practices. The *Katha Upanishad*, an early Hindu teaching text, states: "The Tree of Eternity has its roots in Heaven above and its branches reach down to earth below. It is pure Brahma, the Immortal Spirit, on which all worlds rest. By knowing this, Immortality can be found."

This enigmatic statement is directly linked to the Yoga headstand (*shirsasana*), to the accompanying *visualization* for correct practice of this posture. It also tells of the Tantric method of controlling life energies by reversing their autonomic involuntary flow. The Yoga headstand requires the support of a triangular shape made by the hands and elbows, reminding the Yogi that three forces underlie all phenomena. If you visualize an equilateral triangle with a central focal point, the Yoga headstand will be easy to hold; a natural resonance is created between the form held by the mind and the physical triangular shape, or

Yantra, which is the outer support for the posture.

The *Tree of Eternity*, with "its roots in Heaven above and its branches reaching down to earth below," is a very evocative symbol and is found in several metaphysical traditions. A similar meditation on the microcosm as an inverted tree, with roots in Heaven and branches extending to the Earth, is part of Kabbalistic lore.

Throughout this book we have illustrated simple visualizations that are part of the Tantric and Taoist traditions. The only way to understand the "how" and "why" of visualization is to try it. The remarkable faculty of imagination will reveal more about the true nature of mind than a whole library of psychology books. Transcendental visualization requires only a relaxed and willing mind uncluttered by worldly thoughts or mental chatter. Once the mind is stilled, it can be focused and concentrated on internal imagery.

Try erotic visualization as an energizer. Tantra teaches that visualization must proceed from conscious awareness, which, in turn, makes a kind of subtle channel through which the natural energies reveal themselves in forms, colors and symbols. A Tibetan text known as *The Yoga of Psychic Heat* outlines a simple erotic visualization for generating an inner transcendental passion:

Visualize yourself as an erotic red goddess in the full bloom of youthful vigor, dancing, surrounded by flames of Wisdom. Visualize her as yourself, externally in the shape of a deity and internally altogether vacuous, like the inside of an empty sheath, transparent and radiant; empty inside, like a tent of red silk or a tube distended with breath. First let the clear visualization be your own body size, then as large as a house, then as big as a hill. Finally, make it vast enough to contain the entire universe. Concentrate your mind on this projection and become it. Then reduce it.

The *Chakrasambhara Tantra* gives another version of this type of erotic visualization:

The goddess is to be visualized as red, which is symbolic of dedication and passion. Her single face indicates the essential nature of all things, her two hands symbolize that truth is both "Absolute" and "relative." Her three eyes blaze with passion, her tongue is lustful, devouring all poisons and purifying them with her inner fire. She is naked, with disheveled hair, symbolic of freedom from all bonds of delusion. She is the symbol of the intuition, reminding us that phenomena do not last forever. Blazing like fire, she expresses her Wisdom-essence by embracing her partner without restraint.

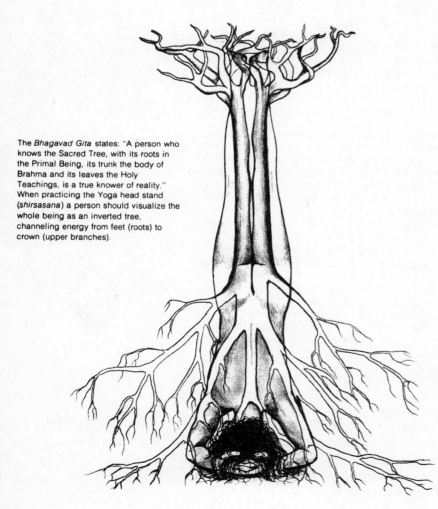

The *Bhagavad Gita* states: "A person who knows the Sacred Tree, with its roots in the Primal Being, its trunk the body of Brahma and its leaves the Holy Teachings, is a true knower of reality." When practicing the Yoga head stand (*shirsasana*) a person should visualize the whole being as an inverted tree, channeling energy from feet (roots) to crown (upper branches).

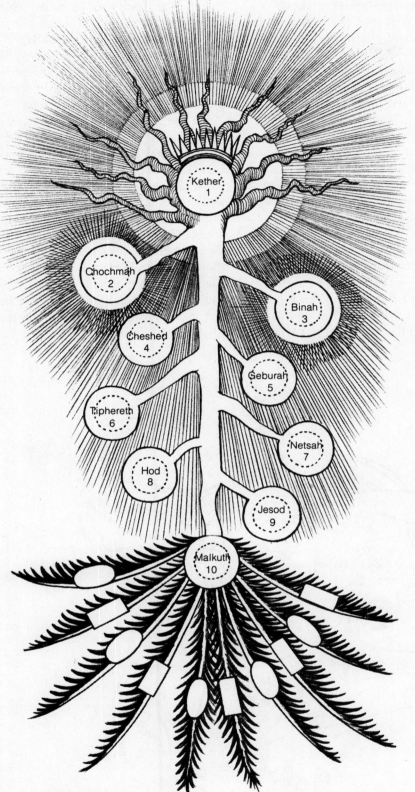

Mystical Tree of Kabbalism, with its roots in God and its branches reaching to the microcosm of man. The ten major divisions, known as *Sephiroth*, refer to parts of the body and higher qualities of the mind. From an engraving, R. Fludd, *Divine Numbers*, 1626.

Dancing Yogini wearing traditional Tantric symbolic ornaments. Erotic visualization is an important aid to conscious spiritualization.

Relationships

1	KETHER	Heaven	Godhead
2	CHOCHMAH	Wisdom	First Motion
3	BINAH	Understanding	The Zodiac
4	CHESHED	Mercy	Right Side
5	GEBURAH	Severity	Left Side
6	TIPHERETH	Beauty	Heart
7	NETSAH	Victory	Right Leg
8	HOD	Glory	Left Leg
9	JESOD	Foundation	Generative System (Male Energy)
10	MALKUTH	The Kingdom	The Senses (Female Energy)

BRAHMA

the creative

Throughout the Tantric teachings similar visualizations are described, with commentaries on the symbolism of the component parts. All mystical traditions make use of visualization for psychic transformation. By doing away with verbal explanations and concentrating instead on symbolic forms, Tantra makes use of the higher faculties of the mind to speed an understanding of the nature of reality.

Meditation on simple colors or colored lights can be very helpful in developing the capacity for complex visualization. Imagine yourself emitting colored light through the pores of your skin and try to focus your mind on creating a consistent tone and quality for the visualization. You'll find that the light will be more intense during the period of breath retention. This type of technique has many practical applications, the most useful of which is psychic healing.

Holding the hands over an injury, while prolonging the period of breath retention and visualizing blue light extending outward from the fingers, effectively heals many physical disorders. Such ancient techniques can be of great service for both physical and psychological problems.

For the couple, the most important visualization is of each other's exalted or higher natures as god and goddess. If you think of your partner in an idealized way, you'll effectively aid the realization of this ideal. Think of each other as *Shiva* and *Shakti* and create an alternate inner reality that can withstand the changes of day-to-day life. Tantra teaches that concentrated visual thoughts are truly eternal; they cannot be affected by the time-bound laws of decay and change. Impelled by the force of faith and transcendental love, visualization can be a vehicle of Liberation.

Tantric representation of Kurukulla, the enchantress, depicted as a dancing erotic goddess garlanded with red hibiscus flowers and shooting love-arrows of flowers from her flowery bow. From a Nepalese painting of the sixteenth century.

Tantric visualization for a couple in embrace, showing the emanation of an eight-petaled lotus from a central syllable "OM" at their conjoined Heart Chakra. Eight scepters, each with the syllable "OM" at its center, emerge from the tips of the petals and encircle the lotus. A ring of water and one of fire create psychic insulation around the visualization. From a Tibetan woodblock print of the seventeenth century.

After one has meditated on Brahma, one should visualize one's chosen deity with all the force of one's soul. By constantly thinking, "This is I," one becomes the deity. A complete consecration of oneself as the deity takes place after the offering of a flower to oneself. "I am god; all instruments of worship, such as eatables, perfume, incense and flowers, become divine through visualization of them as such. I am the abode of god, I am god." Thus one should meditate, bringing god to god and making everything pure and eternal by the re-creation of god in oneself.

KALIKA PURANA

First one should contemplate love, then compassion, followed by joy and non-differentiation. Then in one's heart one should visualize the seed-syllable "HUNG," located upon a lotus, moon and solar orb. One should visualize materializing in front of one the tutelary deity Chandamaharosana, composed of rays of light emanating from one's heart. A wise person should make imaginary offerings to the deity, with flowers, incense and so on. Finally, having paid homage to Chandamaharosana, one should dissolve the deity into the rays of light and focus once more on the voidness, out of which everything emerges.

CHANDAMAHAROSANA TANTRA

psychic protection

BRAHMA

the creative

Learning to confer psychic protection on yourself and your lover is an integral part of Tantric training. Psychic protection prevents energy leakage from the "inside" and the intrusion of polluting influences from the "outside." You can do it for yourself, but ideally it should be done by lovers for each other as a preliminary to love-making. Psychic protection plays a major role in all ritual acts and endows the person with a feeling of self-confidence and invulnerability.

Energy can be lost through the nine body orifices: the mouth, nose, two eyes, two ears, the top of the head, the anus and the sexual organ. Energy may also be dissipated through the pores of the skin, the fingertips, toes, the navel region and especially through the Subtle Body. Tantric Yogis developed simple techniques for preventing such energy losses. The main principle is the concentration or focusing of consciousness on the various parts of the physical and Subtle Body, "seeing" the body and imagining the Subtle Body as a field of force, with energy vortexes at the psychic centers. By an act of Will, linked to the touching of parts of the body lightly with the fingertips,

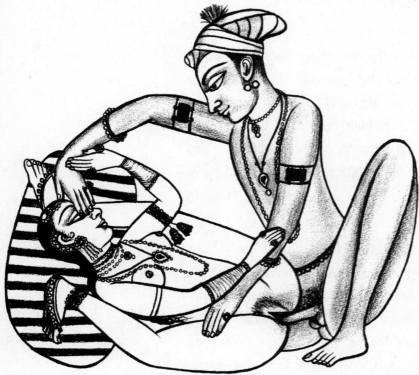

Psychic protection is achieved by consciously focusing the mind while touching parts of the body in turn. Magical acts require *intention* to be truly effective. From an Indian miniature painting of the mid-eighteenth century.

all openings can be "sealed." This ritual of touching the various body parts is known as *Nyasa*, which means "placing," and should be accompanied by visualization of the "openings" being sealed. Any protective Mantra, such as "OM" or "OM—BHUR— BHUWAH—SWA," can aid the concentration of the mind in performing this act.

The ritual of psychic protection provides an ordered awakening of consciousness throughout the body. The parts identified in the ritual correspond to the erogenous zones. The effect is twofold: first, energy loss or "psychic pollution" is guarded against; and second, there is an overall excitation that generates an increase in erotic energy. Various traditions differ in the order of the parts of the body to be touched. Some advise starting at the feet and moving up to the head; others, beginning at the head and touching parts of the body until reaching the feet. Still other traditions suggest beginning at the right foot and advancing up the right side of the body until the top of the head is reached, and then reversing the procedure until the left toe is reached. The following typical but rather complex ordering is found in the *Mahanirvana Tantra*, a late Hindu work: top of head, forehead, eyes, ears, earlobes, nostrils, cheeks, lips, teeth, chin, neck, fingertips, palms, wrists, lower and upper arms, shoulders, chest, heart region, navel, thighs, ankles, insteps, toes and finally, the sexual organ. A simplified version—top of head, throat, hands, navel, feet, and sexual organ—is equally effective, provided the mind is correctly focused. It is, above all else, the *mental attitude* that creates a potent protective field.

The establishment of a field of psychic protection should be part of every love-act, and is ideally suited to foreplay. Many couples experience sudden and unaccountable feelings of fear or loss during particularly passionate love-making. Simple psychic protection will prevent this.

A positive aura or golden cosmic egg should be visualized surrounding you both, protecting you against the entry of polluting or disturbing forces from the outside, and at the same time conserving your inner vitality. This mystic "circle" or "sphere of protection" is taught in all magical traditions. It should be visualized by both partners and made more real by moving the hands in such a way that its limits are clearly defined in the mind's eye. This can take place in the mind or can be externalized through ritual, using sweeping gestures of arms and hands to create a protective field around you both. Touching of various parts of the body should be incorporated into this rite for the stimulation and release of erotic energy.

One of the simplest methods of self-protection is to move your arms in circular sweeps from the navel outward while visualizing the flow of energy and imagining that it is protecting the whole psycho-organism. This type of protective "dance of the hands" can also be performed on your partner's body. Given a positive mental attitude, you'll both experience an immediate feeling of invulnerability and energization. When touching any part of the body, do so with the consciousness focused and the attention directed. Dance can be a form of psychic protection, and many cultures use dance in this way, as a prelude to rites of initiation.

The kiss, the scratch and the embrace are all aspects of psychic protection. The *Kama Sutra* lists the forehead, eyes, cheeks, throat, breasts, lips, mouth, thighs, arms, and navel as places particularly suited to kissing. Kissing with the intention of conferring psychic protection is an effective measure and helps distribute the energies of love in a balanced and harmonious way. Couples often find themselves unconsciously wishing "psychic protection" on each other during foreplay or before separation. Try to incorporate psychic protection into your relationship, without self-consciousness or exaggeration. It's a wonderful means of increasing intimacy and ensuring that the energies of love are not dissipated. Psychic protection effectively guards against negative influences and increases the potency of love-making.

Touching of parts of the body prior to or during love-making is referred to as *Nyasa* and has the power to confer psychic protection.

Saliva has a natural protective power. In Taoist and Tantric traditions saliva is used for psychic protection and for empowering amulets. From a Japanese woodblock print of the early eighteenth century.

May the head be protected, and the face, the heart, throat, the two eyes, ears, nose, lips, teeth, cheeks, chin, neck, nape, arms, hands, shoulders, back, sides, hips, navel, thighs, feet, sexual organ and all bodily parts. May the Supreme Power protect these thoroughly.

MAHANIRVANA TANTRA

With the first two fingers, touch the partner's head, forehead, eyes, throat, earlobes, breasts, upper arms, heart, navel, thighs, feet and sexual organ. Charge these places with the vital energy of transformation.

YOGINI TANTRA

Bending all fingers, except the forefinger, into a fist, the adept should make a circular movement with the hands, as if to encircle the sacred fire. This confers psychic protection and aids the devotee.

LAKSHMI TANTRA

the sensual elements

The *Prana Upanishad*, an early Hindu scripture, states: "The powers that hold together this body and support it through life are known as space, air, fire, water and earth." These *Five Great Elements* are familiar to all ancient metaphysical systems. Unfortunately, modern science has misunderstood the original meaning and significance of these five elements, as well as their subtle relationship to the microcosm and macrocosm. With the advent of atomic theory and the compartmentalization of science, the Five Great Elements have ceased to have any meaning to the scientist.

The *Sushruta Samhita*, an important Hindu medical work of about the third century B.C., states: "The five fundamental principles of space, air, fire, water and earth enter into the composition of all substances. A predominance of any one of these principles determines the characteristic of a particular substance." The element of *space* is, in Yogic texts, related to subtleness and diffusion, *air* to formation and movement, *fire* to heat and expansion, *water* to cohesion and contraction, and *earth* to density and solidification. The space element dominates the faculty of hearing, the air element the sense of touch, the fire element the sense of sight, the water element the sense of taste and the earth element the sense of smell.

In Tantric symbolism eroticism is often used to conceal cosmic truths. Here, a maharaja makes love with five women simultaneously. They hold a musical instrument, a mirror, fruit, a flower and touch his body, symbolizing the five senses of hearing, seeing, tasting, touching and smelling. Tantra teaches that Liberation can be attained through the conscious evocation of the sensual elements. From a Rajasthani miniature painting of the mid-eighteenth century.

In the Tantric view of the human microcosm the *inner fire* and *inner water* are conceived of as complementary and are related to the principles of expansion and contraction; Taoism refers to these forces as Yang and Yin. The faculties of sight and taste are, according to Tantra, expressions of the cosmic principles of expansion and contraction, which characterize the male and female sexual organs when aroused. The inherent orgasmic nature of the fire and water water elements serve as a potent symbol of transcendental eroticism. Tantric cosmology suggests that in the formation of worlds, the water element plays an important role in cooling the fire element sufficiently to allow life forms to emerge. Sexual union causes a harmonization of the inner fire and the inner water, creating the potential for life.

According to Tantra, the five elements are actually created in the body during love-making. The *Hevajra Tantra*, an important Buddhist text of about the ninth century, states: "Through the harmonization of the male and female sexual organs, hardness and erection are produced, which calls up the earth element. From the flow of sexual secretions, the water element emerges and the fire element is evolved through the passion and friction of love-making. The air element is produced from the movements of love and the space element corresponds to the ecstatic Bliss."

Each of the Five Great Elements is linked to a color, shape, sound and taste. Visualization of these attributes can help evoke and focus specific elemental principles, creating a change in the psycho-organism. According to important Yogic texts such as the *Patanjali Yoga Sutras*, the *Gheranda Samhita* and the *Shiva Samhita*, paranormal powers are developed by focusing these elements individually within the Heart Chakra. Elements can be focused by visualization and breath control and channeled into precise areas of the physical or Subtle Body. The chart below indicates the traditional view of the relationship between the Five Great Elements and their attributes.

Tantra teaches that the breath contains the subtle aspects of the Five Great Elements. By focusing the mind on the shape, color and sound of the elements it's possible to consciously extract specific elements from the air. If the senses are unrestrained during abandoned love-making, the breath will naturally balance the elements in the body. Oriental medical texts declare that the sexual secretions change according to the dominance of one or another element. The whole being becomes balanced and harmonized by ecstatic love-making, and at the same time gains the power to heal itself.

The *Shiva Samhita* declares that "The inner being is of a pulsating nature, now expanding, now contracting, essentially composed of a mixture of Potent Voidness and Creative Energy, living in the Temple of the Body." It is the sensual elements that nourish and transform the inner being, allowing evolution to take place. The human body contains all the elements essential for Self-realization and there are no limits to individual potential once this is recognized.

Element	Sense Organ	Faculty	Seed Sound	Shape	Color
Space	Ears	Sound	Hang	Flaming point	Outer space
Air	Skin	Touch	Yang	Crescent	Dark
Fire	Eyes	Sight	Rang	Triangle	Red
Water	Tongue	Taste	Vang	Circle	White-blue
Earth	Nose	Smell	Lang	Square	Yellow

Heaven and Earth have their opening and closing; Yin and Yang develop from each other. Mankind is modeled after Yin and Yang and embodies the sequence of the seasons and elements. If one abstains too much from sexual union, then one's Spirit will not develop, since the interchange of Yin and Yang will have come to a halt. It is possible to derive great benefit from the enjoyment of the senses through sexual intercourse, so substituting new elements for old ones.

I-HSIN-FANG

The five subtle elements, the ego, the intellect, the mind, the five sense organs and their objects are the principles that make up the phenomenal universe.

BHAGAVAD GITA

The best means of stimulating virility is an exhilarating sexual partner. When the desired sense objects yield great pleasure, even if singly experienced by the senses, then what need to be said of the woman in whom the delectable objects of the senses are found established together! Such a combination of sense objects is only found in the person of woman. Hence it is that man's pleasure is mainly in woman and that in her is established the source of all progeny. A woman who is good-looking, young, endowed with auspicious marks and who is amiable and skilled in the Sixty-four Arts is the best virilific.

CHARAKA SAMHITA

commitment

Commitment implies absolute trust. The bond of commitment keeps a couple together. Once established, commitment helps the couple overcome many of life's difficulties by providing a storehouse of strength upon which to draw. Whether commitment is made formally or informally, in the bedroom or a law court or a church, it must be sincere and each partner must have absolute confidence in its validity. Mutual commitment is an essential ingredient of the sexual secrets.

In the Tantric tradition commitment must precede serious effort and is itself an opening into potency. Commitment is also an integral element in every initiation along the way. For the Tantric lover, commitment means *being true* to one's inner reality and sharing this truth with the beloved.

The couple should share their innermost feelings about each other, within the context of their sacred bond of mutual trust. Dispense with self-reproach and feelings of guilt and let yourselves experience the joyous release of sharing. Verbalizing your innermost feelings will create a mystic bond of trust. Explicit commitments can be made without any verbalization whatsoever, merely by "opening up the heart" and letting it commune directly with the heart of the partner.

Love-making is the perfect opportunity for establishing a lasting bond of commitment. During the love-act, the life-force enters the central Subtle Nerve and ascends to the region of the head. According to Tantric teachings, whatever the mind visualizes at such an occasion will inevitably come about. A wish made at the heights of ecstasy is said to have a very good chance of success. People often find themselves unconsciously wishing and fantasizing while making love. If this tendency is made conscious, it will be possible to use ecstatic love-making to create lasting commitments of a liberating nature.

Commitment can take many forms but ideally it should transcend worldly values and selfish desires and be oriented to higher ideals. Commitment to a high spiritual ideal helps to unify the couple and exalts love to a higher dimension. Commitment strengthens self-confidence and leads to increased awareness of spirituality in oneself and the other. True love implies an absolute commitment based on a couple's desire for spiritual evolution *together*.

In the Tantric tradition commitment is formalized in various ways. Commitment to a teacher implies selfless service. Commitment to a spiritual path or specific teaching requires unquestioning faith and patience. Sexual commitment is of two kinds: lifelong, and just for the duration of a particular rite. The lifelong commitment is similar to Western marriage, except that in the Tantric belief structure it is sustained beyond death. Hindus believe that if a couple are truly committed to each other, they will share Eternity.

Commitment "for the duration" means that a couple get together for an agreed period and for a specific purpose; they commit themselves to each other and undergo a brief "marriage ritual" that formalizes their agreement to give the most of themselves to each other. The sexual rites of Tantra generally require a formal commitment by the partners, even if they are not married and do not intend to become married. A kind of mini-marriage takes place. The woman receives a new sari, some ornaments and jewelry, flowers, perfume, fruit and other symbolic items. She is worshipped as an embodiment of the Goddess. Then the woman and man hold hands and are covered by a cloth. They make a statement of commitment to each other and together say *Swasti*, meaning "It is well." Then they recite the following: "It is Kama [love] who gives and Kama who accepts. It is Kama who is taking the Kamini [woman] for the satisfaction of Kama. Inspired by Kama, I take thee. May both our Kama be fulfilled." The man then lights a fire. A small quantity of food is prepared and some of it is offered back into the fire.

Then the couple circumambulate the fire together and meditate on Brahma, Shiva and Vishnu in union with their goddesses, identifying themselves with them. The "bride" then takes seven steps accompanied by her partner, both are garlanded and the ceremony is complete.

Commitment strengthens a relationship and gives it meaning. Whether formal or informal, commitment is very much a part of the Tantric lifestyle. Sexual ritual requires commitment to ensure lasting success. When commitment is motivated by true love, a couple is ready to explore the sexual secrets.

Commitment implies absolute trust and mutual service. Both Taoism and Tantra teach the importance of commitment to achieving Liberation through sexual acts. From a Chinese painting of the Kang-hsi period (1662–1722).

Generally speaking, there is commitment if one does not counteract that which one has taken upon oneself to do. Commitment plays a role in Mantra teaching, and especially in the Tantric discipline, when, having obtained the initial confirmation, one does not fail in one's commitment to look upon the world as a divine mansion and upon all beings as gods and goddesses. In the highest application of commitment one should try to live in such a way that the unitary experience does not fall to pieces, one never becomes separated from service and attention, one partakes of spiritual nourishment, one retains its mystic character, and one guards the authenticity of one's being. NARO CHOS DRUG

Marriage under the Law of Shiva is of two kinds. One is terminated at the conclusion of the rite, and the other is lifelong. Both require a high level of commitment. When it is stated aloud; "Approve our marriage according to the Law of Shiva," a marriage commitment is truly made. MAHANIRVANA TANTRA

BRAHMA

the creative

service

Selless service is truly a sign of spirituality. Radically different from subservience or "bowing to the will of another," it is the genuine desire to give service as an act of love. Service means giving without preconditions or selfish motivations. It should be cultivated, particularly in an intimate relationship.

If a couple cultivate service within their relationship, they will become an integrated interdependent unit. Loving service leads to deeper commitment, which in turn strengthens the relationship. Service should be joyously rendered and accepted, without feelings of resentment or expectancy.

It's essential to maintain equilibrium between the "server" and the "served." This doesn't mean that one should automatically *expect* something just because one has given something; there will inevitably be different needs and situations. Service should be spontaneous, true giving, from the heart. If one of you comes home from work tense or exhausted, the other may offer service in the form of massage; this will relieve tension and also bring you into touch with each other. Similarly, some *unexpected* help with housework will lead to a more spontaneous experience of freedom than any rigidly worked out system of duties or chores. If every part of one's relationship becomes infused with the spirit of selfless service, communication will be greatly enhanced and love will grow.

Selfless service creates a positive aura or psychic atmosphere that becomes charged with uplifting spiritual energy. Suddenly things begin to work out right of their own accord; this is the spiritual effect of real service. Sexual service is the ability to intuit the sexual needs of the other and to give freely, without any thought of return. True service is an act of worship, and as such is a potent tool for lovers.

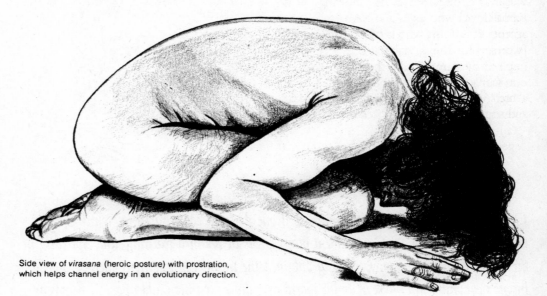

Side view of *virasana* (heroic posture) with prostration, which helps channel energy in an evolutionary direction.

The mind, imbued with love and compassion in thought and deed, should ever be directed to the service of others.

GAMPOPA

People are bound by the shackles of Karma only when engaged in actions other than work performed for the sake of service.

BHAGAVAD GITA

Know that the act is not of the same complexion as its result; a service rendered is not homogenous with something given in return. Everything becomes lovely when it leads you to your beloved.

RUMI

the art of worship

Worship is the *spirit of love* and a sure way of awakening the gods within. A creative attitude is the seed of worship and ecstasy the fruit. The Tantras teach that man and woman should always strive to honor their divine origin. Worship is fundamental to spirituality, regardless of what form it takes.

The Temple of the Body is a place of worship, where you can commune with your original nature. There is no holier temple than the bodily temple with its nine "gateways," its solar and lunar energies, five elements, senses and mind. Flowers, incense, candlelight, music, perfume and food are all used in Tantric worship to gently guide the mind to a knowledge of the spirit.

Worship can, according to Tantra, be of three kinds: external, internal or a combination of the two. The teachings declare: "Those same actions that bind us to worldliness and unconsciousness can, if used correctly, liberate us." Another view is expressed in a popular Tantric aphorism: "One can rise by that same thing by which one falls." This is the criterion for Tantric worship, which involves both external and internal, blended together. The very word "Tantra" implies a conscious weaving together of inner and outer realities.

Such basic activities as eating, drinking, walking and sleeping can be imbued with the spirit of worship simply by performing them consciously and with discrimination. There is no human activity that does not benefit from contact with the spirit of worship. Worship in the Temple of Love, through acts of love, is the most direct route to the experience of ecstatic Oneness.

Tantric and Taoist mystical teachings exalt the initiatory power of the Goddess, the Divine Principle of transcendental intuitive Wisdom. This female force or Shakti exists in both man and woman, as well as in all phenomenal things, animate and inanimate. Symbolized by the female form, the Goddess may take a variety of names—Isis, High Priestess, Divine Mother, Kali, Inner Woman, Anima or simply the Compassionate One. In all cultures, her force has been recognized, and either exalted in worship or decried in fear.

Ritualized worship helps the channeling of energy. In Hinduism idols and symbols are used to help focus the mind on transcendental goals, serving to remind the worshipper of the indescribable nature of godhead. Worship at a Shiva shrine is depicted in this Mughal miniature, *circa* 1735.

Woman's role is multifarious; she is the host and nourisher of every human being who enters this world and the embodiment of eroticism. We spend about nine months inside the womb of our mother, growing and feeding on her pregnant vitality, gradually acquiring organs and senses through her subtle nourishment. Each of us is like a fruit of our mother's womb; when we are ripe, we are born into the world. Entering this world through the Yoni of our mother, we undergo our first sexual initiation and prepare ourselves for the pains and pleasures of life.

Image of Ishtar/Isis, the idealized priestess archetype, naked and with an upturned crescent moon on her head. From Babylon, *circa* third century B.C.

Icon of the Yoni, emanating rays of energy. From a South Indian wood carving of the nineteenth century.

Visualization image of a Wisdom-goddess of the Tantric Kargyudpa sect of Lamaism. Energy flows outward from her Yoni and forms the shape of a Bodhi-tree leaf, under which the Buddha was enlightened. This initiatory image expresses the spontaneous nature of erotic energy. From a Tibetan painting of the late eighteenth century.

Worship of the Yoni, the female sex organ, is found in most ancient cultures, as is worship of the Lingam, the erect male organ. Great insights can be gained from focusing the mind on this mystery of the *original cause* when in sexual union. Although present-day India tends to be puritanical because of Moslem and European influence, it is still fairly common to encounter worshippers of the Lingam and Yoni. Honoring the female principle as embodied in women is a firmly established practice throughout India, as are Tantric rituals such as the *Kumari-puja*, the worship and honoring of young virgin girls. The male principle is also honored in the way a wife treats her husband, or through the worship of *Sadhus*, the holy men who wander over India. The custom of pouring oil and water over the erect Lingam of a Yogi or Sadhu at particular times of the year to ensure prosperity is still practiced. In the Tantric tradition the sexual organs are depicted in amulets. Some of these are worn on the body, others appear as sculptures on the walls of temples.

Meditation on and visualization of the sexual act is a common feature of all pagan and animistic religions. An early Hindu text gives the following beautiful meditation: "Think of the sexual region of a woman as a sacrificial altar, her hairs as the sacrificial grass, her skin as the elixir dispenser, the two lips of her Yoni as the tongues of flame that rise up from the offering." The text goes on to declare that those who respectfully worship "on this altar of love" will be granted their desires. Other texts exalt the power of the Lingam and advise a woman to honor the Lingam as the living embodiment of *Shiva*, the force of Transcendence.

Tantric visualizations commonly begin with highly erotic themes designed to awaken and stimulate the emotions. A secret visualization technique of the Tantric Black Hat sect of Tibetan Buddhism begins thus:

Imagine that your body is in the form of the Wisdom-goddess, a complete virgin-girl, naked, with hair flowing. *Imagine yourself as her*, in the center of an effulgence of light, holding an elixir bowl close to her heart and garlanded with red flowers. Think to yourself that the Guru enters you through your open Yoni and resides in your heart. Then imagine the Wisdom-goddess above the crown of your head, having just consummated the act of love; she is naked, with disheveled hair, and her Yoni is moist and overflowing with sexual secretions. Her three eyes are filled with erotic emotion and look toward the vast expanse of the sky, which, as she begins to dance, becomes filled with similar forms of herself.

This precise and relatively simple visualization serves to identify the Wisdom-goddess with the meditator. A typical example of Tantric inner worship, this visualization is most effective in captivating the emotions and the imagination.

In the Tantric tradition the attitude of worship is referred to as *Sadhana*, meaning "the direct way." Sadhana is an individual's

Erotic visualization serves to awaken and consciously stimulate the emotions. The Third Eye at the forehead symbolizes the attainment of an all-seeing mystic awareness.

art of worship and implies commitment and actual practice. The potential to step aside from purely mundane activities and practice Sadhana is inherent within each of us. For Sadhana to be complete, it should involve *all* activities and should not be seen as separate from one's overall lifestyle. Throughout this first section we have outlined ways in which the individual or couple can learn to recognize and channel energy creatively. The art of worship is essential to the success of these practices. Worshipping the inner spirit during love-making leads to mystical awareness and self-realization. Then love takes on its liberating and truly eternal character.

The Knower of Yoga should always worship the female power, according to the revelation of the Tantras. One should worship mother, sister, daughter, wife and all women. During this kind of worship there should be contemplation of the essential unity of Wisdom and Means, the female and male principles.　　ADVAYASIDDHI

At all times, whether washing the feet or eating, rinsing the mouth, rubbing the hands, or girding the hips with a loincloth, going out, making conversation, walking, standing, in wrath, in laughter, the wise man should always worship and honor the lady.

HEVAJRA TANTRA

The Goddess resides in all women and the Lord abides in all men.

JVALAVALI VAJRAMALA

Hindu shrine showing the Lingam and Yoni; a Kundalini-snake is coiled around the Shiva Lingam and two footprints are at the entrance to the Yoni. This is a glyph of the ideals of worship. The feet symbolize the lineage of teachers, the Yoni the all-powerful energy of femininity, the snake the Kundalini tamed and controlled and the Lingam ultimate transcendence. Stone sculpture from Bagh, India, *circa* fourteenth century.

part two

SHIVA

the transcendental

Shiva is Pure Existence, the immortal Divine Principle. Shiva is Pure Consciousness, Unconditioned and Transcendental. Shiva is the deity of the Mind, the Lord of Yoga, Master of the Three Worlds and the Conqueror of death. The whole universe is created by the Shakti of Shiva.

SHIVA PURANA

Kali is the Liberator. Kali gives protection to those who know her. Kali is the Terrific One, the Destroyer of Time. As the Dark Shakti of Shiva, Kali is space, air, fire, water and earth. Kali performs all the physical needs of Shiva. She is the Possessor of the Sixty-four Arts and increases the Joy of the Lord of Creation. Kali is the Pure Transcendental Shakti. Kali is the Night of Darkness.

KALIKA PURANA

Kali on Shiva. This icon expresses the transcendent power of Tantra. Kali stands on the corpse-like Shiva, extending her tongue in an expression of sensual ecstasy. She is garlanded with heads, representing detachment from the world. Kali is the glyph of the transcendental. Her awesome outer form conceals an inner compassionate nature. Drawing from a stone sculpture of the seventeenth century, Bangla Desh.

SHIVA

High on the peak of Mount Meru, at the center of this universe, Shiva the Supreme Yogi and Shakti, his sensual female counterpart, together view the world and its inhabitants. Freed from all worldliness through selfless sexual communion with each other, the Cosmic Couple are satiated with the transcendental peace that follows ecstasy.

Still embraced by her lover, the goddess turns to Shiva and asks
"O Shiva, for the sake of our love and for the benefit of mankind, will you reveal some secrets on the nature of sexuality?"

Shiva replies
"Dearest, I am intoxicated with love and filled by your passion. How could I refuse such a request? *Sexual secrets* are surely the most significant of all topics worthy of discussion between lovers. No other subject even approaches the sexual secrets in importance. By the power of sex humans and all other creatures enter life. Impelled by sexual energy, beings develop and flourish. Sex is the life-wave, the power of achievement, the force of evolution and transcendence. The whole universe came into existence through the power of sex. With knowledge of the sexual secrets, the primordial power of sex that brought us into existence can be used to achieve Liberation." — THE POWER OF SEX

The goddess asks
"Tell me about the meaning of transcendence. What is its relationship to the creative and preserving functions of Brahma and Vishnu? What is the relevance of the Brahma, Shiva and Vishnu triad of forces to sexuality? Why is it that the sexual secrets are divided into these three parts?"

Shiva replies
"The whole of existence culminates in transcendence, which is the goal of all Yogas. Transcendence means *to go beyond*, to extend beyond phenomenal limitations and the conditioning of dualities. Transcendence is the real goal of evolution and the ultimate destiny of all physical existence. The creative and preserving functions of Brahma and Vishnu are purely phenomenal and dualistic forces unless balanced by the Shiva-function of transcendence. The creative force of Brahma brings all beings into existence, and the preserving force of Vishnu guards their lives. The transcendental force of Shiva is like a doorway leading beyond worldliness; it extends from the mundane to the metaphysical and awakens an understanding of the real nature of existence. On the highest level, transcendence is a total participation in reality beyond both worldliness and death. — THE MEANING OF TRANSCENDENCE

"The force of Brahma manifests through the channel on the right side of the Subtle Body. Known as *Pingala*, this psychic channel controls the flow of solar energy throughout the human organism. Its qualities are fiery, expansive, aggressive and arrogant; when concentrated in the region of the solar plexus, at the Navel Chakra, the creative force of Brahma seeks to fulfill itself through an awakening of its intellectual potentiality. Brahma's force is patriarchal, logical and conventional. — THE FORCE OF BRAHMA

"The force of Vishnu manifests through the channel on the left side of the Subtle Body. Known as *Ida*, this psychic channel controls the flow of lunar energy throughout the human organism. Its qualities are watery, contractive, submissive and modest; when concentrated in the region of the brain, at the Head Chakra, the preserving force of Vishnu serves to instill deep intuitive wisdom into the fiery psyche. Vishnu's force is matriarchal, instinctive and unconventional. — THE FORCE OF VISHNU

"The force of Shiva manifests through the central channel of the Subtle Body. Known as *Sushumna*, this psychic channel controls spiritual evolution. It is the 'highway' that connects this world with the next. Shiva is the penetrating power of pure undifferentiated consciousness. Shiva is the ecstatic transcendental quality of evolution. — THE FORCE OF SHIVA

"Brahma, Vishnu and Shiva together form a triad of forces that can be simply represented by an equilateral triangle with the Shiva-force of transcendence at the apex and the creative force of Brahma and the preserving force of Vishnu at the two base points. This simple glyph symbolizes the penetrating, erect Lingam, rising from a firm foundation.

"This triad of forces manifests on all levels, from the purely physical to the psychological and the spiritual. Every action evokes a reaction; Brahma creates and Vishnu preserves what has been created. Beyond the duality of Brahma and Vishnu, the transcendental force of Shiva acts, resolving all phenomenal limitations. In the physical body, Brahma is food, Vishnu is drink and Shiva is the life energy, the pure vitality, the breath. These three kinds of nourishment, food, drink and breath, are essential to maintaining life in the body. On a psychological level, Brahma is the creative 'psyche,' Vishnu the preserving 'Soma' and Shiva the medium or connecting 'agent.' Spiritually, Brahma is the Creator, Vishnu the Preserver and Shiva the Transcender. From a worldly viewpoint, the forces of Brahma, Vishnu and Shiva cannot exist independent of each other. They are wholly interdependent.

UNDERSTANDING THE SEXUAL SECRETS

"The sexual secrets are best understood in relation to the triad of Brahma, Vishnu and Shiva. Brahma is introduced first, since his creative force causes the birth of all beings. The creative attitude is the first secret of Brahma; it extends outward from its source as a golden protective aura of positive energy and manifests as sixty-four creative energies or 'arts.' Familiarity with these arts harmonizes and uplifts the psyche. The force of Brahma thus creates, extends and exalts reality, providing a fertile ground for the growth of spirituality. From the Tantric viewpoint, understanding the realm of Brahma is extremely important, since it leads to control over all his functions. Sexuality, the passionate fire of the psyche, needs the physicality of Brahma's realm to provide a firm foundation for the achievement of physical as well as spiritual fulfillment. Tantric sex requires both the theoretical understanding and practical application of Brahma's energy. The first part of sexual secrets acts as an initiation into the nature of Brahma and guides the individual to a practical lifestyle in which sex can find its highest applications.

THE REALM OF BRAHMA

THE REALM OF VISHNU

"The third and last part of the sexual secrets evokes the realm of Vishnu, the preserving force. The erotic sentiment is Vishnu's first secret; an eroticism linked to the nourishing, cooling power of Soma, to the watery element and to the natural, intuitive wisdom of the senses. The sensuality of Vishnu's realm cuts through all conventionality and allows for the multifarious roles of woman to be understood and expressed spontaneously. The numerous sexual postures aid in the channeling of sensual energies, and the secret rites of Tantra provide a focus for consciousness to rise from. The third part of sexual secrets serves as an initiation into Vishnu's Paradise on earth and provides couples with the opportunity to explore the true potential of their sexuality.

THE REALM OF SHIVA

"The second and central part of the sexual secrets evokes the transcendental ecstasy of Shiva. This is the spontaneous realm of pure Yogic delight, the timeless joy of selfless love. No words can truly describe the nature of the Shiva-experience. Linked to the central channel of Tantra, Shiva is the one who takes you through. The structure of the sexual secrets is centered on Shiva the Transcendental. This central part should ideally be approached after the first and last parts of the secrets have been absorbed. The three parts that make up the sexual secrets together serve as a glyph of spiritual evolution through the Subtle Body of Tantra."

The goddess asks

"You have mentioned the functions of Brahma, Vishnu and Shiva, but what about their female counterparts? Do they also represent a triad of forces, and if so, how is it related to the triad formed by the forces of creation, preservation and transcendence?"

Shiva replies

"O Sensuous Goddess! Neither Brahma, Vishnu nor I exist without female counterparts, which are best understood as forms of Shakti, meaning 'energy.' Without their Shaktis, Brahma, Vishnu and Shiva would be powerless in the phenomenal world. Though the Shaktis of Brahma, Vishnu and Shiva have numerous different names and forms, the Tantras distill them simply as Saraswati, Lakshmi and Kali, respectively. They also form a potent triad of energies, which can be simply represented by a downward-pointing equilateral triangle, with Kali at the tip and Lakshmi and Saraswati at the other two points.

THE THREE SHAKTIS

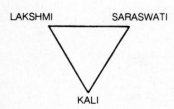

"If the goddess triad, which symbolizes the Yoni of woman, is superimposed on the triad formed by Brahma, Vishnu and Shiva, symbolizing the forces of creation, preservation and transcendence, a six-pointed star is the result. This *Yantra* or mystic diagram formed by the two interlaced triangles symbolizes the unification of the five senses with the mind and is a glyph of male and female qualities in harmonious balance.

"In this all-powerful protective Yantra, Lakshmi is linked to the sense of touch, Brahma to sight, Kali to smell, Vishnu to taste, Saraswati to sound and Shiva to mind. Each of these six 'senses' is visualized as located in one of the six small triangles formed by the six-pointed star, with the presiding male or female function at its apex. This Yantra can be used as an object of meditation, as an aid to the ordering of rituals or as a potent protective talisman. Since ancient times this symbol has been used as a shield against negative influences."

The goddess says

"O Shiva! Please reveal the inner meaning of my mystic form of Kali, she who is black as the limitless night sky, awesome, fearful, yet compassionate. Tell me how she differs from Parvati, my better known form. Tell me how any woman can become one with Kali, and as such, how she can best serve her lover. Tell me, O Shiva, before this night is through!"

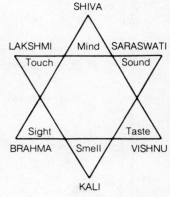

THE GODDESS TRIAD AND THE GOD TRIAD

Shiva and Parvati seated below the peak of Mount Meru, the center of the universe. The Yogi holds a trident, symbol of the power that he has tamed; his consort holds a skull bowl, symbol of renunciation and blissfulness. From a stone sculpture of the tenth century, central India.

THE MEANING OF KALI

HER NAKEDNESS

HER FOUR ARMS

Contemporary representation of Kali. The four arms symbolize the four directions and the four main Chakras of the Subtle Body. The long tongue tells of her all-consuming sensual nature, and the eye in the middle of her forehead evokes the all-seeing consciousness of awakened spirituality.

PARVATI

ONE WITH KALI

The Kali Yantra, symbolizing ascendence over the five elements and senses. From a Rajasthani miniature painting of the late eighteenth century.

Shiva replies

"O Precious Goddess, few are those who truly understand the meaning of Kali. Few are those who can face her terrific form without fearing for their lives. Fewer still are those who serve her as I do you, knowing full well every subtle nuance, every shade of meaning.

"Kali is black because she is the doorway through the voidness of both inner and outer space. Her blackness is made up of all colors and, like the black holes of universes, she ultimately absorbs everything that has ever been created. All brightness eventually recedes into blackness, just as all spirituality eventually merges into Kali-consciousness.

"Kali is absolutely naked, just as your mind was originally naked and will ultimately return to nakedness. Like Shiva's, Kali's nakedness both attracts and repels. In her primordial nakedness, all things are possible. Kali's three eyes tell of her absolute power over the three times of past, present and future and suggest that her inner nature is deeply perceptive. Symbolizing the exalted forces of the sun, the moon and lightning, the three eyes of Mother Kali show her control over this universe.

"Her four arms symbolize the four directions of north, south, east and west, reminding us that the four main psychic centers at the navel, heart, throat and head must be penetrated and harmonized before lasting Liberation can be achieved. Kali's upper left hand holds the sword by which she destroys doubts and dualistic limitations; her lower left hand swings a newly severed head by the hair, symbolizing the severance of the ego and the normally restricting forces of destiny. Her upper right hand makes a mystic gesture to protect and dispel all the fears of her devotees, and her lower right hand makes a gesture that grants wishes.

"Her long-extended tongue tells of her sensual and all-consuming nature. Her garland of severed human heads evokes the fifty letters of the Sanskrit alphabet, and it is their vibrations that hold together the phenomenal world. Kali is pure energy in its original form, the transcendental expression of womanhood. Kali is the awakened Kundalini-energy, the transcendental power of sex, the lustful embodiment of unrestrained, consuming love. Her enemies are hypocrisy, doubt, selfishness and envy; her friends are those who serve and love her dearly. With Shiva as her support, there is nothing in this world or the next that is outside her domain. Though she is externally awesome, her innermost nature is kind and compassionate.

"Parvati is also passionate and sensual. She is the daughter of the Himalaya Mountains, white as the snowy peaks, the embodiment of femininity. Her face shines like the rising sun, she is graced with a beautiful figure, high breasts, full hips and all the qualities of exalted womanhood. Parvati is the godly ideal of the chaste wife, whereas Kali embodies the lustful mistress. Parvati symbolizes the effulgent light of the full moon and Kali the dark lunar night. Though most humans idealize the Parvati archetype and fear the Kali archetype, both are but facets of the one being, which takes different forms for different functions.

"A woman becomes one with Kali by coming to terms with her own awesome power of initiation. As an initiatress into the sexual mysteries of Kali, woman is the ultimate Guru of man. When hypocrisy, self-doubt, selfishness and envy are eliminated from a woman's psyche, the deep intuitive wisdom of Kali emerges. Charged with sexual energy, Kali's wisdom acts as a potent initiation into the nature of reality.

"Kali is fearless and passionate; she does not hold back her favors. For a woman to truly embody Kali, she must get in touch with her own sexuality and dive deep into her unconscious mind. Kali's qualities are of this world and all other worlds. For a woman to become Kali, she must be able to take her man beyond mundane limitations, beyond convention, beyond the expected. During the dark fortnight of the moon and the time of her menstruation, woman naturally takes on some of Kali's qualities. In her Kali role, woman acts as the destroyer of illusion and the fulfiller of desire."

The goddess asks

"What are the best Mantras for evoking Kali in the body of woman, O Shiva? What is Kali's special Yantra and her simplest form? Tell me the best ways of pleasing Kali and the special items for her worship. Tell me also why it is that Kali stands or squats on the reclining form of Shiva."

Shiva replies

"O Insatiable Goddess! Many different Mantras have been used to evoke Kali! Most of them begin with the letter 'K.' The short seed-syllables 'KLING' and 'KRING' are both highly effective, as is the longer Kali Mantra: 'OM-KANG-KALIKA-NAMAH.' Kali's name is a potent Mantra in itself, as is the seed-syllable 'HUNG,' which expresses the transcendental power of the pregnant voidness that underlies all phenomena. 'HUNG' also awakens the Kundalini and helps one become united with Kali.

"Kali's special Yantra, or mystic form, is a series of five equilateral triangles, set one within the other and placed on an eight-petaled lotus. The five triangles of Kali's Yantra symbolize transcendence of the five main bodily senses and elements. The eight-petaled lotus indicates that Kali can be understood by focusing the higher emotions in the Heart Chakra. At the center of this Yantra one should visualize a small point, symbolizing stability of consciousness.

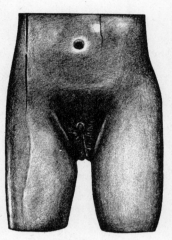

"The Yantra of Mother Kali is a potent symbol of meditation and can also be used as a protective talisman. Kali's simplest form is the Yoni of a woman in intense sexual excitement. The triangular shape formed by the pubic hair is Kali's basic Yantra, the open Yoni is Kali's ever-open invitation; the erect clitoris is like Kali's extended tongue, the sexual odors are her power of enchantment and the profuse moist secretions tell of Kali's all-bestowing nature. The Yoni of woman is unquestionably the original symbol of Mother Kali.

"Kali is pleased by devotion to her ideal qualitites, by repetition of her Mantras, by visualization of her Yantra and her various mystic forms. Kali is pleased when the passionate urge of earnest desire for union with her causes the vitality to enter and rise up the Great Axis, the central channel of the Subtle Body. Kali is pleased by the ecstatic experiences of man and woman in Tantric union. Kali is pleased whenever she is remembered. Kali is pleased with Shiva!"

Yoni of initiation. From a wood sculpture used in the rituals of tribal people, South India, *circa* early twentieth century.

"Kali can be worshipped by anything offered without hypocrisy. Best of all, she likes sensual smells, such as sandalwood, musk, patchouli and camphor. She also likes garlands of red flowers, rhythmic music, sensual dance, pure wine and other intoxicants such as marijuana. Kali likes spontaneous laughter, devotional songs, passionate love and an 'all or nothing' mental attitude. Kali can be worshipped directly through the body of woman. Tantric love-rites are the ideal way of worshipping Kali. During these rites the Yoni should be honored and selfless offerings made. When Kali awakens in the female partner, love takes on a renewed and exalted potency. Kali-power extends from eroticism to the beginning and end of time.

"Kali stands or squats on the reclining Shiva to show that she performs all his physical needs. Standing on Shiva, Kali is well prepared to take on any adversary and come to the aid of those in need. Squatting on Shiva, she sexually serves both her Lord and herself. In the active role of physical love, Kali embodies the lustful mistress, the whore, the sex initiatress, Isis, the High Priestess. In the long Night of Darkness, before the beginning of another Age, Kali sports with Shiva in ecstatic dalliance, serving as a focus for his Yogic power of penetration."

Kali seated on the recumbent Shiva. She is four-armed and holds a skull bowl, a severed head, a snake and a sword. Before her is the Kali Yantra, a series of five triangles within one another. From a Rajasthani miniature painting of the late eighteenth century.

The great goddess asks

"O Lord of All Creatures! Tell me the meaning and different types of sexual initiation! What are the best times for practicing sexual initiations and other sexual rituals? What are the secret rites known as Chakra Puja, Bhairavi Chakra and Yogini Chakra, and how should they be performed? Tell me, O Hero, what is their deepest meaning?"

Shiva, the Supreme Yogi, replies

"Dearest One! Your questions are so direct. Numerous are the sexual initiations that I have given you. Innumerable are those that you have bestowed on me. The true meaning of sexual initiation is empowerment, a selfless act of *giving* from one to the other. The very first sexual initiation of all beings occurs during their exit through the mother's Yoni. The effect of this passage is to cause forgetfulness of past lives. During this first initiation the mother gives the whole world to her offspring, and in return takes away all painful memories of the past. The result of the first initiation normally lasts until death's door.

"Other types of sexual initiation occur both consciously and unconsciously, over the course of a lifetime, during times of ecstatic love-making. Few are those who have not received some kind of sexual initiation from acts of physical love, but those who are consciously *aware* of receiving sexual initiation during love-making are rare.

"Sex has the power of both illusion and Liberation, depending on the participants' degree of conscious awareness. Sexual initiation is the selfless bestowing of one's sexuality on another.

Kali squatting in sexual union with Shiva, who rests on a burning funeral pyre. The transcendental view of Tantric truths is symbolized by this icon. Though the initial impact is terrific, a peaceful effulgence is evoked by this type of image. From a Nepalese painting of the late nineteenth century.

When a person accepts a sexual act as a gift, exchanges take place on several different levels simultaneously. There is a physical exchange and blending of secretions, a psycho-physical exchange of life energies and polarities, a psychological exchange of attitudes, a Karmic exchange through a convergence of destinies—and there is a spiritual exchange, a communion between spirits. On the highest level, all these exchanges add to the quality of the couple.

"In all acts of sexual initiation there is a two-way flow, an exchange of potentialities; the initiator takes on some unresolved energies, conflicts or Karmas, and the initiated receives energies, attainments and positive Karmas. Sexual initiation is thus an act of deep responsibility. During high acts of Tantric sex Karmas and unresolved personality conflicts can be totally transcended. The Yoni becomes an alchemical crucible of transformation, and the Lingam becomes a magical wand with the power of turning one situation into another. Together, the Lingam and Yoni provide all the myriad sexual initiations. In the Tantric tradition, sexual initiation is bestowed by woman on man, by woman on woman or several women, by woman on a couple or several couples, by man on woman or several women, or by a couple on couples or several couples. The person or couple conferring sexual initiation is viewed as a transcendental Guru. True Tantric sexual initiations require the presence and active partici-pation of at least one woman. Sexual initiation is not a free license for wild orgies, but rather the carefully prepared ground from which a transcendental spirituality can blossom.

An elderly woman acts as a sex initiatress, giving spiritual and practical guidance to a much younger couple. From an Indian miniature painting, Jodhpur, circa 1830.

"The best times for practicing sexual initiations and other sexual rituals are during the period between midnight and 3 a.m., during the dark fortnight of the lunar month, especially on the eighth and fourteenth nights of the dark of the moon, during a solar or lunar eclipse and at times of pure spontaneity when there is no doubt of success. A sexual initiation is successful when a person's life suddenly becomes changed for the better as a direct result of the experience. Unsuccessful sexual initiations cause havoc to the psyche of both the initiator and the person who has received the initiation.

"Chakra Puja, Bhairavi Chakra and Yogini Chakra are all ritualized sexual acts performed by more than one couple. They can, however, take place on a purely allegorical level, either by the use of ritual substitutes or by the internalization of the whole process through the power of visualization.

"All sexual Chakras require the participants to form a circle and follow the guidance of a leader couple or Guru. *Chakra Puja* is a simple Tantric term meaning 'circular worship'; it is an evocation of the natural *cyclical* inclination of sexual energy, which seeks to return through repeated cycles of activity. In the practice of Chakra Puja sexual energy is consciously channeled and exchanged among all the participants. As the urge to orgasm is approached by one couple, they are instructed to hold back, while the next couple starts the ascent into ecstasy. A natural buildup of sexual energy is produced, creating an energy vortex that empowers the inner psychic centers or Chakras of the participants and opens up latent psychic powers. Correctly practiced, this type of Chakra Puja imparts spiritual ecstasy and all the participants enter a new dimension, beyond this world.

"*Bhairavi Chakra*, as the name suggests, is the particularized worship of the goddess Kali through a circle of sexually active participants. Three, five, seven or nine are the ideal numbers for a Bhairavi Chakra, though larger numbers sometimes participate in this ritual. When there are nine worshippers in the Chakra, the energies of the nine planets are evoked in turn and are then consciously focused on the resolution of the outstanding Karmas of the participants.

The first initiation of all humans is through the Yoni of the mother. Depiction of the secret form of the goddess as Guhyeshwari, Lady of Mysteries, giving birth to yet another devotee. From a Nepalese wood sculpture of the late seventeenth century.

"Every Bhairavi Chakra should begin and end with the honoring of the female principle. This can be done symbolically by representing the goddess Kali in an image, icon or object associated with her worship. Such a symbolic representation is placed at the center of the circle before the commencement of the rite, and is honored both before and after any sexual activity. The Kali or Bhairavi principle can also be honored through the actual form of a young girl who displays her nakedness at the center of the Chakra, but does not otherwise participate in the rites, except to receive garlands of flowers, sweet scents, incense, fruit, food offerings, jewelry, silks and other honorific offerings. The Kali principle should also be invoked and honored in each female participant. The correct practice of the Bhairavi Chakra is extremely difficult to achieve, largely because of the human tendency to revert to lower instincts at the first opportunity. Therefore a thorough practical knowledge of Hatha Yoga and Tantric sexual techniques is essential to those who wish to participate in this ancient rite.

"The *Yogini Chakra* can be understood on both an actual and a symbolic level. It is similar to the Bhairavi Chakra, except that the participants are a single man with three, five, seven or nine women. The idealized Yogini Chakra outlined in several Tantras has the man with his immediate female partner at the center, surrounded by a circle of eight Yoginis, all of whom participate in sexual dalliance with the aim of releasing and circulating maximum energy. During the actual practice of the Yogini Chakra eight of the women bestow themselves on the man in turn, while the ninth, his principal or most advanced sexual partner, helps bring the eight others to full climax. The man should control his own orgasm until he has absorbed all the energies of the eight Yonis. He then bestows his potentized initiatory seed on the ninth Yogini. In the final act of selflessness the principal Yogini shares the conjoined sexual secretions as a sacrament, to be taken by all participants in the rite.

"The Yogini Chakra was at one time widely practiced by kings and emperors, who used it to acquire extraordinary powers and also to cause the birth of exceptional children. A more elaborate version of the Yogini Chakra was also practiced in the distant past, involving dalliance of a single male with fifteen women, all of whom were adepts of sexual Yoga. Each of the Yoginis embodied a lunar phase and had the power to bestow a particular quality of spiritual effulgence.

"On a symbolic level, the Yogini Chakra is well known to Tantrics. It is a dynamic meditation on the lunar phases, with each phase visualized as a particular erotic goddess with specific qualities and attributes. Furthermore, each of the fifteen lunar goddesses is linked to the individual vowel sounds present in the normal Sanskrit alphabet. Each sound and visualization helps channel and transform the raw energy of the psyche, bringing it into harmonious communion with the deep intuitive wisdom of the Head Chakra."

YOGINI CHAKRA

THE SYMBOLIC LEVEL OF THE YOGINI CHAKRA

The goddess says
"O Beloved! So many questions awaken from within my open heart. So many answers begin to emerge from my expectant mind. Please give clarity and form to these great unknowns. Tell me the mystic meaning of both the consonants and vowels. How do they relate to the lunar Chakra of the Head and to the solar Chakra of the Navel? Tell me also how the fifteenfold Yogini Chakra is structured, O wise and generous lover."

Heaving a great sigh, Shiva replies
"All the consonants are but different aspects of Mother Kali and the vowels are her faithful attendants. The consonants and vowels are the *energy* and *suppport* of the entire phenomenal

Ritual love-making of a maharaja with five women simultaneously, all of whom play musical instruments. This version of the Yogini Chakra was practiced by kings and emperors. Food offerings and ritual items are depicted in the foreground. From an Indian miniature painting, Jodhpur, *circa* 1830.

CONSONANTS AND VOWELS

world. The thirty-five Sanskrit consonants arise from the expanding primordial fire. Ascending through the right channel of the Subtle Body, they are all known as Kali and their function is to provide raw energy waves or quanta, endowing the voidness with their qualities. Reaching the cool inner moon of the Head Chakra, they are distilled and sublimated into crystal-like forms. Taking on physical form they produce a whole realm of biochemical products, glandular secretions and Wisdom-drops.

"The original fifteen Sanskrit vowels originate from the primordial waters, which are the product of cosmic contraction. Descending through the left channel of the Subtle Body, the vowels are known as Ali and their function is to modify the raw Kali wave-pulses, giving form to this dynamic transcendental energy. As this cycle of activity is repeated over and over again, worlds are born and the sensual elements manifest. The consonants and vowels thus serve their cosmic function and are the beginning and end of all phenomena.

"Consonants blend with vowels through the contractive influence of the cooling inner moon of the Head Chakra. Vowels modify consonants through the expansive influence of the blazing inner sun. Contraction and expansion are the original cause of the worlds, just as woman and man are the cause of offspring.

"The Sanskrit vowel sounds are A, Ā, I, Ī, U, Ū, Ṛ, Ṝ, Ḷ, Ḹ, Ė, AI, O, AU and AṀ; each is a seed-syllable of one of the fifteen Yoginis. The fifteen-fold Yogini Chakra is practiced with the participants located as shown. At the center is the Great Yogini, in eternal union with the Great Yogi."

Wide-eyed, the goddess replies

"O Shiva! How wondrous is the nature of your mind! Surely those who practice the Yogini Chakra must be transported to other realms? But tell me, O Great One, what is the role of the Guru? And what are the Guru's mystic forms? How can lovers understand and realize the meaning of the mystic forms for themselves? Tell me also how spiritual longing can bring a person closer to the lasting experience of transcendence."

Shiva replies

"Indeed in your question you intuit the essence of these mysteries. Those who are so initiated can truly travel through time and space. O Beloved, you are right to inquire about the Guru's role. You are wise to draw my attention to mystic forms. As for spiritual longing, it fuels the fire that burns up all psychic obstacles, just as our passion cuts through the limitations of time and space.

"The role of the Guru is total. A Guru is a guide who reveals teachings about the nature of reality and who provides an ideal or touchstone by which one brings oneself to completion. A Guru is a teacher who has perfected a particular attainment and who effectively shares it with others. To people who exist largely in a physical dimension, Gurus are generally parents, ancestors, close friends, teachers, employers, prominent figures or children. Some even take non-human 'Gurus,' such as animals, fantasy ideals, inanimate objects, idols, talismans and discarnate entities, as well as oracles, drugs, possessions, wealth and prestige. Though most of these 'Gurus' have no lasting teaching, deluded beings serve them devotedly.

"Many real spiritual Gurus have lived since the beginning of time. Many live even in this day and their teachings cover the whole spectrum of spirituality. However, not all spiritual Gurus are Tantric Gurus and not all Tantrics are Gurus.

"Tantric Gurus are Yogis or Yoginis who have a high level of attainment and who teach a developed sexual-yogic technology for achieving Liberation within a single lifetime. The sexual-yogic technology taught by true Tantric Gurus is highly practical, direct and transcendental. There are Tantric Gurus who have passed beyond the physical dimension, but who project mystic forms of themselves into the physical realms and teach humans through visions, dreams and other paranormal means. These Gurus are known as Siddhas.

"The role of a Tantric Guru is *to initiate*, to bestow empowerments and blessings, to distribute spirituality and to serve the evolution of other beings until the present Dark Age of Kali comes to an end. Tantric Gurus reveal their teachings in many different ways: through mystical forms, psychic projections, dreams, visions, sexual acts, ritual gestures, transcendental symbols, songs, allegories, music, dance, worship and all the other Sixty-four Arts.

KALI-CONSONANTS

ALI-VOWELS

CONTRACTION AND EXPANSION

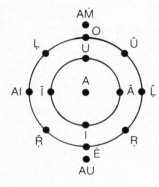

THE 15-FOLD
YOGINI CHAKRA

THE ROLE OF THE GURU

WORLDLY GURUS

SPIRITUAL GURUS

TANTRIC GURUS

THE ROLE OF TANTRIC GURUS

"Tantric mystic forms are highly symbolic initiatory themes that directly express the otherwise hidden path to Liberation. It has truly been said that 'Tantra is continuity, the ultimate participation in the metaphysics of life.' In this sense, mystic forms are *the Guru's continuity*; they are the revealed expressions of the Guru's Tantric attainments. Mystic forms such as *Chakrasambhara* ('The Ruler of the Chakras'), *Hevajra* ('The Indestructible Lord'), *Chinnamasta* ('The Egoless Yogini') and other Tantric 'deities' are but glyphs of specific Tantric teachings perfected by Gurus. In the Tantric way of life mystic forms are earnestly sought as vehicles of Liberation. They provide a transcendental focus for the emotions and the mind; a psychic glyph that is pregnant with meaning based on ecstatic experience, an 'ally' and a secret friend.

"Lovers should try to evolve mystic forms for themselves, using their powers of erotic fantasy to augment their understanding of the Tantric teachings. Beginning with simple Tantric visualizations, they should embody the very principles of transformation. As they open themselves to mystic forms, lovers will find themselves naturally embodying and realizing these forms.

"Since spiritually minded lovers tend to think of each other as Gurus, they should try to develop and nourish their Guru-like qualities. Lovers can then understand the meaning of mystic forms by spontaneously opening themselves to each other, as Gurus do to their most devoted students, and by longing for initiations into life's mysteries.

"Spiritual longing is the driving force of Tantra. It causes mystic forms and ecstasy to manifest through those who are unhypocritical in their attitude to transcendence. Spiritual longing causes Gurus to appear and mystic forms and supernormal incidents to occur. Spiritual longing can bring a person or couple closer to the lasting experience of transcendence by stimulating the natural evolutionary urge to move beyond the purely physical dimension. Spiritual longing attracts ecstasy and fills life with lasting meaning."

VEHICLES OF LIBERATION

MYSTIC FORMS

Mystic form of a Tantric teacher in union with his consort. From a Tibetan painting of the late eighteenth century.

Mystic form known as Chinnamasta, the "Egoless Yogini," the transcendental power of Will and Vision. The goddess sits on the back of lovers in sexual union and severs her own head, symbolizing the ego. Three streams of blood (life energy) flow from her neck, and her body is covered with serpents. This glyph tells of the taming of the Kundalini-energy and the three main channels of the Subtle Body. Two streams of blood are consumed by Varnini and Dakini, Chinnamasta's attendants, and she drinks a third stream herself. Behind, a brilliant sun shows the energy released during this act of psychic transformation. In the Hindu Tantric tradition Chinnamasta is associated with the Chinese mysteries. From a Rajasthani miniature painting of the late eighteenth century.

The goddess Parvati, the Shakti of Shiva, says

"O Lord of my heart, Guru of my soul! There is never a moment when I am not filled with longing for you! Now tell me more. Tell me how erotic fantasy can become a vehicle of Liberation. Tell me how the emotions can be transformed, and also about the role of the sentiments. Then tell me about sexual roles."

Inhaling deeply, the Supreme Yogi replies

EROTIC FANTASY

"Beloved Mistress, erotic fantasy stimulates the emotions and helps lift the sentiments beyond mundaneness. Erotic fantasy is particularly helpful to those who feel restricted and caught up in worldly circumstances. By causing consciousness to expand, erotic fantasy can truly become a vehicle of Liberation.

THE EMOTIONS

"The emotions are *feelings* of ecstasy, love, hate and so forth. When an awareness of the *nature* of emotions is present in the consciousness, nine sentiments manifest. From the original tranquil sentiment, the amorous, humorous, compassionate, furious, heroic, awesome, wondrous and repugnant sentiments arise. Of these, the amorous, humorous, compassionate and wondrous sentiments are naturally uplifting and potentially liberating. The furious, heroic and awesome sentiments play a major role in Tantric evolution because they transcend convention. As for the repugnant sentiment, it serves to repel undesirable influences. All these sentiments evolve from an original ground of tranquility. All have a psycho-cosmic function, leading to transcendence.

NINE SENTIMENTS

CONJURING FORTH EMOTIONS

"The emotions can be channeled by conjuring them from a position of inner tranquility. Different emotions and sentiments are normally linked to an individual's experiences and to psycho-physical processes. The ever-fertile mind of man is a veritable garden of emotions, producing both sweet and bitter fruits. With thought, the mind empowers emotions with meaning. Linked to breathing and the imagination, emotions and the sentiments are the cause behind the endless round of births and deaths.

EMOTIONS ARE FOCUSED IN THE HEART

"Emotions are part of one's being and are generally focused in the region of the heart. They reach all parts of the body and create positive or negative conditions in the senses and organs. Emotions are naturally linked to colors, sounds, forms, worldly phenomena, seasons and planetary motions. For example, there is a color classification based on cosmology; the amorous sentiment is traditionally related to green, the humorous to white, the compassionate to gray, the furious to dark red, the heroic to golden red, the awesome to black, the wondrous to yellow and the repugnant to a certain type of blue. The tranquil sentiment is viewed as translucent, effulgent and shining, yet with hints of all the colors.

SENTIMENTS AND COLORS

CHANNELING EMOTIONS

"By visualizing particular sentiments as colors and using the breathing techniques of Hatha Yoga to give them stability, one can consciously channel and transform emotions. In this process creative imagination and a positive mental attitude are all-important. Generally the inhalation of breath is linked to the amorous and wondrous sentiments, retention of breath to the heroic, awesome and tranquil sentiments, exhalation to the humorous, compassionate and repugnant sentiments, and rapid inhalation and exhalation of breath to the furious sentiment. In most worldly circumstances sentiments are mixed; rarely are they pure.

SEXUAL ROLES

"Sexual roles are directly linked to emotions and sentiments. Within each individual is the potential to play out every kind of role, every aspect of human emotions. Just as an actor takes on different characters, so should couples take on different roles, to deepen their relationship. Staying within a single role is anathema to individual evolution. Different lifetimes are necessary largely because individuals tend to exaggerate particular roles to the exclusion of others.

ROLE PLAYING

"Who is the Self? What is the Other? How many roles do we need to know? These are the questions that come to mind as one plunges into the enigma of identity. Is she Mother, Sister, Daughter, Wife? Is he Father, Brother, Husband, Son? See each other in all of these roles and expand the field of reference to encompass Muse, Mistress, Virgin, Whore, Priestess; Hero, Lover, Don Juan, Shaman, Priest. All these roles prepare one for the great original role of Shiva/Shakti."

Trembling with excitement, the goddess says

"O Shiva, your words bring clarity to the mirror of my mind! Questions arise, needing answers. What kind of sexual patterns emerge for old age and menopause? What is the cure for impotence? Should women make love during pregnancy, and if so, when?"

Taking on a terrific countenance, Shiva replies

"Old age is transcendental, glorious, potentially Divine. Old age can also be pitiful and a time for deep regret. How can one talk about sex and old age without talking first of old age itself? In old age people should renounce worldliness and prepare themselves for their appointment with death. Death is the doorway to transcendence and Liberation. Preparation for death should involve the cultivation of meditation, awareness, fearlessness and spontaneity. The Sixty-four Arts are also aids in coming to terms with death.

"During old age the spirit naturally moves toward transcendence: bodily passions recede, wisdom increases and spirituality emerges. As old age approaches, sexual love becomes less physical than in youth. Male sexuality naturally tends to decline more rapidly than female sexuality, unless counter-measures are taken. Tantric sexual techniques such as conscious retention and mutual absorption should be emphasized in old age, and a healthy Yogic lifestyle should be maintained. Then there need be no fear of sudden loss of sex drive or complex neuroses.

"Menopause, or the change of life, is a perfectly natural function of worldly people. It is the body's way of preparing for transcendence. Menopause occurs in both men and women who, as they get older, become fixed in their worldly roles. It causes a feeling of role loss, often accompanied by deep depression. Physical exercise, Hatha Yoga, healthy diet and Tantric meditation are all helpful in overcoming depression caused by menopause. Once the change of life has passed, the personality undergoes a dramatic change for the better. Those who have gone beyond menopause become initiators, ceremonial leaders and role models of worldly transcendence: they can live out their lives either with or without active sexuality, depending on their preference. Ideally a couple should gradually grow old together, nuturing nature through their selfless love for each other.

"There are many cures for impotence, which is caused by anxiety, physical exhaustion and debility, over-indulgence and old age. Hatha Yoga, correct diet, creative meditation, a positive mental attitude and the use of Tantric sexual techniques are all extremely helpful in overcoming impotence, as are certain drugs, ritual acts and magical invocations. Ginseng root, marijuana and other psycho-active substances can cure impotence if used correctly. A henna poultice applied to the sexual region, the head, the hands and feet is an ancient remedy for such problems, as is the company of beautiful members of the opposite sex. Above all, impotence is cured by an adjustment in mental attitude and lifestyle, as well as by careful use of aphrodisiacs. The sexual secrets contain the panacea for both impotence and sexual problems that may occur at the change of life or during old age, for they concentrate on sexual practices that involve the mutual exchange and circulation of energy throughout the psycho-organism. The Tantric attitude to sexuality removes the onus of 'performance' from both partners and emphasizes instead the importance of harmonization and mutual enrichment. When the fires of youthful passion no longer flare up so quickly, they are easier to control. In old age the practice of Tantric love allows couples to ascend more easily the heights of ecstasy. For the truly Tantric couple, there never need be any fear of impotence.

"Pregnancy has many stages and no hard and fast rules can be made either for or against sex during this time. Common sense and intuition should govern *all* activities during pregnancy, and if there is doubt, advice should be sought. However, it is important not to restrict natural urges during pregnancy, provided they are not detrimental to the growing child. Sex is certainly safe during the first few months of pregnancy, but should be undertaken gently rather than with great activity: positions should be chosen to allow maximum comfort and support. It is important to be aware that a third person, the child, is present within the womb. Since sex takes place on many different levels, care should be taken to ensure harmony. A couple who lie together in close loving embrace can positively affect both the physical and the psychological growth of the unborn child. To express love physically through sexual union is but one of many ways that a couple can share their joy at this time."

Hearing this, the goddess smiles and says

"O Shiva, Lord of All Creatures, how fortunate I am to have such an experienced and thoughtful lover! Perhaps now you will explain the meaning of the expression 'mystic child' and its relevance to the Tantric tradition. Tell me, O Shiva, of the relationship of astrology to sexuality and to the forces of Heaven and Earth. Tell me of the rejuvenating power of sex."

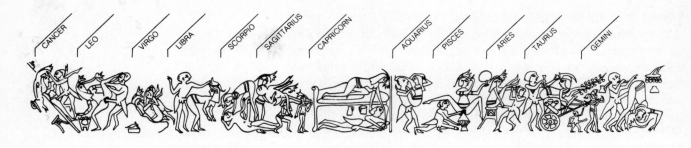

A cycle of sexual mysteries, linked to the sequence of astrological signs. Twelve erotic episodes revolve around initiatory themes. From an Egyptian papyrus, Twentieth Dynasty, now in the Turin Museum.

With a smile, the Lord of Mount Meru replies

"The term *mystic child* refers to the magical field produced by sexual love. This 'field,' or psychic atmosphere, is a potential entity in itself and, when directed by Will, can serve a magical function. Advanced adepts of sexual Yoga can concentrate and focus their converged ecstatic life energies beyond the worldly dimension. A mystic child thus created can be used as an 'ally' or serving entity. Its influence extends beyond physicality.

THE MYSTIC CHILD

"In the Tantric tradition the mystic child is a vehicle of Liberation. The Subtle Body of Tantra is one type of mystic child, as are tutelary deities and other mystic forms. In a way, true disciples are the 'mystic children' of Gurus. A Guru becomes liberated through his disciples, just as disciples become liberated by their Gurus.

ASTROLOGY

"Astrology is the science of Heaven's destiny. In ancient times priests made detailed studies of the influence of planets, constellations and other heavenly bodies on the individual's destiny. Relationships were found between the stars and planets and the repeated cycles of change in humans. Just as Heaven and Earth complete each other, so the motion and qualities of heavenly bodies bring earthly humans to the completion of their outstanding Karmas. This is a process that goes on beyond individual life times. Only when there is conscious control over the life-force can an individual transcend the influence of heavenly destiny.

SEXUAL POSITIONS AND ASTROLOGY

"Sexual positions and roles are directly related to astrological configurations. Both are Yantras, with natural affinities and resonances that interact with one another. In ancient times the subtle relationship between constellations and sexual postures was understood and used to incarnate children with pre-determined qualities. Sexual positions can be used to attain ascendency over astrological influences and thus aid in the conscious control of destiny.

SEX AND REJUVENATION

"Sex is an awesome force that can either rejuvenate or debilitate, depending on whether it is practiced correctly or incorrectly. The old have even become young again through the potent power of sex. Many sexual secrets relate to rejuvenation, and these should be used by those who are in need. The main principle of sexual rejuvenation is to circulate rather than expend sexual energy. By paying attention to the mental, emotional and physical aspects of sexual love and channeling the life energies wisely, total rejuvenation can be brought about."

Laughing to herself, the goddess asks

"What are the different ways of acquiring magical powers? Please tell me also about the correct use of drugs and austerities such as fasting. Tell me the effect of abstinence and celibacy. So many questions and their secret answers race through my thoughtful mind!"

Leaning over to caress her hair, and looking into her eyes, Lord Shiva says to his consort Parvati

MAGICAL POWERS

"Child, though thoughts are many, true answers are few! Though magical powers are part of Tantra, they are not an end in themselves. Known as *Siddhi*, magical powers have been the cause of endless disputes, jealousies, Karmas and lifetimes. They have even caused Yogis to break their vows. For the sake of magical powers many have abandoned common sense and reason.

SIDDHIS
SIDDHAS

"Some forms of magical powers are naturally acquired at birth, from past lives, astrological influences or parents or ancestors. Others are acquired by the practice of austerities, by skillfully withdrawing the senses from contact with the external world and transforming their mode of action. Siddhis can also be achieved by living for prolonged periods in intensely focused meditative absorption, by the constant repetition of potent Mantras and by the correct use of drugs. These five methods are the ways that Siddhis are obtained by mortals. A person who has control over magical powers is known as a *Siddha*. Many are the Siddhas who have passed beyond worldly limitations, becoming the embodiment of magical power.

"Drugs have the power to take one beyond the worldly dimension. Since ancient times many different drugs have been used in magical rites. However, drugs tend to be almost as unpredictable as people and, like sex, can either liberate or enslave. Some say that sex is the greatest drug of all and that there is no intoxicant more powerful than the love of man for woman. Certainly it is true that drugs and sex have much in common. Both can lead to the attainment of magical powers and both have an inherent illusory nature, an ability to greatly alter one's perception of reality. In this sense, drugs and sex are both transcendental.

"There are many different kinds of drugs, with innumerable different actions. Transcendental drugs tend to exaggerate what lies just below the normal threshold of consciousness. They lift or expand consciousness, magnify awareness and can cause the Kundalini-energy to awaken and ascend. In this category are marijuana, charas, bhang, hashish, mescaline, peyote, magic mushrooms, morning glory and other natural organic psycho-active substances. However, if a person takes these drugs when in a negative state of mind or when emotionally unstable, the chances are that the negativity and instability will be greatly magnified. The drug experience then becomes unpleasant, even terrifying, and commonly results in feelings of paranoia. On the other hand, if a person takes these natural drugs with a positive mental attitude and a certain amount of Yogic preparation, transcendental and ecstatic experiences result.

THE POWER OF DRUGS

"There are also drugs that tend to contract or narrow the field of consciousness, block perception and ultimately lead one to oblivion. These are not transcendental drugs and their use has never been endorsed by wise teachers. In this category are the opiates and many synthetic consciousness-altering substances. Such drugs produce a negative effect on both body and mind, regardless of one's mental state. They tend to numb the emotions and cause disharmony within the Subtle Body. In addition, they attract negative influences and entities, and create Karmic obstacles that are difficult to overcome.

"Naturally *uplifting* drugs have a very definite spiritual effect when correctly used as a sacrament. When taken under the guidance of a priest or Guru, they serve to initiate into the experience of transcendence by releasing the individual from self-created limitations. Transcendental drugs can provide a shortcut to Liberation by freeing both Self and ego, and at the same time introducing enhanced receptivity and mystic communion. These drugs should only be taken in the spirit of initiation and with a positive mental attitude. Those who remember to invoke the transcendental qualitites of Shiva while taking such drugs need never fear.

DRUGS AS SACRAMENTS

"Drugs are entities in themselves. The spirit of marijuana, for example, is female. She is alluring, very seductive. In her presence time passes almost without one noticing. Her sweet fragrance intoxicates the senses and uplifts the mind. She is delighted by heroic men and sensual women. When a couple share marijuana, they are allowing her participation in their relationship. Accepting their invitation, the spirit of marijuana adds spontaneity and humor and also acts as a potent initiator. By bringing the couple into her dimension, the spirit of marijuana exalts and magnifies both love and sensitivity.

MARIJUANA

A maharaja smokes a hookah while making love. From a miniature painting in the collection of the King of Nepal, *circa* 1830.

"Austerities alter one's perception of reality by causing the senses to withdraw from their contact with the external world. Austerities help develop the Will and are one of the most ancient ways of obtaining magical powers. However, austerities often require considerable time to bring about lasting benefits and are not an end in themselves. Austerities such as fasting and prolonged exposure to the natural elements cause an increased awareness of the subtle relationship between the microcosm of the body and the macrocosm of the universe. A supersensual faculty emerges through the correct practice of Yogic austerities. If, however, austerities are regarded as a form of self-punishment, they are unlikely to bear any lasting fruit. Rather, they should be practiced in a mood of optimism and creativity.

FASTING

"Fasting increases the inner fire and helps purify the emotions. Many have acquired magical powers by fasting and by the practice of other austerities. Just as you, Parvati, attracted my attention during your time of austerity in the high Himalayas, so humans can awaken their own godly qualities by carefully controlled fasts. Fasting tones the psycho-organism, develops the Subtle Body and helps concentrate the mind. It helps awaken a sense of detachment and opens up an awareness of one's innermost desires. It is part of the true Yogic tradition and is a valuable aid in the understanding of transcendence. In moderation, fasting acts as a potent virilific and aphrodisiac.

"Abstinence is a kind of sexual fasting. Abstinence from sex for up to a month at a time strengthens the body and aids the focusing of life energies and emotions. If after a prolonged time spent together an intimate relationship breaks up, a period of sexual abstinence will help heal emotional and psychological wounds. Abstinence from sex is traditionally a part of mourning; after the death of one's sexual partner, one may abstain for three months or even a year. There is a natural tendency toward periods of abstinence as old age approaches because abstinence helps strengthen and revitalize sexuality.

ABSTINENCE

"Short periods of sexual abstinence, such as for three, five, seven or nine days at a time, can help concentrate sexual energy and increase sensitivity; it may even be recommended prior to the performance of certain sexual rites. Also, if a couple wishes to ensure conception of a strong and healthy child, a few days of abstinence before a prolonged bout of love-making will help them achieve their goal. However, prolonged sexual abstinence is not recommended by the Tantras since it causes unnatural sexual currents to build up within the body.

"During periods of sexual abstinence a person should practice Hatha Yoga and breathing exercises more often than normally. It is very important to eat healthy food and take sufficient exercise during times of abstinence. Sexual energy should be consciously drawn upward through the subtle channels and psychic centers; creative visualization and breath control will help this process of sublimation.

"Sexual abstinence normally means abstinence from all forms of sexual contact. Another way of defining abstinence is to divide it into two types: total abstinence from all kinds of sexual contact, and abstinence from orgasm while maintaining sexual contact. In the latter case Tantric techniques for retention and sublimation of sexual energy should be used. Many have gained magical powers by abstaining from orgasm while drawing in and sublimating sexual energy during physcial contact with the opposite sex. However, this type of sexual abstinence is not advisable for periods of more than a month at a time since physical and subtle energies should be free to exchange and complete each other if true transcendence is to be achieved.

CELIBACY

"Contrary to popular belief, celibacy is not a sign of spirituality. Celibacy is unnatural and is not a suitable practice for healthy individuals. Brief periods of abstinence from sex and total celibacy are completely different in their effect. The celibate lives of monks and nuns are a form of spiritual hypocrisy, since they are denying their natural sexual functions any mode of expression and at the same time separating themselves from the very act that brought them into existence. Celibacy leads to bigotry, fanaticism and narrow-mindedness because of the unnatural restrictions placed on sexual expression."

The goddess Parvati then says

"O Great Yogi, Master of All Austerities! How wonderful it is to hear such clear explanations of life's mysteries. My heart is filled with joy as I reflect on the subtle meanings of sexuality. While your mood is still outgoing and benevolent, please speak to me of Ganesha, the Elephant Lord, whom I created as my son. Tell me the secret Mantras of Ganesha and the meaning of his mystic form. Tell me why Ganesha is linked to the sexual secrets and why his consort is named Siddhi."

Becoming excited, Shiva the naked Yogi draws himself up and says

GANESHA

"Ganesha, the elephant-headed Lord, is the remover of all obstacles. He is to be remembered before starting any work or commencing spiritual rites. Many different Mantras are used to evoke Ganesha. Most of them begin with the letter 'G.' The short seed-syllables 'GAM' and

GANESHA MANTRAS

'GANG' are very effective, as are the longer Ganesha Mantras: 'OM-SRI-GANESHAYA-NAMAH' and 'OM-GANG-GANAPATAYE-NAMAH.' Ganesha's name is a potent Mantra in itself, and it should be called out by those in any kind of difficulty.

GANESHA'S ROLE

"Ganesha is the gatekeeper and Lord of the Sex Chakra. His four arms tell of the four-petaled sexual center and the earth element, symbolized by a square. Ganesha is the remover of physical, emotional and psychic obstacles; his immense body and graceful movements symbolize the blend of inner strength and sensitivity necessary for advancement along the spiritual path of Tantra.

"Elephants are the symbol of kingship and in ancient times they could only be owned by powerful rulers. As the mystic child of my Beloved Parvati, Ganesha is my most precious son. Just as a favored son always has access to his parents, so Ganesha always has access to us. Devotees who wish to know our special secrets should first honor Ganesha, without whose help no magical act bears fruit.

"Ganesha's long trunk reminds one of the Lingam and his sensuous mouth is like a Yoni, delicate yet all-consuming. Ganesha's consort is called Siddhi because magical powers (Siddhi) can only be controlled once sexuality has been understood and used as an aid to individual evolution. Ganesha rules the spirits presiding over the five elements and his large stomach allows him to digest the experiences of his followers. Ganesha brings good fortune and success. He is the symbol of discrimination and entry into the realm of occult power."

Ganesha in dalliance with his consort, Siddhi, the embodiment of magical power. From a stone sculpture, Khajuraho, *circa* tenth century.

THE CREATION OF GANESHA

Parvati says

"O Shiva, it was when you were in Yogic retreat and I was without you that I took the saffron and sandalwood paste from my own body and from it molded a magical child. I made him in the image of a beautiful boy, perfect in every respect, and through my magical power I gave him life. He faithfully guarded the doorway to my inner sanctum, and on my instructions, allowed entry to no one.

"But then all of a sudden you came to visit me, O Great Shiva, and being refused entry by my child, you severed his head from his body with your mighty trident. Such was my sorrow and shame that in your compassionate wisdom you granted a wondrous boon: a royal elephant was beheaded and his head placed on the exposed neck of my child, who then returned to life. Known as Ganesha, this special elephant-headed child of ours was appointed Lord of Obstacles and Ruler over the sex center.

"Ganesha still guards the doorway to the inner sanctum. This is a sexual secret that all women share with me. The Yoni is Ganesha's mouth; the clitoris, his trunk, is my secret Lingam. Truly, Ganesha guards the portal to occult power! For the benefit of those who wish to advance along the path of ecstasy, Beloved Shiva, please explain how sexual climaxes are built one upon another. Tell me the real meaning of the Four Moments and Four Joys and how a couple can practice sex magic without fear. Tell me the secret breathing techniques of Tantra and also how sexual energy can be stored within the bodies of both men and women."

Laughing, Shiva, the Master Yogi, replies

"How insatiable is the appetite of woman! Sexual climaxes are built one upon another by the conscious control of the otherwise involuntary urge to orgasm. During the preliminary stages of love-making both the Lingam and Yoni expand and sexual tension is built up, awaiting release through orgasm. The slower and more gentle the love-movements, the more intense the pleasure-sensations. Sexual climax is approached as the tension/pleasure interface causes both Lingam and Yoni to manifest a series of contractions. These contractions begin in the sexual region and extend throughout the whole body; they create a heightened urge to achieve release through orgasm. Thus, expansion and contraction are the two main factors that bring one to the high experience of sexual climax and are at the beginning and end of all creation.

CLIMAX AND ORGASM

"For sexual climaxes to be built one upon another, there must be a high degree of mutual cooperation between the Yogi and Yogini. The Yogi must strive to control his own climax while maintaining the tension/pleasure experience and bringing his precious partner to the peak of orgasm. On her part, the Yogini should surrender to the rising urge to climax, without any inhibition; she should consciously induce the normally involuntary contractions of her Yoni and her whole body as it approaches climax and focus all her attention on achieving total physical fulfillment.

SURRENDER

"Riding his partner's consciously produced Wave of Ecstasy, the Yogi retains while the Yogini climaxes. In order to achieve total control over retention, he should contract his anal sphincter muscles, draw in his stomach and hold his breath while rolling or turning up his eyes and focusing his mind on the ideal of penetrating transcendence. If necessary, the Yogi should press the secret place between his anus and Lingam to aid in controlling retention.

WAVE OF ECSTASY

"As the climax of the Yogini is achieved, a subtle bio-electrical exchange takes place between the Lingam and the Yoni. In his mind's eye the Yogi should imagine he is drawing in his

EXCHANGE

partner's released sexual charge and blending it with his own unreleased energy. Drawing in and retaining, the Yogi should again stimulate the tension/pleasure experience in the Yogini.

THE DESCENT

"After a brief descent from the heights of climax in fulfillment, the Yogini's Wave of Ecstasy rises again, striving to become one with the cause of her delight. As her climax peaks a second time, roles are exchanged: the Yogini must maintain the high level of ecstasy by stimulating the tension/pleasure experience while the Yogi momentarily abandons control and becomes one with her descending energy wave. At this time the Yogini must maintain the high plateau of impending climax while the Yogi becomes almost overwhelmed by the ebbing tide of orgasm. As the Yogi is about to surrender into descent, the Yogini should draw up the Wave of Ecstasy once again and bring her partner's penetrating sexuality into convergence with her own capacity for ascent to new heights of climax. As the natural convergence of sexual energies takes place, the conjoined Wave of Ecstasy rises higher and breaks through to new peaks of transcendence. No words can truly describe this liberating experience.

THE ASCENT

"This process of ascent by riding the Waves of Ecstasy can be repeated over successive climaxes of the Yogini. In each stage the Yogini stimulates, the Yogi retains, and then roles are exchanged. The Yogini must know how to stimulate the release of maximum sexual energy in both herself and her partner without losing control. Yet she must also surrender herself totally to the urge to climax. For his part, the Yogi must have voluntary control over his own orgasm, yet be able to surrender completely to the descending wave of energy from his partner, just after her climax. In each successive climax of the Yogini the plateau effect of climax is extended and then brought to a higher level by the switching of roles just at the moment of potential descent. Correctly practiced, this leads to the timeless experience of transcendence, the union of Voidness and Bliss.

FOUR LEVELS OF ASCENT

"There are four distinct levels of ascent, which are associated with the four main Chakras at the navel, heart, throat and head, and with the four mystical Moments of Union, called 'variety,' 'development,' 'consummation' and 'transcendence,' and with the evolution of the Four Joys. At the fourth level of climaxes built one upon another, there is feeling neither of self nor of otherness, neither beginning nor end, neither thought nor thinker.

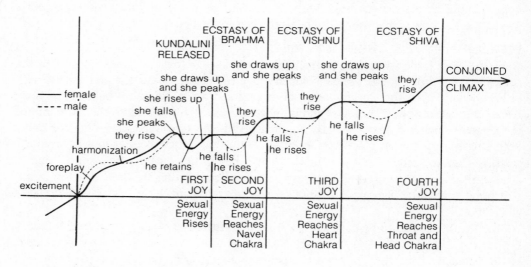

Chart showing the Bliss-wave of the Four Joys. The awakening of Kundalini is depicted by the first ascent and penetration of the Chakras by the subsequent plateaus of ecstasy.

SEX MAGIC

"Sex magic can be practiced without fear only when the emotions are completely understood, purified and consciously controlled. This does not mean that emotions should be suppressed, but rather that they should be directed. If a couple wish to practice sex magic, the altering of life's circumstances through the power of sex, they should strive to resolve conflicting dualities within themselves, strengthening their weaknesses and developing their capacity for creative innovation. An open, quick and flexible mind is essential to achievement of success in sex magic.

SECRET BREATHING

"There are many secret breathing techniques associated with the control of sexuality. The *complete breath* of conscious inhalation, retention and exhalation, drawing in from the lower abdomen, aids conscious control over all body functions; the retention phase is particularly linked to control over involuntary orgasm. The *cooling breath*, which is brought about by inhaling only through the left nostril, calms the urge to orgasm, as does the *crow-beak breath*, inhaling through the rolled-up tongue. Likewise the *heating breath*, which consists in inhaling only through the right nostril, stimulates the sexual drive and brings one closer to climax.

"If one consciously mimics the normal breathing of a person approaching sexual climax, the passions will automatically be stirred up. In the approach phase of her different climaxes the Yogini should thus gain conscious control over her approaching orgasm by using breathing as a potent ally. Similarly, to maintain control over retention, the Yogi should still his breathing and keep his awareness fixed on balancing the solar and lunar forces of his being. Whenever necessary he should emphasize one breath or the other, depending on whether he is in an active or passive role.

"A secret Tantric technique known as *womb breathing* consists of lying in a fetal position and taking only very shallow breaths from the region of the abdomen while imagining nourishment entering through the navel region. This type of breathing is extremely vitalizing and attracts energy from whoever is in close proximity to you.

"Sexual energy is stored in its raw form in the Sex Chakra at the base of the spine. In its transformed state, sexual energy can be concentrated in any of the other Chakras, but especially in the Head Chakra. This is true with both men and women. Sexual energy is naturally transformed and stored in the bodies of man and woman when they make love together harmoniously. Transformed sexual energy is a source of inspiration and insight and can be drawn on in times of need. Though an individual can bring about some degree of transformation of sexual energy alone by the correct practice of Hatha Yoga and creative meditation, it is not comparable to the tranformation of sexual energy that can be brought about by a couple completing each other through succesive heights of ecstasy. That is why it is said, 'Though Yogis can advance far on their own, for them to break through into Immortality they must seek to complete themselves with consorts.'"

With her eyes wide open, Parvati turns to Shiva and says

"O my Husband, with a lover such as you, no woman could remain unfulfilled! You understand so well the infinite capacity of female sexuality. For woman, the experience of orgasm is not finite, but has as many levels, colors and subtle nuances as there are stars in the sky. The techniques that you have outlined for ascending and extending the plateaus of pleasure will surely enable women to reach and explore new heights of ecstasy! Great Yogi, this teaching is surely a secret that can transport lovers to the realm of the gods!

"Hold me closer now and tell me about the secret language of Tantra, that mysterious twilight talk. Please explain to me the different levels of understanding Tantric Truths and tell me also of your secret insights about the central vein of Tantra. Tell me something of ritual gestures and the power of symbolic language. Finally, perhaps you'll feel inspired to clarify the mysteries of the lost fifth Veda and the so-called Great Chinese Rites."

Drawing the beautiful Parvati close to him and whispering in her right ear, Shiva, the Yogi of Yogis and Lord over all creatures, says

"Mistress of my life! Secret language is necessary to avoid diluting the potency of the Tantric teachings. Secret language helps guard the inner meaning of the mysteries from those who are unprepared for them or who would abuse them. By couching the Tantric teachings in a language of multi-leveled meanings, the authenticity of initiation is maintained. Just as a form of secret language naturally develops between lovers and is on occasion used by them in public without others being aware of the real topic of discussion, so the Tantras are protected by double meanings, obscure symbolism, allegory and paradox. Secret language helps express the inexpressible.

"Many different kinds of secret language are used within the Tantric tradition. The teachings can, for example, replace one word with another, like a code. Only initiates who have received oral instruction in the code can ascertain the real meaning of the teachings. In this context, several Tantras refer to the left channel of the Subtle Body as 'the Whore,' the right channel as 'the Tongue,' the universe as 'the Human Skull,' thought as 'the Wild Elephant,' mind control as 'Meat,' breathing practices as 'Fish,' semen as 'Camphor,' the Lingam as 'the Thunderbolt,' the Yoni as 'the Palace' or 'the Lotus,' urine as 'Musk' and this body as 'the Bag.' These are just some of the code words used in the Tantras.

SHIVA

the transcendental

SECRET SIGNS

THREE LEVELS OF TEACHING

REALITY IS PARADOXICAL

The Yoni

The Lingam

Obeisance

Three mystic hand gestures used in the Odissi temple dance and also in Tantric ritual. From traditional sources.

"Some Tantric teachers hide the meaning of their transmission by making use of allegorical songs, riddles or coarse erotic rhymes, the true interpretation of which is only understood by initiates. Others use puns, mime, mystic gestures or secret signs. For example, if a Yogi shows one finger, it implies the question 'Am I welcome?' Stretching out two fingers in reply means, 'You are welcome.' If a Tantric Yogi exhibits his fourth finger to a Yogini, she should indicate that she is proficient in the secret practices by stretching out her little finger; in this exchange of secret signs the Yogi and Yogini are affirming their mutual knowledge of the role of Heaven and Earth, while communicating their desire to perform practices together. Likewise, if a teacher turns over a full bowl of water or food while looking straight at a disciple, it means that that person must empty himself of all clingings or pre-conditions in order to receive the teachings directly.

"Tantric truths should be understood on three levels simultaneously: the literal, the allegorical and the mystical. Ideally, an individual should view these three levels of understanding as complementary and forming a single truth, just as the three main channels of the Subtle Body should be viewed as a complete unit. The potency of Tantric teachings is lost when people interpret them exclusively on the literal, allegorical or mystical level. For example, if the rites of the Yogini Chakra are taken on a purely literal level, they cease to have any significance other than as an excuse for debauchery. If the Yogini Chakra is viewed as purely symbolic or allegorical, it becomes merely an intellectual exercise. If it is viewed as exclusively mystical, it loses both practicality and purpose.

"Reality is paradoxical, multi-faceted and constantly changing. There is no such thing as absolute objectivity; to view truth one must have many vantage points. Those who wish to learn from the Tantras should interpret the teaching from both their own level of attainment and other viewpoints. Above all, a sense of expectancy over and above what fits in with established views should be maintained.

"The central vein of Tantra goes by many different names. The best known is *Sushumna*, meaning 'that which brings one forth with ease.' It is also known as *Avadhuti*, meaning the female adept of sexual Yoga, *Saraswati*, the Mistress of the Sixty-four Arts, and *Nairatma*, the egoless, selfless ecstatic being.

"All subtle veins, nerves or channels are subordinate to the Sushumna. Like the umbilical cord of a newborn child, it pulses with life and reaches from the Base Chakra at the sexual center of the body to the Head Chakra. The Sushumna is itself composed of three progessively more subtle channels, each within the other. Known as *Vajrini*, *Chitrini* and *Brahma Nadi*, they constitute the central vein of Tantra and are expressions of the subtle stages of spiritual refinement. The innermost Brahma Nadi is called the Great Royal Road; only those who know their true origin can travel along it in safety. Gurus, Siddhas and spiritual 'kings' are the only other beings one will encounter along the Royal Road.

"Ritual gestures are a way of expressing the inexpressible. Known as *Mudra*, ritual gestures help bring teacher and disciple closer together. They are one of the most direct and potent ways of awakening and communicating with the deities within. Ritual gestures help break through bariers in communication and are the distillation of wisdom.

"Mudras are used to aid concentration and channel energy through their Yantra or power form. In Tantric high magic, ritual gestures are clearly defined intentional acts that blend emotional and intellectual viewpoints into a single focused mode of expression. In rites of initiation, especially, ritual gestures play an important role.

"The secret meaning of Mudra is woman in her role as a Yogini. Truly the sexual partner helps concentrate the mind and emotions on a single purpose! Known as *Karma Mudra*, the Tantric Yogini is mistress, sex initiatress and high priestess at the same time. In this context the Karma Mudra is a boon, a blessing and a vital aid in the direct experience of ecstatic self-realization. She rapidly brings the Yogi to completion by her selfless service to him, just as he serves to fulfill and liberate her within a single lifetime. As the embodiment of all the senses in their exalted form, the Mudra-woman is the greatest symbol or Seal of Liberation.

"There are five different kinds of Karma Mudra or female consort and they are categorized according to physical and psychological characteristics. They are said to have emanated from the original Five Great Families or root races. The five Karma Mudras or Yoginis are thought of as having five different colors: dark blue, white, red, green and yellow. All have the ability to empower the Tantric Yogi through their special sexual qualities. They are both the cause of the recurring cycle of birth and death and the means of becoming liberated from them. In the Kali Age, when everything is mixed up and truth is turned on its head, the Karma Mudras are not recognizable by their outer appearance but instead must be invoked through the power of visualization.

"Symbolic language takes many different forms in the Tantric tradition. For example, the word *Mudra* may be used exclusively to refer to a mystic hand gesture. On another level it refers to the female sexual partner, and on another level still it indicates a certain type of cereal grain, the seeds of which bear a resemblance to the Yoni and are used symbolically in Tantric ritual.

"The word *Mudra* can be extended by understanding the subtle play of symbolic language. For example, *Mudra* is very similar to the words *Shudra* and *Rudra*, both of which extend its meaning. Shudra means low-caste, unsophisticated, direct. The Tantras do not recognize the validity of caste systems or any other limiting orthodoxies. Yogis are advised to cut through caste conditioning and seek consorts from among the so-called lower castes. One reason for this is that Karma Mudras from the low castes are free of social conditioning and are spontaneous, unpretentious and filled with natural Shakti; furthermore, service comes easily to such a person. The low-caste Karma Mudra is a love partner who is shameless, guilt-free, sexually active, psychologically open and Karmically uncomplex. In choosing such a woman, the Yogi steps aside from the limitations of convention and rapidly attains liberation from dualities. For her part, the Karma Mudra has everything to gain; within a single lifetime she has the opportunity to advance from the lowest to the highest, just by doing what comes naturally.

"*Rudra* means the bestowing of strength or occult power. It also means ruddy, shining, praiseworthy, transcendental anger and the driving away of evil; it is one of my own names, and it refers to those who take after me. In ancient times my mystic Rudra-form sprung from Brahma's forehead and separated into a half-male and half-female being. The Yogi and Yogini in physical union are no different from Rudra, which goes beyond this world. When Mudra, the name of the ritual consort, is extended symbolically to encompass concepts of Shudra and Rudra, the multi-leveled view of Tantric sexuality is revealed. Ideally the sexual partner embodies lustful spontaneity through her caste and bestows strength and occult power through her desire for repeated union with the force of evolution. As such she is known as Rudrani, the Queen of Rudras, and is the Seal of Liberation, my beloved and playful consort. Her names and her delights are many.

"Your question about the lost fifth Veda brings to mind an ancient incident long forgotten by both gods and men. Originally, Brahma had five heads. When he had completed his task of creating the universe, he placed his seed deep within his consort. After a hundred celestial years of pregnancy, she gave birth to the five Vedas, the different branches of knowledge, one from each of his heads. The teachings of the fifth Veda were kept very secret, whereas the other four Vedas were distributed among the Brahmins. Deciding that the secret teachings should be kept safe from the reach of demons, Brahma memorized the fifth Veda, thinking that he would release it to humanity when the time was ripe.

"Brahma the Creator became over-proud with his creation. He became arrogant, possessive and filled with a sense of 'doership.' He forgot to acknowledge the Transcendental and did not bother to invite either you, Parvati, in your form of Sati, or myself to his greatest celebration. In a rage I cut off his fifth head, wherein the fifth Veda was temporarily stored.

"The head reached Mahachina, the Great Country of China, northeast of the Himalaya Mountains. There it was well received; thus began the spreading of the unorthodox teachings, which had been reserved for a time when beings had perfected the other four Vedas. As a result, China became the home of unconventional spiritual practices, especially those with a strong basis in occultism. To this day the secret teachings of the fifth Veda are to be found mixed in with the Chinese mystery schools of Buddhism and Taoism.

"The Sage Vasistha, Brahmin though he was, traveled to China to perfect his spiritual practices, having been advised to do so by the Mother-goddess herself. Reaching China by way of Assam in northeastern India, he was astounded to find Vishnu there in the form of Buddha, his ninth incarnation. To his amazement, the Buddha's eyes were red from the use of wine

A Tantric Guru shows the Mahayoni Mudra, the mystic gesture of the Mother-goddess. From a contemporary photograph.

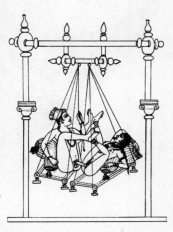

Playful love-making on a swing. From a Bundi Indian miniature of the late eighteenth century.

Shiva and Shakti in ecstatic union. From a central Indian stone sculpture of the eleventh century.

and other intoxicants. Plates laden with meat and fish were in front of him and he was enjoying a number of beautiful women. Vasistha saw other adepts also erotically engaged with exquisite damsels freed from any prudishness.

"Thinking that he was witnessing a mirage, Vasistha said to himself: 'These things are opposed to the teachings of the Vedas. I don't approve of them and will have nothing to do with such despicable practices, which must anyway be the product of illusion.' However, just at that moment the goddess of his devotions revealed herself to him in the form of Tara, a dark-blue emanation of Saraswati. She told him not to lapse into duality or rest his case on bigotry. 'Look,' she said. 'View the total Bliss-experience. A tree should be judged by the taste of its fruit, not by its external appearance. This method of achieving realization is direct and pleasing to me. Take instruction from the Buddha and the other beings and follow their example. This secret method will rapidly bring you to completion.'

"Vasistha stayed in China and participated in the practices of the fifth Veda. He achieved everything there is to achieve and eventually became immortal. Though some people misunderstand them, these practices are dear to my heart and lead to transcendence. The Mahachina practices are an all-or-nothing commitment; everything rests on the acceptance of responsibility and the resolution of dualisms. Only heroes should attempt to ascend the highest peaks. **VASISTHA IN CHINA**

"But, Goddess, I feel somehow reluctant to discuss this topic. Knowledge of the Great **CHINESE RITES** Chinese Rites is dangerous and liable to abuse. Who knows what beings or entities might hear my explanations and take advantage of these secret teachings? Are there no other questions that require answers? Why don't you ask me to expound the fine details of subjects already discussed? Or why don't we just make love and leave this topic until some other time? Too much talk breeds confusion; too many questions lead to too many answers . . ."

Pulling Shiva to her, lowering her eyes and moving her body seductively against him, Parvati entreats her lover

"O Lord of the Three Worlds, do not refuse me this. Only by your grace can knowledge of this subject be revealed! If you won't speak of it here, for fear of being overheard, let us depart at once for Mahachina, and there, seated at ease in a luxurious pleasure garden, we can freely discuss these matters. O Beloved, please grant me this boon. I wish to know more of these Chinese methods of worship!"

Amused by the prospect of erotic play and travel, and moved by her entreaties, Lord Shiva replies

"Very well, we had best transport ourselves. But not to China yet! First I shall become the Buddha and reveal the way these secret teachings became known to him. You should divide yourself after the method of Kameshwari and become the five colored Dakinis of the Directions, Families and Elements. Then we'll go to China and share other intimacies. Only when you are fully satisfied will I bring you back to Mount Meru! Come, before I change my mind!"

So saying, the Master Yogi takes his beautiful consort upon his lap, unites with her and, rising, they move through time and space.

THE BUDDHA

The Buddha sits beneath a large tree, on a hill close to the banks of a river, with a forest in the distance. He is absorbed in meditation and has obviously been without food for a long time. Through exposure to the elements and the practice of austerities, his body has become emaciated; though he is earnestly involved in maintaining his self-discipline, something seems lacking.

The Fasting Buddha, at the time when he had reduced his food intake to just a single grain of rice a day. Stone sculpture from Gandhara, West Pakistan, *circa* second or third century.

The Buddha in the earth-touching position. This incident is associated with his receiving mystic insights from the Earth Mother. Stone sculpture recovered from the site of Ratnagiri monastery, Cuttack, Orissa, *circa* eleventh century.

The Buddha appears to be going through some deep internal crisis. His face looks somewhat strained. All of a sudden he moves his right hand toward the earth and touches it. His lips move slightly. At the very moment that he touches the earth a beautiful young yellow-colored woman appears out of the forest, bearing a small bowl of milk curds. She is obviously from one of the poorer castes and is probably a milkmaid. As she draws close to the Buddha, his countenance clears and a smile begins to form on his lips. Opening his eyes, he looks at her, accepts the offering she places at his feet and becomes filled with radiance. He then proceeds to make four other mystic gestures with his hands. As each gesture is completed, a young woman appears, each of a different color, and cosmic sounds reverberate throughout the universe.

MAMAKI
"My name is Mamaki, the essence of the Earth-element," says the beautiful yellow-colored milkmaid. "I come from the south, but my real home is India. I am but an orphan. Save me with your passionate love! O Great Being, make hard love to me now that I may live and you may achieve your goal!"

LOCANA
"My name is Locana, the essence of the Water-element," says a lovely blue-colored damsel. "I come from the east, but my real home is Africa. I am but an orphan. Save me with your passionate love! O Embodiment of Spiritual Law, come, make fluid love with me now, that I may live and you may achieve your goal!"

"My name is Pandara, the essence of the Fire-element," says an exquisite red-colored lady. **PANDARA** "I come from the west, but my real home is in the land of the midnight sun. I am but an orphan. Save me with your passionate love. O Completely Good One, make expansive, fiery love with me now, that I may live and you may achieve your goal!"

"My name is Tara, the essence of the Air-element," says a gorgeous greenish-colored girl. **TARA** "I come from the north, but my real home is China. I am but an orphan. Save me with your passionate love. O Compassionate One, make all-encompassing love with me now, that I may live and you may achieve your goal!"

"My name is Ishvari, the essence of the Space-element," says a delightful white-colored **ISHVARI** woman. "I come from the Original Center, the Origin of Reality, but my real home is at the peak of Mount Meru. I am but an orphan. Save me with your passionate love. O Heroic One, make expansive, all-pervading love with me now, that I may live and you may achieve your goal!"

The Celestial Buddha in union with the Dakinis of the four directions and center. This incident is recorded in the great *Guhyasamaja Tantra*. From a Tibetan initiation painting of the eighteenth century.

Realizing that all these mystic forms of the Mother-goddess have come to aid him in his search for Liberation from the endless cycle of births and deaths, the Buddha enters the Samadhi state known as "Diamond Glory Partaking of All Desires" and makes love with all of them simultaneously. Practicing the arts of love he had perfected during his youthful years in his father's palace, the Buddha fulfills the desires of each of the Dakinis and they bring him to completion. Ascending in a five-colored rainbow of effulgent light, they are transported to another realm.

THE YELLOW EMPEROR

It is nighttime, the stars move slowly across the heavens and the moon is full. The slight mist clears and the moonlight reveals a Taoist pleasure garden, artfully located among mountains. The scenery is breathtaking. There is a small lake overhung with willow trees; a winding path leads from it through peach and plum trees, past moss-covered rocks, past a goldfish pond, an arbor of roses, beds of peonies and other flowers, to a delightful pavilion strategically located looking down over the lake. In the moonlight the trees and flowers cast strange shadows, some long, some short.

Red lanterns hang from the eaves of the pavilion, which seems to be carved from some kind of precious marble, or perhaps a white jade. The roof is covered with golden tiles and the exquisitely made doors and windows are open, revealing a scene of rare luxury.

Inside, the atmosphere is filled with the odor of sweet orchids, lotuses and other fragrant flowers. Candles and lanterns illuminate the single large room, which has red-colored silk hangings, embroidered curtains, carpets, rugs, painted screens and fine art tastefully arranged. Reclining on a rosewood bed carved in the shape of a dragon is the Yellow Emperor. He appears to be attentively listening to three young Oriental women of unimaginable beauty.

DAUGHTERS OF EARTH

THE DARK GIRL

"Though we are three, in truth we are one," says the damsel with a slighly darker skin than the others. "Just as you are the Son of Heaven, we are the Daughters of Earth. We are called the Plain Girl, the Elected Girl and the Dark Girl; our function is to initiate you into the Supreme Truths concerning sexuality. I am Hsuan-nu, the Dark Girl, the Peach of Immortality, and these are my loving sisters."

THE ELECTED GIRL

"My name is Ts'ai-nu, the Elected Girl," says the one wearing purple silk robes. "I am also called Goddess of Many Colors. Just as the Emperor must familiarize himself with everything in his empire in order to rule it well, so should he know the secrets of sexual love, to enable him to harmonize himself with his Queen and concubines."

THE PLAIN GIRL

"My name is Su-nu, the Plain Girl," says the third young woman, who is completely naked and whose Yoni looks just like a conch shell. "I am also called Queen of the White River. To be quite frank, woman is the only real initiator; man's role is that of a willing student. Just as on the sixteenth day of the fifth month of every year the roles of Heaven and Earth are reversed, so within this Love Pavilion it is my sisters and I who determine the order of events and the Yellow Emperor who complies!"

Pulling the Plain Girl close to him and then placing his head close to her lap, as if in obeisance, the Yellow Emperor says:

"Sensuous One, explain to me the roles of Heaven and Earth! Initiate me into the secret sexual methods pertaining to rulership. Tell me why it is that husbands are but one, whereas wives are many. Reveal to me the inner meaning of polygamy and when, if ever, polyandry is permissible. Tell me also when your precious Conch Shell will be ready and willing to receive my Jade Scepter!"

Laughing mischievously, the Plain Girl draws herself away from the Yellow Emperor and, reaching to one side, she picks up an exquisite multi-stringed musical instrument, something like a zither. The Elected Girl drapes an embroidered housecoat with a phoenix design on

The three sex initiatresses, the Plain Girl, the Elected Girl and the Dark Girl. From a contemporary photograph.

it around the Plain Girl's shoulders, smoothes her hair and moves over to a small table holding a jade bottle and some crystal glasses. The Dark Girl sits next to the Emperor, to his left, and begins to flirt with him.

ROLES OF HEAVEN AND EARTH

"Heaven expands, Earth contracts," says the Plain Girl as she delicately plucks the strings of her instrument. "Expansion and contraction are the roles of Heaven and Earth! Just as Heaven is solitary, whereas Earths are legion, so it is that husbands are one and wives are many. It is truly said that the husband is Heaven and Heaven cannot be shirked!

EMPEROR'S SECRETS

"As Emperor, you are authorized to enjoy one wife of the first rank, three precious consorts, nine wives of the second rank, twenty-seven wives of the third rank and eighty-one concubines. The wife of the first rank is the Queen of Heaven and the three precious consorts are the Daughters of Earth. The nine wives of the second rank symbolize the nine planets and the twenty-seven wives of the third rank echo the twenty-seven constellations in the sky. As for the eighty-one concubines, they lighten the load of years and are for the playful dalliance of Emperors!

Secret dalliance, the multiple love-making of emperors. Woodblock illustration from Kamigata Koishusyo, attributed to Kunisada, *circa* 1840.

EMPEROR'S DUTY

"The Emperor's duty is to rule by maintaining harmony between Heaven and Earth; truly the Emperor is the Son of Heaven! As embodiments of the three Eternal Forces of creation, preservation and transcendence, the Daughters of Earth serve to initiate the Emperor into the ways of man.

"The Emperor should make love with nine chosen consorts every night, proceeding from the lower ranks to the higher. Each of the nine consorts should be satisfied fully, so that the planets are pleased; retaining his semen by proficiency in the Art of Love, the Emperor concentrates powers within. Then, at the full moon, he bestows his seed on the Queen of Heaven.

"Polyandry is permissible between blood brothers and a single woman, since brotherhood implies shared origin. How can those of identical origin in reality be thought of as different? However, be this as it may, it is true of life that brothers often seek to destroy one another through the natural expansive qualities of man, which, in close proximity, manifest as rivalries and petty jealousies. When the force of expansion becomes limited, it is difficult indeed to contain. For polyandry to work successfully, brothers must truly become masters of themselves.

"As for your last question, my Conch Shell is even now ready to receive your precious Jade Scepter! However, by your questions it seems that *you* are not yet ready for *me*! And what of

Multiple love-making between two brothers and their wives. From a Chinese painting of the early eighteenth century.

my sisters? Are you ready for *them*? Here now, Ts'ai-nu, the Elected Girl, has prepared the wine. Drink and look within. See what other questions come to mind."

The Elected Girl holds a glass of warm aromatic wine, the color of cinnabar, to the Yellow Emperor's lips. She takes the place of the Dark Girl, who has got up from the bed and moved over to sit close to the Plain Girl. The Dark Girl hums gently to a melody played on the zither. The tune is made up of five notes, repeated over and over in different sequences.

"Drink your fill, O Noble Lord!" says the Elected Girl haughtily. "Su-nu, your precious Conch Shell, and Hsuan-nu, the Peach of Immortality, are busy composing a song in praise of the Five Elements that originate from the union of Yin and Yang. If you have an immediate use for me, please let me know. Though I prefer purple to the predominance of red in this Love Pavilion, I'll do my best to please you. Perhaps I should rub your head, to aid the effect of the wine? If you have any questions I'll be glad to answer them."

Taken aback by the reversal of roles, the Yellow Emperor drinks some wine and watches the Elected Girl's face as she sensuously moves her body next to him in time with the music. As she nods her head this way and that, her earrings jingle and the Emperor finds himself fascinated by her charms. The wine begins to take its effect.

"Truly you are a Goddess of Many Colors!" says the Yellow Emperor. "If indeed you are also a sex initiatress, initiate me now! Tell me the subtle effect, if any, of illicit affairs and other types of adultery. Explain to me the secret meanings of Self-worship, narcissism, auto-eroticism and forms of bondage. Please explain to me all about fetishism and foot worship. Finally, if you can, tell me the meaning of the Taoist term 'Heavenly and Earthly Net.' In truth, I'm sure these topics are beyond the reach of even the Daughters of Earth herself!"

Pouting erotically, Ts'ai-nu, the Elected Girl, rocks herself back and forth and says:

Taoist love-posture of ritual love-making. From a fragment of a silk scroll of the early sixteenth century.

ILLICIT AFFAIRS

"Yellow Emperor indeed! How is it that illicit affairs and adultery are so close to your mind? Perhaps even now, among your own wives and concubines, there are those who savor such thoughts. Illicit affairs are unfortunate and are the cause of many calamities; their attraction is the thrill of the forbidden. If a woman has illicit affairs, the seed of her lovers will fight and the ancestors will be displeased. If a man has illicit affairs, he loses the respect of those who are devoted to him. So why bother with illicit affairs? Between truly caring people there is no space for deceit.

ADULTERY IN THE HEART

"Adultery does not only refer to acts of the body. Many women commit adultery in their hearts, as do men. At the slightest suspicion of unfaithfulness in their partner, both women and men tend to develop desires for others. Thinking to pay him or her back in kind, they commit adultery with the help of their imagination. While making love with their partner, they make believe they are loving someone else, even bringing to mind a favorite face or name. If such unions produce children, they tend to take after the imagined person.

SELF-WORSHIP

"Self-worship exalts the nobility within and is a secret support for the Spirit. Self-worship implies knowledge of the Self and recognition of its transcendental qualities. Self-worship takes one beyond. In the world all acts of healthy conduct are forms of Self-worship, from bathing to eating to having sex. On the highest level Self-worship is meditation and transcendence.

NARCISSISM

"Narcissism is natural to woman. Striving to realize all her multifarious roles, she draws her narcissism from Nature. For a woman, narcissism can be a form of Self-worship and also a source of nourishment. Though narcissism can also serve the woman within every man, it is an illusory power that has no inherent potential for him. Yin, like water, holds its own mirror; Yang, like fire, throws no reflection back. When male narcissism dominates a culture, it impedes spiritual progress. In extreme, narcissism is a turning away from Bliss.

AUTO-EROTICISM

"Auto-eroticism is a derivation of narcissism. It is a secret circuit of the senses. Auto-eroticism further softens what is already soft. Auto-eroticism is a paradox of Nature, a mystery born of solitude. The Earth is auto-erotic but Heaven is not.

BONDAGE

"Bondage is the Soul's endless round of births and deaths. Bondage is also the body, helpless and confined. Great Emperor, if the sight of a fair maiden trussed and bound excites your passion, be that as it may! There are also those among our Earthly sisters whose blood is quickened by the tug of silken ropes about their delicate wrists and ankles. If both Yin and Yang find pleasure in such diversions, let bondage be practiced as an erotic art, but never should it be employed to degrade the Soul.

"There are those who adopt bondage as an effective means of reversing roles. As an erotic tool, bondage can free the mind by restricting the body. Symbolic of the total surrender prior to release, bondage mirrors the game of life. Those who advocate bondage for their own sadistic or masochistic ends should try warfare instead; then, as captor or captive, destiny is theirs alone, to either confront or flee from. Truly it is said, 'The ropes that bind the strongest are found within the mind.'

FETISHISM

"Fetishism is like a play of ghosts; it is an obsession with specific objects or acts and is brought about by the mind's power of identification. Fetishism is the mind's attempt to endow with meaning that which is not yet fully understood. By the power of fetishism, inanimate objects or ideas appear to be animate. Sexual fetishism occurs when an object or idea associated with sexual pleasure acquires a psycho-spiritual hold over a person. It is the ritual surrounding the fetish that endows it with power and meaning. Sexual fetishes can take the form of such mundane things as silk scarves, stockings, underclothes, bondage ropes, furs, feathers or other items associated with pleasures long past. When the mind is obsessively focused on the fetish, intimate, meaningful memories seem to spring to life on their own. Fetishism is generally associated with nostalgia and morbidity and often conceals an inability to either express or receive love. Although fetishism can be an artificial aid to self-confidence, the ultimate price for this is high.

FEET

"Since ancient times the feet have been recognized as microcosms of the body. Subtle nerves connect the feet with all the inner organs. It is the feet that bear the weight of the body through most of its years. Foot worship is thus a form of honoring the support of Mother Earth and is a custom reserved for those one respects. When the loved one returns weary from battle, his feet should be washed, oiled and worshipped with incense and flowers. When the consort manifests herself as the Goddess of Earth, her lotus feet should be honored and exalted.

FOOT WORSHIP

"Foot worship does not mean foot bondage or foot fetishism, both of which are unnatural. Though in women small feet are taken as signs of refinement and nobility, and are even said to indicate sexual prowess, foot binding is painful and serves no useful purpose. In the practice of the erotic arts the feet can serve as either Precious Crucible or Scepter. When the soles of the feet are placed together, a secret pleasure grotto is formed; at times when the ecstasy of love is rising, the toes curl naturally and can be easily used like the Positive Peak. Truly the feet are the microcosm of both man and woman!

HEAVENLY AND EARTHLY NI

"The Heavenly and Earthly Net is an ancient Chinese Rite designed to avert calamities and natural disasters caused by disharmony between Heaven and Earth. In this rite, performed in the dark of night, men and women make love like birds and beasts, mimicking their sounds, postures and other antics. At times when emperors cannot fulfill their sexual duties, and when Heaven and Earth begin to manifest disorder, the Heavenly and Earthly Net is said to be the last resort. Through this sexual ritual, a natural hierarchy is evolved and the *Tao*, the Cosmic Order, is re-established."

The Yellow Emperor momentarily places his head at the feet of the Elected Girl, who has finished talking and is caressing her left breast. Hsuan-nu, the Dark Girl, suddenly stops humming; a sense of expectancy fills the atmosphere. The Plain Girl puts aside her instrument.

The Dark Girl drinks some wine, leans over to the Plain Girl and kisses her on the mouth. Then, taking her by the hand, she leads her over to join the Elected Girl and the Yellow Emperor on the dragon-shaped bed.

Mimicry of the love-making of animals is a mystic Oriental practice believed to aid the harmonization of Heaven and Earth. From a Japanese print of the eighteenth century.

"So much for serious talk!" she says. "The facts of life are but common sense. Anyone knows that girls menstruate when they're twice seven and that boys can father children when they're twice eight; few, however, can play the Melody of the Five Elements. Everyone recognizes MELODY OF THE FIVE ELEMENTS that clouds and mist are the Yin-juices of the Earth and that Jade is the Yang-essence of the Heavenly Dragon; few, however, understand the real function of the three sex initiatresses!

"Su-nu here is called the Plain Girl, the Queen of the White River; she is Earth's embodiment of all creativity. Ts'ai-nu, who is caressing herself, is called the Elected Girl, the Goddess of Many Colors; she is Earth's natural narcissism, the exquisite eroticism of all preservation. As for myself, Hsuan-nu the Dark Girl, I am called the Peach of Immortality because I bear the sweetest fruits of the Earth and still bestow lasting transcendence!

"The tortoise, unicorn, phoenix and dragon are all creatures with counterparts within the human body. All are called *Ling*, which means 'transcendental.' The tortoise enjoys this Earth without haste, and as a result, lives for a very long time; born of this Earth, the unicorn is much loved by women, and though rarely found, his horn is always hard; the phoenix is born from the ashes of Earth and rises constantly; the dragon, though originally resting in the bowels of the Earth, hides in the Heavens.

"In ancient times I, Hsuan-nu, made magic drums for the Yellow Emperor and so helped him slay the Monster of Time. Now, once again, monsters threaten this age and the sexual secrets have been forgotten. We three young girls have the Son of Heaven to ourselves. Is this the time for 'playing horse' or 'stringing pearls'? Conjoining our complementary forces into One, with our bodies forming the Precious Tripod of Immortality, let us perfect the Elixir THE TRIPOD OF IMMORTALITY right now."

The Elixir of Life was potentized for eighty-one days and nights, during which time all obstacles were easily overcome. Then, rising from the shores of the lake, the Celestial Dragon, bearing a sun and moon in eclipse, flew toward Mount Meru, illuminating it from above.

May it be Auspicious!

part three

VISHNU

the preserver

Vishnu, the Preserver, maintains all things and has the power to manifest in many different forms. In the great Cosmic Ocean he reclines comfortably on the Serpent of Infinity and is the primeval Spirit of Existence, the Lord of the Universe.

VISHNU PURANA

Lakshmi is the consort of Vishnu; she is as beautiful as ten million rising suns and is the embodiment of sensuality. Lotus-eyed and garlanded with lotuses, she is the Eternal Mistress of all beings. She rests upon the thighs of Vishnu and is the patroness of prosperity.

LAKSHMI TANTRA

The King and Queen of Nepal are here depicted as Vishnu and Lakshmi. Seated together in intimate Tantric ecstatic union, they embody the archetypes of preservation and prosperity. The multi-headed cosmic serpent, the tamed vital energy, symbolizes the infinite potency of the cosmos. From a miniature painting in the collection of the King of Nepal, *circa* 1830.

The erotic sentiment is the potent "seed" of mysticism. It is the raw emotion of love, a feeling that stimulates the passions, "fires" the senses and awakens the Kundalini-energy at the sexual center. The erotic sentiment is evoked through the delightful contact of the senses with the external world. When refined and carefully channeled, eroticism leads to the experience of transcendence and ecstasy.

In the Tantric or "secret" tradition, the erotic sentiment correlates with the taste of sweetness. Vishnu, the Preserver, also known as "Lord of the Waters," is said to be the ruler of the erotic; this is supported by the ancient attribution of the watery element to the sense of taste, and by the necessity of saliva in discriminating flavors. Hindu texts recount the many erotic exploits of Vishnu, who in his incarnation as the youthful Krishna is the prototype of the lover. Of his amorous adventures and subtle play, more shall be said later.

Eroticism stirs up the fires of love, in all its varieties. The ancient Indian texts, such as the *Kama Sutra* and *Ananga Ranga*, refer to four distinct types of love: habitual love, imaginary love, natural love and sensual love. Of course such categorization is a simplification, since most loves are a mixture of the different types. However, the importance of this traditional classification of eros is in its bearing on the deeper mystical teachings of the Tantric tradition. We will encounter this fourfold division time and time again as we move deeper into the arcana of the East, most notably in the transformation of sexual energy and the stages of ecstasy.

The erotic sentiment is linked with the element of fire and the sense of sight. Shiva, the Yogic ideal of transcendence, is always associated with fire and mystic eroticism. To understand what this means we have to remember the relationship between the "inner fire" at the navel center of the Subtle Body (the solar plexus) and the "Third Eye" in the head center. This occult eye is brought into action through the distillation and transformation of the inner "fires" in the stomach, liver, spleen, heart, skin and so on; such an effect is brought about by the different kinds of Yoga. In the Western

mystical tradition there is also a knowledge of the spiritual fire, the fire of purified emotion.

In esoteric teachings throughout the world, "fire" and "water" represent the solar-lunar forces of the microcosm. These two great forces can be resolved through the erotic sentiment; whether literally or allegorically depends on the particular context, but always these two elements evoke the erotic. The Tantras declare that the "fires" and "waters" can be experienced through the bodies of both men and women; love-making is the most direct way of realizing their potencies. Solar and lunar breathing, as outlined in the first part of this book, is automatically brought about by the movement of postures during peaks of sexual activity. If consciously channeled, the forces of breath can evoke the solar and lunar energies within and rapidly bring about the prolonged experience of Tantric ecstasy.

Cosmic fire and cosmic water in union. This alchemical concept is found in medieval treatises but originally was developed in the mystery schools of the East. Illustration from an Indian manuscript.

In the East gaiety, joking and laughter are encouraged at funerals, births and marriages, for this spirit, rather than solemnity, fosters love. In the West the concepts of love, lust and the erotic have been greatly confused. This has been due in large part to the influence of the Church, which has chosen to ignore the spiritual dimension of physical love. An old Indian adage declares, "The comic sentiment arises from and is next to the erotic." Another states that the comic is the "mimicry" of the erotic. The mass media have exploited the closeness between the comic and the erotic sentiments. Titillating comedy often serves to relieve the tensions of unfulfilled sexuality. Though laughter is itself healing, it is no substitute for eroticism. Extreme outbursts of laughter can in fact block the flow of energy within the body or force it to flow along unnatural channels.

The recent surge of sexual liberation movements makes this an apt moment to re-evaluate the function of the erotic sentiment in the light of Tantric and Taoist traditions. These teachings repeatedly confirm the most revolutionary discoveries of new-age psychiatry, medicine and cosmology. The remainder of this book outlines important points for consideration. It offers a detailed account of the role of eroticism, particularly as it pertains to the preservation and maintenance of the highest aspects of man and woman.

The wife clasps the husband in her arms. They spread the virile "milk," and, in delivering herself, she milks for herself the potent Juice of Love. RIG VEDA

How delicious an instrument is woman, when artfully played upon; how capable is she of producing the most exquisite harmonies, of executing the most complicated variations of love, and of giving the most Divine of erotic pleasures. ANANGA RANGA

Food is called "Soma," the Waters, which represent the female or Mother-principle, whereas "Agni," the Fire, represents the male or Father-principle. When these two are satiated it is called real spiritual worship. RATISARA

Spiritual worship. The mystic forms of Vishnu and Lakshmi as Radha and Krishna, the embodiments of unconventional love, are portrayed seated on lotuses, wearing lotus petals and holding lotus buds. The lotus is a symbol of spirituality. This icon expresses the ideal of refined eroticism. From an Indian painting of the early eighteenth century.

The Wave of Bliss. From the "36 Views of Fuji" by Hokusai, *circa* 1820, the "Great Wave off Kanagawa," Japan.

Vishnu and Lakshmi

In its role as Preserver, the Divine is called Vishnu. His is the force that maintains all existence. His symbols are the conch shell and discus. Lakshmi is his female counterpart. This archetypal couple, visualized in practice as god and goddess, are identified as higher aspects of the human psyche. To become Vishnu or Lakshmi is to become the Lord or Lady of Preservation, the embodiment of spiritual wealth and material prosperity. In Tantra the couple strives to embody these two principles.

Vishnu "dreams" the play of the world and teaches various methods of preserving the higher self by extracting "Bliss-waves" from the great cosmic Ocean of Existence. Vishnu, the Lord of the Universe, is generally visualized as blue in color. In his original form, he reclines on a great many-headed serpent, the embodiment of infinity, who supports him on the cosmic Ocean. It is said that nine different incarnations of Vishnu have manifested in the world. This myth seems to be an ancient rendering of evolutionary theory; the first incarnation was a fish, then a tortoise, a boar, a man-lion, a dwarf, a warrior, a heroic killer of demons, the Eternal Youth (Krishna), and the Buddha (the intellectual aspect). A tenth incarnation, Kalki, has yet to appear; he is the cosmic horseman of the Apocalypse

who will come to destroy all corruption of this Age.

Many other forms of Vishnu are described in the texts, some of them having four or six arms, which iconographically expresses his multiple roles in a single visualization. Lakshmi, the female counterpart of Vishnu, is conceived as white or red in color, depending on her sentiment, and holding a lotus flower as her special symbol. She too can take many different forms, even multiplying herself to become the different "wives" of her Divine Lover.

The *Prapanchasara Tantra* provides this richly detailed visualization of Vishnu and Lakshmi, which may be practiced by the couple in endeavoring to evoke the divinity within. It states,

Think of a beautiful garden filled with wish-granting trees, fragrant with the scent of flowers and harmonious with the rhythmical humming of large bees. Then meditate on Vishnu, seated upon the great Garuda-bird, who rests upon a red lotus. This form of Vishnu is of a red color, expressive of the erotic sentiment, brilliant like the hibiscus flower and shining with the force of millions of rising suns. He manifests as a handsome youth, exuding sweet-scented nectar and loving kindness; he holds various weapons, including the conch shell, club, bow and discus, and his eyes are gazing upon the face of his consort Lakshmi, who embraces him with the fullness of her love. Encircling this Divine Couple are many beautiful women, with heavy thighs, hips and breasts, smiling erotically, moving voluptuously and sensuously forming their hands into the shapes of lotuses. Their lips are parted, but they are silent in a tremulous kind of passion; with clothes and hair in disorder, their eroticism is openly expressed.

VISHNU

the preserver

Such a visualization evokes the erotic sentiment, which in turn circulates vital energy. Erotic thought has an immediate effect on the rate of breathing, the heartbeat and the flow of energy. Tantra teaches that the role of woman is multifarious; a woman can easily become a number of women. If a woman allows herself to become multiple in her manifestations as girl, wife, mistress, whore, virgin and so on, there will be an immediate increase in the vital sexuality of her man. This happens on a basic energy level; it is biological and psychological at the same time. The expansion of consciousness in a woman naturally creates multiple anima-characters. A man exists primarily in multiple roles, such as hunter, hero,

husband, lover or businessman. Through the expansion of consciousness he naturally distills these into a single entity, which on the highest level of Tantra is the Yogi, or Guru archetype. The ability of a woman to become "all women" for her man is a great source of raw energy and a tremendous vitalizing contribution to a relationship.

Vishnu and Lakshmi together rule over the erotic sentiment, particularly in its function as the sustaining force of existence. Vishnu and Lakshmi also rule over the element of water, without which we cannot maintain our worldly existence. The erotic urge generates profuse and moist secretions; this is essential to our well-being, both in the realm of materiality and that of spirituality. The *Skanda Purana*, a Hindu text, declares, "Everything proceeds by sexual intercourse. Without sexual love all creatures dry up."

A Maharaja in Tantric union with his consort and four other women simultaneously. This form of eroticism should be understood on three levels: as an expression of the multifarious roles of woman within a monogamous relationship; then on the level of a polygamous sexual encounter with energy access and circulation as the criterion; finally and iconographically this form of love-making is known in Tantra as the "union of the five senses." From a miniature painting, Kotah, India, late eighteenth century.

The myths of Hinduism tell us that the son of Vishnu and Lakshmi is the Love god, Kama. A kind of Indian Cupid, he shoots arrows made of flowers on a bow made from flowers and bees. Symbolic of the senses and the erotic play, this account of the "birds and bees" is an interesting variation on the Western concept. Kama is extremely handsome, as Shiva granted him the gift of eternal youth and beauty. Kama embodies the love of Vishnu and Lakshmi; often pictured riding on a dove, he has the cuckoo and bee as his allies. He is especially remembered during Springtime and at the moment of ritual love-making. It is Kama who is evoked in the hearts of lovers; the *Kama Sutra* is his song, the "Melody of Love."

The eighth incarnation of Vishnu is known as Krishna, the playful child or "Eternal Youth," who is depicted in a bluish color and is the popular expression of the erotic sentiment in present-day India. Tantric sexual rites often recapitulate the legends of Krishna, who "sports erotically with the Gopis, the cow-herding women, encircling him, vying for his attention." The Gopis, who milk the cows and churn for butter, are symbolic of the erotic play in life. They also represent the inner swirling of emotion during the process of spiritualization.

The circular erotic dance of Krishna with the beautiful Gopis expresses both the inner swirling of sexual energies in the psychic centers of transformation and the swirling of galaxies in the macrocosm. This "Krishna Lila" or "Krishna's Play" is a psycho-cosmic glyph of energy transformation in the Tantric tradition. It is an erotic dance that evolves from the multifarious nature of woman in her expansive capacity, circulating and constantly changing around the single absolute archetype of God-man, the ever playful Krishna.

The ideal of the Krishna Lila is very popular in contemporary India, despite the tendency to more puritanical religious

The Krishna Lila: The "Play of Krishna." This is a psychocosmic glyph of energy transformation. The beautiful Gopis encircle Krishna. Each one believes that her specific existence is dancing with him alone. From a painting in the collection of the Maharaja of Jaipur, *circa* 1800.

modes of expression. Spiritual sensuality has, in general, been repressed in the East, largely because of the influence of Moslem and Christian invaders. Nevertheless, Indian wives still like to think of themselves as Gopis serving Krishna, and popular devotional songs express this longing for liberation through sensuality.

The Gopis are aspects of Lakshmi, just as Krishna is a manifestation of Vishnu. Each Gopi claims Krishna for her very own; any separation from him creates an intense longing. The Gopis represent refinements of the great emotional force of eroticism. Longing is an essential ingredient in all mystic transformation; it is the emotional surge that can break through all barriers of dualism or conventionality. Without longing and a sense of "specialness," woman ceases to express her multifarious roles. This is a sexual secret that Tantra has utilized as a potent method of increasing the ability for transcendence. Gopis are "Shaktis charged with longing," vying for the attention of a single focused "Lord." In the stories of Krishna he appears to multiply himself into identical aspects and therefore is able to make love simultaneously with all the Gopis. Each feels satisfied that Krishna is hers and hers alone. In this play, Krishna is not unfaithful; he is merely unconventional, projecting his single identity into exact illusory replicas of himself. Each of the Gopis is an aspect of the one Lakshmi. The Krishna Lila is the mythic expression of the Divine Love of Vishnu and Lakshmi, through which the Gopis (representing the emotions) are purified.

Conventional love conforms to predictable patterns; it is the love between husband and wife, believed to produce spiritual fruits through the establishment of the family. This is the way of the world; of service between husband and wife, between parent and child, and of the whole family to the line of ancestors. This path was highly exalted in ancient civilizations such as China and Egypt, and in the West as well until recent times. Marriages were an endorsement to produce children; a man either divorced a woman who could not produce children or took another wife. An impotent man was considered the most unfortunate of all, since he could do nothing to ensure a

blood relative acting on his behalf in the future. Conventional spirituality in all cultures meant blood ties, liberation in the long term through family success, and insisted on the duties of children to their parents even beyond their worldly existence.

The current rise of materialism has perverted the path of conventional love without offering a valid alternative. Conventional love, in the present time, frequently is viewed as limited and lacking novelty. The established conventions have lost their meaning. There is no spiritual activity in present-day Western culture designed to strengthen or add meaning to marriage. A once happily married couple now commonly find that, over the years, they are drifting apart; their marriage contract has become meaningless. Today this is more the rule than the exception, as the ever rising divorce rate testifies.

Unconventional love is unpredictable and spontaneous, based on pure feeling. It is usually deemed illicit, occurring outside the boundary of socially sanctioned love. Eastern mysticism credits unconventional love with enormous potential for transcendence. It is said to lead to Divine Love, if the energy can be correctly channeled.

In the present time unconventional love has almost become conventional, yet rarely is there any mystic fruit reaped from this type of relationship. There has been spontaneity, but without mystical direction. The Tantric teachings can give guidance in this matter.

The boundary between the two forms of erotic love is no longer clearly defined. The categories "unconventional" and "conventional" have lost their meaning. Actually it is a question of attitude rather than of categorization. The Tantras teach that it is possible to bring the unconventional into communion with the conventional; to "have the best of both worlds." This is certainly an attitude to be cultivated in the Art of Love. When love-making becomes predictable and boring, communication breaks down. Self-doubt and lack of faith then dominate the relationship.

Try to introduce the Divine archetypes of Vishnu and Lakshmi into your life. Evoke and become them and try to evolve both conventional and unconventional modes of worship through your love-making. Step into the multiple roles of Krishna and the Gopis. Draw upon the rich imagery of the myth of Krishna to explore your own erotic potential. Each woman is capable of becoming all the Gopis; each man has within him the Divine Lover, Krishna. The practical application of this ancient psychological truth provides a way of life that can fulfill and enhance all expectation. Become Vishnu and Lakshmi, and delight in their Eternal Play.

Vishnu and Lakshmi are ever in love-dalliance together; for this purpose they assume various forms. Their changing outer manifestations tell of their inner communication with each other. They are the Eternal Lovers. VISHNU PURANA

Desire, which is known as Kama or "love," is dangerous only when it is considered as the end. In truth Kama is only the beginning. When the mind is satisfied with the culture of Kama, then only can the right knowledge of love arise.

RASAKADAMVAKALIKA

Unconventional love corresponds to the path of non-involvement in the world and contact with the cosmic principles; it is solely for erotic purposes. Conventional or "procreative" love produces immortality through the line of progeny and the accompanying obligations and ancestral rites. Unconventional or "erotic" love offers immortality through the power of sudden release. DURLABHASARA

Kama and Rati in erotic union. Kama is the Love god, the mystic child of Vishnu and Lakshmi. Rati is his wife, the embodiment of sexuality. A Hindu myth tells how, after Kama was slain by Shiva for using his powers to help Parvati seduce this supreme Yogi, Rati acquired a blessing that restored her husband to life in the form of an Eternal Youth. From an Indian painting of the eighteenth century.

Woman is the Initiatress, the birth-giver, the evoker of
pleasure to the Three Worlds, the kind and compassionate
one. As the object of the five senses, woman is endowed
with Divine Form.

CHANDAMAHAROSANA TANTRA

woman:
the initiatress of love

All ancient cultures with a strong esoteric
foundation have traditions extolling the
initiatory power of woman. Egypt, Greece,
Arabia, India, Tibet and China all shared this
belief. Woman was considered the
embodiment of sensuality and guardian of
the creative potential. Every human being is
born through the Yoni of a woman; every
man strives to re-enter this realm of
womanhood through sexual contact.

Socrates sought instruction in the Art of
Love from Diotima. In initiating him, she
stressed the importance of beauty in a
companion, for its capacity to first stimulate
and then elevate passion from the sensual to
the spiritual plane. The Tantric teachings
make the same point. Though physical
beauty is highly valued, it is not enough in
itself. The power and significance of beauty
of soul surpass superficial beauty, as the
example of Socrates himself testifies.

The ideals of beauty are delineated in
such Indian texts as the *Kama Sutra* and
Ananga Ranga. The different types of

women and men are categorized according
to physical, emotional and mental
characteristics. The *Nayika Sadhana Tika*
declares that the woman with whom one
wishes to practice the Art of Love should
"be of exquisite beauty and have an equal
share of excellence of body and mind. Her
sudden appearance will open the door of
emotion and captivate the mind." Another
text poetically declares that the woman
should be "in the fullness of youth, with
eyes which glance arrows of love, features
expressive of all good things, lips stored
with nectar, a body resembling a delicate
and curvaceous creeper, and dressed in
rich-colored silks."

In the Chinese tradition, women also
guarded and transmitted the sexual secrets.
Taoism refers to three different archetypal
initiatory women: the Plain Girl, the Dark
Girl and the Elected Girl. The most
comprehensive erotic handbooks of China,
such as the *Classic of the Secret Methods of the Plain
Girl*, the *Sexual Handbook of the Dark Girl* and

Kama, the Love god, with his consort Rati as the
embodiment of eroticism and the initiatory power of
woman. From an Indian painting of the eighteenth century.

the *Sexual Recipes of the Plain Girl*, take the form
of an intimate dialogue, where the woman
initiates the man into the arcana of sex.

Concerning the choice of a woman
suitable as a magical and potent sexual
partner, the Plain Girl declares, "Such
women are naturally tender and gentle.
Their hairs are silky, their skin soft and their
bones fine; being neither too short nor too
tall, neither too thin nor too fat, the lips of
their sex organ should be full and their
Pleasure Grotto naturally moist. During the
sexual act, they should exude copious fluid
and move their body in such a way that the
man is continually excited. Their ideal age is
between twenty-five and thirty."

The *Hevajra Tantra*, an important Indian
text, states, "He who is well versed in Yoga
should give honor to the mother and sister,
likewise to the dancer, the washerwoman,
the outcaste woman and the noblewoman
equally. He should combine the Scepter of
his Means with the Lotus of her Wisdom.
From this rite, liberation is obtained." This
seemingly enigmatic declaration actually
points to the initiatory power of
womanhood. Further on occurs the
following clarification: "Gnosis is called the
'mother' because she gives birth to the
world; likewise she is known as 'sister'
because her affection is constant, 'dancer'
because of her tremulous nature,
'washerwoman' because she tinges all beings,
and 'outcaste' because her inner essence is
untouchable."

Even in Christianity, a religion notably
hostile to sexuality and "the flesh," the
tradition of courtly love arose, in which

ideal love of a mistress converges with and
leads to the beatific love of God. To be sure,
this tradition relied on the repression and
sublimation of sexual energy, but this
sublimated energy was put in the service of
a transcendental end. It is curious that
Muhammad the Prophet of Islam, who
himself kept nine wives (his special privilege),
never referred to the initiatory power of
woman. A credible tradition states that he
himself once declared, "I have been granted
four favors which others have not; these are
the qualities of generosity and courage, the
capacity for frequent sexual union and the
ability to very rapidly regenerate my
strength." There is even a recorded instance
when he had sexual union with each of his
nine wives separately in a single night,
performing an act of ritual washing after
successive sexual encounters. Unfortunately,
he never credited his extraordinary capacity
for regeneration to the multiple and
initiatory power of his wives. This feminine
power is very strongly confirmed in many
archaic magical traditions. Chinese Emperors,
for example, were supposed to have nine
ordinary consorts every night and the
Empress for two nights over the full moon.

The initiatory power of woman is
tremendous, resting primarily in the mental
attitude to sensual mysticism. By taking an
active role and exploring the whole range of

The sex-initiatress. Taking the active role
during love-making, she is here depicted
making mystic gestures with her hands.
Energy is being re-circulated by the
positioning of her fingers. From a Chinese
painting of the Ming period.

Woman in the role of initiatress. From a Roman fresco, Naples Museum.

sexual secrets during love-making, a woman can endow transcendental power on her lover. This power, the highest form of Shakti, is a direct expression of the opened-up intuition, a "Wisdom-energy," spontaneous and joyful, which can break down all barriers. A woman should confidently initiate her man into mystical experience. Success rests on pure spontaneity, the ability to trust in and surrender to higher ideals, and the earnest desire to give "something special" to her lover. Self-confidence is the essential ingredient in all rites of initiation, and it is the goddess within each woman who initiates.

A woman initiates through that same Yoni from which, in a previous life, the man was born before. A woman initiates through those same breasts which, in a previous life, suckled the man before. A woman initiates with that same mouth which once gently calmed the man before. A woman is the supreme initiatress of Tantra.

KAULARAHASYA

The Secret Dakini-queen absorbed all the peaceful and wrathful deities into her body. She transformed the Yogi Padma into a seed-sound which rested on her lips, where she conferred the Long-life Blessing. Then she swallowed this seed-sound and inside her stomach Padma received the secret initiation of Boundless Compassion. At the region of the Kundalini, in the sex center, she conferred initiation of body, speech and mind.

PADMA THANG YIG

Woman the Initiatress of Love. Taking the active role, she confers her intuitive awareness and Wisdom-energy on her partner. From a Chinese hand-colored wood print of the Ming period.

the dancer

The dancer is a figure closely associated with sexual energy and the female power of initiation. A mystic song of the Tantric tradition declares that "The dancing-girl has the power to initiate the process of sexual rejuvenation." Many temples of the ancient world housed dancers, whose dancing conveyed the very essence of eroticism. Their presence in the temples of India shocked and offended the puritanical morality of the British, who passed laws forbidding such activities. It is unfortunate that the sexual prowess of the temple dancers caused the British to mistake them for prostitutes.

The temple dancers or "Devadasis" (literally "servants of God") of India were divided into various categories. The highest were experts at the different kinds of Yoga and through years of training developed control over their body functions. As initiatresses of Tantric Yoga, they served an important role. They were considered to be the mistresses of the temple gods, the embodiments of the Gopis, and emanations of Lakshmi. The prosperity of the country was believed to be related to the rites and activities of the temple dancers.

The courts of Kings and Emperors were filled with dancing-girls, whose function was to evoke the erotic sentiment and to engender a mood of spirituality and love. In ancient Egypt, the dancing-girls of the court or temple were believed to have power over life and death; many became influential as priestesses, for dance lends itself to expressing esoteric concepts that cannot be described by words or static pictures. Dance embodies the full range of emotions; thus it can reveal the Subtle Body of Tantra in all its glory.

The following contemporary account by Allen V. Ross stunningly illustrates the sexual role of the Indian temple dancer:

The girl entered softly on bare feet. She knelt before me and kissed my feet. She was good-looking, about thirty, with a face that was at once worldly and childlike. Her body was completely sheathed in a transparant gold silk sari. Her hands, feet and head were bare, except for some gold jewelry that jangled as she moved. She began to dance without any accompaniment at all. This Devadasi conveyed sexuality with every little twitch of her rouged lips, the gestures of her hands, the movements of her head, the stamping of her feet, the roll of her eyes. The opening and shutting of her nostrils, the sinuous twisting of her firm but pliable body, was an amazing performance. I could feel the electrical charges of the girl's erotic magic and it seemed to me that she was using only a fraction of her skills. Her dance, slow and ecstatic, was highly symbolic, displaying various sexual moods, from enticement and arousal to seduction and final rapture. It must have lasted hours and I was completely taken with her. Then she possessed me. There was no vulgar striptease. She daintily slipped out of her clothes, displaying a supple body the color of wild cinnamon. She told me to lie on the mat. After that it was just my Lingam and her Yoni in cosmic union. Her intimacies possessed me. I was devoured. She was what the Hindus call the "sarao-tastryan" or "nutcracker woman," because of the amazing power of her sphincter muscles. I was almost out of my mind. All the while she made murmuring, humming drone sounds that put me into a trance. Suddenly there was an explosion in my brain and I felt myself in another dimension. There were amazing lights and fantastic colors. The walls seemed to be melting and I felt ecstasy in every cell.

An Indian temple dancer. This dance form makes use of erotic body movements and tells a story through gesture and mime. Whole epics were expressed in dance, serving to initiate people into a non-verbal level of understanding. The dance form known as Orissi or "Odissi" is currently closest to the ancient style of Tantric mystic dance.

The dancer: a Yoga posture derived from dance. It is particularly suitable for toning up vitality and circulating energy.

174

VISHNU

the preserver

This description is an accurate account of the potency inherent in the dancer archetype. A dancer needs to gain considerable control over normally automatic responses such as breathing, balance and emotion. This control is similar to the control needed to master the teachings of Tantra. Emotion is the ultimate key; by consciously evoking and channeling the emotions, transcendence can both be achieved personally and transmitted to another person. The emotion of sex is easily evoked through dance. When the body is in a healthy condition and finely tuned, then dance really can become initiation.

The multifarious forms of dance can explicitly or unconsciously convey meaning. All dance forms involving couples present a ritualized, social reflection of the sexual act. The art of spiritual dance has

almost become a thing of the past.

A display of dancing brings out the spectator in everyone. Public dancing and private dancing have distinctly different potentialities. This art form can be performed in solo, for your partner, or improvised together. Let your inhibitions go and indulge your creativity and spontaneity to the limit.

Dance can be many things, an individualistic search for ecstasy, a means of communication, a social activity, a healthful exercise, or a courtship ritual. Of the Sixty-four Arts, dance is one of the most closely related to the Art of Love. The dance of a woman has a unique potential for firing the vitality of man and reviving depleted energies. The tones and rhythms of music incorporated into the erotic dance can enhance and sustain the consummation of love.

Song symbolizes "Mantra" and dance symbolizes meditation. So, singing and dancing, the Yogi always acts with potency. HEVAJRA TANTRA

If in joy, songs are sung, let them be the most excellent Eternal songs. If one dances when joy has arisen, let it be done with release as its object. HEVAJRA TANTRA

There are many delights of visiting dancing-girls. When the dancing is finished he retires to a spacious tower, cooled by the breeze, and there practices the important methods of the Yellow Emperor. He takes the tender hand of a girl as beautiful as Hsi-shih, and the white arm of another one like Mao-shih. Their bodies are beautiful, supple like grass moving in the wind; they put forth all their charms so that one forgets about life and death. PIEN JANG

Some Indian temples had more than five hundred resident dancers in attendance.
They were trained by Yoginis, who had mastered the sexual secrets.

One of the earliest Greek myths on the origins of the gods recounts how the god of Time, Cronus, who was the youngest son of Heaven and Earth, became jealous of his father. Lying in wait, he cut off the erect Lingam of Heaven with a sickle while his father was making love to his mother.

The Lingam of Heaven fell down to the world and a few remaining drops of semen from it impregnated the ocean. Out of the foam of the sea, which broke frothily on the shores of land, the beautiful Love goddess Aphrodite was born.

Aphrodite, who emerged from the water, became the wife of the Fire god, Hephaestus. Though he was the son of Zeus, the Supreme Ruler of the whole world, he was born lame and decidely ugly. Most of his time he spent forging precious metals, making weapons and ornaments. Aphrodite quickly became bored and dissatisfied with her husband and took Ares, the handsome but foolish War god, as a lover.

When Aphrodite's husband learned of her infidelity, he set a trap; with a golden net, forged in his own smithy, he caught her naked in the arms of her lover and called upon the other gods as witnesses. Fleeing in shame, Aphrodite sought refuge on the island of Cyprus, where she gave birth to Eros, the Love god.

The Greek Love goddess Aphrodite is linked directly to Inanna the Fertility goddess of the Sumerians, Astarte the Phoenician Love goddess, Ishtar the Babylonian Love goddess, and Isis the High Priestess and Egyptian Mother goddess. The cult of Aphrodite became famous in Cyprus and influenced Western mysticism considerably. Worshippers came to her island by the thousands from all over the ancient world.

Aphrodite's Phoenician temple at Paphos, Cyprus, showing the sacred black meteorite cone worshipped as the Yoni of the goddess. From a Cypriote coin of the Imperial Roman period, Cyprus Museum, Nicosia.

Women were required to prostitute themselves within the precincts of Aphrodite's temple at Paphos in Cyprus, to any stranger, once, on demand, before becoming eligible for marriage. The money received in this transaction was cherished as a talisman, and no amount was considered too small. Any children born of such unions were brought up in the sanctuary of Aphrodite. Significantly, a woman was still considered a virgin after such ritual prostitution, and children born of this ritual act were said to be "born of a virgin."

We can see that the concept of virgin birth, a central tenet of Christianity, did

Aphrodite as the goddess of Love, Venus, riding on a scallop shell. From a fifteenth-century painting by Botticelli.

not originate with it but was present in Greece, Egypt, India and other ancient civilizations. The twin roles of virgin and whore exerted influence on the sexual expression of women in the ancient world, and made their mark on the female unconscious mind.

Few modern women have not, at some time or other, had fantasies of themselves as prostitutes; others have remained infatuated with virginity. The split in the Western psyche between the archetypes of the "chaste" and "loose" woman is a frequent cause of sexual neurosis in both sexes. The virgin is "pure, unattainable, untouchable outside of conventional marriage, and pristinely spiritual," whereas the whore is "crude, degrading, dissolute and unworthy of respect." Such simplistic ideas still pervade our culture, despite the moves toward sexual liberation.

From earliest times, woman has been associated with the moon, because of her

Sol and Luna, the Sun and Moon, depicted crowned and holding plants, a dove bringing an offering. From a mediaeval alchemical woodcut.

Inanna, the Sumerian Mother-goddess and initiatress into the mysteries. From a terra-cotta sculpture in the Louvre.

monthly cycle, and with the element of water. Man has been associated with the sun and the element of fire. Aphrodite, embodiment of erotic beauty, born out of the water and married to the Fire god, exemplifies the universality of this psycho-cosmic symbolism. The lunar-solar relationship is fully elaborated and refined in the practical sexual Yoga of the Tantric and Taoist traditions.

The art of the Western mediaeval period often represents the Virgin Mary enthroned on the moon. The Greeks had a trinity of virgin goddesses known as Artemis, Hestia and Athena; the first had the moon as her special symbol and was directly associated with Selene, the Moon goddess. The virgin goddesses or *Vestal Virgins* of the Roman tradition were invoked at the beginning and end of all ritual sacrifices. They were believed to be the incarnations of *Wisdom* (Gnosis) and were assigned the task of tending the *Sacred Fire*. One of the three, Hestia, was always depicted wearing a veil, with her right hand resting on her hip. This is, traditionally, the characteristic gesture of the sacred prostitute and even today is regarded as an erotic gesture.

Ishtar, the Babylonian Love goddess or High Priestess, is generally depicted wearing a veil said to "conceal her secrets from the eyes of the uninitiated." The veil was, in ancient times, the traditional mark of both virgins and prostitutes. Ishtar, though also a Mother goddess with children, was addressed ritually and liturgically as "The Prostitute." Similar concepts are found in India, China and other parts of the world, always associated with the Moon mother, who, though a virgin, bore children.

This paradox brings us to the mystery of the *Virgin and the Whore* as exemplified in the Tantric tradition. The initiatory power of woman, dealt with earlier, provides a foundation for understanding these twin sexual roles. The key to this dichotomy lies in the light and dark aspects of the lunar phases that govern the monthly cycle of woman. In Hinduism, the goddess Parvati embodies the moon's bright phases, and the goddess Kali, the dark. In the Greek tradition, Aphrodite and Hecate parallel Parvati and Kali but without so clear a distinction in their mystic attributes.

Stele from Carthage, depicting the goddess Tanit of pyramidic shape and with arms stretched upward toward the crescent moon. To the left is a glyph of an alchemical retort, reminding us that, like the moon, she acts in a renewing and rejuvenative manner.

Parvati and Aphrodite symbolize the white full moon and the principles of preservation and abundance; Kali and Hecate are mystic forms of the dark crescent moon and the principles of dissolution and transcendence. Aphrodite/Parvati represents raw sexual energy in its worldly and productive role, while Hecate/Kali signifies that same sexual energy in its otherworldly and transformative role. The roles of Virgin and Whore may be better understood in the context of the goddesses Aphrodite/Parvati and Hecate/Kali.

As the *Virgin*, woman takes the surrendering role and man acts as the initiator. She is the "clean slate" on which he writes a Karmic message, while she confers and shares her untouchable "pure essence" with him alone. In this role, she embodies conventional love at its most potent level. She is the "pure flower" whose fragrance is his alone to smell.

As the *Whore*, a woman is in the active role; it is she who acts as the initiatress into the mysteries of love. Without any shame or restraint, she is free to give all of herself to him without any restrictions. In this role, woman embodies unconventional love. Sure of her sexuality, she offers herself in service without reservation, guilt or insecurity. She must draw on her own special qualities and confer them on her lover. She is pure Shakti, the power principle of initiation, the *High Priestess*.

Isis, the Egyptian goddess of the Earth and the Moon, symbolizes the productive and preserving principles of Nature. From an ancient Egyptian stone relief.

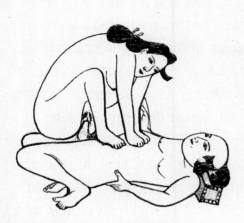

Woman in the active role of an initiatress. From a painted scroll by Yoshida Hamber, Kyoto ukiyo-e school, late seventeenth century, Japan.

performed with a clear and *shared* commitment to a transcendental goal. Frequent concentration on fantasy scenarios during sexual contact commonly leads to boredom and frustration. Sexual union can never be totally fulfilling and consequently unifying unless grounded in a real relationship. The qualities of Virgin and Whore should be incorporated into a relationship for their uplifting and transcendental value.

In much erotic literature, it is the "stolen joys" that taste sweetest; rarely are they shared by the committed couple. However, the bond of true intimacy should add to the capacity for sexual enjoyment rather than restrict it. The key to this seeming contradiction is to bring the unconventional into the shared experience of love.

The women who prostituted themselves in the temple of Aphrodite were ritually acting out what is a fundamental truth to Tantra: the great potency inherent in the spontaneous sexual act. They received their first initiation into eros through contact with a man in this way, and thus became equipped to play the role of Whore for their eventual husbands. Yet they were still considered Virgin. There is certainly an important psychological truth to be learned from this ancient custom. Unconventionality has the ability to *renew* conventionality. When viewed in relation to the light and dark lunar cycle of woman and in relation to the qualities and aspects of Parvati and Kali, the roles of Virgin and Whore take on a deep and mystical significance.

The ancient rites of love were not designed to further promiscuity, but to give meaning to female sexuality. The virgin, muse, whore and goddess can all be embodied in a single woman, just as the boy, hero, lover and god can be found in an individual man. There is today a tendency to separate sexual roles and identify with one to the exclusion of others. This leads to the repression of sexuality and its conversion into fantasy. People then become dishonest about their sexual feelings and instead *cover up* and create complex psychological problems. Fantasy takes over, feelings become atrophied and separation inevitably results.

Though fantasy-inspired sexual role playing is in itself harmless, it rarely produces ecstatic experiences unless

Parvati, favorite of Shiva the Supreme Yogi. As the daughter of the Himalaya Mountain, she personifies abundance and transcendental attainment. She is beautiful like the full moon and holds a trident, datura flower and ritual consecration vase; she makes the gesture of bestowing blessings. From a stone sculpture of the tenth century, Lakshmana temple, Khajuraho.

The extent of a woman's love potential is rarely known, even to those who are objects of her affection. This is because of the subtlety of a woman's love. Women are hardly ever known by men in their true light, though they may love them or become indifferent toward them, may give delight or abandon them, or even extract from them everything that they possess.

KAMA SUTRA

Dancing-girl in the pose of a sex initiatress. Bronze sculpture from the Indus-Valley civilization, Mohenjodaro, *circa* 3000 B.C. After the original in the National Museum, New Delhi.

Passion resides in the woman's right side during the bright fortnight of the lunar month, from new moon to full. The reverse is the case during the dark fortnight. The shifting of passion is believed to take place by the action of light and darkness.

ANANGA RANGA

Each sucks the nectar from the other's lips, breathing lightly, lightly. In those willowy hips the passion beats; the mocking eyes, bright like stars. The tiny drops of sweat are like a hundred fragrant pearls; the sweet full breasts tremble. The dew, like a gentle stream, reaches the heart of the peony; and so they taste the joys of love in perfect harmony. For stolen joys, in truth, are ever the most sweet.

CHIN-P'ING-MEI

Dancing-girl/Yogini in the posture of an initiatress (*ahuyabarada mudra*), inviting the exploration of her mysteries. From a wood sculpture of the eighteenth century, Orissa, India.

active and passive

In "The Virgin and the Whore" we indicated the direct relationship between the submissive and aggressive roles. This flexibility in sexual roles should be fully exercised. Whether the man or woman takes the active role during love-making should depend on spontaneous feeling rather than design.

According to Hindu Tantra, woman by her very nature is the embodiment of Shakti, the active creative principle. It is also said that there is "an inner woman in every man," which refers to the raw energy of Kundalini. A popular Tantric expression states that "Shiva without Shakti is a corpse." It is the Shakti-power of woman that stimulates the erotic sentiment; woman arouses man by channeling this force, whereas man becomes aroused when this Shakti awakens within.

The consummation of love exists at both outer and inner levels. On the outside, in the realm of the sense organs, the play of love is brought about through the contact of the bodies and the senses. On the inside, erotic play takes place in the Subtle Body, the mind and the spirit.

Both outer and inner loving require moments of activity and passivity. The self or *ego* needs to become passive in relation to the Higher Self, one's "spirituality"; and the *will* needs activation and conscious control by the mind in order to awaken the Kundalini and direct it through the psychic centers (Chakras). The Kundalini energy, which is the active principle in sexual union, travels through the psychic centers and finds fulfillment in ecstatic union with the passive Shiva-principle in the Head Center. This is the consummation of inner loving, the goal of Tantra.

Ecstatic sexual orgasm, the outer consummation of love, is a mixture of active and passive, the blending of "fire" and "water," the passions and secretions. Orgasm results from a mutual *giving and taking*, a balance of loss and gain. The inherent bisexuality of both man and woman seeks fulfillment in the exchange of active and passive roles. The mystical, alchemical, Tantric and Taoist teachings

Ardhanarisvara, the androgynous Shiva, with left side female and right side male. The inherent bisexuality of all humans is suggested by this iconographic form. From a stone sculpture of the twelfth century, Bengal.

express this concept in the symbol of the androgyne, the form that is at once both male and female.

The Chinese novel of the late Ming period called *The Way to Holiness through the Flesh* (*Jou Pu Tuan*) contains an illuminating account of how a woman can take the active part during love-making. A bordello madame, who had been taught the technique by a Taoist wizard when she was sixteen, offers the instruction, couching her description in diplomatic terminology:

FIRST PRINCIPLE

It is not the gentleman who should court the lady, but the reverse. If he lies down on his back, she mounts to the saddle and guides his Ambassador into the right channel. When the Ambassador is flushed with enterprise, she holds him tight as a flute in a flute case. When he is listless, she rekindles the flame of his desire with deft finger-play. The wilder the fray, the more active and enterprising she should become; withstanding her adversary's attacks, she should joyously take the counter-offensive. Try as he may, he will be bound to miss certain spots, so the best thing to do is to help him find every sensitive place. Both will benefit. That is what is meant by the Taoist technical phrase "solicitously to lower the Pleasure House [Yoni] toward the Ambassador." That is the first artifice.

SECOND PRINCIPLE

Ready for the fray, the lady takes her place beneath the gentleman. But she does not leave him to do all the work; full of sympathy and understanding, she assists him, taking up his movements and accompanying them. In this way, she turns the game of love into a delightful butterfly chase, giving herself and him a twofold pleasure and at the same time making it easier for the Assailant to arrive at his main goal, her Jewel Enclosure [the womb]. True pleasure must be had in common. The two participants should meet each other halfway. Then their encounter becomes a feast. If the lady does not respond to the gentleman's movements with really sympathetic counter-movements, but remains passive, he might just as well resort to a wooden or cardboard woman with an artificial Pleasure House. Why, then, bother with a living woman of flesh and blood? Every first-class courtesan follows this principle, so gaining the favor of her guests and increasing her own pleasure at the same time. This then is the second artifice, which is designated by the Taoist technical phrase "obligingly to lift her Pleasure House to meet the Ambassador."

THIRD PRINCIPLE

This has to do with something quite extraordinary, something bordering on the magical arts. When there is mutual sympathy between players and they are intimately entangled, a woman should become animated by a desire not to waste the vital essence of her womanhood, not to secrete it for nothing, but to bestow it on her lover for his lasting pleasure. Otherwise she will regret the emission of secretions as a sheer loss, a "loss of capital," so to speak. And so she should resolve that her secretion of vital essence will not be in vain but will redound to her lover's advantage. But how does she go about it?

When she is on the verge of ecstasy, she commands her lover to bring his Tortoise Head close to her Flower Heart [the opening to the uterus], and then to cease all movement. Clasping him in her arms and legs and pressing him close, she gives her belly a very special twist [see "Nurturing Nature"], which causes her Jeweled Enclosure to open and the orifice of her Flower Heart to come to rest precisely on the orifice of his Ambassador. The Ambassador is thus enabled, when ecstasy sets in, to drink her vital essence. It pours directly from her Gateway into his Cinnabar Field [solar plexus] and produces its effect. The wonderful thing about this kind of essence is that it possesses a vitalizing power that no ginseng preparation can approach; moreover, there is nothing like it for prolonging life and rejuvenating the body. This, then, is the third and highest artifice, which is designated by the Taoist technical phrase "sacrificing vital essence for the lover's benefit."

A good lover has no predetermined routine, but can adapt spontaneously to the moment, becoming one with it. An ancient hermetic teaching declares, "As above, so below." As mentioned previously, the person on top echoes the role of Heaven, whereas the one underneath

Taoist love-posture depicting woman "raising up." From a painted scroll of the Japanese school of Hokusai, *circa* 1830.

corresponds to Earth; either the male or the female can fulfill these roles to complete satisfaction. Heaven and Earth "mutually complete each other."

The Moslem teaching on sex, which sought at all costs to keep woman in a subservient position, declares that a woman should "not act the part of a man," adding that this might weaken the man both physically and psychologically.

However, the Indian and Chinese teachings on sexuality emphasize the benefits to be obtained from role switching. In the many postures of love outlined throughout this third part of the book, *active* and *passive* roles are meant to be freely experimented with. Once a natural versatility is gained, the pure joy of intimate love-making can be experienced in the exchange between active and passive.

Though a woman is naturally reserved and keeps her feelings concealed, yet when she gets on top of a man she should show all her love and desire. A man should gather from the actions of the woman above him of what type of disposition she is, and in what way she likes to be enjoyed.

KAMA SUTRA

There is a particularly potent form of love-making that is known as the <u>Method of the Large Bee</u>. In this, the wife, having placed her husband full length upon the bed or carpet, sits squatting upon his thighs and closes her legs firmly after she has inserted his Lingam into her Yoni. Moving her waist in a circular way, churning as it were, she enjoys her husband and thoroughly satisfies hereself. While thus reversing the natural order, the woman should draw in her breath, in the way known as <u>Sitkara</u>; she should smile gently and show a kind of half-shame. Then she should say, "O husband! Today you have become subjected to me, being totally defeated in the Battle of Love." Moreover, she should remember that, without a special exertion of will power on her part, the husband's pleasure will not be perfect. To this end she must ever strive to close and constrict the Yoni until it holds the Lingam, as a finger, opening and shutting at her pleasure, and finally, acting as the hand of the Gopi maiden who milks the cow. This can only be learned by practice and especially by throwing the power of the will into the part to be affected. While so doing, she should mentally repeat the name of the Love god, Kamadeva.

ANANGA RANGA

Woman in the active role. Ancient Greek and Roman love-postures show a wide range of variety. The initiatory power of woman playing the active role was well known. From a Roman marble carving, Naples Museum.

the red and the white

In Eastern cultures, the color red is associated with the female principle and the color white with the male. In ancient China, red always symbolized woman, creative power, sexual potency and a happy, successful life. Brides usually wore red silk under trousers and marriage was referred to as the *Red Affair*. Red lanterns were suspended outside wine-houses and brothels; even burial gifts were painted red in the belief that this would help preserve them from decay.

In India and Tibet, the color red has very similar connotations. It has always suggested dynamic femininity, creative power, passion and sexual energy. Red symbolized fire in the Tantric tradition, and red marks are applied to the forehead of both men and women as a ritual reminder of and a symbolic identification with the Kundalini, the creative energy within. The central point of mystic diagrams, such as the *Sri Yantra*, is usually colored red and is known as the *Shakti Bindu*, the energy point. In Tantra, red is the color code of passion and transcendental delight. The *Red Dakini*, an ecstatic red-colored goddess in the form of a young girl filled with passion, symbolizes in Tantra the refinement of emotion.

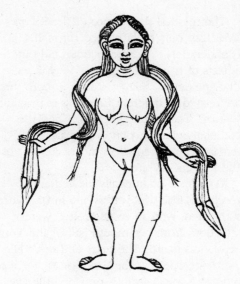

The White Dakini symbolizes the removal of ignorance and worldliness. Her form is visualized as an ideal Yogini, who has the power of initiation into the Wisdom-teachings of Tantra. From a Tibetan painting of the late eighteenth century.

Islam attributes similar qualities to the color red. Moslems use the adjective "red" when describing a beautiful woman. There is a popular Arabic saying that "beauty is red" and red-colored veils are considered particularly seductive: "If ever you go out, my girl, put on a veil of red," declared a famous Arab poet. In the West, we too have sexual associations with the color red; for example, the red heart of Valentine's day, the *Scarlet Woman* and the "red-light district" all have sexual overtones. Red light stimulates the sex hormones of the male, and has long been the color associated with sensuality and pleasure.

In ancient China, the color white symbolized man, the transcendence of all worldly things, death and mourning. Burial ceremonies were always referred to as the *White Affair* and white was worn at funerals; this custom is practiced throughout the East to this day.

In India, celibates traditionally wear white. White is associated with Yoga, meditation and Shiva, who is often described as being "white as camphor." In Tibet, the *White Dakini* is worshipped and identified with for the "removal of worldliness" and Avalokiteshwara, the Compassionate Savior, the symbol of transcendence through the removal of delusion, is depicted as white. Islam strongly identifies white with purity, masculinity, leadership and mysticism.

Sri Yantra, a mystic diagram comprised of nine interlaced triangles; the five upward-pointing ones symbolize Shiva-principles and the downward triangles symbolize Shakti-principles. Depicted as white and red, this *Yantra* evokes the unity of Shiva and Shakti. From a Rajasthani painting, *circa* 1800.

The mystical significance of the *Red and White* can only be fathomed through a consideration of both the inner and outer aspects of man and woman. We will see that the *red and white forces* exist in both, but are related to different functions in man and woman. The natural bisexuality and the complementary attributes of male and female reveal themselves in the context of the Red and White.

Woman is traditionally viewed as receptive, intuitive, watery and lunar. When stimulated, woman emits profuse watery secretions from her mouth (saliva) and Yoni (sexual discharge). The texts of Taoism and Tantra declare that the Shakti or Yin-force of woman is inexhaustible, provided she lives a natural and harmonious life. A woman becomes "fiery" when her passions are stirred up; emotions cause this arousal, altering her rate of breathing, and stimulating her navel center. When a woman has her monthly period, she emits red blood, and after giving birth, she produces white milk to feed her baby.

A Tantric Yogi displaying the centers of the Subtle Body. The cooling moon of the head center distills the psychic heat of the navel center. From a Rajasthani miniature painting of the late eighteenth century.

Woman cries more readily than man when emotionally upset or stimulated.

Man embodies the qualities of aggression and logic. Traditionally associated with the sun and the element of fire, man has a tendency to become dry-mouthed and red-faced when angry. Man rarely cries when upset, but becomes more fiery. When the passions of man are stimulated, his rate of breathing increases; his *inner fire* at the navel center of psychic transformation flares up. In sexual excitement, this awakens the dormant Kundalini-energy, his *inner woman*, which surges up the spinal column in wave after wave and "melts the moon" in the head center. The physical correlate of the head center is the pineal gland, which regulates and controls sexual secretions. Man's sexual stimulation culminates in ejaculation of white-colored semen.

The *Goraksapaddhati*, an important Hindu Yogic text, declares, "The quintessence of the body is of two kinds. These are the *white and red Bindus* [literally "seeds" or "points"], the former of which is of the nature of semen and the latter of which is of the nature of the ovum." The text goes on to say, "Semen is concentrated originally in the *inner moon of the head center*, and is the attribute of Lord Shiva, the Yogi par excellence. The ovum is concentrated originally at the *inner sun of the navel center* and is the attribute of Shakti, the goddess of all becoming." This text presents a clear outline of the twin aspects of lunar and solar forces in the two main bodily centers. It is interesting to note that in this description of the location of the original archetypal sexual forces, the normal "worldly" roles of Shiva as the sun and Shakti as the moon are reversed. Once again, this points to the original hermaphroditic nature of the human psycho-organism.

Every man and woman is the product of the synthesis of sperm and ovum, "seed" and "egg." A Tantric text declares, "Seed is generated inside the body of man and the egg is created in the body of woman. This takes place by virtue of the intake of food rightly digested, which becomes successively transformed into blood, flesh, fat, bones, marrow and vital essence, the whole process requiring exactly twenty-eight days to complete." This one-month period is, of course, identical to the menstrual cycle of woman.

Snakes conjoined and preparing to mate.

In man's body, the most refined sublimation of food is transformed into sperm, which, according to Tantra, contains the man's mental, emotional and physical characteristics in *living* and transmittable form. Modern embryology confirms this concept.

Sperm is a very complex substance, with the capacity to live and retain "consciousness" for a long time after ejaculation. Recent tests by Cleve Backster suggest that sperm that has been released and contained "recognizes" and responds to the presence of the original donor. These tests have been conducted under laboratory conditions, using a technique known as polygraphy. It is logical to suppose that the same reaction occurs when the sperm is inside the body of a woman. The conscious resonance between sperm and donor long after ejaculation is the rationale for magical spells that specify the use of human sperm for empowering amulets and talismans.

Though ejaculated sperm has been observed to remain alive for only a few days under normal conditions, female snakes (the symbol of the Kundalini-energy) have the ability to store sperm from a male snake and use it to impregnate themselves more than six months later. Both Tantric and Taoist texts describe methods of storing and transforming sperm into an inner "lunar effulgence," the *Soma*. A text declares, "The Yogi can cause his seed to rise up to his head

center, where it becomes transformed into *Soma*, the Elixir of gods." In contrast to woman, who has an unlimited supply of vital essence and can therefore have repeated orgasms, man makes sperm from all parts of his body and is limited in how many times he can ejaculate in a single love-session. Sperm is produced from digested food over the period of a month. A man must eat invigorating food in order to replace the loss of vital body elements from repeated ejaculations of sperm. If a man continues to have sex to excess, without eating sufficiently, at a certain point he will ejaculate blood.

The *Red and the White* of Tantric and Taoist teachings are referred to as *materiality-producing forces*. In the outer world, the red force is the *male solar principle*, the fire element, whereas on an inner level, it is the *female inner sun*, the Shakti. Likewise, the white force of the outer world is the *female lunar principle*, the water element, whereas on the inner level, it is the *male inner moon*, the Shiva. This subtle play between external and internal is the key to many practices of Tantric Yoga that lead to the understanding of the relationship of macrocosm to microcosm.

The symbolism of red and white pervades Eastern art and iconography. It is a color coding that indicates the active and passive principles, the "plus" and "minus" of each situation. For example a Japanese Tachikawa text of sexual mysticism includes a colored picture of the sexual cosmogram known as the *Double Mandala of the Two Worlds*, which depicts a man and woman, naked but for their ritual headdress, lying in sexual embrace on an eight-petaled lotus flower. He has his head between the woman's feet and is on top of her, while her head is between his feet. Their legs and arms are stretched out to coincide with the eight petals of the lotus. The man's body is white and the woman is colored crimson. The spot where they join is marked with the magic syllable "AH," which in Tantra is the first vowel sound, the "beginning of all things."

Many similar red and white diagrams exist in Tantra and Taoism. Sometimes they are

Tantric love-posture for channeling and circulating the energies of ecstasy.

figurative, at other times they are abstract. Western alchemical treatises employ the same color symbolism with the identical meaning found in the Oriental texts. For example, texts that refer to the "Blood of the Red Lion and the Tears of the White Eagle," which is said to be the "treasure of the whole earth," are veiled accounts of the making of pure spirituality (the alchemical "gold") by the correct balancing of the red and white forces of woman and man through mystical love-making. A helpful meditation is for a couple to lie together in close sexual embrace, visualizing the man as white and the woman as red. This practice is a powerful tool for awakening and channeling sexual energy. When linked to the more detailed visualization of the inner sun blazing red, and the inner moon cooling white, and to the right and left vital nerves of the Subtle Body, it has the effect of totally transforming sexual union.

By visualizing themselves as red and white, the couple can more easily evoke the inner sun and moon of their conjoined psyches. The right and left vital nerves of the Subtle Body are brought into harmony through this Tantric meditation.

The red and white materiality-producing forces become the unitary creative potentiality. Physically the organism becomes a transfigured body, composed of mentally-spiritually radiant Light, Bliss and Potent Voidness.   NAROPA

A man should imagine that in his Cinnabar Field, just below the navel, there is a bright red essence, golden inside and red with streaks of white outside. He should imagine this essence as dividing itself into a sun and moon that move around in that region and then ascend to a point at the base of his brain, where the two halves are united again. Meanwhile he should let his sex organ be still, deep inside the woman, while above he sucks in the woman's saliva and below he absorbs her sexual secretions. As soon as he senses that his semen is moving and he is about to ejaculate, he should quickly withdraw his sexual organ. Only practiced adepts can achieve this. His Cinnabar Field is located just below his navel and his head center is opposite the two eyes, at the back. He should imagine it as having the form of sun and moon, about three inches in diameter, and joined like one shape. This is what is known as Sun and Moon in Close Conjunction. It is very good to concentrate on this image when making love.   FANG-NEI-PU-I

VISHNU

the preserver

Yin and Yang in union. The balance of Yin and Yang upholds the cosmic order (Tao). Yin symbolizes centrifugal force, movement away from the center, the female principle, passivity, receptivity, night and the watery element. Yang symbolizes the centripetal force, movement toward the center, the male principle, aggressiveness, dynamic activity, day and the fiery element.

harmonization of mood

Both Taoist and Tantric sexological texts stress the importance of complete *harmonization of mood* between the partners. Any forced love-making is potentially damaging to health. An ancient Taoist text emphasizes this: "Yin and Yang, the female and male essential principles, undergo each other's influence. When Yang does not obtain Yin, it is sad, and if Yin does not obtain Yang, then it will not become active. If the man wants to make love but the woman does not feel like it, then it means that their hearts are not yet in harmony and their vital essence is not yet aroused."

The Taoist master Tung gives the following instructions for harmonizing the mood between the lovers:

He should seize her delicate waist and fondle her Jade-like body. Talking of being bound together,

with one heart and a single intent, they should embrace and kiss, suck tongues, press close and caress each other's ears and head. Soothing above and stimulating below, the many coqueteries are revealed. Then the woman should take his Jade Stalk in her left hand, while he strokes her Jade Gate with his right; moved by the life-force of the female element, his Jade Stalk becomes excited; stimulated by the life-force of the male element, her Jade Gate begins to bubble over, like a stream flowing into a valley. When this point is reached, harmonization of mood has been attained.

When they wish to make love, a couple should first engage in gentle foreplay, so their mood becomes harmonized and their emotions become responsive. The stimulation of the senses is essential to inner harmonization. Classical Indian texts suggest that the environment should be used to assist harmonization of mood, along with all the Sixty-four Arts, wherever appropriate. All Eastern treatises on sexuality are unanimous in declaring that love-making should never be rushed, so allowing harmonization of mood to occur naturally.

Taoist love-posture for harmonization of mood. From a woodblock print of the Master Moronobu, *circa* 1680, Japan.

He should loosen her girdle and the knot of her cloth, and turning up her lower garment, should massage her naked thighs. He should teach her some of the Sixty-four Arts and tell her how much he loves her.
                                                                                    KAMA SUTRA

Every time a man wishes to make love, there is a certain order of things to be followed. In the first place, the man should harmonize his mood with that of the woman. Only then will his Jade Stalk rise.
                                                                                    SU-NU-CHING

four moments: four joys

Eastern esoteric treatises distinguish four stages of love-making that are linked to the four main psychic centers where sexual energy is concentrated and transformed. The four stages are expressed through erotic signals: the smile, the erotic gaze, the embrace, and sexual union.

Tantra views the stages of love-making as mirroring a greater cosmology that links the fourfold evolvement of emotion, psychological processes, mystic consecrations, types of consciousness, psychic centers, meditations, primordial sounds, colors, forms, visions and ecstatic joys to four mystical *Moments of Union*, which are called Variety, Development, Consummation, and Transcendence. A recurring statement found in the Tantras is that "everything goes in fours." This is particularly applicable to the psycho-cosmic approach to sexuality found in Eastern mystical teachings.

By understanding the natural genesis of love-making, the couple can control and channel sexual ecstasy in an uplifting, evolutionary direction. Orgasm can be built on orgasm and linked to highly personalized mystic experiences.

The fourfold evolution of ecstasy from the erotic smile through sexual intercourse is linked to biophysical changes in both partners and to psycho-physical experiences. The Bliss-wave of ecstasy passes through four spiritual desire-realms, from physical contact to longing, high passion and transcendence. In these four stages, the sentiment of love is developed and sublimed.

To fully understand the secret teachings of Taoism and Tantra, it is important to learn to recognize the fourfold nature of sexuality in all its manifestations. Tantras teach that the erotic smile, the erotic gaze and the intimate embrace are all worldly levels of sex, whereas actual physical union is non-worldly or "other worldly." Similarly the elements of earth, water, fire and air, which are resolved through the psychic centers of the sex to navel region, heart region, and throat region (see chart of Fourfold Evolution of Ecstasy According to the Tantric Tradition), relate to

The Bliss-wave of Tantric ecstasy. When sexual energy is controlled and channeled consciously, there is no limit to the human capacity for transcendence.

Progressing from state [1] to [4]

VISHNU

the preserver

	[1]	[2]	[3]	[4]
Erotic Signal	Erotic Smile	Erotic Gaze	Intimate Embrace	Sexual Union
Physical Requirement	Honoring	Adoration	Propitiation	Sexual Fulfillment
Spiritual Desire	Physical Contact	Longing	High Passion	Transcendence
Psychic Center	Navel Region to Sex Center	Heart Region	Throat Region	Head Region
Number of Nerve Channels	64	8	16	32
Sound of Center & Color	Ham (White)	Hum (Black)	Om (Red)	Ah (Yellow to Solar Red)
Element	Water and Earth	Fire	Air	Space
Sound of Element	Vang and Lang	Rang	Yang	Hang
Shape for Visualization	Circle and Square	Triangle	Crescent	Flaming Point
Color of Shape	White and Yellow	Red	Dark	Bright Like Full Moon
Type of Consciousness	Waking	Sleeping	Dreaming	Beyond (Fourth Dimension)
Mystical Moment of Union	Variety	Development	Consummation	Transcendence
Type of Joy	Emotional	Perfect	Absolute	Innate

Stages [1] to [3] relate to worldly levels of action. State [4] relates to action out of this world.

preservation of physical existence, whereas the element of space and the head center relate to transcendence and to non-physical existence.

Each of the four stages of ecstasy is linked to a type of consciousness and to a particular kind of mystical experience, and is understood in the Tantric tradition as a separate initiation. Mantras, especially those that are given in the chart, and visualizations can be helpful in blending the shared experience of ecstasy.

The Four Moments and Four Joys cannot be adequately written about or described.

They are to be experienced consciously and joyously by the dedicated couple. By meditating on the fourfold mystery of eroticism, the heart becomes better able to reach out to others.

The Tantras distinguish four types of woman and advise a man to be well versed in the *Four Techniques*, which operate on both the physical and the psychological level: Downward Motion, Retention, Backward Motion and Saturation. These, too, are linked to the production of the Four Joys. A Tibetan text explains them thus:

DOWNWARD MOTION

is like a smith hammering a metal mirror, making the Four Types of Delight descend slowly, like a tortoise, from the head to the sexual region, so realizing the delights in their natural order.

RETENTION

is to hold the delight as one would a lamp in a storm.

BACKWARD MOTION

is like an elephant drinking water, making the Four Joyous Delights ascend to the head region and keeping them stable.

SATURATION

is like a farmer watering his crops, very carefully, to ensure that every pore of the skin is fully saturated with the consummation of love.

By bearing in mind the visual imagery of the Four Techniques, the couple can learn to generate wave upon wave of love and truly channel the Four Moments into Four Joys.

A Hindu maharaja practicing a Tantric love-posture with his consort and two female attendants. This type of posture symbolizes the unity of the three principal subtle channels of Tantra. From a Rajasthan miniature painting of the eighteenth century.

There are four bases of magical power. There is the Heart Base, the Neck and Head Base, the Navel Base and the Sex Base. Each one of these secret bases has a presiding goddess or energy.

ADVAYASAMATAVIJAYA

The Four Joys are known as Joy of Emotions, Perfect Joy, Absolute Joy and the Joy Innate. Their manifestation is known as the smile, the gaze, the embrace and full union. They are also known as Variety, Development, Consummation and Transcendence.

HEVAJRA TANTRA

the kiss

The kiss can express a wide range of emotions, from gentleness, tenderness and consideration, to the heights of eroticism and fiery passion. The ancient texts of Taoism emphasize the importance of deep erotic kissing, placing it second only to the act of love itself. In the East, kissing has always been viewed as a deeply intimate part of love-making. It is still rare to see Chinese or Indian couples kissing in public, and until recently the kiss was banned in Indian movies.

Most cultures make use of mouth contact to express sentiments ranging from casual greeting to erotic exchange. In certain primitive tribes, however, the kiss is practically unknown. Eskimos greet each other by rubbing noses, concentrating on the mutual exchange of breath and the subtle scents of the skin. When a couple exchange passionate kisses, all barriers dissolve, and by gazing into each other's eyes, their spirits become harmonized. The mouth-to-mouth kiss—or "contact of the upper gates," as it is called in Tantra—can be skillfully and pleasurably employed to blend sentiments and harmonize emotions.

VISHNU

the preserver

The kiss is a powerful aspect of foreplay, being the closest approximation to the union of Lingam and Yoni. It is said that the shape and size of a woman's Yoni can be determined from the form of her mouth, and a man's Lingam from the size of his nose. Tantra teaches that the mouth combines the characteristics of both Lingam (the tongue) and Yoni (the mouth and lips). Erotic kissing offers the opportunity to explore both male and female qualities. Active and passive roles are readily exchanged as each tongue enters the mouth of the other. Thus the kiss can be used to experiment and develop actions and rhythms that can be extended to the Lingam and Yoni.

Kissing is explored in the Hindu love treatises, which list the parts of the body especially suitable for kissing. The *Kama Sutra* specifies that the forehead, eyes, cheeks, throat, breasts, lips and mouth are the main places for kissing, along with the thighs, arms, navel and Yoni. The placing of a kiss with conscious intent effectively confers psychic protection and stimulates the psychic centers and channels. Placing the mouth over a sequence of points on the body can bring the Subtle Body to life and awaken the sentiments.

The *Kama Sutra* lists three kinds of kisses particularly suited to a *young* woman, referring to these as the *Nominal Kiss* (when the mouths just touch), the *Throbbing Kiss* (when the woman moves her lower lip as her lover presses his lips to her mouth), and the *Touching Kiss* (when the woman uses her tongue). A number of other types of kisses are then described:

THE STRAIGHT KISS:
When the lips of both lovers are brought into direct contact with each other.

THE BENT KISS:
When the heads of both lovers are bent toward each other.

In the Orient kissing is considered an erotic art form. From a woodblock print of the seventeenth century, Japan.

THE TURNED KISS

When one of the partners turns up the face of the other by holding the head and chin.

THE PRESSED KISS:

When the lower lip is pressed forcefully.

THE GREATLY PRESSED KISS:

When the lower lip is held and touched with the tongue and pressed forcefully.

THE KISS OF THE UPPER LIP:

When a man kisses the upper lip of the woman, while she kisses his lower lip.

THE CLASPING KISS:

When one of the partners takes both lips of the other between his or her own lips.

FIGHTING OF THE TONGUE:

When one of the partners touches the tongue, teeth and palate of the other with his or her tongue.

Deep kissing creates an exchange of vital juices between the partners. Tantra teaches that when a couple make love, their bodies produce subtle secretions that are mutually vitalizing and nourishing. Saliva has a special property that is effective in harmonizing the Yin and Yang forces in the couple (see "Medicine of the Three Peaks"). A Tantric love-making technique suggests that the woman place the tip of her tongue against

Kissing exchanges vital secretions and energies. Taoist and Tantric teachings stress the harmonizing value of deep erotic kissing.

the roof of her mouth, just behind the front teeth, as her orgasm approaches. The tongue is then offered to her partner, so he can gently and lovingly suck the sweet saliva produced from her climax. This is a special secret that has great healing and medicinal value to the couple.

Learn to relax the muscles of the face and mouth when kissing. Remember that kissing allows the essential fluids of ecstasy to mingle and combine in the twin "crucibles" of the mouths. When the art of kissing is cultivated, love-making becomes more intense and fulfilling.

When a woman is excited with passion, she should cover her lover's eyes with her hands and, closing her own eyes, thrust her tongue into his mouth. She should move it to and fro and in and out, with a pleasant motion suggestive of more intimate forms of enjoyment to come.

ANANGA RANGA

Kissing is of four kinds: moderate, contracted, pressed and soft. Different kisses are appropriate for different moods.

KAMA SUTRA

the secret of the upper lip

Tantric treatises point out that a woman's upper lip is one of the most erogenous areas of her body. They explain this special sensitivity by a subtle nerve channel that connects her palate and upper lip to her clitoris. Known as the *Wisdom Conch-like Nerve*, it is so named on account of its form, which at the lower end is encircled many times around, like a shell. Many texts suggest that kissing the upper lip and oral sex create a special kind of circuit through which energy flows.

The kissing of the upper lip is referred to in both the *Kama Sutra* and the *Ananga Ranga*. A man can stimulate the upper lip of a woman by gently nibbling and sucking, while she plays with his lower lip with her teeth and tongue. If the teeth are carefully controlled to create waves of pleasure rather than pain, this practice can be very arousing for both partners.

Japanese finger-pressure (Shiatsu), for relaxing and beautifying the body, correlates the upper lip with the digestive and sexual regions. Massage of the upper lip releases sexual energy and stimulates sexual urges.

An ancient Indian tradition calls for mixing a small quantity of finely ground gold-dust with a little honey and applying it to the tongue and upper lip of newly born children. This practice is especially observed with baby girls as it is believed to confer prosperity and enhance beauty and sensuality. Indian medical texts declare that gold and honey in combination stimulate creativity.

The *Goraksa Vijaya*, an important Yogic text, states, "There is a duct from the moon-center of the head to the hollow in the palatal region and upper lip. It is called the *Shankini Nadi*, and is the curved channel through which the Great Elixir passes. It is like a serpent with mouths at both ends. Below, it descends to the Lotus. This nerve is known as the secret or tenth door of the body, through which a subtle nectar flows."

If a woman can visualize the subtle nerve running from her clitoris to her upper lip, she will be able to awaken it and consciously channel sexual energy through it. This nerve is to be visualized as an empty but vibrant tube, with a conch-like shape at the bottom and a mouth at the top. Deep breathing linked to constriction of the Yoni causes this nerve to become stimulated. By gaining control over this secret Tantric nerve, a woman can enhance the pleasures of love-making, both for herself and for her partner.

Tantra teaches that woman has a subtle nerve connecting her clitoris to the region of the upper lip. Known as the Wisdom conch-like nerve, it channels orgasmic energy.

When a man kisses the upper lip of a woman, it is known as the Special Kiss of the Upper Lip. At such a time, she should kiss his lower lip. KAMA SUTRA

When the woman is full of desire, she should take the man's lower lip between her teeth, gently chewing and biting him there. He should do the same to her upper lip, taking care to suck it gently. In this way they both will become sexually aroused and their passion will produce much heat. ANANGA RANGA

the embrace

All contact between the bodies of lovers is known as a form of embrace. The embrace has a great range of significance, from the friendly hug to the passionate intermingling of limbs. It is not the mere physical contact of bodies that constitutes the embrace, but the intentions and emotions behind that contact. Any physical contact between the couple can be called an embrace when it is motivated by love and the desire to express intimacy. When partners hold hands, their fingers intertwined, the hands can be said to be embracing. The *Kama Sutra* suggests that even shampooing can be considered a form of embrace.

A child experiences love from the mother in the form of loving embraces. Without this body contact, the child feels deprived and begins to exhibit neurotic symptoms. Animals in the wild spend a great deal of time in physical contact with one another, preening, cuddling and playing together. This is a process of "bonding," which ties them together, stimulates recognition and harmonizes the group.

Both the *Kama Sutra* and the *Ananga Ranga* list eight kinds of embrace, which are beautifully described. The following is a synthesis of the different types of embrace according to the Indian tradition.

TWINING LIKE A CREEPER
This is a standing embrace, with the woman clinging to the body of the man, in the same way that a creeper twines around a tree trunk. She should raise one leg and put it around his thigh, kissing him

A prince and a lady in standing embrace. From a miniature painting in the collection of the King of Nepal, *circa* 1830.

repeatedly and drawing his head down to hers.

CLIMBING OF A TREE

This is another standing embrace. The man stands and the woman places one of her feet on his and raises the other leg to the height of his thigh, pressing herself against him passionately. Then, encircling his waist with her arms, in the way that a man prepares to climb a palm tree, she should hold and press him forcibly. She should bend her body over his and kiss him as if she were drinking the Water of Life.

MIXTURE OF RICE AND SESAME SEED

This can be either a standing or a lying embrace. The couple should hold each other so closely that the arms and thighs of one are totally encircled by the arms and thighs of the other, rubbing up against them. Then contact between the Lingam and Yoni can be made and maintained for some time.

MIXTURE OF MILK AND WATER

The couple embrace passionately, as if entering into each other's bodies. The limbs of one touch and are entangled with the corresponding parts of the partner's body. This form of embrace can be practiced in a standing, sitting or lying position.

EMBRACE OF THE THIGHS

One of the lovers forcibly presses one or both of the thighs of the other between his or her own. This can be practiced in a number of different positions.

EMBRACE OF THE MIDDLE

The man presses the middle part, the hips, loins and thighs, of the woman to his own. This type of embrace is very pleasant in a sitting position, with either the woman on the man or the reverse.

EMBRACE OF THE BREASTS

The man places his nipples against the breasts of his partner. He should sit close to her, with his eyes closed, while she presses herself to him. It creates excitement and erotic delight.

EMBRACE OF THE FOREHEAD

This is when forehead touches forehead. Great affection is shown by the close pressure of the arms around the waist and by the mutual contact of brows, cheeks, mouths, breasts and bellies.

These eight variations of the embrace are by no means the full limit of possibilities. However, they do express different sentiments and as such are frequently portrayed in Indian art. The embrace is an important aspect of both foreplay and afterplay. A mere touch or embrace, when consciously employed, can greatly assist in the harmonization of mood and emotions. Any differences or feelings of separateness can be overcome by loving embraces.

Use the embrace to bring yourself and your partner closer together and as part of the preparation for physical union. Unite your bodies and hearts in a melting embrace. Dissolve all worldly problems through a tender or passionate mingling of body and soul.

Those embraces that are not mentioned in the treatises on loving should be practiced at the time of sexual enjoyment if they are in any way conducive to the increase of love or passion. Once the Wheel of Love has been set in motion, there is no absolute rule.

KAMA SUTRA

Whatever thoughts are in their minds, they vanish completely with the onslaught of passionate embrace. When a man and woman are all in oneness, thus clasped together, there is nothing in the whole world to surpass the superb joy of that moment.

KUTTNI MAHATMYAM

There is always a *First Time* for love-making. With the ever increasing liberalization of sexual attitudes in the West, there is a tendency to regard the first act of love-making casually. Yet this is something that has a deep effect on the psyche. Quite a number of people find great difficulty in overcoming their fears or guilts after a disappointing initial sexual experience. Such an experience often has a long-lasting influence, as the psychiatric profession can testify.

The loss of virginity often proves to be a traumatic or disappointing event for the young girl. In the East, marriage traditionally took place just after the onset of puberty. The girl and boy would therefore have the opportunity to explore their sexuality as it dawned, within a committed relationship. Until recently in the West, a woman was expected to remain a virgin until her marriage, which could be quite late in life. She therefore suffered many years of sexual frustration and uncertainty.

In India, and in certain tribes in Africa, girls were ceremonially deflowered with a symbolic representation of the Shiva Lingam, a ritual object kept especially for this purpose, or by squatting upon the Lingam of a statue of Shiva. Often this ceremony would take place in front of the whole tribe and would be an occasion of celebration. In some tribes, the defloration of virgins was performed by an older woman. Strange as this custom may seem to the modern Westerner, it effectively takes the onus of defloration from a man and makes it a ritually significant act. In some ways, this seems preferable to the modern tendency for a girl to either give her maidenhead indiscriminately or to hoard it fearfully.

The Perfumed Garden, an Arabian book of the sixteenth century, states, "A suitor contemplating marriage should choose a virgin, whose love for him will be enduring and who will never forget the man who takes her virginity." There is some psychological truth to this statement, for it is important that the experience of the First Time be as meaningful as possible.

When a man finds himself in the position of being a girl's first lover, he should be sensitive to the honor and responsibility involved. He should gently allay her fears and encourage her to open herself to him carefully.

For a girl, it is a once-in-a-lifetime experience. The man should be aware of this and treat her as a goddess. Envisioning himself as the representative of Lord Shiva, the Supreme Yogi, he should initiate her into sex gently and in the spirit of service.

The First Time for a boy or young man is usually less associated with feelings of "loss" than it is for a girl. A boy's initiation into the wonders of sexuality is often most successful when it is accomplished by an older or experienced woman. If both partners are inexperienced, the problems of sudden loss of erection or premature ejaculation can create obstacles. An experienced woman can take a young man through the stages of love-making with care and consideration, boosting his confidence.

Eastern mystical teachings advise that when a couple make love together for the first time, they should take great care to ensure that the experience is as complete and meaningful as possible. This will potentize their relationship so it can evolve. The custom of considering a marriage formalized only after the first night of consummation was developed by priests who recognized the consequence and deep significance of love-making. The marriage contract was considered "sealed" once a couple had experienced physical union.

If either or both partners have never made love before, it is especially important to make the First Time a memorable and joyous occasion. It is here that sexual ritual makes a major contribution. Everything that leads up to the physical act of love can be understood as ritual, provided it is accompanied by conscious intent.

If it is the First Time, then the partners should each take care to put the feelings of the other first. Casting aside egotism, each should surrender to the divinity within. If they honor the Lingam and Yoni as allies into ecstasy, all doubts and fears will fall away.

Ceremonial defloration was a common feature of priestly cultures. It is still practiced among tribal peoples of India and Africa. From a Rajasthani miniature painting of the eighteenth century.

A Taoist text known as the *Poetry of the Supreme Joy* gives a beautiful description of the consummation of a wedding night:

On a beautiful Spring evening, while enjoying the light of red candles, the groom takes out his Crimson Bird and unties the bride's red silk trousers. He lifts her fair legs and caresses her Jade-like buttocks; she holds his Jade Stalk in her hand and fondles it. The man sucks her tongue, with the result that her mind becomes detached from all worldliness. He then moistens the inside of her Cavern with his saliva and she offers her Field for him to plow. Before she realizes it, her virginity is breached. As she opens herself to him, he inserts deeply and begins to move vigorously; soon his Boy is open and his semen ejaculated. Afterward the couple wipe their sexual parts with the Six Girdles, which are then placed in a basket. From this moment on, they are considered to be truly married. The union of their Yin and Yang energies will continue without interruption from then on.

The text does not elaborate on what the Six Girdles are, but clearly they are part of the ritual of consummation and are kept as talismans. In the Tantric tradition of India, female adepts or Yoginis wore six kinds of ritual ornaments: necklaces, earrings, bracelets, arm-bands, anklets and girdles. These symbolize, respectively, charity, fortitude, fidelity, work, action and energy (according to the *Chandamaharosana Tantra*).

Taoist love-posture, a variation of the classical position known as Jumping Wild Horses. From a woodblock of the seventeenth century, Japan.

The idea that the couple is permanently joined once physical union has been completed ritualistically is expressed in the *Ananga Ranga*: "It is good to know that if a husband and wife live together in absolute closeness, as one soul in a single body, then they will be happy both in this world and in the one to come." This idea is echoed throughout Indian and other mystical teachings.

The *Poetry of the Supreme Joy* goes on to give a fuller description of consummation:

On a moonlit night the couple read the *Sexual Handbook of the Plain Girl*, looking at the illustrations of love-making postures. Screens are placed in a circle around the couch and the pillows are laid out. The beautiful woman then takes off her silk bodice and unknots her red silk trousers, which are embroidered with flowers. Her waist is seen to be as slender as a roll of silk. Her passion has begun to stir; what was previously hidden is now revealed. As the man looks at the exposed lower part of her body, his eyes cloud over. He feels her body and caresses it all over. Then, lifting her feet, he places them on his shoulders.
The man brings his Love-implement close to her belly; they kiss each other, suck tongues and his Weapon begins to rise. Trembling, the Jade Stalk raises its head and is brought into contact with the Golden Furrow; her lower lips open invitingly. His Weapon is as erect as a solitary mountain peak, a rocky crag reaching to the sky. Moist as a shady valley, the movements of the woman's hips cause her Chicken's Tongue [clitoris] to respond; her bodily secretions begin to flow profusely.
The woman lies full out, stretching the middle part of her body. The man rests on his hands, supporting himself on the bed, with his knees bent. His Jade Stalk rises and falls, coming and going, moving to left and right. The Yang Peak enters by the direct route and is brought into contact with the Strings of the Lyre. By moving up and down, the Implement of Love rubs against the Grain-shaped Cave, probing and piercing, pulling and grinding. Buttocks plunge incessantly; it seems as if his Weapon is becoming buried in the burning hot, slippery, deep recess, right to the very bottom. Moving now shallowly, now deeply, now delicately, now vigorously, he pushes his tongue to the very depths of her inviting mouth and penetrates right to her innermost heart.
The limbs of the loving couple become bedewed with sweat; their physical movements produce a sucking sound. The man turns his Implement this way and that, at times letting it grow soft inside the woman and at times swiftly withdrawing the slippery Stalk and then pushing into her again. His Sack swings hither and thither and his Stalk fills her Furrow, right to the bottom of the Inner Stream. Both begin to groan passionately, their chests panting. When she raises up her trembling legs a fragrant odor is smelled. Then, placing her buttocks crosswise on the bed, he employs the *Art of the Bedchamber*, interspersing one short stroke of his Implement between every nine deeply penetrating ones, not stopping until all the signs of satisfaction appear in the woman. He intermixes swift love-strokes with slow ones and freely satisfies his passion and that of his partner. Looking down, he gazes at his Jade Stalk moving in

Make the first experience of sexual union a romantic occasion.

and out of her Golden Furrow and contemplates the sheer joy of such action.

The woman's face begins to change; her voice falters and her hair becomes disarrayed. The side-tresses fall over her languid eyes and her hair comb becomes loosened, to hang like a crescent moon over her shoulder. The man's eyes grow anxious and he exerts himself more fully; his vital juice spurts out. Reaching the innermost part of womanhood, it moistens the Fishpond within her Cinnabar Cave. Then the Jade Stalk is withdrawn, but the woman's Golden Furrow does not close.

The vital essences of both man and woman are combined. Both are relaxed as they quietly enjoy the unity of body and soul. His Love-weapon is slippery and wet with the essence of love; her Jade Cavern exudes moisture and a stream of secretions trickles out between her legs. Their ecstasy is complete.

Another Taoist text declares:

When a man and woman make love together for the first time, the man should sit down to the left of the woman and she should be on his right. He then should sit cross-legged and place her on his lap, pressing her slender waist and caressing her precious body. They should whisper words of passion and endearment to each other, pressing their lips together and drinking each other's saliva.

Indian texts use a similar purple prose to describe the First Time:

He clutches the young girl to his heart, as a maddened elephant seizes a lotus; with the avidness of the Chakora-bird he kisses her moon-like face and takes the border of her sari. As he places his hands on her breasts, which are like lotus-buds, her trembling limbs draw back slightly. Speaking with seductive words, like a bee penetrating the heart of a lotus, he fights the *Battle of Love* with her. Thus in the play of love, with bodies undulating, mad and drunk with love and desire, delirious with passion's nectar, he kisses her mouth and her reddened breasts, which are softer than silk. Lying together, their bodies moving, lips and teeth pressed tight, heart to heart, frenzied and ecstatic, they both are transported into delight. Their biting teeth and lips drink the nectar of love; their two bodies in equal and ecstatic bliss, trembling high on waves of sweetness and desire, quenching the thirst of many years. At last, the god of Love pours his offering into the flames. As the rain clouds cool the earth, the sky becomes clear again.

This typical Indian view of the First Time, from the *Vidyasundara of Bharatchandra*, beautifully portrays the heights of ecstasy available to lovers on their first occasion of union. Mutual trust is extremely important. It is the firm foundation on which a high rite of love can develop and mature.

The fruit of all good marriages is lasting love.

KAMA SUTRA

four types of women

The classical Indian texts categorize women into four distinct types, according to the characteristics of their Yoni. This tradition was maintained in the Tantric era and similar classification systems are found in Taoism. Of course, any system can be misunderstood if taken out of context. Esoteric ideas may be interpreted either literally or allegorically. However, the Tantras stress that the *Four Types of Women* can be understood as archetypes that exist on actual and psychological levels synchronously. These four basic womanly types are:

LOTUS WOMAN

Known as *Padmini*, she is supposed to have originated from the realm of the gods. Her face is beautiful and her body extremely soft, with delicate skin. Her eyes are shining, her breasts full, and she has three folds or wrinkles across her umbilical region. She walks with a swan-like gait, has a low and musical voice, and likes to dress in fine clothes. Her Yoni is perfumed like a newly burst lily and she likes to make love in the daytime.

ART WOMAN

Known as *Chitrini*, she also emanates from the heavenly realm and is extremely beautiful, of medium build. She has a tender body, thin waist, full breasts and heavily made hips. The hair around her Yoni is thin and soft; her Yoni seems raised up. She walks coquettishly, like the swinging gait of an elephant, and has a good voice. The Yoni of the Art Woman has a perfume like honey and is sweet-tasting. She is very fond of pleasure and is particularly proficient in the Sixty-four Arts. She likes to make love at nighttime and is very fond of animals.

CONCH WOMAN

Known as *Shankini*, she emanates from the human realm. Her skin is always warm, her body large, with small breasts and a firm waist. Her head, hands and feet are longer than normal and her voice is at times harsh. She is hard-hearted, and subject to sudden fits of amorous passion that make her head hot and her brain confused. She likes flowers, clothes and ornaments of red, but is addicted to finding fault with others. Her Yoni is always moist and is distinctly salty. Often it is covered with thick hair. She likes to make love in the nighttime especially.

ELEPHANT WOMAN

Known as *Hastini*, she is supposed to emanate from the elemental realm. She is short, stout and walks very slowly, with her neck slightly bent. Her skin is often coarse, of a white color, and she usually has large lips, likes to eat excessively and has a harsh and somewhat choked voice. She is difficult to satisfy and likes prolonged love-making. The juice from her Yoni is slightly pungent, exuding a smell like the muskiness of an elephant in rut. Such a woman likes to make love at any time, regardless of circumstances.

The sexual organs naturally adjust to each other. From a woodblock print depicting a Yoshiwara courtesan, by the Master Utamaro, Japan, *circa* 1800.

These four categories of woman were developed out of a particular lifestyle. Yogic teachings state that a person becomes whatever he or she is able to digest, on the physical, emotional, mental and spiritual levels. With a good diet, a natural lifestyle, a healthy relationship and spiritual direction, the lotus in every woman will bloom.

In women, the lower end of their central pathway has four distinct properties. First, it looks like the tip of an elephant's trunk; second, it is twisted, like the turns on a shell; third, it is closed up, as if by something soft; and fourth, it opens and closes like a lotus flower.

PADMA KARPO

sexual sizes

The West has placed considerable emphasis on the sizes of the male and female sex organs. Indian treatises on love-making categorize both into three classes, according to dimension, and recommend matching sizes as closely as possible. Unions are *equal* or *unequal* according to fit, and specific postures are advised for balancing any imbalance. Wide-open positions allow extra room for a large Lingam to enter a small Yoni. The skillful use of pillows to raise up the buttocks of the woman gives a man with a small Lingam much deeper entry.

A Taoist text declares, "The shape and hardness with which Nature has endowed a man are only external signs. What appears internally is the skill with which he ensures that a woman derives enjoyment from his love-making. If a woman really cares for a man as he cares for her, then it is totally irrelevant whether his organ is long or short, thin or thick." The same text adds, "A long, thick organ is often worse for a woman than a short thin one that is firm and hard. And a firm, hard organ that is pushed in and pulled out in a crude manner is worse than a soft one that is moved about delicately and with tenderness."

Taoist literature sometimes includes medicinal formulas for increasing or decreasing the sizes of both male and female sexual organs. These texts indicate that by using ointments, compresses, powders and potions made from herbs, tree bark, mushrooms and other organic or inorganic substances the desired effect can be achieved. Many texts mention preparations for women who have given birth to children which enable their Yonis to return to normal size quicker and with more ease. All such formulas include sulphur or sulphur in a warm-water solution.

A Taoist master of the Han Dynasty (206 B.C.–A.D. 219), Wu Hsien, prescribes an interesting exercise to enable a man with an unnaturally small Lingam to make it larger.

There is a way to enlarge an unusually small Weapon. In the early hours of the morning, when the Yin-force is diminishing and the Yang-force is increasing, the man should face East and meditate calmly. He should breathe deeply forty-nine times, drawing the breath from his abdomen. Then he should rub the palms of his hands together until they are scorching hot. Next he should hold his Weapon with his right hand, concentrate his mind, and with his left hand he should rub his navel center, encircling it to the left for eighty-one rotations. He then switches hands, rubbing his navel center in the same way, but encircling to the right for eighty-one rotations. He then should roll his Weapon between his hands, as if making a thread from fibers. When making love with a woman, he should nuture his Weapon with the woman's secretions and make a special effort to inhale her breath. This can help him to increase the length of his Weapon.

If a couple are in harmony, then their sex organs will adjust to each other. Rarely is it necessary to resort to artificial means to match sizes. Foreplay is of great help in bringing sexuality into harmony, and is essential to counteract major size differences. Remember always to be considerate of your partner. Then the whole question of sexual sizes will cease to be of significance.

three types of lingam

The *Kama Sutra* and the *Ananga Ranga* both list three types of male sex organs, according to their dimensions. They are:

THE HARE
This is the Lingam that does not exceed six finger-breadths (about five inches) when fully erected. Usually a man with a Lingam of this type is short of stature but well proportioned and of a quiet disposition. His semen is usually sweetish. He is known as being of *small dimension*.

THE BULL
This is the Lingam that does not exceed nine finger-breadths (about seven inches) when fully erected. A man with such a Lingam is usually robust, with a high forehead, large eyes and a restless temperament. He is ever-ready to make love and is known as being of *middle dimension*.

THE HORSE
This is the Lingam that is about twelve finger-breadths (about ten inches) in length when erected. The owner of such an implement is usually tall, large-framed, muscular and has a deep voice. His nature is gluttonous, covetous, passionate, reckless and lazy. He walks slowly and cares little for love-making, unless suddenly overcome by desire. His semen is copious and usually rather salty. He is known as being of *large dimension*.

There is a saying that a man whose Lingam is very long will always be poor. One whose Lingam is very thick will always be in distress. A man who has a thin and lean one will be lucky, and a person whose Lingam is short may well become a king.

ANANGA RANGA

Men are born with as large a variety of Weapons as of faces. It all depends on Nature. A considerable number of short men have long Weapons, while a similar number of tall men have short Weapons. Thin, weak men often have thick, hard Weapons; tall, well-built men often have small, weak ones.

SU-NU-MIAO-LUN

three types of yoni

The *Kama Sutra* and the *Ananga Ranga* both list three types of female sex organs according to their dimensions. These are:

THE DEER
This is the Yoni that does not exceed six finger-breadths (about five inches) in depth. Usually a woman with such a Yoni has a soft and girlish body, well proportioned with good breasts and solid hips. She eats moderately and is addicted to the pleasures of love-making. Her mind is very active and her Yoni juice has the pleasant perfume of the lotus-flower. She is known as being of *small dimension.*

THE MARE
This is the Yoni that does not exceed nine finger-breadths (about seven inches) in depth. Usually this woman's body is

delicate, her breasts and hips are broad and her umbilical region is raised. She has well-proportioned hands and feet, a long neck and a retreating forehead. Her throat, eyes and mouth are broad and her eyes are very beautiful. She is very versatile, affectionate and graceful, and likes good living and lots of rest. She does not easily come to her climax and her love juice is perfumed like the lotus. She is known as being of *middle dimension.*

THE ELEPHANT
This is the Yoni that is about twelve finger-breadths (about ten inches) in depth. This woman usually has large breasts, a broad face and fairly short limbs. She is gluttonous and eats noisily; her voice is hard and harsh. Such a woman is never easily satisfied, but her love juice is very abundant and smells rather like the secretions from elephants in rut. She is known as being of *large dimension.*

Goodness in the female sex organ depends not on its type or position, but in how it is used. High, Middle and Low all have desirable qualities of their own, so long as one knows how to use them. A woman of the Middle type is suited to love-making throughout the year and in every position.

SU-NU-MIAO-LUN

The best among women is one who comes from a spiritual family, is endowed with auspicious signs and freed from the Four Defects of the genital organs; namely, not having the menstrual flow, not of an unpleasant smell, not being diseased, and when filled with sexual desire, not knowing any shame or restraint with the Yogic partner.

CHAKRASAMVARA TANTRA

nine kinds of sexual union

The combinations of sizes of male and female sexual organs produce nine different possibilities or *Kinds of Union*. As the *Kama Sutra* declares, "There are three equal unions between persons of corresponding dimensions, and there are six unequal unions when the dimensions of the sex organs do not correspond. This makes nine in total."

As we shall see later, the number nine has a special esoteric significance. It occurs in the *Nine Apertures of the Body* and in several important metaphysical concepts. Though the classification of sexual sizes is a difficult topic to generalize about, there seems to be a great deal of wisdom in the ancient Indian system. The *Kama Sutra* states, "In *Equal Unions*, there are never any problems. In *Unequal Unions*, positions should be used which create balance."

EQUAL		UNEQUAL	
Men	*Women*	*Men*	*Women*
hare	deer	hare	mare
bull	mare	hare	elephant
horse	elephant	bull	deer
		bull	elephant
		horse	deer
		horse	mare

When the proportions of both lovers are alike and equal, then satisfaction is easy to achieve. The greatest happiness consists in the correspondence of dimensions. Discomfort increases with the ratio of difference.

ANANGA RANGA

Love-postures should be chosen to help compensate for any difference in sexual sizes. From a miniature painting in the collection of the King of Nepal, *circa* 1830.

hindu love postures

Many Hindu books on the Art of Love contain lists of love-making postures. These were added to and complemented in the Tantric tradition.

The *Kama Sutra*, the earliest of the surviving Hindu love manuals, was written around the second century A.D. by a sage called Vatsyayana. This book, which was translated into English by Sir Richard Burton in 1883, contains a wealth of information on sexual matters including lists of numerous love postures. Other later texts, such as the *Ananga Ranga* and *Koka Shastra*, drew their inspiration from the *Kama Sutra*. We have retranslated passages from the *Kama Sutra* and *Ananga Ranga* for this book, with an eye to restoring their original purity and presenting them as part of the Tantric tradition.

The *Kama Sutra* and *Ananga Ranga* were originally illustrated with the various postures. As examples of these early illustrated texts are no longer available, we have re-created the flavor of the originals by gathering together the finest examples of Hindu erotica and redrawing them. In ancient India, it was customary to give a love manual such as the *Kama Sutra* to girls approaching puberty. This was done to help them understand their sexuality and prepare them for womanhood.

Widely Open Position. From a Rajasthani miniature painting, *circa* eighteenth century.

Variation of Yawning Position. From an Orissan miniature painting, *circa* nineteenth century.

postures of the kama sutra

WIDELY OPEN POSITION
The woman lies back, lowers her head and raises up her middle parts. In this position, the man should take care to make his entrance easy.

YAWNING POSITION
The woman lies back, raises her thighs and keeps them wide apart during love-making.

Approach to Indrani Position. From a Deccani miniature painting, *circa* seventeenth century.

INDRANI POSITION

The woman lies back and draws up her thighs so that her knees are against each of her two sides. This position allows a woman to accommodate a man with an unusually large Lingam.

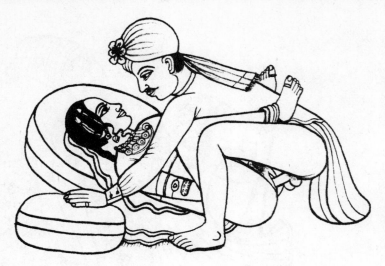

The three positions described above are particularly suitable when the man's Lingam exceeds the woman's Yoni in size. These positions are useful to a Deer Woman to help her widen her Yoni.

Indrani Position. From a Rajasthani miniature painting, *circa* eighteenth century.

CLASPING POSITION

This is when the legs of both the man and the woman are stretched straight out over each other. It takes two forms, the *side position* and the *supine position*, depending on the way in which the couple are lying. In the *side position*, the man should lie on his left side and the woman should lie on her right.

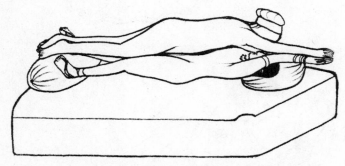

Clasping Position. From a Rajasthani miniature painting, *circa* seventeenth century.

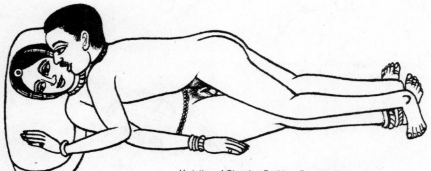

Pressing Position. From an Orissan miniature painting, *circa* nineteenth century.

Variation of Clasping Position. From an East Indian miniature painting, *circa* nineteenth century.

PRESSING POSITION

After love-making has commenced in the *clasping position*, the woman should press her lover by bringing together her thighs to hold his Lingam tightly. This is called the *pressing position*.

TWINING POSITION

Continuing from the *pressing position*, the woman should place one of her thighs across the thigh of her lover. This is known as the *twining position*.

Twining Position. From an Orissan miniature painting, *circa* nineteenth century.

THE MARE'S POSITION

This is when the woman brings her legs tightly together, in the *twining position*, and then forcibly holds the Lingam in her Yoni.

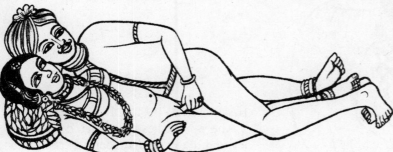

Mare's Position. From an East Indian miniature painting, *circa* nineteenth century.

The preceding four positions are particularly suitable when the woman's Yoni exceeds the man's Lingam in size. They are useful to the Elephant Woman to help her constrict her Yoni.

RISING POSITION

When the woman lies back and raises her two thighs, it is known as the *rising position*.

Rising Position. From a Rajasthani miniature painting, *circa* eighteenth century.

ALTERNATE YAWNING POSITION

This is when a woman lies back, raises both her legs and places them on the shoulders of her lover.

Variation of Alternate Yawning Position. From an Orissan miniature painting of the nineteenth century.

Alternate Yawning Position. From a Rajasthani miniature painting of the nineteenth century.

PRESSED POSITION

The woman lies back, draws up her legs and places them in front of her lover's chest. This is known as the *pressed position*.

HALF-PRESSED POSITION

The woman lies back, stretches out one leg and draws up and contracts the other one as in the *pressed position*.

SPLITTING A BAMBOO

This is when a woman lies back, places one of her legs on her lover's shoulder and stretches the other leg out, and then reverses the procedure, placing the stretched-out leg on the other shoulder and bringing down the first leg, stretching it out, and so on alternately. This procedure is known as *splitting a bamboo* and requires great concentration to perfect.

Pressed Position. From an East Indian miniature painting of the nineteenth century.

Half-pressed Position. From an East Indian miniature painting of the nineteenth century.

Splitting a Bamboo Position. From an East Indian miniature painting of the nineteenth century.

Variation of Splitting a Bamboo Position. From a Rajasthani miniature painting of the eighteenth century.

FIXING A NAIL

This is when a woman lies back and places one of her legs behind her head and stretches out the other leg. This is known as *fixing a nail* and is a difficult posture. It should not be forced; it should be perfected by practice.

THE CRAB

This is when a woman lies back, pulls up and contracts both legs, placing her feet on the region of her stomach.

Variation of Fixing a Nail Position. From a Rajasthani miniature painting of the nineteenth century.

PACKED POSITION

The woman lies back, raises her thighs and crosses one leg over the other. This position creates a tight fit between the Lingam and Yoni.

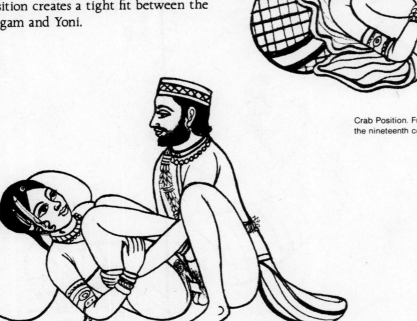

Crab Position. From an East Indian miniature painting of the nineteenth century.

Packed Position. From an East Indian miniature painting of the nineteenth century.

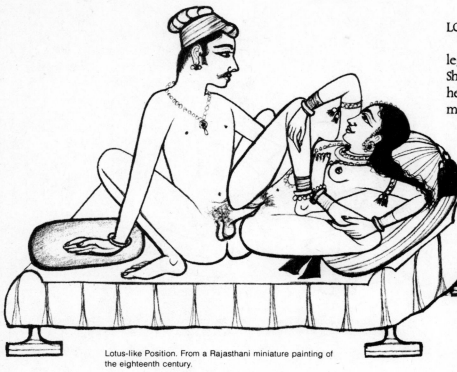

LOTUS-LIKE POSITION

The woman lies back and crosses her legs in the *lotus posture* of a Yogi (*padmasana*). She raises her thighs, bringing them up to her breasts. Entry is then effected, with the man kneeling or lying upon her.

Lotus-like Position. From a Rajasthani miniature painting of the eighteenth century.

TURNING POSITION

When the man turns around and enjoys the woman from behind, without withdrawing from her Yoni, it is called the *turning position*. It can best be learned by practice.

Variation of Turning Position. From an East Indian miniature painting of the nineteenth century.

Variation of Turning Position. From a Rajasthani miniature painting of the nineteenth century.

Turning Position. From a Rajasthani miniature painting of the eighteenth century.

SUPPORTED POSITION

When a man and woman make love while standing, supporting themselves on each other's bodies or on a wall or pillar, it is known as the *supported position*.

SUSPENDED POSITION

This is when the man supports himself against something and the woman, sitting on his joined-together hands, throws her arms around his neck, puts her thighs alongside his waist and moves herself up and down by pushing her feet against whatever the man is leaning on.

POSITION OF A COW

When a woman stands on all fours, with her hands and feet on the ground like a quadruped, and her lover mounts her like a bull, from behind, it is known as the *position of a cow*. At this time, everything that is normally done on the breasts of woman should be done on her back.

Supported Position. From a Rajasthani miniature painting of the eighteenth century.

Suspended Position. From a Rajasthani miniature painting of the early nineteenth century.

Position of a Cow. From an East Indian miniature painting of the nineteenth century.

Variation of Position of a Cow. From a Rajasthani miniature painting of the late eighteenth century.

The love-making of elephants. From an album miniature, Kotah, Rajasthan, *circa* 1780.

OTHER ANIMAL POSITIONS

The characteristics of the different animals should be manifested by acting like them. The couple should produce sounds like the various animals. These auspicious positions are known as: *position of a dog*, *position of a goat*, *position of a deer*, the *forceful mounting of an ass*, the *union of cats*, the *jump of a tiger*, the *pressing of an elephant*, the *rubbing of a boar* and the *mounting of a horse*. Many love-making postures, like Yoga postures, evolved from the observation of animals. The indication is that the different natures of the animals should be emulated. Tantra teaches that this produces a sympathetic, magical bond with specific animals, whose particular powers and qualities (such as strength, quickness, sense of smell or sight) can be assimilated by the couple. In this way, animals become *allies* or extensions of the human personality.

Love-posture from an erotic manual, Kashmir, nineteenth century.

Animal-derived love-posture. From an erotic manual, Kashmir, nineteenth century.

Hindu love-posture in mimicry of that of animals. From an Indian stone sculpture, Lakshmana Temple, Khajuraho, *circa* tenth century.

Love-positions evolved from and were named after the different postures of animals.

UNITED POSITION

This is when a man makes love to two women at the same time, both of whom love him equally. It requires great self-control on the part of the man, who must ensure that each woman reaches her climax.

Variation of United Position. From a Jodhpur miniature painting *circa* 1830.

United Position. From an Indian miniature painting of the mid-eighteenth century.

THE HERD OF COWS

This is when a man makes love with a number of women simultaneously. There are other variations—the *union of many goats,* the *union of a herd of deer,* the *union of a bull-elephant with many females* (which takes place in water)—all of which are imitations of these animals enacted by humans.

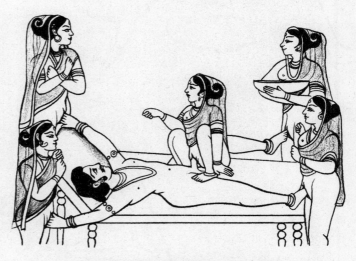

The Herd of Cows. From a Rajasthani miniature painting of the late eighteenth century.

WOMAN ACTING THE MALE ROLE

During love-making, the woman turns around and gets on top of her lover and continues to make love to him. Or the woman can take up this position from the beginning. There are three variations of her movements in this position:

Woman Acting the Male Role. From an East Indian miniature painting of the nineteenth century.

PAIR OF TONGS

The woman sits on top of the man, draws his Lingam into her Yoni, holds it in by the action of her thighs, presses it, moves against him and keeps the Lingam in her for a long time.

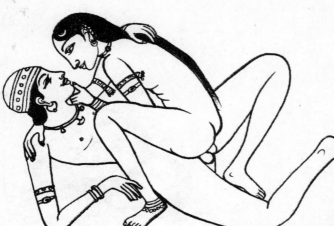

Pair of Tongs Position. From a Rajasthani miniature painting of the eighteenth century.

Variation of Pair of Tongs Position. From an East Indian miniature painting of the nineteenth century.

Variation of Spinning Top Position. From a Rajasthani miniature painting of the late eighteenth century.

SPINNING TOP

The woman sits on top of the man and takes care to maintain contact between the Lingam and Yoni. She turns round and round, like a wheel above him, swinging her body to create the momentum. This is called the *spinning top* and can only be learned by practicing.

Spinning Top Position. From a Rajasthani miniature painting of the eighteenth century.

THE SWING

The woman sits on top of the man, who lifts up the middle part of his body. She then turns around so her back is facing him and rocks backward and forward. This is called the *swing*.

Many of the postures listed in the *Kama Sutra* can be practiced in sequence. Though some of the descriptions are abbreviated and by no means comprehensive, the *Kama Sutra* presents the entire range of love-making variations. The text suggests that lovers should practice love-making postures in water, since this makes bodies much lighter and more maneuverable.

An ingenious person should multiply the kinds of love-making after the example of the many different kinds of birds and beasts. For these different ways of loving, performed according to the traditions of different countries and the preference of individuals, generate love, friendship and respect.

KAMA SUTRA

Beginning stage of the Swing Position. From a Rajasthani miniature painting of the late eighteenth century.

nine movements of the man

The *Kama Sutra* enumerates nine distinct categories of male sexual movements during love-making. This ninefold division, along with the tradition of Nine Kinds of Sexual Union (according to sexual sizes), is a constant feature of metaphysical systemization (See "The Yang Number" for a detailed description of the subtle meaning of the number nine and its multiples). The *Nine Movements of the Man* are:

MOVING FORWARD

The Lingam is moved forward, directly into the Yoni.

CHURNING

The Lingam is held by the hand and turned and churned around in the Yoni.

PIERCING

The Yoni is lowered, and the upper part of it is then struck with the Lingam.

RUBBING

This is the same action as *piercing*, done to the lower part of the Yoni.

GIVING A BLOW

The Lingam is removed some distance from the Yoni and then brought back to forcibly strike it. This is known as *giving a blow*.

BLOW OF A BOAR

This is when only one part of the Yoni is rubbed by the Lingam.

SPORTING OF A SPARROW

This is when the Lingam is deep in the Yoni and is moved up and down repeatedly, without being taken out. This takes place at the approach to climax and should be a playful movement.

PRESSING

This is when the Lingam is inside the Yoni and is pressed deep within.

TOGETHER PRESSING

This is when the man and woman press the Lingam and Yoni alternately, without any withdrawal. It creates a rapid climax.

When a woman is acting the part of a man, she can enact his nine movements. The classical texts state that a man should always make a point of pressing or focusing on those parts of her body on which she turns her eye. A man should learn from the actions and sounds of a woman during love-making so that he becomes aware of her disposition and the way she best likes to be enjoyed. The *Kama Sutra* states that when a woman is enjoying love-making, she shows increased willingness to join the Lingam and Yoni as close together as possible.

Taoist texts list ten different ways for a woman to act during love-making. We enumerate these in the section entitled "Secrets of the Plain Girl," under the subhead "Ten Ways of Moving." This type of categorization is helpful, since it indicates the order in which passion is physically manifested. Tantric texts attach great significance to stages of sexual excitement, seeing them as reflections of a greater cosmology, the order of the evolution of universes. The *Hevajra Tantra*, for example,

states, "From the union of Lingam and Yoni, the earth element arises out of contact with the quality of hardness. From the flow of secretions, the water element arises, and the fire element is evoked by the friction of love-making. The air element arises from the movements of lovers approaching ecstasy, and the space element corresponds to the all-pervading Bliss."

A couple should be aware of their movements during love-making and should try to manifest them as artistically as possible. This helps to focus the minds and emotions of the partners, enabling the channeling of energy and the transformation of ecstasy into the visions of unity. When lovers hold in mind and enact the multifarious sexual roles, they can build up to orgasm consciously. This is one of the secrets and goals of Tantric love-making.

One of the man's chief duties is to learn to withhold himself as much as possible and at the same time to hasten the enjoyment of his partner. The desires of the woman are cooler and slower to rouse than those of the man; she is not easily satisfied by a single act of love-making. Her slower excitement demands prolonged embraces, and if these are denied her, then she often feels irritated. By the second love-act the passions of a woman become thoroughly aroused and she has a full orgasm; then she can be said to be contented. This state of affairs is reversed in the case of a man, who approaches the first act burning with love-heat, which cools during the second, often leaving him languid and disinclined for a third.

ANANGA RANGA

postures of the ananga ranga

The *Ananga Ranga* is a relatively late Hindu work, probably of the sixteenth century. Known as the *Stage of Love*, it is an analysis and compilation of earlier love treatises such as the *Kama Sutra*. The text shows some Moslem influence, and has been translated into Arabic under the title *Pleasures of Woman* (*Lizzat-al-Nisa*.) The different love-making postures are systemized quite effectively into

six categories. These are, first, with a woman on her back in a supine position; second, with the woman lying on her left or right side; third, the various sitting postures; fourth, the standing positions; fifth, with the woman prone, on her stomach; and sixth, with the woman on top, acting the part of the man.

Yogic, alchemical and animal terminology are used to describe the positions in the *Ananga Ranga*. Many can be related directly to Taoist equivalents. We will consider each of the categories individually.

WOMAN LYING SUPINE
eleven variations

EQUAL-LEGGED POSITION

The woman lies on her back, raises both legs, placing them on his two shoulders. Sitting close to her body, he inserts his Lingam into her Yoni. The couple then proceed with their love-making.

BIRD POSITION

The woman lies on her back and the man sits between her legs, raising them both and keeping them on either side of his waist. In this manner, they both enjoy their love-making.

Equal-Legged Position. From a Rajasthani miniature painting of the nineteenth century.

Bird Position. From a Rajasthani miniature painting of the eighteenth century.

Beginning stage of the Bird Position. From an East Indian miniature painting of the nineteenth century.

THE THREE STEPS
or STEPPING BEYOND

One of the woman's legs is left lying on the bed while the other leg is placed on the man's head. He should support himself upon both hands.

Stepping Beyond Position (The Three Steps). From an East Indian miniature painting of the nineteenth century.

VISHNU

the preserver

FEET IN THE AIR

The woman lies on her back and raises both legs, holding them with her hands and drawing them back as far as her head. The man then sits as close to her as possible, places both of his hands on her breasts, and the couple make love joyfully.

Beginning stage of the Feet in the Air Position. From a Rajasthani miniature painting of the eighteenth century.

Advanced stage of Feet in the Air Position. From an East Indian miniature painting of the nineteenth century.

Full Feet in the Air Position. From a Rajasthani miniature painting of the late eighteenth century.

REMEMBRANCE WHEEL

This is also known as the *Wheel of Kama* (the Love god) and is a method much enjoyed by voluptuous lovers. In this position, the man sits between the legs of the woman, who is on her back. He extends his arms as far as possible on both sides of her, holding her legs wide apart. He should move and turn her body with his arms.

Remembrance-Wheel Position. From an East Indian miniature painting of the nineteenth century.

THE INEXHAUSTIBLE KINDNESS or FAVORITE SPLIT

The woman lies on her back and raises both her legs so that they touch the chest of her lover. He should sit between her thighs, embracing her closely and loving her passionately.

THE ELIXIR POSITION

The woman lies on her back and the man squats on both feet. He places both hands under her lower back and draws her to him in close embrace. She returns his affection by tightly grasping his neck. In this position, they make love by gentle rocking backward and forward.

THE BOW

The woman lies on her back. The man places pillows beneath her hips and head, raising her seat of pleasure and rising to it by kneeling on a cushion. With the woman's body now bent into the shape of a bow, he should aim his *arrow of love*. This is a particularly fine love-making position which is much enjoyed by both partners.

Variation of Inexhaustible Kindness Position. From a provincial Mughal miniature painting, *circa* 1775.

Variation of Elixir Position. From a Rajasthani miniature painting of the late eighteenth century.

Elixir Position. From an East Indian miniature painting of the nineteenth century.

Humorous depiction of love-posture. From a nineteenth century Rajasthani miniature painting.

The Bow Position. From an East Indian miniature painting of the nineteenth century.

ALL-ENCOMPASSING POSITION

The woman lies on her back with legs crossed and raised. The man carefully inserts his Lingam into her Yoni. This posture is very well suited to couples burning with desire.

All-Encompassing Position. From an East Indian miniature painting of the nineteenth century.

Variation of All-Encompassing Position. From a Rajasthani miniature painting of the late eighteenth century.

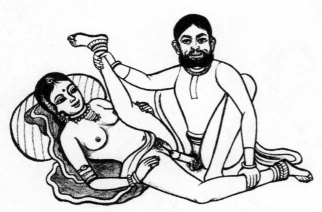

Splitting a Bamboo Position. From an East Indian miniature painting of the nineteenth century.

SPLITTING BAMBOO

This is a position with the woman lying on her back, with one leg upon her lover's shoulder and the other leg straight out on the bed. It is a very effective method for bringing on a woman's sexual climax.

OPENING AND BLOSSOMING POSITION

The woman lies on her back. The man inserts his Lingam into her Yoni and penetrates deeply. He then raises up her legs, joins her thighs closely together, and presses and releases them rhythmically.

WOMAN LYING ON HER SIDE
three variations

OBSTACLE-REMOVING POSITION

The man places himself alongside the woman, who is lying on her right or left side. He raises one of his legs over her hip, and leaves his other leg lying on the bed. This position is only suitable for love-making with a fully-developed woman. With a young girl it is unsatisfactory.

Variation of Opening and Blossoming Position. From a miniature painting in the collection of the King of Nepal, *circa* 1830.

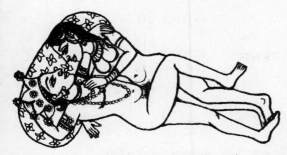

Variation of Obstacle-Removing Position. From a Rajasthani miniature painting of the nineteenth century.

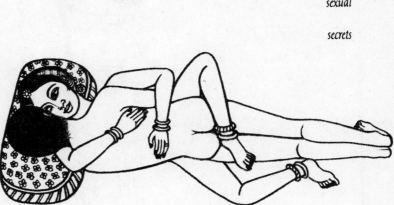

The Crab Position. From an east Indian miniature painting of the nineteenth century.

THE CRAB

The man and woman both lie on their sides. The man lies between her thighs, with one of her legs under him and the other thrown over him, just below his chest.

BALANCE POSITION

The man and woman lie straight on their sides, without any movement or change in the position of their limbs. Love-making is gentle and focuses on rhythm and breathing. This posture is also known as *double hemisphere*, and echoes the process of alchemical distillation.

Balance Position. Contemporary.

SITTING POSITIONS
ten variations

LOTUS POSITION

The man should sit cross-legged in this favorite posture of Yogis. He should seat the woman upon his lap, wrapping her legs around his waist and placing his hands upon her shoulders. She gently inserts his Lingam into her Yoni. In this love-posture, the sexual organs are in closest contact and there is little need for movement.

Lotus Position. From a Nepalese miniature painting of the eighteenth century.

VISHNU

the preserver

Self-Created or Upper-Leg Position. From an East Indian miniature painting of the nineteenth century.

SELF-CREATED or UPPER-LEG POSITION

The man sits in the *lotus position* and the woman is on his lap. She should slightly raise one of her legs by placing her hand under that foot. By moving this leg back and forth, she can create exquisite love-sensations.

Reverse Variation of Upper-leg Position. From a Rajasthani miniature painting of the eighteenth century.

Conjunction of the Sun and Moon. From a Rajasthani miniature painting of the eighteenth century.

CONJUNCTION OF THE SUN AND MOON

The man sits in the *lotus position*, with the woman on his lap. He embraces her neck very closely and she does the same to him. Their movements of love are coordinated by the movements of their arms.

HAND-HOLDING or QUENCHING POSITION

The man sits with the woman on his lap. When Lingam and Yoni are in close contact, he should hold on to both his partner's feet; she reaches behind her and holds his two feet. Sexual energy is released and circulated by this position, invigorating and delighting both partners.

Variation of Hand-Holding or Quenching Position. From a Rajasthani miniature painting of the late eighteenth century.

GAINING-RESTRAINING POSITION

The man sits with the woman on his lap. She passes both of her legs under his arms at the level of his elbows. He holds her neck and shoulders with his hands and rocks her back and forth to climax.

Development of Gaining-Restraining Position. From a Rajasthani miniature painting of the nineteenth century.

Variation of Gaining-Restraining Position. From a Rajasthani miniature painting of the nineteenth century.

TORTOISE POSITION

The man sits with the woman on his lap, and the Lingam and Yoni are in close union. He places his mouth, arms and legs exactly touching the corresponding parts of his partner's body. This position helps circulate and exchange energy. It holds one of the secrets of longevity.

Tortoise Position. From a Jodhpur miniature painting, *circa* 1830.

ALL-AROUND POSITION

This is like the *tortoise position*, but in addition to the mutual contact of mouths, arms and legs, the man should move both legs of the woman under his arms in the region of his elbows.

Variation of All-Around Position. From a Jodhpur miniature painting, *circa* 1830.

PAIR-LEGGED or GEMINI POSITION

The man sits with his legs wide apart and the woman sits between them. Inserting his Lingam deep into her Yoni, he should press her thighs together.

Variation of Pair-Legged Position. From a Rajasthani miniature painting of the nineteenth century.

Pair-Legged or Gemini Position. From an East Indian miniature painting of the late nineteenth century.

ROARING POSITION

This is a posture suited to a strong man and a light woman. The man sits, with the woman on his lap. He raises her up by passing both her legs over his arms, and uses his elbows to move her about from left to right and back again, and so on, until the *Supreme Moment* arrives. This gives great pleasure to the woman.

Roaring Position. From an East Indian miniature painting of the nineteenth century.

Variation of the Roaring Position. From a Rajasthani miniature painting of the early nineteenth century.

MONKEY POSITION

This is very similar to the *roaring position*, except that the man should move the body of the woman in a straight line, away from his face, backward and forward, but not from side to side. This posture requires great strength.

Monkey Position. From an East Indian miniature painting of the nineteenth century.

Reverse Monkey Position. From a Rajasthani miniature painting of the eighteenth century.

STANDING POSITIONS
three variations

KNEE AND ELBOW POSITION

This posture requires great strength on the part of the man. The couple should stand facing each other. The man then places his two arms under the woman's knees, supporting her on his inner elbows. He raises her up as high as his waist, she inserts his Lingam into her Yoni and clasps his neck with both hands. Swinging and rocking, this way and that, the couple should make love with abandon.

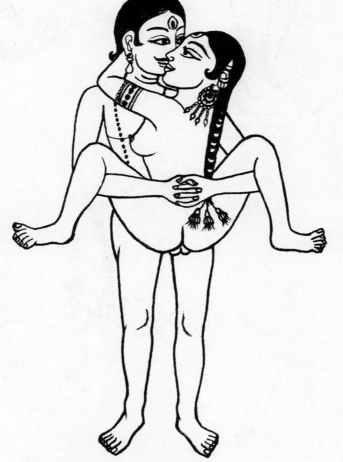

Knee and Elbow Position. From a Nepalese miniature painting of the eighteenth century.

THREE STEPS OF VISHNU

The couple stand facing each other. The man raises one of the woman's legs, clasping it with his hand. Her other leg supports her body from the ground.

Three Steps of Vishnu. From a contemporary photograph.

Three Steps of Vishnu Position. From a stone sculpture, Puri, Orissa, *circa* twelfth century.

Glorious Position. From a Nepalese miniature painting of the eighteenth century.

GLORIOUS POSITION

This posture requires the man to exert great strength. The couple stand facing each other. Then the woman clasps her hands behind the man's neck and jumps up to place her legs around his waist. She hangs on to him, squeezing his waist with her thighs, while he supports her weight by holding his hands and forearms under her hips. Rocking this way and that, they bring each other to ecstasy.

WOMAN ON HER FRONT
two variations

THE COW POSITION
  The woman places herself on all fours, supported by her hands and feet. The man approaches from behind, falls upon her waist and enjoys her as if he were a bull.

Cow Position. From a Rajasthani miniature painting of the late eighteenth century.

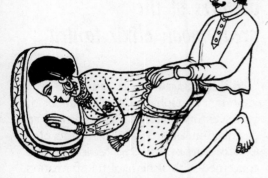

Elephant Position. From an East Indian miniature painting of the nineteenth century.

THE ELEPHANT POSITION
  The woman lies down so that her face, breasts, stomach and thighs all touch the bed. The man then extends himself over and upon her body. Bending himself like an elephant, with the small of his back much drawn in, he works his way underneath and inserts his Lingam into her Yoni. She should raise up her lower parts and encourage him with her movements.

Elephant Position. From a Kangra miniature painting of the nineteenth century.

WOMAN ACTING THE PART
OF THE MAN
three variations

INVERTED POSITION
  The woman lies straight out upon the outstretched body of her lover, her breasts pressed against his chest. She should caress his waist, then reach down and insert his Lingam into her Yoni. Moving her hips vigorously, she should enjoy him.

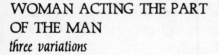

Inverted Position. From a Rajasthani miniature painting of the eighteenth century.

Bee Buzzing over Man. From a Mughal painting of the seventeenth century.

BEE BUZZING OVER MAN

In this posture, the woman plays the role of a large bee, coaxing honey from a flower. Having placed the man full length upon the bed, she squats over his thighs, closing her legs together once his erect Lingam is deep within her Yoni. Then, moving her waist in a circular motion over him, churning and milking, she should thoroughly satisfy herself, bestowing unimaginable enjoyment upon her lover. (This is also known as the *Kali posture*.)

The Elevated Rising or Resurrection Position. From a Rajasthani painting of the eighteenth century.

THE ELEVATED RISING or THE RESURRECTION

A woman whose passion has not been fully gratified should ask her man to lie on his back. Then, sitting cross-legged upon his thighs, she should seize his Lingam and insert it into her Yoni. Moving her waist up and down, lifting up and sinking down upon him, advancing and retiring, she should make love to him in this way.

This completes the thirty-two postures listed in the *Ananga Ranga*. Though it is by no means the complete range of postures possible, it is an easy-to-follow categorization of love-making variations. The author adds one very notable piece of practical advice for lovers. He states, "Fully understanding how love quarrels sometimes arise, I have in this book shown how the man, by varying the enjoyment of his woman, may live with her as if with thirty-two entirely different women, ever changing his enjoyment of her and thus making boredom an impossibility."

postures of the great moon elixir tantra

In the *Chandamaharosana Tantra*, an important metaphysical work of about the ninth century, thirteen sexual postures are described in some detail. The secrets of *Chandamaharosana* (the *Great Moon Elixir*) are concerned with alchemical transformation through the power of sex. Specifically, this Tantra outlines the correct psychological stance necessary to transmute all future possible lifetimes into a single lifetime culminating in Liberation. Most of the text concerns initiation, ritual, Mantra, and meditation, but there are important sections on women, sex rites and postures. The thirteen sexual postures that follow are presented as linked in a series. The Yogi is instructed to perform these postures with great concentration, aiming at generating the most pleasure possible. He may ejaculate or retain, as seems appropriate, but if he does ejaculate, he should engage in oral sex afterward and also feast on special food and wine (see "The Rite of the Five Essentials").

PLEASURE-EVOKING

The woman squats before him and clasps her hands on his shoulders or behind his neck. He places his arms around her waist, draws her to him and inserts his Lingam into her Yoni.

SWING-ROCKING

This evolves from the *pleasure-evoking position*. With their arms wound around each other like braids of hair, the man and woman both lean back and use their weight to create a rocking motion, back and forth like a swing.

KNEE-HOLDING

With the couple holding their arms as in the *swing-rocking position*, he should pull her knees against his chest and use the extra leverage to create exquisite love-rhythms.

THIGH-RUBBING

He should rest the soles of her feet on the base of his thighs and put his arms around her waist. Her arms should clasp his neck. She should than raise and lower herself, pressing her Yoni to him and rubbing his thighs with her feet.

FOOT-MOVING

She leans back and he places the soles of her feet on the navel and heart region of his body. Moving her feet up and down against him, they rock backward and forward with arms wound around each other like braids of hair.

GROUND-PRESSING

He places her buttocks on the ground and clasps her around the waist. She pulls him over her, holding him behind the head with her two hands. He should press down on her forcefully.

EQUAL PEAKS

With the woman drawn up to a squatting position, he should then have her stretch out her legs, each one alternately. This movement produces great ecstasies.

VARIEGATED

She turns around to be enjoyed from behind and draws up her legs, and he places his chest next to her back. She should move to the left, to the right, and up and down, while he rubs her body all over, beginning with the palms of her hands. This helps to circulate and magnify the joys of release.

HONEYCOMB

Turning her around into the *pleasure-evoking position* and placing her squatting before him, with his right hand he should reinsert his Lingam into her Yoni. He should catch her underneath her knees with the crooks of his elbows and wind his arms around hers. Leaning back and moving forward, they should make love passionately, generating sweet Elixir.

MOUNTED YANTRA

With the woman lying back, he should have her place a leg on each of his shoulders. Advancing and retreating, the lovers should use this posture to create great passion.

Mounted Yantra Position. From a Rajasthani miniature painting of the eighteenth century.

Variegated Position. From a central Indian miniature painting of the nineteenth century.

Ground-Pressing Position. From an Orissan miniature painting of the nineteenth century.

Swing-Rocking Position, ideally suited to prolonged love-making. From a Rajasthani miniature painting of the eighteenth century.

Foot-Moving Position. From a Rajasthani miniature painting of the eighteenth century.

232

VISHNU

the preserver

One Leg Up Position. From a Rajasthani miniature painting of the late eighteenth century.

ONE LEG UP

He should have the woman keep her right leg on his left shoulder and bring her left leg down to his upper thigh. As she presses against him and rocks, this position creates ecstatic pleasure and destroys physical and psychological problems.

TANTRIC TORTOISE

From the *one leg up position*, he should have her place both soles of her feet together in the middle of his chest, visualizing *Chandamaharosana* as being born within his heart. He should press her knees with his arms and control his breathing. This position can bring the couple to realize *Chandamaharosana* within themselves.

TOTALLY AUSPICIOUS

He should draw up the soles of her feet to touch his eyes, ears, nose, mouth and the top of his head. This action is in every way auspicious and grants all desires held by the mind at that moment.

Chandamaharosana, the Great Moon Elixir, in sexual union. From a Nepalese painting of the sixteenth century.

Squatting Position, ideally suited to the love-rites of Chandamaharosana. From a contemporary photograph.

The thirteen positions of *Chandamaharosana* are similar to some of the positions described in the *Kama Sutra*. The text advises the adept to gradually arouse passion in his partner, all the while meditating on her Yoni. He should think to himself, "Just as I am now entering this Yoni, so, too, have I emerged numerous times. This Tantric Path which I am following is straight as an arrow, but if I travel along it without knowledge, it becomes the path to countless rebirths. When I enter with knowledge, it becomes the success of *Chandamaharosana*, the Great Moon Elixir." This Tantric mystic form symbolizes the full moon, in the macrocosm and microcosm. The success of *Chandamaharosana* occurs when sexual energy is distilled in the head center, producing subtle hormonal changes and the opening of intuitive wisdom.

Totally Auspicious Position. From a Rajasthani miniature painting of the late seventeenth century.

Approach to Tantric Tortoise Position. Contemporary rendering.

lingam linguistics

VISHNU

the preserver

Eastern erotic writings have the charming custom of using poetic names to refer to the male and female sex organs. This is rather a relief from the popular Western approach, which makes a point of using crude language. The only Western alternatives seem to be in Latin, which unfortunately is a dead language. In the evocation of the erotic sentiment, it is helpful to use positive language to describe the sex organs. Lovers throughout the world tend to nickname each other's sex organs, just as children do. Since the male organ is *external* and visibly changes its appearance according to mood, it is conceived of as having a character. The female sex organ is *internal* and subsequently its character is not visible; therefore its names are often mystical or allegorical.

The terms *Lingam* and *Yoni* have become known in the West through the publication in English of the *Kama Sutra* and other Eastern sex books. There are also less familiar terms used in the Tantric tradition, such as Jewel / Lotus , Scepter / Bell and Wand / Cup. Chinese literature abounds with poetic names for the sexual organs. The variations are too many to enumerate, but we mention the following popular terms:

THE LINGAM

The Jade Stalk, Positive Peak, Mountain Crag, Yang Pagoda, Crimson Bird, Unicorn, Jade Scepter, Weapon of Love, Diplomat, Ambassador, General, Tiger, Serpent, Frog, Cockerel, Tortoise, Boy, Henchman, Warrior, Hero, Monk, Adept, Flute.

THE YONI

The Honey Pot, Jade Gate, Pleasure Grotto, Shady Valley, Precious Gate, Jade Chamber, Mysterious Room, Purple Chamber, Purple Mushroom, Anemone, Grotto of the White Tiger, Valley of Joy, Cinnabar Crevice, Golden Crevice, Secret Cabinet, Golden Furrow, Grain-shaped Cave, Crucible, Oyster, Pearl, Lotus, Open Melon, Peach, Knot, Shell, Lyre, Phoenix.

If a couple endow the Lingam and Yoni with their own personalities, this will help increase their intimacy as a couple and bring them both into deeper communication with their own seats of pleasure. A man can communicate with his Lingam in a firm and affectionate manner, getting to know "him" as if he were a separate individual. This is a way for him to develop an understanding with his Lingam, and assists him to gain conscious control over its function.

A woman can do likewise with her Yoni, establishing a rapport with its inner workings. She will be able to receive information from her Yoni region, become more aware of her lunar cycles and better understand how to control her pleasure portal.

In the Indian tradition, the male organ is viewed as the Shiva Lingam, the embodiment of cosmic creativity. "He" is approached with reverence and awe. The Yoni is viewed as the entrance to the original Sacred Shrine, the embodiment of receptivity. Together, the couple can bring creativity into the shrine and worship the gods within.

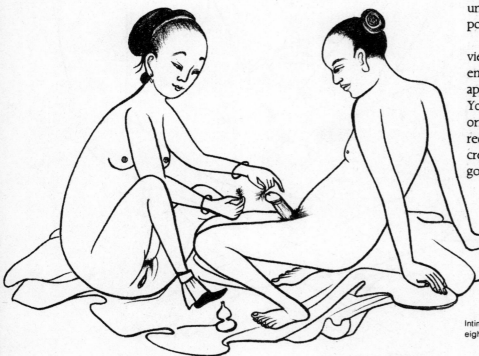

Intimate foreplay. From a Chinese painting of the eighteenth century.

At night it was very different; then his naughty, his sinful, his mutinous Henchman did everything it could to attract attention. Under the coarse wool blanket it would stretch and sprawl, rise up in defiance, or saunter haughtily about. . . . Lord in Heaven, how impetuously his eternal Disturber of the Peace had risen up, how conspicuous his rebellious Henchman was making himself! All stiff and proud, it could be seen holding up the blanket with its head; peering eastward and leering westward, obviously searching for one of its customary hiding places.

JOU PU TUAN

By endowing the sexual organs with personality, control of sexuality is more easily achieved. From a contemporary photograph.

VISHNU

the preserver

The mind is the foremost *erogenous zone*. The two main functions of the mind are *thought* and *imagination*. Thought is generally considered a male attribute and imagination a female one. This division into two categories is both revealing and potentially confusing. Confusion in this context can be avoided if we recall the basic fact of our inherent bisexuality. The categorization of mind into thought and imagination refers to archetypal principles and in no way limits the roles either sex may play.

Thought is associated with *logic* and imagination with *intuition*. If the imagination can be stirred up, then the body will respond through the sense organs. *Subtle channels* connect the mind with the eyes, ears, nose, mouth and skin surface; the hands, feet, sexual region and head are the main *terminals* of the subtle channels. The so-called erogenous zones are in fact all the points and places that lead directly to the psychic centers and, through them, to the mind itself. A close study of the illustrations of the pressure points and acu-meridians will give a clear idea of the distribution of erogenous zones throughout the male and female body.

The *Ananga Ranga* lists the following erogenous zones on the body of woman: the head, mouth, eyes, lips, cheeks, ears, throat, nape of neck, breasts, nipples, belly, back, arms, hands, thighs, Yoni, knees, ankles, feet, big toes, as well as the waist, buttocks, top of the head, space between

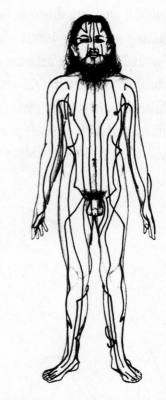

Acu-meridians, front view. These are the subtle channels through which energy circulates.

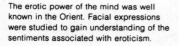

The erotic power of the mind was well known in the Orient. Facial expressions were studied to gain understanding of the sentiments associated with eroticism.

Acu-meridians, back view. By visualizing these channels while retaining the breath, energy is consciously induced into the Subtle Body, charging the whole being with vitality.

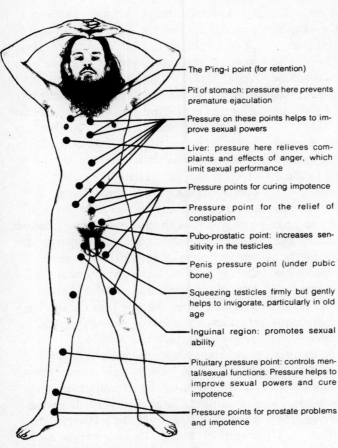

The P'ing-i point (for retention)

Pit of stomach: pressure here prevents premature ejaculation

Pressure on these points helps to improve sexual powers

Liver: pressure here relieves complaints and effects of anger, which limit sexual performance

Pressure points for curing impotence

Pressure point for the relief of constipation

Pubo-prostatic point: increases sensitivity in the testicles

Penis pressure point (under pubic bone)

Squeezing testicles firmly but gently helps to invigorate, particularly in old age

Inguinal region: promotes sexual ability

Pituitary pressure point: controls mental/sexual functions. Pressure helps to improve sexual powers and cure impotence.

Pressure points for prostate problems and impotence

Sex-related pressure points in the male, front view.

Adrenal glands: pressure here tones up the emotional centers

Pressure here helps to improve sexual powers

Sacral vertebrae: pressure points for the prevention of sexual energy loss. Also helps to avoid premature ejaculation.

Pressure on these points can help in cases of impotence.

Prostate: this point, at the tip of the "tailbone," helps to control sex energy.

For control of emission and prevention of "wet dreams"

Pressure point around the anus and between the anus and genitals, helps to stimulate sexual response

Pressure at these points can help to improve sexual performance. These are key meridians, leading to the inner subtle centers.

Sex-related pressure points in the male, back view.

Pressure on these points helps to improve appearance and strength of the eyes; good for relief of headaches

Thyroid glands: pressure on these points helps to stimulate hormone production and keeps skin, face and body both beautiful and healthy. Helps in menopause

Pressure helps to tone up sexual centers

Endocrine glands: massage here helps to stimulate reproductive organs

Knead breasts with palms, to keep firm or enlarge. Stimulates sexual urge

Relieves hysteria

Relieves female sexual organs. Good for the liver

Points which increase the flow of sexual energies. Improves potency

Helps in cases of menstrual irregularities or pains

Pressure points for the ovaries and innermost sexual organs

Inguinal region: pressure here can help to promote sexual ability

Points which help to stimulate the female organs. Gentle pressure relieves tension and helps in menopause problems

Pressure points for vaginal stimulation of sex center and for relaxing that whole area

Pressure point which reaches the pituitary control center.

Pressure points for the relief of menstrual irregularity

Sex-related pressure points in the female, front view.

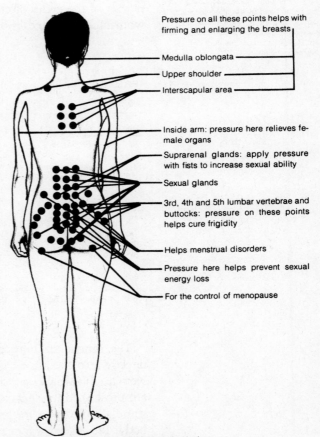

Pressure on all these points helps with firming and enlarging the breasts

Medulla oblongata

Upper shoulder

Interscapular area

Inside arm: pressure here relieves female organs

Suprarenal glands: apply pressure with fists to increase sexual ability

Sexual glands

3rd, 4th and 5th lumbar vertebrae and buttocks: pressure on these points helps cure frigidity

Helps menstrual disorders

Pressure here helps prevent sexual energy loss

For the control of menopause

Sex-related pressure points in the female, back view.

Female figure showing the changing location of erotic passion in woman (known as *Amritakala*), starting with the right big toe on the first day of the bright half of the lunar month, ascending to the top of the head by the fifteenth day, and descending the left side of the body during the dark half of the month. From a Rajasthani miniature painting of the eighteenth century.

the eyes. However, the main and most distinct areas of stimulation are the mouth, Yoni, breasts, neck, navel, buttocks, inner thighs, fingers and toes. In man, the erogenous zones are mostly centered around the Lingam, navel, heart and thighs, though the hands, feet, tongue, ears and breasts are also significantly erogenous.

The Tantric tradition states that passion is located in different parts of a woman's body at different times, according to the lunar cycle. The *Ananga Ranga* concurs, stating, "Passion resides in the right side of woman during the bright half of the lunar month. The reverse is the case during the dark half. The shifting takes place by the action of light and darkness, otherwise the site of passion would remain the same."

This account has some startling scientific implications. We know that the two main glands in the head are the pineal and pituitary, which both secrete subtle essences and hormones. The pineal is activated by light and follows a lunar cycle in women. The signals from the glands in the head reach all parts of the body and govern mood, temperature, and many other delicate and mysterious internal processes.

The *Ananga Ranga* offers us a generalized picture of the cycles of erotic passion in woman, as illustrated in the chart below.

the additional belief that the clitoris of a woman varies in size according to the phase of the moon. Similar ideas are also found in the earliest Indian texts, the Vedas.

In the Vedas, lunar cycles are associated with the Soma plant, a powerful psychedelic drug, which supposedly gained and lost leaves as the moon grew large or small. These plants may have been species of creeper, like the morning-glory plant, or possibly mushrooms or herbs. Tantric commentaries identify the Soma as synonymous with the *Divine Woman*, the *Inner Shakti*, who is externally identified with the female partner. Secret texts, such as the *Chandamaharosana Tantra*, indicate that the Yoni of woman produces Soma-like secretions when she is in high ecstasy. The texts recommend that the adept drink deeply from this fount of life.

All the texts stress that the Bright and Dark Cycle of Woman only operates when she is living a totally natural existence. Even artificial light upsets and alters the periodic cycles of woman and varies the centers of passion. There is a rejuvenation rite that requires a woman to remain in darkness for a full month before sexual activity. This rite has the effect of altering

BRIGHT HALF OF THE LUNAR MONTH (Right Side)		DARK HALF OF THE LUNAR MONTH (Left Side)	
Day	Place	Day	Place
15th	Head and Hair	1st	Head and Hair
14th	Right Eye	2nd	Left Eye
13th	Lower Lip	3rd	Lower Lip
12th	Right Cheek	4th	Left Cheek
11th	Throat	5th	Throat
10th	Right Side	6th	Left Side
9th	Right Breast	7th	Left Breast
8th	Middle of Chest	8th	Middle of Chest
7th	Navel	9th	Navel
6th	Right Buttock	10th	Left Buttock
5th	Yoni	11th	Yoni
4th	Right Thigh	12th	Left Thigh
3rd	Right Knee	13th	Left Knee
2nd	Right Foot	14th	Left Foot
1st	Right Big Toe	15th	Left Big Toe

The Tantric teachings on sexual love tie directly into the lunar cycle of passion in woman. Rituals and sexual Yoga postures are prescribed for specific days, with stimulation advised for precise areas of the body. Taoism has a similar tradition, with

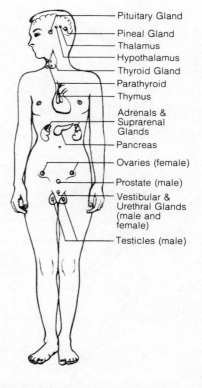

- Pituitary Gland
- Pineal Gland
- Thalamus
- Hypothalamus
- Thyroid Gland
- Parathyroid
- Thymus
- Adrenals & Suprarenal Glands
- Pancreas
- Ovaries (female)
- Prostate (male)
- Vestibular & Urethral Glands (male and female)
- Testicles (male)

The glands of the endocrine system. These all have influence on sexuality and control hormonal secretions.

her hormonal secretions, and at the same time, her *seats of passion*. During this rite, the woman is instructed to focus her mind on her sexuality, drawing up energy from her sex center to her head center and flooding it down throughout her body. She is told to meditate on herself as a waterfall, nourishing her own inner world. Lovemaking practiced after this month of preparation is vitalizing and transcendental.

Try to bring the power of both thought *and* imagination to awaken the erogenous zones throughout the body. Explore the natural relationship of lunar cycles to the seat of passion in the Shakti. With the intuition open, share the secrets of sensual ecstasy.

A Taoist couple making love. The woman looks in a mirror so the sentiments shown in her facial expression can be examined. From a Chinese water color on silk, *circa* seventeenth century.

By understanding the influence of the phases of the moon on the passion of woman, satisfaction can very easily be achieved. Without following these teachings, a person becomes liable to all kinds of sexual difficulties, such as love quarrels.

ANANGA RANGA

The Yogis and Yoginis should meet together on the <u>eighth</u> and <u>fourteenth</u> days of the <u>Dark Fortnight</u>, for the rite of helping all beings.   HEVAJRA TANTRA

By contemplating the vowel sounds in the lunar center of the head region, sixteen Joys arise. These are established according to the phases of the moon.

KALACHAKRA TANTRA

beds and pillows

A comfortable bed or extra pillows can make a great difference to successful lovemaking. Some erotic postures require a bed or couch at a particular level above the ground, whereas others can be practiced anywhere.

A bed should be firm yet soft. The East has always favored low and large couches, which serve as beds in the nighttime and seats during the day. Emperors and kings in ancient times would often conduct their court business from such "beds."

Taoist teachings prescribe different alignments of the bed according to the seasons. A text of the tenth century states, "In the Spring season, it is best to lie with the head pointing eastward; in the Summer, pointing south; in the Autumn, toward the west; and in Winter, with the head to the north."

Eastern beds often had columns and curtains, which made them into small rooms. They were arranged to delight the senses, with flowers and fruit discreetly placed nearby. Such a love-making environment was surely quite different from the modern bedroom. An ancient Indian text describes beds that, by air pressure, "could be made to move up and down in a soft, delightful action, like the undulation of a serpent." It also refers to *resonating beds*, which were set into rhythmic vibration by the intonation of specific musical notes. One Arabian text refers to "a bed with a mattress filled with mercury," rather like our modern water-bed.

A couple should take care to see that their bed is both comfortable and large enough to allow the full play of eroticism. We advise against using synthetic sheets or blankets, as they tend to create static electricity and alter the body polarity. A mattress should be firm yet soft. One text suggests "a mattress stuffed with soft sun-dried straw, flowers and sweet herbs." Feather beds and covers are warm and comfortable, but unfortunately, rather expensive. Once you've set up a bed or mattress, you'll find it easy to hang drapes, silks or curtains according to your own taste.

Pillows and cushions are tremendously important for lovers. Used knowledgeably, they can help create or maintain love-making positions. In ancient China, a certain type of horned pillow, shaped like a half-

moon, gained great popularity, becoming almost a necessity in every love nest. It could be used to support the buttocks of the woman as well as for her head or side. A well-equipped bedroom has cushions and pillows, both large and small.

Typical type of "horned pillow" placed under a woman's buttocks during love-making. Known in Chinese as *chueh-chen*, the pillows were believed to have a magical affinity with the lunar power of women. As well as being a practical aid to deep penetration, they also served a talismanic function.

Consider this instructive description of the correct use of pillows from an erotic novel of the Ming period (1368–1644), known as *The Way to Holiness through the Flesh*:

The use of a pillow is a simple and widely known trick; but few men are considerate enough to bother, and still fewer know how to do the thing properly. In addition to supporting the buttocks with a pillow, most men leave the other under the lady's head; this is a big mistake, for her body becomes bent through being raised at both ends. His weight will cause her discomfort and hinder her movements. Generally it is best to eliminate the head pillow if placing one under her buttocks.

One Hindu love-posture described in the *Ananga Ranga* (The Bow) does specify placement of pillows under buttocks and head simultaneously, but this is an unusual feature. A number of small pillows can be very useful in creating comfortable sexual positions. Imagination is an important ingredient in successful love-making; beds and pillows should be chosen to allow innovation and a variety of positions to develop freely. Then love-making can ascend to the highest level.

Love-making on a traditional Chinese bed. The woman holds her left hand in a gesture used to channel sexual energy and prolong orgasm. From a Chinese painting of the eighteenth century.

Love-making with a horned pillow in use. From a Chinese print of the nineteenth century.

The bed should have a canopy above it, with garlands and bunches of flowers all around. There should be at least two pillows, one at the top and the other at the bottom. Ideally, there should also be a separate couch, as well as perfume, musical instruments, fruits and games.

KAMA SUTRA

Once Shiva said to Parvati, "Dearest, here is a lovely house. Go anoint yourself with sandalwood paste, and while the bees hum and the sun sets, we two will make love on a delightful bed strewn with flowers. I shall take much pleasure in kissing your bright red lips and caressing your body."

PADMA PURANA

cosmetics and ornaments

From the most ancient times, cosmetics and ornaments have played a major part in sexual ritual. The application of makeup to the face can become a personal encounter between the self that one *is* and the self that one wishes to *become*. A "new face" can generate self-confidence and at the same time be a stimulating experience for the partner. Many mystical rites make use of this potential and specify makeup that stimulates particular sentiments. The importance of cosmetics in the present day can be gauged by the enormous worldwide sales of these products, even in the poorest areas.

Egyptian ladies with elaborate cosmetics and ornaments. They wear head-pieces of fragrant perfumes and flowers. From an Egyptian painting.

Tantric makeup, showing the Third Eye of awakened consciousness. From a contemporary sculpture, Crafts Museum, New Delhi.

No woman feels complete without her face makeup and personal jewelery, however simple it may be. Even the most natural look is usually cultivated painstakingly. In all cultures, cosmetics helped make the beautiful look more beautiful, and the ordinary "presentable."

In China, it was customary for a woman to place a red mark in the middle of her forehead. A similar practice still exists in India and Nepal, where it signifies spiritual or religious commitment. In Tantric rites, both the man and woman can wear this mark, to evoke the memory of the *Third Eye* of awakened consciousness.

Many different designs have evolved from basic floral patterns. From a contemporary photograph of an Indian marriage ceremony.

Artful application of cosmetics and ornamentation is a beautiful and significant practice that the couple can share. Obviously, natural cosmetics are preferable to synthetic ones. Many commercial preparations can cause skin problems, so makeup should be carefully chosen or created for oneself. There is no need to buy expensive formulas when Nature provides organic ingredients in a readily usable form. Most women take pleasure in choosing their own special combinations and experimenting on themselves. When properly applied, makeup and ornaments can transform a woman.

Painting the hands of women with henna or red dye is common to many Oriental cultures. It is particularly associated with marriage rites and ritual love-making. From a contemporary photograph.

Tantric rites sometimes specify body makeup. The reasons for this are aesthetic, psychological, symbolic and, on occasion, physiological. Gentle application of colored cosmetics to various parts of the body stimulates and concentrates energy there. Tantric cosmetic preparations incorporate a number of different substances, such as cinnabar, sandalwood powder and paste, sulphur paste, rice paste, saffron, nutmeg, tumeric, arsenic, soot from various substances, camphor, conch shell and ashes, some of which undoubtedly have a physical effect on the body. Particularly potent body makeup is made of crushed drugs such as datura (jimsonweed), marijuana, opium and other intoxicating substances mixed with fragrant oils and colored with pigments. European witches used similar body makeup in some of their rites.

One common custom of the East involves reddening the soles of the feet and palms of the hands of the woman. This is part of the ritual of *honoring the Shakti* (the female principle) and natural pigments such as henna are used for this purpose. In more elaborate rites, the feet of the woman can be completely painted with beautiful designs of flowers and symbols. Other parts of the body, especially the areas where forces are concentrated, like the navel, heart, throat, forehead and palms of the hands, may also be ornamented. Such practices are both aesthetically pleasing and erotically stimulating, helping to capture the imagination. They add magic and intimacy to the relationship. Furthermore, the degree of concentration necessary to successfully apply body makeup will assist in gaining ascendency over the ever-wandering mind.

For Tantric rites of high magic, the body is bathed and lightly oiled, and then dusted all over with ashes. Wood ash contains valuable trace minerals in a finely divided state, easily absorbed through the skin. Pure ash from selected hardwoods (for example, oak) has an invigorating and insulating effect on the body, protecting it against psychic disturbances. Once the wood ash is applied, exact marks (usually groups of three parallel lines) are made on the lower legs, thighs, forearms, upper arms, between the sexual region and the navel, across the navel, the middle of the chest, the throat and the forehead—usually with a powder or ointment made from crushed sandalwood, herbs, cereal grains or intoxicating ingredients. Then the Third Eye, or another symbolic mark, is painted right in the middle of the forehead, rising upward to the middle parting of the hair. The female partner may also have these marks applied, together with the ashes, but the most common custom is for the man to look terrific (with ash and marks) and the woman to look seductive and sensual (face makeup, with parts of the body such as the forehead, throat, nipples, navel, Yoni, hands and feet colored red). The potential inherent in the union of male aggression and female receptivity is activated by the careful and dramatic use of makeup, prior to and during ritual love-making.

The color red is known to effectively stimulate the male sex center. This explains the predominance of red in female facial cosmetics. The Chinese and Japanese, among other evolved cultures, saw in the natural contrast between the skin's pallor (often itself accentuated by white makeup) and the rosy tinge of cheeks and lips, a reminder of the symbolic interplay of *Red and White materiality-producing forces* and accentuated this in their theatrical masks.

Eye shadow also originally had a purpose that has been largely forgotten. Besides accentuating the eyes' natural brightness, shape and beauty, dark colors absorb

The archetypal Tantric couple, Shiva and Shakti. Shiva is depicted with snakes and a garland of skulls and his body is white as ashes. Shakti is shown as sensuous, with red cosmetics and ornaments dominating. Dramatization of sentiments aids ritual love-making by stirring up the emotions. From a Basohli miniature painting, Punjab Hills, *circa* 1690.

reflected light. Kohl, an Eastern product used for this purpose, if properly prepared, has a cooling and therapeutic effect on the eyes. The correct preparation is made from the soot of precious medicinal substances, such as camphor. Recent pharmacological research suggests that camphor stimulates the respiration, heart and cerebral cortex, and has a powerful effect on activating memory. Furthermore, scientific tests show that special preparations of camphor can increase clairvoyance. Tantric texts include special formulas for preparing extra-potent

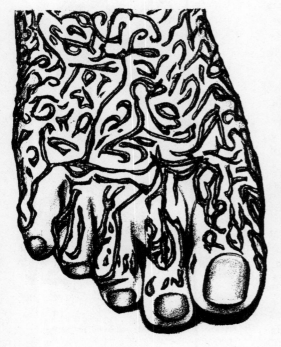

The feet of women are colored with henna or red dye. Patterns are drawn with great care and are considered an essential part of bridal ceremonies in India. From a contemporary photograph.

The Living Goddess of the Tantric tradition. As the embodiment of Shakti, her face is whitened and her lips and brows colored bright red. Kohl is applied to her eyes, flowers and jewels to her hair, and a Third Eye affixed to the middle of her forehead. From a contemporary photograph of the Living Goddess of Kathmandu, Nepal.

kohl by burning camphor with other volatile substances, sublimating the smoke on the outside of a metal pot filled with cold water. The Tantric kohl is scraped off the pot and used on the eyes, forehead and other regions of the body.

Tantric evocations of god and goddess archetypes often make dramatic and aesthetic use of makeup. In Nepal, for instance, there is an annual *Festival of the Living Goddess*, celebrated by decorating and parading a selected virgin girl to whom offerings are made. Her face is exquisitely made up, with marks of red, white, yellow and black. Tantra teaches that every woman has her virginity restored after the completion of her menstrual period. Some rituals specify celebrating this by preparing the female partner as the embodiment of the Living Goddess, using makeup, essential oils, fine clothes and jewelery.

Moles or mouches are presently out of fashion, but no doubt changing trends will bring them back in once again. In the past, women commonly created these beauty marks on their faces and bodies by application of black makeup. In Eastern cultures, the beauty marks subtly communicated by their shape, size and placement the suitability and status of a woman as an initiatress into the secrets of love.

Most women feel an attachment to their ornaments and personal jewelery. These hold special significance, serving as reminders of a particularly potent experience and linking her to the person who either made or bought them. A woman should carefully choose ornaments for a special occasion, considering not only their aesthetic effect, but also their value as amulets. The amuletic view of jewelery is of great significance in both ritual and daily Tantric lifestyle, acting on both conscious and unconscious levels of awareness. An amulet is imbued with emotional and magical qualities, and works through the powers of association and resonance.

Jewelry adds to the beauteous vision that a woman can create through a skillful blending of makeup, clothing and ornaments. Flowers should also be included in the category of body ornaments; it is amazing how stimulating a woman can look by carefully blending their colors and scents with her own.

In the Tantric tradition, a woman's ornaments are meant to symbolize her personal cosmology and evolutionary direction. Five categories of Tantric jewelery (necklaces, earrings, bracelets, head ornaments and girdle ornaments) symbolize the *Five Elements* and five distinct psychological types. By emphasizing particular ornaments, a Tantric Yogini signals her special qualities. In wearing symbolic jewelery, a woman makes contact with an idealized vision of herself.

In Tantric ritual, and especially during the *Secret Rite*, a woman is expected to wear her most symbolic jewelery. A beautiful woman, artfully made up and arrayed in full ornamentation, is a sight sufficient to stimulate any man, particularly if he knows that she has prepared herself in this way just for him. Try to make use of cosmetics and jewelery to empower your relationship and increase aesthetic delight.

Tantric Yogini with body ornaments symbolic of the Five Elements (space, air, fire, water and earth). From a Pala stone sculpture of the ninth century, Hirapur Yogini Temple, Orissa.

By means of oiling, dry massage, bathing, perfumes, garlands, ornaments, comfort, beds, seats, pleasant clothes, the warbling of birds, the tinkling of a woman's ornaments, and by having the body massaged by a beautiful woman, a man's virility gets stimulated.

CHARAKA SAMHITA

Her hair was black as a raven's plumage; her eyebrows as mobile as the kingfisher and as curved as the new moon. Her almond eyes were clear and cool and her cherry-colored lips seemed so inviting. Her nose was noble and exquisitely modeled and her dainty cheeks beautifully powdered. Her face had the delicate roundness of a silver bowl. As for her body, it was as light as a flower, her fingers as slender as tender shoots and her waist narrow like the willow. Her white belly was both yielding and rounded, her breasts soft and luscious.

CHIN P'ING MEI

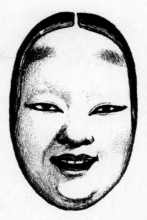

Noh mask from Japan, used in the theatre to exaggerate sentiments. This female face is painted white, with lips dominantly red. From an eighteenth-century original.

biting and scratching

Eastern treatises on the Art of Love always include a section on biting and scratching. As part of the *Battle of Love*, careful biting and scratching of the partner are a way of expressing ecstatic emotions. Sexual energy can be channeled into specific parts of the partner's body through lovesome biting and scratching. Teeth and nails can be consciously used to stimulate erogenous zones, pressure points and acu-meridians, helping to release and circulate energy.

Stimulating the skin surface by lightly using the nails like feathers causes the hair to bristle and goose pimples to form. This acts as a potent energizer and mood changer, and can help awaken the *Kundalini*. Light nibbling of the ears is a stimulating part of foreplay; gentle biting of the nape of the neck, in the way that a tiger grasps a tigress,

Tiger and tigress in love-play. From a contemporary photograph.

is also arousing. The fleshy *Mount of Venus* of the *Yoni* region, and the base of the spine, are both places where playful nibbling can evoke joyous experiences.

The kind of love-bite best known in the West is made by sucking or lightly nipping the partner's skin. It leaves a red mark resembling a small bruise. Such marks are potent reminders of a particularly ecstatic love experience long after the event. Especially during the early stages of a love affair, passionate love-marks can be of great significance to lovers.

The *Kama Sutra* states, "The places that can be bitten are the same as those that can be kissed, except for the very sensitive areas such as the upper lip, the interior of the mouth, the eyes and so on." Eight distinct love-bites are enumerated, classified according to the marks left on the skin. They are known as the *Hidden Bite*, when the skin becomes excessively red; the *Swollen Bite*, when the skin is pressed down on both sides; the *Point Bite*, when a small portion of the skin is bitten with only two teeth; the *Rosary of Points*, when small portions of the skin are bitten with all the teeth; the *Coral and Jewels*, produced from bringing together the teeth and lips (the lip is the coral, and the teeth are the jewels); the *Rosary of Jewels*, when biting is done with all the teeth; the *Broken Cloud*, produced from biting on the breasts with an open mouth; and the *Boar's Bite*, many broad rows of marks near to each other, with red intervals, impressed on the breasts or shoulders. The *Kama Sutra* adds that the lower lip is the best place on which to make the *Hidden Bite*, the *Swollen Bite* and the *Point Bite*; the *Rosary of Points* and the *Coral and Jewels* are suited to the throat, armpit and joints of the thighs; and the *Swollen Bite* and the *Coral and Jewels* are suited to the left cheek in particular. The left, in Tantra, is always associated with the intuition and the moon.

Hindu texts declare that biting should only be incorporated into love-making if it is pleasing to the woman. As a variation on the *Battle of Love*, the woman should "bite her partner in return, with double force." If biting is carefully woven into love-play, there is no need for any fear of excess.

The Art of Scratching is mentioned in both the *Kama Sutra* and the *Ananga Ranga*. In ancient India, the nails were sometimes specially shaped to enable their precise use during love-bouts. The *Kama Sutra* states, "Those with intense passion should have their left-hand fingernails made like a small saw blade, with two or three points. People with middling passion should shape and paint their nails to resemble the beak of a parrot, while those with little passion should paint a crescent shape on their nails."

Eight different kinds of nail marks are described in the classical texts: *Sounding* (pressing, leaving only a slight indentation), *Half-moon* (a curved mark, made with one nail), *Circle* (when two *Half-moon* marks are impressed opposite each other), *Line* (a straight mark, made by drawing a fingernail across the skin), *Tiger's Claw* (a curved line), *Peacock's Foot* (an impression of the five nails simultaneously), *Hare's Jump* (when five nail marks are impressed close together), and *Blue Lotus-Leaf* (resembling a leaf pattern, made with the fingers of one hand).

Eastern erotic art sometimes portrays nail marks on the bodies of lovers, a device used to communicate the mood of fulfilled passion. Long nails have always been associated with eroticism. They can be used to create exquisite sensations for the loved one and energy can be channeled through them. As in all aspects of the Art of Love, it is the mental attitude that determines the success or failure of any particular technique. Biting and scratching are powerful allies which can be used to show feelings of intimacy and passion.

When a man bites a woman, she should do the same with double force. Thus a Point should be returned with a Rosary of Points, *and a* Rosary of Points *with a* Broken Cloud, *and if she feels chaffed, she should immediately begin a love quarrel with him. At such times she should take hold of her lover by the hair, bend his head down, kiss his lower lip, and then, in the intoxication of her love, she should shut her eyes and bite him in various places.*

KAMA SUTRA

The lover, by applying the nails with love and affection, can bring great comfort to the woman. In fact, there is nothing, perhaps, more delightful to both husband and wife than the skillful use of the nails.

ANANGA RANGA

noises of love

People make a great variety of sounds while making love. These *Noises of Love* are ways of releasing emotional blockages, and can be either spontaneously or consciously created. Noises are also produced by the exertion of passionate breathing and by the physical action of bodies. Indian and Chinese texts attach great significance to these love-noises and categorize them in detail. They are all considered aspects of the Battle of Love.

A Chinese erotic novel of the seventeenth century gives a threefold classification for love-noises:

At the beginning of the *Battle*, before passion has really taken hold, a woman utters certain superficial cries of affection, such as "my dearest," "my life," whose purpose is to stir up her partner and arouse his desire. When these sounds issue from her mouth, it is still possible to understand each word plainly.

The second variety of sound is made when, as the *Battle of Love* proceeds, passion reaches deep inside her, tingling and throbbing through all her five inner organs and her four limbs, to the tips of her toes and fingers. Her breathing quickens and becomes irregular, her *Upper Breath* misses contact with her *Lower Breath*; consequently these sounds are confused and indistinct.

Finally, in the third and last phase of ecstasy, at the peak of passion, the woman is so utterly exhausted that her mind as well as her limbs refuses to function; in this state, all sounds stick in her throat and she becomes quite inarticulate. Her *Noises of Love* then have no recognizable meaning.

Some people spontaneously find themselves whispering endearing words or phrases, moaning, crying, laughing or shouting during passionate love-making. Others like to talk, verbalize fantasies, or even swear. Taoist and Tantric teachings do not recommend any kind of abuse of the partner since such practices tend to limit the potential of love-making to ascend to transcendent heights. However, sentiments are better expressed than repressed, and love-making is a great opportunity for sharing emotions through sound. Animal noises are sometimes spontaneously sounded during intense loving and these are given mystical significance in Eastern texts. When animal noises are *consciously* created, emotional blockages can be released effectively. Through animal noises, personality limitations are more easily transcended and the switching of active and passive roles is aided.

In the *Ananga Ranga*, there are references to particular kinds of sound known as *Sitkriti*: "An inarticulate sound produced by drawing in the breath between the closed teeth." This type of love-sound is said to be the particular prerogative and privilege of women and is divided into five distinct kinds likened to the cry of the quail ("Hun! hun! hun!" or "Hin! hin! hin!"), the Indian cuckoo ("Ha! ha!" or "Han! han!"), the spotted-necked pigeon ("Shan! shan!" or " Shish! shish!"), the Hansa goose ("T'hat! t'hat!") or the peacock ("T'hap! t'hap!"). If a woman can bring herself to make these sounds at the time of love, rather than the more usual uncontrolled or worldly sounds and exclamations of Western habit, then she can gain control over her ecstasies and channel love energies in a meaningful way. The imitation of bird sounds creates a sympathetic bond with these airborne species and helps send the energy flying upward.

Two gulls making love.

Tantric texts refer to the use of subtle sounds and Mantras for controlling and channeling the sex energy. The powerful Tantric Mantra "OM—AH—HUM" can be used for this, either externally as love-sounds or internally (in the mind) for protective and focusing purposes. This Mantra can be used a number of ways: linked to alternate shallow and deep strokes ("OM" shallow, "AH" deep, "HUM" focusing of energy becoming more and more subtle), to the breath ("OM" inhale, "AH" retain, "HUM" exhale), or just verbally intoned by both partners as a harmonizing influence. These sounds can also be visualized as opening up the psychic centers of the head, throat and heart, respectively. When used internally (in the mind), this Mantra should follow the rhythm of breath, and when sounded, the strokes of Love. In practice, the couple can find their own system of correlations between the elements listed below.

When using this Mantra, both partners should imagine spirituality descending into the centers of the head, throat and heart. In the heart center, the sound "HUM" emanates outward, vitalizing every part of the physical and Subtle Body. Visualized as dark blue waves of ecstasy, the sound "HUM" nourishes the unity and spiritual integrity of the couple. Tantric texts refer to

humming should be modulated, like that made by a flying insect approaching flowers. It serves to focus the mind and initiates a state of resonance with the Kundalini-power within. Let this humming become your carrier wave through the alchemy of ecstasy.

There are many Mantras that can be used to help control and focus sexual energy. The Mantra "OM—BHUR—BHUWAH—SWA" is an evocation of the *Three Realms* (this world, the next world, and Eternity), and is effective in establishing spiritual direction in a love-rite. The Mantra "OM—AH—HUM—VAJRA—GURU—PEMA—SIDDHI—HUM" evokes the magical power inherent in the union of Lingam and Yoni, and also connects those who use it with the ancient occult lineage. The seed sounds "LANG," "VANG," "RANG," "YANG" and "HANG" are correlated with the elements earth, water, fire, air and space, evoked in that order for the resolution of bodily imbalances or impurities and for opening up the psychic centers.

The sounds "EH" (the transformatory power of the navel center) and "VANG" (the distilling power of the water element) combine together as a single Mantra, "EH—VANG," which expresses the unity of the solar and lunar powers of the psyche. Imagine the sound "EH," blazing up at the navel center, burning up all negativity and physical impurities. Visualize the sound "VANG," cooling and flooding from the head center, washing away all psychic and intellectual limitations. The Mantra "EH—VANG" is effective in resolving dualities and empowering the couple with pure transcendental emotion. This powerful Mantra evokes the unity of Wisdom-energy and spirituality. As the *Advayavajra* states, "EH—VANG comprises everything. A person who understands the meaning of this Mantra has understood all and everything."

Tantra teaches that the emotions can be purified and exalted by correct use of Mantras. It really is very simple to perfect these Mantras and apply them to the Art of Love; there is no surer way to consciously

Tantric love-posture, effective for prolonging ecstasy. From a Rajasthani miniature painting of the eighteenth century.

humming sounds that a female Yogi (a Yogini) can make to release transcendental energy from the sexual center. They are particularly effective when woman takes the active role during love-making. This

Sound	Breath	Stroke of Love	Visualization Color	Meaning
"Om"	Inhale	Shallow	White	Purity of Spirit
"Ah"	Retain	Deep	Red	Divine Love
"Hum"	Exhale	Still	Dark Blue	Eternal Union

generate ecstasy. The movement of the breath during love-making finds release through Noises of Love, which may be either loud or soft, depending on temperament. Some people hardly make any sounds when making love, preferring to bask in silence; others derive great pleasure from expressing Noises of Love consciously or spontaneously. Try to incorporate natural sounds, Mantras and positive endearments into love-making, transforming the Noises of Love into ecstatic harmonies.

It is my view that all movements, sounds and utterances made by a copulating couple in the course of their performance greatly heighten their rapture and whet their sexual appetite.
SHAYKH NAFZAWI

There are noises of love that have actual meaning, such as "Mother," "Father," "Lover," and those that express prohibition, sufficiency, desire for liberation, pain, praise, ecstasy and so on. To these may be added sounds like those of the dove, cuckoo, pigeon, parrot, bee, sparrow, flamingo, duck, quail and other animals. KAMA SUTRA

The sacred syllable "EH," adorned by the syllable "VANG," is the abode of all delights. From "EH–VANG" the Four Joys arise. HEVAJRA TANTRA

In Oriental cultures the Yoni is considered the most sacred part of a woman's body, and is not viewed as unclean. In this Japanese illustration of oral-genital sex, the man honors the Yoni and at the same time channels energy through the feet of his partner, so increasing her enjoyment. From a painted scroll, Nakamura Tei-i, *circa* 1930.

oral erotics

Westerners have only recently begun to view oral sex as acceptable and natural. Yet mouth kissing has always been taken for granted in the West. In India and China, the kiss is considered the epitome of eroticism.

As such, it is practiced in absolute privacy. Indian movies have only just started to show mouth-to-mouth contact on the screen.

The love, comfort and nourishment we receive as babies suckling at our mothers' breasts initiates the chain of association between oral gratification and sex. The relationship of eating to sex is also well

The Yoni-kiss is an erotic theme common to all cultures where mystic sexuality is considered important. From a stone carving in the Rajarani Temple, Bhubaneshwar, Eastern India, *circa* twelfth century.

known to psychology. That Westerners have recently become infatuated with oral-genital sex may well be due to the modern tendency to switch from breast to bottle feeding of children. Nevertheless, the mysteries of oral-genital sex, so well developed in the East, warrant exploration from a transcendental viewpoint.

The subtle and unforgettable aroma of the sexual organs and their secretions should be appreciated and enjoyed. In the animal kingdom, the sense of smell is an important element in mating rituals. Nature designed the musky sexual odors as a virilific and for encoding emotions. The combination of love-juices with saliva produces a unique, chemically charged bond that has both physical and magical properties. When oral-genital love-making is practiced, the *Upper and Lower* energies can be successfully exchanged and circulated. This is the Tantric and Taoist view of oral eroticism, which has much to add to our limited Western viewpoint.

When uniting the mouth with the Yoni, try to meditate on yourself as drinking from the fount of immortality, the inexhaustible *Source of Life*. View the Yoni as the original location of *Shakti*, the potent Kundalini-energy. When you excite Her, She will become pleased and grant every ecstasy; when the *Kundalini* rises upward, all the psychic centers of the *Subtle Body* become illuminated. By giving the best, you receive the most; the Yoni opens herself up and reveals all her secrets.

Hindu texts state that the different ways of kissing the Yoni should be learned from the methods of mouth kissing. Shaykh Nafzawi, author of *The Perfumed Garden*, points out that, like the mouth, the Yoni has two lips and a tongue. The *Kama Sutra* states, "Mouth congress is allowed by the lawbooks, but should be correctly practiced. Just as the udder of a cow is considered exalted at the time of milking, so should the Yoni be viewed at the time of bringing the mouth to it."

The Yoni is always highly honored in Tantric rituals. As the doorway through which all humans must pass, the Yoni is also considered as entrance to both the past and the future. In the *Chandamaharosana Tantra*, the sex initiatress is instructed to squat naked before the man and indicate her Yoni with her forefinger, and say to

him, "I am your royal mother, your formal wife and mistress. Look at this lotus-flower of mine, decorated with a stamen at the center. It is the *Pleasure Field of Heaven*. Numerous are the times that you have emerged from it. Can you kiss and lick this secret place without disgust or lust? Are you prepared to taste the *Red and White*? Are you a hero, or a newborn child?"

Tantrics declare that since all human beings are born through the Yoni, they should honor this part of the female anatomy as the Gateway to Life. From a contemporary photograph.

The "Tantric Yoni-kiss." From a contemporary photograph.

Female sexual secretions are believed to be invigorating and harmonizing to the whole physical system. From a nineteenth-century Chinese painting.

Oral sex performed on the Lingam is categorized in detail in the *Kama Sutra*. Eight variations are listed:

CAUSING or OMEN-MAKING
The Lingam is held in the hand, placed in the mouth and moved in between the lips.

SIDE BITING
The Lingam is covered by the fingers collected together like the bud of a flower. The sides are then pressed with the lips, using the teeth very slightly.

OUTSIDE PRESSING
The Lingam is pressed between the lips and kissed as if drawing it out.

INSIDE PRESSING
The Lingam is pushed further into the mouth, pressed by the lips and then pulled out.

KISSING
The Lingam is kissed as if it were the lower lip of the lover.

RUBBING
After kissing, the Lingam is touched all over by the tongue, which is passed over the head of it.

SUCKING A MANGO
The Lingam is put halfway into the mouth and then forcefully kissed and sucked.

SWALLOWING UP
The Lingam is drawn completely into the mouth, as far as it will go, and then pressed in to the end and sucked, as if being swallowed.

When the *Kama Sutra* was written, the eightfold Lingam kiss was considered a special feature of the massage art. Orthodox Hindus viewed it with suspicion since there was always a possibility of semen emission. There was a taboo against "careless loss of life essence." In the *Vasisthadharmashastra*, a Hindu lawbook, it is stated, "When sexual intercourse is performed in the mouth of one's wife, then it is the ancestors who eat the seed that is emitted." The Tantric view is that semen can be potentized through having sex without ejaculation, and that every emission of semen should be a conscious rather than an involuntary act.

Semen contains amino acids, trace elements and minerals. When a man follows a healthful diet and lifestyle, the semen takes on a sweet taste and has a pleasant, palatable consistency. A woman should honor the Lingam of her lover as the Original Shiva Lingam, the *Male Principle*. Approaching in the spirit of awe and reverence, she should use her mouth as a second Yoni. Rhythmically sucking the Lingam in a relaxed and spontaneous way, she will be able to take it deep within her throat without fear of gagging. Through this practice, a woman can honor and please her lover, receiving his emission as a bodily sacrament.

The *Kama Sutra* lists eight types of oral sex performed on the Lingam. From a contemporary photograph.

Oral sex should never be rushed or be allowed to become mechanical. From a contemporary photograph.

Behold the Shiva Lingam, beautiful as molten gold, firm as the Himalaya Mountain, tender as a folded leaf, life-giving like the solar orb; behold the charm of his sparkling jewels!

LINGA PURANA

She should have him suck her Lotus and show his pleasure. Inhaling the odor, he should enter with his tongue, searching for the Red and White secretions. Then she should say to him, "Eat my essence! Drink the Waters of Release! O Son, be a slave as well as a father and lover!"

CHANDAMAHAROSANA TANTRA

the crow/"69"

The sexual position commonly referred to as "69" in the West is termed *The Crow* in Hindu texts. This is an inverted position, with oral-genital contact between man and woman. It can be practiced with the woman lying down and with the man on top; with the woman on top; in a standing position; and in a number of side postures. It is a pleasant aspect of foreplay and has a harmonizing effect on the body. The Crow is also a potent sexual posture of the Tantric tradition, used for potentizing and circulating sexual energy.

In the enigmatic language of alchemy, the crow symbolizes the transcendental power of dissolution. Crows have always been

viewed as mystic birds and omen-carriers; their unique metabolism allows them to digest poisons without harm. Tantric Yogis consider crows metaphysical allies, able to convey information through their movements and sounds. Crows are commonly depicted as "aides" of Kali (the archetype of transcendence) and Mahakala (the Lord of Time). The sexual posture known as The Crow is, according to Tantra, most effective for mutual subtle nourishment, energy circulation and exchange. It has a potentizing effect on the sexual center of both partners and awakens the transcendental faculties of the mind.

Tantra teaches that the tongue is an important body terminal through which metaphysical energies can be channeled. When The Crow posture is practiced, the tongue of a man is to be used like a second Lingam. The Yoni-essences secreted during oral love-making are easily absorbed by the mucous membranes of the mouth and tongue. Psycho-magnetic Yoni-waves emanate when a woman is sexually excited; these produce a "field of force" that polarizes and discharges with the head

This type of posture is known as the Crow. It is an important aspect of Tantric love-play. From a Rajasthani painting of the mid-eighteenth century.

Taoism teaches that mutual oral-genital sex creates a special energy circuit that can help harmonize vital body elements. From an eighteenth-century Japanese painting.

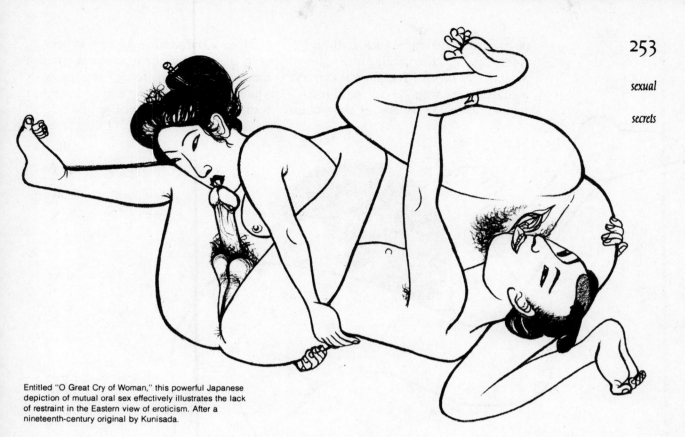

Entitled "O Great Cry of Woman," this powerful Japanese
depiction of mutual oral sex effectively illustrates the lack
of restraint in the Eastern view of eroticism. After a
nineteenth-century original by Kunisada.

center of the male partner practicing The
Crow. The polarizing effect of Yoni-waves
causes the pineal and pituitary glands of
the brain to release powerful secretions,
which help to open up and focus the Third
Eye. This is the mind's inner eye, the
faculty of clairvoyance, which gives insight
into both past and future. The polarizing
power of Yoni-waves has been recognized
since the dawning of Tantric occultism. It
is a great secret, which the modern Tantric
couple can use to open up the latent
powers of the psyche.

When a woman is practicing The Crow
with her partner, she should use her
mouth as a second Yoni, imitating the
contractions of her actual Yoni. Psycho-
electrical Lingam-waves emanate when a
man is sexually excited; a woman should
endeavor to stimulate these waves and
bring them to peak potential by the action
of her mouth. This will cause her Kundalini
to rise up to the head center, which will
be experienced as an ecstatic thrill rushing
up her spine. By bringing her partner to
orgasm at this point, the Kundalini is
nourished and fortified. An energy
exchange takes place, invigorating the
partners. The sexual secretions of the male
are easily absorbed by the mucous
membranes of the mouth and tongue of

the woman; they are rapidly assimilated by
the head center, causing a change in
glandular secretions throughout the body.
Correct use of The Crow for oral-genital
intercourse creates lasting and beneficial
changes in the organisms of both partners.

Tantric erotic art sometimes portrays The
Crow love-posture practiced with the man
standing and the woman inverted. This
difficult position is used for intense energy
channeling and requires great strength in the
man. The woman should keep relaxed and
allow energy from her Yoni to flood to her
head; the man should try to draw the
copious mouth secretions into his Lingam by
breath and diaphragm control, and directly
absorb them through the delicate
membranes of his sex organ. His role is to
build up the peaks of his partner's ecstasies
while controlling his own emission of semen.
The inverse position of the woman enables
her sexual energies to become internalized
and directed to her head; this acts as a great
tonic, invigorating her subtle and physical
body and strengthening her powers of
concentration. The man should use his
tongue like a Lingam, *giving* rather than
taking. By circulating the sexual energy in this
way, a simultaneous and prolonged peak
orgasm can be consciously created. Prior to
ejaculation, the man should transform the

position so he lies on his back, with the woman on top. Then both partners can obtain equal benefit. The physical exertion required of the man, coupled with the absolute relaxation required of the woman, produces a transcendental effect. When both are at rest in the supine position, their minds are opened up to new dimensions. This is a potent moment, empowering meditation and spiritual release.

According to Tantra, this type of Inverted Crow Posture is useful in directing sexual energy to the head center of the female partner, and can enhance clairvoyance. After a contemporary photograph.

When a man and woman lie down in an inverted order, with the head of the one toward the feet of the other, and in this position carry on with their love-making, then it is called The Posture of the Crow.   KAMA SUTRA

With his head resting between her thighs, the Adept drinks deeply from the Source of Life. Above, the goddess causes his power to grow and transform into Buddha-fields within her mind. Below, the Adept endows each Wave of Wisdom with his means. Each meditating on the transcendental experience of non-duality, the confluence of rivers swells and bursts its banks; there are no limitations anymore.

CHANDAMAHAROSANA TANTRA

When Parvati drinks the seed of Shiva, she acts as a snake goddess coiled around the Lingam. She drinks the Soma elixir directly from its mouth.

SATCHAKRANIRUPANA

playing the flute

Chinese erotic literature has many references to Playing the Flute, another name for contact between the mouth and Lingam. The mouth of a woman can "play" the Lingam in an infinite variety of ways, from gentle licking, brushing with the lips and kissing, to deep, prolonged sucking. She should take care to avoid over-zealous use of her teeth, as the delicate membranes of the Lingam can be injured. Playing the Flute is a delicate and stimulating practice by which a woman can come to know the character and subtle delights of the Lingam.

The "living instrument" of the male has to be "played" with care. From a Chinese print of the Ming dynasty.

In Chinese erotic literature the term "playing the flute" is commonly used to describe the contact between mouth and Lingam. It is especially used to evoke the sexual control necessary to achieve the heights of ecstasy. From a Chinese painting of the mid-eighteenth century.

In the Chinese classic The Golden Lotus, there is the following amusing and sensitive passage:

The lovers took off their clothes and sat side by side within the silken net on coverlets of the rarest silk, perfumed with orchids and musk. They laughed and played together until the flush of desire mounted to their brows and the passion in their hearts made them tremble. Then they performed the Mystery of the Clouds and the Rain and did whatever the wine inspired. He sat on the bed and made the Lady of the Vase place herself on the cushions and Play the Flute for him:

Not from bamboo or stone, not played on strings,
This is the song of an instrument that lives,
That makes the emerald tassels quiver.
Who can say what the tune is, or the key?
The red lips open wide,
The slender fingers play their part daintily.
Deep in, deep out; their hearts grow wild with passion. There are no words to tell of the ecstasy that thrills.

nine positions of the dark girl

There is a Taoist text of the Sui Dynasty (*circa* A.D. 590–618), known as the *Sex Handbook of the Dark Girl*, which takes the classic form of a dialogue between a Sex Initiatress and the Yellow Emperor. The Dark Girl is one of a triad of Initiatresses, all of the Taoist tradition, who teach the sexual secrets. The Yellow Emperor is a mythic Chinese ruler who taught mankind the various skills necessary for civilization. He ruled during the Golden Age, when there was no war or sickness; it is said that he ascended to Heaven in broad daylight, after perfecting the Sexual Arts with his twelve hundred wives and concubines. The Dark Girl taught him various other arts, including military strategy and magic, but it was for her sexual wisdom that she was best known.

The *Nine Positions of the Dark Girl* are specifically prescribed for balancing imbalances within the body. Taoism and Tantra both teach that sexual intercourse can have a very beneficial effect on health. Specific postures, like Yoga positions, release and channel energy. If postures and love-rhythms can be correctly chosen, all physical ailments can be easily overcome. The therapeutic value of love-making is a topic that we shall be viewing over the next few sections of this book. The Dark Girl here emphasizes love-positions, strokes of love and the power of rhythm:

The Dark Girl is one of a triad of sex initiatresses in the Taoist tradition. From a contemporary photograph.

TURNING DRAGON

The woman lies on her back and the man lies upon her, with his knees resting on the bed. She raises up her Jade Gate and inserts his Jade Stalk into her mysterious cavern, while he caresses the upper part of her body. He then begins to move slowly, interspersing two deeply penetrating love-strokes between every eight shallow ones. Retaining his semen, his Jade Stalk should ideally be inserted when it is not completely hard and withdrawn while still stiff. If the man performs his movements vigorously and strongly, his health will flourish, the *Hundred Ailments* (all sickness) will vanish and the woman will experience full gratification and joyfulness.

Turning Dragon. From a painting on silk of the K'ang-Hsi period (1662–1722).

TIGER'S TREAD

The woman gets down on her hands and knees, with her buttocks raised and her head down. The man kneels behind her and embraces her waist. Then he pierces her innermost center with his Jade Stalk; it is very important that he penetrate deeply, interspersing five shallow love-strokes with eight deep ones. Retaining his semen, he should continue until the woman's Grotto contracts and expands to release copious Yin-essence. Then he should rest. This method of love-making will prevent the Hundred Ailments, and at the same time increase virility.

Tiger's Tread. From a nineteenth century Chinese painting.

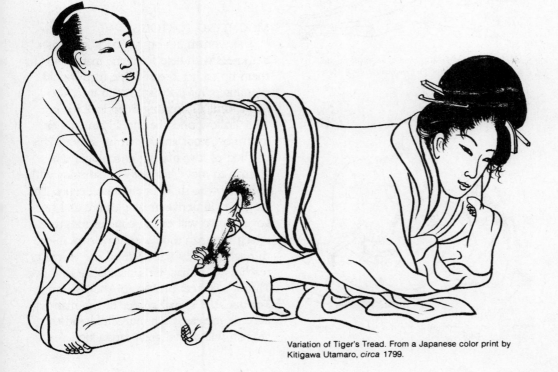

Variation of Tiger's Tread. From a Japanese color print by Kitigawa Utamaro, *circa* 1799.

Approach to Monkey's Attack. From a Japanese Shunga scroll, *circa* 1640.

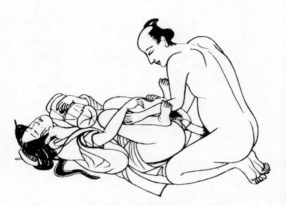

Monkey's Attack. From a Japanese color print by Katsukawa Shunsho, *circa* 1788.

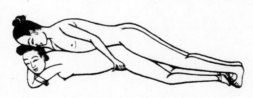

Splitting the Cicada. From a Chinese engraving for the erotic novel *Su Wo P'ien* (The Moon Lady), *circa* 1610.

Mounting Tortoise. From an anonymous series of Japanese prints, *circa* 1680.

MONKEY'S ATTACK

The woman lies on her back and raises up her buttocks and lower back, The man draws up her legs until her knees touch her breasts. Inserting his Jade Stalk into her Perfumed Mouse, he should move rhythmically until her emissions fall like heavy rain. The man should forcefully place the woman in this posture, as if angry with her. As soon as she experiences her climax, the man should stop his movements, retaining his semen. By practicing love-making in this way, the Hundred Ailments will vanish.

SPLITTING THE CICADA

The woman lies flat out on her front and extends her body. The man stretches out over her back, lifting her buttocks so as to insert his Jade Stalk into her Red Pearl. He should make love with her, interspersing six shallow love-strokes with nine deep ones, until she is very excited and her Love Grotto becomes moist. The man should retain his semen, gradually bringing her to full climax, when her Grotto will expand and contract rhythmically. Then he should stop moving. This method of love-making is effective in curing the Seven Bodily Aches (all bodily pain).

MOUNTING TORTOISE

The woman lies on her back and raises her knees with help from the man, who lifts them up to her breasts. The man should then insert his Jade Stalk deep into her Infant Girl. Alternating deep love-strokes with shallow ones, he should aim at her innermost Knot and retain his semen. This method of love-making encourages the woman to move her body in harmony with the man, who should penetrate deeply. The woman will derive great pleasure and her Love Grotto will exude copious moisture, which the man should endeavor to absorb through his Jade Stalk. When the woman reaches her climax, he should cease to move. Through correct practice of the Mounting Tortoise, the sexual power of the man will become increased a hundredfold and the woman will derive great satisfaction.

FLUTTERING PHOENIX

The woman lies on her back and raises her legs. The man kneels between her thighs, supporting himself by resting his hands on the bed. He inserts his Jade Stalk deeply, penetrating into her innermost Precious Stone and moving vigorously. Harmonizing his body with hers, he should intersperse three shallow love-strokes with eight deep ones, pressing himself firmly against her buttocks, so that her Anemone of Love expands and contracts, naturally exuding moisture. He should retain his semen and bring the woman to climax. This method of love-making cures the Hundred Ailments.

Fluttering Phoenix. From a painted scroll, Hokusai school, Japan, *circa* 1830.

RABBIT SUCKING ITS HAIR

The man lies on his back, with both legs stretched out. The woman straddles him, her knees outside the man's legs, her back turned on him and facing his feet. She inserts his Jade Stalk into the Strings of her Lyre and moves voluptuously. When she has reached the zenith of pleasure, profuse moisture will flow from her like a spring. Then her face will become filled with great joy. The man should retain his semen while practicing this love-making method, which prevents the Hundred Ailments.

Variation of Fluttering Phoenix. From a Japanese color print by Kikugawa Eizan, *circa* 1810.

Rabbit Sucking Its Hair. From a series of Japanese prints by Moronobu, *circa* 1682.

OVERLAPPING FISH-SCALES

The man lies on his back and the woman sits on top of him, with her legs stretched out in front of her. The man gently inserts his Jade Stalk slightly, and then stops. He should continue to lightly sport inside her with his Jade Stalk, like an infant playing with its mother's breast. All love-movements should be done by the woman, who should prolong her climax for as long as possible. The man should retain his semen and bring the woman to fulfillment. This love-making method cures all imbalances of temperament.

Variation of Overlapping Fish Scales. From a Chinese print of the Ming dynasty.

CRANES WITH JOINED NECKS

The man sits comfortably. The woman sits on his lap facing him, with her legs apart. She embraces his neck with her arms, while he inserts his Jade Stalk deep into her Wheat-shaped Cave. The man should aid her movements up and down, by placing his hands under her buttocks. He should retain his semen while she brings herself to climax and her moist secretions flow profusely. When the woman is completely fulfilled, they should rest together without making any bodily movements. This delightful method of love-making is effective in curing the Seven Bodily Aches.

All of the Nine Positions of the Dark Girl clearly emphasize the sexual fulfillment of the woman. The man is instructed to retain his semen and maintain a conscious awareness of the circulation of sexual energy throughout his being. Sexual intercourse creates very specific energy currents and has a marked effect on respiration, heartbeat and blood circulation. The Yin-essence of woman fortifies the Yang-force of man, nourishing and invigorating his whole body. This is a sexual secret, known to both Taoist and Tantric traditions. The *Shiva Purana*, an Indian treatise of metaphysics, states, "He who burns his body with the fire of Shiva

and floods it with the Elixir waters of his consort quickly gains immortality."

In the *Sex Handbook of the Dark Girl*, the Love Initiatress explains to the Yellow Emperor that if a man passes through four stages of ecstasy during his love-making, he will receive benefits from the *Nine Spirits* of woman. During the four stages of ecstasy, he should be sure not to emit semen, because if he does, the full benefits will not be received. The Dark Girl declares, "If the Jade Stalk does not seem angry, then the *harmonious spirit* is not attained. If it seems angry but not large, then the *flesh spirit* is not attained. If it is large but not hard, the *bone spirit* is not attained. If it is hard but not hot, then the *heart spirit* is not attained. Therefore it is said that anger is the dawning of the sperm, largeness is the beginning, hardness is the "shutting-off," and hotness is the gate of love. If the above four spirits are controlled correctly, then the duct of sperm will not open before its time and there will be no ejaculation." Taoism teaches that these four spirits are essential to the formation of sperm. Control of them is attained by causing the Jade Stalk to manifest anger, largeness, hardness and heat.

Taoist sexual practices undoubtedly produce a healthful physiological effect. Conscious retention allows the man to give the most to his partner, while benefiting from her nourishing Yin-essence.

Cranes with Joined Necks. From a Japanese print attributed to Tsukioka Settei, *circa* 1760.

If one should resolve to abstain from sexual intercourse, one's innermost spirit will not develop, since the interchange of Yin and Yang will come to a halt. How could one thus supplement one's vital essence? Blending the vital essence during frequent sexual intercourse, substituting the new energies for the old, is the way to derive real benefit. If a man knows how to make love without emitting semen, then his vital essence will return within. This is the secret of life, which greatly benefits the system.   SU-NU-CHING

The Dark Girl personifies the transcendental initiatress into the arcana of sex. From a contemporary photograph.

If a man engages in the sex act just once without emitting semen, then his vital essence will become strong. If he does so twice, his hearing and vision will become very clear. If three times, all bodily diseases will disappear. If four times, an inner peace will become attached to his spirit. If five times, then his blood circulation will be greatly improved. If six times, his loins will become very strong. If seven times, his thighs and buttocks will increase their power. If eight times, his whole body will become shining and radiant. If nine times, his life expectancy will increase.   YI-FANG-PI-CHUCH

the nine spirits of woman

According to classical Chinese traditions, nine *spirits* together make up one *Great Soul*. This tradition occurs throughout occult teachings in China, Tibet, India, Egypt and ancient Persia. The *Sex Handbook of the Dark Girl*, which lists nine love-making positions, gives an interesting account of the *Nine Spirits of Woman* and suggests ways of recognizing their action by understanding of female body language. Eight of the nine spirits are described as directly related to sexual symptoms. The Dark Girl explains:

The *Nine Spirits of Woman* can be easily known by studying their symptoms. If a woman breathes deeply and swallows the saliva that she is profusely secreting, then it is her *lung spirit* that is aroused. If she starts whispering loving words and kisses her partner, then it is her *heart spirit* that has awakened. If she holds her lover in her arms, then her *spleen spirit* has come to life. If her Sexual Cavern becomes moist and slippery, then her *kidney spirit* is excited. If she begins to suck her partner's tongue, then her *bone spirit* is animated. If she hooks her partner's lower body with her feet, then her *muscle spirit* has arrived. If she begins to handle her lover's Jade Stalk, then her *blood spirit* has become stimulated. And if she caresses the nipples and chest of her beloved, then her *flesh spirit* has become delighted. If all these eight spirits do not arrive and harmonize, then the woman will be harmed by love-making. But if the spirits evolve in sequence, she will derive great benefits.

The ninth spirit of woman is brought into action when she makes love with abandonment. She then feels her lover with her lungs, heart, spleen, kidneys, bones, muscles, blood, flesh and her whole being. All her inner spirits become involved and harmonized. Then the innermost ninth spirit is elated and an inner fulfillment takes place. At this point, the overall Great Soul, which came into existence at the moment of conception, can be intimately known.

Such an experience, a natural product of exalted love-making, can even inspire intuitions of past lives. Once a person has returned his or her consciousness to the point of origination, there is a great potential for rediscovering the links in the "chain of causality" (Karmas and lifetimes). Particularly potent love experiences can produce sudden and unexpected glimpses into the past.

The experience of pure joy through knowing the completeness of the Self is referred to in Tantra as the *Fulfillment Stage*. In the *Secret Teachings of Naropa*, an important Buddhist Tantric text of the eleventh century, it is stated:

The person who practices the *Fulfillment Stage* of Yoga, which is one of the finest methods of developing spirituality, should be eager to experience his authentic Being within a single lifetime. The sign

A Tantric master in union with his consort. Their ecstatic union expresses the fulfillment stage of Tantric Yoga, when full spirituality is achieved within a single lifetime. From a Tibetan painting of the sixteenth century.

of this is a feeling of ecstatic dissolution traveling through the central *Subtle Nerve*. Such a person should endeavor to fully experience the meaning of Self and Other. This is experienced by stimulating one's sexual power and vitality, not allowing it to decrease, and by absorbing the woman's secretions, so as to produce a constant feeling of blissful spontaneity.

The Fulfillment Stage of Yoga involves the physical, emotional and mental aspects of the Self; it is the full expression and joy of harmonious love-making. The experience is ecstatic, orgasmic and totally satisfying. Tibetan teachings liken it to the moment of Genesis, created by our primordial ancestral spirits, the cosmic Father/Mother, in ecstatic union. The iconographical representation of this moment is a seated couple locked in sexual embrace, the male aspect colored dark blue and the female milky white.

The overall Great Soul, which is known in Chinese as the *Po*, comes into existence with conception. It is formed by the union of the parents and is directly responsible for establishing the vital organs of the newly forming body. As we mentioned previously, it has nine parts, conceived of as vital spirits, which are delineated in the "Nine Spirits of Woman." These spirits are normally dormant in the body of a woman, but manifest themselves when stirred by eroticism.

Complementary to the Great Soul, is the *Hun*, the *Great Spirit*. The *Hun* enters the body of a child at the moment when the first breath is taken. When a person dies, this Great Spirit leaves first.

The same distinction between Soul and Spirit is found in all ancient religious systems. The *Ba* and *Ka* of ancient Egypt, for example, parallel the Chinese *Po* and *Hun*. The Great Soul (*Po*) and Great Spirit (*Hun*) relate to the solar and lunar forces in both microcosm and macrocosm. They are the *cosmic connection* between this world and the next. By cultivating an awareness of these two principles and enacting their roles consciously during love-making, the couple will be able to nourish each other's deepest Self. This powerful and meaningful secret has many practical applications.

For example, if a person has developed an imbalance in his or her personality, such as being too aggressive, that person can benefit by acting out a passive (lunar) role during love-making. By the same token, someone who has the problem of weakness and passivity can strengthen his or her solar forces by assuming the dominant, active role during love-making. Ultimately, the couple can experience the essence of the Great Soul and Great Spirit in union. This is the constant goal of Taoist love practices.

If Yin and Yang are balanced, the Spirit and Soul obtain a place in which to merge. The Yang is the Hun-Spirit of the sun and the Yin is the Po-Soul of the moon. If they can come together in mutual coexistence, then an appropriate situation for conception will be established. The nature of man is regulated from within and develops a definite shape. The passion of man is regulated by outside factors. Passion accomplishes the union of Heaven and Earth; when "hard" has shed its semen, "soft" dissolves into moisture. The man is white, the woman is red. When the climax is reached, the water element will extinguish the fire element. This blending constitutes the first link in the sequence of all the elements. So it is that the foundation for the embryo is laid.

TS'AN-T'UNG-CH'I

During the love-making of man and woman, their passions should blend together harmoniously. If, at the moment of fertilization, the Yin blood [the ovum] arrives first, the Yang semen will meet it and be enveloped by it. Thus the bone spirit will develop a male embryo. If, on the other hand, the semen arrives first, the ovum of the woman will become mixed with it and be enveloped by it. The "blood" of the woman will stay near to its origin and a female embryo will be created.

CH'U-SHIH-I-SHU

The Cosmic Father in union with the Cosmic Mother. Known to Tibetans as Kuntu Zangpo and Kuntu Zangmo (the All-Good Father–Mother), they are invoked as archetypal ancestors filled with benevolence toward humanity. They are meditated upon as the ideal of the couple, and are visualized as the apex of ecstasy. From a woodblock print of the late nineteenth century, Sherpa, Eastern Nepal.

the yang number

In esoteric traditions throughout the ancient world, the number nine was credited with magical potency. Odd numbers are associated with the male force and even numbers with the female force. The numbers one, three, seven and nine are generally considered magically important, and by multiplying them with each other, a whole series of magical numbers are created. Among these the most significant are the numbers twenty-one, twenty-seven, forty-nine, sixty-three and eighty-one.

Ancient Egypt knew an *Ennead* of gods (a combination of nine), formed from three *Triads*. A typical magical triad would be the concept of father-mother-child, or the triad of principles that forms the structure of this book: creation, transcendence and preservation. China possessed similar traditions of the power of three and its exalted potency as the number nine. On the ninth day of the ninth Chinese month it was customary to ascend the peaks of hills and mountains, as this practice was believed to enhance personality and develop longevity. Contemporary European magical practices make much use of units of three and nine; George Gurdjieff introduced a mystical diagram based on the number nine, and termed it the *Enneagram*. This has since had a significant influence on Western occultism and magical ritual in particular.

Other examples of the significance of the number nine are the already mentioned Hindu *Trinities of Forces*, grouped three together, the *Nine Apertures* of the human body and the *Nine Rulers*, or *Nine Spirits*, which influence the destiny of a person. For the follower of the Tantric tradition of *Shakti* (the evocation of female creative energy), the rites and symbolic forms of the *Nine Goddesses (Nava Durga)* have paramount importance. The mystic diagram known as *Sri Chakra*, popular in Hindu Tantra, consists of nine interlaced triangles, which are directly identified with the Nine Apertures and the relationship of microcosm to macrocosm.

Taoism specifies *Nine Styles of Moving the Jade Stalk* when inside the "female crucible." The master Tung declares:

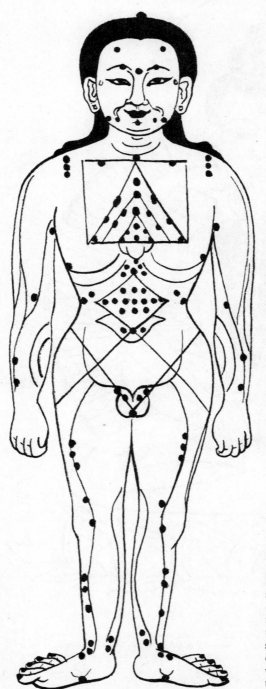

Medical diagram showing 108 points on the body where moxibustion is effective in restoring the psycho-physical equilibrium. Moxibustion is a technique whereby aromatic herbs are burned on the skin surface, or on acupuncture needles affixed to the body. Moxi-points are grouped in triads and are linked to ancient traditions of spiritual healing. Moxibustion is especially suited to the curing of sexual problems. From a Tibetan manuscript of the seventeenth century.

There are the following distinct styles of moving the Jade Stalk: first, by flailing to the right and left, in the same way that a brave warrior breaks up the ranks of the enemy; second, by moving up and down, like a wild horse bucking through a swiftly running stream; third, by pushing in and pulling out, just like a flight of sea gulls playing in the waves; fourth, by alternating deep and shallow love-strokes, swiftly, in the way that a sparrow picks out the grains of rice that have been left in the mortar; fifth, by making deep and shallow strokes, steadily, in the way that large stones sink when thrown into the sea; sixth, by pushing in slowly, in the way that a snake enters its hole when about to hibernate for the winter; seventh, by swiftly pushing and moving, in the way that a frightened rat rushes into its home;

eighth, slowly, as if dragging the feet, in the way that a hawk clutches an elusive rabbit; ninth, and last of all, by first rising up and then plunging down, in the same way that the full sail of a boat braves a heavy gale.

At another point in the text the master declares:

Deep and shallow, slow and quick, straight and slanting—all these are to be known by their own special characteristics. A slow thrust should be like the movement that a carp makes when caught on a hook. A quick thrust should be like the flight of birds against the wind. Inserting and withdrawing, moving up and down and from left to right, interspersed by intervals or in quick succession, all these movements should be properly correlated. One should apply each at the proper time, with a joyful spontaneity, rather than clinging to a single style that suits only personal idiosyncrasies.

According to Taoism, the multiple of the number seven by nine, which totals sixty-three, is the *Number of Sexual Union*. In the I-Ching, (the Chinese *Book of Changes*), the sixty-third hexagram is known as *After Completion*. Composed of alternate broken and unbroken lines, it symbolizes the time of climax—a state of perfect equilibrium. The hexagram pictures the union of water and fire. The normal interpretation is, briefly, "Strong lines in strong places and weak lines in weak places. Favorable outlook, with reason for thought. When perfect equilibrium has been reached, then any movement may cause order to revert to disorder. There is the need to maintain the right attitude." At the time just after climax, as in the hexagram, the male and female elements are in a natural state of harmony. Any movement away from this state of harmony has to be initiated with great care.

Nine multiplied by itself produces the number eighty-one. This is known as the *Yang Number* and has particularly deep implications. Chinese books on sexual techniques emphasize the cycle of nine strokes as the rhythm peculiar to love-making. The Chinese emperors, who were the supreme exponents of sex magic, were supposed to have nine ordinary consorts every night and were advised to make love with each of them without ejaculating semen. Then they were considered to be fully potentized and able to create spiritual children. The Taoist text known as the *Secret Prescriptions of the Bedroom* details the method of "completion of the Yang Number":

In love-making, the semen must be regarded as a most precious substance; by saving it, a man protects his life. After each ejaculation, the loss of semen should be compensated for by absorbing the essence fluids of the woman. There is a method of saving the semen that consists in pausing nine times after every series of nine strokes of the Jade Stalk; the emission of semen can also be prevented by pressing a point underneath the Jade Stalk with the fingers of the left hand. This technique helps to stop the external emission of semen and makes it return inward, strengthening the whole body. Absorbing the woman's essence is brought about by alternating nine shallow thrusts with one deep penetration. Placing one's mouth over that of the precious partner, one inhales her breath and drinks her saliva. When the juices are swallowed, they will descend into the stomach, where they will change from Yin-essence into Yang. When this has been accomplished three times, one should again deliver shallow thrusts, alternating every nine of them with one deep penetration, until nine times nine has been reached. This number, eighty-one, is the high completion of the Yang.

Nine plays a role in Western homeopathy, where the method of potentizing substances involves a nine-to-one dilution, which is repeated over and over in successively smaller proportions of medicine to the inert base material. The more potentized a homeopathic remedy, the finer the dilution. Yet a high potency produces very quick and effective results.

The mystical dances of the Sufis use units of nine as measure bars of their movements. Many breathing practices of Tantric Yoga are also based on a ninefold method of potentization. The mysteries of the number nine are frequently dismissed as "primitive superstition," but actually they have a cosmic foundation and a subtle mode of action. We spend the first nine months of our life cycle within the womb. This is the period when we take on form. To consciously create cycles of nine has a deep influence on our psycho-physical formation.

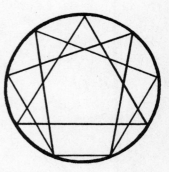

Enneagram diagram showing the inter-relationship of nine points around the circumference of a circle. Each point corresponds to a planet and to a bodily aperture.

Sri Chakra diagram showing nine interwoven triangles as a glyph of the relationship of microcosm to macrocosm. From an Indian painting of the eighteenth century.

The sixty-third hexagram of the *I Ching*, known as *After Completion*, symbolic of the time of sexual climax.

The Dark Girl and the Plain Girl compared the sexual act with the intermingling of water and fire, stating that these two elements can kill people, but can also give them new life. All this depends on whether or not a person has learned the correct methods of sexual intercourse. The Yellow Emperor successfully distilled the <u>Ninefold Elixir</u>, and having partaken thereof, he ascended into Heaven riding on a dragon.   KO HUNG

When I was twenty years of age I became infatuated with Taoist studies. Enrolling in a monastery, I was taught the practice of strengthening the life-force according to the Yellow Book. I learned the secret three—five—seven—nine method of love-making. In pairs of four eyes and two tongues, we practiced the Tao in the Cinnabar Field.

HSIAO-TAO-LUN / CHEN LUAN

Nine times returning, seven times resuming, eight times coming back and six times remaining inside. When thus the climax has been reached, then the "metal" blends with the "fire."

TS'AN-T'UNG-CH'I

playful variations

   The Taoist master Tung once declared, "Of all the things that make mankind prosper, none can be compared to sexual intercourse. It is modeled after Heaven and takes its form by Earth; it regulates Yin and rules Yang. Those who understand its significance can nurture their nature and prolong their years. But those foolish people who cannot understand its true significance harm themselves and die before their time. Truly, Heaven revolves to the left and Earth revolves to the right. Thus the four seasons succeed each other; man thrusts, woman receives; above, there is action; below, compliance."

   Man and woman must move according to their cosmic orientation. The man should thrust from above and woman receive from below. United in this way, they are called *Heaven and Earth in Even Balance*. In his hand-book, the master Tung lists a series of *Playful Variations* evolving from four basic positions linked to the four seasons; Spring, Summer, Autumn and Winter. He lists and describes a total of thirty love-making positions, which he claims cover the whole range of possibilities. Of these, the following twenty-six Playful Variations of love-making are beautifully described:

Standing love-posture. From a seventeenth-century Chinese watercolor.

REELING-OFF SILK

The woman lies on her back and embraces the man's neck with her arms, gripping the middle part of his body with both her legs. The man leans over and embraces her, pressing his lower body against the back of her thighs. He gently inserts his Jade Stalk.

Reeling Off Silk. From a Chinese print of the nineteenth century.

Variation of Reeling Off Silk. From a Japanese woodblock print by Hishikawa Moronubu (1618–1703).

Variation of Reeling Off Silk. From an eighteenth-century Chinese painting.

TURNING DRAGON

The woman lies on her back and lifts up her legs. The man kneels between her thighs and with his left hand pushes back her feet until they are above her breasts. With his right hand he inserts his Jade Stalk into her Precious Gate.

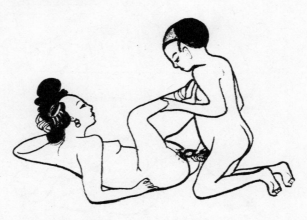

Approach to Turning Dragon. From a nineteenth-century Chinese painting.

PAIR-EYED FISH

The man and woman lie side by side, facing each other. She places one leg on top of his side. Their mouths together, they kiss and suck, languorously. Extending and moving his legs, the man raises his partner's uppermost leg with his hand. Advancing, he inserts the Jade Stalk and rocks her back and forth.

Variation of Pair-Eyed Fish. From a Chinese painting of the late sixteenth century.

Pair-eyed Fish. From a Chinese painting of the late eighteenth century.

VISHNU

the preserver

Variation of Pair of Swallows. From a Chinese painting of
the nineteenth century.

PAIR OF SWALLOWS

The woman lies on her back, extending
and spreading her legs. The man squats and
moves between her thighs; leaning
forward, he embraces her neck and breasts.
She embraces him tightly as his Jade Stalk
enters her Cinnabar Crevice.

Kingfisher Union. From a Japanese print by Torii Kiyonobu,
circa 1703.

KINGFISHER UNION

The woman lies on her back, her legs
raised and holding her ankles from the
outside; in this way, she is suitably open.
The man kneels or squats between her
thighs and embraces her waist with both
hands. Advancing forward, he inserts his
Jade Stalk carefully through the Strings of
her Lyre.

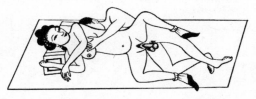

Mandarin Ducks. From a Chinese painting of the mid-
eighteenth century.

MANDARIN DUCKS

The woman lies on her side and bends
both legs. She places her own left leg on
top of the man's kneeling right thigh. He,
partly lying behind her back, puts his own
left leg on top of his partner's right calf.
Raising her left thigh with movements of
his left knee, he inserts his Jade Stalk.

Fluttering and Soaring Butterfly. From a Chinese painting of
the nineteenth century.

FLUTTERING AND SOARING
BUTTERFLY

The man lies on his back with both legs
spread and extended. The woman squats
over him, straddling his thighs and facing
him. With her feet resting on the bed, she
moves over him, delicately and vigorously,
supporting herself with her hands. She
plays upon his Positive Peak with her Jade
Gate.

Reversed Flying Ducks. From a Chinese
painting of the late eighteenth century.

Variation of Reversed Flying Ducks. From a Chinese
watercolor of the mid-seventeenth century.

REVERSED FLYING DUCKS

The man lies on his back with his legs
extended and spread apart. The woman sits
over him, facing his feet and straddling him.
Bending her head downward, she grasps his
Jade Stalk and inserts it into her Cinnabar
Crevice. She flies and moves above him, this
way and that.

LOW-BRANCHED PINE TREE

The woman lies on her back with her legs crossed and raised. The man embraces her waist, while she holds him around his back and neck. The Jade Stalk is then inserted into her Jade Gate.

Low-Branched Pine Tree. From a Japanese print by Okumura Masanobu, *circa* 1735.

BAMBOO NEAR THE ALTAR

The man and woman stand face to face, embracing and kissing each other. As they draw closer and closer together, he presses his Positive Peak into her Cinnabar Crevice, reaching and submerging into her Inner Terrace.

Variation of Low-Branched Pine Tree. From a Japanese Makimono painting of the seventeenth century.

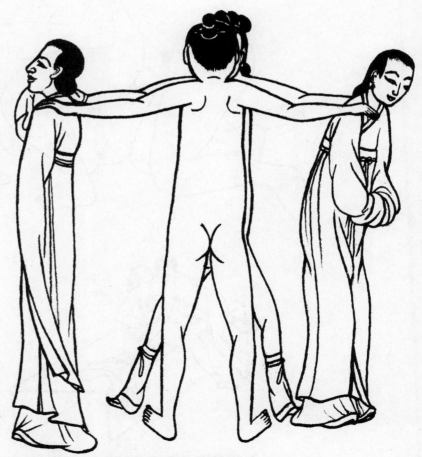

Bamboo near the Altar. From a Japanese Makimono painting of the late seventeenth century.

Variation of Bamboo near the Altar. From an engraving in the Chinese novel *Su Wo P'ien* (The Moon Lady), *circa* 1610.

270

VISHNU

the preserver

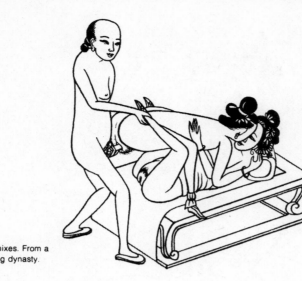

Two Dancing Female Phoenixes. From a
Chinese painting of the Ming dynasty.

TWO DANCING FEMALE PHOENIXES

In this posture, a man makes love with
two women simultaneously. One woman
lies on her back with her legs open and
raised. The second woman lies over her,
drawing her own legs up and spreading her
thighs so both Jade Gates are close to each
other. The two women make love together
as the man kneels between both their
parted thighs and enters the upper and
lower Jade Gates in turn.

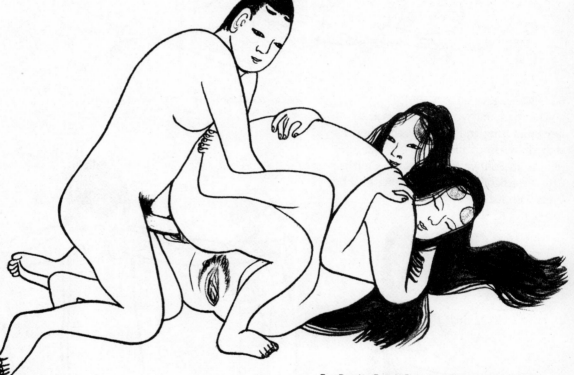

Two Dancing Female Phoenixes. From a Japanese print of
the seventeenth century.

Phoenix Holding Its Chicken. From a Chinese painting of
the late eighteenth-century.

PHOENIX HOLDING ITS CHICKEN

This posture is not described in the text,
but refers to a particular form of love-
making between a large fat woman and a
small man.

SOARING SEA GULLS

The man approaches the side of the bed on which the woman is lying with her thighs open. He draws her to him, lifts her legs and inserts his Jade Stalk deep into her Precious Gate. Standing firm and holding her by the legs, he makes her soar up into the heavens.

Soaring Sea Gulls. From a Chinese painting of the mid-eighteenth century.

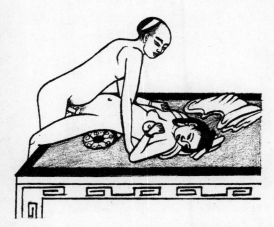

Variation of Soaring Sea Gulls. From a Chinese painting of the nineteenth century.

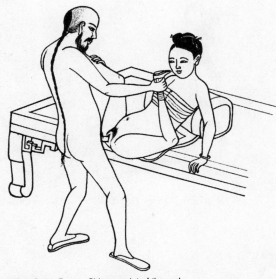

Soaring Sea Gulls. From a Chinese print of the early nineteenth century.

JUMPING WILD HORSES

The woman lies on her back. The man lifts her legs and places her feet on his shoulders, left and right. He then inserts his Jade Stalk deep into her Jade Gate and moves her about.

Jumping Wild Horses. From a Chinese watercolor of the seventeenth century.

Jumping Wild Horses. From a series of Chinese paintings of the late Yuan period (1280–1367).

272

VISHNU

the preserver

Humorous depiction of Galloping Wild Horse. From a Mongolian painting of the late eighteenth century.

GALLOPING WILD HORSE

The woman lies on her back and lifts her right leg. The man kneels and approaches, lifting her right leg higher and supporting her neck with his left hand. With his right hand he holds her right foot, moving it this way and that. Together they should generate movements like the galloping of a wild horse across the grasslands.

Galloping Wild Horse. From an eighteenth-century Chinese painting.

Pawing Horse. From a Japanese print, *circa* 1680.

PAWING HORSE

The woman lies on her back, lifts up her right leg and places it on the man's left shoulder as he kneels close to her Grotto. Turning her with his upper thigh, he inserts the Jade Stalk deep into her Cinnabar Crevice. The other leg of the woman moves freely, rather like a pawing horse.

JUMPING WHITE TIGER

The woman is on her hands and knees, bending her head downward. The man kneels behind her, embracing her waist with both hands. He inserts his Jade Stalk into her Precious Gateway.

Pawing Horse. From a Japanese print, *circa* 1640.

Jumping White Tiger. From a Japanese print by Sugimura Jihei, *circa* 1680.

DARK CICADA FIXED TO A TREE

The woman lies face downward, with legs extended and open. The man approaches from behind, moves between her thighs and lifts her lower body slightly. He thrusts his Jade Stalk into her Precious Gate and embraces her neck with his hands.

Dark Cicada Fixed to a Tree. From a Chinese painted scroll of the eighteenth century.

MOUNTAIN GOAT FACING A TREE

The man sits comfortably and has the woman sit on his lap, her legs astride and her back to him. She bends her head and considers how to insert the Jade Stalk into her Treasure House. Reaching down, she effects entry; the man embraces her waist and thrusts upward. Rhythmically they move their bodies this way and that.

Variation of Dark Cicada Fixed to a Tree. From a Japanese print of the early eighteenth century.

Mountain Goat Facing a Tree. From a Japanese woodblock print of the series known as Koshodu-zue juni-ko, Edo, *circa* 1780.

THE JUNGLE FOWL

The man squats or sits on the bed and his partner stretches her legs wide, facing him. A second woman is in attendance and helps by inserting his Jade Stalk into his partner's Precious Gate, uniting them by bringing their bodies together. Standing or sitting behind, the second woman aids the movements of the first woman, pushing her backward and forward. This brings the greatest of pleasure.

Continuation of Jungle Fowl. From a Chinese print of the Ming dynasty.

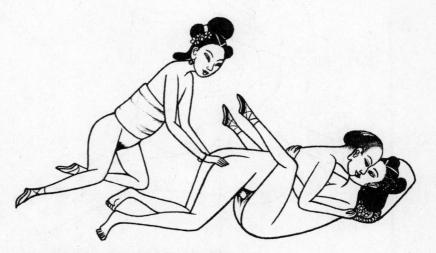

Jungle Fowl. From a Japanese scroll of the seventeenth century.

274

VISHNU

the preserver

Phoenix Playing in the Cinnabar Crevice. From a Japanese print by Sukenobu, early eighteenth century.

PHOENIX PLAYING IN THE CINNABAR CREVICE

The woman lies on her back, raising her legs and holding them under her thighs. The man kneels facing her and inserts his Jade Stalk into her Cinnabar Crevice. This love-making position very quickly brings gratification.

MYSTIC BIRD SOARING OVER THE OCEAN

The woman lies on her back and the man rests her legs over his upper arms. Leaning over, the man embraces the woman's waist and then inserts his Jade Stalk.

Mystic Bird Soaring over the Ocean. From a Japanese anonymous print, *circa* 1680.

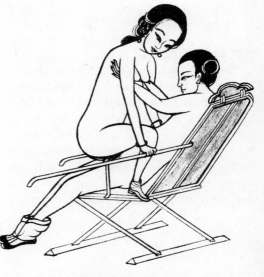

Variation of Shouting Monkey Embracing a Tree. From a Chinese painting of the eighteenth century.

Shouting Monkey Embracing a Tree. From a Chinese painting of the Ming dynasty.

SHOUTING MONKEY EMBRACING A TREE

The man sits with legs outstretched, with the woman riding on his thighs. She embraces him with both hands and he supports her buttocks with one hand and inserts his Jade Stalk with the other. Then, supporting himself on the bed, he moves rhythmically.

CAT AND MOUSE
SHARING A HOLE

The man lies on his back, with legs extended and apart. The woman lies down on him and inserts his Jade Stalk deep within her. A variation is for the man to lie on the woman's back and introduce his Jade Stalk into her Precious Gate from above.

Cat and Mouse Sharing a Hole. From a Chinese painting of the Ch'ien Lung period (1736–1796).

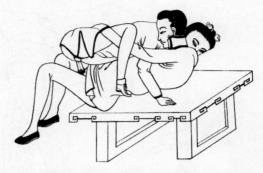

Variation of Cat and Mouse Sharing a Hole. From a Chinese painting of the early nineteenth century.

DONKEYS IN THE
THIRD MOON OF SPRING

The woman crouches on hands and knees, or with her legs straight. The man stands behind her and embraces her waist with his hands. Then he inserts his Jade Stalk into her Precious Gateway and moves her body to climax.

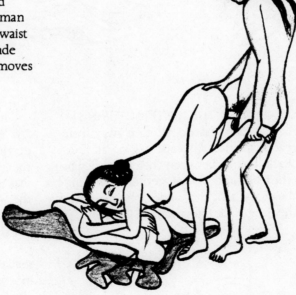

Variation of Donkeys in the Third Moon of Spring. From a Mongolian painting of the mid-eighteenth century.

Donkeys in the Third Moon of Spring. From a Chinese color print of the Ming dynasty.

Variation of Donkeys in the Third Moon of Spring. From a Chinese painting on silk, K'ang Hsi period (1662–1722).

HOUNDS OF THE NINTH AUTUMN DAY

The man and woman face away from each other, both crouching on all fours. Each looking between their legs, they bring their buttocks close together. Lowering his head and reaching under, the man inserts his Jade Stalk into the Jade Gate.

Hounds of the Ninth Autumn Day. From a Japanese print, *circa* 1680.

The Taoist master Tung of the Sui Dynasty (A.D. 590–618) places great emphasis on the need for absolute harmonization of the couple's mood. He states, "If the man shakes and the woman doesn't respond, or if the woman moves and the man doesn't follow, not only is there injury to the man, but there is also damage to the woman." He goes on to explain that, by correct use of sexual positions, "The man attains an increase of life-force and the woman eliminates all illness. Sex should be leisurely; smoothly inserting and languorously moving, rarely fast and vigorous."

Long ago in the Orient, before her marriage a bride was traditionally given books illustrating love-making positions. There are accounts of these sexual guidebooks in all Oriental cultures. A poem of the later Han Dynasty (*circa* A.D. 25–220) refers directly to the use of illustrated sexual guidebooks:

While the precious girl spends the night
You feast and play with her;
Pointing out the pictures of love,
You observe and enact their sequence.

In an erotic novel of the Ming period, *The Way to Holiness through the Flesh*, the hero introduces his prudish new wife to the joys of sex. The story tells how he purchased a book of love-postures, which were accompanied by beautifully poetic texts. From reading and viewing them, he managed to introduce her to the Art of Love. Five postures are illustrated, which our hero describes:

FLUTTERING BUTTERFLY
SEARCHING FOR FLOWERS

In this picture, the woman is shown with parted thighs, seated on a rock by the side of an ornate pool. The man carefully "feels out the lay of the land." Gently he inserts his Proboscis into the depths of her open Flower. Since the love-battle has only just begun, both have relatively normal expressions on their faces. Their eyes are open.

QUEEN BEE MAKING HONEY

The woman lies on her back, with pillows all around and under her delicate body. Her legs are parted and raised, as if hanging in mid-air. Her gentle hands press against his Fruit, guiding him directly to the entrance of her Flower. Her face has an expression of hunger and thirst, while he looks intensely excited.

BIRD FINDING ITS WAY TO THE NEST

The woman lies slightly to one side, one leg stretched high, supported by cushions; she clutches at his thigh with both hands. It is as if his Faithful Servant has finally reached her Sensitive Cave, and she fears that it might move away and get lost. This is the reason why a slight shadow of anxiety is depicted on her otherwise blissful face. They are making love passionately.

GALLOPING HUNGRY HORSE

The woman lies flat on her back and presses her partner's body with both hands. Her feet rest on his shoulders as he enters to her right, up to the hilt. That they are approaching ecstasy is depicted by their eyes, which are as if veiled beneath half-closed lids. Their tongues are in intimate union.

DRAGONS WEARY OF BATTLE

The woman's head rests sideways on one of the many pillows. Her arms droop, looking like silken threads. The man rests his head on the side of her neck and looks very relaxed. Their *Perfumed Soul* (ecstatic spirit) has fled; only the barest thread of life is discernible. This depicts Bliss savored to the very end.

These beautiful and poetic descriptions of love-making are clear indications that sexuality was viewed as a high art form in the East. Most of the postures depicted in Chinese art are relatively easy to practice. Many are identical to postures described in Indian and Arabian texts, though the names differ. If modern couples explore these ancient love-postures, they will find their lives are enriched and self-confidence will pervade their relationship.

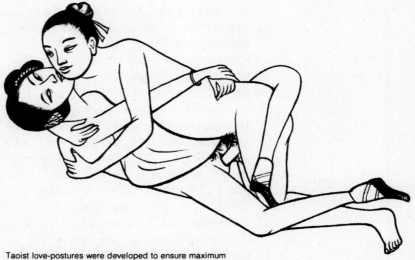

Taoist love-postures were developed to ensure maximum comfort and intimacy. From a Chinese print of the Ming dynasty.

A depiction of the Plain Girl initiating a nobleman into the Taoist posture known as Jumping White Tiger. From a Japanese print by Sugimura Jihei, *circa* 1680.

secrets of the plain girl

An ancient Chinese tradition tells of a river goddess who took the form of a shell, from which she was incarnated as a woman. The shell's resemblance to the Yoni has caused it to become a symbol of fertility in Eastern culture. The *Goddess of the Shell* was also known as the *Plain Girl*, one of a triad of sexual initiators of the mythical Yellow Emperor.

Legend has it that the Plain Girl designed a fifty-stringed zither, which she played for the Emperor. One day her music so affected him that he declared the instrument too dangerous for human ears. He ordered it split in two, each half left with twenty-five strings. This story takes on an added dimension in light of the importance of the number fifty in Tantric teachings. For fifty is the number of the original sound vibrations from which all worldly things emerged. Fifty are the heads on Kali's garland, and fifty the number of letters in the Sanskrit alphabet. The English alphabet of twenty-six letters has just over half this number.

The Plain Girl taught the Yellow Emperor the secret methods of love-making. The books known as the *Secret Methods of the Plain Girl* and the *Sex Recipes of the Plain Girl* are two of the works that bear her name. They contain a wealth of information, which, since it is attributed to a woman, is of particular importance today.

In one text, the Plain Girl declares, "Woman is superior to man in the way that water is superior to fire. People who are expert in the Art of Love are like excellent cooks, who know how to blend the different flavors into a tasty meal. Those who know the Art of Yin and Yang can blend the pleasures of the senses; but those who do not know it will have an unexpected death, without ever having enjoyed love-making." She then goes on to describe the symptoms, desires and passionate movements of the woman. We quote from her at length.

FIVE SYMPTOMS

The Plain Girl declares that there are *Five Symptoms* by which a man can tell when a woman is sexually excited:

First, she grows flushed or red in the face; at this point, the man should draw close to her. Second, her nipples grow hard and her nose becomes slightly moist; then he should insert his love-weapon. Third, her throat becomes dry and she begins to swallow profuse saliva; this indicates that the man should begin slow movements of loving. Fourth, her Jade Gate becomes moist and slippery; then the man should plunge into her very deeply. Finally, copious emissions from her Inner Heart begin to exude outward; at this stage, the man may move freely inside her body.

FIVE DESIRES

The Plain Girl enumerates *Five Desires* by which the response of a woman can be gauged:

First, if in her mind she desires to make love, then her breathing will become irregular. Second, if her Jade Gate desires to make love, then her nostrils will become distended and her mouth will open. Third, if her vital essence wishes to be stirred up through love-making, she will begin to move her body up and down rhythmically. Fourth, if her heart's desire is to be completely satisfied, then profuse moisture will be emitted from her Jade Gate, sufficient even to wet her clothes. Fifth, if she is ready to reach orgasm, then she will stretch her body like an animal, and close her eyes.

TEN STAGES OF LOVING

The Plain Girl lists *Ten Stages of Loving:*

First, by embracing the man with her arms, a woman shows that she wants him to draw her body close and possess her in love. Second, by stretching out her legs, a woman shows the man that she wants him to rub the upper part of her Jade Gate [the clitoris]. Third, by stretching her stomach, she shows that she wants him to make short love-strokes in her body. Fourth, by beginning to move her buttocks backward and forward, she shows that she senses she will soon be experiencing great pleasure. Fifth, by raising her legs, she shows that she wants him to penetrate into her body with deep love-strokes. Sixth, by squeezing her thighs together, she shows that her Jade Gateway is emitting love-juices. Seventh, by moving her body from left to right, she shows that she wants the man to penetrate into her body from the side. Eighth, by raising the upper part of her body and pressing her breasts against the man, she shows that she has almost reached her zenith of pleasure. Ninth, by relaxing her limbs, she shows that she has reached her climax. Tenth, by the emission of a copious flow of love-juices from her Precious Gateway, she shows that her vital essence has been released.

therapeutic love-making

The *Discourse of the Plain Girl* lists the *Eight Benefits* from particular rhythms of love-making. These rhythms are mostly combinations of magical numbers, taking the Yang Number as their inspiration. The Yang, or male force, is represented by odd numbers and the Yin, or female force, by even ones.

Therapeutic love-making, by controlling the rhythms and positions of intercourse, is a topic unique to Oriental medicine.

According to Eastern medical observation, the blood, flesh, fat, bones, marrow and semen (or ovum) are links in a chain that evolves according to a natural order and rhythm. The *Sushruta Samhita*, a major Hindu medical text, states, "Life-essence produces blood, from blood is produced flesh, from flesh originates fat, which gives rise to bones. From bones originates marrow, which in turn goes to generate semen or ovum." This sevenfold generation of bodily elements is a natural process that can easily be upset by over-exertion or unhealthful habits. Likewise it can be reinforced by a careful choice of actions.

Therapeutic love-making draws its inspiration from the fact that specific postures channel energy in different ways, enabling the body to focus on and correct imbalances. Love-making is always linked to changes in respiration, heartbeat, circulation, glandular secretions and brain waves. Since the body has the ability to create antidotes for any disease or condition, it is just a matter of triggering the correct metabolic process. Hatha Yoga postures and breathing have proved very effective in bringing the body to cure itself of even the most serious illnesses. Sexual Yoga can do this even more efficiently since both male and female principles are working in harmony and complementing each other.

Therapeutic love-making was an ancient Taoist science. Through control of the rhythms and positions of love, vital elements of the body become harmonized. From a Japanese color print by Isoda Koryusai, *circa* 1772.

Hatha Yoga by itself can be a lengthy and difficult discipline to perfect, whereas Taoist and Tantric love-making naturally generates vitality and energy.

Taoist and Tantric therapeutic love-making both emphasize rhythm and posture. These actions can benefit all parts of the male and female body and have a strengthening and lightening effect on the spirit. Though basically simple, this discipline does require that the man perfect his powers of retention. Woman's role in therapeutic love-making is that of an Initiatress invoking the nourishing powers of nature. Her emotional energy and subtle secretions are essential in bringing about harmonization of body and mind in her partner. While the man concentrates on retention, it is the woman's role to abandon herself to "giving," opening up the healing energies of her spirit. By so "giving," she also "receives"; her Yin-force is stengthened and her restorative and vitalizing powers are enhanced. The sexual secrets declare that if a woman truly opens up her awesome powers of rejuvenation, there is no limit to her healing potential. The following eight postures, rhythms and benefits all depend on the man's ability to control ejaculation and the woman's willingness to circulate healing energies.

Taoist love-posture particularly suited to prolonged love-making. From a Chinese print of the Ming dynasty.

Therapeutic love-posture for the concentration of semen. From a Chinese painting on silk of the K'ang-hsi period (1662–1722).

Variation of a therapeutic love-posture for the concentration of semen. From a Chinese painting of the eighteenth century.

THE EIGHT BENEFITS

CONCENTRATION OF SEMEN

To achieve this benefit, the woman is asked to lie on her side, with her thighs spread wide. The man lies alongside, between her legs, and inserts his Love Weapon carefully. He should cease making love with her after giving eighteen strokes of love. This method helps to concentrate the semen, and at the same time cures any bleeding of the woman. It should be practiced twice daily, for a period of fifteen days. (Note: 18 is 2 × 9)

RESTING THE SPIRIT

To achieve this benefit, the woman lies on her back, with legs stretched out and a cushion under her buttocks. The man kneels between her open thighs and inserts his Weapon. He should cease making love with her after giving twenty-seven strokes of love. This method will rest the spirit of the man, and at the same time cure any chills in the sexual region of the woman. It should be practiced three times daily for a period of twenty days. (27 is 3 × 9)

BENEFITS FOR
THE INTERNAL ORGANS

To achieve this benefit, the woman lies on her side and bends or lifts both legs. The man, laying his body at right angles across her, inserts his Weapon from behind. He should cease making love with her after giving thirty-six strokes of love. This method benefits the internal organs of both the man and the woman. It should be practiced four times daily, for a period of twenty days. (36 is 4 × 9)

STRENGTHENING THE BONES

To achieve this benefit, the woman lies on her side, with her left knee uppermost and bent. She should stretch out her right leg. The man lies on top of her, resting his weight on his arms and legs. Inserting his Weapon, he should give exactly forty-five strokes of love. This method harmonizes the joints of the man and at the same time cures any congestion in the body of the woman. It should be practiced five times daily, for a period of ten days. (45 is 5 × 9)

HARMONIZATION OF
BLOOD CIRCULATION

To achieve this benefit, the woman lies on her side, bending her right leg and extending her left leg. The man lies over her, resting on his hands, and she inserts his Weapon. He should give exactly fifty-four strokes of love. This method will help promote the circulation of blood and harmonize the life conduits. At the same time, it is effective in curing any pains in the sexual region of the woman. It should be practiced six times daily, for a period of twenty days. (54 is 6 × 9)

Therapeutic love-posture for resting the spirit. From a Japanese print by Okumura Masanobu, *circa* 1708.

Therapeutic love-posture for benefiting the internal organs. From a Japanese color print by Utamaro, *circa* 1800.

Therapeutic love-posture for strengthening the bones. From a Chinese painting on silk of the K'ang-hsi period (1662–1722).

Therapeutic love-posture for the harmonization of blood circulation. From a Chinese print of the eighteenth century.

VISHNU

the preserver

Therapeutic love-posture for increasing the blood. From a Chinese painting on silk, *circa* early nineteenth centruy.

Variation of a therapeutic love-posture for increasing the blood. From a Chinese painting of the nineteenth century.

Therapeutic love-posture for balancing the elements. From a small white porcelain bowl, K'ang-hsi period (1662–1722).

Therapeutic love-posture for adjusting the whole physical system. From a Japanese print by Sugimura Jihei, *circa* 1690.

INCREASING THE BLOOD

To achieve this benefit, the man lies on his back and the woman kneels on top of him. When her buttocks are raised, he inserts the Jade Stalk deeply. The woman moves up and down, making love with him until she has received exactly sixty-three strokes of love. An alternate method is for her to squat over him. This method of love-making increases a man's strength and stores up his blood. It is also very effective in curing any irregularities of the woman's menstruation. It should be practiced seven times daily, for a period of ten days in succession. (63 is 7 × 9)

BALANCING THE ELEMENTS

To achieve this benefit, the woman lies flat out on her front, with face down and buttocks raised; a cushion can be effectively used to support her. The man lies on top of her and inserts his Love Weapon from the rear and gives exactly seventy-two strokes of love. This method balances the elements in their bodies and increases the production of bone marrow. It should be practiced eight times daily, for as long as it takes to produce the benefits. (72 is 8 × 9)

ADJUSTING THE WHOLE PHYSICAL SYSTEM

To achieve this benefit, the woman lies on her back, with both legs folded under her in such a way that her buttocks rest on her feet. The man leans over her, with his legs apart, and mounts her, inserting his Weapon. He should give her exactly eighty-one strokes of love. This method will strengthen his bones and vitalize his whole being. Furthermore, it effectively cures sexual problems of the woman. It should be practiced nine times daily, for a period of nine days in succession. (81 is 9 × 9)

Therapeutic love-making should be practiced without any emission of semen. Similar techniques exist in the Indian Tantric tradition, though rarely are they so simply outlined. The *Sushruta Samhita*, an early Hindu medical work, declares that "Love-making with a beautiful and generous woman, performed with careful attention, is the best medicine of all."

Measured strokes of love have a direct

effect on breathing and concentration, and have the added benefit of stimulating the vital "fires" within. It is important that love-strokes not be counted out loud or in the mind. Rather, they should be *measured* against a rhythm, such as background music, or *recorded* by the use of a rosary, beads, or any other mnemonic device as portrayed in many Taoist and Tantric paintings. Love-strokes can also easily be recorded on the fingers without actually counting.

Therapeutic love-making is not difficult and is certainly one of the most direct ways of balancing physical and mental imbalances. Since these techniques are valid for the twentieth century, any couple can benefit tremendously from practicing this ancient tradition.

If one moves but does not emit semen, the life-force and vigor are in excess. The body absorbs the energy and all the senses are sharpened. P'ENG TSU

A man should learn to control his ejaculation. To be greedy for feminine beauty and emit beyond one's vigor injures every vein, nerve and organ in the body, and gives rise to every illness. Correct practice of sexual intercourse can cure every ailment and at the same time open the doors to Liberation. YANG-SHENG-YAO-CHI

ejaculation

The Plain Girl informs the Yellow Emperor that a man should regulate the frequency of ejaculation, according to his strength or weakness, but should never *force* himself to ejaculate. She states categorically that every time a man forces himself to ejaculate, his whole bodily system is harmed. Indian works and Tantric treatises share this position.

The Plain Girl declares:

Every man should regulate the emission of semen according to his store of vital essence. He should never force himself to ejaculate. If he should do so, then his body will be harmed. A young and strongly built man can afford to ejaculate twice daily, but thin ones only once. A strong man of about thirty years of age can afford to do so once daily, whereas a weak man the same age should only do so once every two days. A strong man of forty years can ejaculate once every three days, but a weak man this age should do so only every four days. Strong men of fifty can safely do so every five days, whereas a weak fifty-year-old needs a rest of ten days. Strong men of sixty may healthily ejaculate every ten days, but weak men of this age need twenty days in between. A strong man of seventy years can ejaculate once a month without harm, but a weak one that age should not ejaculate anymore.

The Taoist master Peng describes the symptoms of forced ejaculation as "buzzing in the ears, tiredness of the eyes, worn-out limbs and a very dry throat." He advises restraining ejaculation, stating that this practice strengthens the vital essence and increases clarity of hearing and acuteness of vision. He adds, "Through the repression of his passion during love-making, the man's love for the woman will increase. It is as though he could never get enough of her." Another text takes the extreme position that a man should "make love scores of times in one day, without ejaculating even once, since this will cure all disease and increase longevity."

The choice of whether or not to ejaculate is best left to the man. A woman should be able to intuit the physical needs of her lover as well as her own. She should not demand that he "come" every time they make love together, but rather should adapt herself to experience love in new and different ways. Both Taoist and Tantric teachings stress that the Western view of sex as a race to climax and physical collapse is both physically limiting and psychically damaging. In contrast, the East sees in physical love the

Taoist love treatises teach that the older the man, the less frequently he should ejaculate. Here a younger woman acts out the role of a sex initiatress, bestowing longevity on her partner. From a Chinese painting of the mid-eighteenth century.

potential for bringing both partners to new heights of ecstasy time and time again.

Toward the end of the nineteenth century, Alice Stockham proposed a love-making technique that she termed *Karezza*. She wrote:

The ordinary hasty spasmodic method of co-habitation, for which there has been no previous preparation, and in which the wife is passive, is alike unsatisfactory to husband and wife. It is deleterious both physically and spiritually. It has in it no consistency as a demonstration of affection, and is frequently a cause of estrangement and separation. *Karezza* so consummates marriage that through the power of will and loving thoughts, the crisis is not reached, but a complete control by both husband and wife is maintained throughout the entire relationship, a conscious conservation of Creative Energy.

Her book *Karezza: Ethics of Marriage* is an enthusiastic endorsement of ancient Taoist and Tantric love techniques. Like the Taoist Initiatresses, she states, "Although woman has not the semen to conserve, yet equally with man she has the thrilling potency of passion, that when well directed, heals sensitive nerves, vitalizes the blood and restores tissue. In this deeper, truer union, the very heart of *Karezza*, woman as well as man prevents and cures disease. *Karezza* has a therapeutic value not equaled by any remedy of pharmacopoeia, or by any system of healing." The techniques that Alice Stockham taught were no different from basic Eastern practices of semen retention (we shall be examining these over the next few sections of this book).

A couple can certainly benefit from learning how to control their physical orgasms. However, it is by no means necessary, or even advisable, to refrain from ejaculation indefinitely. A balanced sexual relationship implies "giving and taking." Bearing this in mind, the couple should endeavor to share and exchange vital essences, as seems appropriate. Potentization through sexual retention then takes on a transcendental meaning and purpose.

If a man repeatedly misses the right rhythm of love-making, his vital essence will be drained. The effect of incorrect rhythm is forced ejaculation, which rapidly causes exhaustion. As a result of this, over a period of time, the Hundred Diseases develop in the body.

YU-FANG-PI-CHUH

Both the Original Semen and that which is ejaculated during sexual union are essentially the same. Before the sex act, the semen is distributed over the entire body; it has no fixed location, but dwells in a condensed form within the Original Spirit. It is this aspect that is referred to in classical texts as the Original Semen. When a man and a woman make love, the semen is drawn down from all parts. A place in the inner part of the head [the pituitary gland] causes the semen to descend along the spine to the lower region. Other aspects of semen are drawn from the different organs of the body, such as the kidneys and bladder.

TS'UNG-SHU-CHI-CH'ENG

One should not eject this "camphor" [semen] casually. It is from this substance that the Yoginis have their origin. Its nature is that of the Supreme Joy. It is indestructible and luscious, as pervasive as the sky.

HEVAJRA TANTRA

One of the most important contributions of the East to the mysteries of sex is its thorough understanding of interconnections between three seemingly separate processes: breathing, thinking and the production of semen. Tantric and Taoist teachings provide precise and practical information on this subject.

According to Tantra, the stabilization of breath, thought and semen is one of the most important of the sexual secrets. By gaining control of these three, it is possible to ascend the evolutionary path of transcendental love. Many of the more advanced Yoga practices deal exclusively with this threefold task.

During normal love-making, the *sensual elements* (the senses and their organs) are stirred by the force of emotion. Breathing becomes quickened and the imagination is excited. As the movements of love proceed, the metabolism of each partner becomes changed: the heartbeat and circulation alter, and the glands begin to secrete sex hormones. The natural links between the increased rate of breathing, the excitation of the mind and the sudden sexual climax with ejaculation give us the clue to understanding how to control and separate these different functions. In this lies one of the fundamental secrets of Tantric sex.

Tantric love-making implies conscious control of breathing, thinking and ejaculation during physical union. Breath control is actually very simple, depending mainly on conscious *awareness* of the rate and depth of breathing. By directing our attention to or contemplating our breath, we bring an unconscious, parasympathetic process under conscious control. Tantric love-making is best accomplished when the breath is deep, rhythmic and drawn through the nose. Once the breath is brought under control, love-making and energy circulation can continue almost indefinitely.

Meditation stabilizes thought. One-pointedness of mind, the goal of all Yogis, is, paradoxically, both simple and difficult. Tantric Mantras ("protectors of mind") and Yantras (forms for the mind to grasp) can greatly assist in stabilizing the mind. A stabilized mind leads to total absorption, the merging of the individual with the transcendental.

During Tantric love-making, meditation plays an important role in assisting the stabilization of thought. During normal intercourse, it is the "thought of orgasm" that brings one to it. Tantric sexual techniques emphasize the importance of controlling and transforming thought. This, in turn, leads to transcendental ecstasy. As the popular Tantric axiom states, "One may rise by that same thing by which one may fall."

Stabilization of semen is directly linked to stabilization of breath and thought. Semen is also stabilized by correct diet, healthful lifestyle and therapeutic love-making. If a man can consciously control breath, thought or (preferably) both, he will never be subject to involuntary ejaculation, or meaningless loss of life essence, but rather will realize his full potential for conscious *giving*.

Breath, thought and semen are the three constituents of the Enlightenment Potential. They should be harmonized and consciously controlled. The Yogi who brings together breath, thought and semen becomes the Indestructible One, endowed with transcendental spontaneity.

KALACHAKRA TANTRA

So long as the breath is in motion, the semen moves also. When the breath ceases to move, then the semen remains at rest.

GORAKSA SAMHITA

VISHNU

the preserver

retention

The retention of semen and the conscious control of ejaculation are dealt with at length in Eastern treatises on sex. Various techniques, some complementary, are utilized. All are based on the knowledge of the relationship of breath, thought and semen. We will describe certain methods that are both simple and practicable.

A Taoist book of the Tang Dynasty (*circa* A.D. 618–907) clearly states:

When a man feels he is about to ejaculate semen, he should close his mouth and open his eyes wide. In particular, he should try to stabilize his breath, holding it if possible, but without forcing anything. By moving his hands up and down and breathing only with movements of the lower abdomen, he will gain control over breath and semen. The spine should be kept straight. If necessary, he should press the *Ping-i* acu-point [one inch over his right breast] with the *index and middle finger of his left hand*, then let out his breath, at the same time gnashing his teeth. This action will definitely cause the semen to be retained, so that it can freely ascend and benefit the brain. If semen is emitted freely, it will cause harm to the spirit.

Notice that in this account, both physiological and psychological techniques are employed. Any conscious movement, such as the hand motion described above, helps to control and circulate energy and focus the mind. Pressure of the acupuncture point above the male right breast creates a "short circuit," which aids retention. The index and middle finger of the left hand are connected to the large intestine (the region of the navel center) and the sex energy/circulation meridians, respectively. Gnashing the teeth produces profuse salivation, which cools down and nurtures the system. Retention and control of breathing helps gain control of ejaculation.

Another text, known as the *Classic of the Immortals*, declares:

Taoist love-posture for causing semen to rise while practicing retention. From a Chinese engraving for the erotic novel *Su Wo P'ien* (The Moon Lady), *circa* 1610.

The way to make the semen return, to thereby nourish the brain, is as follows. When a man feels that he is about to ejaculate, he should firmly press *the place between the scrotum and anus* with the *fore and middle fingers of his left hand*, at the same time inhaling deeply and gnashing the teeth, without holding the breath. This practice will cause the semen to be activated but not ejaculated. It will instead return from the Jade Stalk, ascend, and stimulate the brain. This method was taught by Lu the Immortal, but he ordered his disciples to swear an oath that they would not divulge this potent secret to the uninitiated.

Once again we have a technique for retention that makes use of knowledge of the acu-meridians to short-circuit the energy flow. The place between the scrotum and anus is the location of the duct through which semen must pass if ejaculated. Pressure there will divert any emission back into the prostatic region. This practice is common to both Taoist and Tantric teaching; many sexual Yoga postures advise the adept to "press his heel into the space between scrotum and anus."

A master of the Han Dynasty, Wu Hsien, gives a concise account of ejaculation control. He first advises the man not to get too excited while making love so as not to lose control. He suggests that a man first learn to regulate his rhythm, trying one deep followed by three shallow love-strokes, for eighty-one total cycles. He next advises the man to follow this rhythm with one deep and five shallow love-strokes, again for eighty-one repetitions. Finally the man should try one deep and nine shallow love-strokes. The master adds that if the man feels he is about to ejaculate, he should stop his movements and withdraw his Jade Stalk so that only the tip remains within his partner's Jade Gate. After his passions have calmed, he can begin to resume deep insertion. He stresses that the man's main concern should be that the woman reach orgasm quickly and frequently.

Wu Hsien advises a man to close his eyes and breathe in deeply but gently *through his nose* if he wishes to control his ejaculation and focus his mind. He points out that a man should never start panting while making love, because if he does, he'll lose control and ejaculate. His final word is that a man should practice the art of conscious retention for at least five thousand love-strokes before ejaculating, as then his whole being will become potentized.

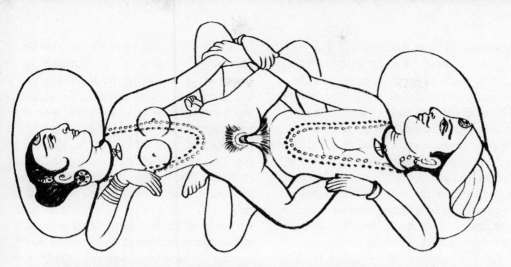

Love-posture showing a *bandha* (lock) for aiding retention. The bodies of the couple make a *Yantra* (a power-form), which potentizes sexuality. From a Nepalese painting of the eighteenth century.

The teachings of the Taoist master Tung add further information:

A man should always ensure that the woman reaches her climax of pleasure. When he feels that he is about to ejaculate, he should make repeated short strokes with his Weapon, sporting between the Strings of her Lyre and the Grain-shaped Cave [the lips of her vulva and her inner Yoni]; these movements should be just like a child plucking with its mouth at the nipples of the mother. The man should close his eyes and concentrate his thought. Pressing his tongue against the roof of his mouth, he should bend his back and stretch his neck. Opening his nostrils wide and drawing back his shoulders, he should then close his mouth and draw in his breath through his nostrils. This will stop him from ejaculating and cause his semen to ascend upward. It is quite possible for a man to consciously regulate his ejaculations. When he is making love to a woman, he should ideally only release his semen two or three times in every ten sessions.

By partly withdrawing his Lingam and playfully moving it around the entrance to the Yoni, a man is able to absorb the Yin secretions and be "mothered by his partner"; this gives him added strength. One Tibetan secret text calls this act "milking the Heavenly Cow." Pressing the tongue against the roof of the mouth, just behind the upper front teeth, is another device for controlling the urge to ejaculate; it causes another "short-circuit" and helps cool the passions. Sucking in the breath through the rolled-up tongue also has a cooling and stabilizing effect.

Tantric teachings outline the same ejaculation-control techniques as Taoism, with the exception of the use of the *Ping-i* (acu-meridian above the right breast). The main emphasis of Tantra is on the need to learn control over breath and thought. Since

Yogic sex presupposes a thorough practical knowledge of breath control (*Pranayama*) and meditation, it is not surprising that specific *external* devices are rarely mentioned. However, one special feature is the emphasis given to anal sphincter control, which, when perfected, creates the same effect as applying pressure to the region between the scrotum and anus. Anal sphincter control is a technique of Kundalini Yoga that consists in repeated constriction of the muscles around the anus, drawing up the downward-moving energies. Anal sphincter control, known as *Mula Bandha*, is best perfected as part of the Yoga Asanas and meditation training.

Some Yogic and Tantric texts emphasize a technique known as *Vajroli Mudra* ("Diamond Seal"). This is an advanced Yogic practice of drawing up liquids through the Lingam by contractions of the lower diaphragm. Such practices can be dangerous and are hardly necessary for most lovers. Other Yogic techniques known as *Bandhas* ("Locks") affect retention by constriction or physical blocking of life-energy conduits. The *Mula Bandha*, or "Root Lock" already mentioned, is one such device. Some of the more complex Yoga Asanas naturally create *Bandhas* that aid the retentive process. Many complex sexual postures have a similar effect in controlling ejaculation. These are better discovered spontaneously during love-making than rehearsed without passion.

Tantra specifies that certain love-making postures are effective in helping to control ejaculation. Sitting and squatting postures are particularly suitable, since they naturally cause sexual energy to flow upward. Difficult Tantric postures, where the man is in reverse (such as the head stand or back stand), are also used to cause sexual energy to flow back to the head center. In the versions used in sexual Yoga, the woman makes all the movements while the man maintains his posture and retains his semen. One of the most suitable of all the postures for retention is practiced with the man lying flat on his back, without moving. With such a posture, it is the woman who has the responsibility of ensuring that he does not ejaculate; it is for her to act out the normal movements (and restraints) of the man.

Mental repetition of Mantras (see "Noises of Love") and visualization-meditations (see Part I) are very effective in stabilizing breath, thought and semen. If the man can also visualize the process of energy sublimation, he will find it easier to exert control over ejaculation. The process of sublimation is conceived of and visualized as life energies ascending the central channel, opening up and nourishing the psychic centers, one after the other. When the life energies reach the head center, they invigorate the whole psycho-system. The subtle nerves, the body meridians, the psychic centers and the flow of sexual energy through them should all be held in the mind's eye. When breathing in, try to visualize life energy permeating your whole being, and see it transformed and refined on its journey upward through the psychic centers. At the same time, hold in mind a vision of your female partner as the Living Goddess and dedicate your emotions to her complete fulfillment.

He should retain the breath and contract the lower stomach. Visualizing the Divine Buddha Chandamaharosana in union with the Goddess Wisdom-energy, he should press his heel against the base [the scrotum] and his tongue against the roof [the palate]. By concentrating his wavering thoughts and controlling his breath, he will prevent the semen from moving outward. Thus he should practice the Yoga of Liberation.

CHANDAMAHAROSANA TANTRA

At the moment that the man is about to ejaculate, he should raise his head and hold his breath. Glaring angrily and rolling his eyes from left to right, he should contract his stomach, causing the semen to return and enter his veins. This excellent practice has the effect of improving the vision and strengthening the spirit. YU-FANG-PI-CHUH

Neither passion nor absence of passion is found in the excellent union of Hevajra with his consort. Controlling his emission by the power of Yogic sound, the adept should evoke fourfold waves of ecstasy in his partner. As the Joy Innate arises, he should glare angrily and gnash his teeth—"Ha-hā, Hi-hī, Hu-hū, Hé-hai, Ho-hau, Hāng-hāh!"—thus he should control and transform the Stages of Ecstasy. There is no beginning, middle or end to this practice!

HEVAJRA TANTRA

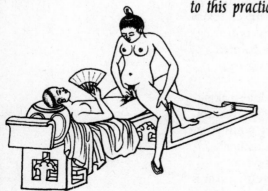

Taoist posture of sexual Yoga used to aid retention and empower the libido. From a Chinese print of the late eighteenth century.

mutual absorption

The Tantric and Taoist texts stress the importance of "absorbing your partner's equivalent" whenever there is an emission of vital juices. The loss of semen, which is drawn from all parts of the body, can weaken and shorten the life of the man. The way to counteract loss through ejaculation is to consciously absorb the womanly secretions. Various techniques are suggested, all of which we shall deal with in detail. Both the male and female viewpoints are important and helpful.

First of all, the Lingam should remain within the Yoni as long as possible without ejaculation. This enables the man to absorb Yin-essence from woman's inexhaustible supply of lunar energy, so strengthening his vital force. Taoism declares that every ejaculation of semen has the potential to diminish the vital force of man unless compensated for by the absorption of an equivalent Yin-essence from the woman.

An early Chinese text of the Han Dynasty states, "The Yellow Emperor learned the Art of Sex from the Dark Girl and other Sex Initiatresses. This consists simply of suppressing the ejaculation of semen and absorbing the essential fluid of the woman." But too much suppression of semen is

Mutual absorption takes place on both physical and psycho-physical levels. From a Chinese painting of the late eighteenth century.

unnatural and debilitating. A Chinese medical book declares, "The passion of man naturally has great periods of abundance. At this time, even the most controlled man cannot bear prolonged abstention from ejaculating. If a man abstains too long from emitting semen, he will develop boils and ulcers. Man cannot do without woman, and woman cannot do without man. If a man does not make love with a woman for a long period of time, his mind will grow very unmanageable. If this happens, his Spirit will suffer; and if the Spirit suffers, then his span of life will be shortened."

The seasons and weather influence sexual urges, as do astrological configurations. It is essential to consider the strength of the body and the state of the psyche before deciding whether to ejaculate or not. If the body is weak and the spirit is low, it is obviously a time to retain. The main points are that ejaculation should never be forced and that man should always consciously absorb the woman's sexual secretions. When the sexual secrets are understood in the heart, the choice of ejaculation or retention will become spontaneous, based on, and the product of, the couple's mutual atunement.

Mutual absorption is achieved in part by slightly withdrawing the Lingam and visualizing the absorption as taking place. The head of the Lingam easily absorbs sexual secretions through the membranes of its skin. Likewise the Yoni of woman can absorb secretions directly through the inner walls and womb. When a woman gains

Taoist love-posture particularly suited to mutual absorption. The mental attitude should be brought to bear on exchanging vital essences with the partner. From a Chinese painting of the late eighteenth century.

conscious control over her Yoni, she can absorb and transform her own and her partner's emissions. Once mastered, this practice will enable her to bestow the potentized Yin-Yang love essence on her partner.

Just as man benefits from absorbing Yin-essence, so can a woman benefit from absorbing Yang-fluid. If a woman selfishly and repeatedly extracts semen from her partner, she is in fact engaging in a form of vampirism.

Chinese tradition tells of a legendary Queen of the Western Paradise who liked to copulate with young men, from whom she extracted vitality. It was said that every time she did this, the young man would become ill, whereas she would look more and more beautiful. Taoism teaches that if a woman practices sexual vampirism, she runs the risk of losing her female qualities. She begins to become hardened and thinks like a man. Tradition has it that such a woman actually can become physically transformed.

A Taoist treatise on sexual alchemy declares; "If a woman knows the way to nurse her potency and to effect the harmony of the twin essence of Yin and Yang, she can transform herself completely. If, during the sex act, she can prevent her sexual secretions from being absorbed by the man, then these will flow back into the complexion of her body; her Yin-essence will become nurtured by the man's Yang-essence, provided he ejaculates. A woman who has learned this secret will be able to feed on her lovers." Male sex hormones (which are secreted in semen) actually have a transforming effect on women. In excess, male hormones cause a woman's voice to deepen and create other disturbing physiological changes. Semen can only be replaced by drawing vital ingredients from the bodily organs, a process that takes some time. The *Rig Veda*, an ancient Hindu work, states, "Though the wife should entice the man, it is a foolish woman who sucks dry the wise man."

Of course, the most beneficial sexual technique for the couple is *mutual absorption*. A woman should not "milk her man dry," nor should he "demand all of her resources." The bond of love presupposes a two-way exchange. Fulfillment of the woman is all-important, as only then can she bestow her full initiatory potential on her lover; but "coming" or "not coming" should not be the sole criterion for whether the act of love is considered successful or not.

Man should take care to adapt his sex life to the Yin and Yang forces of the cosmos. He should not make love when it is excessively cold or hot, when there is a strong wind or heavy rain, when there is an eclipse, during an earthquake, or when there is thunder and lightning. These are all taboos of Heaven. He should not make love when over-intoxicated, neither when over-elated or angry, when feeling depressed or when in great fear. These are the taboos of man. He should not make love near places sacred to the spirits or such special sanctuaries of Heaven and Earth, nor near a well or close to the kitchen fire. These are the taboos of earth.   PENG TSU

Master Jung was an adept at nurturing and controlling his physical functions. He absorbed new essences from the Mysterious Valley of woman. The main point of this art is to prevent one's potency from dying. The "returned semen" strengthens the vitality and nourishes the brain.
                    LIEH-HSIEN-CHUAN

medicine of the three peaks

According to both Tantric and Taoist esoteric teachings, woman produces three distinct types of sexual secretions, from her mouth, breasts and Yoni. By absorbing these *Threefold Elixirs*, a man can compensate for ejaculation of semen and can nurture his spiritual essence.

A book of the Ming period describes the three types of female secretions, calling them the *Great Medicine of the Three Peaks*:

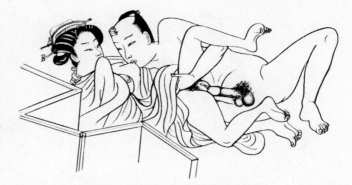

According to both Taoist and Tantric traditions, the breasts of women secrete subtle essences that have a beneficial effect on the whole organism. From a Japanese print by Isoda Koryusai, *circa* 1775.

The upper peak of woman is know in Taoism as the *Red Lotus Peak*. The medicine that emanates from it is called *Jade Fountain*, *Jade Liquid* or *Sweet Spring*. It emanates from beneath the tongue of woman and is of a very light color almost transparent. When it is produced in abundance, the man should endeavor to swallow it, transforming it in his *Cinnabar Field* [the navel center] at his solar plexus. This medicine imparts fluidity to his five internal organs. Reaching his left side, it will nourish his intuition and strengthen his *Mysterious Gate* [the sexual center]. Reaching his right side, it will effectively increase the potential of his solar *Cinnabar Field*. This will have the effect of generating vital essence and strengthening the blood.

The middle peak of woman is known as *Double Lotus Peak*. The medicine that is produced from it is known as *White Snow*, *Essence of Coral* or *Immortality Peach Juice*. It emanates from the two breasts of a woman, particularly from one who has not produced a child and who hasn't any milk. Its color is white and it has a slightly sweet and very agreeable taste. A man should suck and drink that special medicine. When it reaches his *Cinnabar Field* [the navel center], it brings nourishment to his spleen and stomach. When the

White Snow is sucked out of a woman, her blood circulation will be greatly improved, and both partners will experience delightful feelings of pleasure. When deeply sucked, this precious fluid reaches as far as the *Flowery Lake* [the head center] above and descends to the *Mysterious Gateway* [the sex center] below. It has a beneficial effect on the whole organism. Of the *Three Peaks*, this one should first receive the attention of the lover.

The lower peak of woman is known as *Purple Mushroom Peak*, *White Tiger's Cavern*, or *Mysterious Gate*. The medicine that is produced from it is known as *Moon Flower* or *White Metal*, and exudes from her *Palace of Yin*, deep inside her womb. Its doorway is usually closed, but when a woman is aroused during love-making to such an extent that her cheeks become flushed and her voice catches in her throat, then this inner *Doorway* of hers is opened. When she reaches the climax of pleasure, the moisture exudes, flowing freely downward. If a man wishes to absorb this womanly secretion, he should withdraw his *Weapon* until it is only at the depth of a thumb tip. This has the effect of benefiting his *Original Yang-force* while at the same time nurturing and harmonizing his Inner Spirit.

During erotic kissing the couple exchange saliva. Taoism credits female saliva with life-giving properties. From a Japanese print by Shimokobe Shusui, *circa* 1760.

292

VISHNU

the preserver

Taoism teaches that female sexual secretions can be effectively absorbed through the head of the Lingam by slightly withdrawing to the entrance of the Yoni. From a Chinese painting of the nineteenth century.

The drinking of the *Jade Fluid*, the saliva produced by the mouth of a sexually excited woman, is frequently mentioned in Taoist treatises as "one of the best ways of strengthening the Yang." Occult traditions throughout the world credit saliva with magical properties. It is used on talismans and for "absent healing" as a way of making contact with a patient who is not present in person. Modern radionics, a branch of homeopathy, uses saliva for diagnosis, and also as a "target" at which healing energies can be directed.

Western allopathic medicine has an incomplete understanding of the salivary glands and their secretions. The current theory states that "Stimulation of the cerebral cortex and the hypothalamus evokes salivation." Interestingly enough, in Tantric love-rites, substances such as camphor and incense are burned and placed near the female partner. Camphor and other related volatile odoriferous substances have the effect of stimulating the cerebral cortex and thus evoking salivation in the Shakti.

The quantity and composition of saliva vary considerably, depending on the type of stimulation producing it. Edible substances produce semi-fluid enzyme-rich saliva, whereas inedible substances placed in the mouth stimulate very watery secretions. If an acid substance is eaten, the saliva becomes very rich in protein; milk causes profuse salivation, rich in organic material. Homeostatic saliva is usually acid, and when flowing freely, it becomes alkaline. The tonic properties of oral secretions are widely accepted by Western medicine, but the special nature of saliva produced by sexual stimulation is still relatively unknown to the Occident.

The drinking of *White Snow* from the breasts of a woman is a mysterious concept to Westerners The text clearly refers to it as a physical rather than a subtle secretion. It is made quite clear that White Snow is not the normal breast milk produced by a woman with child, but rather a secretion spontaneously generated by sexual excitement.

An early Taoist text refers to a man who lived to the age of one hundred and eighty by sucking the secretions from women's breasts. In India, one occasionally hears of Yogis producing milk-like breast secretions. Indian medical texts declare that "mother's milk is the best of all foods and can rejuvenate an old person." Interestingly, there have been a number of cases of *men* spontaneously producing milk to feed a baby whose mother suddenly dies, illustrating that within man, woman lies latent.

There are subtle connections between a woman's breasts and her uterus. When her breasts are sucked, the womb contracts, and this in turn affects glandular secretions. Tantric teachings declare that breast secretions are often activated by particular sounds, especially those similar to the first cry of a baby. A woman without child can certainly produce physical milk-like breast-essence (*White Snow*) during sex, provided she freely experiences the desire to give. This mother-like and nurturing desire creates an emotional message to the glandular system which in turn causes the snow to fall. Breast secretions can also occur on a purely subtle, non-physical level.

During intense sexual excitement the breasts of woman sometimes secrete subtle essences that are invigorating and rejuvenating. From a Chinese painting of the nineteenth century.

A sexually excited woman secretes fluids in her Yoni. Taoist refers to these special secretions as *Moon Flower Waters*; Indian and Tantric texts speak of *Moon Fluid* or quite simply *Love Juice*. The *Kama Sutra*, the classical Hindu love treatise, states: "Women do not emit like men do. The fall of semen from the man takes place only at the end of his love-making, while the juices of the woman are secreted continually."

The emissions from the Yoni of woman vary considerably, depending on temperament, general health, diet, the moment in the monthly cycle, and the level of sexual passion. Ovarian hormones, minerals and tissue salts, as well as amino acids and other essential body-building substances, are but some of the highly potent substances contained in Yoni-juices. Only recently has Western sexology accepted the fact that when a woman has an orgasm, she actually does produce secretions other than those termed "merely sexual lubricants." It seems that these emanate from the uterus and "dormant prostate" region.

Tantra considers the *Love-juice* or *Lotus-nectar* of woman most beneficial when it has a sweetish taste. This accords with Oriental medical treatises, which relate sweetness to assimilation and nourishment. The *Ananga Ranga* declares, "The Lotus-type of woman produces love-essence perfumed like a lily that has just burst open. The Art woman emits hot juices that have the perfume and taste of honey; a Conch woman secretes distinctly salty love-fluid."

An important Taoist alchemical book declares that woman has a Yang-essence in her uterus, which is emitted as menstrual blood once a month. Referred to as *Red Snow*, it is said to be "The true essence of the woman's blood, which creates the embryo in the womb." It is this original Yang-essence that is drawn upon when a woman produces her *Moon Flower Medicine*, and it is this which is credited with the power of strengthening the Yang-force in man, through a process of direct absorption.

Various techniques, such as those given in the "Mutual Absorption" and "Nurturing Nature" sections of this book, are taught in both Tantric and Taoist traditions for the absorption of the threefold *Peak Medicine* of woman. An account in a Taoist alchemical

A Tantric love-posture specifically for mutual absorption and nurturing nature. Movement should be gentle and rhythmic. From an Indian miniature painting, Rajasthan, eighteenth century.

work advises, "When the Tortoise [the male organ] has entered, one should await the coming of the *Essence of Woman*, produced from her climax. Then the Tortoise should turn its head, holding back its own semen, and drink up the juices of the woman."

Such absorption can take place either by advanced Yoga techniques (*Uddiyana Bandha*), which create a vacuum or negative pressure in the bladder of the man, thereby "sucking up the woman's Yoni-emissions," or quite simply by the natural absorptive capacity of the head of the Lingam. The membranes of the Lingam become erect by absorbing a tremendous quantity of blood. In the same way, when the Lingam becomes soft within the Yoni, it naturally absorbs its secretions.

Taoist love-posture for absorbing female secretions directly through the head of the Lingam. From a Japanese print, *circa* 1680.

Absorption of the Yoni secretions can also take place directly through the mouth. Then there is a direct exchange between saliva and Yoni-juices. This type of oral sex helps to integrate the two "poles" of the body (the "Upper and Lower") and creates a healthful exchange of secretions, energies and potentials. Tantrics declare that the absorption of female secretions through the tongue, lips and mouth is beneficial to the whole system and is "pleasing to the Kundalini." (This aspect of sexuality is discussed in detail in "Oral Erotics" and "The Crow: '69.'")

The Medicine of the Three Peaks has the potential for nourishing and revitalizing the body and spirit. Any practice based on this fact should not be abused; a bond of love is essential for there to be any lasting exchange of potency. The distillation or alchemization of love takes place primarily in the heart center, from which the highest emotions derive their strength. It would be a big mistake to view the secrets of womanly secretions only on an external level. Love must "charge" the physical with the spiritual. Only then can true sexual alchemy take place.

Why trouble with the Pill of Immortality when one is welcomed to drink from the Jade Fountain?

HSU-HSIAO-MU-CHI

The man makes his semen return and prevents any emission. He absorbs the juices from the woman's Precious Gateway, while above he drinks her saliva. This special practice is known as Completing Nature; it endows a person with good health and long life.

TA-LO-FU

When he has embraced his female partner, inserted his Scepter into her Lotus, he should drink heavily from her lips; they seem as if sprinkled with milk. As the full richness of delight is enjoyed, her thighs begin to quiver and her first fulfillment is reached. This is the way of becoming One with the Imperishable, by absorbing each other selflessly. These practices should not be abused, or else they'll push one into the hells of sickness and confusion. Adepts should take care to act correctly in these potent practices.

KALACHAKRA TANTRA

Mutual oral sex allows vital secretions to be circulated and exchanged. From a Rajasthani miniature painting of the mid-eighteenth century.

the battle of love

Taoist teachings frequently refer to love-making as a "battle." The Dark Girl, whom we previously mentioned as an Initiatress of the Yellow Emperor, is credited with authoring several books on military strategy as well as works on the Art of Love. The idea of considering the sexual partner as an "enemy whom one must defeat" may at first seem strange and contrary, but is actually based on a profound insight. This psychological technique should be undertaken in the spirit of gamesmanship and not allowed to degenerate into egotism. Victory belongs to the one who succeeds in obtaining the partner's vital essence first.

In an early Taoist text, the Plain Girl declares, "When engaging the 'enemy,' the man should consider her as worthless as a stone and himself as precious as gold. As soon as the man senses that he is about to ejaculate, he should stop all movement. Making love to a woman is like riding a galloping horse with a frayed rein, or like staggering on the brink of a dangerous precipice." This technique, in essence, is a psychological trick to help assist retention.

A later Ming Dynasty treatise states:

A superior "general" should concentrate on drawing out the opponent. He should cultivate a detached attitude of indifference [the term "superior general" refers to the Taoist adept]. When he is about to make love, he should fondle the Jade Gateway of the woman with his hand, and suck her tongue. He should squeeze her breasts and suck in her pure breath; in this way, she will become very excited. All this time the man should keep himself under control, detaching his mind as if it were floating in a clear blue sky. He is advised to imagine that his body is sinking into nothingness. Closing his eyes, the man should not look at the woman, so that his own passion does not become stirred up; an inner feeling of nonchalance is necessary.

This kind of sexual attitude is hardly compatible with a lasting relationship, unless both partners are aware of what is happening and play it as a game. The same text gives an account of how to "defeat the enemy" by preventing ejaculation and "making the semen return." It takes the form of an allegory: "The turtle withdraws internally, the dragon inhales, the serpent swallows, and the tiger waits." The commentary gives an interpretation of this cryptic instruction:

Closing the eyes and mouth, withdrawing the feet and hands, and pressing the point between the scrotum and testicles with the fingers, while at the same time concentrating the mind, is the "way the turtle withdraws into itself." By drawing in the *True Fluid* [the Yoni-emissions], by making it flow steadily upward [by absorbing it through the Lingam] until it arrives at the secret place in the brain, in this way "the dragon inhales." The serpent "swallows its victim" by first nibbling at it until it is powerless, then swallowing it completely. The tiger "waits and catches its prey stealthily."

The allegory of a battle is commonly used in Taoist texts to describe love-making. The theory is that the "enemy" uses up his or her reserve of strength, thereby having to "surrender." The above text continues:

The enemy surrenders and I gather the spoils of victory. This is known as "already completed," which guarantees peace for a full generation. Withdrawing from the battlefield, I regain strength and place the booty in the storeroom, so increasing my reserves. "Gathering the spoils of victory" means that when the woman has reached her climax of pleasure, I continue to move my Weapon in and out, varying deep strokes with shallow ones, withdrawing it completely from time to time. By sucking her tongue and squeezing her breasts, I induce her to shed her *True Fluid*, which then can be absorbed by me. The term "full generation" means twelve years; the "storeroom" is the bone-marrow.

This description is an account of alchemical love-making, designed to strengthen male potency. It suggests that every time a man receives the *True Fluid* or *Inner Yang* of woman, he has the possibility of increasing his life expectancy by twelve years. It is interesting that recent gerontological research into methods for preventing aging have established that the bone marrow is a determining factor in aging. Experiments on animals, which have involved the direct transplantation of new bone marrow, effectively increased their life span. Bone marrow and semen are

Aggression can be used to channel sexual energy. In Taoism love-making is compared to a battle. From a Japanese painting by the lady painter Uemura Shoen (1875–1949).

A wrathful Tantric visualization of Mahakala and consort in ecstatic union. Visualizations of such angry forms are helpful in transmuting personality limitations. From a Tibetan painting of the late eighteenth century.

intimately connected; both are generated in related glandular cycles.

There is certainly psychological efficacy to considering the partner "worthless and ugly" in order to avoid premature ejaculation, or

to retain semen. But such a viewpoint is hardly compatible with the Tantric objective of envisioning the partner as a god or goddess, and could lead to false or potentially damaging results. Taken to the extreme, this activity leads to sexual aberrations such as sadomasochism. Tantra seeks to elevate, not to subjugate, the partner. In the Tantric Battle of Love, the victory belongs to the couple and is not the exclusive right of one or the other.

Tantric texts frequently describe terrific or ugly forms for visualization as a way to transform negative psychological traits. The wrathful sentiment is the simplest passion to generate. Visualizations of angry forms are, in fact, easier to maintain than peaceful ones. However, in Tantra, all the terrific mystic forms are conceived of as being "internally beautiful and deeply compassionate." In the mind of the Tantric adept Initiatory Guardians, Dakinis or Tantric Yoginis often appear as terrifying visions, which are ultimately transformed into beautiful ones.

It is a strange aspect of our psyche that the things we are repelled by—terror, wrathfulness or ugliness—fascinate us and are easier to visualize than those we are attracted to. Because the emotions are more readily aroused by aspects of personality that are repressed or remain unconfronted by the inner spirit, the motive power for the visualization is more easily summoned. Psychic obstacles and negative emotions can best be removed by visualizing them as the awesome wrathful forces of the psyche and transforming them during sexual union. In this mysterious timeless battle the forces of darkness are summoned, subdued and sublimated through the power of Tantric visualization. When the Battle of Love takes place on an inner dimension, the process of spiritual transformation is greatly accelerated. True victory lies with the dawning of the inner light.

The Battle of the Sexes is not unlike the art of warfare; before the opening of hostilities, the two contestants spy upon each other, feeling out their strengths and weaknesses. Success in battle depends on this.   JOU PU TUAN

Every man who has obtained a beautiful Crucible [woman] will naturally love her with all his heart. But when he makes love with her he should force himself to visualize her as ugly and hateful. With a calm mind he should insert his Jade Stalk into her Crucible, moving it slowly backward and forward. When he has done this a few times, he should stop, so as to calm his lust. A little bit later he should begin again and so continue until the woman reaches the point where she can scarcely contain herself. The man should be careful to move slowly, so that the woman is the first to arrive at the climax. As soon as he senses that his semen is about to be ejaculated, he should withdraw his Jade Stalk and employ the art of retaining his semen.   HSUI-CHEN-YEN-I

The longer the battle raged, the more imposing became the stature of his Warrior, and with it his courage; no longer was her Pleasure Grotto a bottomless pit. Both on the sides and in the depths the desired contact was made. Her body began to quiver and writhe voluptuously, and moans of pleasure issued from her lips. The grass and bushes around her Gateway grew moist with the dew of ecstasy. He reached for the cloth, to wipe away some of the juices, but she restrained him. A Battle of the Sexes, she felt, should be a wild frenzy, an ecstatic temple dance with a rousing accompaniment of gongs and drums.

JOU PU TUAN

nurturing nature

Woman has a limitless amount of Yin-essence, provided that she is in tune with nature. Spontaneous loving experiences revitalize and replenish her Yin-essence. However, if she is forced to engage in routine, mechanical sexual activity, she risks the danger of depleting her vital energy.

A Taoist alchemical treatise states:

> When a woman makes love with a man, it is very important that her heart be quiet and her thoughts composed. If the man has not reached the highest joy when the woman feels close to her climax of pleasure, she should try to contain herself. If she senses that she will respond to the man's movements by involuntary orgasm, she should stop the movements of her own body and in this way will nurture her essence. If her Yin-essence becomes depleted through repeated *involuntary* orgasms, then a kind of vacuum is created in her body, which is then prone to attracting disease.

Taoism emphasizes that "a woman should not allow herself to become sad or jealous, even if she should see her man making love with another woman, for this will cause her Yin-essence to become over-excited. Then the woman will be afflicted by physical pains while sitting or standing, and her female secretions will flow out on their own, so causing her to wither and age before her time."

In order to call forth her natural responsiveness and awesome sexual potency, woman must cultivate harmony with her environment and her partner. The nature of woman can be nurtured by making contact with Yin elements—by walking in flower gardens, or with bare feet on dew-laden grass. Contact with beautiful women is said to be one of the most effective ways of nurturing the Yin, and for this reason, Sapphic love was considered quite natural in cultures that recognized this power in femininity.

A woman's nature is nurtured when she gains ascendancy over her emotionality, allowing this primal energy to transform her personality. If a woman can learn to control and channel her emotional energy, she can become an inexhaustible source of psychic nourishment to her partner. Both Taoism and Tantra teach that emotional maturity is the key to understanding the alchemy of ecstasy.

Nature is nurtured by uninhibited love-making. This is the rationale behind ancient pagan sexual rituals. Lovers can nurture nature spontaneously, provided they maintain the balance between "giving" and "taking."

The mystery teachings on sexuality emphasize that a woman should never allow herself to become jealous or overly possessive. In the polygamous society of ancient China co-wives learned to accept one another as sisters rather than as rivals. From a Chinese painting of the Ming dynasty.

Normally, in a healthy relationship, any loss of female Yin-essence is compensated by absorption of the male Yang-essence. However, if a man repeatedly forces himself on a woman, he may extract her vital energy. If she is not living a natural lifestyle, she will have no way of compensating for what has been "taken" from her.

Alchemical texts, such as the *Chandamaharosana Tantra*, describe the Yoni of woman as "a crucible, a vessel of transformation." It is in this vessel that the Yin and Yang essences combine, transform and nurture the couple. This process takes place in both a physical and subtle dimension.

One of the foremost physical techniques for absorbing and transforming sexual vitality is the Tantric *Vajroli Mudra*, the "Diamond Seal," a method that aims at reversing the flow of sexual energy. Both men and women can practice this technique for consciously absorbing their partner's love-secretions and drawing sexual energy upward, to empower spiritual evolution.

Woman practices the *Vajroli Mudra* by creating suction through the rhythmic constriction of the walls of her Yoni. At the same time, she visualizes the energy drawing upward and swallows her saliva.

The physical technique involves two distinct movements. The first is a conscious constriction of the urethral sphincter muscles, just below the clitoris. These muscles are very closely related to the anal sphincter, which governs excretion. The urethral sphincter controls and regulates urination. If a woman locates and contracts this muscle while urinating, then the flow will be interrupted, and continue when released. Once the location is known, practice can develop this muscle and prepare it for the Art of Love. While practicing this contraction, the woman should pull up the lower part of the abdomen, alternating contractions with relaxation.

A woman can check the effectiveness of her sphincter movements by gently inserting one or two fingers into her Yoni while performing the exercise. When correctly done, the contractions will clasp and unclasp her fingers. The *Ananga Ranga* states:

The woman should ever strive to close and constrict the Yoni until it holds the Lingam as with a finger, opening and shutting at her pleasure, and finally, acting as the hand of the Gopi girl, who milks the cow. This can only be learned by practice, and especially by throwing the power of the will into the part to be affected. While so doing, she should mentally repeat the name of the Love god, Kamadeva (whose seed Mantra is the sound "KLING"), in order that a blessing may come to her. And she will be pleased to know that this art, once learned, is never lost. Her husband will then value her above all women, nor would he exchange her for the most beautiful queen. So lovely and pleasant to man is she who can constrict her Yoni in this way.

The second movement of the woman involves a simple Yogic exercise known as *Uddiyana Bandha*, or "Flying-up Restraint." This exercise helps draw vital energy from the sexual region and channel it upward. *Uddiyana Bandha* is effected by exhaling the breath and contracting the stomach muscles, producing a negative air pressure or vacuum in the lower part of the abdomen, which takes on a concave appearance. An additional movement known as *Nauli* or "Surging Wave," consists in churning the abdominal muscles, which helps to draw up and transform sexual energy. These two movements are cultivated by belly dancers, who probably derived the technique from Indian temple dancers instructed in these Tantric methods.

Through gaining control of her Yoni and abdominal muscles, a woman can nurture her nature while at the same time giving an exquisite experience to her partner. This very special twisting movement of woman during love-making is considered an important sexual secret in both Taoist and Tantric teachings, as it is one of the most effective ways of drawing up, concentrating and transforming sexual energy.

A man can also perform the *Uddiyana Bandha*, which enables him to draw up sexual secretions through his Lingam. The constriction of the man's urinary sphincter during love-making creates an internal vacuum, aiding in the absorption of secretions while causing a hardening of the Lingam along with an exhilarating experience for the woman. The whole process, known as *Vajroli Mudra*, has the effect of circulating and exchanging energy between the partners and is the key to mutual absorption.

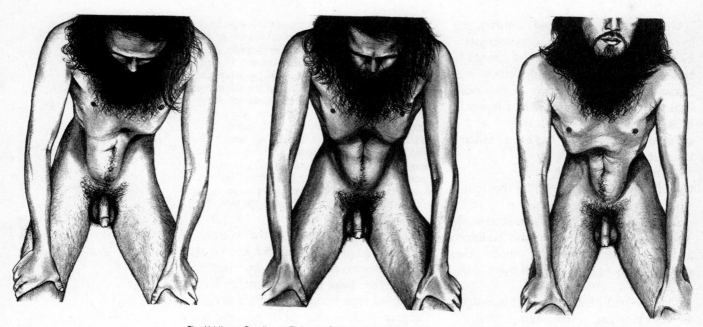

The *Uddiyana Bandha*, or Flying-up Restraint, was named after an ancient kingdom in eastern India where Tantric Yoga first developed. The exercise is performed with the hands resting above the knees and the breath exhaled. First the right and left abdominal muscles should be isolated, followed by the stomach, which is then churned, a process known as *Nauli*. The *Gheranda Samhita* declares that "whoever practices the *Uddiyana Bandha* conquers death. The Great Bird of Vitality is drawn up through the Central Axis, raising the consciousness." This exercise can be used to help absorb sexual secretions and energies.

Nature is nurtured by the harmonious blending of male and female sexuality. The ancient teachings state that when two people make love with the whole of their physical, emotional and spiritual being, there is an exchange of psychic energy between them and a harmonization with the evolutionary energy of nature. The couple become "in tune" with natural forces. Taoism declares that when Yin and Yang are in balance, mankind is brought back into direct communion with the forces of Earth and Heaven, nature is nurtured and humanity prospers.

Those who want to nurture nature and prolong their lives should meditate deeply on their ultimate aim and consider the source of their origin. TS'AN-T'UNG-CH'I

Above the Lingam and below the navel is the region that is known as Uddiyana or "flying up." There is a great secret of the restraint [Bandha] of this area, which produces the most effective way of overcoming death. GORAKSASHATAKAM

Entering the median nerve at the Navel Center, from the sexual region, the vital force moves through the middle of the other nerve centers. Becoming the Fire force of Wisdom-energy, it rises upward and pervades all the nerve channels, untying all the psychic "knots." From this process there are five supernormal signs that appear to the practitioner of this Yoga. These are the "flaring," the "moon," the "sun," the "lightning" and "saturn." The "flaring" appears as a yellow radiance, the "moon" as white, the "sun" as red, the "lightning" as pink and "saturn" as blue. Within each of these radiances, in turn, one's own body will be enhaloed. SIX DOCTRINES OF NAROPA

transforming the true

A very interesting Taoist text, which bears directly on our previous section, concerns the secret methods of mutually absorbing and transforming sexual energy. It instructs neither the man nor the woman to reach an outer climax or orgasm, but instead to keep their experience on the brink of ecstasy, all the while controlling the emotions and channeling energy upward. Known as the *Secret Teachings of Transforming the True*, this practice nurtures the spirit and invigorates the body, providing equal benefits to both partners.

According to ancient Eastern teachings, subtle inner channels or "ducts" connect the breasts of woman with her sexual center. These channels distribute vital energy; when a woman's breasts are sucked, the nipple erects and the womb contracts. As we have mentioned, Taoism declares that the breasts of woman secrete a subtle medicine that is a great source of potency for her lover. The same teaching is found in Tantra, where some texts prescribe the sucking of virgin breasts as an effective procedure for rejuvenation. It is noteworthy that Leonardo da Vinci's famous anatomical drawing of sexual intercourse depicts descending ducts from the breasts of woman to her uterus, as well as a subtle connecting nerve between the Lingam and the lower part of the spine. This nerve serves as the ignitor of the Kundalini.

The Tang Dynasty (A.D. 618–907) Taoist text of the master Teng gives a detailed account of an alchemical love-making technique known as *Transforming the True*. In this text, the subtle channels connecting the breasts of woman with her uterus are mentioned. The master states that the couple should mentally repeat a power phrase during love-making and suggests that:

A man and woman may together practice the art that leads to longevity. Known as *Transforming the True*, it is a secret method that should only be transmitted to adepts. It allows a man and woman to activate their life-essence at the same time; the man nurtures his semen and the woman her secretions. The Yin-essence of the woman becomes activated and the man's Yang-essence becomes strengthened. If this discipline is practiced in the right way, then the vital fluid will spread like clouds throughout the entire body, their spiritual essences will be harmonized and both partners will become rejuvenated.

Both partners should begin by meditating, deliberately detaching their minds from all worldly things. Then they should grind their teeth seven times, to produce much saliva, while mentally repeating the following power phrase: "May the Golden Essence of the Original White Light bring my five Inner Flowers [psychic centers] to life. May the Supreme Lord of Evolution harmonize my innermost Soul and fortify my Spirit. May all the six vital energies be bound together as One, so that their spirits return to strengthen the Head Center. May the two of us unite completely and blend harmoniously. May the fruit of our loving be sweet and may our innermost Treasure be conserved." Having completed this verse, the couple should proceed with their love-making.

The man should refrain from ejaculating. If he controls his thought and his breath, the semen will become transmuted and will ascend the spinal column until it reaches the secret center in his brain [the pituitary gland]. This is known as the *Return to Origin*.

The woman should control her emotions so that she does not complete her climax; this nurtures her Spirit. She should let the vital force of her two breasts descend through the subtle channels to her sex center and then ascend from there until the energy reaches the secret place in her brain. This is what is known as *Transforming the True*. The Elixir formed in the bodies of the couple should be nurtured for one hundred days; then it will truly become transcendental. This practice, if prolonged, confers Liberation.

All alchemical practices require psychic and physiological stability. The alchemy of love-making presupposes that physical and emotional energies are already under conscious control. Once stability is achieved, it is the power of love that truly transforms the fires of passion into the ecstasy that endures.

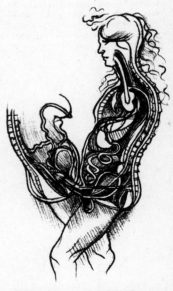

By my inner firmness I have caused my seed to remain stationary in the middle of the Lingam. Thus it is always fruitful, ever ready. This is the power of self-transcendence.

SKANDA PURANA

Leonardo da Vinci believed that there are subtle connections between the breasts and the uterus of woman, and between the Lingam and spinal column of man. From a drawing by Leonardo, in the collection of Queen Elizabeth of England.

The Way of Enjoyment depends on the nurturing of body and soul. The best resolution is to keep to the <u>Golden Mean</u> of neither too much nor too little. There are physical ailments that can develop from over-indulgence in sex or from a man's <u>forcing</u> himself to ejaculate. Those wise people who know how to nurture nature do not make the mistake of over-indulgence.

YIN·SHAN·CHENG·YAO

As between Heaven and Earth, movement must be balanced between the male and female elements. The male element absorbs the female one and is converted; the female element receives the male one and is transformed. The female and male elements must operate in complementary ways. If the Jade Stalk feels firm and strong and the Precious Grotto moves open and extended, two life-forces exchange emissions and flowing liquids penetrate mutually.

CLASSIC OF THE EXALTED GIRL

Anatomical chart of body according to ancient Taoist alchemical tradition. The navel center is depicted as a cauldron. The heart center is connected directly to the central spinal axis, which ascends to the head center. From a print of the Ming dynasty.

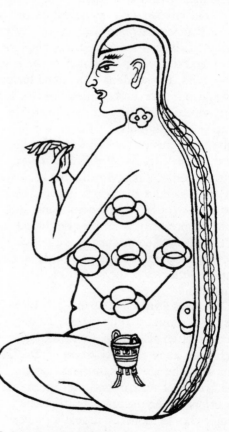

Taoist alchemical teachings declare that the Elixir of Life is made within the body, by circulating sexual energy and distilling it into the heart center. This diagram depicts the circulation and transformation of sexual energies according to Taoism. From a print of the Ming dynasty.

The central axis of the body is conceived as a great pathway through which sexual energy can ascend. From a print of the Ming dynasty.

Ritual love-making implies the subtle weaving of the known with the unknown. A couple are depicted in Tantric union; they are surrounded by imaginary protections of themselves, acrobatically entwined. For any ritual to be successful, the power of the imagination must be brought to bear on the unknown. From a Rajasthani miniature painting of the late eighteenth century.

ritual love-making

Ritual love-making is central to both Taoist and Tantric traditions. Ritual implies an understanding of the order of events best suited to the fulfillment of a goal. A definite *intention* must impel the performance of any ritual act. Ritual love-making elevates the mundane to the spiritual. It empowers the sexual act with a meaning that lasts beyond life itself. Ritual can also be spontaneous, but spontaneous ritual requires conscious intuitive awareness and *emotional constancy* to be effective. Above all, a ritual act has a magical or transcendental energy and is a bridge between the known and the unknown. Sexual rituals can open the soul to a deeper experience of ecstasy. Ritual love-making in both Taoism and Tantra is considered the most direct way to achieve Liberation within a single lifetime.

Accounts of sexual rites and rituals exist in all ancient religious traditions. Paganism was born out of sexual ritual and recognition of the power and joy inherent in the sexual act. Folklore, folk dances and fairy tales often conceal ancient teachings and rituals of love-making. Christianity and Islam absorbed some of these pagan teachings on sexuality and transformed them into allegory.

It is fortunate that the Eastern tradition of sexual ritual has survived in a practical form to the present day. Western sexual rituals are found only in magical cults such as the Wicca (witch covens), the O.T.O. (Ordo Templi Orientis, founded by Karl Kellner, after learning the sexual secrets from two Hindu Tantric Yogis and an Arab; this order was later taken over by Aleister Crowley) and other occult organizations. These cults draw their inspiration directly from Tantra and Taoism, often in a distorted way. In the East, there are Yogis practicing authentic sexual rites that have been handed down in direct succession for over a thousand years. It is to them that we owe much of the material in this book.

All the basic principles of ritual love-making have been dealt with individually in the previous sections. Weaving together these parts into a complete and meaningful whole is the endeavor of all true practitioners of Tantra. The very word

304

VISHNU

the preserver

Mystic sexual dance of *Siddha Jalandhari*.
Many ancient ecstasy teachings point to
the harmonizing power inherent in mystic
dance. Here the man holds a scepter and
bell (symbolic of the male and female sex
organs), while his consort holds a skull
bowl and drum (symbolic of
compassionate wisdom and primordial
sound vibrations). From a Tibetan painting
of the late seventeenth century.

Tantra in Sanskrit is associated with
weaving, an art demanding a sense of
synthesis, care and attention. It is also
linked to the concept of expansion. Thus,
Tantric sexual ritual implies the weaving
together of the *Sixty-four Arts* into an all-
expansive ecstatic experience.

Many kinds of sexual rituals exist and
not all of them have to do with love-
making per se. The East has traditional
rituals associated with birth, childhood,
puberty, defloration, marriage and sexual
consummation, as well as seasonal,
religious, mystical and oracular rites; all of
these have a certain element of sexuality,
either concealed or manifest.

In the Taoist text known as *The Yellow
Book for Passing over to the Other Side*, an ancient
sexual ritual is beautifully described in
which couples enact a drama of cosmic
dimension. The ritual was devised to help
couples to unify their Yin and Yang
essences, which would enable them to

enter the timeless realm of Immortality.
First the participants had to undergo a
retreat of purification for several days:

Then the couples stand, face to face and holding
hands, the man's index finger between the index
and middle finger of the woman. Standing thus, the
couples meditate on the gods and goddesses of the
body, the spirits of the season and the purpose of
the ritual. Then each couple separates and singly
meditates on the gestures and postures of the rite.

The master instructs the participants to undress,
pair off, and begin a slow mystic dance. First
standing, then seated and finally reclining, the
couples perform a series of mystic movements and
gestures, imitating animals, birds, natural forces and
celestial bodies. Every move that the man makes is
mirrored exactly by his partner. If he lifts his left
arm or leg, she must raise her right arm or leg. This
is called *Cosmic Harmonization*. Gradually the
movements accelerate and spontaneity prevails.
Intoning a prayer that expresses their desire to
move both Heaven and Earth, the couples lie down
and touch each other on the head, the heart and
the sexual region, all the while controlling their
breathing and holding in mind the concept of
Cosmic Harmonization.

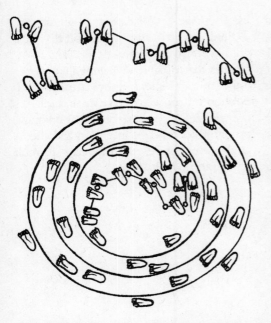

Footprints to illustrate the movements of a couple in ritual dance. Earth is represented by a spiral of three and a half turns (reminding us of the three and a half turns of the Kundalini at the sexual center). Heaven is represented by the constellation shape of the Great Bear. From a Chinese diagram of the late thirteenth century.

The man then places his left hand on his partner's left breast and caresses her body, moving his hand three times downward as far as her leg, intoning an invocation to *The Supreme Force of the Left*. He then does the same to his partner's right side, invoking *The Mysterious Old Man of the Right*. Then using his left hand, he caresses the woman's body from her throat center to her sexual center, all the while honoring the *Supreme Being of All Becoming*. He should then repeat this with his right hand.

Three times he should touch the woman's Jade Cavern, placing his right hand on her Door of Life and opening the lips of her Golden Doorway. With his right hand he should insert his Jade Flute into her Gateway. He should touch the top of his partner's head with his left hand and caress her Door of Life in a downward movement, from left to right, using his right hand and intoning the following power phrase of transcendence: "Water flows toward the East [the male side], clouds return to the West [the female side]. Yin nourishes the forces of Yang; how subtle and transcendental is this cosmic truth. Let the Life-essence rise up! May our vitalities be joined!" The woman then also declares, "From Yin and Yang all creation emerged. Heaven covers, Earth supports. Remembering this, I fill my whole being with blissful strength!"

This ancient sexual ritual has many elements that can be incorporated into modern love-rites. The linking of fingers helps channel energy. Meditation on the *beings* within the body, seasonal spirits and the purpose of the ritual all help to direct sexual energy along the path to fulfillment. Mystic dance, made up of natural movements and gestures, mirrored in each partner and increasing in tempo, greatly aids the harmonization of mood; personality limitations are quickly overcome by this joyous "opening." Breath and mind control are essential to any concept of *Cosmic Harmonization*.

Touching the body at precise points with the right or left hand is an ancient magical technique for channeling sexual energy. By invoking archetypes such as *The Supreme Force of the Left* (the Original Female Principle) or *The Mysterious Old Man of the Right* (the Ancestral Patriarch), energy is identified with and channeled back to its source. In this ancient text we see a very early example of the principle of identification of the couple with god and goddess archetypes. When sexual union is empowered by the invocation of power phrases and accompanied by consciously ordered movements, the limitations of individual personalities dissolve and the spirit is free to explore its deeper

Visualization of *Kalachakra* in male/female union as the Lord and Lady of Time. The twenty-four-armed male figure holds his eight-armed female counterpart in ecstatic embrace. Such complex visualizations help to concentrate all mental functions in a single transcendental direction. From a Tibetan painting of the sixteenth century.

Footprints to illustrate the steps of a ritual sexual dance. This diagram is based on the seven-star constellation known as the Great Dipper. From a Chinese diagram of the Tao-tsang, *circa* 1116.

dimensions. Power phrases or Mantras add direction to ritual acts. The power of the word has, since ancient times, been viewed as the source of creation itself. Indeed, during ritual love-making, any word that is declared impresses itself deep within the psyche and takes on a lasting significance.

Such high rituals of love-making are really quite simple. It is not a matter of learning dogma, but rather of understanding how to use the most basic elements of life in an exalted way. It is not "what you do" but "how you do it" that matters. Tantra teaches that ritual love-making, like all important acts, should grow naturally and develop out of self-confidence and self-knowledge. A synthesis of sexual union, proper practice, right intention and the guidance of the heart is the secret formula of all Tantric high ritual.

The dancing ecstatic union of Hevajra and Nairatma ("The Indestructible" and "Egoless Compassion"), according to the mystery teachings of the *Hevajra Tantra*. The male figure is visualized as of dark color, with nine heads symbolic of the nine sentiments. From a Tibetan painting of the eighteenth century.

The Emperor practiced the Secret Method known as Discipline in Pairs, performed with girls of good families. He selected the most beautiful of his concubines and had them perform the Dance of the Sixteen Dakinis. Their hair was plaited in long tresses and braided with gold thread. They wore long red robes, ivory crowns studded with jewels and held bowls in their hands. The brothers of the Emperor all engaged with these sixteen dancers, two to each, making love in the great hall known as Everything without Obstacle. The Emperor found his joy in this cosmic drama.

YUAN SHIH-YEH-TING-CHI

High is the mountain of the spinal column, and at the top of it, there sits the Bliss-bestowing girl in the form of a huntress. She is all covered with peacock feathers and a beautiful garland of flowers is around her gazelle-like neck. "O exalted hunter! O mad hunter!" So exclaims the girl on the mountain peak. "I am your dearest mistress; my name is Spontaneous Wave of Bliss!"

Many are the trees on the mountain. The huntress-girl, decked with beautiful earrings of lightning and thunder, plays alone in the forest. The bedstead of the Three Essentials of Body, Speech and Mind is made ready. In expectant Bliss, the hunter spreads the bedclothes. Then the serpent-like hunter and the selfless goddess pass their night of love on that bed.

MYSTIC SONG OF SIDDHA SARAHA

the secret rite

Most accounts that present the Tantric love-rite are highly complex, and likely to confuse a Westerner unaccustomed to Eastern ritual. For this reason, we will give here a version that, though direct and complete, is greatly simplified.

It is important that the *Secret Rite* not be rushed or interrupted. Put aside plenty of time, and take care that you won't be disturbed. Try to ensure that the environment is "just right," enhancing it with flowers, fruit, incense and gentle music. It is best for the couple to make all these preparations beforehand.

Ideally there should be only a candle or an open fire burning. The couple should be located so that only subdued light falls on their bodies. A castor-oil lamp, made by placing some castor-oil in a small container and inserting a wick made by rolling up some cotton wool, is particularly suitable

since it burns steadily with a bright, slightly purplish light.

Sexual ritual—or *Maithuna Sadhana*, as it is known in Tantra—commences with both partners taking a bath or shower, preferably in cold water. This has the effect of vitalizing and toning up the psyche. Then the couple should lightly oil and massage each other. This should be followed by a brief period spent in stretching exercises, to relax the muscles and free the circulation of vital energies. Dance serves the same purpose and can be a most effective way of harmonizing mood and circulating energy between the couple.

In the next stage, the couple sit down, preferably with legs crossed in the lotus posture, and with the woman to the *right* of the man. They should practice simple meditation, clearing their minds of any worldly or habitual thoughts and regulating their breath by gentle alternate-nostril or *Solar-Lunar Breathing*. When both feel completely relaxed and harmonized, they

Radha and Krishna in dalliance. The consort places herself to the right of her lover at the commencement of love-making and moves over to the left as the rite proceeds. Tantric texts declare that this mirrors the order of energy flow in the right and left sides of the Subtle Body. From a miniature painting, Kulu, *circa* 1720.

serpentine energy wave uncoiling at the base of their spines. The powers of fantasy and imagination should be drawn on to make the Kundalini excited. Conceived of as a primordial ecstatic female being, the Kundalini should be endowed with emotional energy. From this point on in the ritual, the partners must forget their personal, human identities and know themselves only as Shiva and Shakti, the Supreme Couple.

Starting with her right side, the man should gradually move his hands up the woman's body, gently touching her with his fingertips, in this sequence: right toe, right foot, right knee, right thigh, Yoni, right buttock, navel, middle of chest, right breast, right side, right side of throat, right cheek, lower lip, right eye and top of her head. Then he should descend to her left eye, upper lip, left cheek, left side of throat, left side, left breast, middle of chest, navel, left buttock, Yoni, left thigh, left knee, left foot and left toe. This sequence links directly into the lunar cycle of passion in woman. Gently vibrating his hands as he touches these erogenous zones, the man should visualize energy streaming out of his fingertips, exciting passion in his partner.

She should visualize herself as a *Living Goddess*, a receptacle of love, his *Precious Crucible*. Concentrating upon the release of erotic energy, she should stimulate her sexuality by deep breathing and by gently rocking her body backward and forward. Feeling the Kundalini vibrating within, the woman should empower her whole being with a sense of expectancy.

The man should contemplate the flame of a candle or lamp and then return his gaze to his partner's body. He should gently apply perfumed oil (of musk, patchouli or sandalwood, preferably) to her pubic hair, navel, heart region, throat, forehead and top of her head, while mentally invoking the following ancient saying: "Woman is fire. Sexual energy is the fuel; her Yoni is the flame; her pubic hair, the smoke; penetration, the offering; pleasurable feelings, the sparks. In this fire, the gods offer up their semen. From such offerings, every being is born."

The man should apply additional perfumed oil to her hair, behind her ears and to the palms of her hands, all the while controlling his mind by the use of

are then ready to proceed with the Secret Rite itself. A simple aid to harmonization of breath and mood is shared singing, which can accompany a recording. The main point is that it should be devotional or transcendental in nature.

The first part of the Secret Rite is the honoring of the female principle, the *Shakti*, both externally and internally. The man performs external honoring by seating his partner on a pillow or cushion in front of him, lightly wrapping her body with a red or violet shawl of cotton, wool or silk. Imagining her as the most beautiful goddess in the whole universe, he should bring to mind her best qualities and gently massage her feet with perfumed oil. This massage should be concentrated on the region around and between her largest toes. Humming a Mantra gently to himself, the man should endow this moment with potency and expectation.

The couple should both perform inward honoring by remembering the purpose of the ritual, which is to become totally unified with one's origin. Evoking the Kundalini-power within each of them, they should visualize a molten-gold

Ritual love-posture. From an Orissan miniature painting of the nineteenth century.

Mantra and meditation. For this ritual, the
Mantra "OM–AH–HUM," as expounded in
"Noises of Love," is particularly suitable. He
should honor his partner, placing flowers
in her hair or a garland around her neck.
He can apply body makeup to her, or do
anything that is exalting and stimulating
to his partner in her role as a Living
Goddess. During this time, it is most
important that the man remain steady and
controlled, his consciousness focused on
the intention of the ritual.

The woman now moves slightly to the
left of her partner and should begin to
arouse him with movements of her hands
and lips over his body. In so doing, she
should think of her lover as Lord Shiva
himself, the Supreme Yogi; she should
honor his Lingam as the Shiva Lingam,
anointing it with oil. Once the female
partner is located to the left of the man,
she takes on the role of sex initiatress.

She should perform self-worship by
lighting some incense sticks and moving
them in a circular or undulating
serpentine motion around herself and her
partner, in a clockwise direction. While
doing so, she should imagine that all
negative influences are excluded; that she
is insulating herself and her partner from
the rest of existence.

The couple can now commence the act
of love-making, either in a seated or lying
position. Seated positions are generally more
effective for prolonged intimate contact,
and can be aided by the skillful use of
cushions and pillows. All Eastern texts are
unanimous in saying that sexual rites should
begin with the woman sitting on the right
of the man and then moving over to his left
side for the stage of sexual fulfillment. The
right side is associated with the Solar breath,
logical thought processes, the lineage of
ancestors, and so on, whereas the left side is
associated with the Lunar breath, intuition,
and the mystic lineage of teachers and
initiators. When a Hindu woman is married,
she sits to the right side of her partner, but
for sexual rites she moves over to his left.

Love-making should be gentle, sensual and
reciprocal. With the Lingam inserted into
the Yoni, the couple should explore the
peaks and plateaus of loving. Alternating
moving with stillness, the Tantric couple
should endeavor to anticipate the approach
of climax in each other, coordinating their

309

secrets

A maharaja in Tantric union with a lady. Once seated to his
left side, she opens herself up to him as an initiatress into
the mysteries of love. From a Basohli miniature painting of
the early eighteenth century.

In Tantric sexual rites, when the woman moves to the left of the man, she takes on an active role. Here
a couple are depicted as god and goddess. The man holds a scepter, symbolic of the Lingam, while
his consort holds a ritual bell, symbolic of the Yoni. From a Nepalese painting of the late fifteenth century.

loving so as to release surges of energy that mutually enrich their whole being. The longer they can maintain heightened sexual excitement without climax, the more transcendental the experience will be.

Seated postures aid prolonged love-making and assist the upward movement of sexual energy. From a contemporary photograph.

Postures can be varied to create new forms for sexual energy to flow through. Posture changing aids retention and empowers the love-rite with new potential. Ideally the couple should discuss and work out beforehand a basic sequence of love-postures, or even a strategy for their love-making, as this will enable them to avoid physical misunderstandings and allow them to elevate love-making to its highest form. However, ultimately a spontaneous awareness should supersede any predetermined order of love-making. Once the basic fabric of ritual is integrated into the consciousness of the couple they must draw on their inner resources to add depth and dimension to the ritual.

Stimulating the passions to release waves of ecstasy, the couple should nurture each other's nature and explore the transcendental power of love. Visualizing the sexual energy rising upward through their conjoined *Subtle Body*, both man and woman should give and receive, circulating vitality throughout their whole being.

Opening up their mind's eye with the power of Kundalini, the Tantric couple should endeavor to experience mystic initiation from the realms of the Immortals. Look into the ecstatic mind for illuminating and meaningful visions. Look into the open heart for a deeper understanding of life itself. Tantras teach that there is nothing out of reach of the couple who practice Tantric love with dedication and commitment.

A love-rite can be practiced with a specific purpose in mind, such as physical healing, the resolution of a problem, or the taste of Liberation. If there is a specific objective, it should be held in the mind of both partners, particularly as the climax is approached. To make love *with* or *without* mutual physical orgasm is a matter of personal preference, physical condition or pure spontaneity. Tantra emphasizes that if there is ejaculation of semen, the man should compensate by leaving the Lingam in the Yoni for some time, absorbing the secretions directly. Prolonged Tantric love-making should incorporate oral sex, as this is effective in ensuring that each partner receives the product of his or her ecstasy and does not suffer any physical loss. Control of sexuality comes through familiarization with the various techniques of retention and mutual absorption, and also through intuitive exploration.

Seated posture well suited to ritual love-making. This type of Taoist posture can be used to create waves of ecstasy by rocking backward and forward. From a Chinese painting of the Ming dynasty.

There should always be some fresh fruit, sweets and a beverage readily available. Partaking of food during love-making has symbolic significance and is stimulating to the sense of taste and to the vitality of the body. Passion increases thirst, and it is quite natural to want to quench it. All the five senses come into play in evolved erotic activity; conscious evocation of the senses potentizes the whole experience of love.

When the man is about to ejaculate, he should make a big effort to draw the energy upward, tracing the flow in his mind's eye. He should mentally intone the seed Mantra "SWAHA" (or "OM SWAHA") at the moment of ejaculation, and touch the top of his partner's head, or between her eyes, as an act of empowerment.

There is a tradition of choosing particular times of the month for the practice of sexual rites. The fifth or eighth day after the cessation of a woman's menstrual period is considered particularly efficacious, as are the full moon and solstice nights. The time between midnight and two o'clock in the morning is much favored both for meditation and sexual ritual.

Parts of the Secret Rite can be incorporated into every act of loving. Mainly it is the mental attitude of exaltation that is important, as well as the sense of expectancy. Once there has been a shared orgasm, or a prolonged plateau of ecstasy, try to open yourself up to new dimensions. Let your creative imagination be fed by the intuition and, while still in intimate union, you will find that there are many secrets that will dawn of their own accord. Love-making is a doorway to transcendental ecstasy. The doorway of Tantric love is ever open to those who bring their highest qualities and intentions as a ritual offering.

Sexual energy should be consciously circulated and the contact between Lingam and Yoni maintained. By changing postures, retention is more easily controlled, allowing the couple to prolong the peaks of ecstasy. From an East Indian painting of the nineteenth century.

A couple in love-dalliance. The woman reclines while holding her fingers in the energy-circulation gesture, with thumb and forefinger linked. Ritual love-making should never be rushed. From a Rajasthani miniature painting of the eighteenth century.

Idealization of the Tantric couple in seated sexual union. The two extra arms of the male are shown holding a sword (symbolic of wisdom) and book (symbolic of knowledge). His other two hands hold scepter and bell, indicating that Lingam and Yoni are in union. From a Nepalese painting of the eighteenth century.

At the commencement of the rite, the woman should be placed in a comfortable seated position. Her feet should be carefully washed and perfumed; then sandal paste and oils are to be applied to the various parts of her body. Flowers and light should be offered, together with incense and music. She should then be seated on the left side and kissed and touched so as to inspire the mind.

NAYIKA-SADHANA-TIKA

In a pleasing place, free from all distractions or disturbances, in secret, he should take a woman who has desire. "I am the Buddha, the Perfected One, Immoveable; she is the Precious Wisdom-initiatress." Thus the wise man should meditate with fixed thought. Then the man and woman should meditate on their respective divine forms. They should carry out the practice of uniting Lotus and Scepter, patiently and according to what should be done. Here, indeed, there is great pleasure. Here, indeed, Chandamaharosana, the Great Moon Elixir, is situated.

CHANDAMAHAROSANA TANTRA

The Lotus-flower, the sex organ of the partner, is an ocean filled with Bliss. This Lotus-flower is also a transparent place, where the Thought of Enlightenment can rise up. When it is united with the Scepter, the male organ, their mixture is compared to the Elixir produced from the combination of myrrh and nutmeg. From their union a pure knowledge arises, which explains the nature of all things.

KALACHAKRA TANTRA

the rite of the five essentials

One Tantric sexual rite is both well known and often misunderstood. The *Ritual of the Five M's* or the *Five Essentials* has come to be referred to as the Tantric Eucharist. Each of the five main ingredients has a Sanskrit name beginning with the letter "M": cereal grains (*Mudra*), fish (*Matsya*), wine (*Madya*), meat (*Mamsa*) and sexual union (*Maithuna*). These are believed to be the essential ingredients of the phenomenal universe and are related symbolically to the five elements of earth, water, fire, air and space, respectively. Cereal grains, fish and meat together evoke the vegetable, aquatic and animal realms of existence, which are called upon as "allies" during the rite itself. Wine and sexual union in combination elevate the senses and foster mystical release.

SPACE	Sexual Union	*Maithuna*
AIR	Meat	*Mamsa*
FIRE	Wine	*Madya*
WATER	Fish	*Matsya*
EARTH	Cereal grains	*Mudra*

Small amounts of cooked fish and meat should be prepared beforehand and beautifully arranged on plates, together with some bean sprouts or cereal. A good red or white wine, or champagne, is ideal; brandy or other kinds of liquor can also be used. In present-day Bengal, as in the past, marijuana is prepared for smoking, taken in drinks (*Bhang*), or prepared with sweets.

The rite usually takes place at midnight, during the dark of the moon. An open fire is considered essential. Candlelight helps create a suitable atmosphere, as does the color scheme of the environment. Red light or reddish colors effectively stimulate the male sexual center, and violet or purple, the female's. Any sexual ritual is heightened when performed in a natural ambiance; if there is an open fire, offerings of food should be put into the flames, with the intention of feeding the gods. Taking a small amount of each foodstuff, it should be offered to the fire while intoning the Mantra "SWAHA." This ritual oblation serves to separate the mind from greed, selfishness and attachment.

The participants prepare themselves in the same way as described previously for the

Symbolic diagram of the Rite of the Five Essentials. At the center is a depiction of a transcendental goddess, the idealization of Shakti. The five petals making up a lotus shape show sexual union (*Maithuna*), the eating of special meat (*Mamsa*), the drinking of wine (*Madya*), the eating of fish (*Matsya*) and a man making a gesture of controlling his vitality (*Mudra*). From a Rajasthani painting of the nineteenth century.

Tantric painting of Kundalini as a goddess. At her feet are shown sacrificial offerings, food and drink. From a Rajasthani miniature painting of the eighteenth century.

314

VISHNU

the preserver

Tantric painting illustrating the ascent of sexual energy through the Subtle Centers (Chakras). A Yogi is depicted as a five-faced Shiva seated in lotus posture, with the elephant-headed Ganesha (symbolic of sexuality) on his lap. The hands make mystic gestures of Yogic control; above, a goddess covers the eyes of the Yogi to indicate that an inner transformation is taking place. From a Kangra miniature painting of the early eighteenth century.

Secret Rite. Sweet-smelling incense is suitable for burning, and if possible there should be some soft, sensual music. We recommend natural rhythmic music rather than highly verbal aggressive tunes or rock and roll, and have found Indian sitar, tabla, vina or similar sounds most appropriate. The fundamental frequency of all Hindu sacred music is between seven and eight cycles per second. This is identical to the resonant frequency of the earth's globe, to the frequency of the Kundalini when activated, and to human brain waves when in a state of deep meditation. In Tantric ecstasy, the whole body resonates at this frequency.

The couple sit together, with the woman on the left side. After the initial preparation, the food and wine should be empowered by encircling it with burning incense sticks, then, after offering a part to the fire, the participants share the remainder. Tantric texts admonish not to debase this holy rite into an excuse for feasting and orgying, but to respect it for what it is: a unique opportunity to identify and merge with the different elements and life-forms partaken as sacraments in the ritual.

A nobleman performing the Rite of the Five Essentials. His consort offers him a cup of wine. From a Kangra painting of the eighteenth century.

First the wine is drunk, not for intoxication, but for the delight and stimulation of body and mind. Meditate on the wine as an Elixir, an Ambrosia of the gods, symbolic of the primordial fire out of which all life emerged and by which all existence is ultimately reduced. Each may offer the drink to the other, transferring it from mouth to mouth.

Next, while meditating on the animal world, the participants consume the meat, symbolic of the air element, without which we would all immediately die. This is followed by fish, symbolic of the water element and evocative of the aquatic realm of life. Then the cereal grains or fruit are shared, the couple all the while remembering that our bodies are largely dependent on the vegetable kingdom and the earth element. After this ritualized acknowledgment of the elements, the couple should make love with passion.

Love-making symbolizes the element of space, which is all-pervasive and undefinable. Space is inherent in all the other elements. Tantras equate the element of space with the ecstatic blissful feeling of love-making, stating that "space touches all the other elements." Practically this means that love-making should be exalted as an *uplifting all-pervasive experience* and not "grounded" to a worldly level. The *Hevajra Tantra* declares, "By passion this world is bound, by passion, too, it is released. When passion courses through the blood, it brings with it the nature of Bliss, which is ultimately resolved into the space element. The world is prevaded by Bliss, which pervades and is pervaded."

Ritual love-making should be free from inhibition or restraint. From a contemporary photograph.

The Rite of the Five Essentials is most effective when performed as a sacrament, linking the partaking of each of the ingredients with a higher goal. Thus, the cereal grains (*Mudra*) symbolize the earth element and *detachment from worldliness*, fish (*Matsya*) symbolizes the water element and *control of breath*, wine (*Madya*) symbolizes the fire element and *purification of senses and mind leading to the inner secretion of nectar* (*Soma*: the hormones from the pineal gland), meat (*Mamsa*) symbolizes the air element and *control of sound* (both speech and subtle Mantric sound), and sexual union (*Maithuna*) symbolizes the space element and the *correct use of sexual energy*.

THE FIVE SACRAMENTS

SACRAMENT	ELEMENT	YOGIC ACTIVITY
Sexual Union	Space	Control of sexual energy
Meat	Air	Control of sound
Wine	Fire	Purification of senses
Fish	Water	Control of breath
Grains	Earth	Detachment from worldliness

While practicing this rite, the Kundalini should be visualized as an ascending wave of pure energy, undulating like the body of a snake, or a sensuous beautifully red-colored woman, the embodiment of eroticism. The Kundalini rises up to partake of the Tantric feast, passing through the psychic centers and illuminating them with her primordial energy. Reaching the head center, the Kundalini Shakti tastes the nectar of bliss. Satisfied, she empowers the couple with her limitless wisdom-energy and confers psychic protection.

The *Mahanirvana Tantra* states, "Fish, meat, cereal grains, roots, fruit and anything suitable that is ritually offered up to the higher realms together with wine are all known as *ingredients of worship*. Let each person take up his or her own cup and meditate on the Kundalini. She is *Pure Energy* and she reaches from the sexual center to the tip of the tongue. When the Kundalini is excited, she rises up and reaches the head center. Bliss issues from the meeting of Kundalini with the *Moon of Full Consciousness*."

The Rite of the Five Essentials is most effective when it is performed "heroically," without fear; emotions direct the flow of Kundalini. Kundalini Yoga is an aggressive spiritualism that does not allow human weakness to gain control. Traditionally this rite is performed as an act of confrontation with one's innermost fears, as a means of transcending them. Performed with care and insight, the Rite of the Five Essentials reestablishes contact with the motive powers of evolution, which then can be drawn upon to perfect both spirit and soul.

Tantras teach that the Kundalini moves up and down the spine of both partners during ecstatic union. The Kundalini, a wave of pure delight, can be controlled by breathing, repetition of Mantras and visualization of her energy. In the bodies of the couple the Kundalini establishes benign brain waves; this causes the body to produce biochemical changes and glandular secretions, which contribute to the spiritual evolution of the couple. At the same time, the Kundalini can be viewed as an echo of the deep primordial pulse emanating from the core of the earth, planets, suns and stars to the nucleus of the atom. During sexual climax, the Kundalini resonates and harmonizes with the original creative impulse (the Logos) of the Universe. It is this resonance that opens the couple to the grand ecstatic experience of Tantra, the mystic feeling of cosmic unity.

Taoist ritual love-posture. Seated positions allow ecstasy to be much prolonged. From a Chinese painting of the late Yuan period (1280–1367).

Ritual love-making involves enjoyment of all the sensual pleasures in the belief that liberation naturally comes to those whose physical desires are fully satisfied. From a Jodhpur miniature painting of the early nineteenth century.

The Lord and Lady of Secrets in Tantric union. This exalted mystic form of the couple is an idealization of the qualities necessary for the spiritualization of sexual love. The lotus, sword, wheel and flaming jewel symbolize the ascent of sexual energy, the need to surrender personal ego to higher Wisdom, the inevitable cycles of Karma and the shining ideal of attainment. From a Tibetan painting of the mid-seventeenth century.

We eat meat and drink wine. The true Tantrics come together, but the frauds are kept far away by fear. We take the fourfold preparations and use musk and camphor; herbs and special meats we eat with relish. Then, uniting Scepter and Lotus, we establish rulership over the whole of existence. HEVAJRA TANTRA

I follow the cult wherein there is enjoyment of wine, fish, flesh, grains and woman. In the Goddess I seek refuge. To the line of Gurus, I am devoted. I am Shiva, the terrific, the transcendental! She is Shakti, the sensual, the liberator.

RUDRA YAMALA TANTRA

He should eat meat and fish, drink wine or milk, and partake of intoxicants with concentrated mind. When he has satisfied his partner and himself, the Yogi and Yogini should then make love with passion. Transforming the five poisons into Elixirs, they should reach out into the great beyond. This powerful practice is by far the best; it can produce Liberation within a very short time. CHANDAMAHAROSANA TANTRA

before and after

A common mistake that occurs during love-making is an intense outpouring of attention and energy up to the time of orgasm, followed by disinterest or apathy once it has been achieved. Generally the man is responsible for this, as he tends to come to climax quickly, often without fully satisfying the woman.

Foreplay should be mutual to create total harmonization of mood and bodily elements. From a Japanese print in the style of Shusui, mid-eighteenth century.

Love-making should not be treated as a "hundred-yard sprint" ending in total collapse. This tends to create feelings of emptiness or resentment in the partner— the phenomenon known as post-coital depression. When a couple become familiar with each other's sexual needs, mutual adaptation is natural and easy.

Everything that is sexually stimulating is part of foreplay and effectively harmonizes the physical and subtle natures of the couple. Eastern teachings state that woman, like water, is slow to come to a boil and slow to cool down afterward. The reverse is true of man, who is compared to fire, which is quickly ignited and speedily extinguished. However, if the two are correctly balanced, one will transform the other. Fire and water in balance produce steam, which naturally rises upward. This movement is analogous to the ascent of vital energy through the subtle channels and centers. During sexual union, this ascent takes place spontaneously when there is harmony and consideration in the love-play.

If passion is bubbling over in one but just beginning to stir in the other, then the couple should try to blend and harmonize these two states rather than going their separate ways. Love-play should always be undertaken with an earnest desire for the other's absolute fulfillment rather than for selfish gratification.

Afterplay is equally as important as foreplay. The *fruit of love* will only ripen with

Mutual foreplay. From a Japanese painted scroll of the Tosa school, *circa* late sixteenth century.

careful nurturing of the tree on which it grows. After the couple has reached climax, they should continue to remain in close union for some time. This allows for the mutual exchange of subtle energies and the absorption of vital juices, which revitalize them. This is the time when the couple can come to know each other better in a non-verbal, mystical way. Having shared an ecstatic experience, they have much to digest. Meditation is completely natural when lying in close embrace, the Lingam within the Yoni.

After the intense physical exertion of love-making and the release of orgasm, the body finds itself in a unique state of relaxation. This state is highly conducive to meditation and mutual absorption. Lying together, immobile, limbs entwined, the sexual organs remaining in union, the couple can experience a complete blending of their separate identities. Use this time to focus the mind with *Mantra* and allow the waves of ecstasy to continue flowing.

Try to avoid sudden entry without foreplay. The ancient texts insist that the partners' bodies need to become gradually harmonized; otherwise complications can develop, especially in the case of older people. Sexual union affects all organs of the body. Correctly accomplished, it is truly invigorating, but if abused, it leads to debilitation.

Avoid jumping up immediately after orgasm and rushing off to the bathroom for a bath, douche or shower. Lie together and savor the touch, taste, smell and sight of each other. Try to consciously blend your sexual secretions and absorb their full potency. Caress each other, play, talk, laugh or meditate, and you will suddenly feel ready for another shared ecstasy. Above all, try to permeate the experience of sex with *love*; bring out love from the depths of your being and offer it to your partner. In the Temple of Love there is no *before* or *after*, only the *Eternal Now*.

The foreplay of love. From a Japanese print by Sukenobu, *circa* 1710.

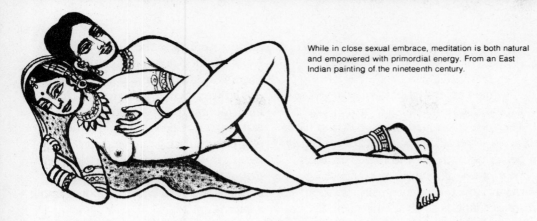

While in close sexual embrace, meditation is both natural and empowered with primordial energy. From an East Indian painting of the nineteenth century.

At the first time of love-making, the passion of the male is intense and his time to ejaculation is short, but in subsequent unions on the same day, the reverse is the case. With the woman it is the contrary, for at the first her passion will be weak and her time until orgasm long, but on other occasions of love-making on the same day, her passion will become more intense and her time until orgasm very short. KAMA SUTRA

Correct love-making should not culminate in total physical exhaustion. From a Japanese print of the mid-eighteenth century.

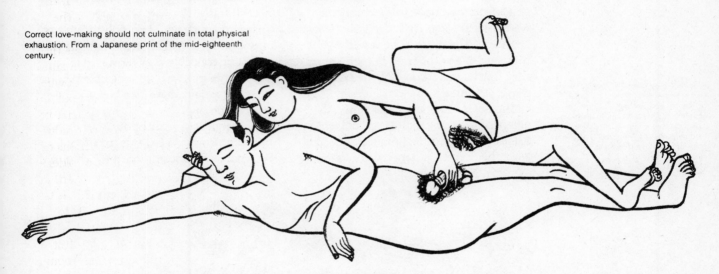

When a woman is tired, she should place her forehead on that of her lover and should take rest, without disturbing the union of their sex organs. When she has rested herself, the man should turn around and begin to make love with her again. If the lovers spend time playing with and caressing each other both at the beginning and at the end of their loving, then their ecstasy and confidence increase. Love-play enhances pleasure.

KAMA SUTRA

Try to empower the partner with intuitive initiation. Allow spontaneous feelings to be expressed by ritual acts of endearment. From a contemporary photograph.

the secret dalliance

VISHNU

the preserver

In the East, sexual practices evolved that extended beyond the unit of the couple. The ancient cultures of Egypt, Arabia, India, Nepal, Tibet, China and Japan were largely polygamous. Unlike the Judaeo-Christian view of sexuality, with its insistence on monogamy, the Oriental teachings about sex are not limited to the couple. Sexual practices were developed to enable a man to fully satisfy the needs of his wives or concubines, while at the same time acquiring an increase in magical power. This power was accessible to all participants and could be used for either worldly or transcendental purposes.

Chinese texts refer to the love-making of a single man with more than one woman as *The Secret Dalliance*. A Taoist saying declares, "The pleasures enjoyed in the company of a number of women are secret; very few come to know of the potential of these pleasures."

The Secret Dalliance was generally practiced by emperors, kings, noblemen or adepts. The sexual techniques associated with the Secret Dalliance were carefully

guarded to enable the ruling classes to maintain their position of authority. That there is a potent magical power to be gained from Secret Dalliance is a tenet fundamental to Taoist and Tantric teachings. It is believed to be an effective way of stimulating the vital force in both men and women, and of gaining access to magical powers over and above those normally available within a monogamous relationship.

The teachings of Secret Dalliance, outlined in Taoist and Tantric texts, deal almost exclusively with a single man enjoying the pleasures of more than one woman. Rarely does one find mention of a single woman in love-dalliance with more than one man. The reasons for this are cultural, physiological, and metaphysical.

Culturally, the East was largely polygamous rather than polyandrous or monogamous. A man could have as many wives or concubines as he was able to support. A girl was brought up to expect that she would share her husband with other women.

Consequently, sexual possessiveness, so prevalent in the West, was minimized. Polyandry was uncommon, and when it did

A nobleman in playful sexual dalliance with seven women. In ancient cultures polygamy was common. Multiple sexual encounters were believed to endow the ruling classes with magical power, longevity and wisdom. From a Japanese color print attributed to Kitao Shigemasa, *circa* 1780.

take place, it was usually restricted to men within a single family—for instance, two brothers might share a wife.

The physiological reasons are extremely interesting. According to Taoism, woman is believed to have an inexhaustible supply of Yin-force. The secret teachings state that when two or more women are in close contact, they nurture and stimulate the supply of Yin, creating a magnetically charged field of psychic energy. The effect of this on a man practicing the Secret Dalliance is a "doubling of potency" and a resultant strengthening and elevation of his Yang-force. On the other hand, where there is a predominance of Yang—that is, two men with a single woman—the Yang elements are inclined to cancel each other out. This is demonstrated most dramatically by the fact that if sperm from *unrelated* males are brought together, they naturally fight. If the sperm of two men "meet" within a single Yoni, they will be antagonistic to each other and will battle until one gains ascendency. The Yoni will become a battleground rather than a creative retort.

The metaphysical view of Taoism and Tantra stresses that woman is the embodiment of Nature, which is conceived of as multifarious. She has a natural narcissism, which inclines her to look for her reflection in other women and in the beauteous things of the world. She strives to express her multifarious roles through the power of Shakti, which is narcissistic and ultimately compassionate. A woman's body is soft, yielding, receptive; it evokes sensuality. When two or more women are in harmony, they have the power to transform the sensual into the supersensual.

The nature of man is aggressive rather than receptive. Narcissism is not an inherent characteristic of man, who is, however, very territorial. The transcendental power of Shiva lies in the resolution of all dualities. In the realm of the Secret Dalliance it is the single, unitary, focusing faculty of the male principle that is of paramount importance.

Indian texts declare that two sentiments can be exalted by the presence of a third sentiment (*Bharata*). The *Kama Sutra* states, "When a man makes love with two women at the same time, both of whom love him equally, then it is known as the

The Secret Dalliance of a single man with three women. From a Japanese woodblock print by Sugimura Jihei, *circa* 1680.

Taoist threesome. From a Japanese woodblock print by Sugimura Jihei, *circa* 1680.

An intimate love-dalliance. From a Japanese print by Sugimura Jihei, *circa* 1680.

322

VISHNU

the preserver

According to Hindu Tantras great power is inherent in carefully controlled multiple love-dalliance. From a Rajasthani miniature painting of the eighteenth century.

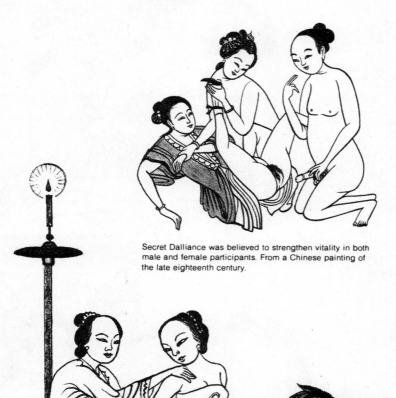

Secret Dalliance was believed to strengthen vitality in both male and female participants. From a Chinese painting of the late eighteenth century.

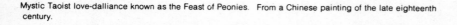

Mystic Taoist love-dalliance known as the Feast of Peonies. From a Chinese painting of the late eighteenth century.

United Position." In the *Chandamaharosana Tantra* there is the following explicit account of Secret Dalliance:

> One woman, coming from the disc of the moon, is enjoyed by another similar one. The third person is different from these two and should balance their forces. By enjoying together, they all become free from decay and death. The right and the left blend together in the Central Pathway. He stimulates both; they arouse each other and combine with him. The two moons are always filled with nectar; the sun is ever burning.

Throughout pagan cultures there are instances of sexual rites centered around troilism. For example, among the Walindi, an African tribe living in the Lake Chad region, the women form partnerships with each other soon after reaching puberty. They live together as "husband and wife," and when they are ready, together they select the single man who will become their real husband. During an elaborate ceremony in which the female moon-spirit is evoked, each woman has oral-genital intercourse with the chosen man. As soon as he ejaculates into the mouth of one woman, she immediately transfers the semen from her mouth into the sexual organ of the woman who is her partner. Having done so, she says three times, "All your children are also mine." From that time on, both women are free to make love with the man.

A Taoist text states, "A woman should never be jealous or sad when she sees her lover making love with another woman, for then her Yin-essence will become agitated and she will be liable to sickness, even withering and aging before her time." This is an important truth to be remembered by those who wish to explore Secret Dalliance together.

Westerners often think that Taoist and Tantric sexual practices focus on unconventional sexual encounters, promiscuity and wild orgies. This view is inaccurate and misleading. Free sex or group sex as we understand it in the West is far removed from the highly evolved, self-disciplined practices outlined in Tantric and Taoist teachings.

Tantra stresses the importance of the *couple*, which is idealized as a cosmically complete entity—the male and female in balanced union. Tantric rites evolve from the view of the *couple within* (which recognizes the inherent bisexuality of everyone, whether externally male or female), to the ideal of the couple made up of separate but complementary sexual beings. The couple, allegorical or actual, is the firm foundation of Tantra.

The sexual teachings of Tantra are always to be understood on three levels: the allegoric/symbolic, the literal/physical and the secret/transcendental. According to Tantra, the *Union of Three* is a rite that can be internalized and practiced symbolically through the power of fantasy and visualization. In the *Kaula Tantra* there is a meditation that teaches the couple to identify with the *Kundalini Shakti*—the raw sexual energy, visualized as a serpent-like fire rising up from within a red triangle. The Kundalini-energy of the man and the woman is to be imagined as conjoined in ecstasy, rising up through the subtle centers (*Chakras*) to the head center, where it is ecstatically transformed into a single form, a beautiful girl, a sensual Red Dakini with many magical attributes. In their mind's eye the couple should merge and identify with her as a wish-granting transcendental Wisdom-being. This merging is one of the goals of high magic.

If Tantric practices are extended to encompass troilism or forms of group sex, the participants should be aware that they are entering a new and highly volatile dimension. The Tantric Union of Three is a giant step away from the predictable or the conventional. It involves considerable responsibility, for such a rite can release energies more powerful and potentially more dangerous than those normally experienced by a couple. These energies can be manifested creatively or destructively, and must be carefully channeled and transformed. Positive energies can be nurtured by breath control, by visualization, and by controlling and prolonging orgasm. Creative energies released during the Union of Three should be recirculated among the participants by maintaining as much contact as possible between the *sex terminals* of the bodies: the sexual organs, breasts, mouths, hands and feet. The flow of energy within the Union of Three should be focused in the minds of all the participants. Energy loss from the region of the navel or the top of the head is to be avoided. Selflessness must pervade the experience, and pure ecstatic

Oriental traditions credit love-dalliance with the power of rejuvenation. From a Japanese painting, Kangyo, nineteenth century.

Taoism teaches that when correctly performed, the love-dalliance of a single man with two women can double sexual potency and increase the power of the psyche. From a Chinese painting of the early nineteenth century.

In Eastern cultures it was common for a wealthy man to marry a woman *and* her sister. This was believed to enhance longevity and increase the male Yang-essence, so enabling the birth of many sons. From a Chinese scroll painting of the nineteenth century.

Chinese Union of Three, of the type known as the Feast of Peonies. From a color print of the Ming dynasty.

consciousness, as Bliss-waves, should be maintained and circulated throughout the *Yantra of Union*.

In the Union of Three the man should meditate on himself as *Shiva*, the Lord of Transcendence. His main role is to keep alive the fire of concentration by correct use of *Mantra* and *Yantra*. He should always keep the circulation and transformation of energy in his mind's eye. As *Shiva the Transcendental*, the man should endeavor to maintain the balance of forces, using his control of breath, thought and semen.

The third person should only be invited into the Union of Three if there is a bond of mutual trust. She should be given every consideration and honored equally. Both women must visualize themselves as pure expressions of the *Primordial Shakti*, the potent power of eros. Each woman should stimulate and evoke the innermost Shakti of the other, endeavoring to experience the power as her own, without any feeling of separateness. By nurturing each other's nature spontaneously, the women experience a doubling of potency at each peak of ecstasy.

A rite such as the Union of Three should not be embarked upon without due consideration. Sharing one's partner with another is a supreme act of generosity. Unless jealousy and egotism are completely put aside, the couple may suddenly find themselves opened up to forces of negativity. The Union of Three has the potential for Tantric liberation, but it can be extremely dangerous if carelessly used. If any of the participants is emotionally unstable, selfish or unfamiliar with the esoteric principles of spiritualization through sexual transcendence, there is the danger of personality conflicts. Clarity of heart, presence of mind and spiritual consideration must always be present if the Secret Dalliance is to produce sweet rather than bitter fruits.

In the Tantric Union of Three both women should generously bestow their Shakti on the man, worshipping him as Lord Shiva, the Yogi whose Lingam is always erect. They should give to him, and to each other, offering up the ecstasy of their union to the Divine Principles within. The earnest desire for liberation and spiritual transcendence should be held within the hearts of all participants.

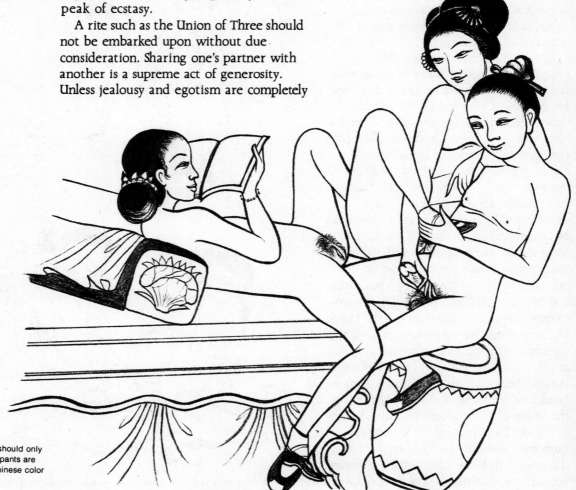

Practices of Secret Dalliance should only be undertaken if all the participants are emotionally mature. From a Chinese color print of the Ming dynasty.

The three cousins lay down head to head and the Master was encouraged to roll and sport over and between them to his heart's content, taking pleasure with this one and that one. When he had satisfied the middle one, he honored her right-hand neighbor, and then he visited the neighbor on the left. Everyone found the experience so exciting that all four of them were appeased.   JOU PU TUAN

There is a Secret Dalliance known as the Heavenly and Earthly Net whereby people indulge in sexual play like the birds and beasts, many females with a single male. It is believed to be a method of averting calamities and potentizing the whole country.

TAO AN

According to Tantra, the Union of Three is a rite that can be internalized and practiced symbolically with help from the powers of fantasy and visualization.

posture of the gobbling fishes

Posture of the Gobbling Fishes. From a contemporary photograph.

Chinese texts describe an erotic love posture for Secret Dalliance known as *The Gobbling Fishes*. It is an exercise of selflessness, designed for complete satisfaction of all the participants. We quote directly from an ancient text that is primarily concerned with the therapeutic benefits of this form of love-making:

The two women lie down in the most normal position for sexual union: one woman on her back and the other on top of her, in such as way that both their Pleasure Places are in direct contact with each other. They should embrace closely, passionately rubbing their Grottos together until their lower lips open of their own accord, like the mouths of fishes gobbling up water plants while swimming.

The man should kneel between their thighs, waiting until both the women are very excited and approaching their climax. He then separates their Pleasure Grottos with his hand and inserts his Jade Stalk between them. In this way, both women can simultaneously benefit as he moves in and out. This method of love-making is pleasurable and beneficial. It helps strengthen the sinews and bones, at the same time effectively doubling the potency. It also cures physiological and psychological afflictions. This posture reminds one of the fish playing among the water plants as they suck in the clear and blow out the murky water.

There is a posture known as Two Dancing Female Phoenix Birds. *It takes place with one man and two women. He should tell one of the women to lie on her back and the other one to sit on top of her. The woman underneath raises her legs, while the upper woman moves her own legs apart in such a way that their two Jade Gates are in close contact. The man should kneel, facing them. In this way he will be able to enter the upper and lower Jade Gates in turn.*

MASTER TUNG

sisterhood and sapphism

In ancient India, it was considered normal for women to have intimate relationships with each other. In a wealthy household, a girl would be brought up with one or more *Sakhis*, female companions from poor families, who would live together with her like a sister. Close physical contact between women has always been considered normal and healthy in Eastern cultures. Sisters or woman friends would commonly share the same bed.

The word *Sakhi* or "girl friend" is related to *Shakti*, the vital female power principle, the raw Energy of Tantra. To have a Sakhi as a companion was considered vitalizing, auspicious and "special." It was widely believed that such sisterhoods strengthened the femininity of all participants. A Sakhi added her own qualities and experiences to those of her "sister." Often a woman and her Sakhi were inseparable; when a noblewoman married, her Sakhis became co-wives and assisted in ritual love-making. Sapphic activities within such sisterhoods were considered normal and are frequently portrayed in Indian art.

Sisterhoods evolved naturally in a polygamous society. Wives and concubines usually lived in close proximity, often sharing the same bed. Mutual caressing was never considered perverse; it was

Women bathing and embracing each other. From an Indian miniature painting of the eighteenth century.

encouraged and idealized as an expression of real caring. The natural narcissism of woman was exalted in Oriental cultures.

The *Ramayana*, an important Hindu epic, contains an account of a ménage in which Sapphic sex is poetically described:

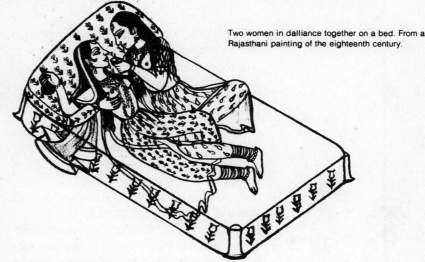

Two women in dalliance together on a bed. From a Rajasthani painting of the eighteenth century.

There were innumerable women lying on rugs, who had fallen asleep after spending the night in sensual play. Their breath was subtly perfumed with sweetened wine. Some of the girls savored each other's lips as they dreamed, as if they were their master's. Their aroused passions drove these lovely sleeping women to make love to their companions. Some slept in their rich garments, propped up on bracelet-laden arms; some lay across their companions, on their bellies, their breasts, their thighs, their backs; clinging amorously to one another, with arms entwined, the slender-waisted women lay together in sweet intoxicated sleep.

A wealthy Indian woman would normally employ a number of female attendants, whose duties included bathing, oiling, massaging and generally beautifying their mistress. In contemporary India this is still the custom. Close contact with maidservants or Sakhis commonly develops into a Sapphic relationship, particularly with single, lonely or widowed women.

The *Kama Sutra* describes how women can use their mouths on each other's Yonis and ways of satisfying sexual desires by the use of bulbs, roots or fruits having the same shape as the Lingam. Unlike male homosexuality, Sapphism was not considered sinful and was not an offense under Hindu law. In miniature paintings of the mediaeval period, woman are often portrayed fondling each other intimately. Pictures illustrating themes of Krishna and the Cow girls commonly depict Gopis in sensual dalliance together.

A noblewoman with six female attendants. They are busy in the bathing, drying, anointing and decorating of their mistress. From a Rajasthani miniature painting of the eighteenth century.

VISHNU

the preserver

Egyptian girl in attendance on a lady.
From a painting of the Eighteenth Dynasty
(1567–1320 B.C.).

In Buddhist and Hindu Tantric literature, there are references to the transcendental and regenerative power inherent in sisterhoods. Taoist teachings particularly emphasize this view. Five distinct categories of Sapphism are known to contemporary Hinduism. The common form of Western lesbianism, largely aggressive and replete with sexual role playing, is the lowest type. Indians view it as degenerate and far removed from the higher, more spiritual forms of sisterhood practiced in the East.

There was considerable contact between Egypt and South India, which was famous for its rich silks, spices, women and temple dancers. In ancient Egyptian society, there was no law condemning Sapphism. Archaeological evidence shows that women were brought up in close contact with one another. Tomb paintings depict female attendants caressing their mistresses and show ménages in the Indian manner. In temple communities dancing girls lived together and sisterhoods were encouraged.

Hebrew law does not condemn Sapphism. In Islamic society, where polygamy was very common, lesbianism has always been popular, both inside and outside the harem. It is curious that Muhammad is believed to have declared lesbianism an unlawful practice, particularly since the thirteenth-century Arab historian Abd-al-Latif al-Baghdadi wrote, "The woman who has not tasted repeatedly of the delights of another woman's body does not exist in our lands." The Arab fear of women gaining power may account for the contradiction. To the Arab mind, women are possessions and status symbols, to be controlled rather than exalted or liberated through the power of mystic sex. The enlightened view of femininity expressed in Tantras is not a part of Arabian thought.

In many pagan cultures throughout the world, intimate sexual contact between women is considered natural. This is particularly so in matriarchal societies. Most tribal groups in Africa, Asia, the Pacific

Female musicians and dancing-girls. From an Egyptian
painting of the Eighteenth Dynasty (1567–1320 B.C.).

Islands and South America include Sapphism as an integral part of the socio-religious system. For example, a woman of the Paia, a Bantu tribe of Africa, is only allowed to have her virginity taken by another woman. This woman is carefully chosen by her and becomes her "sister," living with her for three days every month, during which time they practice Sapphism. Luduku women of the Congo also pair off together early in life. Among tribes in New Guinea it is customary for a girl to perform oral love-making with her older female friends, in the belief that by so doing she absorbs some of their feminine wisdom.

In China and Japan, Sapphism is also very common. According to Taoism, woman has an unlimited supply of Yin-essence, which is

Sappho lived on the island of Lesbos during the sixth century B.C. The words *lesbianism* and *Sapphism* derived directly from her reputation as a lover of women. According to Socrates, she was uncommonly beautiful. Plato regarded her as the "Tenth Muse," and Ovid recommended that all girls read her works. Only with the advent of Christianity did her name become infamous.

Sisterhoods need not involve sex between women. However, if sexual contact evolves spontaneously, there are a variety of ways in which women can satisfy one another. Esoteric teachings emphasize the importance of the kiss between women. The watery element evoked during kissing is associated with the moon, which governs womanly cycles. Taoist teachings emphasize oral stimulation of the mouth, Yoni and breasts as the way for woman to nurture their natures.

Eastern teachings endorse and encourage

According to Taoist teachings, Sapphism allows women to nurture each other's nature. From a Chinese painting of the nineteenth century.

Two Oriental ladies sharing intimacies. From a Japanese print by Suzuki Harunobu, *circa* 1760.

regenerated every month with the completion of her menstrual cycle. The concept of women nurturing each other's vital essence is a fundamental principle of Taoist teaching.

Sisterhoods have been greatly misunderstood in the West. Recent polls indicate that a large proportion of Western women have some form of Sapphic experience during their lifetime. Nonetheless, it is common in the West to associate Sapphism with perversity and to make no distinction among the forms of lesbianism. The most renowned of Western female homosexuals was the Greek poet Sappho. The majority of her writings were destroyed in A.D. 1073 on the orders of Pope Gregory VII.

Two Oriental ladies in Sapphic embrace. From a Japanese print by Katsushika Hokusai, *circa* 1810.

loving relationships between women. However, the modern Western woman seeking to explore her sexuality with another woman should be aware that Sapphism is not an *alternative* to heterosexual love. The exclusive practice of Sapphic love is not promoted by Taoist or Tantric teachings, which give supreme significance to the male/female unit, the cosmic couple.

A Sapphic or sisterly relationship requires real caring and generosity. The modern woman is conditioned to view other women as competitors rather than allies. Women of the ancient East knew sisterhood and solidarity. Contemporary women can gain insight into the real meaning and practice of women's liberation from the Tantric tradition.

According to Taoism, "When softness is in close proximity with softness, the female Yin-essence is enhanced." This thought was basic to the argument in favor of Sapphism.

My source of happiness is a soft-skinned girl, her smile adorned with pearls. The moisture of her mouth is sweet and fresh. Between her legs there is a fissure, as pretty and alluring as the neck of a young gazelle. That night we spent in sucking mouths and other parts. If to love my girl friend in such a way is "sinful," then to love a man is indeed "unlawful."

A woman's thoughts to her lady-love, from

THE PERFUMED GARDEN.

Women are peonies, spring flowers, lotuses and bowers.
Women are pomegranates, peaches, melons and pearls.
Women are receptacles, crucibles, vessels and worlds.
Women are the fruit of life, the nourishing force of Nature.

YUAN-SHIH YEH-TING CHI, TAO TSUNG-I

masturbation/ self-gratification

Until recently, open discussion of masturbation was taboo. Masturbation was referred to euphemistically as *self-abuse*, *playing with oneself*, the *solitary vice* or *self-gratification*. Many are the children who have endured lectures about the "sinful dangers" of this practice. Such warnings, at an early and impressionable age, often cause neuroses later on in life.

The atmosphere of "sin" or "guilt" surrounding the act of masturbation can produce a kind of vicarious thrill or *rush*, rather like that felt in committing a punishable crime. Fear can be immediately stimulating, but its long-term effect is debilitating.

During the last several years, there has been a tendency to bring sexual matters out into the open. Masturbation has emerged as a topic that people are willing to discuss. An analysis of popular sex-oriented magazines indicates a groundswell of interest in this particular aspect of sexuality. The once "solitary vice" has been elevated into a "therapy," a "variation of love-making" and an important part of the repertoire of sexually liberated lovers. What do Eastern teachings have to say about this volatile subject?

First of all, a clear distinction is drawn between male and female masturbation. Second, *mutual masturbation* between a man and a woman is not considered masturbation per se. Since it is not looked on as an end in itself, it is categorized as foreplay. A different view is taken of mutual masturbation between two men or two women. We shall examine each of these situations thoroughly.

Both Taoist and Tantric teachings agree that "semen is a man's most precious possession." It is not to be carelessly wasted. The medical texts state that ejaculation of this vital essence by a male who has not yet reached maturity is potentially detrimental to his health, since important body elements are dispersed. The *Charaka Samhita* says, "If a young boy, whose body elements are not yet fully formed, practices masturbation, he is liable to lose vitality. If he continues to do so, then his body will become weakened

and his internal organs damaged. This is particularly true up to the age of sixteen years, by which time the male body is completely formed."

Masturbation involves the physical, emotional and mental aspects of an individual. If practiced as a solitary exercise, the breath and imagination perform a major role. Though self-gratification can be momentarily stimulating, there is no long-term benefit to a man. His physical reserves become depleted without an opportunity for replenishment; that is, there is no opportunity for "compensating" by absorbing vital fluids or energies from a partner. Any ecstasies are short-lived without the support of a shared experience and an exchange of energies. Solitary sexual practices produce a particular kind of *psychic field* that remains fixed within the sensation realm of the sexual center, without either ascent or transformation of the raw creative energy.

Many factors may stimulate the desire for masturbation. As the sexual center becomes activated, a young boy is inclined to explore his sexuality by playing with his Lingam; in this way, he becomes familiar with the workings of his body. This form of sexual exploration is harmless, provided the urge to ejaculate can be controlled. Autoerotism *without ejaculation* can help a young man gain control of his sexual energy and introduce an awareness of the interrelationship of breath, thought and the emission of semen. This helps strengthen sexual confidence, which is a major ingredient of a healthful sex life. Familiarization with the stages of arousal prior to ejaculation can teach a man how to gain control of his sexuality; he is then adequately prepared for transcendental heterosexual experiences in the Taoist or Tantric tradition. Retention of breath and visualization of the sex energy circulating and nourishing the body are the key to the control of ejaculation.

Eastern teachings unanimously advise against the practice of male masturbation with ejaculation. The texts advise that a man living segregated from women should practice Yogic postures, breathing and meditation, so as to internally transform his sexual energy. The Yoga head stand, deep breathing, visualization of the *Subtle Body*, and repetition of Mantras all help the male sublimate his sexual energy.

The medical treatises cite instances when *masturbation with ejaculation* is condoned. For instance, an unhealthy diet can create "devitalized" semen, which cannot be successfully sublimated. If sublimation is not possible, then it is better to ejaculate than to "hoard morbidified life-essence." Another medical reason for ejaculation is if the *Subtle Pathways* of the body have become "blocked"; a symptom of this is extreme lethargy. The Taoist and Tantric view is that only lustrous, healthy semen is fit for internalization, and that this is built up by Yogic diet and lifestyle.

A single man who is not having sex may find that sexual pressures build up to the point where physical release is advisable. It is certainly unnatural for a young man to suppress his sexuality; if he cannot find release through the Yogic disciplines of sublimation and transformation, or through heterosexual contact, then masturbation with ejaculation is the final resort. In the ancient world, men married early and the Art of Love was cultivated almost from the onset of puberty. Masturbation was therefore unnecessary. The physical symptoms normally associated with "growing up," such as pimples, boils and skin eruptions, are an indication of sex energy striving for release. The alchemical view of this is that the vital "mercuric" energy (the semen) is polarized into a "sulphurous" substance that the body rejects through the skin. For those who are unable to practice the Yogic teachings of sublimation and transformation, or who are unwilling to radically change their lifestyle, heterosexual love-making with emission of semen is far better than release through masturbation. If sex with a woman is not possible and sublimation is impracticable, then masturbation with ejaculation may be resorted to. It should not become a habit, however. Healthy semen contains vital nutrients, trace elements, amino acids and vitamins in purified form. Sperm should never be carelessly discarded because it is the *living essence*, containing all the physical and spiritual attributes of man.

Ejaculated sperm can live outside the body for quite some time. It should not be treated disdainfully. Tantras state that sperm should be honored; there is a psycho-physical link between a man and his sperm long after ejaculation. The *Kaulavali Tantra* advises that "sperm ejaculated through masturbation should be positively endowed by one's mental attitude to it. Sperm should be ritually returned to the elements of its origin, or used for a magical purpose such as the empowering of amulets." The term "elements of its origin" means the earth, water, fire or air. Ancient pagan customs such as the scattering of semen on fields, under trees, into waters, or into the sacrificial fire, or of rubbing preparations mixed with semen onto the body, echo this view.

The Eastern teachings regard female masturbation as a phenomenon totally different in its effects from male masturbation with ejaculation. The primary difference is woman's "unlimited supply of Yin-essence" as compared to man's finite Yang-essence. The female body is replenished and its vital elements balanced after the completion of each lunar cycle. In the course of a month, a woman is revitalized and nourished by her natural harmony with the forces of the moon.

Woman embodies all the senses in their exalted form and narcissism is natural to her. The *Nine Spirits of Woman* are nourished by the release of erotic energy through the female body. Autoerotism in woman increases the flow of Yin-essence and helps her gain control over sexual reflexes. Women have many effective methods of self-gratification; for example, simple rocking movements stimulate the sexual center. Some women can reach orgasm by gently caressing parts of their body, the breasts and Yoni in particular. Deep rhythmic breathing can bring a woman to orgasm, as can erotic fantasy. The Yoni is the gateway to her Temple; masturbation is a way for woman to nourish her own eroticism and learn to please the deities that dwell within her.

Once the Yin-essence is awakened in the body of woman, it needs appeasement. A woman requires longer than a man to become sexually excited; yet once stimulated, she can have many orgasms in succession. The mental attitude is most important. *Bliss-waves* can be built up within the body of woman, carrying her *Transcendental Spirit* to new heights. The peaks of ecstasy are more easily scaled in the body

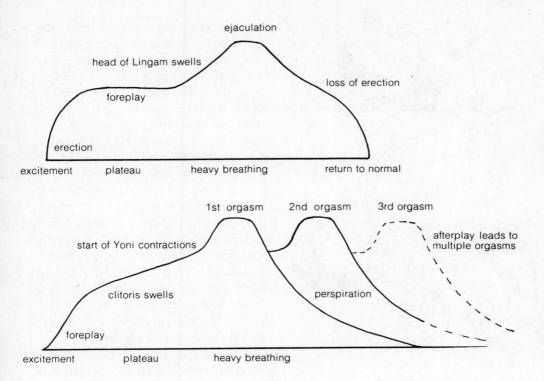

ejaculation

head of Lingam swells

loss of erection

foreplay

erection

excitement | plateau | heavy breathing | return to normal

Chart showing the stages leading to male orgasm. There is a steep increase in sexual excitement during early foreplay, which levels off and then rises as ejaculation is approached.

1st orgasm | 2nd orgasm | 3rd orgasm

start of Yoni contractions

afterplay leads to multiple orgasms

clitoris swells

perspiration

foreplay

excitement | plateau | heavy breathing

Chart showing the stages leading to female orgasm. Excitement is steady, rising to a peak during climax and creating a series of peak experience waves over subsequent orgasms.

of woman than in man. The chart above illustrates the multiple orgasmic nature of woman and shows a comparison with male orgasm.

Solitary satisfaction for a woman does not require the introduction of a Lingam substitute into the Yoni. Ancient Indian texts suggest that natural organic substances such as fruits or vegetables are better than fabricated substitutes; one text recommends the stalk of a plant, which, when soaked in hot water, swells up and takes on agreeable warmth and texture. In China and Japan a variety of sexual aids were developed for female self-gratification. We describe these fully in the section entitled "Sexual Aids."

The importance of the mental attitude toward masturbation cannot be overstressed. Guilt must not enter the exploration of this form of sexuality. Remember to circulate and dedicate the energy to a higher purpose than mere sensualism. Offer your pleasure to Lord Shiva, visualized in the mind's eye. Offer the Bliss-waves of orgasm to feed the gods and goddesses within the body. Mentally resolve a desire for transformation and spiritualization. Let the sex energy ascend to the sublime. This strengthens the Subtle Body at the same time that it vitalizes the physical body.

Fantasy is an important element of masturbation. Perverse fantasies can

damage the psyche and induce complex psychological problems. Positive creative fantasy should be cultivated during masturbation; a woman can visualize Shiva the Yogic ideal, or hold in mind a "view" of herself making love with an idealization of her Lover-archetype.

Traditionally in Japan and China, a wife would have a replica of her husband's Lingam made of tortoise shell, horn or wood, with his name beautifully inscribed on it. Such an object was greatly cared for and kept in a specially made box. The woman used this object, known as *Harikata*, for masturbation or for sex with co-wives of the household, the principal wife taking the male role. Thus during the prolonged absence of the husband, a means of self-satisfaction was available that incorporated his actual form. If you insert anything into the Yoni, first "empower" it by meditating upon it as the ever-erect Shiva Lingam, the

Chinese lady using an artificial Lingam affixed to her foot. From a Chinese print of the Ming dynasty.

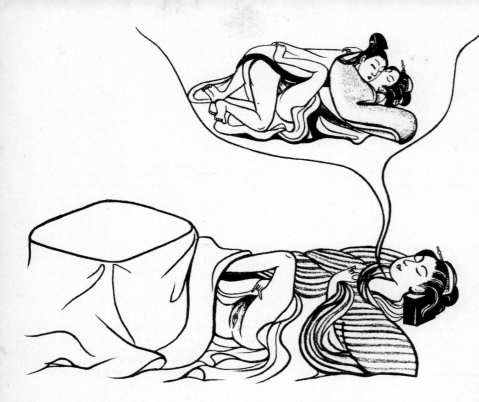

Sexual fantasy or dream, depicted as arising from the throat region. From a Japanese print of the eighteenth century.

cosmic symbol of transcendence. Mutual masturbation between women can be used to potentize the vital essence. Sexuality is enhanced, provided the mental attitude is nourishing rather than vampiristic. When the Yin-essence is circulated and exchanged between women, there is a doubling of potency, a feminization that manifests itself throughout the body. The women involved become more generous, selfless and compassionate, and their bodies take on enhanced female qualities. Between women there is a natural intimacy, a sharing of innermost feelings, rarely found among men. Taoist texts state that when women share, their "complexion becomes very clear, shining like the full moon, and their eyes sparkle brightly." A Tantric saying declares, "Soft things become softer when brought together, as in women; hard things blunt each other, as with men."

Mutual masturbation between boys or men is associated with initiation rites in certain primitive tribal societies. These rites of initiation are believed efficacious in establishing patriarchal unity. Aggression is commonly played out, accompanied by forceful verbalization or chanting. A *Karmic bond*, or sense of sharing, is brought about. In various African tribes mutual masturbation is allowed between boys as part of their puberty rites. However, it is condemned after adolescence. Secret societies are sometimes founded around masturbatory

rites celebrating the power of death. None of the higher Eastern mystic teachings requires such an activity, since the real transcendental bond is with the female force, the Shakti, which is considered paramount. Though it is true that instances of mutual masturbation between males occur in the context of magical occultism, these are of a very low order and are associated with black-magic rites performed for selfish rather than transcendental ends.

What has been referred to as "mutual masturbation" in a heterosexual situation is not really masturbation at all, but *foreplay*, leading up to penetration and mutual orgasm. Often it is linked to oral sex, in which case the emission of vital essence should be absorbed by the partner's mouth. When the male Yang-essence is absorbed within the body of a woman, it is transmuted into Yin. When the female Yin-essence is absorbed by the man, it is transformed into potentized Yang. Mutual masturbation in a heterosexual context is one of the most important ways of harmonizing mood and body essences.

Various modern so-called Tantric works deal almost exclusively with learning to prolong orgasm through disciplined masturbation. The idea is to masturbate until reaching the moment of orgasm, and then exercise self-control by "holding back." Ancient Tantric texts do not in any way support this view. Orgasm control is best achieved within the context of a couple, as part of the *Battle of Love*. Breathing exercises, Yoga postures and meditation all serve to transcend the limitations of an over-abundance of sexuality, without the need to cultivate masturbation as an outlet.

Mutual masturbation and love-play. From a Chinese painting of the nineteenth century.

Semen gets diminished by old age, anxiety, diseases, strain of labor, fasting, excessive
sexual intercourse and masturbation. By wasting, fear, suspicion, grief, seeing deformities
of others, by lack of response in a woman, by not bestowing sufficient thought on the
subject of sex, and by abstention from sex, a man is rendered incapable of mating.

CHARAKA SAMHITA

The male is moved by the life-force of the female, and his Jade Stalk is excited to action.
The woman is moved by the life-force of the man, and the liquid of her Secret Cavern
begins to flow. These are the arousals caused by the natural qualities of the male and
female forces of the cosmos. They are something that cannot be duplicated by human
Will alone.

ISHIMPO

Do not expel your semen needlessly. Do not expel your semen forcefully, as if dashing
something down from the heights. You'll upset the five main bodily organs, injure the
life-energy channels and give rise to every kind of ailment as a consequence.

ISHIMPO

brotherhood of man

There is a natural feeling of brotherhood
between men. Authentic commitment and
love can exist between men without any
need for sexual contact. Tantra tells of the
need for feelings of brotherhood, as such
feelings help men to share their problems
and shared experiences lead to
understanding.

Nothing binds men more effectively than
shared participation in dynamic, *fiery* types of
activity. In the past, men hunted, worked
and made war together and many
brotherhoods were created as part of these
activities. Nowadays there is a decreasing
emphasis on physical activity, though men
still participate in aggressive sports and
cooperate in business activities. However, it
seems that there are fewer opportunities for
a man to externalize or transform sexual
energy on a physical level.

Freud's term *libido* refers to emotional
cravings that prompt any specific human
(and especially sexual) activity. The libido is
the *sex drive*, the "fire coursing through the
blood." Throughout history it has had the

power to bind men. When the potent fire
of *Kundalini-energy* is untransmuted, it is
externalized as aggression. Sex and aggression
often manifest themselves in the formation
of brotherhoods between men. Many
primitive people use sexual bonds between
men to establish commitment and reinforce
reliability. This is done through rites of
initiation, sometimes centered around group
or selective homosexual activity. Among the
Pueblo Indians of New Mexico, for example,
initiation rites revolve around masturbation
of a single selected male who is held in great
honor. Circumcision rites of some African
tribes are closely linked to concepts of
brotherhood.

The result of strenuous physical exertion
is always *watery*; perspiration pours from all
parts of the body. Love-making also
produces watery secretions. The symbolism
of fire and water permeates occult traditions
and is an integral part of rites of initiation
leading to the establishment of
brotherhoods. Even war has the potential
for the exchange of fire and water: fiery
aggression creates sweat, blood and, often
enough, tears. Wars often evolve from the
need to express aggression externally. When
the libido of men is high and is not

channeled through transcendental sex practices, men create excuses to go to war. Emotional cravings have to be expressed; they cannot be bottled up forever. In the past, many brotherhoods were formed around shared participation in battle, the real causes of which were often forgotten. Islam is one of the more recent cultures that revolves around the desire to externalize sexual energy. The brotherhood of Islam lost track of the original emotional *mystic* craving of its principal prophet, Muhammad. Over the course of history its women came to bear the burden. Though the brotherhood created by Islam transformed the face of the globe, it is still unable to recognize the sexual basis of its own phenomenon. Islam can only cease to be a religion of force and evolve into a truly transcendental experience if it breaks away from its long-established custom of relegating women to a subservient role.

Tantric brotherhood implies shared beliefs and shared emotional longings. The desire to be liberated from the endless round of births and deaths, to be freed from suffering and the fear of death, is the germinal requirement for true Tantric brotherhood in this Dark Age of materialism. Shared participation in Hatha Yoga, Tantric meditation and ritual can lay the ground for a Tantric brotherhood, working as an all-powerful transformative energy in the New Age.

There is a brotherhood of Tantrics waiting to be brought to life. This brotherhood will awaken as the end of the Kali Age approaches. Recognizing the potent Female Principle of life, the Brotherhood of Tantra will transform this polluted world. Then at the ecstatic moment when one Age transforms into the next, those faithful followers of the selfless path will reach their goal.

KAULA TANTRA

male homosexuality

Some prehistoric cave paintings depict men engaged in what appears to be ritual homosexuality, wearing masks of animal heads. The mimicry of animals in order to gain magical power over them is a common practice of primitive peoples. It seems very likely that male homosexuality first developed among groups of hunters who copied and ritualized animal copulation (mounting from behind). Such acts were considered the essential ingredient for assuring a successful hunt.

The Prairie Indians of North America practiced male homosexual rituals during their Bison Dance, the purpose of which was to empower the hunt by a process of imitative magic. The Indians believed this process was necessary before their ancestral protective Spirit would send bison into their territory. In this ritual, the shaman played out the role of a demon who first had to fail in his attacks on the women of the tribe and then was overcome and homosexually raped by male dancers disguised as bison.

There is an ancient Egyptian myth that tells how Set, a son of Isis and Osiris, once invited his brother Horus to spend the night in his house. They shared the same bed and in the night Set tried to sexually abuse Horus, who awoke in time to stop Set's sperm from entering him. Set was taken to court and tried for the offense committed on his brother, an abuse that was considered only allowable as an outrage for those vanquished in battle. The Horus-Set conflict is portrayed as an eternal dispute between the powers of good and evil. In Egypt, the figure of Set personified the principle of evil; with the body of a dog, a long nose, sharp ears and a stiff tail, Set was evoked in rites of black magic. The Greek writer Plutarch states that Set's testicles were torn from him by Horus, effectively limiting his future powers. He adds, "The Egyptians raised a statue to Horus in commemoration of this event. It showed Horus holding Set's sex

Rock carving showing a male mounting an animal. From a prehistoric cave, Val Camonica, Italy.

organ in his hands, stopping him from his attempted abuse."

Male homosexuality was condemned in ancient Egypt, although there are some indications that it was practiced by the military as a ritual for ensuring the subjugation of prisoners. It began to appear more frequently with the degeneration of the priesthood, and was blamed for the weakening of their occult power. Cults that promoted male homosexuality as a secret rite of high magic developed. Homosexual practices were also promoted among the Babylonian priesthood and are blamed for their loss of magical power. In the *Avesta*, the sacred book of Mazdaism (the ancient Iranian religion), the prophet Zarathustra relates his conversation with Ahura Mazda, the god of Light, where the latter declares, "A man who sexually enters a male or who receives the male is a demon. Such a man thus sacrifices to the demon, is the incubus of the demon, is the succubus of the demon and is no better than a demon." The Hebrews had a similar view of male homosexuality, regarding it as originating in the land of Canaan and considering it "the vice of dogs."

In ancient Greece, male homosexuality was elevated almost to the status of an institution. A kind of military pederasty existed in Greece from ancient times, linked to warlike activities. In Sparta, it was considered part of the educational system and an essential initiation into soldiery. In Crete, the law protected male homosexuals, even outlining procedures for "correct abduction of young boys." In Athens, homosexuality was reserved for free men and forbidden to slaves. Though the Greek philosophers attempted to promote the sublimation of male homosexuality, it developed into magic cults often based on misunderstandings of the Egyptian mystery rites. Homosexual freedom can be associated with the decline of Greece. From the first century onward, homosexuality flourished in Rome; male prostitution developed to an extraordinary extent and another great empire fell.

The destruction of Sodom and Gomorrah is described in identical terms in the Bible and the Koran. Early Christianity took a strong anti-homosexual position, using Rome as an example of the effect of licensed homosexuality on a nation. Though the Koran specifically condemns male homosexuality, it became firmly entrenched in Moslem culture. Practically all Turkish, Arab or Persian poetry is tinged with male homosexual themes. Arab conquests were always associated with the forceful rape of women and the abduction of young boys. Saladin, the adversary of Richard Coeur de Lion in a Crusade for the Holy Land, was a homosexual whose cruelty in battle has seldom been surpassed. The Islamic brotherhood spread widely through the power of the sword. In so dominantly a patriarchal society, the creative *Female Principle* was relegated to a lowly status. Tantric esoteric teachings declare that if a woman is treated very aggressively and degraded during sexual union, then any male child produced will have strong homosexual tendencies. Anal intercourse with a woman, followed by normal intercourse, is said to be one of the ways in which homosexual males are conceived.

The biological function of male sexual aggression is to impress females, while at the same time keeping away rival males. Its purpose was never to degrade the creative Female Principle. Aggression may be incorporated into love-making in the spirit of erotic play, but consideration for the sanctity of woman must never be forgotten.

The Freudian theory hypothesizes that male homosexuality results from the combination of a dominant, over-protective mother and a weak, uninterested father. The child is thus deprived of a masculine role-model and both overwhelmed and frightened by the company of women. Though it may be that early traumatic experiences with women *can* create homosexual tendencies in a man, rarely is this a sufficient cause. These tendencies more often develop from an imbalance of sex hormones, which can be brought about by fear. Hormone secretion is *controlled* by the pituitary gland, which is situated in the head. Levels of the male sex hormone are increased with exposure to sexual stimuli. Fear, stress and anxiety cause the testosterone hormone level to diminish. When testosterone is produced in excess, it triggers aggressive sexual urges. It has been substantiated that violent

The dog of Set. From an ancient Egyptian carving.

Set, the brother of Horus. From an ancient Egyptian carving.

criminals produce much higher levels of this substance than do non-violent ones. Sex hormones are secreted by various glands in the body, by the gonads or sex glands in particular. Estrogen and progesterone are the female counterparts to testosterone. All hormones, however, exist in both sexes, in varying proportions.

Male homosexuality seems to be largely determined by imbalances between sex-hormone levels in the body. The cause of this biochemical imbalance may originate in the unconscious, but the biological effect is a powerful reinforcement. Studies of homosexual men suggest that they are, in fact, "men with the hormonal chemistry and minds of women." Generally they have a low sperm count and low levels of the male sex hormone in their body, though dominant and highly aggressive male homosexuals have excessively high levels of these.

It would appear that the aggressive male homosexual, who usually has a younger, passive lover, is trying to balance out and "externalize" the consuming inner fire of Kundalini-energy. When the Kundalini-fire is untransmuted, it usually is expressed as worldly aggression. This is an intriguing clue to the relationship between sex and aggression, and explains why aggressive male homosexuality is always linked with military conquest. If aggression is carried to the extreme, it creates hormonal imbalance, which in turn leads to sexual problems. A man should reserve real aggression for physical work, sports, business and, ideally, Yogic transformation. The Tantric texts outline many visualizations of violent, wrathful entities whose inner natures are always conceived of as compassionate and loving. This symbolizes the way in which the raw Kundalini-energy can be tamed by psychological and physiological processes. It is a major tenet of Tantra that can give practical help to male homosexuals who wish to change their sex habits.

Male homosexuals are either very aggressive (taking a male role) or very passive (playing a female role). Usually, as the man gets older, he goes from playing the passive role to taking the aggressive role. Studies indicate that the average homosexual male is extremely promiscuous, often having as many as one thousand different partners during the course of a lifetime, most of whom are total strangers. The main parts of the male anatomy that are admired by homosexuals as sexually exciting are the chest, buttocks and genitals, in that order. A recent opinion poll among *women* also listed these among the features that they first looked at in a man. The prime difference between the tastes of homosexual men and normal women was that the women were *most* attracted to the eyes of a young man, whereas this aspect of the body was considered *least* interesting by male homosexuals. This is an interesting distinction that suggests that male homosexuality is essentially an aesthetic of surfaces rather than of inner qualities. Certainly it is true that narcissism is a major characteristic of male homosexuals.

Kinsey, in his famous report on *Sexual Behavior in the Human Male*, found that about four percent of all men are exclusively homosexual throughout their lives. He also noted that about twenty-five percent of his cross section of the male population had had more than incidental homosexual experiences, thirty-seven percent had had some kind of homosexual experience leading to orgasm, and that this figure became as high as fifty percent among those who had remained bachelors until the age of thirty-five.

There are four distinct types of physical exchange between men: mutual caressing without orgasm, masturbation with orgasm, oral sex and anal sex. The Eastern view is that the first two categories are not necessarily to be viewed as homosexuality, and a man who has had such experiences should not view himself as a homosexual. Oral sex between men is taboo according to Hindu and Buddhist law, though there are references to masseurs in ancient India sometimes relieving their customers in this way. The *Kama Sutra* lists ways for oral sex between men, but adds that priests and high-caste Hindus should not allow themselves to become "polluted in this way." Furthermore, the Hindu lawbooks condemn a man who swallows the semen of another. Anal sex between men was unheard of in India until the Moslem invasions and is not a traditional sexual practice of the Chinese or Japanese. The

Taoist and Tantric texts unilaterally condemn anal sex between men as unnatural, unhealthy and potentially damaging to the psyche.

Male homosexuality in the West normally features oral-genital sex, including absorption by the partner of the ejaculated semen. According to Taoism, this causes the Yang-essence to be transformed into "male-Yin-essence." Though an exact translation of this process into modern scientific terminology would be difficult, the idea may shed some light on the paradoxes of male homosexuality. Semen contains hormones that, when ingested, undoubtedly help to transform the passive partner into an active one. Anal sex involves the absorption of male hormones through the rectum.

According to recent biological theories, *all* fetuses are female internally, even if they have male sex organs partly or completely formed. It is believed that they are female, until and unless the sex glands release hormonal instructions to the contrary. Though this is not exactly in accordance with the Eastern teachings on this subject, there is an interesting similarity that will help explain some of the factors determining male homosexuality. In an important Tibetan medical work, the *Gyud-zhi*, the following illuminating account of the conception process occurs:

Three things are needed for the formation of a body. These are potent male semen, a fertile female egg, and the mind of a being already existing in the *Intermediate State* between death and birth, impelled by the right *Karma*. It depends on the predilection of the being, whether its body is going to become male or female. If it identifies with the semen and is attracted by the mother, at the same time disliking the father, then it will be born a boy. If it identifies itself with the sexual secretions of the mother, but feels anger toward her, then a girl-child will be born.

This shows a remarkable correlation to Freud's oedipal theory.

The same text goes on to state that "During the third week after conception, it is still possible to influence the sex of the future child. In general, births and subsequent fates are dependent on *Karma*, but sometimes one can influence this by adding an additional cause. If someone wishes for a son, then during the third or fourth week the method known as *Changing the Center* can be practiced. It can only be

done before the sex organs of the fetus have formed completely." The method referred to involves ingestion by the pregnant woman of specially prepared products that have high male hormone content. Among those listed are the milk from a cow that has had male calves, menstrual blood from a young girl mixed with semen from a virile boy, a special preparation of purified mercury and other substances that must be prepared in a ritual way and according to astrological requirements.

Yogic teachings state that the movement of the breath in the body is a primary determining factor of gender in children. When there is no harmonization of mood before and during love-making, the breath of the couple may become locked and dominant to the same side of their body. Tantra teaches that this can cause the birth of children with unbalanced sexual identity and, in extreme cases, can lead to homosexuality. Eastern teachings emphasize the use of postures to control and harmonize the flow of breath; it is taught that gender of offspring can be predetermined by such techniques. Recent scientific research into the ancient Hebrew tradition of using particular postures to control the sex of offspring is just one indication of the validity in these practices.

Negative aggressive fantasy while having sexual union is another way that sexual problems may develop in offspring. Parents create Karma, which their children must take into their identity. In turn, children "bring Karma to their parents." The intertwinings of destinies passed on from life to life is the basis of continuity between this world and the next. An active, aggressive male homosexual is in a great position of responsibility. By practicing oral or anal sex with his male lover, he "transmits" his Karma as well as his hormones and vitality. The links in a chain of destiny are established and invariably passed on to others. The *Chain of Karma* exists on physiological and metaphysical levels simultaneously. We should not consider one aspect without duly taking note of the other. Homosexual men transform one another physically but pay the price of complex metaphysical entanglement. J. G. Bennett, a student of the Russian metaphysical scientist George

Gurdjieff and teacher of Oriental philosophy, expresses an interesting viewpoint on male homosexuality. He says:

A homosexual who thinks himself special or superior to others cannot even enter the deeper aspects of self-work. It is equally necessary here to put aside any sense of guilt or inferiority. I have myself observed the way that Gurdjieff dealt with homosexuals. He was at pains to give them confidence that they could work on themselves, and he never allowed them to feel that they were special. The homosexual who cannot restrain his sexual impulses, and yet seriously wants to work on himself, may have to wait until he reaches an age at which the sexual function begins to lose its force, when a wonderful change can come and a remarkable progress occurs. Many homosexuals are indeed exceptionally perceptive and sensitive to other people, including those of the opposite sex, and they can, therefore, do a great deal of good even if their own transformation is delayed.

Male homosexuality is only rarely mentioned in the archaic periods of Chinese history. During the Ch'in and early Han Dynasty (221 B.C.–A.D. 24), there was a series of homosexual princes and emperors who were recorded in Chinese history as being exceedingly sadistic and who actively promoted male homosexuality. The last emperors of the early Han Dynasty became weak and degenerate. Eunuchs gained control and the people were heavily taxed. A disastrous epidemic ravaged China and it is recorded that an unusually high proportion of children with homosexual characteristics were born. The people revolted under a powerful Taoist leader and the dynasty fell. From this time until the advent of Moslem influence much later, male homosexuality was viewed with suspicion. It was only condoned when associated with the production of especially sensitive art works. The high incidence of homosexuality among male artists suggests that if the sex energy is sublimated and expressed through activities requiring extreme sensitivity, a male homosexual can make real spiritual progress.

Aggressive male homosexuality has long been linked to the decline of civilizations. It is particularly common at times when a nation appears to be losing its spiritual direction. When associated with degeneracy in the priesthood, it gives rise to pseudo-occultism, which is far removed from the transcendental spirituality of the higher Tantric and Taoist traditions. It is

unfortunate that occultism in the West has since the time of the Knights Templar been tainted by homosexuals masquerading as mystics. C. W. Leadbeater, one of the founding members of Madame Blavatsky's Theosophical Society, and Aleister Crowley (an active bisexual), the expounder of the secret rites of the O.T.O. (The Ordo Templi Orientis, an occult Templar organization) and founder of his own magical fraternity, were individuals who used mysticism to promote their own sexual proclivities. In recent years, there has been a sudden surge of occult and mystic organizations centered around sex magic with strong homosexual leanings. Coupled with this has been the new "acceptance" of homosexuality in Western society. It is the view of Eastern masters that when male homosexuality dominates a society, it signals the end of real civilization.

It is completely natural for young men to explore their own or other young men's bodies, and this should not be confused with homosexuality. Science has recorded numerous instances of exploratory "homosexual" advances between animals such as rats, mice, bats, hedgehogs, dogs, goats, pigs, sheep, horses, lions and monkeys. If aggressive male animals are kept together for long periods without the company of females, a certain proportion will become actively homosexual. This does not suggest that male homosexuality is either natural or unnatural, but indicates the multifarious aspects of humanity to be found in Nature. Tantra teaches that *evolution*, rather than devolution, is to be encouraged *by correct choice of action*. The elevation of male homosexuality almost to the status of a new religion is a potential threat to society and to humanity's spiritual evolution.

An excessively homosexual society will quickly annihilate itself. No amount of theorizing can alter this fact, which has been demonstrated throughout history. Over the past two thousand years the Occidental view of male homosexuality has radically changed. Surely it is time for homosexuals themselves to wake up to the reality of their situation and seek solutions to their problems, rather than campaigning for more acceptance of homosexuality. Eastern teachings offer practical techniques for overcoming the wiles of destiny. Yoga postures, breathing practices, visualization and meditation techniques can help balance imbalances in the subtle and physical body. Aggressive energy can be used to transform the psyche, even to the extent of transforming sexual polarity. Tantra teaches that when the creative attitude is brought to bear on any problem, there are no obstacles that cannot be overcome.

Many a poet, unawakened to the Light of Truth,
Has, through his ignorance, persisted in misguided ways,
Extolling in his lines the superiority of boys.
His poetry and that of others of his kind astound me.
He claims that boys have coquetry and can be trusted
Not to menstruate or find themselves with child.
Anyone, I say, who flees from girls
And has his needs supplied by catamites

Has little need for folly . . . he already has enough.
No lecher slyly sunk in sodomy, eschewing righteous ways,
Can be compared with some gallant
Who makes himself a slave to girls, and loving,
Never wakes from the rapturous dreams of love.
There is no lad, I say, to compare with a tender girl,
One half of whom is a sandy dune,
And the other half a curving branch. . . .
For us did God contrive and wondrously create
The other sex, and make their lovely eyebrows into bows,
Wherewith to shoot the shafts of love.
A young she-camel is the camel's natural mate—
No other male for him.
And so do not, in folly, heed the Devil—
For sodomy is just another of his tricks.

THE GLORY OF THE PERFUMED GARDEN

Angry form of Mahakala, the Protector of Tantric Buddhism in Tibet. The wrathful outer form, conceived of as dark and fearful as outer space, conceals a deep transcendent essence that rests on the tranquil ground of compassion. From a contemporary sculpture in the Rumtek monastery, Sikkim.

VISHNU

the preserver

The anus has a beauty and sensitivity of its own. No part of the human body should be considered unclean. It is an Eastern custom to wash the anus with cold water as part of the daily ablutions. Tantra teaches control of the anal sphincter muscles, indicating that sexual energy can be conserved in this way. When this muscle is contracted, the *sexual center* is stimulated and the sex glands produce hormones. Anal intercourse is not recommended by Tantric teachers because, among other things, it tends to stretch and weaken the sphincter muscles, producing energy loss.

Anal penetration disturbs the balance of vital forces in the body. The *downward-moving vital principle*, one of the five *Prana vitalities*, is reversed. This can create digestive problems, leading to constipation, irregularity and, ultimately, cancer of the rectum.

As an organ of excretion, the anus and rectal passage always contain traces of bacterial waste. A person is in danger of infection through anal insertion and can also suffer severe tissue damage or soreness. If normal sex is engaged in afterward, the dangerous possibility exists that bacteria will be transferred from the anus to the innermost parts of the Yoni of woman.

In ancient India, anal sex with a woman was called *lower union*. It was not considered normal. Some medical works mention it briefly, claiming it sometimes has the effect of an enema and at other times causes constipation. The Chinese tradition takes a similar position, and though anal sex with women was practiced on occasion, it was uncommon until the period of Moslem influence.

Anal sex with another man, or *sodomy*, has already been dealt with in the section on homosexuality. It was an essential ingredient of Moslem culture, despite the fact that Muhammad condemned the practice. Christianity always linked the Devil to anality, and he was commonly depicted as showing his behind. One of the accusations leveled by the Church against the Knights Templar was that they had "anal knowledge of each other." During a public inquiry into the un-Christian activities of the Templars, it was asserted that a member of the mystic society, after having been made a prisoner by the Turks, had introduced anal-oriented practices into the cult.

Anal sex is increasingly common today, partly because of the lack of understanding of its ramifications and partly because of the contemporary tendency to do *everything* that was once considered taboo. It is natural for someone who desires to become sexually liberated to explore the possibilities of new types of experience. A definite "no" is a closed door, which can block the inner potential for self-knowledge. If anal sex is considered relevant to a heterosexual relationship, it is the responsibility of the man to understand the physiological and psychological nature of this practice. A man should never *demand* this kind of surrendering from a woman.

A premeditated act and a spontaneous one have very different psychic effects, and penetration can happen in a totally organic way, almost by mistake. In such circumstances, pleasure can be experienced by both partners because of mutual openness.

At the location similar to the prostate gland in men, women have a similar but smaller gland, the cervix, the *flower of the uterus*. A thin membrane separates it from the anal passage. Conceivably an unusual

Arabian couple practicing anal sex in imitation of animals. From a Persian miniature painting of the nineteenth century.

placement of the cervix may be a physiological reason why certain women prefer anal to normal sex. We mention here an interesting extract from a Ming Dynasty erotic novel, which introduces this aspect of heterosexual sex rather beautifully:

Porphyry loved one form of sport above all others. After joining with the man in various modes of love-making, she desired him to pluck the flower of her bottom, while she herself touched the innermost flower of her womb with her delicate fingers. He told her, therefore, to raise herself on hands and legs, like a horse, and then he thrust himself into the flower of her posterior. She, reaching down with her hands, played with the heart of her other flower.

Some women find it necessary to offer every bodily orifice to their lovers as a symbol of their complete surrender and commitment. This desire, however, should not be exploited by a man. A preference for regular practice of anal intercourse indicates the desire for domination and power over the partner and perhaps the inability to love. According to the Yogic medical viewpoint, the body of woman has three main openings: the mouth, the anus and the Yoni. Among these, the mouth is created for things to enter *in* and for sounds to come *out*, the anus is for excretions to

come *out* and the Yoni is for the Lingam to enter *in* and a child to come *out*.

Anal sex can be frightening, painful and degrading for a woman. The "surrendering" aspect and the fear factor are intimately linked. Surrendering induces a sense of timelessness and fear releases strong emotional feelings. These factors together produce psychological and physiological changes; fear releases particular body secretions, can "put the ego in its place" and even induce the Kundalini-energy to enter and rise up the Central Pathway. But putting another person in a state of fear is a grave Karmic responsibility and not something to be taken lightly. Though no act is inherently "right" or "wrong," the mental attitude and quality of consciousness must be considered before endorsing anal sex as a new variation of love-making. The majority of women do not enjoy this practice, and those who are addicted to it may well have cause for regret later on in life. Enjoyment of anal sex may be brief, but the effects are lasting. Rather than turning to anal sex to add variation to one's love life, it is far better to perfect the techniques of transcendence. Tantra offers numerous exciting ways to stimulate and explore sexuality without the need for anal sex. The Yoni offers every facility for self-liberation.

Away with sodomy, and all will perfect be;
For making-love, use a woman's parts,
By far they are the best.
Two males beneath the clothes,
Are greater trouble than they're worth.

SHAYKH NAFZAWI

reverse kundalini

Ancient Chinese erotic texts refer to normal heterosexual love-making as the "Union of the Clouds and Rain" (*yun-yu*). Male homosexuality is commonly referred to as "Reverse Clouds and Inverted Rain" (*fan-yun-fu-yu*), particularly when anal intercourse is implied. In the Tantric tradition of India, male homosexuality is called *Reverse Kundalini*, a term that is also

used to describe retrogressive, degenerate or perverse sexual practices.

Reverse Kundalini, as the name suggests, refers to any sexual practice that reverses the natural upward flow of sexual energy. Anal sex invariably reverses the flow of sexual energy in the passive partner. Many ancient texts warn against anal sex or Reverse Kundalini, and state that the sensation accompanying this practice is a tingling chill that is both terrifying and exciting. Eastern traditions declare that the experience of Reverse Kundalini is psychically damaging and physically debilitating.

In order to understand Reverse Kundalini, it is necessary to take a look at traditional Yogic anatomy and then compare it with modern Western anatomy. The Yogic text *Goraksashatakam* refers to the existence of a special sexual gland:

Above the Lingam and below the navel there is a bulbous-like root [Sanskrit: *Kanda*], rather similar to the egg of a bird. It is the source of seventy-two thousand subtle life-carrying nerves. Over this "root" lies the all-powerful Kundalini, folded eight times and always closing the entrance to the Central Nerve with her "mouth." When awakened by the Inner Fire and consciously fanned by the Vital Breath, the Kundalini rises up the Central Nerve [Sanskrit: *Sushumna*], taking the Life Force with her as if it were a thread of light.

Gray's Anatomy, a standard Western medical work, describes an important sexual gland, the prostate, in the following way:

The prostate gland resembles a chestnut in size and shape. It is placed in the pelvic cavity and rests upon the rectum, through which it may be distinctly felt, especially when enlarged. Its base is directed upward and is situated immediately below the neck of the bladder. Its apex is directed downward to the deep layer of the triangular ligament, which it touches. The prostate consists of two lateral lobes and a middle lobe and is perforated by the urethra and the ejaculatory ducts. It is immediately enveloped by a thin but firm fibrous capsule, distinct from that derived from the *recto-vesical fascia*, and separated from it by a plexus of veins.

Anal sex between men can stimulate the prostate gland through the rectal wall,

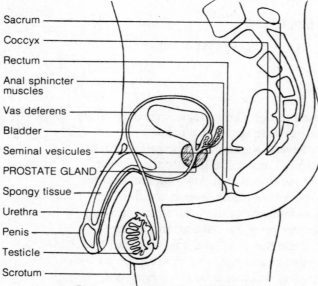

Sacrum
Coccyx
Rectum
Anal sphincter muscles
Vas deferens
Bladder
Seminal vesicules
PROSTATE GLAND
Spongy tissue
Urethra
Penis
Testicle
Scrotum

Diagram showing position of prostate gland.

producing spontaneous ejaculation of semen. Tantric teachers view such activity in the following way: The natural ascent of the Kundalini, awakened by sexual excitement, becomes blocked; the pressure created then causes the Kundalini-energy to turn back on itself and move in a downward direction. The only subtle nerves that the sexual energy can enter are those leading to the lower part of the body. The long-term effect of Reverse Kundalini is a devitalizing of the upper part of the body, a morbidity and heaviness in the lower body and limbs, and psycho-spiritual lethargy throughout the whole organism.

Anal sex is not the only cause of Reverse Kundalini. Fear can induce it, by causing the body to constrict itself, cool down and drain vitality from the upper regions. Reverse Kundalini can also occur through strenuous physical exertion, sudden shock, or a neurotic obsession, which can create separation and imbalance in the flow of life energy through the body. One of the most common causes of Reverse Kundalini in a sexual context is when a man and woman indulge in strenuous love-making on a full stomach. The vital fires of the body become concentrated on the digestion of food in the stomach and intestines, inhibiting and blocking the free flow of energy, and therefore causing drowsiness and heaviness, feelings that are the antithesis of the uplifting experience of union. The symptoms of Reverse Kundalini are a sense of separation from the Higher Self, fixation on morbid fantasy, sadomasochistic obsession, hot and cold chills, shortness of breath and weakness in the limbs. Reverse Kundalini can be counteracted by living a natural life, by deep breathing (which will help reverse the downward flow of energy) and healthy sexual practices. A Yogic exercise that also helps is known as *Mulabandha*, the rhythmic contraction of the anal sphincter muscles, which should be accompanied by visualizing sexual energy rising upward, invigorating and vitalizing the whole organism.

According to Shaykh Nafzawi, the Moslem author of *The Perfumed Garden* and a well-known sexologist of the early mediaeval period:

All authorities on religious law are agreed that a man may use any part of a woman's body for sexual gratification, *the rectum excepted*. Anal sexuality is a matter on which there is no complete agreement. Most exclude it on the grounds that it is forbidden by certain traditions of the Prophet, but quite a large body of opinion allows it. In his writings Ibn Sha'ban attributes the permissibility of the practice of anal sex to the Prophet's Companions and Successors. It is, however, a well-known fact that in Muhammad's community anal sex was considered unlawful.

The base or sexual center is complex and all its elements are interconnected. The Western anatomical view is interesting since it tends to support many of the ancient Yogic descriptions of this center and how it functions. There are remnants of glandular structures around the base of the spine, in the region of the coccyx, a bone-like structure formed from four *coccygeal elements* and *coccygeal horns*, which articulate with the "horns" of the *sacrum* (a composite triangular bone forming the back of the pelvis). This whole area is believed by some to be the remnants of an animal-like tail, which became atrophied during the process of evolution.

The *perineal body* is a complex structure between the anus and sexual organ made up of four interrelated parts, known in medical terminology as the *bulbocavernosus muscle* (in the front), the *sphincter ani externus muscle* (behind), and the two *superficial perineal muscles* (at the sides). The first of these expels the last of the urine and also serves as "an accessory muscle of erection for the penis," helping to ejaculate the semen. In a woman, this muscle constricts the vaginal orifice. Conscious control of this muscle is a goal of considerable importance in the Tantric tradition.

The *pudendal nerve* is the main neural connection with the muscles of the *perineal body*. Control of this nerve gives absolute control over erection and ejaculation in the man, and over Yoni contractions in the woman. Its three branches arise in the pelvis by roots from the *sacral nerves* and eventually connect with the *sciatic nerve*. The pudendal nerve finally emerges out of the perineal body as the *dorsal nerve* of the Lingam or Yoni.

The equivalent Tantric description tells of a fourfold lotus within which is a second fourfold "base" ruled over by an elephant-headed deity (Ganesha), above which is an inverted triangle containing a Lingam shape (the prostate) enveloped by the Kundalini. A central duct rises upward

The Base or Sexual Chakra as described in recent Hindu Tantric works. The Kundalini is shown coiled around the Lingam-shaped prostate. The elephant with multiple trunks symbolizes the many different paths through which sexual energy can flow.

from it, to the other Subtle Centers.

In the prostate gland of the male are located the *seminal vesicles*, sometimes referred to as "blind pouches" or *prostatic utricles*. Each is roughly the size and shape of a small finger. The seminal vesicles are directed backward and upward into the prostate and are believed by Western medicine to be the "male homologue of the female uterus and vagina." They secrete an alkaline constituent of the seminal fluid, analogous to the secretions produced in the Yoni of a sexually excited woman. In this area is the *ejaculatory duct*, which leads from the region of the prostate and directly adjoins the rectum.

At a location similar to the prostate in men, women have a *cervix*, the "flower" of the uterus. A thin membrane separates it from the anal passage. Conceivably, an unusual placement of the cervix and mouth of the womb may be a physiological reason why some women enjoy anal sex.

The blocking of the prostate gland in men, and pressure on the cervix through the inner rectum in women, can cause an unnatural current of sexual energy to build up and be released in a downward-moving direction. Such *Reverse Kundalini* commonly leads to neurosis and personality problems, and sensitivity to humor becomes replaced by cynicism. The physical symptoms are a sudden thickening in the lower part of the body: the waist, hips and legs become heavier, without any appreciable change in dietary habits. Similar symptoms often occur during the "male menopause" and are especially associated with the surgical removal of the prostate gland. A healthful diet, lifestyle and sex habits all contribute to overcoming problems of Reverse Kundalini.

When sexual energy is directed upward and circulated throughout the whole body, psycho-physical morbidity is replaced by transcendental spiritual radiance and well-being.

Arabian couple practicing anal sex. From a Persian miniature painting, early nineteenth century.

Close the anal orifice by the heel of the left foot, press that heel with the right foot carefully, move the muscles of the rectum slowly and gradually contract the muscles of the Yoni or perineum [the space between anus and scrotum]. Restrain the breath by using the Jalandhara Bandha [pressing the chin into the chest and contracting the throat]. This is called Mahabandha and is effective in destroying decay and death. When a person knows how to use it correctly, it helps that person accomplish all desires.

GHERANDA SAMHITA

The Great Goddess Kundalini, the Pure Energy of the Self, sleeps close to the rectum in the region known as Muladhara; she has the form of a serpent having three and a half coils. So long as she is asleep in the body, the Soul is a mere animal and true knowledge does not arise. Contract and dilate the anal sphincter again and again. This is called Asvini Mudra and is the most effective way of awakening the Shakti within.

GHERANDA SAMHITA

arabian nights

The very words "Arabian Nights" evoke sensuous and exotic imagery: a man in a harem reclining on cushions and carpets, water-pipe in hand, a beautiful woman on each arm and attendants offering delicacies to the accompaniment of dance and music. Such are the popular ideas associated with Arabia. Shaykh Nafzawi in his classic *The Perfumed Garden* gives a typical description:

He arrived then at the curtain hanging at the entrance; it was of red brocade. From there he examined the room, which was bathed in light, filled with many chandeliers and candles burning in golden sconces. In the middle of this saloon played a jet of musk-water. A tablecloth extended from end to end, stretched out over the floor and covered with sundry meats and fruits.

The saloon was provided with gilt furniture, the splendor of which dazzled the eye. In fact, everywhere there were ornaments of all kinds. On looking closer, the King ascertained that round the tablecloth there were twelve maidens and seven women, all like moons; he was astonished at their beauty and grace. His attention was above all attracted by a woman like the full moon, of perfect beauty, with black eyes, oval cheeks, and a lithe and graceful waist; she humbled the hearts of those who grew enamored of her. Stupefied with her beauty, the King was as if stunned. He then said to himself, "How is there any getting out of this place? O Spirit, do not give way to love!"

Continuing his inspection of the room, he perceived glasses filled with wine in the hands of those who were present; they were drinking and eating. He heard one of the women saying to one of her companions, "Oh, let's go to bed; sleep is overpowering us. Come, let us light a torch and retire to the other chamber." Later the King hid himself. The two women returned from their ablutions and shut the doors of the room. Obscured by wine, they passionately pulled off each other's clothes and began to caress each other.

In the harem, Moslem women commonly entered into sisterly or even Sapphic relationships. The ritual of bathing, with mutual washing, shampooing, massage and depilation, fostered an ambiance of sensuality, so often associated with polygamy and Oriental sexuality.

According to the Koran, a man is allowed up to four wives simultaneously, as well as any number of concubines. As J. G. Bennett, the interpreter of Gurdjieff's teachings, so clearly points out, "The rule made by Muhammed specified three conditions of polygamy. First, there must be the means to supply the needs of more than one family. Second, there must be sufficient virility to satisfy more than one woman. Third, there must be sufficient inner authority in the man for more than one woman to accept him. These conditions somewhat diminished the incidence of polygamy."

Richard Burton, translator of *The Arabian Nights* (first published in 1885 in a private edition), cites traditional sources for the following reasoning: "If a man has only one wife, she holds herself as an equal, answers back and gives herself airs and graces. Two wives are always quarreling. Three wives are no real company, since two of them will invariably team up together against the nicest of the three and will cause havoc. Four wives are the best solution, since if they quarrel they can more easily make things up between themselves in equality. The husband thus enjoys comparative peace." Burton further states that the Moslem restriction of four wives to one husband is derived from an even older Jewish custom.

Though the popular view of Arabian Nights is linked to polygamy and overt sensuality, most modern Moslems do not have more than one wife and tend to be conservative in their sexual habits. Women are beginning to take an active role in Islamic society, and some of the restrictions on them are being lifted. Nevertheless, Arabic culture remains patriarchal and essentially chauvinistic. The traditional Hollywood version of "Arabian Nights" is hard to find in the real world.

Islam is riddled with primitive superstitions about the sex act, which, when analyzed, can be reduced to a paranoiac dread of women "gaining ascendancy" over men. Sexual postures with the woman on top and taking the active role are viewed with suspicion and said to be "detrimental to health" for the most illogical reasons. Shaykh Nafzawi, for instance, declares that "If you do it with the woman bestriding you, your dorsal chord will suffer and your heart will be affected; and if in that position the smallest drop of the usual female secretions enters your organ, then a painful problem will result."

Moslems attach a certain amount of guilt to sexual intercourse, as evidenced by

Ghazali (the eleventh-century Sufi mystic): "It is a good marital practice for a man to turn away from the direction of Mecca while engaging in sexual intercourse, out of respect for the Holy Places." Ghazali advises that the first, middle and last days of the month are unsuitable for sexual intercourse since "on such nights the Devil himself attends the union." Arabic women are generally forbidden to sleep on their backs, except when in sexual embrace, for it is believed that "If they openly lie in such a way, the Devil will forever try to possess them."

There is a great deal of male chauvinism in Moslem teachings on sexuality. Women have the status of property and are envisioned as less than second-class citizens. A popular Moslem saying is that "A man's shame [*aurat*] extends from his navel to his knees, whereas a woman's is from the top of her head right down to her toes. Even Ibn Arabi, the Sufi mystic of the twelfth century, gives a bigoted view of woman:

Woman occupies an inferior degree to that of man, confirming the Koranic Word that "As for men, they precede women by one degree." There is a ternary of God, man and woman; man reaches out toward his Lord, which is his origin, as woman reaches out toward man. When man loves woman, he desires union, that is to say the most complete union that can be possible in love; and in the form composed of elements, there exists no union more intense than the act of physical love. Voluptuousness spreads through every part of the body; therefore Moslem sacred law prescribes total ablution and purification of the body after the conjugal act, just as the extinction of the man in the woman has been total after the voluptuous rapture of sexual union. For God is jealous of His servant, He does not tolerate that the latter may enjoy anything but Him.

According to Ghazali, there is a tradition that the prophet Muhammad once said, "Let none of you fall on his wife like a brute beast, but let there be some prior communication between husband and wife." He was asked what kind of communication was meant, to which he replied, "A kiss and gentle words." On another occasion, known as the Sermon of the Farewell Pilgrimage, Muhammad is alleged to have declared, "I commend to you fair treatment of your women, for they are your captives. Of themselves they possess nothing. You have them on trust from God,

and have lawful access to their bodies by God's own command. Men and women have rights over one another. Women have the right to decent food and clothing, and it is your right as husbands that no one whom you find distasteful should tread your carpet. Your womenfolk should allow no one access to your house without your permission or knowledge. If they do, then avoid them in bed, and beat them, though not too severely." When asked, "What kind of woman is best?" the Prophet Muhammad replied, "One who is pleasing to her husband's eye when he looks upon her, who obeys him when he gives an order and gives him no displeasure by what she is or has." Aisha, Muhammad's favorite wife, once said, "Women are men's dolls. A man must make his doll as pretty as he can." As an afterthought she added, "As a plaything, a man should treat you well."

The typical Moslem approach to sexuality is very worldly and physical. Male dominance and the power of the patriarchy are given priority almost to the exclusion of consideration for women. The idea that a man "owns" his woman, or women, is typical of obsessive patriachal values. The demand of absolute and unquestioned "service" from the woman is the unbalanced result of such male dominance. True service between partners can only be realized if mutually undertaken, with consideration for each other. Islam distorts and inflates the value of male sexual aggression and, almost without exception, is devoid of insight and respect for the needs and rights of women.

In Islamic society the popular saying that "Large is beautiful" applies particularly to women; bride-prices were often paid according to the weight of a girl about to be married. In men, large sexual organs are highly prized and sexual success is equated with overt aggressive masculinity. According to Shaykh Nafzawi, "Coitus is highly beneficial to strong, full-blooded persons of heavy build, but harmful to those who are the exact opposite. A man who works a woman younger than himself acquires new vigor; if she is of the same age as he is, there will be no advantage from it; and if she is older than himself, then she will take all his strength." He adds, "If you are lying with a woman, do her business several times if you feel inclined, but take care not to overdo it, for it is a true word that 'He who plays the Game of Love for his own sake, and to satisfy his desires, feels the most intense and durable pleasure; but he who does it to satisfy the lust of another person will languish, lose all his desire, and finishes by becoming impotent.'" An early tradition states that Muhammad advised his followers to "select virgins when seeking wives, for they have the sweetest mouths, the most fertile wombs and the fairest complexions." Shaykh Nafzawi states that "Sexual intercourse with girls under thirteen is bad, since it can harm or deaden the brain and bring on depression and morbid fantasy."

Many love-making positions depicted in Islamic erotic art are taken directly from the ancient illustrated love manuals of the Hindus. Both the *Kama Sutra* and the *Ananga Ranga* have been presented in abbreviated or edited forms in the Arabic language. However, these translations have been grossly distorted to emphasize the Moslem view of male dominance and superiority.

In all fairness, Muhammad's teachings on sexuality were perhaps suitable as an improvement on the very primitive and aggressive culture that dominated Arabia. It is curious that the Kaaba, the cube-shaped building in the Great Mosque of Mecca, contains a black stone or meteorite that was once worshipped as a symbol of exalted femininity. The ancient Meccans worshipped mother-goddesses in the form of stones, which were ritually circumambulated as the Kaaba of Mecca is today. The pre-Islamic pantheon is made up of names and images of pious men and a triad of goddesses, Allat, Al-Uzza and Manat, who ruled throughout Arabia. All shrines and images of goddesses were destroyed on the orders of Muhammad, who associated them with the ancient Babylonian mystery cults. It seems that Muhammad distrusted the power wielded from such ancient seats and chose to elevate the patriarchy to a position of absolute supremacy.

Islam does not present us with any overall mystic view of sexuality. If we make comparisons with Indian and Chinese teachings in this area, we find Arabic culture lacking in sexual sensitivity. However, Islam has nurtured some of the world's greatest mystics in the spiritual lineage of the Sufis, whose love-inspired poetry and mystic songs have become quite well known in the West. Sufism, however, drew a great deal of inspiration from ancient Indian mystic teachings. Hazrat Inayat Khan, for example, who did much to introduce Sufism to the West in recent times, drew almost exclusively from Hindu sources to illustrate his thoughts. Sufi poetry exalts womanhood through allegory, keeping to the letter of Islam while carefully hinting that the absolute love of a man and woman for each other mirrors the love of God for his creations.

Though the popular and romantic idea of Arabian Nights is far from the actuality of love in the Middle East, modern couples can learn something from it as it was idealized and practiced in the past. In Richard Burton's mammoth work *The Arabian Nights* there are richly sensuous descriptions of love-making that can provide inspiration. In the twenty-sixth of the stories we encounter the following description:

When I entered and took a seat, the lady at once came in crowned with a diadem of pearls and jewels; her face dotted with artificial moles in indigo, her eyebrows pencilled with Kohl and her hands and feet reddened with Henna. When she saw me she smiled and took me to her embrace and clasped me to her breast; then she put her mouth to my mouth and sucked my tongue and I did likewise. Then we sat down to converse and I hung my head earthwards in bashfulness, but she delayed not long ere she set before me a tray of the most exquisite viands, marinated meats, fritters soaked in bees' honey and chickens stuffed with sugar and pistachio nuts, whereof we ate till we were satisfied. Then they brought basin and ewer and I washed my hands and we scented ourselves with rose-water musk'd and sat down again to converse. Then we fell to toying and groping and kissing till nightfall, when the handmaidens set before us meats and a complete wine service, and we sat carousing till the noon of night, when we lay down and I lay with her; never in my life saw I a night like that night.

The rich imagery associated with Arabian Nights can be incorporated into one's environment. Instead of limiting the love-nest to Western standards of décor, a couple can learn to expand their intimate settings to encompass more exotic cultures. When this is coupled with the Tantric approach to honoring the creative principle, the bedroom, like a stage, become a setting for the play of eroticism.

Arabian love-making. From a Persian miniature painting of the nineteenth century.

Be to him a plot of land, and he will be your Heaven above; be to him a place of rest, and to you he will be a mainstay; be to him a bondmaid, and to you he will be a slave. Do not cling to him, lest he rid himself of the burden of your weight—yet do not keep away from him too much, lest he forget you. If he comes toward you, then you move close to him; but if he moves away, then keep your distance also. Pay careful heed to his nostrils, ears and eyes so that he may never smell anything but fragrant perfume from your body and never hear of you anything but what is of good report, and never see anything in you but beauty.

GHAZALI

If you rule your wife outwardly, yet inwardly you are ruled by her whom you desire, this is characteristic of man; in other animals love is lacking, which shows their inferiority. The Prophet said that woman prevails over the wise, while ignorant men prevail over her; in them the fierceness of animals is immanent. Love and tenderness are human qualities; anger and lust are animal ones. Woman is a ray of God; she is not the earthly beloved. She is creative; you might say she is not created.

RUMI

circumcision

Circumcision is a very ancient custom, found in diverse cultures. There are indications that circumcision was practiced in pre-dynastic Egypt. During the Old Kingdom (*circa* 2780—2270 B.C.), circumcision was common, as is attested by bas-reliefs depicting this rite. The regular Egyptian hieroglyphic sign for the Lingam shows the mark of circumcision. It has been suggested that early in Egyptian history circumcision was reserved for the nobility, and that only later was it extended to the whole male population. Perhaps the excessively hot climate, which could create irritation and sweat rashes around the foreskin, was a significant factor in bringing this practice into popular use.

Supposedly the Jews were adopting an Egyptian custom when they incorporated ritual circumcision into their religion. There are, for example, numerous affinities between ancient Egyptian rituals and those outlined for Jewish ceremonial use. The tabernacle is specifically made from Egyptian shittim wood, and it seems likely that the Ark of the Covenant was derived from the Sacred Boat of Egyptian pharaohs. The tradition is that Jews have been circumcised since the time of Abraham. The Kabbalist view is that male circumcision symbolizes a covenant with Yahweh and is an initiation into the suffering of the world. The Jewish *Moyel*, or circumcising priest, is generally very skillful and uses chanting and ritual to give the act meaning.

The Moslems also incorporated circumcision into their culture. During their invasions of India they were horrified to find that Hindus and Buddhists were uncircumcised. Circumcision became a prerequisite for acceptance as a convert to the new religion; the same swords used in battle were used for this purpose.

In the Orient circumcision is very rare. The Indian and Tibetan teachings on the subject stress that it is only useful for medical reasons, such as when a foreskin cannot be retracted and sexual intercourse is impaired. Concerning China, R. H. Van Gulik, the celebrated Orientalist and sexologist, writes: "It is worth noting that there are no traces of painful manhood or womanhood initiation rites for either boys or girls, and that circumcision for boys and clitoridectomy for girls were both completely unknown."

In the past, circumcision has always been the culmination of an initiation rite, either into a patriarchal group or into the tribe. Many primitive African tribes use the rite of circumcision as a test of endurance and as an initiation into a cult. Although circumcision is a very minor operation, its psychological effects can be devastating. This is particularly true in the modern setting, where circumcision is often carried out as a purely clinical rather than a ritual act. Babies are extremely impressionable, and although the pain is relatively slight, there is a danger that circumcision may create psychological and sexual problems unless the right attitude is brought to bear.

If the father is circumcised, more often than not his son will also be. If a family wishes to maintain a tradition of circumcision, it is advisable to have the operation performed as a meaningful ritual and to employ a circumcising priest. If the family is hesitant, then the decision should wait until the boy is able to decide for himself. We feel that it is best to wait until the child is old enough to understand exactly what is transpiring and why. Since the operation can be carried out at any age, and painlessly with anesthetics, there seems little point in early circumcision, unless it is dictated by custom or medical necessity.

Male circumcision consists in the surgical removal of part or all of the foreskin. Generally, there is a tendency to over-circumcise. This is particularly easy with an infant, since it is difficult to judge the precise amount of skin to be removed. Therefore it is preferable to half-circumcise in such cases, by removing only the outermost tip of the foreskin. Even in a grown man the circumcision wound is not particularly painful; it heals in about nine days, and normal sexual intercourse can be resumed after three weeks.

Circumcision is by no means necessary for hygienic reasons. An uncircumcised boy, however, should be taught how to keep his Lingam clean. Parents should explain how to carefully retract the foreskin and wash the inner Lingam at least every few days. In an uncircumcised boy the foreskin should not be fully retracted until after the age of three.

Some medical conditions make circumcision advisable. The persistent recurrence of itching, soreness and redness of the inner surface of the foreskin and the head of the Lingam is one such indication. If in doubt about whether or not to circumcise for medical reasons, it is best to consult a specialist.

Some have suggested that premature ejaculation can sometimes be cured by circumcision, even at a relatively late stage in life, since it results in a decrease in the Lingam's sensitivity. On the other hand, some consider this decrease in sensitivity one of the disadvantages of the operation. Medical opinion is divided about equally for and against the general practice of circumcision, though in most hospitals it is performed routinely on male infants. We feel that a clinical hospital environment for

circumcision is the most unpleasant aspect of this operation, and as such is best avoided.

As for female circumcision (the surgical removal of all or part of the clitoris), it must surely be one of man's most cruel inventions. It is first referred to in the late Ptolemaic period of Egyptian history (*circa* 300–30 B.C.) and is still practiced in some Arab and African cultures. It was introduced to the West in Victorian times, supposedly to stop young girls from playing with their Yonis. Fortunately female circumcision has been discontinued in the West.

The choice for male circumcision is an aspect of sexuality best left to the individual or family. Outside the hospital setting, it can be a meaningful ritual, with some possible physical benefits. However, there is a strong case for delaying the decision to circumcise or not until the boy is of an age to decide for himself.

She asked him through the interpreter why it is that Moslems demanded circumcision and caused so much suffering to their boys. "Besides," she concluded, "it is interference with God's manner of creation and useless at that." "Ah," said the Moslem Ruler, "tell her that circumcision is of the greatest value, for a branch, if pruned, grows strong and thick and sturdy. So long as this operation is not carried out, it will remain thin and weak."

IBN HAYYAN

menstruation: the red snow

A Chinese tradition speaks of menstruation as the *Monthly Affair*, the *Monthly Guest*, *Regular Fluid*, the *Red Flood*, *Peach-flower Flow*, or the *Red Snow*. As in most other ancient cultures, in China it was customary for a woman to separate herself from her normal wordly activities during this time. During menstruation, a woman was not supposed to cook or take part in any family duties or religious rites, and her forehead was generally marked with a red spot to indicate her condition.

The taboos associated with menstruation are practically universal. They exist in both primitive and sophisticated cultures, from

India to China, Japan, the Pacific Islands, North and South America, Africa, the Middle East and parts of Europe. In all these areas of the world special arrangements are usually made for women at the time of their monthly bleeding.

During her monthly period a woman is more open, receptive and vulnerable than usual; she is often prey to moods and emotions that a man finds hard to understand. All the signs associated with the onset of menstruation, such as moodiness, sudden irritability, listlessness, fits of passion, swollen breasts and stomach, sudden weight gain, skin irritations, flushing and so on, are caused by hormonal changes accompanied by the excretion of toxic elements from the body. It is a time of complete purification, when a woman prepares to become "new again," just as the moon does every month.

The association of menstruation with the moon and lunar cycles is culturally universal. There are even common taboos against "looking at the moon when menstruating." Ishtar, the Moon goddess of the ancient Mediterranean cultures, was believed to menstruate during the time of the full moon. Hindus believe that a menstruating woman is under the moon's influence and should be treated with respect and care. Orthodox Hindus are very paranoid about the touch or even the glance of a menstruating woman. Both are supposed capable of causing food to spoil or milk to curdle. Traditionally, a woman is not to bathe at all during the time of menstruation. However, once her period is completed, she is supposed to have a thorough wash, or even a full mud bath, letting the mud dry on her body and then washing it off afterward. Her hair is shampooed and, in Moslem cultures, treated with henna. She is then viewed as being *totally renewed*, a "virgin" once more.

In the Hindu tradition, menstrual blood is considered a form of Agni, the Fire god. It is the fiery and sulphurous aspect of menstrual blood that, according to Tantra, is both dangerous and potent. Tantric teachings state that during her monthly period woman is virtually the embodiment of the downward-moving Vital Energy (the *Apana*), which governs the eliminative functions of the body.

Menstrual blood contains the remains of the uterine lining, together with amounts of discarded egg cells, estrogenic hormones, lecithins, arsenic compounds and rich concentrations of essential minerals such as iron and phosphorus. It is these that Eastern mystical and alchemical teachings refer to under the single grouping "sulphurous." The *Golden Treatise of Hermes Trismegistus*, the seminal work of Western alchemy, views menstrual blood similarly, referring to it as "brimstone," "unguent" or "hidden wisdom." "Know that the fatness of our earth is sulphur," states the *Golden Treatise*. "Sulphur tinges and fixes and is the connection of all alchemic tinctures."

From a worldly standpoint, a woman is shedding waste material when she menstruates. Moslems greatly fear the power of menstrual blood, as do orthodox

Brahmins. In many cultures a man will not even walk on ground that has been trod by a menstruating woman. In primitive societies menstrual blood is used in Black Magic rites and for empowering negative charms and amulets.

Tantric Yogis view a menstruating woman as the very embodiment of Mother Kali, the Transcendental Power, linking this world to the next. A mystic form of this female principle, known as the goddess Vajravarahi, is described in Tantric texts as "dripping with blood and passionately pressing the thighs of her partner with her legs and lower body."

According to Tantra, a woman is "very special" at the time of her menstrual period. She is a "doorway to the other worlds." Yogis understand the invigorating and rejuvenating powers of menstrual blood. In rituals designed to tap these powers a menstruating woman takes the active role and becomes Kali the Initiatress into transcendence.

Making love in the standard "missionary" or "woman supine" position with a menstruating woman is not considered beneficial, since the movements of love will push the woman's downward-moving energy and excretions back upward. The natural flow is thwarted, and at times menstruation may even stop as a result of such love-making, causing a reabsorption of bodily residues that can jeopardize a woman's health.

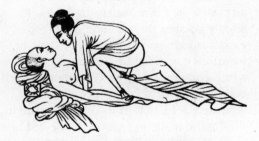

Taoist love-posture with woman in the active role. Such postures are particularly suited to love-making when a woman is menstruating. From a Chinese painting of the late eighteenth century.

The Tantric form is for the man to lie down on the bed or carpet, while the woman sits above him. Taking the active role, without shame or sexual restraint, she makes love to him, pouring the downward-moving energy and the libation of the menstrual flow on his erect Lingam. From her he receives the invigorating essence of her ova-rich blood, which would have been the basis for supporting the life of a fetus, and she experiences a loss of menstrual pains and cramps. Many Tantric texts credit such love-making with the power of physical rejuvenation and initiation into the wisdom-teachings.

The menstrual cycle is mainly controlled by the female hormones estrogen and progesterone, though the male hormone testosterone is continuously secreted throughout the female cycle. Birth-control pills are made from synthesized female hormones, which regularize the period. However, such benefits may be offset by the fact that they alter a woman's natural cycle.

A recent study of menstruation found that the monthly periods of women living together tend to synchronize. According to the scientific paper published at the conclusion of the study, "the longer the women lived together, the more their periods tended to occur on the same days, even though most of the women claimed that they were not aware of when the others were menstruating." A secondary finding was that girls with regular boy friends tended to have shorter menstrual cycles and more regular periods.

There are many factors in modern life that adversely influence the natural cycle of woman. Emotional upset, tension, dieting and excessive travel can all make a woman miss her periods or upset their regularity.

The view that a woman is renewed after the cessation of her menstrual period is supported by many ancient traditions. In priestly cultures the tradition is that menstruation *renews* virginity. The cycle of woman is compared to that of the moon, which changes and creates different influences at the different periods, ultimately returning to its original status. In the Tantric tradition a woman is viewed as a virgin (*Kumari*) just after menstruation, as a young wife (*Saraswati*) during the week following menstruation, as a worldly mistress of the house (*Lakshmi*) during the next week, and as a wise lady (*Kali*) during the approach to menstruation. During menstruation itself she is "beyond worldliness," "dead to the world and its responsibilities," and therefore freed from household duties. It is during this time that she serves as a link between this world and the next.

In her role as mother and sustainer of the family, a woman spends the majority of her time caught up in a web of worldly activities. By the time her period approaches, she has become more like a man through her contact with worldliness and her husband or lover.

Many of the rules governing a menstruating woman, such as that she should not cook for others or take part in religious practices or wash in the common bathing place, are based on the knowledge that her psychic atmosphere at this time is quite different from that during the rest of the month. It is not that she is dirty, but that she is "different" and is exceedingly open to non-worldly forces. This is one of the main reasons why, in evolved ancient cultures, special places—parts of buildings or even a whole house—were set aside for women to live while menstruating.

Traditionally, such a place was overseen by one or several elderly woman, already past their menopause. These "wise women" would have the job of looking after the needs of the younger menstruating women, using the time to instruct and initiate them into various arts, sciences, crafts, ritual songs, music and spiritual traditions, all of which could later be applied to worldly life. In particular, this was a time to learn the legends of the tribe, the lineage of the family, and to become acquainted with the powers of transcendence. The Kailash tribe of Kafiristan, which resisted Moslem culture until recently, is one group that has preserved this tradition. Many so-called primitive tribes of India and Africa still have a common "menstruation house" for women.

Though it would indeed be difficult for a modern woman to apply this ancient tradition to her life (to do so completely would mean a rearranging of society), some aspects of the ancient wisdom on menstruation can be usefully adapted to suit our present culture.

A man should treat his woman in a more protective way during the time of her menstruation. She should make it a policy not to get involved in worldly activities, but rather to cultivate her "retreat from the world." In this way she will become more familiar with her own sexual identity and its cycles of change.

Voluntary self-seclusion may in fact be very rewarding for a menstruating woman. This retreat allows her to explore the terrain of her psyche, while at the same time permitting her to rest from her worldly duties. The time of menstruation is particularly suited to meditation and contemplation, and can be a great chance to experience transcendence from worldliness.

When a couple are closely knit, it is not unusual for the man to experience some of the menstrual pains of his partner. Even in the Moslem culture, this has been recorded. Abu Abbas Saffah had a single wife with whom he was deeply in love. It was said of him that "If she ails, he ails; and even if she menstruates, he also does the same in his own way." Woman is attuned to the lunar cycle, and man is keyed to the longer solar rhythm; nevertheless, the essential bisexuality of each relates him or her to both cosmic cycles.

Though the orthodox Hindu viewpoint is that the couple should refrain from love-making during the woman's menstrual period, the Tantric approach is that if passion calls, there should be no holding back. With the right mental attitude, a couple can safely and enjoyably use this time of enhanced potency to explore the mysteries of Kali and her renewing powers.

Kali making love to Shiva. She personifies the regenerative power of female sexuality. From a Rajasthani miniature painting of the eighteenth century.

The Tantric Adept should view a menstruating woman with reverence and awe. She is the living embodiment of Kali, the power of transcendence; her menstrual blood [Khapushpa] is the flowery essence of all womanhood, the very blood of life. Possessed of supernormal qualities, it is a potent rejuvenating and transforming force, purifying all poisons through its alchemical fire. By performing sexual rites with a menstruating woman, the Adept can more quickly advance along the Path of Liberation.

KAULA TANTRA

Menstruation is only for a matter of days, and God willed that it be used to totally purify and cleanse the womb. When it's all over, a woman is better than before.

SHAYKH NAFZAWI

conception and contraception

In order to fully understand the Eastern teachings on both conception and contraception, we must examine the ancient, traditional view of how an individual "life" becomes embodied in a womb. All traditions declare that mental attitude is the prime factor in determining both conception and the gender of the child. The time of love-making, with respect to both the woman's menstrual cycle and the hour of the day or night, also plays a role. Finally, health and diet are important considerations.

In the East, there is a general agreement that the first few days immediately after the cessation of a woman's menstruation are conducive to conception. This belief is expressed in Indian, Tibetan, Chinese, Japanese and Arabic sexological works. The Arab writer Abu Bakri, for example, says, "Sexual intercourse in the latter part of the night, shortly after menstruation, and at the beginning of the lunar month, never fails to produce noble children." He adds the interesting view that "Children conceived as a result of nocturnal intercourse are generally nobler than those conceived during the day."

A Chinese text, which quotes some of the *Sexual Secrets of the Plain Girl*, states: "There is the following fixed method for obtaining children. First, one should purify one's heart and put aside all worldly sorrows, meditating and concentrating the mind with the help of a fast. Then, on the third day after the woman's menstruation has stopped, in the period after midnight and before the early morning, the man should excite her passion. There should be considerable foreplay. Then he should unite with her, ensuring that his innermost feelings are adjusted to hers, and carefully blending his own enjoyment with that of his partner."

According to Peng Tsu, the Chinese Taoist master, "In order to obtain children, a man should conserve his semen by not ejaculating too frequently; by this means he will become more potent. Then, if he makes love with his woman on the third or fifth day after her menstruation has finished, she will conceive."

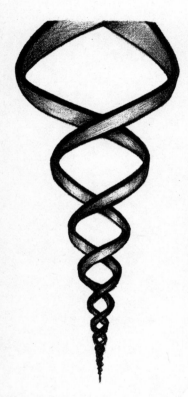

During passionate love-making an energy vortex is created that attracts beings from the Spirit-realm.

The Hindu tradition is very similar. The *Charaka Samhita*, an important early Indian medical work, declares: "If a woman wishes to conceive a child, she should wait until her menstruation has finished. She should then take a bath and be massaged and shampooed. Then both she and her husband should dress in white clothes and wear garlands of flowers; greatly longing for each other, they should make love passionately."

The same text adds that "During such love-making the woman should receive the seed of man while lying on her back, for in that posture all the elements in the body are balanced and retain their correct positions." Many ancient traditions point to the role of love postures in conception, and favor the woman-supine position as most effective for ensuring impregnation. Ancient Hebrew and Chinese texts support this view.

The whole process of conception is beautifully described in the *Charaka Samhita*:

The semen, having been set in motion by the ecstatic Self *and informed by it*, emerging from the man's body, mixed with the sexual secretions of the woman, having entered the inner parts of her Yoni. It reaches the womb, where the Conscious-element [the Spirit], *which has the mind as its instrument*, proceeds first of all to gravitate to itself all the needed ingredients. It gravitates all the Vital Elements to itself, drawing the subtle Space-element before the others [air, fire and so forth].

All the ancient teachings on conception stress that mental attitude is paramount in guaranteeing success. As the great Hindu teacher Atreya so clearly states, "An infant is said to be born of the mother, the father, born of the Spirit, born of concordance and of nourishment. There is, however, always the connecting agent, *the mind.*"

When a couple make love, a "vortex" of swirling ecstatic energy rises up through their Psychic Centers. Esoteric teachings declare that it is this energy vortex that attracts and "draws down" the Spirit of a being *already existing* in the intermediate state between death and birth and impelled by the right Karma. The parents do not "make" the child, but rather "attract" the Spirit into the womb. The physical body is then built up to house the Spirit, drawing from the genetic instructions contained in the sperm and ovum. Biologically, a number of factors are necessary before conception can take place. The woman must be healthy and fertile; the man must have potent semen. The coming together of sperm and ovum must take place during the woman's fertile period of ovulation. Along with the biological factors of conception, a bond of spirituality and love should permeate the union, as otherwise a Spirit will be attracted that will cause disruption in the home. The Karmic elements of conception cannot be overstated. When conceived in love, there will be love generated. When a child is conceived in fear or lust, these same sentiments will ultimately pervade the family. The energy vortex, in creating a condition ripe for conception, carries the dominant sentiments of the couple into the Spirit-realm and attracts a being that reflects these sentiments. Esoteric traditions declare that the energy vortex becomes "colored" by the sentiment of the lovers and it is this "coloring" that attracts the Spirit of the child to be.

The *Charaka Samhita* gives an intriguing view of conception. It states: "A woman gives birth to a child *resembling that person of whom she thinks* at the time of conception." Many children bear little resemblance to other family members. Both women and men commonly fantasize when making love, particularly if the relationship is casual. The fantasy of having sex with a person other than the love-partner creates the possibility that the woman will conceive a child resembling her fantasy-lover. In ancient India this principle was used to attract beautiful and abnormally intelligent children into a family. The woman would visualize herself making love to a divine being, such as Krishna, in the belief that some of the godly qualities would become part of the new child. Several Hindu texts refer to this technique and attest to its success. The Greeks taught that imagination plays an important role in the type of child conceived. Hesiod and Empedocles (*circa* 440 B.C.) both cite the significance of fantasy to physiognomy; later, Hippocrates and the celebrated physician Soranus supported this view, as did Aristotle and Pliny.

In most healthy relationships both partners are deeply in love with each other and look to exalted qualities in the partner; these qualities are manifest in their offspring. In the Tantric approach to love-making the visualization of the couple as god and goddess creates an ideal psychic atmosphere for the conception of beautiful, intelligent and "godly" children.

In the ancient cultures of the East there is a consistent tradition that the sex of a future child can be controlled by careful attention to the diet of the would-be mother in the months before conception. Hindu texts declare that if a woman wants a boy child, then she should eat salty foods, whereas for a girl child, sweet foods should be chosen. Recent experiments in Canada and France (by Dr. Jacques Lorrain and Dr. Joseph Stolkowski) have shown an 80 percent success rate in pre-determining sex of offspring by restricting the would-be mother's diet. Saltier foods increase the mother's potassium and sodium content, and indeed create a higher incidence of male births. Fine wine or beer, as well as most vegetables, provide high concentrations of potassium and sodium salts. Sweet foods, and dairy products in particular, have high calcium and magnesium contents, and if a woman restricts her diet to these items in the two months prior to conception, she is more likely to conceive a female child.

Eastern traditions view contraception primarily as matter of personal choice. If a woman *wishes* to become pregnant while making love with a virile partner, then the Eastern view is that conception is likely; on the other hand, if she does *not* want to become pregnant, her psyche will inhibit and reject the sperm. The *living sensitivity* of sperm, which maintain a subtle or psychic contact with the man, is responsible for their *receptivity* to mental messages from the couple. The time in the woman's periodic cycle is also important since when a woman ovulates, her mental and physical conditions *attract* conception. The Yoni of an ovulating woman contains a mucus that reacts to the sperm and energizes it, thereby increasing the likelihood of conception. A sensitive woman can tell when she is ovulating by distinct changes in her emotions (she becomes more sensual and "motherly"), her body odor, her Yoni secretions and her vision. Recent experiments have shown that during ovulation a woman's vision improves considerably.

The possibility of mental control in conception or contraception is supported by the findings of Verrier Elwin, a theologian and anthropologist who spent many years living with the Muria tribe of India. The Murias believe that "a girl can only become pregnant when she binds herself to a man *in her mind*, and remains physically true to him." According to Elwin, "This conviction that a girl needs to bind herself to a man before she can become pregnant must have anchored itself so deep into the consciousness of the Murias that it is very effective. Until such time as a Muria girl marries, she rarely conceives, even though there is full sexual freedom. But once she commits herself to a man, then she soon becomes pregnant." Many primitive tribal people use this method of birth control exclusively, with up to 96 percent reliability, and see the mental attitude toward conception as an integral part of the process of conception itself.

Contraceptive drugs have been widely known in the East since ancient times; among the ingredients used in contraceptive preparations are carrot seeds, datura seeds, nutmeg, castor-oil plants, camphor, cloves, opium, lemon, sesame seeds and special herbs. Recently some of these have been tested and proved effective. They work through altering glandular secretions in both male and female, through changing the Yoni secretions so that they inhibit the free movement of sperm and through directly influencing the ovulation cycle. In India there are numerous indigenous drugs with contraceptive properties; these are referred to in the extensive Ayurvedic literature and are also known in folk medicine. Though not all these traditional contraceptive drugs are wholly effective, their use should not be discounted as "old wives' tales." Far too few of these traditional Eastern contraceptive drugs have been adequately tested by Western science.

Another form of contraceptive used in the East employs a combination of device and drug. For example, the women of ancient Sumatra molded opium into a cup-like shape and inserted it into their Yonis, fitting it over the cervix just like a modern cervical cap, but with the additional spermicide effect of the opium. Another variation known in the Orient is called *Musgami*, which is an oiled silky paper cervical cap, used in the same way. Other cervical caps are recorded as being made from beeswax and, simplest of all, from a half-lemon squeezed out and inserted over the cervix; the juice of the lemon is also a spermicide.

It may come as a surprise to learn that intrauterine devices were used in Egypt and the ancient East. The *Kamaratna Tantra* states that "If a piece of the root of a datura plant is placed in the uterus before cohabitation, there will be no impregnation." Other texts refer to the effectiveness of placing a coiled-up castor-oil plant root into the uterus prior to love-making.

Astrological birth control has been known in the East since ancient times. However, this is an obscure area, veiled in superstition and certainly fortified by personal belief in a particular astrologer or astrological system. There are no hard and fast rules in this area, and it may be that the effectiveness of some astrological birth control is largely psychological. Also in this category are magical methods of birth control such as the use of charms and amulets, a popular and sometimes effective method known throughout the East. A generally reliable rule in this area is that an *exceptionally charismatic* astrologer or magician *is* able to create contraceptive circumstances consistently, whereas *the method alone* does *not* produce reliable results.

Advanced Tantric couples can develop conscious control over conception, just as the advanced Yogi learns to control ejaculation. It is the mental attitude that is of prime importance. If control of the mind is linked to physical techniques such as retention, reabsorption and breath control, contraceptive devices will play a less important role in loving.

THE PILL

The contraceptive pill is the most popular birth-control method in use in the West. First developed commercially in 1960–61, using synthetic progesterone (produced after natural progesterone was found in great concentrations in a certain species of Mexican wild yam) and estrogen hormones to suppress ovulation, the pill was quickly hailed as the answer to the world's population problem. Simple to use, cheap to produce and highly effective, the birth-control pill seemed to be a panacea.

The advent of the birth-control pill brought with it a revolutionary change in attitudes toward sexuality; no longer would women have to suffer continual anxiety about getting pregnant. The great advantage to the pill is that it enables a couple to make love spontaneously. Another apparent attraction is that a woman who is "on the pill" usually has much lighter and more regular monthly periods and commonly does not have the sudden mood changes normally associated with menstruation.

Unfortunately, birth-control pills were rather hurriedly put on the market. Progesterone and estrogen are ovarian hormones that inhibit the pituitary gland, thus interrupting the natural cycle of hormone production in the body. Though research had shown that estrogen is cancer-producing, this hormone was included in the first birth-control pills in a concentration ten times greater than necessary for the required effect. Not surprisingly, numerous unpleasant and sometimes fatal side effects of the birth-control pill have been recorded. At least 15 percent of all contraception pill users report serious side effects, despite the fact that the last eighteen years of research have produced a marked improvement in birth-control pill formulation.

Some women are more adversely affected than others. One of the most common results of prolonged birth-control usage is an alteration in metabolism that creates unwanted physical changes, such as a sudden increase in weight, larger breasts and hips, and often complex psychological changes.

A woman who is using birth-control pills is cut off from her natural lunar rhythm, both biologically and psychologically. Her whole metabolism changes. A woman on the pill is robbed of her copulins, the powerful scent of her Yoni secretions, which are very specific short-chain aliphatic acids *having a definite stimulatory effect on the male sex drive*. Tantric and Taoist love-making, with its emphasis on natural sexual urges, is thus threatened by the unnatural use of contraceptive pills. Synthetic hormones commonly have the effect of reducing libido. The sexuality researchers Masters and Johnson report that when a woman complains of loss of ability to come to orgasm, the first question to ask is whether or not she has been taking birth-control pills. Frequently the answer is yes. A further disadvantage of birth-control pills is that they greatly change the acid-alkaline balance of the Yoni secretions, making the user more vulnerable to venereal infections. According to Barbara and Gideon Seaman, who have researched birth-control extensively, "women who take the pill with estrogen in it neither ovulate nor menstruate, but have something called 'withdrawal bleeding' which resembles menstruation." In their comprehensive book entitled *Women and the Crisis in Sex Hormones*, the Seamans give valuable advice to women recovering from the cumulative adverse effects of hormone usage. Vitamin therapy, especially vitamins B_6, B_{12}, C and E, is helpful in overcoming adverse symptoms in women who have been on the pill for some time. Vitamin and mineral deficiencies are common in women who use birth-control pills and ginseng is one of the most effective remedies available for counteracting these adverse reactions.

A number of birth-control pills for men are already on the market, though their purported use is to help overcome impotence, senility and various bone diseases. These pills are made of combinations of estrogen with high concentrations of androgen (a male sex hormone), and have the effect of increasing the sex drive while at the same time lowering the sperm count. However, their use in some instances has resulted in loss of virility and marked psychological and physiological changes.

The decision whether or not to use contraceptive pills must rest with the individual and her or his doctor. Some brands are less dangerous than others, and some people can use birth-control pills without adverse side effects. However, in recent years there has been a dramatic and sensible swing away from contraceptive pills and toward other birth-control methods.

OTHER BIRTH-CONTROL METHODS

Birth-control methods apart from the contraceptive pill include intrauterine devices such as IUDs (for example, the "copper seven"), diaphragms, cervical caps, condoms or sheaths, as well as spermicides (foams and jellies), sterilization, lunaception (the "safe period" or "rhythm method"), astrological birth control, Karezza, thermatic method, abortion and other related procedures.

There are many different types of IUDs or "coils." The best-known and smallest coil available in the West is the "copper seven," which is easily fitted and, once inserted, needs no further attention. The disadvan-tages of IUDs are that, if incorrectly fitted, they can cause discomfort or possibly perforate the uterus, or may sometimes be expelled without the woman's knowing. They can also cause intrauterine infection and tend to increase the length and heaviness of the period. IUD users often lose several times the normal amount of iron during their periods, though copper-based IUDs may help control this loss to some extent. When fitted by an expert, the IUD is an effective, unobtrusive birth-control method.

Diaphragms, of which there are numerous types, are made of rubber or plastic. The diaphragm is fitted by a doctor, and thereafter the woman inserts it herself, before intercourse. The fitting must be good, and spermicides must be used to ensure reliability. A woman should be refitted every year or two, or after a pregnancy. The diaphragm is held in place by the inner muscles of the Yoni. It has recently been suggested that a diaphragm may tend to slip if the woman takes a very active and superior role in love-making. Otherwise, the diaphragm is one of the safest and most reliable birth-control methods.

The *Cervical cap* is a thimble-like cap of rubber or polyethylene that fits tightly over the cervix, the neck of the womb. It naturally adjusts to the slight changes in shape and size of the cervix during the monthly cycle and can be kept in place, except during menstruation, or it can be inserted and removed at will. However, the cervical cap is held in place by vacuum suction, and the caps currently available are suitable only for women with prominent cervixes or strong uterine suction. Another drawback is that doctors endorse its reliability only in conjunction with the use

of spermicides. In nineteenth-century Europe women used cervical caps made from beeswax. Perhaps a custom-made cervical cap will emerge that will be suited to every woman and prove reliable without the use of spermicides.

Many different *condoms* or *sheaths* are in use today. All have the disadvantage of cutting off any physical or subtle exchange between the Lingam and Yoni during love-making. A condom or sheath acts as an insulator, preventing the establishment of the natural electro-magnetic field during sexual union, and as a barrier to the blending of vital essences and secretions. Oriental condoms are generaly one half to one third as thick as those in use in the West. Subsequently, there is more sensitivity with these than with Occidental varieties.

Spermicides (foams and jellies) are effective when used in conjunction with other barrier methods, but have the disadvantage of altering the chemistry of love (the subtle secretions) as well as interrupting and limiting love-play. Oral sex and prolonged foreplay are restricted by the use of modern spermicides. Natural spermicides have been known in the East since ancient times. Many unguents and erotic ointments of the Orient are in fact spermicides. Essential oils extracted from plants and blends that incorporate sandalwood and camphor in particular alter the sexual secretions and can produce a natural spermicidal effect.

Sterilization is anathema in the Tantric tradition, and medically suspect as well. Too little is yet known about the true role of the reproductive and related glandular systems. Though sterilization has become quite common, there are disturbing side effects with this form of birth control. The technique for women involves cutting, cauterizing or blocking both fallopian tubes so that the sperm cannot reach the ovum. After sterilization, women sometimes suffer severe menstrual complaints and psychological depression. Male sterilization, or vasectomy, is accomplished by cutting, tying or blocking the small internal tubes (the *vas deferens*) that carry the sperm from the testicles to the Lingam. As a result, sperm leaks into the bloodstream and can produce, in some men, complex physiological and psychological reactions, though it is said that most men eventually develop an "immunity" to their own sperm.

Lunaception is a form of birth control that attempts to understand the lunar cycle and its relationship to ovulation. In ancient times women's cycles were generally in natural harmony with the phases of the moon, with ovulation occurring at the full moon and menstruation at the new moon. Louise Lacey's book *Lunaception* gives a concise account of how she experimented, sleeping in a lit room for three nights (the fourteenth, fifteenth and sixteenth nights of her cycle) to induce ovulation and regulate her periods. She found that by the fourth month her periods and ovulations kept perfect step with the new and full moons. By regulating the menstrual cycle, the "fertile period" can be precisely known and intercourse with ejaculation can be avoided during this time.

A woman has a menstrual cycle of approximately twenty-eight days. If we count the day of menstruation as the first day of that cycle, then by the fifth day (in most women) the period is over. At this time the body temperature is slightly *lower* than normal. By the ninth day the so-called *fertile period* begins, and lasts until about the seventeenth day. The peak days, when ovulation takes place, are around the thirteenth or fourteenth day of the woman's natural lunar cycle, at which time the body temperature is slightly *higher* than normal. After the eighteenth day, through to the onset of menstruation, there is a so-called *safe period*, when love-making with ejaculation very rarely creates pregnancy.

There is some dispute as to whether the days immediately following menstruation (day five) through to the onset of the fertile period (day nine) are another safe period. The Eastern view is that the days immediately after menstruation are in fact the most conducive to conception *provided that love-making is completely harmonious and that the semen of the man is potent*. Since the sperm, which actually effects pregnancy, may require several days to swim up the fallopian tubes, we can clearly see that love-making immediately after menstruation has a high risk of causing pregnancy unless some type of contraceptive measure or retention is employed.

It is difficult to determine precisely when ovulation takes place, particularly if a woman is not living a natural lifestyle. Only about 70 percent of modern women have a clearly discernible mucous or temperature pattern, and far fewer have a reliable twenty-eight-day cycle. Drugs, birth-control pills and tranquilizers can easily throw off ovulation. However, a number of devices and methods have been developed to try to determine ovulation and, as a result, the safe period. These techniques consist in the measuring of temperature changes, electrical potential variations or Yoni secretions. A recent invention is the Ovutimer, a small device into which a woman inserts small samples of her cervical mucus as she approaches ovulation. The Ovutimer measures the thickness of the mucous secretions and thus gives an indication of the exact day of ovulation. One hazard of this method of birth control is that particularly passionate love-making can bring on a woman's ovulation prematurely. Nevertheless, some people successfully use the *safe period* or *rhythm method* of birth control.

The Tantric approach to safe-period birth control is that devices should not be needed to determine ovulation or the likelihood of conception. Conscious body awareness and knowledge of the body cycle should be sufficient for a woman to *know* whether or not she is near ovulation. Mental control is a highly important factor also, and it may be that in the future, with the development of self-hypnosis techniques, this method will become practical for Westerners. Sensitivity is the key to mental control. Parapsychological tests have shown that, during the time of the full moon, ESP scores rise dramatically with sensitive subjects. That ovulation in women was once linked to the full moon gives us an interesting insight into the sexual rites commonly associated with this time of the month.

Astrological birth control is still in its infancy in the West and there is some dispute as to its effectiveness. It was first presented by Dr. Jonas, a Czechoslovakian, who found a constantly repeating cycle that correlates the angles of the sun and moon to periods of fertility. He claims to have found that a woman's *most* fertile period is the twenty-four hours immediately preceding the sun-moon "angle" *at which the woman was born*. Abstention from intercourse for about three

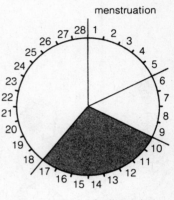

Chart showing the lunar cycle of woman, with menstruation and fertile periods marked.

days during the periods when solar-lunar angles are repeated (which is about thirteen times a year) is said to reliably prevent conception. In 1970 Kurt Rechnitz claimed he had verified Jonas's findings on astrological birth control and, in a study of more than twelve hundred cases, he found the system 97 percent effective. From a Tantric viewpoint, the sun-moon angle of a person's birth *is* tremendously significant since it determines the balance of solar and lunar energies in the psycho-organism. Since the event of birth leaves a powerful psychic imprint, it may be that the recurring cycle of solar-lunar influences programs ovulation. However, too little research has yet been completed in this area to ensure reliability.

Karezza was a technique developed by Alice Stockham and first written about by her in 1896. Her book *Karezza: Ethics of Marriage* outlines the basic Eastern view and teachings on retention. This method of birth control is similar to *coitus interruptus*, with the use of Yogic techniques of breath control, meditation, postures and finger pressure at specific points to aid retention of semen. Used on its own, the Karezza method is not 100 percent effective, since there is the risk

Taoist love-posture and hand movements used to aid retention. From a Chinese painting of the nineteenth century.

that small amounts of semen might be inadvertently released during love-making. Nor is the exclusive use of retention healthful, since it can cause a blockage of subtle channels in the body and lead to a buildup of sexual "pressure" in the body. Another disadvantage of this technique is that it prohibits *mutual absorption*. Karezza is well known in the Orient; the Arabs called it *Imsak* and used it effectively to overcome problems of premature ejaculation or loss of virility. However, Karezza alone is neither a complete love-making technique nor a complete birth-control method.

The *thermatic method* of birth control is an ancient Oriental technique that was rediscovered by Martha Voegeli and has been promoted in India since 1912. This is a temporary method of sterilization that works by elevating the scrotal temperature by just a few degrees; it has proved highly effective in some men. Voegeli's method requires that the man take a daily forty-five-minute bath in water at a temperature of 116° F. for twenty-one days consecutively. The man then remains sterile for six months, after which time normal fertility returns. The treatment can be repeated without danger of total impotence or total sterilization. However, it does create glandular changes that may create long-term side effects. Too little research has been completed to date to assure its safety.

Abortion is not a contraceptive, since it involves the termination of a conception. Some primitive tribes have used it as a birth-control method, and it is becoming increasingly popular in the West today. However, the Tantric view of abortion is that it inevitably creates Karmic problems that are best avoided.

All birth-control methods involve some degree of risk, inconvenience or chance of pregnancy. The choice of method must rest with the individual. Astrological birth control and mental birth control may someday be effective if sufficient research is done on these methods.

Of all the devices outlined, the IUD is the method least likely to interfere with the experience and chemistry of love. Further research may yield reliable organic IUDs or perhaps new types of cervical caps that will prove to be more effective, practical and acceptable than those currently available.

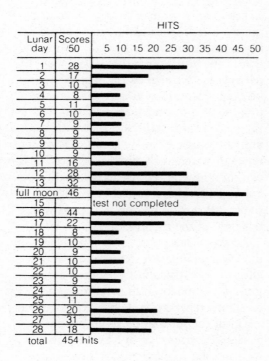

Lunar day	Scores /50	HITS 5 10 15 20 25 30 35 40 45 50
1	28	
2	17	
3	10	
4	8	
5	11	
6	10	
7	9	
8	9	
9	8	
10	9	
11	16	
12	28	
13	32	
full moon	46	
15		test not completed
16	44	
17	22	
18	8	
19	10	
20	9	
21	10	
22	10	
23	9	
24	9	
25	11	
26	20	
27	31	
28	18	
total	454 hits	

Chart showing how ESP scores vary according to the phases of the moon. The highest scores occur during the full and new moon. From *Beyond Telepathy* by Andrija Puharich.

sexual aids

Sexual aids are mentioned in the *Kama Sutra* as well as in a number of Indian and Chinese texts. They are divided into two distinct categories: *drugs* and *implements*. We deal with the former category in the section entitled "Aphrodisiacs," which follows.

Implements, or *love instruments*, are devices used to augment or substitute for the sexual organs. Ancient texts describe various devices to be put on or over the Lingam to supplement its length or thickness. These were made of gold, silver, copper, ivory, horn, wood, cane or even jade; many different types are described in Chinese, Japanese and Indian literature. There are accounts of special rings, often of jade, that fitted around the base of the Lingam and had a protruding part, which was used to stimulate the woman's clitoris during love-making. Such sexual aids were considered "innovations" to be used when needed. They were by no means presented as the ideal way to make love, and were generally considered desensitizing and unnecessary.

Orthodox Hindu lawbooks prohibit the use of substitute Lingams or "dildos," on the grounds that they are "insults to Shiva, whose Lingam is ever-erect." Hindu medical texts state that if hard inanimate objects are inserted into the Yoni, they are liable to cause long-term physical problems for the woman. The *Kama Sutra* suggests that only *natural* objects be used as dildos, and cites bananas, mangoes, carrots, radishes, cucumbers, the stalks of plants or mushrooms, gourds and other fruits or vegetables that resemble the erect Lingam in shape and texture. The same text adds that "a reed made soft with oil and tied to the waist with ribbons may be used in connection with or in the place of the Lingam."

Chinese and Japanese texts refer to the double-dildo, an implement made of treated roots, horn, wood or ivory, with two silk bands attached to the middle. One woman could insert an end of it into her own Yoni, fastening it with ribbons tied around her waist. She then could satisfy a girl friend with the prominent end of the shaft, while herself enjoying the friction produced from the movement of the other end inside her.

Chinese Lingam ring, with dragon motifs, *circa* eighteenth century.

Japanese artificial Lingam for use as a dildo (*Harigata*). Made from horn, *circa* eighteenth century.

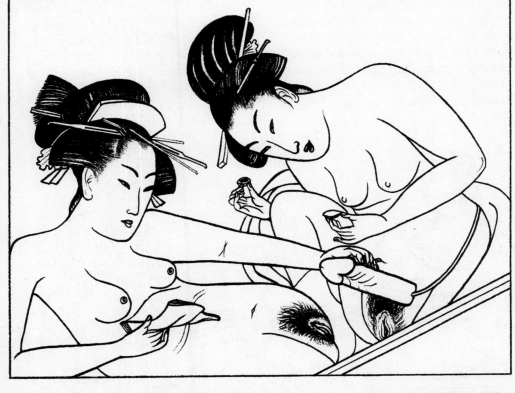

Japanese women using an artificial Lingam (*Harigata*) to satisfy each other. From a color print by Chokyosai Eisho, *circa* 1800.

Two ladies making love with a substitute Lingam between them. From a Chinese painting of the eighteenth century.

Playful sexual dalliance on a swing. From a Chinese painting of the eighteenth century.

Lovers using belt or sling as a sexual aid. From a Japanese painted scroll of the early seventeenth century.

Another Oriental innovation, used by women for self-satisfaction, is known as the *Burmese Bell*. This consists of a pair of small hollow spheres made of silver, one containing a drop of mercury and the other having a metal "tongue" that vibrates and produces a tinkling sound when moved. These twin spheres are carefully inserted into the woman's Yoni and held in place by a piece of silk cloth. When she rocks her body or walks around, the movement of the mercury creates a gentle vibration inside her and a pleasant sound is produced. In China this sexual aid was called *Mien-ling* (literally "exertion bell"), and in Japan a similar device was named *Ri-no-tama*. Modern sex shops offer related gadgets as well as a whole range of vibrators. Unfortunately, most of these are mass-produced from synthetic materials and are badly designed, aesthetically ugly and potentially damaging to the human body.

Innovative sexual aid, using a bow. From a late Mughal painting, *circa* 1690.

Love-making is best when it is uncomplicated by external aids. Foreplay is recommended by the *Kama Sutra* and other authoritative texts, especially when a man is unable to satisfy a woman easily. The Yoni of a woman should not be penetrated until she is excited and naturally lubricated. Nowadays many different creams, gels and oils are sold for lubricating the sexual organs. These commercial preparations are really unnecessary. In most cases, the excitement of sexual contact will produce more than sufficient sexual secretions to allow for comfortable entry. Saliva can also be used most effectively, and it has the advantage of containing essential and magical properties.

Anything inserted into the Yoni should be soft enough not to harm its internal parts. A Japanese text advises that if a dildo is used, it should first be warmed by immersing it in warm water or oil. For playful variations of love-making, organic sex aids such as fruits (which can be eaten afterward) should be used.

A complete survey of sexual aids should include playful devices like swings, rocking chairs or beds, water jets and inventions spontaneously conceived of in the ecstasies of loving. The whole environment can be thought of as a sexual aid, so take care to make it beautiful and suitable. The human body itself has a wealth of possibilities in the limbs, hands, fingers, toes, chin, nose,

breasts and tongue. Create your own sexual aids, if you find you need them. But, according to Tantra, the *direct* contact between bodies has a special potency that can never be matched by substitutes.

Furniture can be used as a sexual aid by helping maintain new positions. From a color print of the Ming dynasty.

Sexual aids should be slightly soft, provocative of vigor and well fitted to suit the intended purpose. Made according to the natural liking of the individual, they are always to be used carefully.

KAMA SUTRA

Golden Lotus took his silken gown. Something dropped out of the sleeve and fell tinkling to the ground. She picked it up and weighed it in her hand. It was like a little ball, but very heavy. She looked at it for a long time, but could not imagine what it was for.
"What is it?" she said. "And why does it seem so heavy?"
"Don't you know?" he said, laughing. "They call it the Bell of Fecundity, and it comes from Burma, a country somewhere in the South. A good one is worth four or five measures of silver."
"Where is it to be put?" the woman asked.
"First put it inside you, and then get on with what has to be done. The results are quite indescribable."

CHIN P'ING MEI

aphrodisiacs

In the Orient deer's antlers are valued for their aphrodisiacal properties.

Marijuana; the secretions from the female plant have strong aphrodisiacal properties.

Many aphrodisiacs are listed in Eastern sexological works. Some of them have merely a placebo effect, but others are actually effective on the physical level. Many foods can be prepared in such a way as to release vitalizing forces. Healthy food and a natural lifestyle are by far the most effective aphrodisiacs. Fresh air, water and fire all have the power to stimulate sexuality, as does the harmonious contact of the senses with objects of enjoyment. An often quoted Oriental saying is, "The most natural aphrodisiac for a man is a beautiful woman, passionately asking to be enjoyed."

Fasting can have an aphrodisiacal effect on the body, provided it is practiced in moderation. Yoga and breathing exercises can greatly help to stimulate the natural vitality of the body; if these are combined with meditation, so that the mind is freed of anxiety, then there will rarely be any need for physical aphrodisiacs. A healthy mind and a creative imagination together produce a "climate" in which all things are possible.

Aphrodisiacs are normally included as topics in works pertaining to the Art of Love. Generally it is taught that a substance that *resembles the sexual organs* is likely to act as an aphrodisiac if correctly prepared. This concept is known as the *Doctrine of Signatures*, and evolved from the observation that herbs, plants or other substances with a particular appearance, color, shape or smell were effective in curing ailments linked by similar characteristics. An example of this is the Indian mango, which resembles the kidneys in shape and is an effective natural cure for some cases of kidney disease.

Correct preparation is very important when using any aphrodisiac. A specialized branch of Indian medicine is devoted to this study. Aphrodisiacs may be broadly categorized under three main headings: the animal, the vegetable and the mineral. These categories are kept separate or combined to produce the whole range of aphrodisiacs that are suited to the condition and temperament of the individual.

Animal substances include eggs (of various birds), different kinds of milk (but especially goat milk), wild fowl, sparrows, peacocks, the flesh of vigorous animals, mussels, oysters, sea horses, fish eggs (caviar), especially vigorous fish (salmon) and animal parts such as deer horn, musk pods, ambergris from whales, rhinoceros horn, and a whole range of animal sex organs. For these products to be effective, they must come from animals in the wild, hunted in the right season and when the animals are in good health.

Vegetable aphrodisiacs are even more numerous, and their preparation requires even more care. Among those included in traditional Eastern works are: ginger root, fennel, ginseng root, mushrooms, black beans, particular kinds of onions, gourds, carrots, wild asparagus, wild rhubarb, figs, licorice, almonds, pistachio nuts, pine kernels, sesame seeds, cinnamon bark, nutmeg, saffron, black pepper, raisins, walnuts, honey (from particular flowers), glutinous millet, tree bark, orange seeds, aconite root, opium husks, damiana, datura, marijuana, as well as fortified "wines" made from grapes, pomegranates, wild flowers and herbs. As is the case with animal substances, these should be of high quality and gathered in the correct season.

Mineral aphrodisiacs listed in Eastern medical works include mineral pitch ("Shilajeet"), stalactites, mercury, sulphur, mica, arsenic, conch shell, cowries, pearls, calcinated gold, silver, copper, iron, amber, coral, emerald, sapphire, ruby and diamond. The preparation of mineral aphrodisiacs is extremely complex and a science in itself, known in India as *Rasayana*.

Ginseng has been used for thousands of years for its regenerative and aphrodisiac properties. Recently it has been tested by Western science and shown to have a real effect. The red ginseng root gives the best results, but it should not be taken continually. A forty-day course of ginseng extract (or powdered root), followed by three months without its use, is a typical prescription that works in most cases. The exact dose is determined according to the strength of the individual root and the physical condition of the person.

An aphrodisiac tea can be made from a combination of select spices and dried ginseng root. Equal amounts of cinnamon bark and green cardamom should be pounded together with pestle and mortar. An amount of fresh ginger root equal to their combined volume should be added and crushed. Then about nine black peppercorns, two or three cloves, some ground nutmeg (not too much) and a pinch of saffron should be added. The whole mixture should then be boiled gently for nine minutes. When the decoction is complete, it should be strained and a tea should be made from it in the normal way, but with the addition of crushed ginseng root. The tea should be allowed to stand for some time and can be served either hot or cold, with or without milk. Honey can be added as a pleasant and stimulative sweetener.

There are many aphrodisiacs that can be applied directly to the sexual organs. They are effective mainly through their heating or cooling qualities. Sandalwood oil mixed with a little crushed ginger and cinnamon is one of the most effective of these recipes. Oil of cloves diluted with a base oil, or camphor and oil in combination, can produce invigorating results. However, considerable care should be taken in using such preparations. Particularly dangerous are aphrodisiacs that work through irritation of the sex organs: "Spanish fly" or cantharides, the powder of blister beetles or insects, has been recorded as causing many casualties by this means.

It is worth repeating that a healthy lifestyle is the most consistent of all aphrodisiacs. It really is preferable not to have to rely on external aids for a satisfactory sex life. Then the use of aphrodisiacs on very special occasions can make a real difference.

The ginseng root has long been valued as a powerful aphrodisiac.

The use of aphrodisiacs should be learned from a study of the science of medicine, from the religious texts, from those who are learned in the art of magic, and from confidential relatives. No means should be tried that are doubtful in their effects, or that are likely to cause injury to the body, that involve causing the death of animals, and that bring a person into contact with impure things.

KAMA SUTRA

There is a limit to what aphrodisiacal ointments can do. At the most they can stretch one's endurance for a bit. If you apply an aphrodisiac to a naturally powerful instrument, it is as if a gifted and well-prepared candidate should take a ginseng stimulant just before his examination. He will feel doubly fresh and alert, and his dissertation will pour out on its own accord. On the other hand, a lover whose implement is naturally feeble will no more be fortified by aphrodisiacs or ointments than an ignorant and untalented candidate would be helped by drugs, even if he consumes whole pounds of ginseng before his examination.

JOU PU TUAN

sex education

Children have an eager curiosity and mental flexibility that enable them to learn new things easily. A child's degree of understanding should never be underestimated. Sexual education can begin at a very early age. Sexuality is best introduced to the child as part of a loving and truthful family relationship. Nakedness within the home should not be discouraged and the child's body awareness should be cultivated. If parents express a lack of inhibition and guilt about nakedness and sexuality, their attitude will be reflected by the child.

Secrecy and stories concocted to shield the child from the truths of sexuality will only confuse the child and lead to guilt and neurosis. Children see through hypocrisy and are sensitive to, and affected by, the guilt feelings of others. A child should learn to view the body as a Temple of Love, a shrine to be shared only with those who are trusted and loved. Children can readily learn all the basic Tantric practices outlined in Part I of this book—the creative attitude, self-examination, Hatha Yoga, breathing, food awareness, diet, hygiene, bathing, Dream Yoga, massage, meditation, visualization and so on—and this can constitute the basic grounding of their sex education. Example and shared participation in these activities are by far the best teaching method. Feelings of sexuality are an integral part of the experience of growing up, and should be explored in an atmosphere of openness, rather than viewed as a hidden or unmentionable experience. In this way the sudden traumas often associated with "revealing the facts of life" can be avoided. These "facts" should form the basis of what will be, for the child, a gradual familiarization with the full spectrum of love.

Children should be made familiar with depictions of sexual and sensual love, so that they develop a positive and healthy attitude to the images of love. Children have an innate sense of the truth; the best teaching method is direct and sensitive, incorporating sex education into the child's initiation into the greater mysteries of life.

Intimacy should pervade the family atmosphere. Encourage mutual bathing and massage, as well as shared participation in Yoga, dance, music, song and household chores. "Sharing" is one of the most important factors for healthful intimacy in the family. Everyone has a selfish streak, and it is important to evolve out of selfishness and into a deep and compassionate awareness of the needs of others. Any situation that creates jealousies between children should be confronted early on, through a family "sharing" of all facets of the problem. This is the test of real love and is the ground for a healthful approach to sexuality.

Boys and girls are essentially very different; they should therefore be treated differently. A boy is interested primarily in the *logic* of life and looks for *answers* to every kind of question. Sex is a fascinating topic, even at an early age. Therefore logical and direct answers should be given to questions pertaining to sexuality. A boy should be taught sexual hygiene, how to wash his Lingam properly and also the importance of keeping the anus clean. He should be told about erections, so he doesn't feel guilty when they manifest. A boy-child represents a dominant Yang-force, the Solar Power, the Heavens, the aggressive and expansive qualities of consciousness. All these have to be refined and developed by right upbringing and education.

A girl is interested especially in the *emotions* of life and desires to *intuit* answers to life's questions. If parents recognize this basic difference in the approach to learning in males and females, there will be a discernible change in the child's attitude to education. A girl-child represents a dominant Yin-force, the Lunar Power, the Earth, the submissive and contractive qualities of consciousness. A girl tends to experience the world largely through sensory impressions. For a girl, the best introduction to sexuality is through refinement in the arts. A girl should be told to expect menstruation and be familiarized with her mother's menstrual procedures. She should be prepared, so that she can look forward to the time when she "becomes a woman."

Though there are male and female sides to each individual, sexuality springs from the dominance of one or the other gender. Thus, an enlightened approach to sex education pre-supposes that the inherent psycho-physical differences between the sexes are made use of. One of the most recurrent findings of psychology is that there is an inherent difference in the abilities of the two sexes. Boys naturally build towers while girls build enclosures; boys are better at spatial thinking, numbers and logical problems, whereas girls generally learn to read earlier, speak earlier and are better at perceiving emotions. Boys are generally more successful than girls in solving problems that require manipulation, have better daylight vision and are able to withstand greater extremes of heat than girls, who usually have better night vision, are able to tolerate greater extremes of cold and can process information more rapidly.

Children should be taught firmly and generously. It is quite common for a child to try to "gain ascendancy" over one or the other parent in an attempt to monopolize the family environment. All children respect authority if it is consistent and direct. Discipline in the home is important to all aspects of education, including sex education. Children should not be given unlimited access to everything all at once, just as in Tantra the mystery teachings are reserved for those who are adequately prepared. It is the duty of parents to prepare their children *for the world*, rather than use them as vehicles for their own self-indulgence. Too often we see children mirroring parental neuroses with a naive innocence that often leads to deep-seated emotional problems later in life. Most of these problems are rooted in a lack of correct sex education, either through the bad example of parents or through a breakdown in family communication.

In most families, it is inevitable that children will overhear or see their parents making love. Though the mystery and magic of sexual union should be reserved as something to look forward to, as something sacred and special, children should not be kept unaware of the actual mechanics of sex. Rather than being left completely in the dark about "how mommy and daddy do it," or pushed into voyeurism to satisfy their natural curiosity, children should be gradually introduced to the realities of love-making. A door can be deliberately kept open, the child can be asked to light incense and bring flowers and refreshments while parents are

In the Orient children learn about sexuality very early in life. From a Japanese color print by Suzuki Harunobu, *circa* 1766.

expressing intimacy. There need not be blatant exposure, but rather a subtle sharing of the atmosphere of sexuality, so that the child naturally becomes aware of "what it's all about." It is completely natural for a mother to bring her baby into bed with her and husband, even to nurse a child while making love. Likewise, children should be invited into the bedroom when a couple are in intimate embrace, since the atmosphere of love can only be healthful. By entering the magic circle of love, children can receive a deep initiation into sexuality.

Since ancient times illustrated sex manuals have played an important role in Oriental cultures. We have endeavored to make this book both an education into the nature of sexuality and an initiation into the real meaning of the creative function. Love-making is *the most natural* of all activities, and one in which shame has no part. The whole history of sexual neurosis in the West is rooted in the repression of sexuality and inadequate sex education. With the right approach to sexuality, life will become a more meaningful and joyous experience, the alchemy of ecstasy itself.

Sex is not a taboo topic in Oriental cultures. The most natural of human acts, it should not be treated as a secret vice. From a Chinese print of the Ming dynasty.

VISHNU

the preserver

summary of secrets

Intimacies in the Love Pavilion. From a Japanese Chuban color print by Koryusai, *circa* 1770.

Both Tantric and Taoist teachings present an enlightened view of sexuality that has much to contribute to Western culture. These teachings do not simply ask you to reconsider your *attitude* toward sex; rather, they offer a practical and evolutionary way of life in which sexuality is given a spiritual purpose. Now that social hierarchies have lost their meaning and rulers have abandoned their function as ambassadors of the gods, the Sexual Secrets are finding their way into the mainstream of thought. No longer limited to the select few, these secrets offer deep insights into the real nature and purpose of existence. The teachings are eternal, optimistic and transcendental; the holistic view of sexuality that they describe reaches from this world to the next, beyond even the limitations of life and death.

In the East sex was traditionally regarded as a high art form worthy of respect. Instead of viewing sexuality as a taboo topic, with all the inevitable negative associations, people saw this most natural of all acts as auspicious, venerable, even "lucky." In practicing the Sexual Secrets, a couple will find an ideal vehicle for realizing the true equality between man and woman. Freed from sexual frustration, inhibitions and feelings of guilt, couples will experience themselves moving closer and closer together, rather than further apart.

Both Tantra and Taoism teach that incorrect sexual attitudes and practices are the underlying cause not only of psychological but of physical and spiritual problems as well. Positively oriented sexuality offers the most direct and harmonious method of resolving these problems.

We hope that this book will provide a fertile ground of reference for individuals and couples wishing to participate in the universal nourishing force of sensual ecstasy. When one's sexuality is brought into harmony with one's natural spirituality, a whole new dimension of reality opens up. It is our contention that the acceptance of guilt-free, creative sexuality is a panacea for many modern psychological ills.

Don't be distressed if it seems that progress is slow. Sudden breakthroughs can be expected, once there is a high level of commitment and the earnest desire to succeed. Try to develop a dynamic sense of expectancy as well as an openness and awareness of both your own and your partner's sexuality. Though both the theories and practical techniques outlined in this book are of great help, it is the *wisdom of the heart*, the higher aspects of love, that reveal the Sexual Secrets. This intuitive wisdom is accessible to all who recognize the interrelationship between sexuality and spirituality.

Sexual liberation implies the liberation of the whole being: body, mind and spirit. This holistic viewpoint is an essential ingredient to the understanding of the Sexual Secrets. Once viewed in this way, the secrets will help you become better lovers as well as initiate you into the beauty, spirituality, science and mysticism of sex.

It is not necessary to abandon one's religious beliefs in order to practice the Sexual Secrets, nor is it necessary to adopt Hindu, Buddhist, Tantric or Taoist viewpoints. The Sexual Secrets are to be found in all great religions, but many of the teachings have been obscured or lost; only in Tantra and Taoism are the Sexual Secrets preserved intact. It is the *principles* described in this work that are important. The Sexual Secrets are not a dogma; rather, they are a collection of truths about sexuality that have withstood the test of time. We hope they serve you well!

All physical and psychological debility must ultimately be attributed to the faulty practice of sex. The Art of Love is to be considered foremost of all the arts in that, correctly practiced, it brings one toward the goal of Immortality.   SU-NU-CHING

The joy of sexual love, manifested in so many attractive and delightful ways, makes the human condition truly blessed.   SMARADIPIKA

Indian composite erotic elephant, the symbol of sovereignty. A sexual amulet in the form of a miniature painting, Rajasthan, late eighteenth century.

glossary

Skt. = Sanskrit word
Tib. = Tibetan word
Ch. = Chinese word
Jap. = Japanese word

Adi Shakti (Skt.) The original Shakti, the Creative Principle of Divine Energy in its female personification.
Agni (Skt.) The Fire god of the Hindu pantheon. Portrayed as two-headed, seven-tongued and red-colored. As the celestial fire, he is also known as Surya, the sun; in the microcosm, he dwells in the Navel Chakra (solar plexus).
AH (Skt.) The first vowel-sound of the Sanskrit alphabet. A Tantric sound-syllable signifying the beginning of all creation. In the Subtle Body of Tantra, "AH" is focused in the Throat Chakra.
Ahuyabarada Mudra (Skt.) Gesture of mystic invitation. Posture of a sex initiatress, with one hand on the hip.
Ajna Chakra (Skt.) The Third Eye or Brow Chakra of the Subtle Body of Tantra, depicted as a two-petaled lotus. A glyph of the pineal gland, which controls the psycho-organism.
Akarna Dhanurasana (Skt.) "Akarna" means near to the ear, "*dhanu*" is a bow and "*dhanur*" an archer. This Yoga posture makes the legs and back very flexible and aids the control of sexual energy. Literally the "near-ear bow posture."
Ali (Skt.) The fifteen Sanskrit vowel-sounds, which the Tantras equate with the left channel of the Subtle Body. The seed syllables of the fifteen Yoginis, linked to the phases of the moon. Intimate female friends and the zodiacal sign of Scorpio.
Amritakala (Skt.) The changing location of erotic passion in the body of woman, linked to the phases of the moon.
Apana (Skt.) The downward-moving life current, one of two main vital airs of the body. The *Apana* is focused in the lower digestive region and extends to the anus. Associated with the color orange-red, it governs the eliminative function.
Aperture of Brahma
See Brahmarandhra.
Ardhanarisvara (Skt.) The androgynous Shiva where left side is female and right side is male. Symbol of the balanced union of Shiva and Shakti, the resolution of inner and outer dualities. The hermaphrodite, a glyph of mysticism and sensuality. An alchemical archetype.
Asana (Skt.) A position that is both firm and pleasant. A Yoga posture or method of sitting, employed to harness and control the psycho-physical energies of body, and mind.
Asvini Mudra (Skt.) The contraction and dilation of the anal sphincter muscles. An effective way of awakening sexual energy and channeling it upward. Asvini literally means "mare."
Avadhuti (Skt.) The female adept of sexual Yoga. A secret name for the central channel of the Subtle Body of Tantra, otherwise referred to as *Sushumna*.
Avalokiteshwara (Skt.) The embodiment of compassion. A Bodhisattva, one who is freed from the notion of self and who works for the Liberation of others. A savior and symbol of transcendence through the removal of delusion. His Mantra is "OM–MANI–PADME–HUM."

Bandha (Skt.) Literally, to contract, lock, knot, bind, catch or restrain. Refers to Yoga postures that constrict or control particular body organs or energies; postures that channel back normally outward-flowing energy. Good for aiding the retention of semen and the involuntary urge to orgasm.
Bandha Padmasana (Skt.) The bound lotus posture. From Padmasana (the cross-legged lotus pose) the arms are crossed behind the back, each hand catching and holding the opposite toes. This posture enhances flexibility in the neck, shoulders and back and is used to awaken the latent Kundalini.
Base Chakra See Muladhara.
Bhagasana (Skt.) A Yoga posture in which the feet are placed together, as if in prayer, below the genitals. This posture is assumed to honor the cosmic Yoni, the all-encompassing female energy of creation. An advanced posture for ecstatic equilibrium.
Bhairava Chakra (Skt.) The worship of the goddess Kali through a circle of sexually active couples; the "divine orgy" common to pagan religions. In the Tantric tradition, the Bhairavi Chakra is practiced to gain occult powers.
Bhakti (Skt.) Faith or spiritual devotion. Homage, piety, love as a religious principle. The uplifting force of faith.
Bhujangasana (Skt.) The cobra posture. A Yoga position that exercises the spine and tones up the internal organs. It improves circulation and respiration and stimulates sexuality.
Brahma (Skt.) The creative aspect of the Hindu triad of forces governing all phenomena. Brahma corresponds to the birth process and rules over destiny; his symbol is the golden egg or aura. The creative force of Brahma brings all beings into existence. His female counterpart is Saraswati, the patroness of the Sixty-four Arts. In the microcosm, Brahma resides in the Navel Chakra.
Brahma Nadi (Skt.) The innermost subtle channel of the *Sushumna*, the central channel of the Subtle Body. Known as the Royal Road, it is the expression of the most subtle level of spiritual refinement.
Brahmanda (Skt.) The "egg" or aura of Brahma, said to contain the whole universe. A term used to denote the Subtle Body in its role of microcosm to the macrocosm of Brahma.
Brahmarandhra (Skt.) The "Aperture of Brahma." The fontanel opening at the top of the head, which is visible at birth but closes during the first year of life. According to Eastern occult tradition, the soul normally enters or leaves the body through this opening.
Buddha (Skt.) The Enlightened One. The historical Buddha was a prince who renounced the royal life and became an ascetic. He was called the Buddha after he achieved Enlightenment.
Buddha Body The human body transformed into an enlightened or superhuman body through the practice of physical and mental Yoga.
Buddha Field The psychic atmosphere created by the presence of an Enlightened person.

Chakra (Skt.) Mystic circle, literally "wheel." A psychic center or focal point within the Subtle Body. The Chakras are located primarily at the sexual region, spleen, navel, heart, throat and head. Each Chakra, or plasma field, acts as a transformer of energies, converting impulses from one frequency to another. Often referred to as "lotuses," the Chakras open and close according to psycho-physical conditions. Each Chakra has a specific number of divisions or "petals" that connect to parts of the Subtle Body. A gathering of Tantrics is also known as a Chakra.
Chakra Puja (Skt.) A Tantric term meaning "circular worship," normally referring to ritualized sexual acts performed by more than one couple seated in a circle. This term can also mean the conscious focusing of devotional energies to open up the Chakras of the Subtle Body.
Chakrasambhara (Skt.) "The Ruler of the Chakras." A Tantric mystic form (*yidam*) symbolizing mystic truths. An expression of dynamic teachings. The name of an important Tantra that treats the transforming effect of solar (as opposed to lunar) energy. A vehicle of Liberation, personified by a couple in sexual union.
Chandamaharosana (Skt.) "The Great Moon Elixir." A Tantric mystic form (*yidam*) and tutelary deity. The name of an important Tantra that concerns itself with the conscious control of lunar energy. Chandamaharosana is symbolized by the full moon, both in the macrocosm and the microcosm, and personified by a couple in sexual union in a squatting or half-kneeling position.
Chinnamasta (Skt.) A Tantric goddess or secret mystic form, the "Egoless *Yogini*" or female adept of sexual Yoga. She is depicted having severed her own head (the ego) and holding it in her hand. Three streams of blood (symbolizing the three principal channels of the Subtle Body) flow from her exposed neck and nourish her own severed head as well as her two attendants, Varnini and Dakini. The mysteries of Chinnamasta are said to have originated in China.
Chitrini (Skt.) A category of woman referred to in the ancient Hindu love treatises. Known as the "Art woman," she emanates from the heavenly realm. The same term is used to refer to one of the very subtle channels making up the *Sushumna*, the central channel of the Subtle Body.
Chueh-Chen (Ch.) Chinese horned or crescent-shaped pillows used to support the buttocks during love-making.
Cinnabar Field/Terrace Taoist term designating the solar or transforming plexus. Texts refer to it as located just below the navel.
Complete Breath A Yogic breathing practice in which conscious control of the breath's threefold division into inhalation, retention and exhalation is developed. The complete breath is the first step in using the breathing function as a means to Liberation.
Cooling Breath A Yogic breathing technique in which the breath is inhaled through the tongue formed into a tube. It helps cool the whole body, reduces high blood pressure, soothes the eyes and ears, and is beneficial to the liver and spleen. Also known as Crow Beak or Kaki Mudra.
Crow Beak See Cooling Breath.
Crow Posture A sexual posture for mutual oral-genital intercourse. Referred to as Sixty-nine in the West.
Crucible Taoist and Tantric term designating the female sexual partner and, especially, the Yoni. Also the instrument through which the transformations take place.

Dakini (Skt.) The personification of the cosmic feminine energy as an erotic Wisdom-archetype sometimes creative, sometimes dissolutive. A guardian of the esoteric teachings, a heavenly goddess, the expression of the exalted intuition. A muse.
Dark Girl See Hsuan-Nu.
Devadasi (Skt.) Literally "Servant of God." A temple dancer, of whom there were several categories. The highest were great Yoginis who exercised control over their body functions. They were initiatresses of Tantric Yoga, considered to be mistresses of the temple gods and embodiments of the Gopis. The Sexual Secrets were taught by them.
Dhanurasana (Skt.) Literally "bow posture." It stretches and strengthens the abdominal and back muscles, aids digestion and invigorates the gonads, which control sexuality.
Do-In (Jap.) Oriental self-massage, aimed at bringing the body into harmony with the cosmos.
Dorje (Tib.) The Imperishable, the Adamantine or "Diamond Scepter." A Tantric symbol for the male sexual organ (the Lingam) and a ritual implement used in high magic.
Double Lotus Peak A Taoist mystic and sexological term for the breasts of woman.
Dyaus (Skt.) Heaven, the sky, the supreme firmament. Dyaus, the sky father, covers the earth and fertilizes her with rain, his seed. An ancient Vedic term, equivalent to the "ether," the connecting agent between elements.

Eh (Skt.) Tantric seed-sound or syllable representing the transformatory power of the Navel Chakra. A natural sound expressed during passionate love-making.
Elected Girl See Ts'ai-nu.
Enneagram A mystic diagram based on the number nine. Popularized by George Gurdjieff, it shows the interrelationship between nine points around the circumference of a circle. Each point corresponds to a bodily aperture (in the microcosm) and planet (in the macrocosm). A symbol used by occultists as a glyph of the psyche.
Essence of Coral See White Snow.
Essence of Woman Taoist term for the sexual secretions produced in the Yoni of woman during the heights of climax.

Fan-Yun-Fu-Yu (Ch.) Literally "reverse clouds and inverted rain." A term used to denote male homosexuality and anal intercourse.
Flowery Lake Taoist term for the Head Chakra of the Subtle Body.

Gam (Skt.) Tantric seed-syllable of Ganesha, the elephant-headed Lord of Obstacles. Pronounced "gang" or "gung."
Gandapa (Tib.) The name of a famous Tantric teacher who, after years of celibacy, achieved Liberation through spontaneous erotic contact with a Yogini. Also known as Ghantapa.
Ganesha (Skt.) The elephant-headed deity of the Hindu Pantheon. Several myths tell how he was magically created by Parvati and through a boon became the first deity to be worshipped in all Hindu rites. Also known as Ganapati, he is referred to as the Lord of Obstacles and is associated with the Sexual Chakra of the Subtle Body. He brings good fortune and success.
Gang (Skt.) See Gam.
Garuda (Skt.) A great mythical bird, the vehicle of Vishnu. He devours physical and psychological poisons and is portrayed holding a snake. Identified with dynamic occult power. A protector deity and guardian of the Tantric mysteries.
Gayatri Mantra (Skt.) A Sanskrit Mantra or power phrase, "OM–BHUR–BHUWAH–SWA," which evokes the Three Realms (this world, the next world and Eternity). Used in magical acts and rites and for psychic protection and focusing healing energy. It represents the surrender and offering of the self to higher forces and helps confer spiritual direction. An appropriate Mantra for love-making.
Goldasana (Skt.) The crane posture. Helpful in developing balance and posture, it strengthens the hips and legs and stimulates the internal organs.
Gomukhasana (Skt.) The head of a cow, a Yoga posture that creates an energy circuit beneficial to the upper Chakras.
Gopi (Skt.) Cow-girl or milk-maid. The Gopis are all manifestations of Vishnu's consort, Lakshmi. They express the power of longing (both erotic and spiritual) and represent the emotions refined. The Gopis vie for Krishna's attention, participating with him in a circular erotic dance that channels the emotions through the Chakras.
Goraksasana (Skt.) The cow-herder posture. A difficult balancing pose that aids the control of sexual energy. Named after a famous Yogic teacher.
Great Axis/Pathway/River The subtle "psychic pathway" that runs from the region of the perineum to the fontanel at the top of the head. Tantra teaches that the Great Axis connects the individual with the cosmos. See also Holy Mount Meru.
Guhyasamaja (Skt.) "The Assembly of Secrets." A Tantric mystic form (*yidam*) and tutelary deity. The name of an important Tantra, personified by a seated couple in sexual union.
Guhyeshwari (Skt.) A secret form of the goddess known as the Lady of Mysteries. A name of the Tantric sex initiatress.
Guna (Skt.) Quality or attribute. A constituent of Nature and a manifestation of consciousness. The three principal *gunas*, referred to as Sattva (the creative),

Rajas (the preserving) and Tamas (the transcendental), permeate all that exists.
Guru (Skt.) Teacher, spiritual master, guide. Literally "the dispeller of ignorance," a Guru is also a touchstone, an ideal to which the discipline aspires. A Guru's role is to initiate.

Halasana (Skt.) The plow posture. A simple Yoga posture that stretches and strengthens the muscles, stimulates the thyroid and parathyroid glands and helps one gain control over sexual energy.
Hamsa (Skt.) Literally "Great Swan" or "Bird of the Soul." A power word, or Mantra, derived from the sounds made by the breath while exhaling ("HAM") and inhaling ("SA"). Used as a meditation device to gain ascendency over the normally involuntary breathing process. See HANG.
Hang (Skt.) A Tantric seed-sound or syllable associated with the space element, the ears, the sense of hearing and the shape of a flaming point. Sometimes pronounced "ham."
Harikata (Jap.) A dildo or artificial Lingam. Often a replica of the husband's Lingam, used for self-satisfaction during periods when he is absent. Kept in a special box and treated with honor.
Hastakara Yantra (Skt.) A Yantra, or mystic diagram of the hands, illustrating the relationship of subtle forces influencing individual destiny. The symbols relate to cosmological forces and are used by palmists to help focus on archetypes.
Hastini (Skt.) A category of woman referred to in the ancient Hindu love treatises. Known as the "Elephant woman," she emanates from the elemental realms.
Hatha Yoga (Skt.) The physical practice of Yoga based on *Pranayama* (the science of breath). Hatha Yoga refers to the HA-breath of the sun (through the right side of the body) and the THA-breath of the moon (through the left side of the body) in harmonious balance. The word "Yoga" means to yoke or join together. Physical postures help harmonize the breathing process. See Solar-Lunar Breathing.
Head Chakra The uppermost center of the Subtle Body, visualized as a downward-pointing lotus of thirty-two petals. The focal point for the lunar forces of the microcosm. Popularized Tantra refers to the Head Chakra as "the thousand-petaled lotus."
Healing Breath A Yogic breathing practice whereby a fixed 1 : 4 : 2 ratio of the times taken up by inhalation, retention and exhalation is consciously induced. This is known as the Healing Breath, which has the effect of slowing the breathing and relaxing and healing the body.
Heart Chakra The middle center of the Subtle Body, visualized as a downward-pointing lotus of eight petals. The focal point for the emotions.
Heavenly and Earthly Net An ancient Taoist love-making rite in which couples make love in imitation of animals and birds in the belief that this helps restore Nature's order and averts calamities.
Heroic Posture See Virasana.
Hevajra (Skt.) "The Indestructible." A Tantric mystic form (*yidam*) that symbolizes the mystery teachings of the lunar cycle. As a tutelary deity, Hevajra is portrayed dancing ecstatically in sexual union. The name of an important Tantra.
Holy Mount Meru The mythical center of the universe according to Hindu and Buddhist cosmology. The abode of Shiva and Shakti. A great pilgrimage place, identified with Mount Kailash, in western Tibet. One of the names of the central channel of the Subtle Body. See Great Axis/Pathway/River.
Hsuan-Nu (Ch.) "The Dark Girl." Instructress in the Taoist arcana of sex. She is credited with authoring three books on military strategy and is identified with the Taoist "Peach of Immortality." One of three sex initiatresses of the mythical Yellow Emperor.
Hun (Ch.) The Great Spirit. According to the Taoist view, the Hun enters the body of the child at the moment when the first breath is taken and is associated with the Yang or male solar force. The Great Spirit co-exists with the Great Soul (Po), and as death approaches, leaves the body first.
Hung (Skt.) Also referred to as "HUM." A Tantric power-syllable or Mantra that expresses the transcendence inherent in voidness. By uttering this sound, one awakens the Kundalini.

Ida (Skt.) One of the three principal channels of the Subtle Body. From the left nostril the Ida rises to the crown of the head and descends to the base of the spine, crossing over the central channel at each Chakra. Sometimes referred to as the "Force of Vishnu."
Immortality Peach Juice See White Snow.
Indra (Skt.) The Hindu king of the gods according to the Vedas. The ever-young, heroic ruler of the world, whose magical weapon is the thunderbolt. The embodiment of virility and the cause of fertility.
Inner Yang A Taoist term used to describe the subtle glandular secretions produced in the Yoni of the sexually ecstatic woman. Credited with powers of rejuvenation.
Ishvari (Skt.) A name of exalted femininity. A Wisdom goddess or Dakini of white color, associated with the space element and the center of the universe.

Jade Fountain/Liquid A Taoist sexological term for the saliva produced in the mouth of a woman during the heights of sexual ecstasy. Credited with a vitalizing and strengthening effect on the partner who absorbs it. Also called Sweet Spring.
Jalandhara Bandha/Mudra (Skt.) A Yoga posture whereby the neck and throat are contracted into a hook shape, the chin resting on the top of the chest. An aid to sense withdrawal, this technique stimulates the thyroid gland and helps develop the powers of visualization.
Jiva (Skt.) The Immortal Soul. The Individual Soul united with its Eternal Unchanging Source. Individual consciousness.

Kaki Mudra (Skt.) See Cooling Breath.
Kalachakra (Skt.) "Time Wheel." A Tantric mystic form (*yidam*) that symbolizes the relationship between inner and outer realities, especially the correlation between astrology and physiology. Also, the cycles of change in both microcosm and macrocosm. The name of an important Tantra, said to have been introduced from the magical kingdom of Shambhala by the master Pito. Kalachakra is depicted colored red, white and blue (symbolizing the three principal channels of the Subtle Body), with twenty-four arms and standing in ecstatic sexual union with his eight-armed consort.
Kali (Skt.) The dark awesome Hindu goddess of Transcendence. The transcendental power of sex.
Kali Yuga (Skt.) The present eon. The age of darkness and materialism. One of a repeated cycle of four eons.
Kama/Kamadeva (Skt.) The Hindu Love god, similar to Cupid. The son of Vishnu and Lakshmi, Kama is said to be invisibly present during all acts of love. Eternally youthful and handsome, he is the deity who presides over the mind and the liberator of desires. Rati, his wife, is the embodiment of sensual love.
Kameshwari (Skt.) A name of Shakti, particularly in her role as lustful mistress. Kameshwari embodies the original power principle of Tantra. She is portrayed holding a noose (attachment or the power of desire), an elephant hook or goad (knowledge or the intellect tamed), a sugarcane bow (the mind) and an arrow (the sense objects). Together, the bow and arrow symbolize the power to act.
Kamini (Skt.) The embodiment of desire. A Love goddess or a loving woman. A term used in connection with sensuality, intoxicants and transcendental beauty.
Kanda (Skt.) Male sexual gland, probably equivalent to the prostate. Located above the Lingam and below the navel.
Kapala Randhra Dhauti (Skt.) Literally "head cavity purification." A Yogic massage technique that consists in rubbing the area close to the bridge of the nose. Helps clear the sinuses, invigorates the liver and induces clairvoyance.
Kargyudpa (Tib.) One of the ancient sects of Tantric Lamaism. Founded by Marpa "the Translator" in the eleventh century, this sect emphasizes the importance of the Tantras, oral transmission and Yogic practices. Its present hierarch is the Karmapa Lama.
Karma (Skt.) The natural law of action causing reaction. The workings of destiny and that which shapes reality. According to the Eastern view of reality, what we are experiencing now is a direct result of our past actions, either in this life or a previous one. Karma motivates reincarnation.
Karma Mudra (Skt.) The female sexual partner who is adept at sexual Yoga. A Tantric Yogini. Traditionally, there are said to be five different kinds of Karma Mudra, categorized according to physical and psychological characteristics. A Karma Mudra is free from any guilt or shame about her sexuality.
Karmapa (Skt. and Tib.) The hierarch of the Kargyudpas.
Khapushpa (Skt.) Literally "womb flower." Menstrual blood.
Khechari (Skt.) Literally "ski flier" A Yogic technique in which the tongue is gradually elongated and turned backward until it reaches the nostril openings inside the head. Correct practice of the Khechari Mudra is said to free one from hunger, thirst, disease, old age and death.
Kling (Skt.) A seed-syllable or Mantra, associated with the goddess Kali, the love god Kamadeva and Krishna. A power word that contains the secret of attraction. Sometimes called Kring.
Kohl (Skt.) Eye balm or eye makeup, black in color, beneficial to the eyes if correctly prepared.
Kring (Skt.) Seed-syllable, particularly associated with the goddess Kali. See Kling.
Krishna (Skt.) "The Dark One," the eighth incarnation of Vishnu, usually blue in color. Krishna is the ideal of the playful, all-potent child, the Eternal Youth who can take many different forms. From the Tantric point of view, Krishna represents the spontaneous power of unconventional love. An embodiment of male eroticism.
Krishna Lila (Skt.) The circular erotic dance of Krishna with the milkmaids (Gopis), symbolic of the swirling of sexual energies through the Chakras. A term used to describe the paradoxical nature of reality. An annual festival of Hinduism. A general term for erotic play.
Kumari (Skt.) A virgin girl.
Kumari Puja (Skt.) The worship of virgins. A Tantric ritual that consists in honoring a virgin girl, viewing her as the embodiment of a goddess.
Kumbhak (Skt.) A container or pot. A term used in Yoga to describe the method of retaining the breath by forming the lower abdomen into the shape of a pot. Used to refer to the retention of breath.
Kundalini (Skt.) The normally latent psycho-sexual power that, when awakened, ascends through the central channel of the Subtle Body. The root word "kunda" means a pool or reservoir of energy. Kundalini is likened to a coiled snake, ready to strike at any moment. When the Kundalini-energy is correctly directed, it can cause cosmic consciousness to manifest and Liberation to be achieved. Also known as the Kundalini Shakti or Inner Woman.
Kundalini Yoga (Skt.) A form of Yoga intended to awaken and channel Kundalini-energy. Sometimes referred to as Laya Yoga.
Kuntu Zangmo (Tib.) The Cosmic Mother, the "all-good" archetype of compassionate femininity.
Kuntu Zangpo (Tib.) The Cosmic Father, the "all-good" archetype of transcendental masculinity. Often depicted in union with Kuntu Zangmo (the Cosmic Mother). This united form is invoked as a benevolent mystic "ancestor" and meditated on as the ideal couple. Depicted seated in sexual union.
Kurukulla (Skt.) A Tantric form of the goddess Tara in her role of enchantress. Depicted holding a bow and arrow made of flowers. A symbol of the power of love.

Lakshmi (Skt.) The female counterpart or Divine Energy of the god Vishnu, who fulfills a preserving function in the Hindu triad of forces. Lakshmi, who is also called Shri, is the embodiment of prosperity and good fortune.
Lang (Skt.) A Tantric seed-syllable, or Mantra, associated with the earth element, the sense of smell, the square shape and the color yellow.
Lao-tse A Chinese philosopher of the sixth century B.C., the author of the *Tao Te Ching*.
Ling (Ch.) Transcendental. A word used to refer to a type of mushroom said to confer immortality and also to the male sexual organ. Possibly derived from the Sanskrit word Lingam.
Lingam (Skt.) The male sexual organ. A symbol of Lord Shiva, the cosmic principle of transcendence. A sign or mark that "proves that existence is real." The male gender.
Locana (Skt.) A name of exalted femininity. A Wisdom goddess or Dakini of blue color, associated with the water element and the eastern part of the universe.
Lotus/Lotus Flower A Tantric term for the female sexual organ, the Yoni.
Lotus Nectar A Tantric term for the sweet-tasting love-juices of the female partner.
Lotus Posture See Padmasana.

Madya (Skt.) Sweet wine, one of the ingredients used in the Secret Rite of Tantra. Symbolizes the fire element and the purification of the senses.
Mahabandha (Skt.) Literally "the Great Lock or Seal." A Yoga technique whereby the anal orifice is covered by the heel of the left foot while the anal muscles are contracted. An aid to controlling the flow of subtle energies in the psycho-organism.
Mahachina (Skt.) The great country of China.
Mahakala (Skt.) Literally "Great Time." The Lord of Time. A Tantric protector or idealization of transcendental compassion. The guardian of the deeper mysteries. A name of Shiva.
Mahayoni Mudra (Skt.) The mystic gesture of the Mother-goddess. A hand gesture in which the fingers are interwoven so that they make a form resembling the Yoni. A subtle energy circuit.
Maithuna/Maithuna Sadhana (Skt.) Sexual union. The ceremonial union of Shiva (the male principle) with Shakti (the female principle). An auspicious rite aimed at raising the Kundalini through physical love. In the Rite of the Five Essentials, Maithuna represents the space element and corresponds to the control of sexual energy. Correctly practiced, Maithuna endows the couple with occult power and Liberation.
Mamaki (Skt.) A name of exalted femininity. A Wisdom goddess or Dakini of yellow color, associated with the earth element and the southern part of the universe.
Mamsa (Skt.) Meat. One of the five ritual elements used in the Rite of the Five Essentials. Mamsa represents the air element and corresponds to the control of inner sound.
Mandala (Skt.) A mystic circle. An enclosed space used for magical or ritualistic purposes. A symbol and expression of the psychological processes of unfolding and integration. A circle of psychic protection, a cosmogram.
Mantra (Skt.) A protection of mind. A power phrase or mystic sound-syllables

composed of vowels and consonants. Used for controlling and focusing the mind. An aid to spiritualization, Mantras can be used to control and channel sexual energy.

Marjariasana (Skt.) The cat posture. A simple Yoga posture that helps strengthen the back and aids in overcoming lethargy.

Matsya (Skt.) Fish. One of the five ritual elements used in the Rite of the Five Essentials. Matsya represents the water element.

Matsyasana (Skt.) The fish posture. A simple Yoga posture that is ideal for relaxation and meditation. It helps concentrate the mind and prevents the involuntary loss of sexual energy.

MAYURASANA (Skt.) The peacock posture. A difficult Yoga posture that tones up the whole abdominal area, improving the digestion and stimulating the sexual glands.

Mien-Ling (Ch.) Known as the "exertion bell" or "Burmese bell," it is an Oriental sexual aid consisting of a pair of hollow silver spheres, one containing a drop of mercury and the other a metal tongue that vibrates. Once it is inserted into the Yoni, exquisite sensations are produced whenever the woman moves. Called Ri-no-tama in Japanese.

Mitra (Skt.) Solidarity and friendship. The foremost of the sovereign principles and one of the Vedic gods. Mitra protects the codes of honor.

Monthly Affair/Monthly Fluid Chinese term for menstruation. See also Red Snow/ Red Flood.

Moon Flower Waters/Medicine Taoist term used to describe the love-juices produced in the Yoni of woman during arousal. Also referred to as White Metal, this secretion is said to strengthen, nurture and harmonize the inner spirit of the man who absorbs it.

Moon Fluid Tantric term for female sexual secretions produced during the heights of eroticism.

Mount Meru See Holy Mount Meru.

Mudra (Skt.) Mystic hand gesture used to focus subtle energy, transmit teachings through symbols and confer psychic protection. An aid to Tantric meditation. Mudra can also mean woman in her role as Yogini. The same term is sometimes used to refer to cereal grains used in Tantric rites.

Mula Bandha (Skt.) See Mahabandha.

Muladhara (Skt.) The Base or Sexual Chakra of the Subtle Body, physically located between the anus and the sexual organ. Visualized as an upturned lotus of four petals.

Musgami (Ch.) An Oriental birth-control device made of oiled silk paper. A kind of cervical cap.

Mysterious Gateway A Taoist term for the Sex Chakra of the Subtle Body. Also refers to the Yoni.

Nabho Mudra (Skt.) A Yogic technique in which the tongue is turned upward toward the palate, behind the front teeth, while the breath is restrained. This exercise is used in conjunction with the Jalandhara Mudra and aids the circulation of vital energies.

Nadi (Skt.) An energy channel of the Subtle Body. An invisible conduit through which psychic energy is distributed to the different parts of one's being. Yogic texts state that the channels of the Subtle Body are composed of 72,000 nadis.

Nairatma (Skt.) A Wisdom Dakini, the embodiment of the "non-self," the egoless ecstatic Yogini. The consort of Hevajra and a secret name for the central channel of the Subtle Body.

Nauli (Skt.) Literally "surging wave." A Yogic technique in which the abdominal muscles are churned and contracted to draw sexual energy upward.

Nava Durga (Skt.) Nine goddesses of the Hindu pantheon, associated with the mythology and rites of the Mother-goddess. Their names are Mahalakshmi, Nanda, Ksemankari, Shivaduti, Mahatunda, Bhramari, Chandramandala, Revati and Harsiddhi. During the Durga Puja rites (in the month of October) these goddesses are invoked.

Navel Chakra The transformation center of the Subtle Body, visualized as an upward-pointing lotus of sixty-four petals, effulgent like the sun. The focal point for the solar forces of the microcosm. The solar plexus.

Nyasa (Skt.) The touching of parts of the body with the intention of conferring psychic protection. Usually accompanied by a Mantra.

OM (Skt.) The Supreme Mantra, the manifestation of spiritual sound.

Original Semen A Taoist term that refers to the constituents of semen, which is made up of elements produced in all parts of the body.

Padma (Skt.) Lotus. Either actual or mystical, such as a center of the Subtle Body. A symbol of femininity and spirituality. The Yoni.

Padmasambhava (Skt.) Literally "self-created from a lotus." The name of a great Tantric master of the eighth century who established Tantric Buddhism in Tibet. The founder of the Nyingmapa sect.

Padmasana (Skt.) The lotus posture. A comfortable, well-balanced, seated position, with both legs crossed. This posture is an aid to meditation. One of the most important asanas.

Padmini (Skt.) A category of woman referred to in the ancient Hindu love-treatises. Known as the "Lotus woman," she is said to originate from the realm of gods. An ideal Tantric consort.

Palace of Yin A Taoist term for the sexual center of woman, deep within the womb. This center produces profuse secretions when stimulated.

Pandara (Skt.) A name of exalted femininity. A Wisdom goddess or Dakini of red color, associated with the fire element and the western part of the universe.

Parvati (Skt.) The daughter of the Himalaya Mountains. The benign consort of Shiva and the embodiment of sensuality. She personifies transcendental abundance and the delight of Tantric union.

Paschimottanasana (Skt.) A stretching position that helps strengthen the spine, abdomen, heart and internal organs. Also known as Ugrasana.

Peach-Flower Flow Taoist term for menstrual fluid.

Pingala (Skt.) One of the three principal channels of the Subtle Body. From the right nostril the Pingala rises to the crown of the head and descends to the base of the spine, crossing over the central channel at each Chakra. Sometimes referred to as the "Force of Brahma."

Ping-I (Ch.) An acu-pressure point located one inch above the right breast of man. If pressed, it aids in the control of involuntary orgasm.

Plain Girl See Su-Nu.

Playing Horse A Taoist term for sexual games in which one partner "rides" on the other.

Playing the Flute A Taoist term for oral sex between the mouth and Lingam.

Po (Ch.) The Great Soul. According to the Taoist view, the Po comes into existence at conception, being formed by the union of the two parents. It is said to have nine parts, conceived of as vital spirits. The Po is associated with the Yin or female lunar force.

Prana (Skt.) Literally "Life-force." A Yogic term for vitality and breath, which has a fivefold division. The name of the upward-moving breath, which causes the spirit to evolve. Normally the *Prana* rests in the region of the heart.

Pranayama (Skt.) The science of *Prana*. Yogic breathing practices that are aids to Liberation.

Prithivi (Skt.) The Earth. The most ancient of all goddesses, the original Mother-goddess, sometimes represented by a cow in Hinduism.

Purple Mushroom Peak A Taoist term for the Yoni. Also called White Tiger's Cavern or Mysterious Gate.

Queen of the Western Paradise A legendary Chinese queen who attained immortality by nurturing her Yin-essence through controlling her climax each time she made love with young men.

Radha (Skt.) Success, achievement, the presiding goddess of the life energies. A manifestation of Lakshmi, the goddess of Prosperity, she is the principal consort of Krishna and is Queen of the Gopis.

Rajasic (Skt.) The preserving constituent of Nature. Rajas means mobility, activity and induces the passionate sentiment and is arousing. Related to the power of Will.

Rang (Skt.) A Tantric seed-syllable, or Mantra, associated with the fire element, the sense of sight, the triangular shape and the color red.

Rasayana (Skt.) One of the eight branches of Indian medicine. An ancient Hindu science that uses precious metals and gems for rejuvenation.

Rati (Skt.) The wife of Kama, the Love god. She is the embodiment of eroticism and portrays the initiatory power of woman in the active role. A term meaning love-play or sensual desire.

Red Lotus Peak A Taoist term for a woman's mouth. Also referred to as Jade Fountain, it secretes a sweet, invigorating saliva during sexual ecstasy.

Red Snow/Red Flood A Taoist term for the menstrual flow. Sometimes referred to as the Yang-essence, Peach-Flower Flow, the Monthly Affair or the Monthly Guest.

Reverse Kundalini A Tantric term for unnatural, retrogressive, degenerative or perverse sexual practices. It refers to any sexual practice that reverses the natural upward flow of sexual energy, such as anal sex.

Ri-No-Tama (Jap.) See Mien-Ling.

Rite of the Five Essentials The secret Tantric sexual rite in which five ingredients (cereal grains, fish, wine, meat and sexual intercourse) are combined as a kind of Eucharist. An aid to the attainment of occult powers and Liberation.

Royal Road See Brahma Nadi.

Rudra (Skt.) One of the ancient names of Shiva, with many levels of meaning. Rudra is the celestial fire, the bestowing of strength, fierce, transcendental anger, the driving away of evil.

Rudrani (Skt.) The Queen of Rudras. The name of a form of Shiva's consort.

Sadhana (Skt.) The "direct way," the attitude of worship. An individual's art of worship, implying commitment and practice. The spiritual quest. Adherence to a particular spiritual discipline.

Sadhu (Skt.) An Indian holy man, ascetic or Yogi.

Sa-Ham/So-Ham (Skt.) Literally "I am she," "I am he." The natural sound made by the breath entering and leaving the body. See Hamsa.

Sakhi (Skt.) Girl friend; a woman's female companion or attendant.

Salamba Sarvangasana (Skt.) The supported shoulder stand. One of the simplest and most effective Yoga asanas that benefits the whole glandular system and thus vitalizes the whole being. A reverse posture.

Samadhi (Skt.) A state of complete Yogic absorption. Profound meditation, deep concentration on transcendence. A state of non-duality. Peaceful bliss.

Samana (Skt.) One of the five main divisions of the life-force. The Samana is largely focused on the navel region and aids digestion and metabolism. Associated with a solar red color, with the faculty of sight and with the assimilative function.

Saraswati (Skt.) The female counterpart or divine energy of Brahma the Creator. Saraswati is the patroness of the Sixty-four Arts and is the goddess of Learning. Her symbol is the vina, a seven stringed musical instrument. Also a secret name for the central channel of the Subtle Body.

Sati (Skt.) A form of the goddess associated with faithfulness. The daughter of Daksa (ritual skill), one of the original seven sages created by Brahma. The pilgrimage places of the followers of the Mother-goddess are all associated with parts of Sati's body. Sacrifice.

Sattvic (Skt.) The creative and illuminating constituent of Nature. Sattva means clarity, the higher nature of the mind. That which leads one to union with the Divine.

Secret Dalliance A Taoist term that refers to the love-making of a single man with more than one woman. Viewed as a way of gaining magical powers.

Seed-Sound A primordial sound or Mantra. See Seed-Syllable.

Seed-Syllable Letter(s) of the Sanskrit alphabet representing one of the primordial vibrations of the phenomenal world. Seed-syllables are the essential components of all Mantras.

Sexual Chakra See Muladhara.

Shakti (Skt.) The active creative energy of femininity. The female creative force. The power of Tantra.

Shakti Bindu (Skt.) The central point of a mystic diagram (either a Yantra or a Mandala), usually colored red. Seed, energy point, the symbol of the conjoined sperm and ovum.

Shankini (Skt.) A category of woman referred to in the ancient Hindu love treatises. Known as the "Conch woman," she emanates from the realm of humans.

Shankini Nadi (Skt.) A subtle channel that connects the clitoris of woman with the upper lip and palatal region. Known as the "tenth door" of the body, it is an important sexual secret.

Shavasana (Skt.) The corpse posture. One of the simplest of all Yoga postures, it consists in lying flat on one's back and totally relaxing every part of the body.

Shirsasana (Skt.) The Yoga head stand. One of the most important of all Yoga asanas. A reverse posture that increases the supply of blood to the upper glands and thus helps overcome old age, loss of memory and senility.

Shiatsu (Jap.) Japanese finger-pressure massage therapy.

Shilajeet (Skt.) A natural mineral pitch that is a tonic and a powerful aphrodisiac. Contains many minerals, including gold salts.

Shiva (Skt.) The transcendental aspect of the Hindu triad of forces governing all phenomena. The Yogic ideal and "Lord over Death." The Supreme Yogi, whose consort, or Shakti, is referred to as Parvati in her benign aspect and Kali in her awesome aspect. The Eternal, Immortal Spirit, the penetrating power of focused energy.

Shiva Lingam (Skt.) The Lingam of Shiva. The ever-erect sexual organ, often idealized in sculpture or stone. See Lingam.

Shudra (Skt.) Low-caste, unsophisticated, direct. A type of Karma Mudra.

Shitali (Skt.) See Cooling Breath.

Siddha (Skt.) A perfected being. A seer, saint or great Yogi who has mastered both inner and outer realities.

Siddhi (Skt.) Magical or paranormal powers. Yogic attainments. Also a name of Ganesha's consort.

Simhasana (Skt.) The lion posture. A simple Yoga posture that is highly effective in stimulating psychological strength.

Sitkara (Skt.) A method of drawing in the breath through closed teeth, so producing a hissing sound. A type of Cooling Breath.

Sitkriti (Skt.) Love-sounds produced by drawing in the breath through closed teeth. Referred to in the Hindu love treatises as a prerogative and privilege of woman.

Six Girdles Taoist ceremonial items associated with the physical consummation of marriage. Colored silks used as love-cloths.

Solar-Lunar Breathing A Yoga breathing technique in which air is inhaled and exhaled through alternate nostrils, the right nostril being associated with solar energies (heat and expansion) and the left nostril with lunar energies (cold and contraction). This important technique helps the Yogi gain control over normally involuntary body processes. See Hatha Yoga.

Soma (Skt.) The Hindu lunar deity, worshipped as the bestower of physical beauty and clairvoyance. Also the name of various types of psycho-active plant drugs derived from creepers, herbs or mushrooms. Twenty-four varieties of Soma are described in the Vedas, most of which were composed under states of heightened consciousness attained through the use of these drugs. Soma is also the "Nectar of Ecstasy," the subtle bio-physical secretions produced from the pineal and pituitary glands during focused sexual Yogic practices. Soma is the name given to sexual energy.

Spleen Chakra The assimilative center of the Subtle Body, visualized as a downward-pointing lotus of thirty-two petals. Later Hindu Tantras refer to this Chakra as the Svadhisthana.

Sri Yantra (Skt.) A mystic diagram (Yantra) comprised of five upward-pointing and four downward-pointing triangles interlased in such a way that forty-three small triangles are produced. This glyph symbolizes the divine unity of Shiva and Shakti. The word "Sri" means beauty and is one of the names of Lakshmi, the female archetype of prosperity and preservation.

Stringing Pearls A Taoist term for the love-making of a single man with several women, who bring their Yonis close together to allow penetration in turn. Derived from the Chinese character "chuan," meaning "to string together."

Su-Nu (Ch.) "The Plain Girl." An instructress in the Taoist arcana of sex. She is credited with authoring several sexual handbooks as well as treatises on music. One of three sex initiatresses of the mythical Yellow Emperor.

Subtle Body A Yogic term used to describe the normally invisible body of bio-vibratio present within and around the physical body. Also called Brahmanda (the aura of Brahma), it is composed of plasma energies and vortices, ever-changing and interacting.

Surya (Skt.) The Sun god of the Hindu Pantheon, usually depicted as a golden shining being riding a celestial chariot pulled by seven horses. As the visible representative of the Supreme Creative Principle, the sun is viewed as the oversoul of the world. The true Yogi aims to awaken and channel the energies of his own "inner sun," located at the navel region.

Sushumna (Skt.) The principal and central channel of the Subtle Body. It is also known as the Path of Brahma, the Road of Evolution, and connects this reality with a higher one. The *Sushumna* itself contains three progressively more subtle channels, known as Vajrini, Chitrini and Brahma Nadi.

Swasti (Skt.) A Tantric power phrase meaning "It is well," "May it be auspicious." A solar swastika symbol.

Sweet Spring See Jade Fountain Liquid.

Tai Chi (Ch.) An ancient Chinese system of calisthenics based on the natural flow of energies in the body and in the world. Tai Chi movements tend to be graceful and often mimic animals and birds.

Tamasic (Skt.) The destructive constituent of Nature. Tamas means inertia, ignorance, excessive physicality, "that which obstructs sensitivity." On the highest level, Tamas means transcendental.

Tantra (Skt.) Spiritual method or system that takes into account both "inner" and "outer" realities. Derived from root words meaning "to expand," "weave" or extend consciousness," Tantra implies a continuity beyond physicality. Tantric teachings evolved in India and spread to Nepal, Tibet, China, Japan, Thailand and Indonesia. These teachings are said to be particularly relevant in this time of materialism and narcissism since all human activities can be used as tools in the Tantric route to Liberation. Tantras are

texts that outline specific Tantric practices.

Tao (Ch.) The ancient Chinese philosophy that views Nature and Spirit as interdependant and mutually sustaining. Tao is "the way," the Cosmic Truth, conceived of as the path trodden by the wise. Two philosophical works are of particular importance, the *Tao Te Ching* by Lao-tse and the *Book of Chang Tzu*.

Tara (Skt.) A Savior and an embodiment of motherly compassion, generally viewed as the counterpart of Avalokiteshwara. Representing the air element and the northern direction, the goddess Tara is venerated in both Hindu and Buddhist traditions. Her name means "star."

Third Eye Awakened consciousness. The mind's inner eye and its faculty of clairvoyance. See Ajna Chakra.

Throat Chakra The communication center of the Subtle Body, visualized as an upward-pointing lotus of sixteen petals. One of the four major centers of the Subtle Body.

Tika (Skt.) A mark made on the forehead to signify commitment to a spiritual ideal. Part of daily Hindu ritual.

Transformation Chakra See Navel Chakra.

Trataka (Skt.) A Yogic and Tantric technique of "gazing," used to strengthen the eyes and to awaken powers of clairvoyance.

True Fluid A Taoist term for female sexual secretions. Life-essence.

Ts'ai-nu (Ch.) "The Elected Girl." An instructress in the Taoist arcana of sex, she represents the narcissistic quality of Nature. One of three sex initiatresses of the mythical Yellow Emperor.

Twilight Language A Tantric term for the secret language of allegory and paradox, used to convey esoteric teachings. Twilight language should be understood on three levels: the literal, the allegorical and the mystical.

Udana (Skt.) One of the five main divisions of the life-force. The Udana is mainly focused in the region of the throat and controls metabolism, aging and communication. Associated with a red-violet color, the faculty of touch, the process of swallowing and salivation.

Uddiyana Bandha (Skt.) An advanced Yogic technique that helps draw up sexual energy. Named after the ancient Tantric kingdom of Uddiyana in Orissa (eastern India), it can be practiced by either man or woman and consists in contracting the stomach muscles, thus creating a vacuum effect in the lower abdomen and bladder.

Ushas (Skt.) The Dawn goddess, wife of Agni, the Fire god. Ushas is portrayed as a young woman exposing her breasts for the admiration of man. She is said to be an "awakener of beings."

Ushtrasana (Skt.) The camel posture. A simple Yoga asana that stretches the muscles of the back and arms while stimulating the glandular system.

Vajravarahi (Skt.) A Tantric guardian goddess of occult secrets. Depicted as sow-headed, she is identified with the central channel of the Subtle Body, with the transcendental power of menstruation and with sexual abandon. An initiatress of the Tantric mysteries.

Vajrini (Skt.) One of the very subtle channels making up the central channel of the Subtle Body (the *Sushumna*).

Vajroil Mudra (Skt.) An advanced Yogic and Tantric practice of drawing up liquids (water, milk or sexual secretions) through the sexual organ by contractions of the lower diaphragm (using the Uddiyana Bandha technique).

Vang (Skt.) A Tantric seed-syllable, or Mantra, associated with the water element, the sense of taste, the circular shape and the color light blue.

Vasistha (Skt.) The name of a great Brahmin sage who engaged in Tantric practices and attained Liberation.

Veda (Skt.) The sacred Hindu scriptures

of the Brahmanic tradition. There are four principal Vedas, known as the *Rig, Yajur, Sama* and *Atharva*. There is an ancient tradition of a lost "fifth" Veda.

Vina (Skt.) A seven stringed Indian musical instrument, normally with gourds at each end of a fingerboard. Symbolizing the play of the senses, the vina is associated with Saraswati, the consort of Brahma.

Viparitakarani (Skt.) Literally "reverse system." A Yogic term used to refer to the inverse postures of Hatha Yoga and the Tantric philosophical/practice viewpoint, which aims to reverse the outward and downward flow of life energies. Viparitakarani is said to be the best method of overcoming old age and destiny.

Virasana (Skt.) The heroic posture. A comfortable and straightforward Yoga asana ideal for meditation and sexual activities.

Vishnu (Skt.) The preserving aspect of the Hindu triad of forces governing all phenomena. Vishnu rules over the life function and is the Lord of cosmic play. His role is to stimulate eros and satisfy Lakshmi, his consort. Vishnu's force is matriarchal, unconventional and intuitive. Normally visualized as blue in color, he "dreams the world;" his symbols are the conch and the discus. In the microcosm, Vishnu resides in the Heart Chakra.

Vyana (Skt.) One of the five main divisions of the life-force, the Vyana pervades the whole body, circulating the energies derived from food, breath and the mind. Controls both the expansive and contractive aspects of the being. Associated with a light blue color, with the faculty of hearing and with body posture.

White Metal See Moon Flower Waters/Medicine.

White Snow A Taoist term referring to subtle secretions produced from the breasts of woman during sexual arousal. Also known as Immortality Peach Juice and Essence of Coral.

White Tiger's Cavern See Purple Mushroom Peak.

Womb Breathing A secret Tantric and Taoist breathing technique used to attract virility and vital energy. The person lies in a fetal position, drawing only shallow breaths from the lower abdomen while "abstracting" the mind and visualizing energy entering through the navel region.

Yab (Tib.) Father. The animus, the original male principle.

Yab-Yum (Tib.) The combined male and female principles viewed as the ideal. The resolution of all dualities. Cosmic one-ness.

Yang (Ch.) The Force of Heaven. The positive, male principle, linked to the qualities of expansion, heat, lightness and dryness. Also a Sanskrit seed-syllable or Mantra associated with the air element, the sense of touch, the crescent shape and the dark color of space.

Yang Fluid Semen. Sometimes portrayed as celestial dragons in the Taoist tradition.

Yang Number The number eighty-one (nine multiplied by nine). A magical number according to Taoism.

Yantra (Skt.) A mystic diagram, pattern, magical design or meditation symbol. A way of focusing the attention through visual means. The root word "yan" means to retain. Tantric love-postures are said to be Yantras since they focus and channel energies. The term "Yantra" can be used to refer to any machine or device. The body is one's personal Yantra, just as one's method of breathing makes one's personal Mantra and one's lifestyle and belief structure determines one's "Tantra."

Yellow Emperor Known as Huang-Ti, he is said to have ruled in the Golden Age (we are presently in the Iron Age or Dark Age of Kali) and was known as the Son of Heaven. He figures prominently in the medical and sexological teachings of Taoism and is said to have ascended to Heaven in broad daylight, having perfect-

ed himself through practicing the Sexual Secrets.

Yidam (Tib.) Tutelary deity or idealized representation of esoteric truths. The mystic protector and benefactor. The secret form of the Tantric teacher. One's personal deity, referred to as Isthadevata in Sanskrit.

Yin (Ch.) The Force of Earth. The negative, female principle, linked to the qualities of contraction, cold, heaviness and wetness. According to Taoism both man and woman embody Yin and Yang qualities; the predominance of one of the other determines gender.

Yin-Essence Female sexual secretions. The ovum.

Yoga (Skt.) Literally "to join together." Union. The communion of the individual self with the greater Self or godhead. Sexual union is one form of Yoga.

Yoganidrasana (Skt.) Vishnu's sleep posture. Also known as the posture of the intermediate state, it is a Yoga asana requiring flexibility of the back, arms and legs. It warms the body and releases latent energies.

Yogi (Skt.) A person who practices and is proficient in Yoga. One who has mastered himself, who is in control of his senses.

Yogini (Skt.) A female Yogi.

Yogini Chakra (Skt.) A Tantric secret ritual practice in which a single man makes love with a number of women, each of whom is adept at sexual Yoga.

Yoni (Skt.) The female sexual organ. The original source. The doorway into this world. A fountain, receptacle or container worthy of veneration.

Yoni Mudra (Skt.) A Yoga technique in which the apertures of the head are closed or sealed with the fingers so that the sensual energies associated with ecstasy are not dispersed.

Yuga (Skt.) An age or eon of time. Hindu writings refer to four yugas, which repeat themselves over and over again.

Yum (Tib.) Mother. The anima, the original female principle.

Yun-Yu (Ch.) A Taoist term denoting physical sexual union. Literally "the Mystery of the Clouds and the Rain." The secrets of sexuality.

SUPPLEMENTARY GLOSSARY OF TERMS USED TO REFER TO THE SEXUAL ORGANS

CHINESE TERMS

MALE
Ambassador
Assailant
Boy
Crimson Bird
Faithful Servant
Fruit
Henchman
Implement
Jade Flute
Jade Scepter
Jade Stalk
Love Weapon
Positive Peak
Proboscis
Tortoise
Weapon
Yang Peak

FEMALE
Anemone of Love
Cavern
Chicken's Tongue (clitoris)
Cinnabar Cave (womb)
Cinnabar Crevice
Conch Shell
Door of Life
Female Crucible
Fishpond (womb)
Flower
Flower Heart (opening to womb)
Golden Doorway
Golden Furrow

Grain-shaped Cave
Grotto
Heart of the Peony (womb)
Infant Girl
Inner Heart
Innermost Knot (entrance to womb)
Inner Stream
Inner Terrace
Jade Cavern
Jade Gate
Gade Gateway
Jewel Enclosure (womb)
Love Grotto
Mysterious Cavern
Mysterious Valley
Perfumed Mouse
Pleasure Grotto
Pleasure House
Pleasure Place (clitoris)
Precious Crucible
Precious Gate/Gateway
Precious Stone
Red Pearl
Secret Cavern
Sensitive Cave
Sexual Cavern
Strings of the Lyre (lips of vulva)
Treasure House
Wheat-shaped Cave

Indian/Tibetan Terms
MALE
Arrow of Love
Bull
Jewel
Scepter
Scepter of His Means
Wand

FEMALE
Bell
Cup
Lotus
Lotus Flower
Lotus of Her Wisdom
Pleasure Field of Heaven
Seat of Pleasure

bibliography

Bibliography of works consulted in the writing of Sexual Secrets. Texts which have been translated from Sanskrit, Tibetan and Chinese specifically for this book are not included.

Agarwal, U. Khajuraho Sculptures and Their Significance. Delhi, 1964.

Agrawala, S. Vasudeva. Shiva Mahadeva: The Great God. Varanasi: Veda Academy, 1966. An exposition of the symbolism of Shiva.

Allgrove, G. Love in the East. London: Panther Books, 1964

Anand, Mulk Raj. Kama Kala. Geneva: Nagel Publications, 1958.
——— and Mookerjee, Ajit. Tantra Magic. Delhi: Arnold Heinemann, 1977.

Arbuthnot, F. F., and Burton, Sir Richard. The Kama Sutra of Vatsyayana. Edited by W. G. Archer. London: George Allen & Unwin, 1963. Introduction by K. M. Panikkar.
———. The Kama Sutra of Vatsyayana. Edited by John Muirhead Gould. St. Albans, Eng.: Panther Books, 1963. Introduction by Dom Moraes.
———, ed. and trans. Ananga Ranga: The Hindu Art of Love by Kalayana Malla. New York: Medical Press, 1964. With Indian Pharmacopeia by Gabers and Rama.

Ashe, Geoffrey. The Virgin. St. Albans, Eng.: Paladin Books, 1977.

Avalon, Arthur, trans. The Greatness of Shiva (Mahimnastava of Puspadanta). Madras: Ganesh & Company, 1963.
———, trans. Wave of Bliss (Anandalahari). London: Luzac & Company, 1917. Reprint. Madras: Ganesh & Company, 1961.
———, trans. Hymn to Kali (Karpuradi-Stotra). Madras: Ganesh & Company, 1965. Commentary by Swami Vimalananda.
———, trans. The Great Liberation (Mahanirvana Tantra). Madras: Ganesh & Company, 1927, 1963.
———, trans. Kulacudamani Nigama. Madras: Ganesh & Company, 1956.
———, ed. Kalivilasa Tantra, Vol. VI of Tantrik Texts. Translated and edited by P. C. Tarkatirtha. London: Luzac & Company, 1917.
——— and Avalon, Ellen, trans. Hymns to the Goddess. Madras: Ganesh & Company, 1964.

Ayer, V. A. K. Sariraka Sastra: Indian Science of Handreading. Bombay: Taraporevala Publishers, 1975. Sanskrit text with translation and commentary.

Baba, Bengali. Patanjali: Yoga Sutras. Poona, 1949.

Baba, Pagal. Temple of the Phallic King: The Mind of India. Edited by E. Rice. New York: Simon & Schuster, 1973.

Bagchi, P. C. Studies in the Tantras. Calcutta: University of Calcutta Publications, 1939.

Banerjea, A. K. Philosophy of Gorakhnath. Gorakhpur, 1962. Foreword by Gopinath Kaviraj.

Banerjea, J. N. The Development of Hindu Iconography. Calcutta: University of Calcutta Publications, 1956.
———. Pauranic and Tantric Religion. Calcutta: University of Calcutta Publications 1966.

Banerji, S. C. Tantra in Bengal: A Study in Its Origin, Development and Influence. Calcutta: Prokash Publications, 1977.

Barber, T. Biofeedback and Self Control. Chicago, 1971.

Basu, Manoranjan. Tantras: A General Study. Calcutta: Basu Publications, 1976.

Bataille, G. Eroticism, London, 1962.

Bedi, B. P. L., trans. The Art of the Temptress (Kuttni Mahatmyam of Damodar Gupta). Bombay: Pearl Books, 1968. A Sanskrit classic on the art of seduction considered as a discipline.

Bergson, Anika, and Tuchack, Vladimir. Zone Therapy: A Step-by-Step Guide to Applied Pressure Therapy. New York: Pinnacle Books, 1974.

Bernard, Theos. Hatha Yoga: The Report of a Personal Experience. London: Rider & Company, 1968.

Beurdeley, Michel, in collaboration with C. Fu-jui; J. Pimpaneau; and K. Schipper. The Clouds and the Rain: The Art of Love in China. London: Hammond & Hammond, 1969.

Bharati, Agehananda. The Tantric Tradition. London: Rider & Company, 1965.

Bhattacharyya, Benoytosh. An Introduction to Buddhist Esoterism. Varanasi: Chowkhamba Sanskrit Series, 1964.
———, trans. Nispannayogavali. Baroda: Oriental Institute, 1949. Translation and commentary.

———, trans. The Indian Buddhist Iconography. Calcutta: Firma Mukhopadhyay, 1968. Based mainly on the Sadhanamala and cognate Tantric texts of rituals.
———, trans. Two Vajrayana Works. Baroda: Gaekwad Oriental Series, 1929.
———. Sadhanamala. 2 vols. Baroda: Oriental Institute, 1968. English introduction and Sanskrit text.
———. Guhyasamaja Tantra. Baroda: Gaekwad Oriental Series, 1931. Text and commentary.

Bhattacharyya, N. N. Indian Puberty Rites. Calcutta, 1968.

Bhavnani, Enakshi. The Dance in India. Bombay: Taraporevala, 1970.

Bhishagratna, Kaviraj, trans. The Sushruta Samhita. 3 vol. Varanasi: Chowkhamba Sanskrit Series, 1963.

Bird, Christopher, and Tompkins, Peter. The Secret Life of Plants. London: Allen Lane, 1973.

Bloch, I. Sexual Life in England Past and Present. London, 1958.

Blofeld, John. The Way of Power: A Practical Guide to the Tantric Mysticism of Tibet. London: George Allen & Unwin, 1970.
———. Mantras: Sacred Words of Power. London: George Allen & Unwin, 1977.
———. Beyond the Gods: Buddhist and Taoist Mysticism. New York: E. P. Dutton & Company, 1974.

Bose, D. N. Tantras: Their Philosophy and Occult Secrets. Calcutta, 1965.

Bowie, Theodore, and Christenson, Cornelia V., eds. Studies in Erotic Art. New York: Basic Books Inc., 1970.

Briggs, G. W. Gorakhnath and the Kanphata Yogis. Delhi: Motilal Banarsidass, 1973.

Bryk, Felix. Voodoo-Eros: Ethnological Studies in the Sex-Life of the African Aborigines. Translated from the German by M. F. Sexton. New York: United Book Guild, 1964.

Buckley, Edmund. Phallicism in Japan. Chicago, 1895.

Burang, Theodore. Tibetan Art of Healing (English translation from the German). London: Watkins, 1974.

Burton, Sir Richard, trans. The Book of the Thousand Nights and a Night (Arabian Nights). Benares: The Burton Club, 1885.
———, trans. Hindu Art of Love (Ananga Ranga) with The Symposium of Plato (translated by B. Jowett). London, 1963.
———. The Perfumed Garden of the Shaykh Nefzawi. London: Neville Spearman, 1963. Introduction by A. H. Walton.

Burton, Robert. The Mating Game. Lausanne: Elsevier/Phaidon, 1976.

Cabanes, A. The Erotikon: A Treasury of Scientific Marvels of Human Sexuality. Translated from the French by R. Meadows. New York: Book Awards, 1966.

Caprio, Frank S. Variations in Sexual Behaviour. London: Calder Books, 1970.

Cerney, C. V. Acupressure: Acupuncture without Needles. New York: Cornerstone Library Publications, 1974.

Chakravarti, Chintaharan. The Tantras: Studies on Their Religion and Literature. Calcutta: Punthi Pustak, 1963.

Chand, Devi, trans. The Yajur Veda. Delhi: Paul & Company, 1965.

Chandra, Lokesh. The Esoteric Iconography of Japanese Mandalas. Delhi, 1971.
———. Mandalas of the Tantra Samucchaya. Delhi, 1969.
———. Japanese Mysteries of Ganesha. Delhi, 1971.

Chandra, M. The World of Courtesans. Delhi: Vikas Publications, 1973.

Chang, C. C. Garma. Teachings of Tibetan Yoga. New York: University Books, 1963.

Chang, Jolan. The Tao of Love and Sex: The Ancient Chinese Way to Ecstasy. London: Wildwood House, 1977. Foreword and Postscript by Joseph Needham.

Chatterji, J. C. Kashmir Shaivaism. Srinagar, 1962.

Cheng, W. C. Erotologie de la Chine. Paris, 1963.

Chew, W. C. The Goddess Faith: A Religion of the Mind. New York: Exposition Press, 1977.

Chattopadhyaya, S. Evolution of Hindu Sects. Delhi, 1970.
———. Reflections on the Tantras. Delhi: Motilal Banarsidass, 1978.

Colaabavala, F. D. Tantra: The Erotic Cult. Delhi: Orient Paperbacks, 1976.

Comfort, Alex, trans. and ed. The Koka Shastra: Medieval Indian Writings on Love (Ratirahasya of Kokkoka). New York: Stein & Day, 1965. Preface by W. G. Archer.
———. The Joy of Sex: A Gourmet Guide to Lovemaking. New York: Simon & Schuster, 1972.
———. More Joy of Sex. New York: Simon & Schuster, 1978.

Culling, Louis T. A Manual of Sex Magic. St. Paul, Minn.: Llewellyn Publications, 1971.

Cutner, H. A Short History of Sex Worship. London: Watts & Company, 1940.

Danielsson, Bengt. Love in the South Seas. New York: Reynal, 1956.

Danielou, A. Yoga: The Method of Re-integration (its Origin, its Aims, its Methods). London: Johnson Publications, 1973.
———. Hindu Polytheism. London: Routledge & Kegan Paul, 1964.

Dasgupta, R. An Architectural Survey of the Kamakhya Temple. Gauhati, 1960. Foreword by S. K. Bhuyan.

Dasgupta, Shashibhusan. Obscure Religious Cults. Calcutta: Firma Mukhopadhyay, 1969.
———. Introduction to Tantrik Buddhism. Calcutta, 1950. Reprint. Introduction by H. V. Guenther. Berkeley, Cal.: Shambhala, 1974.

Dastur, J. F. Everybody's Guide to Ayurvedic Medicine. Bombay: Taraporevala, 1960.

Datta, B. N. Mystic Tales of Lama Taranatha. Calcutta: Ramakrishna Vedanta Math, 1957.

David-Neel, A. Initiations and Initiates in Tibet. Translated from the

French by Fred Rothwell. London: Rider & Company, 1970.

———. *With Mystics and Magicians in Tibet*. London, 1931.

———. *Secret Oral Teachings in Tibetan Buddhist Sects*. San Francisco; 1968.

De, Sushil Kumar. *The Early History of the Vaisnava Faith and Movement in Bengal*. Calcutta: Firma Mukhopadhyay, 1961.

———. *Ancient Indian Erotics and Erotic Literature*. Calcutta, 1959.

———. *The Treatment of Love in Sanskrit Literature*. Calcutta, 1929.

De Beauvoir, S. *The Second Sex*. Translated and edited by H. M. Parshley. New York: Bantam Books, 1961.

De Becker, R. *The Other .Face of Love*. Translated by M. Crosland and A. Daventry. New York: Grove Press, 1969.

De Langre, J. *The First and Second Books of Do-in*. Megalia, Cal.: Happiness Press, 1971, 1974. The art of rejuvenation through self-massage.

D'eon, C. *The Science of Regeneration or Sex Enlightenment*. Cal.: Health Research Publications, 1968.

Delacourt, M. *Hermaphrodite: Myths and Rites of the Bisexual Figure in Classical Antiquity*. London, 1961.

Desai, Devangana. *Erotic Sculpture of India: A Socio-Cultural Study*. Delhi: Tata McGraw-Hill Publishing, 1975.

Devi, Kamala. *The Eastern Way of Love: Tantric Sex and Erotic Mysticism*. New York: Simon & Schuster, 1977.

Dimock, E. C. *The Thief of Love: Bengali Tales from Court and Village*. Chicago: University of Chicago Press, 1963.

Douglas, Kenneth. *The Life and Liberation of Padmasambhava*. 2 vols. Emeryville, Cal. Dharma Publishing, 1978. From the French version by G. C. Toussaint.

Douglas, Nik. *Tantra Yoga*. Delhi: Munshiram Manoharlal, 1970.

———. *Tibetan Tantric Charms and Amulets*. New York: Dover Publications, 1978.

———. *The Book of Matan: Automatic Writings from the Brink of Eternity*. Sudbury, Eng.: Neville Spearman, 1977. Foreword by Lyall Watson.

———, Ed. *Chakra Magazine: A Journal of Tantra and Yoga*. 4 issues. Delhi: Kumar Gallery Publications, 1969–71.

——— and Slinger, Penny. *Mountain Ecstasy*. Paris and Rotterdam: Dragon's Dream Publications, 1978.

——— and Slinger, Penny. *The Secret Dakini Oracle*. New York: Destiny Books, 1979.

———; Slinger, Penny; and White, Meryl. *The Secret Dakini Oracle Deck: A Tantric Tarot*. New York: U.S. Games Systems, 1978.

——— and White, Meryl. *Karmapa: The Black Hat Lama of Tibet*. London: Luzac & Company, 1976.

Downing, George. *The Massage Book*. London: Wildwood House, 1973.

Droscher, Vitus B. *The Magic of the Senses: New Discoveries in Animal Perception*. London: W. H. Allen, 1969.

Dubois, Abbe J. A., *Hindu Manners, Customs and Ceremonies*. Translated by Beauchamp. London, 1936.

Dutt, M. N. trans. *Garuda Purana*. Varanasi: Chowkhamba Sanskrit Series, 1968.

Edwardes, A. *The Jewel in the Lotus: A Historical Survey of the Sexual Culture of the East*. New York, Julian Press, 1959. Introduction by Albert Ellis.

——— and Masters, R. E. L. *The Cradle of Erotica: The Definitive Study of Exotic Afro-Asian Sexual Behaviour*. New York: Lancer Books, 1962.

Egerton, Clement, trans. *The Golden Lotus (Chin P'ing Mei)*. 4 vols. London: Routledge & Kegan Paul, 1972.

Eliade, Mircea. *Shamanism: Archaic Techniques of Ecstasy*. London: Routledge & Kegan Paul, 1964.

———. *Yoga: Immortality and Freedom*. Translated by W. R. Trask. New York: Pantheon Books, 1958.

Elisifon, E., and Watts, A. *Erotic Spirituality: The Vision of Konarak*. New York: Macmillan, 1971.

Elwin, Verrier. *The Kingdom of the Young*. London: Oxford University Press, 1968.

Ellis, Havelock. *Studies in the Psychology of Sex*. New York: Random House, 1968.

Etiemble. *Yun Yu: An Essay on Eroticism and Love in Ancient China*. Translated from the French by James Hogarth. Geneva: Nagel, 1970.

Evans, Tom, and Evans, Mary. *Shunga: The Art of Love in Japan*. New York: Paddington Press, 1975.

Evans-Wentz, W. Y., ed. *The Tibetan Book of the Dead*. Translated from the Tibetan by Lama Kazi Dawa Samdup. London: Oxford University Press, 1960.

———. *Tibetan Yoga and Secret Doctrines*. Translated from the Tibetan by Lama Kazi Dawa Samdup. London: Oxford University Press, 1965. Foreword by R. R. Marett and Yogic commentary by Chen-chi Chang.

———. *The Tibetan Book of the Great Liberation*. Translated from the Tibetan by Laden La and the Lamas Karma Sumdhon Paul; Lobzang Mingyur Dorje; and Kazi Dawa Samdup. London: Oxford University Press, 1965. Contains a psychological commentary by C. G. Jung.

Feng, Gia-fu. *Lao Tsu's Tao Te Ching*. London: Wildwood House, 1973.

Fielding, W. J. *Strange Customs of Courtship and Marriage*. New York, 1956.

Filliozat, J. *The Classical Doctrine of Indian Medicine: Its Origins and Its Greek Parallels*. Translated from the French by Dev Ragpj Channa. New Delhi: Munshiram Manoharlal, 1964.

Fischman, Walter, and Warren, Frank Z. *Sexual Acupuncture: A Dramatic New Technique to Intensify Your Pleasure*. New York: E. P. Dutton, 1978.

Fiser, Ivo. *Indian Erotics of the Oldest Period*. Praha, 1966.

Ford, C. S. *Patterns of Sexual Behaviour*, New York: Harper & Row, 1951.

Foucault, M. *The History of Sexuality*. Vol. I. Translated from the French by R. Hurley. New York: Pantheon Books, 1978.

Foucher, Max-Pol. *The Erotic Sculpture of India*. London: George Allen & Unwin, 1959.

Fremantle, Francesca, and Trungpa, Chogyam, trans. *The Tibetan Book of the Dead: The Great Liberation through Hearing in the Bardo* (translated from the Tibetan). Berkeley: Shambhala, 1975.

Fulder, Stephen. *About Ginseng: The Magical Herb of the East*. Wellingborough, Eng.: Northants, 1976.

Garrison, O. V. *Tantra: The Yoga of Sex*. New York: Julian Press, 1964.

Gendron, Jacques. *Poesie de la Pierre Indienne*. Paris: Noumea 1971.

George, Chris S., trans. *The Chandamaharosana Tantra* (translation of Chaps. I–VIII). New Haven, Conn.: American Oriental Society, 1974.

Gerhard, P. *Pornography or Art?* Harrow, Eng.: Words and Pictures, 1968.

———. *The Pillow Book or History of Naughty Pictures*. Bishop's Stortford, Eng.: RBW Press, 1971.

Getty, Alice. *Ganesha: A Monograph on the Elephant-Faced God*. Delhi: Munshiram Manoharlal, 1972.

Ghalioungui, Paul. *Magical and Medical Science in Ancient Egypt*. London: Hodder & Stoughton, 1963.

Ghose, A. C. *The Ratishastra of Nagarjuna Siddha*. Calcutta, 1904.

Ghosh, D. P. *Kama Ratna: Indian Ideals of Feminine Beauty*. Delhi, 1973.

Ghurye, G. S. *Indian Sadhus*. Bombay, 1964.

Gichner, L. E. *Erotic Aspects of Hindu Sculpture*. Washington, D.C., 1949.

———. *Erotic Aspects of Japanese Culture*. Washington, D.C., 1953.

———. *Erotic Aspects of Chinese Culture*. Washington, D.C., 1957.

Goldberg, B. Z. *The Sacred Fire: The Story of Sex in Religion*. New York: University Books, 1958. Introduction by Charles Potter.

Gordon, A. K. *The Iconography of Tibetan Lamaism*. Rutland, Vt.: Charles Tuttle & Paragon Reprint, 1972.

Goswami, Hemchandra, trans. *Kamaratna Tantra*. Shillong, 1928.

Govinda, Lama Anagarika. *Foundations of Tibetan Mysticism*. London: Rider & Company, 1969.

Graves, Robert. *The White Goddess: A Historical Grammar of Poetic Myth*. London: Faber & Faber, 1961.

Griffith, F., and Thompson, H. *The Leyden Papyrus: An Egyptian Magical Book*. New York: Dover Publications, 1974.

Griffith, R. T. H., trans. *The Hymns of the Rgveda*. Delhi: Motilal Banarsidass, 1973. With commentary.

———, trans. *The Hymns of the Samaveda*. Varanasi: Chowkhamba Sanskrit Series, 1963. With commentary.

———, trans. *The Hymns of the Atharvaveda*. 2 vols. Varanasi: Chowkhamba Sanskrit Series, 1968. With commentary.

Grigson, G. *The Goddess of Love: The Birth, Death and Return of Aphrodite*. London: Constable, 1976.

Grosbois, Charles. *Shunga: Images of Spring*. Geneva, 1964.

Grove Press, ed. *Fille de Joie: A Book of Courtesans, Sporting Girls, Ladies of the Evening, Madams, a Few Occasionals and Some Royal Favorites*. New York: Grove Press, 1967. An anthology of Eastern and Western sources.

Guenther, Herbert V. *The Tantric View of Life*. Berkeley: Shambhala, 1972.

———, trans. *The Royal Song of Saraha: A Study in the History of Buddhist Thought*. Seattle: University of Washington Press, 1969. With commentary.

———, trans. *The Life and Teaching of Naropa*. (translated from the Tibetan). London: Oxford University Press, 1963.

———, trans. *sGampopa's Jewel Ornament of Liberation* (translated from the Tibetan). London: Rider & Company, 1970.

——— and Trungpa, Chogyam. *The Dawn of Tantra*. Berkeley: Shambhala, 1975.

Gulabkunverba Society. *The Charaka Samhita*. 6 vols. Translated by a board of scholars. Jamnagar: Sri Gulabkunverba Ayurvedic Society, 1949.

Gupta, Sanjukta. *Lakshmi Tantra*. Leiden: E. J. Brill & Company, 1972. Contains the entire translated text.

Gupta, Shakti M. *Loves of Hindu Gods and Sages*. Bombay: Allied Publishing, 1973.

Gurdjieff, George. *All and Everything*. London: Routledge & Kegan Paul, 1962.

Hall, Manly. *The Secret Teachings of All Ages*. Los Angeles, 1973.

Hamada, K., trans. *The Life of an Amorous Man*. Rutland, Vt.: Charles Tuttle, 1964. A translation of the Japanese classic by Saikaku.

Harding, M. E. *Woman's Mysteries: Ancient and Modern*. New York: Harper & Row, 1976.

———. *The Way of All Women: A Psychological Interpretation*. London: Rider & Company, 1971. Introduction by C. G. Jung.

Harner, M. J. *Hallucinogens and Shamanism*. New York: Oxford University Press, 1973.

Heilbrun, Carolyn G. *Toward a Recognition of Androgyny*. New York: Alfred A. Knopf, 1973.

Hibbett, H. *The Floating World in Japanese Fiction*. London: Oxford University Press, 1959.

Hofmann, A., Ruck, C. A. P., and Wasson, R. G. *The Road to Eleusis: Unveiling the Secret of the Mysteries*. New York: Harcourt, Brace & Jovanovich, 1978.

Hoyle, Rafael L. *Checan: An Essay on Erotic Elements in Peruvian Art*. Geneva: Nagel, 1965.

Humphries, R., trans. *Ovid's The Art of Love*. Bloomington: University of Indiana Press, 1960.

Illing, R. *Japanese Erotic Art, and The Life of the Courtesan*. New York: St. Martins Press, 1978.

Ingham, Eunice D. *Stories the Feet Can Tell*. New York: Ingham Publications, 1976.

———. *Stories the Feet Have Told: Zone Therapy and Gland Reflexes*. New York: Ingham Publications, 1959.

Inkeles, G., and Todris, M. *The Art of Sensual Massage*. San Francisco: Straight Arrow Books, 1972.

Irwin, Yukiko, and Wagenvoord,

James. *Shiatzu: Japanese Finger Pressure for Energy, Sexual Vitality and Relief from Tension and Pain.* London: Routledge & Kegan Paul, 1977. Foreword by Dorothea M. Kerr.

Ishihara, A., and Levy, H. S. *The Tao of Sex: An Annotated Translation of the 28th Section of the Essence of Medical Prescription (Ishimpo).* Yokohama: Shibundo Publications, 1968.

Iyengar, B. K. S. *Light on Yoga.* London: George Allen & Unwin, 1976.

Jacobs, Hans. *Western Psychotherapy and Hindu Sadhana.* London: George Allen & Unwin, 1961.

Jacolliot, L. *Occult Science in India and Among the Ancients, with an Account of Their Mystic Initiations.* Translated from the French by W. L. Felt. New York: University Books, 1971. Foreword by O. V. Garrison.

Jaggi, O. P. *Yogic and Tantric Medicine.* Vol. V of *History of Science and Technology in India.* Delhi: Atma Ram & Sons, 1973.

Jhavery, M. B. *Comparative and Critical Study of Mantrashastra.* Ahmedabad: Sarabhai Manilal Nawab, 1944.

John, Bubba Free. *Love of the Two-Armed Form: The Free and Regenerative Function of Sexuality in Ordinary Life and the Transcendence of Sexuality in True Religious or Spiritual Practice.* Middletown, Cal.: Dawn Horse Press, 1978.

Johnson, O. S. *A Study of Chinese Alchemy.* Shanghai, 1928.

Jung, C. G. *Archetypes and the Collective Unconscious.* London: Routledge & Kegan Paul, 1959.
———. *Man and His Symbols.* London: Aldus Books, 1964.
———. *Mandala Symbolism.* Translated by R. F. C. Hull. Princeton, N. J.: Princeton University Press, 1972.
———. *Psychology and Religion.* Collected Works, Vol. 11. Translated by R. F. C. Hull. London: Routledge & Kegan Paul, 1958.
———. *Psychology and Alchemy.* Collected Works, Vol. 12. Translated by R. F. C. Hull. London: Routledge & Kegan Paul, 1968.
———. *Alchemical Studies.* Collected Works, Vol. 13. Translated by R. F. C. Hull. London: Routledge & Kegan Paul, 1967.

Jung, Emma. *Animus and Anima.* Zurich: Spring Publications, 1972.

Jyotirmayananda. *Meditate the Tantric Yoga Way.* Translated and edited by Lillian K. Donat. London: George Allen & Unwin, 1973.

Kakati, B. K. *The Mother Goddess Kamakhya.* Gauhati: Lawyers Publication, 1967.
———. *Visnuite Myths and Legends: In Folklore Setting.* Gauhati: Lawyers Publications, 1952.

Kale, Arvind, and Shanta. *Tantra: The Secret Power of Sex.* Bombay: Jaico Publications, 1976.

Kannan, S. *Swara Chintamani: Divination by Breath.* Madras: Kannan Publications, 1967.

Karambelkar, V. W. *The Atharvaveda and the Ayur-veda.* Nagpur: Usha Kara, 1961.

Kaviraj, Gopinath. *Aspects of Indian Thought.* Burdwan: University Press, 1966.

Kaye, Anna, and Matchan, Don C. *Mirror of the Body.* San Francisco: Strawberry Hill Press, 1978. Foot pressure therapy.

Keith, A. C., trans. *The Veda of the Black Yajus School (Taittiriya Sanhita).* 2 vols. Delhi: Motilal Banarsidass, 1967.

Keswani, N. H. *The Science of Medicine and Psychological Concepts in Ancient and Medieval India.* Delhi: All India Institute of Medical Science, 1974.

Khanna, Madhu, and Mookerjee, Ajit. *The Tantric Way: Art, Science, Ritual.* London: Thames & Hudson, 1977.

King, Francis. *Sexuality, Magic and Perversion.* London: Neville Spearman, 1971.

Kinsey, Martin, and Pomeroy. *Sexual Behaviour in the Human Male.* London: W. Saunders, 1948.
———. *Sexual Behaviour in the Human Female.* London: W. Saunders, 1953.

Kinsley, D. R. *The Sword and the Flute: Kali and Krishna.* Berkeley: University of California Press, 1975. Dark visions of the terrible and the sublime in Hindu mythology.

Kleen, Tyra. *Mudras: The Ritual Hand-Poses of the Buddha Priests and the Shiva Priests of Bali.* London, 1942.

Krishna, Gopi. *Kundalini: Paths to Higher Consciousness.* Delhi: Orient, 1976.

Krishnamurti, Y. G., and Shrama, Chandrakanta. *Samudrika: The Hindu Art of Sex and Body Sign Predictions.* Delhi, 1971.

Kronhausen, Phyllis, and Kronhausen, Eberhard. *Erotic Art.* London: W. H. Allen, 1971.
———. *The Complete Book of Erotic Art.* New York: Bell, 1978.
———. *Catalogue of the International Museum of Erotic Art.* San Francisco, 1973.

Kuhn, F. *The Before Midnight Scholar: The Jou Pu Tuan.* Translated by R. Martin from the German rendering of Li Yu's classic. London: André Deutsch, 1965.

Kumar, Pushpendra. *Sakti Cult in Ancient India: With Special Reference to the Pauranic Literature.* Varanasi: Bhartiya Publishing House, 1974.

Kushi, M. *An Introduction to Oriental Diagnosis.* Edited by William Tara. London: Red Moon Press, 1976.

La Barre, W. *The Peyote Cult.* New York: Schocken, 1969.

Lacey, Louise. *Lunaception: A Feminine Odyssey into Fertility and Contraception.* New York: Coward, McCann & Geoghegan, 1974. Introduction by Barbara Seaman.

Lal, Kanwar. *Immortal Khajuraho.* Delhi, 1965.
———. *The Cult of Desire.* Delhi, 1966.
———. *Kanya and the Yogi.* Delhi: Arts & Letters, 1970.
———. *Temples and Sculptures of Bhubaneshwar.* Delhi, 1970.
———. *Miracle of Konarak.* Delhi, 1967.

Lalita. *Choose Your Own Mantra.* New York: Bantam Books, 1978.

Leadbeater, C. W. *The Chakras.* London, 1972.

Leeson, Francis. *Kama Shilpa.* Bombay: Taraporevala, 1962.

Legeza, Laszlo. *Tao Magic: The Chinese Art of the Occult.* New York: Pantheon Books, 1975.
——— and Rawson, P. *Tao: The Chinese Philosophy of Time and Change.* London: Thames & Hudson, 1973.

Lessing, F. D., and Wayman, Alex, trans. *Fundamentals of the Buddhist Tantras.* The Hague: Mouton, 1968.

Levy, Howard S. *Chinese Footbinding: The History of a Curious Erotic Custom.* London: Neville Spearman, 1966. Foreword by A. Waley and introduction by W. Eberhard.
———. *Harem Favorites of an Illustrious Celestial.* Taichung, 1958.
———, trans. *Warm-Soft Village.* (from the Chinese and Japanese). Tokyo, 1964.
———, trans. *The Illusory Flame.* (from the Japanese). Tokyo, 1962.

Licht, Hans. *Sexual Life in Ancient Greece.* London: Routledge & Kegan Paul, 1932.

Llewellyn. *Gnostica Magazine.* Issues 1–49. St. Paul, Minn.

Luk, Charles. *Taoist Yoga: Alchemy and Immortality.* London: Rider & Company, 1970.

Malinowski, Bronislav. *Sex, Culture and Myth.* London: Hart-Davis, 1963.

Marcade, Jean. *Eros Kalos: An Essay on Erotic Elements in Greek Art.* Geneva: Nagel, 1962.
———. *Roma Amor: An Essay on Erotic Elements in Etruscan and Roman Art.* Geneva: Nagel, 1961.

Marr, G. S. *Sex in Religion: A Historical Survey.* London: George Allen & Unwin, 1936.

Mascaro, J., trans. *The Dhammapada: The Path of Perfection* (translated from the Pali). London, 1973.

Masters, R., and Johnson, V. *Human Sexual Response.* Boston: Little, Brown & Company, 1966.

Mathers, E. P. *Eastern Love.* London, 1927.

Mathur, G. L., trans. *Erotic Indian Tales* (from the Sanskrit classic *Suksaptati*). Delhi: Hind Books, 1971.

Mead, Margaret. *Male and Female: A Study of the Sexes in a Changing World.* New York: William Morrow & Company, 1949.
———. *From the South Seas: Studies of Adolescence and Sex in Primitive Societies.* New York: William Morrow & Company, 1930.

Mehta, R. J. *Konarak: The Sun Temple of Love.* Bombay, 1971.

Meyer, J. J. *Sexual Life in Ancient India.* London, 1930.

Mishra, R. S. *Yoga Sutras: The Textbook of Yoga Psychology.* New York: Doubleday Anchor, 1973.

Mookerjee, Ajit. *Tantra Art: Its Philosophy and Physics.* Basel: Ravi Kumar, 1971.
———. *Tantra Asana: A Way to Self-Realization.* Basel: Ravi Kumar, 1971.
———. *Yoga Art.* London: Thames & Hudson, 1975. With a contribution by P. Rawson.

Morris, I. *The Pillow Book of Sei Shonagon.* London: Penguin Books, 1971.

Mukherji, B. *Rasajalanidhi: An Indian Alchemy.* 3 vols. Benares, 1938.

Murti, G. S. *The Science and Art of Indian Medicine.* Madras: Theosophical Publishing House, 1948.

Muses, C. A. *Esoteric Teachings of the Tibetan Tantra.* Lausanne: Aurora Press, 1961.

Nafzawi, Shaykh. *The Glory of the Perfumed Garden: The Missing Flowers.* Translated by H. E. J. London: Neville Spearman, 1975.

Narayanananda, Swami. *The Kundalini Shakti.* Rishikesh, 1950.

Nebesky-Wojkowitz, R. *Oracles and Demons of Tibet.* Graz: Akademische Druck, 1975.

Needham, Joseph. *Science and Civilisation in China.* Cambridge: University Press, 1954–74. Thus far 7 vols have been published; Vol. V, sect. 2, is of especial interest.

Neumann, E. *Art and the Creative Unconscious.* Translated from the German by R. Manheim. London: Routledge & Kegan Paul, 1959.
———. *The Great Mother: An Analysis of the Archetype.* Translated from the German by R. Manheim. Princeton, N. J.: Princeton University Press, 1972.

Neven, A. *Le Tantrisme dans l'Art et la Pensée.* Brussels: Palais des Beaux-Arts, 1974.

O'Flaherty, Wendy Doniger. *Asceticism and Eroticism in the Mythology of Shiva.* London: Oxford University Press, 1973.

Olsen, Eleanor. *The Tibetan Collection at the Newark Museum.* Catalogue in 5 vols. Newark, 1950.
———. *Tantric Buddhist Art.* New York: China Institute in America, 1974.

Oman, J. C. *The Mystics, Ascetics and Saints of India.* London: Fisher Unwin, 1905.

Pal, Pratapaditya. *The Sensuous Immortals: A Selection of Sculptures from the Pan-Asian Collection.* Los Angeles: County Museum of Art and MIT Press, 1978.
———. *The Art of Tibet.* New York: Asia Society and New York Graphic Society, 1969.
———. *Nepal: Where the Gods Are Young.* New York: Asia Society and John Weatherhill, 1975.

Palos, Stephan. *The Chinese Art of Healing.* New York: McGraw Hill, 1971.

Pandit, M. P. *Lights on the Tantra.* Madras: Ganesh & Company, 1957.
———. *Kundalini Yoga.* Madras: Ganesh & Company, 1962.
———. *Thoughts of a Shakta.* Madras: Ganesh & Company, 1965.
———. *Sri Aurobindo on the Tantra.* Pondicherry, 1967.
———. *Studies in the Tantras and the Vedas.* Madras: Ganesh & Company, 1967.
———. *Gems from the Tantras.* Madras: Ganesh & Company, 1969.

Pathak, V. S. *History of Saiva Cults in Northern India (A.D. 700–1200).* Varanasi, 1960.

Payne, E. *The Shaktas: An Introduction and Comparative Study.* Calcutta, 1933.

Pott, P. H. *Yoga and Yantra: Their*

Interrelation and Their Significance for Indian Archeology. Translated from the Dutch by R. Needham. The Hague: Nijhoff, 1966.

Prakash, Om. *Food and Drinks in Ancient India*. Delhi, 1961.

Puharich, Andrija. *Beyond Telepathy*. London: Darton, Longman & Todd, 1962.

Rafaelli, R. *Rapture: Thirteen Erotic Fantasies*. New York: Grove Press, 1975. With text by Steve Hull.

Raghavan, V. *Yantras or Mechanical Contrivances in Ancient India*. Bangalore, 1956.

Raglan, L. *The Temple and the House*. London: Routledge & Kegan Paul, 1964.

Rawson, Philip. *Tantra: Catalogue of the Hayward Gallery Show*. London: Arts Council of Great Britain, 1971.
——— *The Art of Tantra*. London: Thames & Hudson, 1973.
——— *Tantra: The Indian Cult of Ecstasy*. London: Thames & Hudson, 1973.
——— *Erotic Art of India*. London: Thames & Hudson, 1977.
——— *Erotic Art of the East: The Sexual Theme in Oriental Painting and Sculpture*. New York: Prometheus Press, 1968.
———, ed. *Primitive Erotic Art*. New York: Putnam's, 1973.

Ray, P. C. *History of Chemistry in Ancient and Medieval India*. Calcutta: Indian Chemical Society, 1956.

Ray, Tridibnath, trans. *Ananga Ranga of Kalyanamalla* (translated from the Sanskrit). Calcutta, 1944.

Reich, Wilhelm. *The Function of the Orgasm: Sex-Economic Problems of Biological Energy*. Translated from the German by P. Wolfe. New York: World Publishing, 1971.

Rele, Vasant G. *Mysterious Kundalini*. Bombay: Taraporevala, 1927.

Reynolds, Valrae. *Tibet: A Lost World*. Bloomington: Indiana University Press, 1978

Rinpoche, Rechung. *Tibetan Medicine*. London: Wellcome Institute of the History of Medicine, 1973.

Riviere, J. M. *Tantrik Yoga: Hindu and Tibetan*. Translated from the French by H. E. Kennedy. Northants, Eng.: Aquarian Press, 1973.
———, trans. *Rituel de Magie Tantrique Hindoue*. Milan: Arche Publications, 1976. French translation, the *Yantra Chintamani*.

Roerich, G. N. *The Blue Annals*. (from the Tibetan). Delhi: Motilal Banarsidass, 1976.

Rosenblum, Art. *The Natural Birth Control Book*. Philadelphia: Aquarian Research Foundation, 1976.

Ross, Allen V. *Vice in Bombay*. London: Tallis Press, 1969.

Roy, A. T. *Nervous System of the Ancient Hindus*. Hazaribagh, 1930.

Ruegg, D. Seyfort. *The Study of Indian and Tibetan Thought*. Leiden: E. J. Brill, 1967.

Sahu, N. K. *Buddhism in Orissa*. Orissa: Utkal University, 1958.

Samdup, Lama Kazi Dawa. *Chakrasambhara Tantra*. London: Luzac, 1910.

Saraswati, Swami Janakananda. *Yoga, Tantra and Meditation in Everyday Life*. Translated by Sheila Le Farge. London: Rider & Company, 1978.

Saraswati, Swami Pratyagatmananda. *Sadhana for Self-Realization: Mantras, Yantras and Tantras*. Madras: Ganesh & Company, 1963.
——— *Japasutram: A Study in Mantra Shastra*. Madras: Ganesh & Company 1971.
——— *The Metaphysics of Physics: The Background of Modern Cosmological Conception in Vedic and Tantric Symbolism*. Madras: Ganesh & Company, 1964.
——— *Science and Sadhana*. Calcutta, 1962.

Saso, M. *The Teachings of the Taoist Master Chuang*. New Haven, Conn.: Yale University Press, 1978.

Sastry, K. *The Veda and the Tantra*. Madras, 1951.

Saunders, E. *Mudra*. London, 1960.

Sawa, Takaaki. *Art in Japanese Esoteric Buddhism*. New York: Weatherhill, 1972.

Schmidt, Toni. *The Eighty-five Siddhas*. Stockholm, 1958.

Schroeder, L., and Ostrander, S. *Psychic Discoveries Behind the Iron Curtain*. Englewood Cliffs, N. J.: Prentice-Hall, 1970.

Scott, G. R. *Far Eastern Sex Life*. London: Swan, 1949.

Seal, B. *Positive Sciences of the Ancient Hindus*. Delhi, 1958.

Seaman, Barbara, and Seaman, Gideon. *Women and the Crisis in Sex Hormones*. New York: Bantam Books, 1978.

Seidensticker, E., trans. *The Kagero Nikki: Journal of a 10th Century Noblewoman*. Tokyo, 1955.
———, trans. *The Tale of Genji by Shikibu* (translated from the Japanese). New York: Knopf, 1978.

Sen, R. K. *Aesthetic Enjoyment: Its Background in Philosophy and Medicine*. Calcutta: University Publications, 1966.

Seth, B. R. *Khajuraho in Pictures*. Delhi, 1970.

Shankaranarayanan, S. *The Ten Great Cosmic Powers*. Pondicherry, 1952.
——— *Glory of the Divine Mother (Devi Mahatmyam)*. Pondicherry: Dipti Publications: distributed by Ganesh & Company, 1968.

Sharma, S. *Yoga and Sex*. Delhi: B. I. Publications, 1973.

Sharma, Y. S. *Sri Kundalini Sakthi: Serpent Power*. Bangalore, 1971.

Sharpe, E. *The Secrets of the Kaula Circle*. London: Luzac & Co., 1936.

Shastri, M. N., trans. *The Garuda Purana* (translated from the Sanskrit). Varanasi: Chowkhamba Sanskrit Series, 1968.
——— and others, trans. *The Linga Purana* (translated from the Sanskrit). Delhi: Motilal Banarsidass, 1973.
——— and a board of scholars, trans. *The Shiva Purana* 4 vols. (translated from the Sanskrit). Delhi: Motilal Banarsidass, 1973.

Shendge, M. J., trans. *Advayasiddhi* Baroda: Oriental Institute, 1964.

Shivananda, Swami. *Kundalini Yoga*. Sivanandanagar, 1968.

Shukla, D. N. *Shilpa Shastra: Hindu Achievements in Aeronautics and Fine Arts*. Lucknow: Vastuvanmaya, 1967.
——— *Six Fine Arts*. Lucknow: Vastuvanmaya, 1967.

Shukla, S. A., trans. *The Goraksashatakam* (translated from the Sanskrit). Bombay: Lonavla Publications, 1969.

Sierksma, Fokke. *Tibet's Terrifying Deities: Sex and Aggression in Religious Acculturation*. Rutland, Vt.: Charles Tuttle, 1966.

Singer, Irving. *The Goals of Human Sexuality*. London: Wildwood House, 1973.

Singer, June. *Androgyny*. New York: Doubleday, 1976.

Singh, Lalan Prasad. *Tantra: Its Mystic and Scientific Basis*. Delhi, 1976.

Sinha, J. *Sakta Monism: The Cult of Shakti*. Calcutta, 1966.
——— *Schools of Saivism*. Calcutta, 1970.

Sircar, D. C. *The Sakta Pithas*. Delhi: Motilal Banarsidass, 1973.
——— *The Shakti Cult and Tara*. Calcutta: University of Calcutta Press, 1967. A collection of articles.

Sivin, Nathan. *Chinese Alchemy: Preliminary Studies*. Cambridge, Mass.: Harvard University Publications, 1968.

Slater, P. E. *The Glory of Hera: Greek Mythology and the Greek Family*. Boston: Beacon Press, 1971.

Slinger, Penny. *Fifty Percent the Visible Woman*. London: Villiers Publications, 1971.
——— *An Exorcism: A Photo-Romance*. London: Villiers Publications, 1977.

Snellgrove, D. L., trans. *Hevajra Tantra*. 2 vols. London: Oxford University Press, 1959.
———, trans. *The Nine Ways of Bon* (translated from the Tibetan). London: Oxford University Press, 1967.

Spink, Walter M. *The Axis of Eros*. London: Penguin Books, 1975.

Stekel, W. *Auto-Erotism*. New York, 1950.

Surieu, Robert. *Sarv-e-Naz: An Essay on Love and the Representation of Erotic Themes in Ancient Iran*. Translated from the French by James Hogarth. Geneva: Nagel, 1967.

Suryanarayanamurthy, C. *Sri Lalita Sahasraranamam*. Madras: Ganesh & Company, 1962.

Tabori, Paul. *Pictorial History of Love*. London, 1962.

Taimni, I. K. *The Science of Yoga*. Illinois, 1965.

Tantrik Order. *International Journal of the Tantrik Order in America*. External Issue, Vol. V, No. 1. St. Louis: Tantrik Press, 1906.

Taylor, G. R. *Sex in History*. London, 1965.

Thera, Nanamoli. *Mindfulness of Breathing*. Kandy, Ceylon, 1964.

Thirleby, A. *Tantra: The Key to Sexual Power and Pleasure*. New York: Dell Books, 1978.

Thomas, P. *Epics, Myths and Legends of India: A Comprehensive Survey of the Sacred Lore of the Hindus, Buddhists and Jains*. Bombay: Taraporevala, 1961.
——— *Kamakala: The Indian Ritual of Love*. Bombay: Taraporevala, 1963.

Tisserand, Robert B. *The Art of Aromatherapy: The Healing and Beautifying Properties of the Essential Oils of Flowers and Herbs*. New York: Inner Traditions International, 1977.

Trungpa, Chogyam. *Meditation in Action*. Berkeley, 1970.

Tucci, Giuseppe. *The Theory and Practice of the Mandala*. Translated by A. H. Broderick. London: Rider & Company, 1974.
——— *Rati Lila: An Interpretation of the Tantric Imagery of the Temples of Nepal*. Geneva: Nagel, 1969.

Tulku, Tarthang. *Kum Nye Relaxation: Theory, Preparation, Massage*. Berkeley: Dharma Publishing, 1978.

Unwin, J. D. *Sex and Culture*. London: Oxford University Press, 1934.

Upadhyaya, S. C., trans. *Hindu Secrets of Love (Rati Rahasya of Kokkoka)* (from the Sanskrit). Bombay: Taraporevala, 1965.

Van Gulik, Robert H. *Sexual Life in Ancient China: A Preliminary Survey of Chinese Sex and Society from 1500 B.C. to 1644 A.D.* Leiden: E. J. Brill, 1974.
——— *Erotic Color Prints of the Ming Period*. Tokyo, 1951.

Van Kooij, K. R. *Worship of the Goddess According to the Kalikapurana*. Leiden: E. J. Brill, 1972.

Vander, A., and others. *The Encyclopaedia of Sex Practice*. London, 1972.

Vasu, S. C., trans. *The Shiva Samhita* (translated from the Sanskrit). Delhi: Oriental Books Reprint Company, 1975.
———, trans. *The Gheranda Samhita: A Treatise on Hatha Yoga* (translated from the Sanskrit). London: Theosophical Publishing House, 1976.

Veith, Ilza, trans. *The Yellow Emperor's Classic of Internal Medicine* (translated from the Chinese). Los Angeles: University of California, 1972.

Velde, H. van de *Ideal Marriage*. London: Heinemann, 1965.

Vijnanananda, Swami, trans. *The Srimad Devi Bhagawatam* (translated from the Sanskrit). Delhi: Oriental Books Reprint, 1977.

Vira, Raghu, and Taki, Shodo. *A Dictionary of the Secret Tantric Syllabic Code: Daksinamurti Uddarakosa*. Lahore, 1938.

Volin, Michael, and Phelan, Nancy. *Sex and Yoga*. London, 1967.

Waddell, L. A. *The Buddhism of Tibet or Lamaism*. London: Heffer & Sons 1959.

Waley, A. *The Nine Songs: A Study of Shamanism in Ancient China*. London: George Allen & Unwin, 1956.
——— *The Pillow Book of Sei Shonagon*. London, 1928.

Walker, Benjamin. *Sex and the Supernatural*. London: Macdonald, 1970.

Walton, A. H. *Aphrodisiacs: From*

Legend to Prescription. Westport, Conn.: Associated Booksellers, 1958. Introduction by H. Goodman.

Wang, Chi-chen, trans. *The Dream of the Red Chamber* (translated from the Chinese) London, 1929.

Wasson, R. G. *Soma: Divine Mushroom of Immortality.* New York: Harcourt Brace Jovanovich, 1973.

Watson, Lyall. *Supernature: The Natural History of the Supernatural.* London: Hodder & Stoughton, 1973.
———. *The Romeo Error: A Matter of Life and Death.* London: Hodder & Stoughton, 1974.

Watts, Alan W. *Nature, Man and Woman: A New Approach to Sexual Experience.* London: Thames & Hudson, 1958.

Wayman, Alex. *The Buddhist Tantras: Light on Indo-Tibetan Esotericism.* London: Routledge & Kegan Paul, 1973.
———. *Yoga of the Guhyasamaja Tantra: The Arcane Lore of 40 Verses.* Delhi: Motilal Banarsidass, 1977.

Wedeck, H. E. *Love Potions Through the Ages: A Study of Amatory Devices and Mores.* New York: Philosophical Library, 1963.

Westermarck, E. A. *The History of Human Marriage.* London, 1891.

Wickler, Wolfgang. *The Sexual Code: The Social Behavior of Animals and Men.* Translated by Francisca Garvie. New York: Doubleday Anchor 1973.

Wilhelm, Richard. *The Secret of the Golden Flower: A Chinese Book of Life.* London: Routledge & Kegan Paul, 1962.
———. *The I Ching or Book of Changes.* Translated by Cary F. Baynes. London: Routledge & Kegan Paul, 1965.

Woodroffe, Sir John, trans. *The Serpent Power.* Madras: Ganesh & Company, 1922. 2 works on Laya Yoga translated from the Sanskrit.
———. *Sakti and Sakta.* Madras: Ganesh & Company, 1965.
———. *Mahamaya: The World as Power/Power as Consciousness.* Madras: Ganesh & Company, 1964.
———. *The World as Power.* Madras: Ganesh & Company, 1966.
———. *The Garland of Letters: Studies in Mantrashastra.* Madras: Ganesh & Company, 1963.
———. *Kamakala Vilasa* (translated from the Sanskrit by Punyananda Natha). Madras: Ganesh & Company, 1961.

Yogananda, Paramahansa. *Autobiography of a Yogi.* Los Angeles: Self-Realization Fellowship, 1969.

Zimmer, H. *Myths and Symbols in Indian Art and Civilization.* Edited by J. Campbell. New York: Pantheon Books, 1963.

Zvelebil, K. V. *The Poets of the Powers.* London, Rider, 1973.

index